Success With
Gardening Collection

® Landoll, Inc.
Ashland, Ohio 44805
® The Landoll Apple Logo is a trademark owned by Landoll, Inc.
and is registered with the U.S. Patent and Trademark Office.

TABLE OF CONTENTS

Success with

Climbers & Creepers

CLAUDIA KRINNER

Series Editor:
LESLEY YOUNG

Contents

Nasturtiums are ideal for covering a fence with greenery and flowers.

Kiwi fruit flowers.

Morning glory requires plenty of sun.

7

Foreword

Houses and other buildings may be made of concrete and brick but all around them carefully cultivated flower beds, patios, and balconies and lovingly tended rockeries and hedges bear witness to a human longing to be close to nature. Nowadays many gardens are quite small and patios and balconies do not often provide enough space for all the pots, containers, and boxes one might wish. The best way to overcome this lack of lateral space is to make good use of the vertical by letting plants grow and flower on a façade and, at the same time, cover boring buildings, concrete walls, and plain fences with greenery. If permitted, in time plants will creep and climb up several storeys, filling the space between a balcony and a roof, above an entrance door and around windows.

This colorful guide will tell you how to make the outside of your house more attractive by using climbing plants. Here you will find numerous ideas for greenery to cover any structure.

Author Claudia Krinner, an expert on climbers and garden design, explains which plants are particularly suited to covering a house or balcony with greenery. She supplies detailed, individual instructions on plant care and reveals which plants will flourish both in the garden and also in large containers. Popular climbing plants, like clematis, ivy, Virginia creeper, grapevine, cathedral bell, climbing roses and many others, are shown to full advantage in the lovely color photographs.

Most plants need some form of climbing aid and in order to help the reader to choose and construct the best one for each plant, this volume supplies precise instructions and step-by-step illustrations on the use and securing of the right support. Enchanting flowers in the spring and juicy apples, pears, apricots or peaches in the fall offer a splendid return for the effort of establishing espaliers. All you need to know about planting and caring for fruits grown in this way against a house wall can be found in a separate, detailed chapter.

To ensure success in the planting of new climbers, the author has provided useful advice on choosing the right position, the best compost and growing mediums, the right way to plant, both in open soil and in large containers, and on watering and fertilizing. Notes are also given on the use of biological plant protection agents, while step-by-step, full-color illustrations help to convey practical gardening knowledge.

One point that often concerns the amateur gardener is the danger of damage to a house wall or other structure when climbers are grown and the author has covered this topic fully, so that you can feel free to go ahead and cover an entire wall with climbing roses, ivy or a grapevine. Finally, do not forget that "green" walls not only create beauty and a special atmosphere around a house, they also provide shelter and food for many fascinating creatures.

The author
Claudia Krinner has a diploma in landscape gardening and is an expert on garden design and the use of climbing plants.

Author's notes
This volume deals with the planting and care of climbing plants and creepers on the outside walls of buildings. Some of the plants described here are toxic and the instructions for individual care indicate this by means of a special symbol. Please make absolutely sure that children and domestic pets are not able to eat toxic plants as they may seriously damage their health.
Also make certain that all climbing aids and espaliers are well secured to avoid the risk of accidents or injury.

A house smothered in luxuriant greenery
Many climbing plants, like the Virginia creeper shown here, manage to cover entire walls in a relatively short time.

Plants and climbing aids

There is no finer sight than a house wall covered by the leaves of a fiery-colored creeper or enveloped in a mass of green foliage, unless it is a balcony adorned with a colorful, scented cloud of flowers or a patio that is reminiscent of the warm Mediterranean. It may be every gardener's dream but it is an ambition that is easier to turn into reality than you might believe. The range of suitable climbing plants is huge and the right climbing aids are easy to install.

Planting climbing plants around the outside of your home will give it a completely new appearance. The widespread use of climbers can also play a part in improving the general atmosphere of a town and will provide both a habitat and food for many small creatures. Without the need for a great deal of equipment or even special knowledge, you can disguise an ugly corner or adorn the shady side of a building with flowering climbing plants, evergreen ivy, or Virginia creeper, covering every surface, from house façades, balconies and patios to above entrance doors and around windows, right through to gutters and composting sites.

Plants for housewalls

The success of your "green" house exterior will largely depend on your selection of the right plants.
Climbing plants: With only a little effort, and in a very short time, some climbers will completely cover ugly façades or large expanses of unsightly wall. Such plants are also suitable for providing greenery on a balcony, on fences, and in the garden. One important point to note is that plants have different ways of climbing and will, therefore, require different types of climbing support. Relatively few climbing plants can manage without this.
Fruit espaliers have long been a popular way of growing fruit trees against a wall or fence.
Bushes and hedges: Planted along a fence or the side of a patio, bushes and hedges are excellent for providing shelter or a visual screen. Many species make a home for birds, small mammals, and insects, and thereby contribute to the protection of nature and encourage wildlife in the garden.
Large container plants are an ideal way of providing greenery in positions where you cannot plant directly into the ground.
Many climbing plants are also suitable for planting in large containers or pots.
Summer flowers can be planted in balcony boxes to create greenery and color anywhere. These are usually annuals which can be sown as seed or planted as young plants obtained from garden centers or nurseries.

Buying plants

Growing in the right position is particularly important for the healthy development and growth of plants. The mini-climate will vary in different spots so that different conditions will be experienced by plants growing outside, in garden flower beds or against a house wall than by plants grown in a large container or balcony box.

Climbing plants which flourish in large containers
black-eyed Susan (*Thunbergia alata*)
cathedral bell (*Cobaea scandens*)
clematis (*Clematis*)*
convolvulus (*Convolvulus sepium*)*
cucumber (*Cucumis sativus*)
hop (*Humulus lupulus*)
ivy (*Hedera helix*)*
kiwi fruit (*Actinidia chinensis*)
morning glory (*Ipomoea tricolor*)*
nasturtium (*Tropaeolum*)
ornamental gourd (*Cucurbita pepo var. ovifera*)
rose (*Rosa*)
Russian vine (*Fallopia baldschaunica*)
scarlet runner bean (*Phaseolus coccineus*)*
spindleberry (*Euonymus fortunei*)*
sweet pea (*Lathyrus odoratus*)*
Virginia creeper (*Parthenocissus quinquefolia* and *P. tricuspidata*)
(*toxic plants)

Wisteria will flourish in a sheltered position on the south- or west-facing side of the house.

The most important points to consider when choosing plants are light, temperature, soil, and water.

You will find detailed information on the individual requirements of many climbing plants.

Perennial climbing plants or woody plants do not die back in the winter. Instead, they form woody shoots. These plants are usually sold as young plants in containers or pre-grown in pots. Shrubs can also be obtained as rooted plants and are usually cheaper when bought this way as they do not have a firm rootstock. They may take rather longer to become established than plants bought with a proper rootstock.

My tip: Before planting, make sure that you undo the twine securing the cloth around the rootstock so that it cannot strangle the neck of the root.

Annual climbing plants or summer flowers can be pre-grown in pots or bought as seed. They will not survive the winter and will have to be re-sown or bought as young plants again the following spring.

Summer-green, deciduous woody plants (like Virginia creeper), whether bought as a small plant in a pot or with a rootstock and protective covering, are best acquired when they have no leaves. This will help the plant to establish itself more easily as it does not lose so much water through evaporation when it is leafless.

11

Unfortunately, you will not be able to tell at this stage whether you have purchased a healthy, robust plant. Plants like hops or bindweed, which have a rootstock and have been pre-grown in a pot, are also obtainable from garden centers. The parts of the plant that are above ground will die off in the winter; the underground parts will form new shoots in spring.

When purchasing **plants for espaliers**, it is important to consider the height of the trunk of the plant. This is the distance between the neck of the root to the beginning of the crown which is where the plant begins to branch out.

Remember where the windows are in a house wall when working out where to plant an espalier.

Climbing techniques
Hops (left) and other winding plants require vertical supports; plants which have adapted their leaf stalks for climbing, like the clematis (right), grow best on grid-like frames.

Climbing techniques
Virginia creeper (Parthenocissus quinquefolia, left) is a plant with suckers. The climbing rose (right) is a rambler which holds on with its thorns.

How to recognize healthy plants

● By their leaves. In the case of large container plants and summer flowers, a good healthy green color will generally indicate that the plant is not suffering from any deficiencies.

● By the bark which should be completely undamaged. Cuts in the stem that are the result of work done to improve the shape of the plant do not fall into this category. However, any such marks should look clean and some protective tissue should already have grown over them.

Pests and diseases
should never occur on quality stock.

When purchasing woody plants, remember to check for rust. This is recognizable by tiny, bright red bumps on the bark. Even healthy plants can be infected.

Where to purchase plants

The best place to go is a reputable plant or tree nursery run by professional gardeners. Here, in addition to quality stock, you will also be able to obtain expert advice. You will find the addresses of local nurseries in your telephone directory. You can also purchase a directory of nurseries and plant specialists in most good bookshops, or write to the inquiries page of a reputable gardening magazine (enclose a stamped, self-addressed envelope).

Garden centers: In addition to offering a similar selection to tree nurseries, good garden centers should also have a large selection of accessories for sale.

Mail order companies also offer a wide selection of plants. Whenever you order something from a catalog, do make sure that it will come from a reputable source so that you will be certain to receive genuinely fresh stock.

Markets and other venues often offer interesting opportunities to stock your own garden or balcony with new plants, but do check such plants carefully for signs of disease or pests.

How plants climb

Whatever support plants find in nature to help them to climb from the shady ground up to the light, is what you will have to provide artificially around your house or on your balcony.

NB: The type of climbing aid should be chosen to suit the individual climbing technique of the plant. There are plants that wind, plants with tendrils, plants with root suckers and those that ramble.

NB: Various kinds of climbing aid can be obtained to suit these respective climbing techniques. These climbing frames or grids must be fixed to the wall before planting. The minimum space between the house wall and the climbing aid should be at least 4 in (10 cm).

Plants that wind
Most climbing plants belong to the group of winding plants which climb up the support by using the whole shoot. These plants always wind around their support in one direction only, so a distinction must be made (when viewed from above) between:
● left-winding plants which grow anti-clockwise and are most common, and

● right-winding plants (only a few) which grow clockwise, such as hops and honeysuckle.

Climbing aids for winders:
Plants that wind require vertical supports such as sticks, strings, or wires.

It is important to choose a support with the correct diameter. Support sticks with a diameter of 1¼-2 in (3-5 cm) are suitable for most winders. A support with a much larger diameter, from about 4 in (10 cm) upward, would be too big for the winding shoot of *Wisteria* to encircle, for example. If the climbing aids are too thin, on the other hand, very vigorous winders, like Russian vine, may strangle themselves.

Vertical crosspieces between the individual support sticks are merely intended to strengthen the frame and to prevent the plants from sliding down the smooth surface of the support. If you wish a shoot to grow sideways, it will have to be trained and tied.

Plants with adhesive pads and root suckers
Virginia creeper (Parthenocissus tricuspidata "Veitchii," left) climbs with the help of adhesive pads; ivy (right) uses root suckers.

My tip: Winders require enough space to encircle their support. Wall spacers will ensure the necessary gap between the wall and the frame (minimum distance 12 in/30 cm).

Plants with tendrils

These plants climb by using specially adapted organs, for example, either with the help of specially adapted long leaf stalks, like the clematis (*Clematis*), or by using tendrils which evolved through an adaptation of the shoots, as in the case of the grapevine (*Vitis vinifera*).
There are:
● plants which climb by means of long leaf stalks that are sensitive to pressure
● plants with suckers, which use their slender shoots purely for climbing
● plants with tendrils, which have developed additional adhesive pads on the tips of their shoots to help them to climb without any other kind of aid. These include some forms of Virginia creeper (*Parthenocissus tricuspidata* "Veitchii" and *Parthenocissus quinquefolia* "Engelmannii") which only grow a few adhesive pads.

When stimulated by pressure or touch, these pads secrete minute quantities of an adhesive which hardens on exposure to air.

Climbing aids for plants with tendrils: Net or grid-shaped climbing aids made of wood, wire, twines, or builders' reinforcing mesh. Grids, wire mesh, and wires may be arranged vertically, horizontally or even diagonally.
● The individual sticks of a grid or frame should not be too thick as the tender shoots would find it too difficult to wind around them.

Annuals with tendrils
cathedral bell (*Cobaea scandens*)
nasturtium (*Tropaeolum majus, T. peregrinum*)
ornamental gourd (*Cucurbita pepo var. ovifera*)
sweet pea (*Lathyrus odoratus*)*

Perennials with tendrils
clematis (*Clematis*)*
grapevine (*Vitis vinifera*)
Virginia creeper (*Parthenocissus quinquefolia, P. tricuspidata*)
(*toxic plant)

● In the case of delicate plants, for example those that use extended leaf stalks, like nasturtium, the mesh gauge of a grid should not be more than 2 by 2 in (5 by 5 cm).

Plants with root suckers
Plants may also climb with the help of their roots, for example ivy. As soon as it comes into contact with a firm base, ivy produces special adhesive roots straight out of the shoots just beneath a leaf stalk.
Being "true climbing plants," plants with root suckers do not require any kind of climbing aid.

Annual winders
black-eyed Susan (*Thunbergia alata*)
morning glory (*Ipomoea tricolor*)*
scarlet runner bean (*Phasaeolus coccineus*)*

Perennial winders
Akebia quinata
Celastrus orbiculatus
Dutchman's pipe (*Aristolochia macrophylla*)
honeysuckle (*Lonicera*)*
hop (*Humulus lupulus*)
kiwi fruit (*Actinidia chinensis*)
Russian vine (*Fallopia baldschaunica*)
wisteria (*Wisteria sinensis*)*

(*toxic plants)

My tip: Young plantlets like to use a short piece of twine or a stick leaning diagonally against the wall as a means of getting started in the right direction.

Ramblers

Ramblers like the climbing rose (Rosa) are not equipped with specially adapted climbing organs. Instead, they produce long, flexible shoots, usually also equipped with thorns or prickles, to help them to climb up the larger supporting plants that they hold onto. If they cannot find enough support themselves or their own weight pulls them down, however, it will be necessary to supply them with additional climbing aids.

Honeysuckle covering an arch
This vigorous climber soon covers an arched climbing frame with a profusion of summer flowers.

Climbing aids for ramblers: Use grids or frames with as many vertical battens as possible, for example, diagonal grids. These plants cannot climb by themselves so their new shoots have to be woven into the frame or tied up from time to time.

Ramblers
blackberry (Rubus)
rose (Rosa)
winter jasmine (Jasminum nudiflorum)

Materials

As a rule, erecting climbing aids is not something for which you will need planning permission but it is always a good idea to ask your landlord if you are renting a home. The case is different if the building is an historic one and this point should be checked with the relevant authority.

Support sticks

Support sticks made of wood, plastic, metal, or plastic-coated metal are among the simplest types of climbing aid. They can be arranged in a pattern or woven together with the help of wire or twine, or you can stand several sticks in such a way that they meet at the top.
Use: These are ideal for winding plants, like scarlet runner beans, black-eyed Susan or Russian vine.
Securing: Lightweight sticks for supporting annual winders should be driven about 20 in (50 cm) deep into the soil. More stable sticks can be set in holes 20-32 in (50-80 cm) deep, perhaps even cementing them in if they are intended to

support very vigorously growing climbing plants like Russian vine. Drive the sticks into the compost in a pot or large container if the plants are to grow in pots.

Ropes or twine made from natural fibers

Ropes made of hemp, sisal or coconut fiber can be obtained from gardening suppliers. They are plant-friendly and provide a firm grip as they have a rough surface. Their durability will be somewhat limited, however, if they are used outdoors. They tend to expand in increased humidity so the support they give to the plants can become too loose.
Use: For annual winders.
Securing: Knot them to screw-in eyes or to rings that can be dowelled into the house wall.

Plastic rope

It is essential to use twine or rope with a rough surface as a climbing aid in order to prevent the plant from sliding down. Nylon hop ropes, ¾-in (15-mm) thick, can be obtained in the trade. These ropes have a rough surface, are cheap, can be straightened out quite easily with a simple stretcher (obtainable from hardware stores), and will last a long time.
NB: Vigorously growing winders may become too heavy for these ropes.
Use: For perennial winders like kiwi fruit and hops.
Securing: Fasten them to the house wall in the same way as rope made of nylon (see above).

Wire rope

Because of their strength, wire ropes can be used to bridge larger gaps. Galvanized or plastic-coated stainless steel wire will have sufficient anti-rusting qualities.

To prevent winders from sliding down smooth surfaces of vertical supports, provide horizontal supports, install screw-on wire rope clamps at regular intervals to act like "knots," or rough up the plastic coating.
Use: For winders like hops and Dutchman's pipe.
Securing: These must be fixed securely because of the load on the support. A tripod dowelled into the wall at the top end of the rope/wire should be sufficient. Anchoring the rope/wire in the soil can be achieved with the help of a point anchor made of concrete or heavy, galvanized metal plates. Use metal eyelets that have been cast in, welded on or screwed on (see illustration above).
Use various kinds of stretchers to pull the rope taut (obtainable from builders' merchants or from hardware stores; remember to indicate the gauge of wire you are using):
● simple wire stretchers for ropes less than 10 ft (3 m) long; these can only be tightened by a maximum of 10 in (25 cm).
● locking stretchers for use with thicker wire and rope to a length of over 10 ft (3 m). Thinner rope ends should be tidily twisted together using pliers at the junction point with the stretcher. Thicker wire ropes are best taken to a professional ropemaker where the ends are placed in soft metal capsules and then sealed together under great pressure.

Plastic-coated grids
Garden centers can supply a good stock of plastic grids and plastic-coated metal wire, including tools, as ready-to-buy items. They are easy to assemble and are normally treated against rusting by the manufacturers.
Uses: For plants with tendrils and

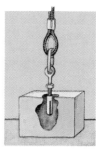

Fixing wire supports
At the top end, a tripod has been dowelled into the wall (left). A point anchor made of concrete is used to anchor the wire into the ground.

winders like *Clematis* or smaller climbing roses. These grids would rapidly end up being too small for vigorously growing plants like *Wisteria* or Russian vine.
Securing: Hang on wall spacers with dowelled wall hooks.

Builders' reinforcing mesh and wire-mesh grids
Builders' reinforcing mesh can be bought in sections of 8 by 17 ft (2.5 by 5 m) in builders' merchants. Use a strong metal saw or a bolt cutter for cutting the mesh to size. This mesh is easy to shape into arches or pergolas or to fix to walls as a flat climbing aid. Note that it will need a coat of anti-rust paint.
Wire-mesh frames are also suitable as climbing aids. The wire mesh is very cheap and is usually galvanized. It will be even stronger if it is set into a strong wooden frame and fixed with U-shaped steel nails.
Use: For winders like *Clematis*, sweet peas or nasturtiums.
Securing: Install in the same way as plastic grids (see above).

Wood
Wooden frames or grids are still the most popular element for

supporting green climbing plants because of their natural look, plant-friendly qualities, and the multitude of possibilities for use.
Use: For perennial winding plants and plants with tendrils.

My tip: The diameter of wooden battens may sometimes be too large and additional horizontal twines or thinner wooden battens will have to be provided as climbing aids.

NB: Climbing frames made of wood should not be in direct contact with the soil which might cause the wooden parts to start to decay from the bottom up (it is a good idea to secure them in concrete with a "metal shoe").
Wood protection agents:
Treating the wood with a protection agent before installation is recommended. Try to use biological wood protection agents as they are less harmful to humans and plants. They include: linseed oil, wood oil, wood tar, soda, and natural resins. You can also obtain pigments (in powder form) for mixing with the agent to obtain a colorful finish.
Pressure-treated woods (the protection agent is driven into the wood under high pressure) are good for use as posts or weight-bearing supports with a larger diameter. They should not, however, contain substances that are harmful to plants, such as phenols, chlorine, or ammonium hydroxide. When purchasing wood, ask which agents have been used to treat it.
The most important points to remember when using wood are:
● Use high-quality wood with few knotholes.
● Cover up exposed ends with plastic or metal strips to protect them against rain.

● The use of planed wood will decrease the risk of the wood becoming soaked right through.

● The unprotected ends of posts should be cut off at an angle so that water can run off more easily.

Grids made of wood: These can easily be made out of roof battens which can be obtained from a lumber yard or builder's merchant in a range of diameters from ¾ by 1½ in (2 by 4 cm) to 1½ by 2½ in (4 by 6 cm) and in lengths of 7-20 ft (2-6 m), either rough-cut or planed, in a natural, untreated state or pressure-treated. Even without any experience of woodwork, you will find them easy to assemble into the desired grid pattern and they are very cheap to buy. When constructing a wooden grid, nail, screw, or glue the battens together both horizontally and vertically. Use rustfree wire pegs or a weatherproof glue or screws.

Securing: Use dowels for fixing hooks into the wall. Use metal or plastic capsules as spacers. Pieces of cork will do equally well if the spaces are small.

Climbing frames made of metal

Metal structures, made from steel pipe, for example, and properly treated against rusting, are very durable and strong. They are especially useful for creating free-standing, three-dimensional or curved climbing frames.

It will be necessary to tie the plants on. Such elaborate climbing frames will have to be made in a metal workshop.

Use: For rose arches, gateway arches, bowers, and covered walks; for annual and perennial climbing plants, plants with tendrils and ramblers.

Securing: This should be carried out by the manufacturer.

Planting containers

Fortunately, many climbing plants do not make great demands with respect to space, so they will flourish just as well in large containers, pots, and balcony boxes.

The most important points to consider when choosing plants are:

● All containers, no matter what material they are made of, must be equipped with drainage holes so that excess water can run away. Very few plants can cope with waterlogging.

● All large plant containers require a drainage layer.

● Containers for climbing plants must be sufficiently spacious as the plant will require plenty of room for the development of its roots if it is to produce large amounts of leaves and flowers. Annuals will make do with an ordinary balcony box but perennials require a container that is at least 12-16 in (30-40 cm) deep, and wide enough to leave space for an insulating layer made of polystyrene.

● Before purchasing any large, heavy containers, troughs, or urns, find out the carrying

capacity of your balcony or patio. Even if the plants themselves are not that heavy, the weight of the containers increases dramatically when filled with wet compost.

Clay containers: The porous material from which these containers are made makes an exchange of air possible among the roots of the plant and the risk of waterlogging is also reduced as excess water can evaporate through the walls of the vessel. On the other hand, rapid evaporation will also cause the soil to cool quickly around the roots, which many plants dislike. Clay pots and containers are not suitable for overwintering outside.

My tip: Before using them, clay and terracotta pots should be soaked in water long enough so that no more tiny air bubbles are seen rising to the surface. This means that the clay is now saturated with water and, to begin with at least, chalky deposits will be avoided. When they do appear, scrub them off with a tough scrubbing brush and a vinegar and water solution (1:4).

Wooden containers:

● Always stand wooden containers on a base to prevent the rapid decay of the wood.

A wire grid with a wooden frame

Lay the wire mesh on the wooden frame (left), use U-shaped nails to fix the edge of the wire (center) and hang up the frame using spacers (right).

Nasturtiums quickly produce a mass of colorful flowers on a fence.

Black-eyed Susan is a very undemanding summer-flowering plant.

● Wooden containers are subject to weathering. Make sure they have been painted inside and out with a plant-friendly wood protection agent.

Plastic containers: The advantages are fairly obvious. They are cheap to buy, long-lasting, and do not weigh much and are, therefore, ideal for balconies and windowsills. They are also practical and easy to clean as the smooth surface will not encourage the growth of algae.

Troughs made of natural stone: Usually, no drainage holes have been provided so the container will require a good drainage layer. Carefully choose the position in which you are going to keep the trough as its weight will prevent it from being moved about too easily.

Plant containers with a water reservoir: Recently, plant containers with inbuilt water reservoirs have become more widely available. The reservoir is at the bottom of the plant container and, depending on the size of the container, can hold up to 2½ gallons (10 liters) of water. Fertilizer can also be introduced in this way.

NB: These containers should also be equipped with a properly functioning water-level indicator. Too much water in the container would cause the roots to rot as they would be standing in water all the time. Even when using this method, you will not be able to dispense with watering for more than a few days as plants in large containers will require lots of water, particularly if they are placed in a sunny position.

Creating greenery

Walls covered in green foliage are not only an aesthetically pleasing adornment of houses and other buildings in towns, they also provide a habitat for birds and other wild creatures. In this way, foliage and flowering plants, grown against a house wall or in pots and containers, can be used to create a natural haven all around the outside of your house.

A green façade

Before buying plants to cover a wall you should give some thought to what you intend to achieve.

● Will you wish to influence the direction in which the plants grow or do you not mind which way they climb up the wall? You could choose climbing plants which require climbing frames that merely need fixing to the wall in the right position for the plant to cover the wall with greenery. Or you may wish to let plants with root suckers, which do not require any climbing aids, grow unhindered up a wall.

● Do you want the wall to be covered in greenery as soon as possible and up to what height do you wish the plants to climb? Hops and Russian vine, for example, are recommended as fast-growing climbers; ivy and spindleberry (*Euonymus fortunei*) are much slower, at least for the first few years.

● If you wish to cover the entire façade with a uniformly dense, green tapestry, the best plants are ivy and Virginia creeper. If, however, you wish only part of the façade to be hidden or even a particular area of it, for example to emphasize the importance of the entrance, clematis, roses, Dutchman's pipe and honeysuckle would be most suitable.

The advantages of greenery on a façade

Houses covered in climbing plants are not only ecologically beneficial, they also profit from many favourable effects created by the woven covering of plants. Plants growing on a wall provide a kind of protective covering for the house.

A habitat for birds and insects: Green façades create new living spaces which offer many creatures shelter and nesting facilities, and also food in the shape of flowers and fruit. In addition to bees, beetles, butterflies, and spiders, birds, and bats will also join the community on the house wall, where both prey and predators will feel at home.

A temperature equalizer: Plants let water evaporate through their leaves. This process leads to a slight cooling in temperature of their immediate surroundings, which is why outdoor seating in many warm countries is often surrounded by climbing plants.

Due to this effect, houses covered in greenery enjoy a more temperate climate. The temperature is lowered slightly in hot summer weather, while the cold of winter is alleviated a little by an evergreen plant covering. The difference in the daytime and night-time temperature is also decreased.

Protection from rain and weather: A thick plant covering will protect a house wall from rain. There is still plenty of ventilation behind the protective covering of leaves, so the wall will not be covered in condensation. Thickly covered house walls will be shielded even from heavy showers.

Increase in humidity: Plants on a house wall lose water through evaporation to the immediate environment without the moisture condensing on the wall.

Damage to the façade

Very often, damage to a house wall is ascribed to climbing plants which are not the culprits at all. Instead, already damaged or damp masonry is responsible for the problems. The reputedly damaging effect of ivy or Virginia creeper on a façade just does not happen so long as the façade was undamaged to begin with as the adhesive pads and roots will not harm sound rendering or cement. Plants with tendrils and adhesive pads, like Virginia creeper, secrete a sticky substance to let them adhere to the wall and this does no damage to the wall. Climbing plants never bore holes or make cracks in walls, they only take advantage of already existing uneven places and cracks. This means that damaged walls should be properly repaired before letting plants climb up them.

Grown in a sunny position, a Virginia creeper will produce beautifully colored fall foliage.

How to avoid damage to a façade

● Ivy or Virginia creeper should not be planted right beside wooden walls that require regular painting. Old sheds or garage walls will suit these plants.

● Façades treated with water-repellent paint are not suitable for plants with root suckers. The root suckers of ivy may penetrate the top layer of paint and continue producing roots underneath this. The consequence will be peeling paint.

● Gutters and the surfaces of roofs should not have plants climbing across them. Self-climbing plants on roof surfaces will push their shoots under the roof tiles and even lift them up.

NB: Gutters that are blocked with growing plants will lead to dampness in walls.

The right side of the house

Different plants have different requirements as to position. The section on care
will tell you which side of the house is suitable for which plants.

The south-facing side: This is the ideal position for kiwi fruit, grapevines, or espalier fruit (the south-facing side is too warm for apples) and deciduous climbing plants like wisteria, roses, honeysuckle, or morning glory.

The west-facing side: This is often the side which receives most rain in northern areas, although it also enjoys the full warmth of the afternoon sunshine and can therefore support espalier fruit. A dense, evergreen covering will protect the fruit against heavy rain.

The east-facing side: Here, the morning sun will still provide enough warmth for active growth and this side is also often more protected than the west-facing side. However, late frosts in spring may damage the flowers of espalier fruit on this side, which may mean a lack of fruit later on.

The north-facing side: Here, it is better to plant evergreen plants which cover the whole surface, like ivy. The north-facing side is not suitable for planting espalier fruit.

Decorative design

Deciding to cover your house with greenery will still leave plenty of scope for your own ideas, whether this is the choosing and combining of different plants, the building of suitable climbing aids, or the optimal utilization of existing surfaces.

Climbing roses and Virginia creeper.

The fall colors of Virginia creeper.

A green and flowering balcony

A sufficient screen from neighboring balconies can be obtained with tall-growing climbing plants like scarlet runner beans which can be trained on simple twines or wires.
(Always check about attaching fixtures with your landlord.)
Green and flowering climbing plants on horizontal wires or twines will transform your balcony into a densely covered, flowering summer bower. Annual winders and plants with tendrils are most suitable for this and will manage quite well in flower boxes or pots. Charming contrasts can be created with a combination of climbing plants and annual summer flowers in a pot. Perennial species (in containers with a height of at least 14 in/35 cm and a diameter of 12-16 in/30-40 cm) which need to overwinter on a balcony, should be hardy.

Make sure to consider the following points when establishing plants on a balcony:

● Balconies that are open to strong winds require protection from the wind to let young plants acclimatize themselves; for example, by using bamboo matting as a screen.
● Plants on a balcony are more susceptible to attack by pests which means more time spent on care.
● Boxes fixed to the outside of a balcony railing must be secured properly.

Doorways and entrances

You can create greenery around your entrance door with honeysuckle, Russian vine and Virginia creeper – sometimes these plants will end up supplying a covering of greenery over the entire façade. The way to set plants directly into the soil beside a doorway is shown.
A green archway above an entrance doorway, for example in the garden of a terraced house, can be covered with roses, honeysuckle, or clematis. Large container plants, like bay and box trees, can look very charming beside a rather grander doorway. Climbing plants can also be trained on frames or taut wires (see pp. 11 and 12) on both sides of a doorway, and may be planted in large containers or boxes. The entrance to a house may not always be in a sheltered position, so only choose plants that are not too sensitive to wind and weather.

Color around a window

Windows can be transformed into mini-balconies.

● If there is an outside window ledge, you can utilize the depth and width of the embrasure and stand a box on the ledge. Secure it well, so that it cannot tip off!

● Use lightweight boxes as window ledges cannot cope with a great amount of weight.

● Never install window boxes on the side of the house that is most exposed to wind or rain.

● Hardy, perennial climbing plants, like ivy or clematis, may be allowed to cover a façade from a window by using sufficiently insulated window boxes. Draw taut wires or twines along the wall beside the window to provide a climbing frame for the plants. These supports should be secured to the wall with wall hooks that have been dowelled in. Make sure to check with your landlord first.

Clematis alpina "Francess Rivis."

Metal drainpipes as supports for climbing plants

If a vertical drainpipe is anchored properly and is a sufficient space out from a wall, it may be used as an ideal support for less hefty winding plants like Dutchman's pipe, hops, black-eyed Susan or scarlet runner beans. Wisteria, for example, should never be allowed to climb up a drainpipe; its yard-long shoots will become woody and tough in time and are quite capable of "strangling" a drainpipe. Very delicate winding plants, on the other hand, will not be able to use such large pipes.

● If no place for planting is available at the foot of a drainpipe, you can create a planting pit or set the plants (preferably annuals) in a pot or container.

● In order to prevent the shoots from slipping down the smooth surface of a drainpipe to begin with, you may carefully tie the plant to the pipe or draw a hop twine from the ground to the top.

NB: Remember to cut the plant back so that it cannot block the top of the drainpipe.

My tip: Do not let plants with tendrils and adhesive pads climb up drainpipes and do not plant them near pipes as their adhesive pads tend to create rust spots on metal surfaces.

Plastic drainpipes should not be used for climbers as they will not bear the weight.

Climbers on a patio

A patio will provide plenty of room for a multitude of different combinations of plants.

Large container plants, like oleander, bougainvillea, or hibiscus, will feel particularly at home on a patio on the south-facing side of the house. (Advice on growing plants in large containers is given on pp. 20-9.)

Climbing plants on patios or fences can turn boring party walls or wire fences between adjoining gardens into a living screen.

● Honeysuckle, clematis, or roses, planted in beds beside patios or along walls, will produce a riot of summer flowers, particularly if planted in a south-facing position.

● If you want to hide a patio wall or an adjoining wire fence with a covering of green foliage even in winter, the best species to plant are ivy or *Euonymus fortunei* which will also flourish on a north- or east-facing patio.

Clematis montana "Rubens" is a profusely flowering variety.

● If there is no room on a house wall, perennial climbing plants can be grown in a large trough in front of a patio wall.

Simple builders' steel mesh or twines that have been secured to wall hooks will be sufficient as a climbing aid.

Shrubs will also provide a wonderful visual screen beside a patio or along a fence. Hedge maple, lilac, forsythia, or spiraea will provide cheerful accents with their flowers, fruit, or colorful fall foliage. Most shrubs will require planting in open soil on account of their size and the extent of their root systems.

Fences

If you do not have enough room for a proper hedge, fences constructed of different materials, such as wire or wood, are absolutely ideal as climbing aids.

Climbing plants will produce enchanting flowers in the summer and Virginia creeper will decorate your fence with a wealth of wonderful, glowing-red leaves in the fall.

● Vertical fence posts are ideal for supporting winding plants like convolvulus, black-eyed Susan or morning glory. Any missing horizontals needed can easily be added by drawing rope or wires from post to post.

● Plants with tendrils, like nasturtium, clematis or sweet peas, will climb effortlessly on small-gauge wire fences.

● Using annual plants, you can create a different look along a fence every year and also have the time to provide wooden posts with a regular protective coat of paint.

● Vigorously growing perennials, like wisteria or hops, require a fence height of at least 7-8 ft (2-

2.5 m). The fence must also be very strong.

● You can find out just how many plants you will need for the length of fence, and the proper spacing of these plants.

● Plantations of shrubs or other plants along fences not only provide an attractive visual screen, they are also high on the list of ecologically beneficial improvements: hazelnut, hedge maple, or cornelian cherry (*Cornus mas*) provide shelter and food for birds and small mammals like hedgehogs or dormice.

NB: Make sure there will be enough space between your plants and any neighboring property when planting beside fences. Find out how large the plants will grow when you buy them.

Covering garbage can shelters, fuel stores, etc.

Even such unattractive objects as these can be use to support plants if you choose the right ones.

● Virginia creeper will soon obscure garbage can shelters and other structures. Ivy will also cover such ugly eyesores with its green foliage but will do better in less sunny positions.

● Instead of going for a complete covering, you could also stand plant troughs of summer flowers, like patience-plants, pinks or daisies, or climbing plants with hanging shoots, like Virginia creeper (*Parthenocissus quinquefolia*), on top of a garbage can shelter and thereby improve its appearance.

Other sites

Even the composting corner of the garden can be brightened up as the bars or grid of the composting container itself can provide an excellent climbing frame for plants.

Flowering, climbing plants, like sweet peas or nasturtiums, which will cover a container with their bright flowers in no time at all, will cheer up any dull corner of the garden. Planting soft fruit bushes, such as red/black/whitecurrants or gooseberries, or other low-growing shrubs, like lilac or forsythia, in front of a composting station will also aid the compost to ripen as maturing compost does not like to receive too much direct sunlight.

Shrubs that are ecologically beneficial
barberry (*Berberis vulgaris*)
broom (*Genista tinctoria*)
buckthorn (*Rhamnus catharticus*)*
cornelian cherry (*Cornus mas*)
elder (*Sambucus nigra* and *S. racemosa**)
hedge maple (*Acer campestre*)
*Frangula alnus**
hawthorn (*Crataegus crusgalli*)
hazelnut (*Corylus avellana*)
holly (*Ilex aquifolium*)*
hornbeam (*Carpinus betulus*)
juniper (*Juniperus communis*)
privet (*Ligustrum vulgare*)*
Prunus mahaleb
sloe (*Prunus spinosa*)
snowy mespilus (*Amelanchier lamarckii*)
spindleberry (*Euonymus europaea*)*
whitethorn (*Crataegus monogyna*)
willow (*Salix*)

These bushes provide shelter and food for numerous species of birds and small creatures. (*toxic plants)

Position, planting, and care

Your plants will thrive better if you create the best conditions for healthy growth right from the start. In order to do this you will need to know the individual requirements of the plants with respect to position and soil, when and how to plant them, and how to care for them properly. If all of these conditions are met, your plants will flourish and be the envy of all who see them.

Planting

The right time to plant
The best time is in spring when the plants will have enough time to form proper roots and to grow well before the first frosts in late fall.
Container plants or plants sold with a rootstock can be planted all year round but will require a great deal of care and attention. High temperatures during the daytime will inhibit growth.

Position
Light: Not all plants have the same requirements with respect to light. Generally, a distinction is made between:
● positions in full sunlight
● semi-shady positions, and
● shady positions.
Examples of climbing plants which require lots of light include roses and wisteria. However, most native American climbing plants normally grow wild in semi-shady positions on the fringes of woodland; for example hops. Ivy is a good shade provider in the wild.
Temperature: Sufficient warmth is essential to the survival of many plants. Sunny, and therefore warm, positions are ideal for frost-sensitive plants like woody espalier plants or large container plants. Flowering climbing plants will also thrive here. Evergreen climbing plants prefer positions with a more balanced temperature (even north-facing).
Soil: Depending on their requirements, individual plants will thrive in various different kinds of soil. Even if the soil has been improved , you should not try to grow plants that require a rich soil in a very poor one.
Water: Most climbing plants require a plentiful supply of water to help them to absorb the nutrients in the soil.

Planting in open soil
The work involved in planting and care is less involved if you plant directly into open soil as, here, climbing plants will find the kind of conditions that most closely resemble those of their natural habitat:
● They are growing directly in the soil, so they have plenty of space for their roots to grow.
● They will be supplied with plenty of rainwater.

On a patio

Depending on the site of the patio, you may have to provide protection from the wind in order to obtain a really sheltered position for Mediterranean plants or espalier fruit trees. As most patios are situated on the south side of the house, the plants planted or kept there are subject to intense sunlight and considerable differences in temperature during the course of the day. More watering by the gardener will therefore be needed than for plants planted in open soil.

The soil in beds along the sides of new patios is often mixed with builders' rubble and will have to be improved before you plant anything.

On a balcony

Balconies share many features of a patio but the amount of light received may be impaired by neighboring balconies or shadows created by other nearby buildings. During the summer, balconies may turn into real heat traps for plants, as heat reflected from road surfaces or house walls may collect there. It is, therefore, particularly important to provide suitable shading and to water the plants adequately.

Virginia creeper will provide a protective covering for your house.

25

Planting beside walls

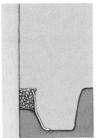

Dig a planting hole, lay a piece of filter fabric in it and fill the space between the hole and the wall with gravel. Mix dug-out soil with improving substances. Insert the plant, lean the support stick against the wall, and fill up the hole with soil.

Types of soil and how to improve them

As a rule, climbing plants demand fairly loose, nutrient-rich soil such as humus-rich garden soil. As most soils do not possess all the features of an ideal plant soil, they have to be improved with loosening or binding substances and should receive basic fertilization before planting commences.

Sandy soils generally contain very little humus.

● Characteristics: A fine, crumbly structure, therefore very water-permeable and easy for roots to penetrate, but with a decreased capacity for storing nutrients.

● Improvement: Use organic fertilizers and binding substances like loam and organic compost.

Loamy soils often contain plenty of humus.

● Characteristics: If there is a high clay content, it may be difficult for roots to penetrate. A loamy soil should have a good capacity for retaining nutrients. If it dries out severely, large cracks may cause damage to roots.

● Improvement: Use sand for loosening and compost or stable manure as fertilizer to turn it into an ideal growing medium.

Chalky soils, depending on their situation, will naturally tend to contain a thin or thicker layer of humus.

● Characteristics: Usually lumpy or gravelly so very permeable for water and nutrients.

● Improvement: Use sand and compost for loosening, and stable manure and mineral fertilizers for fertilizing.

Peaty or marshy soils will have either a thin or thick layer of humus on top.

● Characteristics: As a rule, poor in nutrients, loose and easy for roots to penetrate when drained; not a good growing medium.

● Improvement: Add mineral fertilizers and lime.

Soil exchange: An exchange of soil is necessary if climbing plants are to be planted beside a wall where soil is often full of builders' rubble or is very compact (very difficult for roots to penetrate). In some cases, you may even have to remove flagstones, tiles, or similar coverings beforehand. Unwanted material like chunks of concrete, stone chippings, or coarse gravel, should be completely removed. The remaining soil should be improved with humus, fertilizer, and, depending on the type of soil, with loosening or binding substances.

Compost for plants in large containers and boxes

Plants which have to make do with small volumes of soil or compost must be supplied with compost that is adapted to their requirements.

Ripe garden compost is very rich in nutrients and very suitable for growing plants. It can be taken as waste matter from a kitchen garden or made from vegetable and plant kitchen scraps etc. in a compost heap in your own garden. You can buy special composting bins in garden centers.

Suitable growing mediums are also sold as ready-to-use products in garden centers etc.

Standard compost, which is sold in bags, usually consists of loamy soil and peat. Often, loosening substances like polystyrene fragments and fertilizer are mixed in with it so that this compost can be used for planting without further preparation.

Peat consists of the dead parts of marginal plants. Due to its very fibrous structure, peat acts as a loosening agent in compost and soil. It absorbs and stores water well and is contained in many commercial composts.

Despite this, environmentally aware gardeners are now recommended to avoid using peat as much as possible as producing it contributes to the destruction and loss of large areas of natural wetlands and moors.

Ordinary garden soil is rarely suitable for large containers. Depending on its consistency, soil-improving substances will probably have to be added to it.

Pruning

Climbing plants which can be bought in tree nurseries and are sold with roots but without soil around them, should be cut back

immediately before planting. The above-ground shoots should be cut back by about one-third of their length, and the roots by about ½-¾ in (1-2 cm).
Damaged roots or those that have obviously dried up should be cut back to where they look healthy. Thicker main roots (more than a finger-wide) should be left.
Container plants should not have their roots cut back and the shoots should be pruned only sparingly as plants with a properly covered rootstock should not suffer shock from being replanted.
Shrubs and annual climbing plants that are almost exclusively obtainable as container plants should not be cut back before planting.

The correct way to plant

The way a plant is planted affects the way it will grow. It is, therefore, particularly important to observe a few basic rules when planting in a well-prepared position so that the plant is sure to thrive.

Planting in open soil
When preparing a planting hole, you should check, even before buying the plant, that the soil is loose, easy for roots to penetrate and not too sandy. A small "trial hole" of about two spades' depth can be dug to check this point. If the soil is too stony or contains too much clay, you can buy the necessary improving substances at the same time as the plant. Exchanging the soil later on, after planting, is both difficult and usually harmful to the plant.
NB: The size of the planting hole depends on the size of the rootstock which should have enough room in the hole to expand. As a general rule, be guided by the standard dimensions of 24 by 24 by 24 in (60 by 60 by 60 cm).

Method
● Dig the planting hole.
● When digging, make sure that the darker soil on top is not mixed with the lighter soil underneath; if possible, pile them up separately.
● The bottom of the planting hole should be loosened up with a spade, shovel or a pick, to a depth of at least 8 in (20 cm).
● Carefully remove the plant from its container, stand it in the planting hole and check the position.
● Take the plant out again and place some of the lighter undersoil, mixed with soil-improvement substances or compost (mixing ratio 1:1), in the hole so that, when placed in the hole, the neck of the root of the plant will be level with the top edge of the hole.
● If the plants have been bought with the rootstock tied in a covering such as sacking, make sure you loosen the cloth at the neck and remove any tight twines. The cloth should remain around the roots as it will decay in time.
● Now, shovel in the rest of the dark topsoil, mixed with controlled-release fertilizer (hoof and horn chips or mineral fertilizer), making sure that you follow the manufacturer's directions. Place this around the plant and tread it down firmly.
● Use the remaining soil to create a shallow gulley around the plant for watering purposes.

Care after planting
● Water the plants well (about 1¼-2½ gallons/5-10 liters or more, depending on the size of the plant).
● Self-climbing plants should be trained toward the wall using the stick to which the young plant was tied when bought, in order to give the plant some hold.
● Remove the support sticks of plants with tendrils and winding plants and immediately tie the plant to the climbing aid which you have already installed.
● After watering, protect the planting area from drying out by mulching (using straw, grass cuttings, or bark mulch). This will also prevent the growth of weeds.

Planting directly beside a wall
If the planting area is right beside a house or garage wall that would be damaged by moisture or water splashes, the wall should be given a coat of insulating paint. If this cannot be done, a layer of gravel, approximately 16 in (40 cm) wide, should be laid between the wall and the planting area.

Drainage in a large container

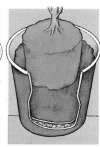

Place a 2-4-in (5-10-cm) thick layer of drainage material in the container. Lay filter fabric on top and draw it up to the inside edge of the container. Add the compost. Stand the plant in the container, shovel in compost between the pot and the rootstock, and press down firmly. Water well.

Spindleberry.

Clematis hybrid.

Honeysuckle.

You will require: gravel (⅔ in/16 mm in diameter) and filtering fabric.

Method

● To protect the wall, dig a trench 12-16 in (30-40 cm) wide and 8 in (20 cm) deep along it.
● Dig out the actual planting area adjacent to it (approx. 24 in/60 cm wide and 24 in/60 cm deep). Then treat the dug out soil in the same way as when planting in open soil.
● Fill the shallow pit along the wall with a layer of gravel.
● Lay the filtering fabric between the gravel and the planting area.
● Insert the plant and then fill up the planting area with soil.
NB: All work carried out outside the boundaries of your property will require permission from your local council or neighbor.

Planting in large containers and boxes

When choosing the height of the container, consider the eventual height of the plant and the size of its rootstock. The plant will need enough space for its roots to spread out and should not be squeezed into its container.
NB: To give protection against freezing in winter, an insulating liner should be placed in the container before inserting the drainage layer.
Drainage: To prevent waterlogging or a blockage of the drainage holes, before planting, larger containers should first be filled with a 2-4 in (5-10 cm) layer of gravel (of about ⅓-⅔ in/8-16 mm diameter) or with Hortag. Hortag is much lighter than gravel and is therefore ideal for large plant containers. Cover the

drainage holes with broken pieces of pot beforehand. Over the drainage layer spread a layer of fabric filter which should then be pulled up around the sides to the top edge of the container. This will prevent compost or soil being washed down the sides of the fabric and into the drainage layer.
Planting
● After planting, carefully water the plant but do not flood it.
● It is better to water several times sparingly on a daily basis.
● If the planting medium has sunk down a little after a few days, top up the container with extra compost and form a watering gulley.
● Do not fertilize plants bought in garden centers until about six weeks after planting, as they will already have been provided with controlled-release fertilizer.

Morning glory and ornamental gourd.

Russian vine.

Climbing rose.

Plants from other sources can have controlled-release fertilizer mixed in with their compost. Once you have done this, do not fertilize again for another four weeks.
Balcony boxes with summer flowers planted in them will not require a drainage layer as they are not very deep. They should, however, still have drainage holes which should be covered with fragments of broken pot.
● An ordinary balcony box that is only 4¾ in (12 cm) wide, 6 in (15 cm) deep will be too small for perennial climbing plants. They require containers with a capacity of 7½-10 gallons (30-40 liters).
● Annual climbing plants, on the other hand, will manage in standard-size balcony boxes as long as they are given the right amount of water and fertilizer.

● Adequate protection from frost will also be necessary for balcony boxes if the plants are expected to overwinter in them.

Planting annual climbing plants
Annuals that are pre-grown in pots or large containers often have a headstart with respect to growth but, having begun life in a greenhouse, are also often more sensitive than hardened, home-grown plants.
Sowing and raising: The seed of many climbing plants can be bought or collected and sown in pots (larger seeds) or seed trays. The seed compost in the seed tray should be moistened slightly (use a spray bottle) and the tray should be covered with a transparent lid or plastic wrap. Also cover pots with plastic wrap.

From time to time, lift the film or lid for ventilation.
Pots or seed trays should be placed in a warm, light but not too bright spot; the seeds require a temperature of about 68°F (20°C) to germinate. During this time, keep the surface of the seed compost slightly moist. The germinating seeds are usually too densely packed in a tray to develop fully. The tiny plantlets have to be thinned out to provide more space when two germ leaves are fully developed. The space between rows should be 4 in (10 cm) and the spaces between individual plants 2 in (5 cm).
Sowing in open soil: You can obtain the seeds of many annual climbing plants from garden centers. These can be sown straight into open soil.

Particularly robust species, like scarlet runner beans, nasturtiums, and convolvulus, are well suited to this method:

● Soak larger seeds in lukewarm water overnight to speed up germination.

● Make a 2-in (5-cm) deep drill in loose garden soil (for several plants growing beside each other) or a 2-in (5-cm) deep hole for each seed (check the directions for depth on the package).

● Lay the seeds in the hole (if there are several, ensure correct spacing which should be indicated on the package, probably three to five seeds) and cover them with soil.

● The seeds will germinate sooner if you lay a piece of plastic sheeting over the planting area, weighted down with stones around the edges. When the seedlings appear, the sheet can be removed or raised on wooden or wire sticks so that the plants have room to grow. It is advisable not to plant seeds before the last cold snap toward the middle of the last month of spring as the young plants will not cope with frost.

Planting in open soil: Annual climbing plants have very special soil requirements because of their rapid growth and they also require a good supply of nutrients. The hole should be dug as described. However, a hole with a depth of 12 in (30 cm) will be sufficient.

Planting in large containers and boxes: If your home-grown or bought annual climbing plants are to be planted in a large container or balcony box, proceed as for planting in large containers.

Sowing seed in a seed tray and pricking out
Sow the seed evenly, using a folded piece of paper. Cover the seed tray with plastic wrap. Loosen the seedlings from the growing medium with the thin end of a pricking-out tool. Make a hole with the thick end of the pricking-out tool and plant the seedling deep enough for the first leaves to lie on the surface of the growing medium. Press down lightly.

Care

If you know what a plant's requirements are, you can ensure that it has the best possible care. Every plant has to be supplied with an adequate amount of water and nutrients. There are also other measures of care to attend to for climbing plants, such as tying up shoots, the occasional pruning, and, if necessary, providing protection against cold and frost. Plants which are not growing in open soil, but are planted in large containers or boxes, are particularly dependent on regular and sometimes intensive care.

Watering

Water is essential for all plants. The amount of water that plants lose daily through evaporation from their leaves depends on the temperature on that day, the humidity, and the amount of direct sunlight. The following rule applies: the cooler the day and the higher the humidity, the less water the plants will require.
NB: Do not water plants during midday or in intense direct sunlight.
Plants in open soil need not be watered quite as often as plants in large containers or boxes on account of their widely spreading root systems.

● It is important that you water thoroughly so that even the deepest roots are adequately supplied with moisture.

● Young or recently planted plants need more frequent watering. For the rest, it will be sufficient to water every eight to ten days during the main growth period (from the second month of spring to the second month of fall).

● Annual climbing plants that are situated in a sunny position should be watered more often.

● During the winter, water evergreen climbing plants like ivy only occasionally and only on frost-free days.
Plants in large containers and boxes, which contain relatively little compost, will use up water rapidly.
How often you water will depend on the individual requirements of plants, the size of the planting container, and on the weather. The basic rule is:

● Plants in pots should be watered more often than those growing in open soil.

- Large, vigorously growing plants in pots require more frequent watering as the supply of water in the rootstock will be used up more quickly.
- On hot summer days, water plants growing on a patio or balcony twice daily, preferably in the morning and evening.
- Consider what type of containers the plants are in: water will not evaporate quite so quickly from plastic containers as from clay containers.
- You can usually tell by looking at the leaves whether plants need water: if they are drooping or the leaves are rolled up, they are in desperate need of water.

The "finger test" will determine whether a plant is thirsty. Push a finger about ½ in (1 cm) deep into the top of the compost. If it feels damp, you will not need to water that day; if it feels dry, water well.

Rainwater is still to be recommended for watering, despite the increase in pollution, and is still better for plants than hard, lime-rich main water. Main water should be left to stand for a few days before using it.

Watering during holidays: Watering large container or balcony plants can be a problem if you are to be away from home for any length of time. Irrigation systems are sold in garden centers but you should always test these thoroughly before you go away to make sure that they work properly. If you are going away for a brief vacation, you should be able to manage by using plant containers with inbuilt water reservoirs. The most reliable "system," however, is still a friend or accommodating neighbor who will follow your written instructions!

My tip: Watering balcony boxes that are attached to the outside of a balcony railing may cause inconvenience to neighbors with balconies under yours. If you do not have very tolerant neighbors below you, it is better to hang the boxes on the inside of the railing.

Fertilizing

Plants require certain nutrients for growth and well-being. Particularly during the vegetative period, while the plant is growing and flowering, it should be provided with sufficient nutrients. Nutrients that are lacking in the soil or compost must be replaced and this is done by fertilizing. Some species like a lot of fertilizer, such as scarlet runner beans or ornamental gourds, while other, less demanding, plants, such as wild forms of clematis and ivy, manage on very little.

The frequency of fertilizing during the growth period depends on the individual plant species and is described in the instructions for care.

Types of fertilizer: Fertilizers are available in solid, dried or liquid form.
- Liquid fertilizers do not need to be dissolved in water first and are particularly suitable for plants in large containers or on balconies.
- Solid fertilizers are mixed with the soil or compost and will gradually release nutrients to the plant as these nutrients must first be broken down through the action of water.

The nutrient composition of fertilizers: In addition to the three main nutrients of nitrogen (N), phosphorus (P), and potassium (K), plants also need lesser quantities of trace elements like magnesium, iron, sulphur, copper, boron, and manganese.

- Nitrogen supports the upward growth of plants and the development of leaves. Nitrogen deficiency is recognizable by yellow leaves and stunted growth.
- Phosphorus is necessary for the formation of roots, flowers, and fruit.
- Potassium builds up the plant's resistance to disease and pests.

Compound fertilizer (mineral and inorganic fertilizer) contains all of the main nutrients. However, the nutrient composition is not the same for all fertilizers. The proportions of main nutrients in any fertilizer are always expressed as the abbreviation N P K, and given as a ratio in that order on the outside of the packaging. Thus, 7:7:7 means equal proportions of nitrogen, phosphorus and potassium are included, each nutrient comprising 7 percent of the total content.

NB: 2 tablespoons (20 g) mineral fertilizer per 40 sq in (1 sq m) is enough.

Types of fertilizer
- Mineral fertilizers or inorganic fertilizers contain nutrients in the form of soluble salts. When given to the plant as granules, they are dissolved by water and washed down among the roots. Controlled-release fertilizer contains nutrients in the form of small beads which release the nutrients very gradually aided by the action of moisture.
- Organic (or biological) fertilizers consist of animal products like ground hoof and horn, horn chips, dried blood, animal dung, or plant extracts. This type of fertilizer often provides only one nutrient: animal manure and horn chips, for example, provide nitrogen; bonemeal provides phosphorus. Organic fertilizers are generally not compound fertilizers and it takes a relatively long time for the nutrients to become effective.

An attractive visual screen – a wire fence covered with ivy and Virginia creeper.

How often to fertilize

Plants growing in open soil need not be fertilized quite so often as plants in large containers or boxes, as they can draw on a natural reservoir of soil nutrients. Large container plants and balcony plants have to be supplied with fertilizer on a regular basis in order to balance the disadvantages created by their positions.

● One or two doses of fertilizer will be sufficient for perennial climbing plants during the vegetation period.

● Annual climbing plants that are growing in open soil require regular fertilizing at intervals of about four to six weeks over their short growing period.

● A weekly dose of fertilizer is recommended for plants in smaller containers or pots; fertilizing every two weeks will be sufficient for larger containers (from 12-16 in/30-40 cm high).

● Large container plants should not be fertilized after the end of summer so that they can prepare themselves for winter.

As a basic fertilizer for woody plants: mix the main nutrients NPK (ratio 10:10:15) with the planting medium if you are not using compost that already contains fertilizer.

Plants sold with a rootstock, or container plants, will welcome a starter boost from an organic fertilizer. Plants in pots should be fertilized again about six to eight weeks after planting. Plants in open soil should be fertilized about two to three months after planting.

The right way to fertilize

● Only provide fertilizer if the plant is able to absorb nutrients; that is, during the growth phase from spring to fall.
● Always read the manufacturer's directions regarding dosage.
● Never strew the fertilizer on dry soil or compost as the roots would soon suffer burns from such a high concentration of nutrients.
● Always mix controlled-release fertilizer with the soil or compost.

Mistakes in fertilizing

● Signs of a lack of fertilizer: Meager growth, lack of flowers, light-colored or discolored leaves. An immediate dose of compound fertilizer will help, preferably in liquid form.
● Signs of an excess of fertilizer: Brown spots on leaves or burned edges to leaves, unnaturally long shoots, very large, limp leaves. Remedy: In the case of potted plants, thoroughly drench the area of the roots in running water. This is best done in a bath. Do not water the plant again for about three days. In the case of plants growing in open soil, all you can do is water very thoroughly.

Tying up

It is sometimes necessary to tie parts of climbing plants to a support as, occasionally, the plants will not manage to find the support provided on their own or will simply send their shoots out in another direction.

Even self-climbers like ivy or Virginia creeper are grateful for initial help in training them toward a wall or fence.

Ramblers, like climbing roses, will need to have their new shoots tied up regularly.

In the case of espalier fruit, tying up is very important as it serves to anchor the new growth, determines the direction in which the plant will continue to grow and stimulate fruit production.

Plant-friendly tying materials

include garden twine, hemp string, or rope and rubberized wire.
NB: When tying up plants, give consideration to the potential thickness of the shoots; the tie should not be too tight around the shoot as this will interfere with transportation of water and nutrients and the outer skin of the shoot may be rubbed raw or damaged. The best way to proceed is to make a loose loop around the shoot, tie a second loop around the support stick etc., and then finish off this loop with a knot, making a figure of eight.

Pruning

Generally speaking, climbing plants do not require much pruning but will cope with it quite well as a rule. Otherwise, only frost-damaged shoots need cutting back to green, healthy wood in the spring.

Winter protection

By late fall sufficient winter protection should be provided against severe frost. The first step toward this is made by choosing hardy plants in the first place and then planting them in the right position, for example somewhere sheltered.

Frost protection in open soil:

It is mainly young plants that are at risk here but roses and warmth-loving climbing plants will also be very grateful for some form of protection when the temperature drops below zero.

How to protect your plants

● Heaping up soil around the stem, to a height of 8-12 in (20-30 cm), and covering this with brushwood, straw, or conifer branches (also to a height of 8-12 in/20-30 cm) will protect the plants from freezing to death.
● Climbing roses or more sensitive climbing plants like wisteria can also be wrapped in bundles of straw or brushwood along the length of their longer shoots.
● In the case of evergreen climbing plants, frost damage can be avoided by watering the plants during the fall and on frost-free days in winter. Lack of water will increase susceptibility to damage.

Frost protection for plant containers:

If you wish to overwinter perennial climbers in large containers on a balcony or patio, you will have to provide adequate insulation of the containers against frost.

Method

● Before planting or inserting a drainage layer, line the inside walls of the container with ¼-½-in (5-10-mm) thick polystyrene sheeting. The drainage layer will protect the floor of the container against freezing.
● If the container is round, draw the filter fabric up to about 2 in (5 cm) below the upper edge of the container and insert a ½-¾-in (1-2-cm) layer of coarse sand or grit between the wall of the container and the layer of fabric.
● Always choose containers that are frost-proof for overwintering outside.
● Cover plants in large containers with brushwood or straw.
NB: Large container plants, for example oleander or fuchsia, cannot be overwintered outside and will require particular conditions in their winter quarters, so it is important to find out about any such requirements before you purchase sensitive plants in order to avoid disappointment later.

Fruit espaliers

One of the reasons why espaliers are so popular is their dual blessing of attractive foliage and a harvest of fruit. Espalier fruit trees bear enchanting blossoms and you can also fulfil your ambition of picking fresh pears, apples, peaches, or apricots straight from your own house wall. Some most decorative forms of espalier can be created, even by novice gardeners.

Points to note about fruit espaliers

The difference between espalier fruit trees and fruit trees grown in open soil is that an artificial shape of growth is produced by tying up and judicious pruning. This makes it possible to produce tasty, fully ripened fruit in a small space, for example on a house or garage wall.

Growing aids for espaliers

There are various different possibilities for growing espalier fruit on a wall. All methods involve directing the shoots into the desired shape by fixing them to a growing aid. The following are suitable growing aids:
● Wooden frames made of sticks.
● Horizontally and/or vertically stretched wires (depending on the shape of the espalier) which have to be fixed to the wall with the aid of dowelled wall hooks.
● Horizontal wires drawn tautly between two wooden posts which are about 3-4 in (8-10 cm) thick. At each end of the planting area you should drive the wooden posts into the soil slightly at an angle and at least 28 in (70 cm) deep. Depending on the height of the espalier, the posts may protrude up to 7 ft (2 m) above the soil.
NB: All growing aids should be a minimum distance of 4-12 in (10-30 cm) from the house wall (see p. 11) and should be erected and fixed to the wall before planting.

Shapes of espaliers

These fruit-bearing woody plants can be used to enhance a façade in many different forms. Both stems and branches can be trained into geometric shapes. The average height of growth of individual plants is important in determining the final shape of the espalier; vigorously growing varieties, such as pears, for example, can be trained to cover an entire house wall with greenery.
The most commonly seen espalier shapes are:
● A cordon which is the simplest espalier shape. It consists of a vertical stem or trunk without any lateral branches and is, therefore, very suitable for narrow spaces, for example between a door and a window. The distance between two such trees should be no less than 20-24 in (50-60 cm); only plant varieties with similar speeds of growth beside each other.
● A U-shape, which forms a "double" cordon without a continuous main shoot. The space between individual branches should be 24-32 in (60-80 cm).
● A palmette with a broad fan shape and much branching; this is particularly suitable for vigorously growing varieties in larger areas.

● A high espalier, for which a long, vertical stem is first grown and lateral branching is allowed to begin at a certain height (for example around windows on the ground floor). This shape may grow right up to the gable of a house and is often used for vigorously growing pear trees.
NB: When choosing the shape of an espalier you must always consider the speed and final extent of growth of the fruit tree.

Suitable fruit species

Species suitable for planting as espaliers are: apples, pears, peaches, apricots, and grapevines. Growing fruit against a house wall in this way brings the benefit of extra warmth, so that, even in regions with a rougher climate, gardeners can still grow their own fruit.

Planting and care of espalier fruit trees

Fruit grown on espaliers requires more intensive care than that given to perennial climbing plants in open soil: in addition to fertilizing and watering, careful pruning and regular tying up are essential if you want to obtain a worthwhile harvest.

The best position

Fruit growing requires special climatic conditions. Before you decide on the varieties you intend to buy, do make a realistic assessment of your normal climate and temperature. If you give this information to the nursery from which you are ordering plants, their expert staff will be able to advise you if your choice is unsuitable and suggest alternatives.

A house wall that you intend to use for growing espalier fruit should meet the following requirements:

● The wall should be situated in a sheltered position, as draughts will prevent the plant from benefiting from accumulated warmth.

● It should be well ventilated; that is, there must be adequate space between the wall and the espalier.

● The more sun that reaches the wall, the more demanding the types of fruit you can try to grow on it.

The best side of the house for establishing an espalier is the south-facing one. Even in unfavorable regions (high altitude, areas affected by late frosts), you can often plant particularly warmth-loving varieties of fruit, such as peaches, apricots, or late-ripening varieties, against a south-facing wall.

Planting them too close together may cause the plants to be harmed by temperatures that become too high. Insufficient ventilation between the wall and the espalier will encourage fungal infection, such as mildew, in many fruit varieties.

NB: Many house walls are not adequately protected against the water splashes and rising damp that may penetrate from the adjoining planting area.

The right soil

In many cases, the soil immediately in front of a wall is not suitable for growing espalier fruit unless it has been adequately prepared beforehand. Large items such as tiles, flagstones, asphalt, etc., will have to be removed before planting and the soil underneath must be replaced with suitable soil. The length of the planting hole will depend on the desired width of the espalier, but the minimum depth and width of the hole should not be less than 40 in (1 m).

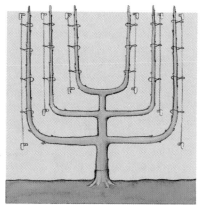

Palmette
This shape can be created with four, six, or more arms. Never choose an uneven number of branches for this palmette as the tree will look unbalanced.

As a rule, *fruit trees* prefer a warm, permeable, crumbly, moist soil. In addition to these characteristics, the right nutrient content is also of great importance . Pure humus soils or garden soils are usually deficient in minerals. By mixing in the right fertilizers, both the nutrient content and the mineral content can be improved.
NB: Information on the soil requirements of popular espalier fruits can be found on pages 56-59.

The correct way to plant

Espalier fruit should be pruned immediately before planting, when all branches should be cut back by about one-third of their length. Before planting, also cut back the fine roots slightly, thereby encouraging renewed root formation. When planting espalier fruit, you should note the following points:

● Soak the rootstock of the young tree in a bucket before planting.

A U-shaped fruit espalier

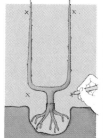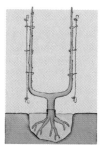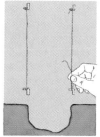

Stand the espalier tree in the planting hole and mark the positions for the wall hooks on the wall. Take the tree out, fix the hooks to the wall, and draw wires between them (corresponding to the shape of the espalier). Insert the tree in the hole. Tie the little tree to the growing aid. Check the ties from time to time to make sure they are not too tight or loose.

Planting trees

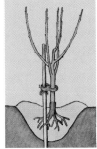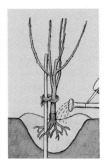

Stand the young tree in the prepared planting hole. Fill the hole with soil and tie the tree to a wooden support stick. The grafting point should end up about a hand span above the soil. Make a gulley for watering and water the young tree well.

● Dig out the planting hole, loosen the soil well, and fill the hole again, to about two-thirds, with soil.

● Drive a wooden stake into the soil as a support for the young tree (diameter 3-5 in/8-10 cm).

● Stand the young tree in the planting hole, shovel in the rest of the soil, and tread it down firmly all around the tree.

● The grafting point (recognizable as a lump at the lower end of the stem) must remain above the soil or roots will start forming from it that will grow into unwelcome wild shoots which will draw energy and nutrients from the grafted fruit variety.

● Tie the young tree to the support stake using a figure of eight loop made of coconut fiber or hemp twine, and then nail the tie to the post so it cannot slip down.

● Leave a gulley for watering around the tree and water well.

● Tie the shoots of the young tree to the growing aid in the desired shape.

Fertilizing espalier fruit
A soil containing a balanced ratio of organic and mineral nutrients is an important precondition for the healthy development of an espalier tree.

Nitrogen will encourage the roots to develop and shoots to grow. If too much nitrogen is supplied, however, the trees will become susceptible to disease and the fruit will rapidly decay.

Phosphorus encourages the formation of fruit and the ripening process and ensures a good flavor.

Potassium strengthens the plant and is important for good wood and fruit formation.

How often to fertilize
Fertilizer mixed in with the soil at the time of planting will last for the first year. Well-established espalier fruit trees should be fertilized two or three times a year; the best times are in the spring when the plant starts growing again and after the harvest, around the time when the wood ripens, to encourage resistance against frost.

Espalier fruit trees like fertilizer such as:
● well-rotted manure
● compound fertilizer
● garden compost that is mixed with organic fertilizer.

● In addition to compost or compound fertilizer, you should also give the plants fermented plant brews in the spring and fall. A combination of fermented nettle and borage brew acts as both a fertilizer and an effective plant protection agent.

NB: Avoid unripened, fresh manure as this can burn the roots.

Water sparingly, but regularly
The area around the plant should be kept fairly moist, although fruit trees do not like "wet feet." Waterlogging in the area of the roots may cause fruit trees to die off.

NB: When fruit espaliers are grown against very sunny walls, you may have to water twice on very hot summer days.

A short-term period of dryness will not damage espalier fruit unduly.

Tying espaliers
Tying performs several functions in the case of espalier fruit. It serves to:
● fasten the shoots to the climbing aid
● train the shoots in the desired direction of growth
● encourage fruit formation.

Tying horizontally encourages the food made by the leaves through photosynthesis to be stored in the flower buds and thereby aids fruit formation. (Vertical shoots tend to produce leaves rather than buds.)

When trained horizontally, espaliers require less pruning as fewer vertical shoots are formed. The general rule is to cut less and tie up more.

How to train for horizontal growth:
Humidity makes wood more

flexible, so the best time to tie up branches is in the morning or evening.

● Persuading the first branches of a young fruit tree to grow in a horizontal plane without breaking is made easier by hanging small metal tags or clay pots on them (tied on with twine around the middle of the branch). The branches will gradually be pulled down by the weight.

● Suitable materials for tying are garden twine, hemp string, package string, or even coconut fiber rope for larger branches.

● The branches should be tied to the growing frame by means of loose figure-of-eight loops.

NB: The branches should not end up drooping downward but should be more or less horizontal.

Grafting fruit varieties

As a rule, espalier fruit trees are grafted onto the stock of another fruit tree, sometimes even on-to another fruit species. Grafting makes it possible to combine very different qualities of two varieties of fruit, for example combining a good yield with hardiness to frost or resistance against fungal infections and a prolific formation of fruit or larger fruit. The grafting point is generally thicker than the rest of the stem on account of the extra tissue that has formed at the point of cutting. It may be either directly above the neck of the root or (in the case of quince or cherry) on the upper end of the stem just below the branches. The grafting of fruit varieties is carried out in specialist nurseries. If you wish to know more about it, you can obtain information from your local gardening society or plant nursery.

A vigorous stock grown from a seedling has the following advantages: it is robust and undemanding; it is suitable for positions where the soil quality is not very good or the climate is rough; it is recommended for wall espaliers, especially high ones.

A less vigorously growing stock is better suited to smaller areas, for example between windows.

NB: Before buying any fruit tree for training into an espalier, you should find out from the nursery whether the stock and the espalier shape you are planning to grow are suited to each other.

Pruning espalier fruit trees

It is not possible within the limited scope of this book to cover the various methods of pruning in great detail and you would be well advised to consult other, specialist literature on this subject (inquire at your local library or garden center). I have, however, included a few basic pieces of information.

When to prune

There are many different opinions on this matter. However, the following basic rule can be applied: *The main time for pruning is in early spring* when the tree has hardly any foliage. At any other time severe pruning carries a risk

Thinning out cut
The old and infertile shoots are removed (see marked cutting points, left) so that light and air will be able to penetrate the crown.

of the tree being badly debilitated or even killed through loss of sap. Spring pruning can include removing branches and shoot tips that died during the winter. Pruning is also simpler at this time as the fruit and leaf buds are better formed and therefore more easily seen.

General rule: Fruit buds are usually larger than leaf buds. If you cannot distinguish them, ask an expert to identify them for you the first time or else simply decide for yourself and wait to see what appears when the bud opens.

Fall is also a time for pruning espalier fruit trees. Do not do this too early, however, as the trees will still be producing too much sap and the wood will not have matured. Ripe wood will survive the winter better. (A sign of ripened wood is when the leaves start to discolor and finally fall off.)

My tip: Prune your trees again after the harvest is over as this will strengthen them.

For pruning you will need a strong pair of secateurs, a wound-sealing substance, a small saw, and a sharp, preferably slightly curved, knife.

NB: The secateurs should be your main tool when pruning. If you have to start sawing away, it usually indicates that you have previously neglected a few necessary duties. Remember that it is better to prune more often and cut away less each time.

Tips on pruning
● Mark the branches with colored wax crayon before cutting as this will help you to take off the right branches.

● Cut the branches off straight, using secateurs. Any ragged or frayed cuts should be cut cleanly with a sharp knife afterwards.

● Cut surfaces that are larger than 1¼ in (3 cm) in diameter should be treated with a wound-sealing substance to encourage growth of new tissue and to prevent the secretion of sap.
● If a large branch is cut right beside the main stem or taken from the crown, make sure that no stumps remain to create a risk of invasion by fungal infection.

Training cut

This can be used to give your espalier tree the right shape of crown during its first year, as this will be determined by the main shoots. As the espalier is basically a flattened shape, you should let only lateral branches remain as main shoots in order to create the correct shape; all other shoots should be cut back to the stem and the cut surfaces treated with a wound sealant. Weaker shoots and those that tend to the vertical should be removed during the training cut. Only the main shoots which will produce the branches that will bear the fruit should be left.

A thinning-out cut

A thinning-out cut should be undertaken in fruit trees for the following reasons:
● To provide the crown with sufficient light and ventilation.
● To maintain a balance between growth and fertility in the tree.

Pests and diseases

Plants die more often as a result of poor care than from diseases or attack by pests. Correct care is the best preventive measure against diseases and pests. When treating sick plants, avoid the thoughtless use of toxic spray in your garden. Very often biological plant protection agents will do the job and they are also kinder toward both plants and the environment.

Damage through the wrong kind of care

This can occur in all plants that are not cared for properly.

Waterlogging
Symptoms: Limp, faded shoots and leaves, often yellow discoloration. Damp soil or compost in large containers. Root tips are brown to black, decayed on the inside (check by pinching the root; healthy roots are light-colored inside).
Cause: Too much watering or too often; absent or blocked drainage holes; no drainage; impermeable growth medium.
Prevention: Water carefully, provide an adequate number of drainage holes and a good drainage layer as well as loose, permeable compost or soil (mix in sand or grit).
Remedy: None.

Drying out
Symptoms: drooping, yellow leaves that dry up at the edges and roll up. Flowers fade and drop off prematurely. The roots turn brown.
Cause: Not enough water on hot

or very windy days; a position that is too hot and sunny.
Prevention: Water more frequently during hot periods. Mix substances that store water with the soil or compost (for example, loamy soil or humus).
Remedy: Stand the rootstock in a container of tepid water for several hours. If damage is severe, nothing will help.

Nutrient deficiency
Symptoms: Nitrogen deficiency: pale leaves; meagre growth. *Phosphorus deficiency*: bluish-violet leaves. *Potassium deficiency*: weak shoots; brown leaf edges that roll up later on. *Magnesium deficiency:* leaves are yellow to brown with clearly marked leaf veins. *Iron deficiency* (chlorosis): leaves are yellow, leaf veins conspicuous.
Causes: The compost or soil contains too much lime (this prevents adequate absorption of nutrients); soil or compost is too compact or hard; not enough fertilizer.

Prevention: Loosen the soil once a month using a rake; water with rainwater; proper fertilizing.
Remedy: Provide the missing minerals. Remove the top layer of soil and replace it with a new layer containing mineral fertilizer.

Clematis wilt
Symptoms: Sudden death of healthy shoots.
Infested plants: Clematis hybrids; wild species are not so susceptible.
Prevention: Ensure adequate moisture during the growth period.
Remedy: None known at present.

Fungal diseases

Black spot
Symptoms: Small, blackish, round spots on leaves which die off after a while.
Infested plants: Often roses.
Prevention: Remove damaged leaves. Spray with mare's tail brew, repeat at intervals of several days.
Remedy: Spray, preferably with a biological preparation, repeat after two weeks.

Pear rust
Symptoms: Orange-yellow spots (like rust spots) on leaves.
Infested plants: Pear trees.
Prevention: Ornamental juniper is an intermediate host for the fungus, so avoid ornamental juniper trees in gardens where pear trees are grown.
Remedy: Spray the pear trees, preferably with a biological preparation, repeat in two weeks.

Powdery mildew
Symptoms: a flour-like, white film on leaves and young parts of plants. Powdery mildew will also occur in dry weather.

This pear espalier has been growing here for many years.

Infested plants: Fruit trees, grapevines, roses, cucumbers. Powdery mildew will only be transmitted between plants of the same species.
Prevention: Ensure a well-ventilated position; spray several times with mare's tail brew at intervals of a few days.
Remedy: Spray with preparations containing dinocap.

Downy mildew
Symptoms: whitish-yellow fungus spots on uppersides of leaves; a white fungus film on undersides of leaves. Occurs mainly in wet summers.
Infested plants: Roses, grapevine.
Prevention: A well-ventilated position. Spray with mare's tail brew at intervals of six weeks.
Remedy: Spray, preferably with a biological preparation (ask at your garden center), repeat again after 10-14 days.

Trumpet vine is a fast-growing climbing plant.

Pests

Aphids
Symptoms: Black or green aphids on shoots and buds. Damage caused through sucking sap visible on leaves, stalks, and branches and can cause them to wilt and die. Rolled-up leaves. Infested plants: Roses, fruit trees, annual climbing plants, honeysuckle.
Prevention: Ensure a balanced nutrient supply as overfertilized plants are particularly susceptible to infestation by aphids. Fermented or fresh nettle brew will strengthen the plant's resistance.
Control: Spray with tansy brew, repeat every few days; spray with agents containing pyrethrum.

Spider mites
Symptoms: The plants look limp, the leaves dry up and drop off. Small white spots on the leaves, gossamer-fine webs underneath.
Infested plants: Nasturtiums, honeysuckle, clematis hybrids, climbing roses, grapevine.
Prevention: Spray with nettle and mare's tail brew.
Control: Spray with an agent containing pyrethrum.

Codling moth and sawfly larvae (in apples)
Symptoms: To begin with, tiny eggs on the fruit, later holes in the fruit flesh and core; red-brown excrement at the entrances.
Infested plants: Apple trees.
Prevention: Remove all windfalls. Spray with tansy brew.
Control: Employ agents containing pyrethrum.

Scale insects
Symptoms: Light to dark brown scales stuck firmly to leaf undersides and leaf stalks. Damage caused by the sucking of sap from branches and stems.
Infested plants: Fruit trees, roses.
Prevention: Spray with tar-oil winter wash or tansy brew, repeating in several days.
Control: Brush down stems; spray with tar-oil.

Biological plant protection

Plant brews can be sprayed as a preventive and to protect against pests and fungal infections. Fermented plant brews are used as additional fertilizer to mineral and organic fertilizers, to strengthen and fortify plants.

Passionflower is a spendid flowering climber.

Plant brews

Preparation: 2¼ pounds (1 kg) fresh, coarsely chopped leaves or 7 ounces (200 g) dried leaves in 2½ gallons (10 liters) cold water. Leave to soak for 24 hours, then boil for 30 minutes. Let cool, remove scum, and use up quickly. Dilute the brew with water in the ratio of 1:2. This method can be used to prepare the following protective and fortifying brews:

Nettle brew has a strengthening and fortifying effect and is good for controlling aphids.

Tansy brew for controlling all kinds of insects (aphids, insect and moth larvae), leaf spot disease, and mildew.

Mare's tail brew for controlling spider mites and mildew.

Fern brew (made from *Dryopteris*), undiluted: use as a prevention against scale insects.

Fermented herbal brews

Preparation: 2¼ pounds (1 kg) fresh, coarsely chopped leaves or 7 ounces (200 g) dried leaves in 2½ gallons (10 liters) cold water (preferably water that has been left to stand or, better still, rainwater). Leave the brew to stand in the sun (in a wooden or plastic container, never in a metal container). Fermentation will begin after two or three days. Stir thoroughly once daily. A fairly bad smell will be produced. The fermented brew will be ready to use after two or three weeks. Remove the scum, dilute the fermented brew with nine parts water and water the plants. This recipe can be used to prepare the following fermented plant brews:

Fermented nettle brew promotes resistance to disease, contains nitrogen and has a soil-balancing effect.

Fermented borage or comfrey brew contains large amounts of nitrogen and potassium. It is good for vigorously growing plants with lots of flowers.

Biological plant protection agents

Several such preparations can be bought from garden centers. They consist of herbal extracts, algae additives, or pure chemical elements like sulphur or boron. The substances contained in these preparations can be present singly or mixed together. They are used mainly as brews for spraying.

Always follow the manufacturer's directions when using them as some biological plant protection agents, for example pyrethrum, are toxic.

Pyrethrum agents contain pyrethrum which is obtained from a species of chrysanthemum. It is used to control aphids and mildew. It is not dangerous to bees.

Sulphur and dinocap preparations are used to control fungal infections.

Other herbal extracts, usually combined with sulphur or dinocap, can be used for controlling pear rust, mildew and scale insects.

NB: Never spray plant extracts in bright sunshine as they may cause the leaves to burn. Preferably spray under a cloudy sky, in mornings or evenings.

Warning: Children and domestic pets should be kept away when any such products are being sprayed.

Popular climbing plants and espalier fruit trees

The following pages present a selection of profusely flowering, easy-to-care-for climbing plants and varieties of espalier fruit, with photographs, descriptions, and special notes on the correct care of each plant.

Glossary of keywords

The first name is the common name, which is followed by the botanical name (genus and species). The introduction gives details of the plant's climbing technique, its appearance, shape of growth, and any individual characteristics.

Origin: An important clue to the correct care of the plant.

Flower/fruit: The main flowering time as well as details of flowers and the formation of fruit.

Position: Information on requirements in respect of temperature, wind, amount of sunlight, and the right side of the house.

Soil: Advice on soil consistency in the open and for compost in containers.

Water: Tips on proper watering.

Fertilizing: Information on how often to fertilize and what to use.

Further care: Special tips on care and details on climbing aids (if necessary).

Diseases/pests: Only given if the plant is particularly susceptible to certain diseases or pests.

Overwintering: Only for plants that can be grown in a large container.

Use: Only given if the plant is particularly suited to a certain manner of climbing/covering.

My tip: Extra tried and tested tips on care.

Key to symbols

 Position for the plant: south-facing, sunny.

 Position for the plant: west- and/or east-facing, semi-shady.

 Position for the plant: north-facing side, shady.

 This plant is also suitable for a large container.

 This plant is toxic.

An arbor with clematis
Arbors covered in greenery create a tranquil atmosphere.

List of plants

Annual climbing plants

Annual plants can be bought in the form of seeds for sowing at home or in pots (seedlings, young plants).
black-eyed Susan (*Thunbergia alata*)
cathedral bell (*Cobaea scandens*)
convolvulus (*Convolvulus sepium*)
cucumber (*Cucumis sativus*)
morning glory (*Ipomoea tricolor*)
nasturtium (*Tropaeolum*)
ornamental gourd (*Cucurbita pepo var. ovifera*)
scarlet runner bean (*Phaseolus coccineus*)
sweet pea (*Lathyrus odoratus*)

Perennial climbing plants

Perennial plants can be bought pre-grown from garden centers.
clematis (*Clematis*)
Dutchman's pipe (*Aristolochia macrophylla*)
grapevine (*Vitis vinifera*)
honeysuckle (*Lonicera*)
hop (*Humulus lupulus*)
ivy (*Hedera helix*)
kiwi fruit (*Actinidia chinensis*)
roses (*Rosa*)
Russian vine (*Polygonum baldschaunica*)
spindleberry (*Euonymus fortunei*)
Virginia creeper (*Parthenocissus*)
winter jasmine (*Jasminum nudiflorum*)
wisteria (*Wisteria sinensis*)

Espalier fruit tree species

Espalier fruit trees can be bought as young trees in tree nurseries
apple (*Malus domestica*)
apricot (*Prunus armeniaca*)
peach (*Prunus persica*)
pear (*Pyrus communis*)

Black-eyed Susan is ideal for balcony boxes.

Cathedral bell is a tireless bloomer.

Black-eyed Susan
Thunbergia alata

This annual winding plant, with heart-shaped, long-stalked, dark green leaves, will grow up to 7 ft (2 m) tall. It is a pretty, delicate summer-flowering plant.
Origin: Southeast Africa, Madagascar.
Flower/fruit: Midsummer to mid-fall, funnel-shaped, yellow to orange single flowers with a dark center, 2 in (5 cm) across. Fruit: Pea-sized, winged capsule with four seeds.
Position: Warm, sunny and sheltered from wind, south-facing.
Soil: Rich in nutrients and humus, standard compost in large container, loose growing medium.
Water: Water regularly but avoid waterlogging.
Fertilizing: In a large container and in open soil, every two weeks with liquid fertilizer; nettle brew also suitable.
Further care: Use twine or a stick as a climbing aid. Tie the shoots to begin with. Pinching out shoot tips once will encourage the plant to branch out. Spacing of plants 24-32 in (60-80 cm).

Cathedral bell, cup and saucer vine
Cobaea scandens

This graceful annual grows up to 13 ft (4 m) tall. Its leaves are feathered and reddish when shooting. The leaf ends have been adapted into tendrils.
Origin: Mexico.
Flower/fruit: Flowers from midsummer to the first frost. Bell-like flower, first whitish-green, later violet. White, red and blue varieties exist. Fruit: 2-2½-in (5-7-cm) long, oval, with three grooves.
Position: Sunny, south- and west-facing walls.
Soil: Rich in nutrients, permeable. Can be grown in compost in a large container.
Water: In open soil or container, water plentifully during the summer.
Fertilizing: In open soil, two to three times during the summer; every two to three weeks with compound fertilizer in a pot.
Further care: Requires taut wires, twines or sticks as a climbing aid. Pinching out shoot tips encourages branching and formation of flowers. Space plants 24-32 in (60-80 cm) apart.
Use: As a visual screen, for covering a wall or in pots on a balcony.

Scarlet runner beans are both decorative and useful.

Nasturtiums will flower all summer long.

Scarlet runner bean

Phasaeolus coccineus

Annual winding plant, up to 13 ft (4 m) tall. The leaves are soft and feathered, with three lobes.
Origin: South America.
Flower/fruit: Red flower, from early summer to mid-fall. Green bean pods, up to 12 in (30 cm) long from midsummer to late fall. Seeds pink to violet, edible.
Position: Sunny to semi-shady; south- and west-facing walls.
Soil: Deep, rich in nutrients. Use fertilized standard compost in a large container.
Water: Water plentifully during the summer; when the weather is very dry, water daily both in large containers and open soil.
Fertilizing: Three times during the growing period, using compound fertilizer. In a large container, every six to eight weeks with compound fertilizer.
Further care: Will require a climbing aid such as wire, a stick, or twine. Space plants 10-12 in (25-30 cm) apart.
Use: Beans for soups, salads, as a vegetable.
Warning: Green beans are toxic if eaten raw.

Nasturtium
Tropaeolum

Plant with tendrils and large, long-stalked leaves (up to 3 in/8 cm across). Hybrids of *T. majus* and *T. peregrinum* are sold.
Origin: South America.
Flower/fruit: *T. majus* has yellow to carmine red flowers from early summer to mid-fall. Fruit: up to ¾ in (2 cm), light green to yellow, ridged. *T. peregrinum* has very feathery, yellow flowers from midsummer.
Position: In full sunlight, on south- and west-facing sides of the house.
Soil: Loose, permeable garden soil, or standard compost in a container.
Water: Water plentifully in a large container; in open soil, daily in summer.
Fertilizing: Potassium- and phosphorus-rich fertilizer encourages flower formation. Begin fertilizing when plants in open soil start flowering; every six to eight weeks in a large container.
Further care: Requires a thin grid or wire fence as a climbing aid. Space plants 40 in (1 m) apart.
Diseases: For aphids, spray plants two or three times with tansy brew.
Use: Excellent for covering composting bins or fences.

Ornamental gourds will cover fairly large areas with greenery.

Cucumbers provide fresh ingredients for salads in the summer.

Ornamental gourd
Cucurbita pepo var. *ovifera*

A fast-growing, summer plant with tendrils (up to 27 ft/8 m tall). Leaves 4-8 in (10-20 cm) long; makes a good visual screen. Colorful fruit.
Origin: South America.
Flower/fruit: Mid-summer to mid-fall; large, funnel-shaped, yellow flowers. Popular with bees. Conspicuous fruit which can be kept for a long time as indoor decoration.
Position: Sunny, south- and west-facing walls.

Soil: Nutrient- and humus-rich soil, best mixed with compost. Use standard compost when growing this plant in a large container.
Water: Plentifully to prevent drying out.
Fertilizing: Every four weeks with compound fertilizer during the vegetative phase in open soil; weekly with liquid fertilizer in a container.
Further care: Requires only twine or another simple climbing aid. Space plants about 7 ft (2 m) apart.
Use: Very good for covering a large area with greenery. Grow on a frame over a compost heap to provide shade.

Cucumber
Cucumis sativus

This plant grows quickly (up to 13 ft/4 m), with green tendrils in summer and large, rough, hairy leaves. Many different varieties.
Origin: Western India.
Flower/fruit: early to late summer, golden yellow flowers ¾ in (2 cm) across with pointed petals. Separate male and female flowers. Popular with bees.
Fruit: A green cucumber.
Position: Sunny, sheltered from wind, south-facing wall.
Soil: Humus- and

nutrient-rich; mixed with compost in a container.
Water: Keep evenly moist. Use water that has been left to stand for a day or more. Dryness will make the fruit bitter.
Fertilizing: In open soil, use diluted, fermented nettle brew two to three times during the vegetation phase or use compound fertilizer. If grown in a large container, use dissolved compound fertilizer every 21 days.
Further care: It will require twine or a frame to hold onto. (Try builder's concrete reinforcing mesh.) Space plants 3 ft (1 m) apart.
Use: For salads.

The flowers of the convolvulus close up at night.

Morning glory needs nutrient-rich, loose soil.

Convolvulus
Convolvulus sepium

This annual, left-winding plant with arrow-shaped leaves will grow 3-10 ft (1-3 m) tall.
Origin: Central Europe.
Flower/fruit: Late spring to early fall, white or pink goblet-shaped flowers (2-2½ in/5-7 cm long). The flowers close at night and in bad weather. Fruit: capsule-shaped, pointed, with four to five seeds.
Position: Sunny, west- and east-facing walls.
Soil: Nutrient-rich tending to loamy. In a large container, mix standard compost with some loam.
Water: Keep moist; water well in both open soil and a large container if the weather is dry.
Fertilizing: In open soil, every eight weeks with compound fertilizer during the vegetation phase; every four to six weeks with compound fertilizer if grown in a container.
Further care: Requires a stick, frame, or twine for climbing. Otherwise fairly undemanding. Space plants 24-32 in (60-80 cm) apart.
Use: Very picturesque as a covering for a fence.
NB: Contains tannins and resins.

Morning glory
(*Ipomoea tricolor*)

This mainly winding species is fast-growing, up to 17 ft (5 m) tall. Broad, heart-shaped leaves, often with three lobes. Well-known varieties: *I. tricolor* and *I. purpurea*.
Origin: South America.
Flower/fruit: Funnel-shaped single flowers, 4 in (10 cm) across, from midsummer to early fall, white with a blue edge. *I. purpurea* has delicate violet flowers. Paper-like, brown fruits, brown seeds.
Position: Warm, sunny and sheltered from wind, south- and west-facing walls.
Soil: Nutrient-rich, loose garden soil with compost; also in large containers.
Water: To protect the soil from drying out, water daily during the summer; twice daily in a container.
Fertilizing: In a large container, once or twice weekly; in open soil, once during the vegetation phase with compound fertilizer.
Further care: Sensitive to wet, cold weather. Spray with tansy brew or pyrethrum preparations as prevention against red spider mites. Space plants 8-10 in (20-25 cm) apart.

Sweet peas come in many varieties.

The flowers are favorites for vases.

Sweet pea
Lathyrus
odoratus

This summer-flowering climber can grow up to 7 ft (2 m) tall. Its paired, feathery leaves end in tendrils. The genus includes about ten climbers and also some low-growing species. It is a very popular plant on account of its delicate fragrance and attractive flowers. Many sweet peas flower best during days with many hours of light, which means that, in the fall, they flower less and less until they finally die.

Open-soil varieties and also some for planting in large containers: Cuthbertson sweet peas, Spencer varieties and Zvolaneks Colossals with particularly large flowers on long stalks.
Origin: Southern Europe.
Flower/fruit: midsummer to mid-fall, colors range from white through yellow and pink to lavender and deep violet. The flower is delicate and usually has spurs and lateral wings. Strongly scented. Fruit: 2-2¾-in (5-7-cm) long pods which turn brown when ripening. They contain spherical seeds.
Position: Warm, sunny and sheltered, cannot cope with draughts.

South-facing wall or fence with sufficient shade from the sun. Cannot cope with direct, intense sunlight at midday.
Soil: Nutrient-rich, permeable garden soil. Chalky soil preferred. In a large container, use loose compost.
Water: Keep evenly moist; sensitive to drying out. Cover the soil with mulch. Never let the planting container dry out.
Fertilizing: High demand on nutrients. In open soil, water with fermented nettle brew once or twice weekly. Always use organic fertilizer. Use liquid fertilizer once or twice weekly in a large container.

Further care: Will require climbing aids like strings, brushwood, sticks, chicken wire, or a delicate frame as the tendrils cannot cope with very thick supports. Always remove all wilted flowers as soon as possible to ensure continuous flowering. Space plants 6 in (15 cm) apart.
Use: For covering a balcony in greenery, in boxes or pots, on a fence, or as a visual screen along the edge of the patio.

My tip: If you cut the flowers early in the morning, they will last longer when arranged in a vase.

48

Dutchman's pipe will also grow quite happily in the shade.

The flowers of the honeysuckle spread their strong fragrance in the evening.

Dutchman's pipe
Aristolochia macrophylla

This tall winding plant has conspicuous leaves, 12 in (30 cm) across, that are soft and heart-shaped. It is green throughout the summer and grows up to 33 ft (10 m) high. It will provide a good visual screen with leaves that overlap like roof tiles. Other useful species are *A. moupinensis, A. tomentosa*. This plant is quite happy in a town.
Origin: North America.
Flower/fruit: Late spring to midsummer, the inconspicuous, small, yellow-green flowers do not appear until about the third to fifth year. They form insect traps. Fruit: a 4-in (10-cm) long capsule.
Position: Shady to semi-shady, north- or east-facing site.
Soil: Loose, nutrient- and humus-rich. Will also cope with chalky soil.
Water: Requires plenty of water; the soil must never be let dry out.
Fertilizing: Young plants two to three times per year with compost and organic fertilizer; older plants twice with compound fertilizer.
Further care: Requires climbing aids. Space plants at 7-10 ft (2-3 m).

Honeysuckle
Lonicera

This vigorously growing winding plant is usually green during the summer and grows 10-20 ft (3-6 m) tall. There are many species.
Origin: Central Europe, western China.
Position: Sunny to semi-shady, south- and west-facing sites.
Soil: Undemanding.
Water: Avoid drying out during the summer, otherwise there is a risk of infestation with aphids.
Fertilizing: Compound fertilizer once a year in open soil; in pots, every four weeks with compound fertilizer.
Further care: Cut back to prevent bareness from below, requires taut wires or sticks as a climbing aid. Space plants 7-10 ft (2-3 m) apart; individual planting preferred.
Overwintering: In large containers with winter protection.
Warning: Toxic berries!
Species: These include(:)
L. caprifolium: yellow/white flowers
L. heckrottii: reddish flower
L. henryi: red/yellow flowers
L. periclymenum: yellow/white flower
L. tellmaniana: orange flowers

"Lawinia" unfolds large, scented flowers.

"White Cockade" is eminently suitable for displaying in a vase.

Climbing roses
Rosa

Depending on the variety, this makes a 7-17 ft (2-5 m) tall rambling plant. The bush is green during the summer and grows vigorously, with annual shoots up to 17 ft (5 m) long. Its thorns are the actual climbing mechanism of the plant. The leaves are shiny, dark green, and slightly serrated. They remain green for a long time in the fall.
Origin: Crosses from cultivars and from Far-Eastern wild species.

Flower/fruit: Single flowering from late spring to early summer; continuous flowering from early spring to mid-fall; no flowers until the second year, singly or in bunches, single or double; white, yellow, pink or red flowers with many yellow stamens. Some varieties are scented. Popular with bees. Red, berry-like fruit (hip) from late summer to early fall with numerous, small, yellow seeds. The fruit can be used to make jelly, tea, wine and syrup cordials.
Position: Sunny, south- and west-facing sites, sheltered but not too sheltered from wind (not enough circulation of air

will create susceptibility to fungal infections).
Soil: Nutrient-rich, loamy humus.
Water: Plenty during the first year and during drought in open soil; water regularly in large containers. Avoid waterlogging.
Leave the rootstock to soak in a bucket for several hours before planting and water well again after planting. When watering, water the roots but not the leaves.
Fertilizing: Regularly in open soil, from spring to late summer with rose fertilizer. In a large container, every four to six weeks during the same period.

Further care: Tie shoots to a climbing aid. Cutting out shoots that have finished flowering will encourage continuous flowering roses to produce further flowers. Cut back well in the spring. Space plants 7 ft (2 m) apart.
Diseases/pests: Susceptible to fungal diseases.
Overwintering: In open soil, heap up soil around the roots and cover shoots with brushwood or straw. For large container plants, line the pot with polystyrene sheeting and also cover the shoots with straw and tie this in place.

"Golden Showers" flowers continuously.

"Rosenresli" is a robust climbing rose.

Varieties:

Red flowers:

"Flammentanz:" blood red, double flowers, flowers once, up to 13 ft (4 m) tall, spreading growth, robust and hardy.

"Gruss an Heidelberg:" blood red, double, like cultivated rose, large flowers, scented, continuous flowering, vigorous growth, up to 7 ft (2 m) tall.

"Sympathie:" velvety dark red, double, flower like a cultivated rose with strong scent, continuous flowering, up to 10 ft (3 m) tall. Robust variety.

Pink flowers:

"Chaplin's Pink Climber:" dark pink, strongly colored, very large flowers, profusely flowering, semi-double, early flowering. Very vigorous growth, cut off shoots that have finished flowering.

"Coral Dawn:" coral pink, double flowers, like cultivated rose, scented, continuous flowering. Up to 10 ft (3 m) tall. Flowers last quite a long time.

"Dorothy Perkins:" cherry pink flowers, small, but profusely flowering, scented. Up to 7 ft (2 m) tall.

"Lawinia:" pure pink, large double flowers, scented. 7-10 ft (2-3 m) tall. Flowers several times, grows vigorously. Very weather-hardy.

"Rosenresli:" To begin with, salmon red, then salmon pink flowers, large, loosely double. Scent of tea roses. Up to 7 ft (2 m) tall. Not susceptible to disease.

Yellow flowers:

"Casino:" yellow, large, double flowers, scented, continuous flowering. Up to 8 ft (2.5 m) tall, strong.

"Coupe d'Or:" golden yellow, large flowers, profusely flowering, for east- and west-facing walls.

"Golden Showers:" lemon yellow, double flower, scented, continuous flowering, up to 7 ft (2 m) tall.

"Goldstern:" deep golden-yellow, similar to cultivated roses, double flower, continuous flowering. Up to 7 ft (2 m) tall, robust.

White flowers: "Fräulein Octavia Hesse:" pure white flowers, early flowering, vigorous growth, cut shoots sparingly.

"Ilse Krohn Superior:" pure white, double, like cultivated rose, continuous flowering, strongly scented, profusely flowering. Up to 7 ft (2 m) tall, robust.

"White Cockade:" white, like cultivated rose. Intense scent. Flowers several times, grows vigorously. Good cut flower.

Ivy can live for hundreds of years.

The flower umbels smell faintly of honey.

Ivy
Hedera helix

Ivy is an evergreen climber that can attain heights of up to 10 ft (30 m) with the help of its suckers. It is the only indigenous European plant with root suckers but it can also grow as a ground cover plant in woodland. The leaves of the young plant have three to five lobes, are dark green with white veins and lose the lobes with age. When very old, the shoots of an ivy may be as thick as a human arm. It can live for several hundred years. To begin with, growth is relatively slow. Recommended species include *H. colchica* "Arborescens," with its early flowers, which will attain a height of no more than 60 in (1.5 m); *H. helix* "Goldheart" with small, yellow leaves; *H. hibernica* which has larger leaves than *H. helix*, is more sensitive to frost and rarely produces fruits.

Origin: Central Europe, North Africa, Asia.

Flower/fruit: Early to mid-fall, inconspicuous, green/yellow, semi-spherical flower umbels that smell faintly of honey. Flowers do not appear until the plant is five to ten years old. The berries are popular with birds.

Position: Semi-shade, shade, north- and east-facing walls. Bright south-facing walls are too hot.

Soil: Humus-rich, slightly sandy, loamy soil; loamy standard compost in large containers.

Water: Water well in a large container and in open soil during dry weather and in the fall, otherwise keep fairly moist. Ivy loves high humidity, so enjoys the shade of trees.

Fertilizing: Not demanding; one to two doses of compound fertilizer during the vegetative phase in open soil. Every eight to ten weeks in summer give compound fertilizer if grown in a large container.

Further care: Train young plants upwards with the help of a stick. No need to cut back; will cope with a shaping cut. Space plants 3-7 ft (1-2 m) apart.

Use: Eminently suitable for covering undamaged walls and façades, or unsightly sheds.

Overwintering: Give winter protection if in a large container.

My tip: Ivy is a ground-covering plant which will not climb until it meets a vertical obstacle.

Warning: The berries are very toxic!

The flowering racemes of wisteria.

Spindleberry will thrive in the shade.

Wisteria
Wisteria sinensis

This is a winding plant that will grow up to 33 ft (10 m) tall, with 3-ft (1-m) long annual shoots and asymmetrical feathered leaves.
Origin: North America, eastern Asia.
Flower/fruit: Mid to late spring, numerous, 6-12-in (15-30-cm) long blue violet racemes at five to ten years. Delicately scented. Occasionally, velvet-haired, 4-8-in (10-20-cm) fruit pods in late spring.
Position: Warm, sunny. South- and west-facing sites.
Soil: Nutrient-rich, permeable and humus-rich. Hates chalk.
Water: Daily during the summer.
Fertilizing: In open soil, once or twice during the vegetation period with compound fertilizer.
Further care: Requires a stable wire as a climbing aid; cut back after flowering; shortening young shoots during the summer will encourage the formation of lots of flowers. Space plants 7-10 ft (2-3 m) apart; it is better to grow plants individually.
Warning: All parts of this plant are toxic!

Spindleberry
Euonymus fortunei

This evergreen shrub climbs with the help of root suckers and can grow to about 7 ft (2 m) tall. Depending on the species, the foliage is light green, variegated yellow or dark green. The leaves are ¾-2½ in (2-6 cm) across and generally red in winter.
Origin: Eastern Asia.
Flower/fruit: Late spring to early summer, greenish-yellow flowers grouped in umbels. It sometimes produces white fruit with orange red toxic seeds.
Position: Semi-shade, shady, north- and east-facing sites.
Soil: Humus-rich, loamy, with a high content of lime. In a container, in loamy standard compost.
Water: Water well during the fall and winter.
Fertilizing: In open soil, two to three times a year with organic fertilizer. In a pot, every six weeks with a compound fertilizer.
Further care: Will need a climbing aid. Avoid cutting back as the plant gets older. Space plants 5-7 ft (1.5-2 m) apart.
Overwintering: In a pot with winter protection.
Warning: The seeds are toxic!

The fall coloring of Parthenocissus tricuspidata ranges from yellow through orange to red.

Virginia creeper
Parthenocissus

A climbing shrub which is green in summer. Some can grow more than 33 ft (10 m) tall without any climbing aid. They anchor themselves to any support, using tendrils that have been converted into adhesive pads. Two species are most common: *P. quinquefolia* and *P. tricuspidata*. Both can cope well with a town or city atmosphere and they are particularly suited to covering large areas of walls and façades with greenery.

Parthenocissus quinquefolia

Fast-growing, 27-40 ft (8-12 m) tall, winding plant, green in summer, with suckers, and sometimes with adhesive pads at the ends of shoots. The leaf is about 4¾ in (12 cm) across, dark green; in autumn an intense carmine red. Also available is *P. quinquefolia* "Engelmanii," 33-40 ft (10-12 m) tall, with adhesive pads at the ends of shoots. Dark red coloring in the fall.
Origin: North America.
Flower/fruit: In summer, inconspicuous flower, whitish-green, with panicles. Strong pleasant scent, popular with bees. Fruit: blue pea-sized berries, much sought after by birds.
Position: Sunny to semi-shady. Fall color will be better in a sunny position. South-, west- and east-facing sites.
Soil: Humus-rich. Use standard compost in a large container.
Water: Water well during drought in any site.
Fertilizing: In open soil, once a year; every eight weeks with compound fertilizer in a pot.
Further care: Young plants require taut wires or a climbing frame. Space plants 7 ft (2 m) apart.
Overwintering: Give protection if in a pot.

Parthenocissus tricuspidata

May grow up to 33-50 ft (10 -15 m) within one to two years. Self-climbing; the ends of shoots have adhesive pads with which the plant is able to hold on by secreting an adhesive. The leaf has three lobes, is 4-8 in (10-20 cm) wide, bronze colored when shooting, then deep green and shiny; fall coloring from yellow to orange to red. The variety *P. tricuspidata* "Veitchii" is widely available from garden centers and is distinguishable from *P. tricuspidata* by smaller, more oval leaves with three lobes.

Food for birds: Parthenocissus quinquefolia berries.

The grapevine bears tasty fruit from the first month of fall onward.

P. tricuspidata "Veitchii Gigantea" has broad leaves. *P. tricuspidata* "Veitchii Aurea" has yellow green leaves with reddish edges; less vigorous than other varieties.
Origin: Eastern Asia.
Flower/fruit: early to midsummer, yellowish-green flower, faintly scented, popular with bees. In late summer pea-sized, bluish-black berries ripen on red stalks.
Position: Sunny, semi-shady, south- and west-facing sites.
Soil: Nutrient-rich, deep; use standard compost in a large container.
Water: During a drought, water plants well in large containers and open soil.
Fertilizing: Undemanding; once or twice annually in open soil. About every four to six weeks with compound fertilizer in a large container.
Further care: *P. tricuspidata* "Veitchii" does not require any climbing aid. It may die back a little due to frost damage but will soon produce new shoots from below. Space plants 7-10 ft (2-3 m) apart.
Overwintering: Give protection to containers.
Use: All forms of *P. tricuspidata* are suited to growing in containers. *P. tricuspidata* "Veitchii" will cover even concrete walls with greenery.

Grapevine
Vitis vinifera

This is a vigorously growing plant with suckers, which grows up to 33 ft (10 m) tall. Its annual shoots can be up to 10 ft (3 m) long. The leaves have three to five lobes, are roundish and change color in the fall. For planting in cooler regions, try white or red "Gutedel," "Früher Malinger," and "Früher Blauer Burgunder." Always plant two plants one beside the other.
Origin: Central and southeastern Europe.

Flower/fruit: Later spring to midsummer, small, yellowish-green panicles, slightly scented. Fruit from early fall; grapes with two to four seeds, light yellow or bluish-red.
Position: Sunny, warm, south-facing site; sheltered from wind.
Soil: Nutrient-rich, sandy, loamy.
Water: Undemanding; protect the soil from drying out.
Fertilizing: As a fruiting vine two to four times annually, with mineral fertilizer.
Further care: Cut back to a few shoots in mid-winter. Space plants 6-17 ft (2-5 m) apart.

Kiwi fruit requires a warm, sunny position.

Russian vine unfolds delicately scented flowers.

Kiwi fruit, Chinese gooseberry
Actinidia chinensis

This is a fast-growing, left-winding plant, green in summer, 13-27 ft (4-8 m) tall. The leaves are undivided, with serrated edges. Plant both female and male plants to obtain fruit. Suitable for a city climate.

Origin: Southeast Asia.

Flower/fruit: During late spring to early summer, white flowers appear, 1¼ -1½ in (3-4 cm) across, pleasantly scented, turning yellow toward the end of the flowering period. The fruit grows to a maximum of 2 in (5 cm), from late summer.

Position: Warm, south-facing.

Soil: Nutrient- and humus-rich with very little lime in open soil; standard compost in a large container.

Water: Never let the soil dry out.

Fertilizing: In open soil during the summer, every six weeks with compound fertilizer. In a large container, every month.

Further care: Requires a climbing aid. Cutting back annual shoots encourages more flowers. Space plants 3-7 ft (1-2 m) apart.

Overwintering: Provide winter protection in a pot.

Russian vine
Fallopia baldschuanica

This climber can reach up to 27-50 ft (8-15 m). It is a winding plant. The young leaves are reddish, later light green, and turn yellowish in the fall, heart-shaped and 1½-3½ in (4-9 cm) long.

Origin: Eastern Asia.

Flower/fruit: Midsummer to mid-fall, white, 6-8-in (15-20-cm) long panicles with a slight scent. Popular with bees. Flowers from the second year onward. Fruit: from early fall, winged brown nut, eaten by birds.

Position: Sunny to semi-shady, south-, west- and east-facing sites.

Soil: Open soil should be humus- and nutrient-rich; standard compost in a large container.

Water: In a large container, daily during the summer; open soil should not be left to dry out.

Fertilizing: In a large container, every second to fourth week until the end of summer. In open soil, twice with annually compound fertilizer.

Further care: Strong climbing aid required. Cut back in spring. Space plants at 7-10 ft (2-3 m).

Overwintering: In a large container provide winter protection.

Winter jasmine will begin to flower from the last month of winter onward.

The fruit of the hop is also much in demand for flower arranging.

Winter jasmine
Jasminum nudiflorum

This rambling plant is green in summer, with bright green leaves and long, arched and trailing shoots. Up to 10 ft (3 m) tall, a lovely early-flowering plant.
Origin: Eastern Asia.
Flower/fruit: Depending on the position, early winter or early spring; star-shaped, yellow flowers, 1 in (2.5 cm) long, after five years. Fruit: rare, black berries.
Position: Sunny to semi-shady, warm, sheltered. South-facing site; west-facing with protection from wind.
Soil: Permeable, humus-rich.
Water: Water well in fall before frosts commence, the shoots lose water through evaporation even in winter. Also water well in summer in dry periods.
Fertilizing: Once or twice annually with compound fertilizer.
Further care: Climbing aids required, such as wires or a climbing frame, needs tying. Prune in spring every two to three years. Space plants 7-10 ft (2-3 m) apart.
Use: Its hanging shoots make it an ideal covering for walls and banks.

Hop
Humulus lupulus

This is a 20-ft (6-m) tall, winding plant. The leaves are heart-shaped, up to 6 in (15 cm) across and have three lobes. There are both male and female plants.
H. scandens does not grow as fast nor is it as hardy as *H. lupulus*.
Origin: Central Europe.
Flower/fruit: Mid- to late summer, greenish, female, strongly scented catkins and male flowers in panicles. Fruit: almost cone-shaped, hanging, from early fall.
Position: Semi-shady, west- and east-facing sites.
Soil: In open soil, nutrient-rich, loamy soil; in a large container, loamy standard compost.
Water: Water well in dry weather. Avoid waterlogging in a large container.
Fertilizing: In open soil, once or twice annually; regularly every six to eight weeks in a large container; with compound fertilizer.
Further care: use a stick or wire as a climbing aid. Cut back in fall. Space plants 7-8 ft (2-2.5 m) apart.
Overwintering: Provide winter protection in a large container.

Clematis montana "Rubens" will produce an abundance of flowers.

Clematis "Jackmanii" bears enormous star-shaped flowers.

Clematis
Clematis
(wild forms)

Almost exclusively at home in the northern hemisphere. This winding plant has green leaves in summer and climbs up to 33 ft (10 m) high. Less vigorously growing clematis species are suitable for large pots.
Flower/fruit: Late spring to early fall, bell-like or open flowers singly or in panicles. The wild forms have abundant flowers. Fruit: feathery.
Position: Semi-shady. The area around the roots must be covered by plants; west- and east-facing sites; south-facing with protection from sun.
Soil: Humus-rich, permeable, moist. Can cope with lime; use standard compost in a large container.
Water: On hot summer days, water daily but avoid waterlogging.
Fertilizing: In open soil, once or twice annually; in a container, every six weeks with compound fertilizer until late summer.
Further care: Requires a climbing aid. Plant deep; the rootstock should be at least 4 in (10 cm) beneath the soil. *C. montana, C.* "Lasurstern" and *C.* "The President" should be cut back after flowering. All other clematis should be cut back in early spring. Space plants at 7-10 ft (2-3 m).
Overwintering: Provide winter protection in a large container.
Protect from frost when plants are young.

Warning: All species are slightly toxic!

Clematis montana

Grows 20-27 ft (6-8 m) tall; leaves reddish-brown when shooting, later dark green. The wild form is generally not available from garden centers, only cultivated varieties. *C. montana* "Rubens" (pink-flowering) or *C. montana* "Superba" (white).
Origin: Central China, Himalayas.
Flower/fruit: Late spring to early summer, white flowers, up to 1½ in (4 cm) across, when the plant is three to five years old; cultivated varieties flower abundantly.

Traveller's joy, old man's beard
Clematis vitalba

This tall-growing wild species grows rapidly to over 70 ft (20 m). The oval leaves are up to 4 in (10 cm) long.

Origin: Central Europe.
Flower/fruit: Mid-spring to mid-fall, white, up to ¾ in (2 cm) across, with slight scent of almonds, produced three to five years after planting. Fruit: from late spring to late winter, silvery seedheads.

Clematis hybrids

The large-flowered cultivars are more suited to growing in large containers. Cultivated clematis varieties have oval leaves 6 in (15 cm) long, and climb to 13 ft (4 m).
Origin: Usually from British and French raisers.
Soil, water, fertilizing and further care: as for wild varieties.
Diseases: Clematis wilt.
"Ernest Markham:" flower: midsummer to early fall, 4-6 in (10-15 cm), brilliant dark violet.
"Jackmanii:" robust and hardy. Flower: midsummer to mid-fall, 4-6 in (10-15 cm), abundantly flowering, violet purple.
"Lasurstern:" Flower: late spring to early summer; again in early fall, 4-6 in (10-15 cm), violet blue.
"Nelly Moser:" Flower: late spring to early summer, again early fall, 6-8 in (15-20 cm), pale pink striped.
"The President:" Flower: early to midsummer, again mid-fall, up to 6 in (15 cm), dark violet.
"Ville de Lyon:" Flower: early summer to early fall, 4-6 in (10-15 cm), deep carmine red.

Clematis "Ville de Lyon" forms a thick tapestry of blossom.

Pear flowers are a delight for bees.

Pears will yield lots of fruit on an espalier.

Pear
Pyrus communis

The pear is a 50-70-ft (15-20-m) tall, pyramid-shaped, deciduous tree. The pear can only be pollinated with pollen from other pear trees, so several trees must be planted in the same vicinity. The leaves are roundish-oval.

Origin: Central Europe.

Flower/fruit: Mid to late spring, white flowers with petals up to 1 in (2.5 cm) across. Numerous reddish-yellow stamens. Fruit ripens from late summer to late fall.

Position: Sheltered, sunny, south- or south-west-facing espalier.

Soil: Deep, nutrient-rich, slightly sandy.

Water: Requires sufficient moisture; water well in dry weather but does not like waterlogging.

Fertilizing: Three times with compound fertilizer (in the spring, summer and fall).

Further care: Do not plant in the vicinity of junipers (risk of pear rust). Space plants 3-7 m (10-23 ft) apart.

Use: Suited to growing as a fan-shaped espalier.

Espalier varieties:
"Alexander Lucas:" Flower medium early; large grass green to yellow green fruit, juicy and sweet. Ripens mid-fall. Storage: until early winter.

"Gute Luise:" Flowering time short; fruit: large, green to reddish-yellow, very tasty and juicy. Ripens: early to mid-fall. Storage: until late fall. Good yield and fruit quality.

"Mme. Verté:" Long-lasting flower, good pollen producer; fruit: small, plump, greenish-brown and pleasantly sweet. Ripens: mid-fall to early winter. Storage: until late winter. Regular yield even in unfavorable positions.

"Napoleon's Butterbirne:" Long-lasting flower, robust; fruit: medium-sized, bottle-shaped, light green to light yellow, very juicy and a little sharp. Ripens: mid to late fall. Storage: until early winter. High yield.

"Regentin:" The flower is slightly sensitive to frost; fruit: medium-sized, whitish-green, juicy and tasty, a wonderful winter pear. Ripens: mid to late fall. Storage: early to midwinter.

"Williams Christ:" Small, robust flower; fruit: large, yellowish-green, very tasty and tender. Ripens: late summer. Storage: one to two weeks. High nutrient requirements; not quite hardy in frost.

Peach trees bloom as early as the first month of spring.

The first fruit is ripe by the middle of summer.

Peach
Prunus persica

This deciduous tree, which grows up to 27 ft (8 m) tall, has dark green, longish, serrated leaves. It grows quickly but does not live for very long. Peach trees are self-pollinating so one specimen is sufficient for producing fruit. Bush forms are usually available in the trade. Grown as a cultivated variety as a peach seedling on light, sandy soils; if the soil is heavy and loamy, a peach scion is grafted on to a plum stock.

Origin: Probably China.
Flower/fruit: From early to mid-spring, ½-2 in (1.5-5 cm) long, dark pink petals. Fruit: midsummer to early fall, varieties with yellow or white fruit flesh. Roundish, yellow to reddish, velvet-skinned fruit with a large, brown kernel. Recently, smooth-skinned varieties (nectarines) are much cultivated.
Position: sunny, warm and sheltered. South-facing site.
Soil: Sandy but nutrient-rich.
Water: Can cope with short-term lack of water but the soil should not be left to dry out.
Fertilizing: Three times during the vegetation period with compound fertilizer, not too late in the fall to guarantee maturing of the wood.
Further care: Cut back in early spring. Space plants 10-17 ft (3-5 m) apart.
Varieties:
"Mamie Ross:" Flower fairly hardy; fruit: medium-sized, light red, striped, slightly sharp taste. Ripens: late spring-early summer. Storage: up to one week. Will still ripen even in cooler areas.
"Mayflower:" Flower, longlasting, early; fruit: small, bright red, striped, greenish-white flesh, velvety skin which pulls off easily. Ripens: mid-summer. Storage: eat fresh. A resistant early variety.
"Proskauer:" Flower small and late, relatively resistant to frost; fruit: medium-sized, flesh yellowish-white, kernel easy to remove, tasty. Ripens: late summer to early fall. Storage: eat fresh. Will still ripen even in regions with a rough climate.
"Weisser Ellerstädter:" flower medium-sized; fruit: large, spherical, yellowish-white with white flesh, kernel easy to remove, tasty. Ripens: early fall. Storage: eat fresh. Resistant to disease; produces abundant fruit.

Apricots, like peaches, bloom early.

The tasty fruit can be frozen.

Apricot
Prunus armeniaca

This deciduous tree grows 10-13 ft (3-4 m) tall, in favorable areas even taller. The wild form was originally a tree of the steppes, so it requires plenty of warmth. The leaves are broad, oval to heart-shaped, dark green with slightly serrated edges. Cultivated trees are grafted onto different kinds of stock, the one most frequently used is the root of a plum tree (advantage: smaller growth). Usually available as a shrubby tree in the trade. Apricots are usually self-pollinating, so only one variety is required to harvest fruit.

Origin: Northern China.

Flower/fruit: Mid-spring, medium risk of frost damage, five white petals up to ¾ in (2 cm) long, numerous yellow stamens. Popular with bees. Fruit from midsummer onward, orange yellow, roundish with a large, brown kernel, fuzzy skin.

Position: Sunny, dry and sheltered. Apart from really warm areas, only recommended as an espalier on the south-facing side of a house.

Soil: Light, sandy but nutrient-rich.

Water: Prefers a dry climate, sensitive to positions that are too moist and which might encourage infestation by fungal diseases.

Fertilizing: Three times during the vegetation period, with compound fertilizer; no later than early fall so that maturing of the wood is not delayed.

Further care: In positions that are at risk from late frosts the flowers can be protected from freezing if they are sprayed with water immediately before the onset of the frost, as the water will then freeze on the flower and the flower will be insulated by its coat of ice. Space plants 10-17 ft (3-5 m) apart.

My tip: The fruit is suitable for freezing.

Cultivated varieties: "Grosse, Wahre Frühaprikose" (early, true apricot): Flower sensitive to frost; fruit: large, oval, tasty. Ripens: midsummer. Storage: eat fresh. Variety with abundant yield.
"Aprikose von Nancy:" Flower medium early; fruit: orange yellow to carmine red, sweet with a fine sharp taste; velvety skin. Ripens: mid- to late summer. Storage: eat fresh. Relatively hardy to frost, high yielding if given a regular pruning.

Apple blossom is enchantingly beautiful with a delicate scent.

Espalier apples are often sweeter than those from a tree.

Apple
Malus domestica

This deciduous tree has been an indigenous European plant for thousands of years. It is grafted onto various stocks for a high yield of fruit. It grows up to 33 ft (10 m) tall but can also easily be grown as an espalier. Numerous varieties. Apples require pollen from another tree, so try to plant two different varieties side by side.

Origin: Central and southeastern Europe.

Flower/fruit: From mid- to late spring, whitish-pink flowers, pink when still closed, up to ¾ in (2 cm) acrsss, with numerous yellow stamens. Popular with bees. Fruit ripens, depending on variety, from midsummer to late fall.

Position: Sunny to semi-shady, east-facing site.

Soil: Nutrient-rich, loose, loamy.

Water: Keep soil moist, protect it from drying out.

Fertilizing: Three times annually with compound fertilizer (spring: for faster growth; summer: growth of fruit; fall: energy loss through harvest). Fertilizing too late in the fall will hinder the maturing of the wood! Also use garden compost as a fertilizer.

Further care: Pruning required. Mulching will prevent washing out of nutrients (use grass cuttings). Space plants 10-17 ft (3-5 m) apart.

Diseases/pests: Guard against mildew by providing a well-ventilated position.

Varieties:
"Berlepsch:" flower slightly sensitive to frost; golden yellow fruit, juicy, tasty. Ripens: mid- to late fall. Storage: until late winter; high yield, resistant.
"Cox's Orange:" late, long-lasting flower; yellow red fruit. Ripens: mid-fall. Storage: until late winter. Wood slightly sensitive to frost.
"Goldparmäne:" flower not very sensitive to frost; red yellow fruit, sweet, tasty. Ripens: mid-fall; Storage: until late winter.: James Grieve": robust flowers; fruit: light yellow to light red, sharp-sweet. Ripens: early to late fall; Storage: six weeks. Rejuvenating cut required!
"Klarapfel:" frost-resistant flower; whitish-yellow, slightly sharp fruit. Ripens: mid- to late summer. Storage: three weeks. Disease-resistant variety.

NOTES

NOTES

Fruit Trees

CHRISTINE RECHT

Series Editor:
LESLEY YOUNG

Introduction

When you plant fruit trees in a garden you can be sure of springtimes filled with fragile blossom and the buzzing of honeybees and a fall harvest of mouthwatering fruit. However, you can only really enjoy your home-grown fruit if you know it does not contain the residue from chemical plant protection agents and that is what this guide to fruit growing is all about. In this book Christine Recht explains in a manner that is easy even for complete novices to follow all the important details about growing organic fruit. The most important point of all is your choice of the right tree for the right position, while selecting the most suitable varieties of fruit can prove just as important as being aware of the type of soil that you have and the climatic conditions on site. Excellent color photographs and detailed instructions on the care of several of the most popular types of fruit will help you to choose wisely. Clear illustrations are used to instruct the reader in the correct way to plant fruit trees, hedges and espaliers. The right way to prune your fruit trees is also demonstrated in simple, step-by-step diagrams. One of the key messages of this volume is the use of organic plant protection which involves using natural remedies in your battle against pests and diseases. Only if you encourage the many useful insects to live in your garden – the organic gardener's first line of defence against pests – will you be able to harvest healthy fruit uncontaminated by chemicals.

Contents

Apricot "de Nancy."

Sweet cherry blossom.

Bitter cherry "Schattenmorelle."

Both beautiful and bountiful

All parts of a tree – roots, trunk, branches, and foliage – have an important job to do and a sound understanding of these functions will help you considerably in the care of your fruit trees. This know-ledge is just as relevant for the giants among the fruit trees as for the smaller trees created by grafting.

It is essential to be aware right from the start that a fruit tree is not always a giant that requires plenty of room. It can just as easily be a small tree that you can pick fruit from without using a ladder. It might even be a bush that begins branching out just above the soil. In principle, all woody plants that bear fruit containing pits can be called "trees" even if they do not quite correspond to the standard image of a tree. A fruit tree in your garden will not only produce nourishing, tasty fruit, it will also prove to be an ornament for the garden at any time of year.

How a tree functions

When you understand how all of a tree's systems work, you will also understand why certain measures of care are necessary.

The roots

The roots anchor the tree in the soil which is its constant source of nutrients. The roots will continue to grow as long as the tree is alive.

Their delicate tips are covered in fine hair-like roots that are responsible for absorbing water and nutrients from the soil. These tiny roots are continually being produced as the main roots grow outward and this is why there is no sense in watering a tree near its trunk because the nutrients and water are absorbed by the fine roots under the ground at a point roughly matching the ends of the branches that form the crown of the tree above ground. The old, woody roots serve only as anchors for the tree.

The trunk and the branches

The trunk and branches contain millions upon millions of little channels that transport water and the nutrients dissolved in it from the root system to the crown and back again. The nutrients are thus carried from the roots through the woody parts of the tree towards the leaves. The channels between the bark and the trunk then carry the nutrients formed in the leaves back down

toward the soil. The cambium is situated between the wood and these conducting channels. Every year, the cambium forms fresh wood containing new channels for transporting the precious water from the roots to the leaves and, on its outer edge, the cambium also ensures the formation of new channels for the downward transportation of nutrients produced by the leaves. This is how the annual "tree rings" are formed so that the branch or trunk gradually becomes thicker. You should always try to ensure that neither the bark nor the cambium is damaged; for example, by tying the tree too tightly to a support stick, through careless handling of a lawn mower, by hammering in nails, or letting deer or rabbits nibble at the bark.

The leaves

The leaves perform several essential functions. First of all, they are responsible for the evaporation of moisture absorbed by the tree. Only in this way can the nutrients dissolved in the water be properly absorbed. They are then replenished from the soil through the fine

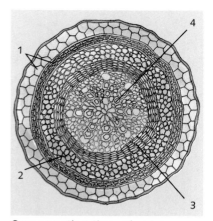

Cross section through a tree
1 bark, 2 conducting channels, 3 cambium, 4 woody part.

How a tree functions
The nutrients and water absorbed from the soil by the roots are transported right up to the leaves. The leaves extract carbon dioxide from the air and, with the help of sunlight and chlorophyll, this is transformed into oxygen and sugars. The sugars nourish the tree; the oxygen is released to the air.

hair roots. Above all, an important chemical reaction takes place in the leaf in a process known as photosynthesis. During this process the leaf transforms carbon dioxide gas into oxygen and sugars with the help of sunlight and water.

The flower

The flower serves to propagate the species after it has been pollinated by insects. From the pollinated flowers fruits are formed which contain seeds to provide the foundation for the growth of a new tree. However, trees grown from the propagated seeds of cultivated fruit trees are unlikely to resemble their parent tree with respect to variety and will often bear small fruit with an inferior flavour. This is because cultivated fruit trees are usually

grafted. In nearly all fruit species, the new flowers are formed during the first month of summer just after the fruit begins to grow. If a tree produces too much fruit, it will hinder the formation of new flowers. This is why fruit trees often carry very little fruit in the year after an abundant harvest.

The right shape of tree for every position

Always choose a stock that will not grow very tall for a small garden, to create a hedge, or for a tree destined to live in a large container. Large, standard trees will only have enough room to grow in a real orchard or as a single tree in front of a house. You still have a wide choice as several different shapes of trees are available within most fruit species. The **dwarf pyramid** shape is most commonly seen in apple and pear trees. The trunk grows up to 28 in (70 cm) tall and the crown remains fairly small. This means that all measures of care and harvesting can be carried out quite easily without a ladder. The yield will be in the region of 22-66 pounds (10-30 kg) which is quite sufficient for the average

household. The dwarf pyramid shape is not suitable for a solitary tree in a small garden but several, planted in a row, will form an attractive hedge to create a useful screen from a neighboring garden. Dwarf pyramids should always be tied to a support post. Apple, pear, peach, cherry, apricot, and quince trees can be grown as **bushes** but other types of fruit trees will form crowns that are too large. The stem of a bush will grow to about 24 in (60 cm) high but the crown will spread wider than in the dwarf pyramid shape. This means that the yield will also be higher. Bushes are suitable for solitary trees or as a hedge but only in large gardens. The **low standard** shape is suitable for all types of fruit. It may attain a height of only 40 in (1 m) but the crown will be as large and spreading as that of a tall standard. This form is also easy to harvest by hand but all work carried out underneath the tree, like mowing and care of the soil, becomes difficult as you cannot stand upright underneath the crown of the tree. Short standards are suitable as solitary trees in a small garden; they can also be planted as a hedge if there is enough room.

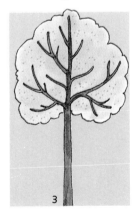

Shapes of trees
1 bush, 2 pyramid, 3 tall standard are the most important shapes of trees. They are distinguished by their height and the width of their crowns.

73

The semi-standard, with a height of up to 5 ft (1.5 m), or the **tall standard** which has a stem that attains a height of up to 8 ft (2.5 m) is the classic form for fruit trees like apples, pears, and plums. The crown may spread out considerably so a tree of this size will require plenty of room. The harvest is measured in tens of pounds (kilos). A semi-standard or regular standard may also be used as a feature in an ornamental garden and not just for its splendid blossom. A tall standard can provide shade for a seat in a garden or even be the centerpoint of a larger garden. Semi- and tall standards live much longer than the smaller forms of trees. These larger trees can attain an age of up to 80 years.

The reasons for grafting

A wild tree takes many, many years to grow from seed. Even if you wish to grow your own fruit, you will probably not wish to wait for decades to enjoy the first harvest and you will also want to be sure that the tree will bear the kind of fruit you like. This is why, as a rule, most fruit trees are grafted. In graft-ing the scion of the desired variety is grafted onto the root (stock) of another strong and fast-growing variety. The grafting point is usually just above the root but in rare cases (cherries and quinces) it may be just beneath the crown. It is visible as a slight thickening of the stem. By choosing a particular stock, both the size and the shape of the tree can be selected as well as its hardiness, suitability for certain soils, and the age to which it will grow. It is the root that determines the quantity of nutrients and moisture a tree can absorb. Stocks that do not grow fast will form small root systems, the intake of nutrients will be modest, and the tree will not grow as tall or as wide as it might. Stocks of varieties that grow vigorously are used for tall standards. They can absorb lots of nutrients and water, and the tree will become a giant. Nowadays, gardens tend to be smaller and there is a greater interest in growing all types of fruit on slow-growing stocks. However, so far this has only been possible with apples and pears.

They can be grown successfully on slow-growing stocks even in small gardens. In the case of plums and cherries, however, so far no satisfactory slow-growing stock that is reliable over longer periods of time has been found. There are also no reliable small-growing forms of apricots or peaches. A walnut tree is always very tall. By nature quinces are bushes, so they are grafted to grow on a taller stem.

Do-it-yourself grafting

When you buy a young tree in a nursery, it will already have been grafted. Many people wonder, however, whether it is worthwhile grafting a tree on to a stock themselves. Generally speaking, probably not. However, certain old varieties of fruit are now coming to the fore again because tree nurserymen and other expert gardeners have recognized that the old varieties are invaluable, not only for their healthy genes but also for their good flavor and resistance to many pests and diseases. To date, though only a very few nurseries have specialized in the grafting of older varieties and this means that it may well be worth a layperson's while to take a scion from a tasty, indigenous apple or pear variety and graft it onto a suitable stock, and thus preserve the old variety for posterity. Stocks can be purchased in good tree nurseries.

The crown sizes of fully grown trees

Apple		**Sweet cherry**	
tall and		tall and	
semi-standard	27-33 ft (8-10 m)	semi-standard	27-33 ft (8-10 m)
bush	13-17 ft (4-5 m)	**Bitter cherry**	
dwarf pyramid	7-10 ft (2-3 m)	bush,	
Pear		semi-standard	13-17 ft (4-5 m)
tall and		**Peach**	
semi-standard	20-27 ft (6-8 m)	bush	13-17 ft (4-5 m)
bush	13-17 ft (4-5 m)	**Apricot**	
dwarf pyramid	7-10 ft (2-3 m)	semi-standard	17-20 ft (5-6 m)
Plum		**Quince**	
tall and		bush	10-17 ft (3-5 m)
semi-standard	17-20 ft (5-6 m)	**Walnut**	
Greengage		tall standard	27-50 ft (8-15 m)
tall and			
semi-standard	13-17 ft (4-5 m)		

A well cared for apple tree in an orchard. The abundant blossom promises a rich harvest of fruit.

Growing your own fruit

Before buying a fruit tree, the following points should be carefully considered: What type of fruit do I like? What type of tree will suit the conditions in my garden? How can I integrate it into my garden? The following chapter will help you to answer these questions and also give useful advice on purchasing.

The right position

Before purchasing any fruit tree you should be clear in your mind about certain important points.

Climate: Not every type of fruit will thrive in every climate. This means that you can choose from among hundreds of apple varieties to find just the right one for a mild, lowland climate or for an altitude of over 3,300 ft (1,000 m). Whether you have cold or mild winters must be taken into consideration and also the length of the summer season and the average humidity. The best plan is to ask at your local tree nursery which variety of fruit is particularly suitable for the conditions where you live.

My tip: Also ask about local varieties of fruit trees. Many nurseries now include old varieties in their range, which were previously unavailable or forgotten. These older varieties are often extremely tasty and most resistant to pests and diseases. In addition, they are adapted to the climate in which they were first grown long ago.

Mini-climate: The exact same conditions of sun, wind, or rain will not prevail everywhere in your garden. The climatic conditions within a limited area are referred to as its mini-climate. Fruit trees grow best in east- and south-facing positions. You can plant an apple tree on the west-facing side of the house, however, as it will prefer moist, cool conditions. Cherry trees prefer a windy position. All other fruit varieties prefer warm, sheltered positions, particularly during blossom time when late frosts can ruin the entire harvest in one night. You must therefore study the mini-climate in your garden carefully. Frost will often form in low-lying hollows while the temperature on a nearby slope will not drop below freezing.

The soil: The soil conditions should also be checked before you buy a fruit tree as not every type of fruit will cope with every type of soil. To be on the safe side, dig up a sample of soil and have it checked at a soil analysis laboratory. (Ask at your local garden center or tree nursery for the address of a laboratory that provides this service. You can also buy a soil analysis kit to use yourself.) If, however, the soil consistency turns out not to be ideal for the fruit you wish to grow, this is no reason to give up. The deciding factor is the right type of stock as the same variety of fruit may be combined with different stocks that grow well on dry, stony, moist, or humus-rich soil. Improving the soil may also help, particularly for small-growing species.

Spatial requirements: The number of trees you can accommodate in your garden will, of course, depend on the size of your garden and also on the size of the trees. In principle, solitary trees should always be planted far enough apart so that the crowns will not touch when the trees are mature. If the crowns do begin to become entangled with each other, the fruit will not receive enough light for ripening.

Distances to neighboring properties: A tree whose branches protrude into a neighbor's garden may become a cause of disagreements. For this reason, make sure that you leave plenty of space between the tree and your neighbor's boundary. Your legal responsibilities regarding the placing of trees must also be considered and you can obtain advice on this from your local council. A sensible general rule is that a tree should be planted as far from your neighbor's boundary as you anticipate the diameter of the crown will extend. This will ensure that, later on, no branches will protrude into your neighbor's space. For example, if the crown of the mature tree is expected to have a diameter of 20 ft (6 m), the tree should be planted at least 10 ft (3 m) from the neighboring boundary.

In the spring, fruit trees are a delight in any garden or balcony – each flower is more beautiful than the one before.

Designing with fruit trees

Fruit trees can form part of the total design scheme of the garden in many different ways.

A solitary tree can look splendid in the center of the garden. We recommend choosing a variety that not only bears good fruit but also produces splendid blossom. Such a fruit tree will be just as decorative as an ornamental shrub in your garden. Both tall standards and semi-standards, as well as not too slender dwarf pyramids, are suitable for solitary planting.

A fruit tree hedge may comprise a single row of fruit trees of the same or different species. More artistic hedges can also be grown on an espalier. The dwarf pyramid and bush shapes are both ideal for creating a fruit tree hedge.

The flowers in the photograph:
1 *peach blossom*
2 *apple blossom*
3 *apricot blossom*
4 *sweet cherry blossom*
5 *quince blossom*
6 *pear blossom*

A fruit espalier on a house wall is always recommended whenever you intend to grow fruit species that like warmth. Among these are pears, peaches, apricots, and bitter cherries. A south- or west-facing wall is the ideal place. Pears, especially, will thrive in such a position, even in harsher climates. Espaliers can be shaped in an informal fashion or in a more strictly formal way. A boring house façade can be turned into an eye- catching feature with an artistically designed espalier. For pears, use a pyramid shape; for bitter cherries, peaches, and apricots use varieties with broad, spreading crowns.

A proper orchard will probably remain just a romantic dream for most people unless they live in the countryside. Most of the commercial, classic, mixed fruit orchards usually grow fruit for producing wines, cider, etc. on tall standard shapes. The better types of fruit, intended for eating, are often grown as hedges or in rows of dwarf pyramids.

Fruit trees in large containers

Nearly all types of fruit trees can be grown in large containers. However, caring for trees grown in containers is not that easy, the yield is low, and the life expectancy of the tree rarely exceeds ten years. Nevertheless, a small flowering apple tree or peach tree in a large container makes a lovely sight, particularly on a balcony in the middle of a city. Generally speaking, all young trees that are grafted on slow-growing stocks can be planted in a large container. Recently, dwarf varieties of apple and peach have been cultivated especially for

Espalier fruit can even be grown in a large container: here, the apple variety "Elstar" is trained in a double-cordon shape.

growing in large containers. Their smaller fruits complement the smaller size of the little standard trees. The dwarf apple "Garden Annie" will grow no taller than 2 ft (60 cm).

Pollination

No tree will bear fruit if it has not been pollinated. Apples, pears, sweet cherries, and some plum varieties will definitely require a second tree or, better still, several other trees, for successful pollination.

Before buying a fruit tree, it is worth finding out what other fruit trees are growing in the vicinity as these may fulfill the pollination requirements. If this is not the case, you may have to buy two or three varieties of one species. If you do not have enough room for this, you may be able to

Before buying a fruit tree, ask the following questions:

● How much space will the tree require?
● How tall will the tree grow?
● What kind of climatic conditions will it require?
● What type of soil will it need?
● Does this variety need a pollen donor?
● Is the variety robust and not very susceptible to typical diseases?
● How old is the crown?
● Has a planting cut been carried out?
● Is the bark smooth and undamaged?
● Are the roots in good condition?
● Is the grafting point free of superfluous growth?
● Will the tree nursery supply a replacement if this tree does not grow properly?

graft several different varieties onto one tree. Bitter cherries, quinces, peaches, and apricots are self-pollinating. In the case of the walnut tree, both male and female flowers are produced on the same tree. It is advisable to ask for advice from a good tree nursery about varieties that are good for pollination. There will also be no pollination without bees and other insects so avoid the use of insecticides to combat pests.

Buying a tree

A fruit tree should last for many years, sometimes for decades, so it should not be a haphazard purchase. It can be bought from a garden center or from a tree nursery, sometimes by mail order. The latter is usually the answer if you want varieties that are not so common. If you are not very familiar with fruit trees, it is a good idea to get expert advice from a local tree nursery. When you buy the tree, it will be one or two years old, which means that you cannot yet tell what it will turn out to look like. The nursery will also be familiar with climatic conditions in the area and should graft onto suitable varieties. Advice should be given while consulting a detailed map of your garden. Only by doing this will the tree nursery expert be able to tell you which stock your tree should be grafted onto, what shape of tree to choose, and which variety would be most suitable. From my experience, it seems that laypersons tend to go for a stronger-looking young tree rather than choosing a "skinny-looking" dwarf pyramid shape on slow-growing stock which might be more suitable for his or her garden. Choosing a tree that grows too big will inevitably result in the gardener having to chop it down in a few years' time because it casts shade all over the garden.

The correct way to plant a fruit tree

The planting of a fruit tree is an important occasion. After all, this tree will be part of your life for years to come, so you should try not to make any mistakes when planting it. The tree will spend its entire life in one position, deriving nutrients from the soil and spreading its roots in the ground.

The right moment to plant

A young fruit tree can be planted either in the fall, (that is, at the end of the vegetation period in the first/second month of the fall), or in the spring before the start of new growth, around the first month of spring.

● Fall planting is better, in principle, as the tree has time to root properly before the winter and will then produce plenty of shoots in the spring. Temperatures may start to become critical during the first month of winter. If the ground should freeze right through, the roots will no longer be able to absorb moisture and the little tree will die.

● Planting in spring is only recommended for species that are sensitive to cold, like peach, apricot, or quince. During a very cold winter, these young trees can easily freeze to death.

● Container trees can also be planted in the summer, when they will quickly adapt and start growing.

Immediately after purchasing

After purchasing, young trees should be planted as quickly as possible in the soil, otherwise the roots risk drying out. If you have bought it from a tree nursery or garden center, the best thing to do is to stand the tree in a bucket of water for several hours. The same goes for a tree that has arrived by mail order.

Do not plant if there is a risk of frost

If frost is forecast, it is better to leave planting the tree until the spring. The following measures should be undertaken to protect it.

● Dig a pit 12 in (30 cm) deep in a sheltered position.

● Stand the tree in the hole with its roots slightly on a slant.

● Cover the roots with the soil that was removed.

● Cover the entire pit with a thick layer of straw.

Checking the soil

If you do not already know what type of soil you have in your garden or what nutrients it contains, then it is time to take a soil sample. It would be better still to have the soil sample analysed before buying your young tree (soil analysis kits can be obtained from garden centers).

The planting hole

The planting hole need not be very deep but should have a fairly large diameter. Apart from pears, which drive a tap root deep down into the soil, all other fruit trees produce flat, long roots just beneath the surface of the soil. These roots should be given the chance to spread their soft tips as far as possible. If the soil is very compacted, it might be a good idea to break it up in several places with a pickaxe; otherwise the tree might end up standing in a pool of water. If the fine roots cannot spread unhindered, the entire tree will not be able to grow properly.

Improving the soil

Before the advent of tractors which could be used to remove large tree stumps from the ground, orchard owners used to let old stumps burn away slowly and the ash thus supplied fertilizer for the new tree. As a rule, it is sufficient to sprinkle a bucket of woodash and two handfuls of bonemeal on the loosened soil of the planting hole, plus one or two buckets of ripe compost. If the soil analysis results show that the soil is deficient in certain nutrients, these will have to be added.

A support post

All trees should be tied to a support post after planting.

● For dwarf pyramid fruit trees, choose a strong post that will last a long time as the young tree needs to be tied to it for as long as it lives. The roots of weaker stocks are so small and fine that the tree could be knocked over in strong wind. The post will have to be replaced after some years if it has rotted away.

● For semi-standard or tall standard trees, a simple tomato cane should be sufficient. It can be removed sometime during the second year.

Planting on a slope

If you plant your fruit tree on a slope, the planting hole should be a little larger and much deeper on the upperside. In this way, the tree will end up standing on a flat area within the slope. To prevent heavy rain from washing the soil away, secure the front edge of the planting area with a few large stones or thick planks.

Planting in a row

If you have planted several pyramid-shaped bushes in a row, for example as a hedge, it is better not to dig separate planting holes but, instead, to dig a 7-ft (2 -m) wide trench and loosen and improve the soil. This will create a planting bed that will let the small trees thrive.

My tip: If you are removing old trees and placing new trees in the same holes, change the species of fruit: plant fruit with seeds where you previously grew fruits with pits and vice versa.

There are many different varieties of plum to suit every type of climate.

Planting

Planting a tree

Before planting, make sure you have the following tools to hand: a spade, hoe, fork, shovel, pickaxe, support post, strong rope or tie, and a watering can or garden hose. Make sure that you have given careful thought to the site. How much sunlight will the tree receive during the day? Does the site get frosted in the winter? Will the garden hose reach far enough?

Planting
(illustration 1)

Digging the hole: The hole should be dug to a spade's depth and to the diameter of 5 ft (1.5 m). Place the soil to one side and loosen the soil on the floor of the planting hole to a spade's depth. This is best done with a fork which should be driven into the soil at intervals of 4 in (10 cm). Moving the handle back and forth will loosen the soil. You will need a pickaxe if the soil is compacted. Afterwards, crumble up the soil with a hoe. Add nutrients to this loosened layer: for example, a bucket of woodash and two handfuls of bonemeal with two buckets of ripe compost on top.
NB: If the plant was not pruned ready for planting when it was purchased, carry this procedure out now.
Planting: The support post should be hammered into the ground before actually planting the tree (see illustration 2). If you were to do it afterward you would damage the roots of the young tree. Now stand the tree in the planting hole in such a way that the grafting point is 4-6 in (10-15 cm) above the surface of the ground. Only in the case of quinces or pears grafted onto quinces should the grafting point be level with the ground. Now shovel

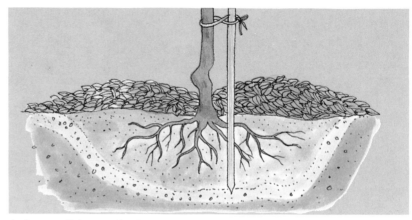

1 Strew a little wood ash and bonemeal on the floor of the planting pit, then add a bucketful of compost. Fill up with the extracted soil. Mulch around the bottom of the tree.

the well-crumbled soil back into the hole. It should be put back in the same sequence as when it was dug out, so that the soil that came out last is the first to go back in. The top layer should go back on top. While doing this, lift the tree up and down slightly several times so that the soil will settle well between the roots. Do not replace a top layer of turf if there was one. The grass would absorb too many nutrients and take water from the tree. When the tree is planted properly in its

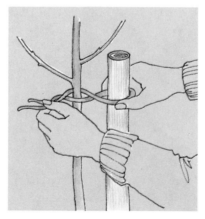

2 Tie the tree to a support stake with a figure-of-eight loop.

hole, you should check whether it is standing straight. Now carefully tread down the soil and then water well. The soil will settle and you will have to add more. A mulching layer of straw, grass cuttings, or bark will protect the tree for the first few months. This will also ensure that the soil remains loose and moist.

Tying the tree to a support post
(illustration 2)

A soft coconut-fiber rope or even an old nylon stocking, if you have nothing else, should be wrapped firmly around the stem and post in a figure-of-eight. During the first few months, retie the rope often as it should never be left to cut into the stem because this would interfere with the flow of sap.
When the tree is planted you may need to provide protection against damage by dogs digging, cats using it as a scratching post, or animals nibbling at the trunk. Wrap sacking or plastic round the young stem.

The planting cut

Any good tree nursery will carry out a planting cut for you at the time of purchase if you ask. If need be, you can also do this yourself before planting.

Cutting level

(illustration 3)

Before planting, all three main shoots should be cut in such a way that the top buds are on the same level, i.e. on one horizontal line. This will ensure that, during the following year, all new shoots and extensions of the main branches will be of the same length and strength. The central shoot should remain about 8 in (20 cm) longer than the lateral shoots.

The branches

(illustration 4)

An unpruned young tree has several branches: the central branch, the lateral branches, and the inferior shoots. The central shoot is easy to identify as it is basically an extension of the main stem. For lateral branches, choose three shoots of about the same thickness, which are situated at an oblique angle to the stem. They should not be all at the same level but distributed along

3 The top buds should all be at the same height; the central leader is 8 in (20 cm) longer.

a 20-in (50-cm) section of the stem. If the lateral shoots are too close together, they may break. All other laterals apart from the main laterals should be cut off close to the stem. You can let two or three unpruned, weaker branches remain as they will produce many leaves during the following year and will help to feed the tree through photosynthesis.

Cutting laterals: The three laterals that you have chosen should be shortened by about half for fruit with seeds (fruit with pits by about two-

thirds). Always cut above a bud that points outward. This will encourage all buds to shoot in the spring.

Training shoots outwards

(illustrations 5 and 6)

The laterals should grow at an angle of about 45 degrees to the main stem. If this is not their natural angle, use a small wooden stick to push the branch outward or weight it with a stone on a short piece of twine. If the angle is too wide, use soft twine to pull the branches closer to the stem.

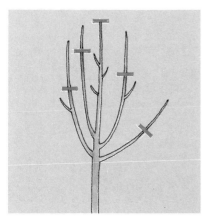

4 Planting cut: shorten the main branch extensions by about a half.

5 Main branches can be pushed apart or tied up.

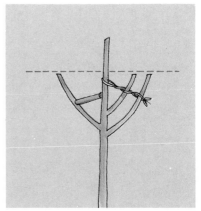

6 This is what a young tree should look like after the planting cut.

Many ways to grow fruit trees

There are many reasons for not just planting solitary fruit trees in your garden: a hedge may take up less space; fruit species that prefer warmth will ripen best on a house wall; a small tree can produce fruit just as easily in a large container on a balcony.

A house espalier

Pear, peach, apricot, and bitter cherry varieties, which all love warmth, will do particularly well on a warm house wall, on the wall of a garage or against a shed where they will be fairly well sheltered from late frosts, drafts, and rain. A well-grown fruit espalier will also provide a house with its own unique character.

NB: Apples are not suitable for an espalier on a house wall as they prefer fresh, cool air all around them.

A grid or trellis is essential for an espalier on a house wall. Unlike ivy or other creepers, fruit trees are not able to hold onto a wall by themselves. They have to be tied on. Build the grid with great care. It will be quite open to view in the winter when the fruit tree has lost its leaves!

The type of tree to choose is one that grows as little as possible. There is a good reason for this as the roots will never be able to spread out properly toward the house wall. Also, the crown of a tree that grows vigorously would not be easy to keep in check.

The planting hole should be prepared in exactly the same way as for a freestanding tree. It should be placed 20-28 in (50-70 cm) away from the foundations of the house. Check the subsoil as, very often, the area around a house is full of builder's rubble in which no tree will thrive. If this is the case, the planting hole should be cleared out completely and filled up with good soil and compost.

Care is almost the same as for a freestanding tree. The area of soil around the bottom of the tree should be kept free of weeds and other vegetation. An espalier tree will require watering throughout the summer months.

Espalier shapes

There are several different tried and tested shapes for espaliers which are more or less easy to grow even by a novice gardener.

A loose espalier is simple to create and looks good. Pears and peaches in particular are suitable for this shape. Apricots are very difficult to train.

A fan-shaped espalier looks good if trained around a window or balcony. Bitter cherry, peach, and apricot are all suitable for this style.

The classic espalier shape needs a lot of work and is probably too difficult for a layperson to build. The formal cordon espaliers and palm-shaped espaliers are usually only seen in a few botanical gardens these days. If you really want to grow one of these espaliers against your house (only pears are suitable for these shapes), you should contact a fruit tree expert who is familiar with the art of creating them.

A fruit tree hedge

If you have a small garden and want to harvest different kinds of fruit, it is worth planting a fruit tree hedge.

The shapes to choose are pyramid shapes for fruit with seeds and small bushes on slow-growing stocks for fruit with pits. Plums, greengage, and sweet cherries are not suitable for growing as hedges because of their large crowns, but apples, pears, quinces, bitter cherries, apricots, and peaches are.

The distances from tree to tree in a hedge should be 7-8 ft (2-2.5 m). If you plant them too close together, the fruit will not receive enough sunshine for proper ripening.

Shapes of hedges

The simple tree hedge consists of a row of pyramid-shaped bushes which are placed side by side. Each one has its own support post and will grow as an individual tree. The hedge requires plenty of room.

An espalier hedge is grown against a freestanding espalier made of wires. It will become very dense and the fruit should still ripen well as it will receive plenty of light from both sides of the hedge.

A safe place to ripen. The pear variety "Tongern" grown as a house espalier.

A Bouché-Thomas hedge consists of trees that have grown into each other and will become extremely dense.

Fruit trees in large containers

Small trees in large containers will not live for very long but they should yield a good harvest. Suitable for this medium are apples on slow-growing stocks; pears grafted onto quince; peach and apricot grafted onto plum; greengages grafted onto blackthorn and bitter cherries. Recently, the market has seen the arrival of dwarf varieties specially cultivated for growing in large containers.

Growing your own trees in large containers

Growing your own fruit trees is considerably cheaper than buying ready-grown small trees.

● Buy a one-year-old grafted tree in the fall, shorten the roots a little, and plant the young tree in a bed in the garden.
● Cut the crown into the desired shape in the spring.
● Pull the lateral branches slightly outward and cut out the shoots that grow inward during the summer.
● During the following spring, plant the tree in a large container.
● For a container, use a suitable compost that should occasionally be fertilized with hoof/horn or bone-meal afterward.

Further care of a tree in a large container

Fruit trees in large containers should be repotted every two to three years. The roots will have to be shortened on that occasion. Trees in large containers should be overwintered outside. The container should be well wrapped up in straw and bubble pack or something similar.

Growing an espalier or hedge

Espaliers on house walls

You must take great care when building an espalier grid as it needs to form an attractive feature on its own during the bare winter months.

Building a grid
(illustration 1)
● Battens that have been planed and treated with linseed oil should be doweled vertically into the façade.
● Place a ½-in (1.5-cm) block of wood as a spacer at each doweling point to keep the batten from contact with the wall. This will keep the back of the espalier ventilated and the battens will last longer.
● Screw or nail further planed, treated battens at intervals of 20 in (50 cm) horizontally onto the vertical battens.
Another method (suitable for a fan espalier and smaller walls):
● Three or four strong battens doweled into the wall with spacer blocks.
● Screw horizontal battens to this at 20-in (50-cm) intervals.

How to train the espalier fruit tree
A loose espalier
(illustration 2)
● Tie the two lower laterals of the crown horizontally to the grid, then cut the middle shoot 20 in (50 cm) above it.
● The tree will produce new shoots below the cut. The two strongest laterals should be tied on both sides to the next highest batten, while one is trained up as a central leader.
● Cut off all other shoots.
● During the following spring cut off the new central leader 20 in (50 cm) above the second fork and tie the new lateral shoots to the grid.
● Continue in this way until the wall is covered. Shoots growing upward from the lateral branches should be tied to the vertical battens and shoots that grow too close together should be cut off. All strong shoots that grow forward and all those that are not the right shape should also be cut off.

A fan espalier
(illustration 3)
● Bend the middle shoot of a young tree to one side until it is almost horizontal and tie it firmly to the grid.

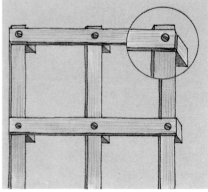

1 A stable trellis made of battens with spacer blocks.

● Strong vertical shoots will grow on this bent shoot and these can then be bent to either left or right and tied to the grid.
● Superfluous shoots can be cut back to the branch.
● Bending laterals in this way can be continued until the entire surface of the wall is covered. The stronger a shoot grows, the more you will have to bend it to train it to the horizontal. When bending shoots, be very careful not to break them. The best time to do it is during the first and second months of summer when the shoots are already strong but still flexible.

2 An open house espalier. This shape can even be trained around a window.

3 Fan espalier: the main shoots are growing on the highest parts of the bent central shoots.

Hedge espaliers
The grid
(illustrations 4a and 4b)

a Drive pressure-treated wooden posts (about 4 in/10 cm in diameter and 7½ ft/2.2 m long) about 24-28 in (60-70 cm) deep into the ground at 17-ft (5-m) intervals to provide vertical supports.

● Instead of wooden posts, you could also use metal posts that are cemented in. They will last longer.

b Galvanized or plastic-coated wire can be drawn between the posts and then pulled tight with a wire stretcher.

● Hammer the two end posts in at a slant and anchor them tightly into the ground with special anchors (available from hardware stores).

● The lowest wire should be 20 in (50 cm) above the ground; the rest spaced at 20-in (50-cm) intervals above this.

Hedge shapes
The hedge espalier
(illustration 5)

● After planting, train one lateral shoot to the right and one to the left and shorten the middle shoot.

● During the following years, in the first and second months of summer, tie the two strongest lateral branches to the right and left on the wire,

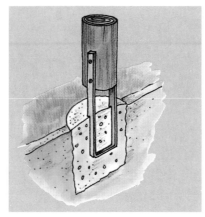

4a Wooden posts last longer if they are inserted in a concrete holder.

shorten the middle branch again, and cut off all other shoots.

● When the tree has attained a height at which all jobs can still be carried out without the help of a ladder, bend the middle branch down to the top wire and tie it up.

Maintenance cut: All shoots that grow strongly to the front and back should be cut off and also any shoots that form in the bend of the middle branch. New shoots on lateral branches can be tied up or thinned out. The hedge is allowed to be fairly dense.

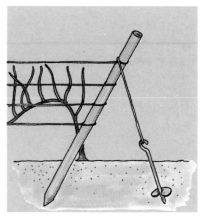

4b Slanting posts are held in position with a screw anchor.

Bouché-Thomas hedge
(illustration 6)

● Plant young trees at an angle of about 30 degrees. In this form of hedge the grafting point should be close to the ground.

● The strongest shoot will now grow upward. It should be bent to the other side where it will meet the main branch of the neighboring tree.

● The shoots should be tied together where they cross. This will form a grid-like hedge that need not be tied up. The roots that grow from the grafting point will give the tree enough stability.

5 Espalier hedge: The fruit ripens very well as it is receiving light from two sides.

6 A Bouché-Thomas hedge supports itself – one tree is supporting the other. It can grow very dense.

A selection of delicious apples, all of which could be grown in your own garden. In addition to the popular varieties, many older, local varieties of apples are now being offered again by good tree nurseries. It could be well worth your while to make inquiries. Many of the old varieties can also be grafted onto a low-growing rootstock.

"Kardinal Bea"

"Ontario"

"Graham's Jubilee"

"Discovery "

"MacIntosh Roger "

"Boskoop "

"Gloster "

"Melrose "

"Gala "

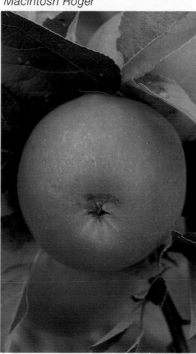

"James Grieve "

"Gewurzluiken "

How to obtain a rich harvest

Only well-cared-for fruit trees will yield a rich harvest. You should make use only of natural fertilizers in your own private garden. This will require some effort but the reward for all your hard work will be very tasty fruit. All other measures of care will depend on the weather, the time of year, and the state of the tree.

Proper fertilizing

Fertilizing does not play the greatest part in ensuring the quality of fruit. Far more important is the choice of the right variety, a suitable stock, the weather, pruning, and soil conditions. In other words, if you have chosen the wrong variety for your climatic conditions or if your cherry tree is growing in wet soil, the very best fertilizer will not help. You need to fertilize if you wish your fruit tree to develop and thrive for many years and to produce plenty of fruit. The tree is quite capable of absorbing nutrients from the soil through its widely spreading roots over many years but, eventually, all these reserves will be used up.

This is particularly true for all smaller varieties whose root systems are less wide-ranging. The task of the gardener is to make sure that there are always plenty of nutrient reserves available. These reserves are made up out of many components.

Nitrogen (N) is needed by the tree for the formation of new shoots and leaves. Too much nitrogen will result in scab and brown spots in the fruit flesh, the fruit will be watery, acidity will be reduced, and the fruit will be tasteless. Too little nitrogen will result in meager growth and less flower and fruit formation.

Phosphorus (P) is required by the tree for the formation of fruit. A phosphorus deficiency will cause inhibited ripening of fruit and fruit that quickly goes bad. The tree will blossom sparsely and the flowers will look pale.

Potassium (K) ensures that the tree is resistant to pests, diseases, and frost. Potassium deficiency leads to fruit that is tasteless and which rots quickly. The leaves will dry up before the fall. The tissue of the shoots is weakened and very susceptible to disease, particularly if, at the same time, the tree is receiving too much nitrogen. Too much potassium will also have a detrimental effect: the tree will be unable to absorb sufficient calcium and magnesium. The fruit will remain small and sour.

Calcium (Ca) raises the quality of the fruit and is a good soil improver, but the right amount must be given. If there is too much calcium in the soil, the tree will no longer be able to absorb essential nutrients. This means that you should check the pH factor before adding lime to the soil: apples and quinces like a pH value around 6; pears and other fruit with pits prefer values from 6-7. If the pH factor is below this, the soil will require extra lime.

Magnesium (Mg) is a very important nutrient that was for years underestimated. Every plant – even a fruit tree – requires this mineral to produce sufficient chlorophyll which, in turn, is responsible for the absorption of nutrients from the air through photosynthesis.

Trace elements like manganese (Mn), zinc (Zn), iron (Fe), copper (Cu), and boron (B) are absorbed by the tree in minute quantities but they are, nevertheless, vital.

When to fertilize

If you are giving your fruit trees natural fertilizers, give them controlled-release fertilizer which takes a long time to become effective but is also available to the tree for a long time. The exact time at which to fertilize is, therefore, not so important. Even so, it is a good idea to stick to a proper fertilizing schedule for young or small-growing trees so that nutrients are available when they are most needed. Older, tall, or standard trees need only be fertilized if they show obvious symptoms of nutrient deficiency. Generally, a layer of compost placed around the tree above the root system will be sufficient.

Fertilizing in the fall will serve to fortify the young tree and strengthen the shoots in the following spring. Both ripe garden compost and horse manure are equally good.

An orchard near the house. You will have to prune regularly if your trees are growing as close together as shown here.

Fertilizing for flowers should be carried out shortly before blossom time. The tree should receive plenty of water, plant brews, or natural liquid fertilizer.

Fertilizer intended to strengthen flower buds encourages the formation of buds for the following year. This should be carried out in the first month of summer for pears and cherries, and in the second month of summer for all other types of fruit. This fertilizing can be done with well-rotted compost, manure from stables, or with liquid fertilizers to which missing nutrients may be added.

Fertilizing for fruit should be done about four weeks after fertilizing for flower buds but, this time, give as little nitrogen as possible. Nitrogen encourages excessive shoot production and the shoots would not be hardy.

What to use

Garden compost is the best fertilizer for fruit trees in a small garden. It should be packed in a 4-in (10-cm) layer on the soil under the tree and covered with straw in the fall.

Manure from stables should be well rotted and spread extremely thinly on the bare soil under the tree.

Organic mixed fertilizer (horn, bone meal, or organic-mineral fertilizer) should be worked shallowly into the soil under the tree. It is used on poor soil or soil that is full of clay. This type of fertilizer is also suitable for flowers and flower buds. You can prepare your own **liquid fertilizer** for flower production. It is used if fertilizing with compost is not adequate.

Fermented herbal brews, mainly made out of nettles and comfrey, are used in the summer. They should be adequate if the right amount of compost has been given during the fall.

Wood ash is particularly good for fruit trees as it contains lots of potassium. Tip a shovelful on the soil around the bottom of the tree two to four times per year (depending on the size of the tree).

"Green" fertilizer, consisting mainly of legumes (for example, lupins, pea foliage, sweet peas) may be used as a substitute for part of the fall fertilizer. A mass of this foliage can be laid on the soil under the tree as mulch.

How to fertilize

You should not work the soil to any depth underneath a fruit tree as the roots lie close to the surface.

Solid nutrients, in the form of compost, manure from stables, wood ash, and organic fertilizers, should only be worked in superficially.

Liquid fertilizers should be applied as follows:

● All round, underneath the far edge of the crown of the tree, use a fork to pierce the soil at intervals of 8 in (20 cm) and move the handle around to loosen the soil.

● Pour liquid fertilizer into the holes produced.

● Then add plenty of water so that the nutrients are thoroughly washed down through the soil.

Further care

A few more tips on care should be observed if you wish to obtain a healthy fruit tree.

The soil around the base of the tree

The circular patch of bare soil around the stem of the tree and stretching to the width of the crown should be kept free of grass or other vegetation as this would draw

---

Homemade liquid fertilizer

Add one of the following ingredients to 12½ gallons (50 liters) water: 4½ pounds (2 kg) wood ash, 2 pounds (1 kg) soot, 11 pounds (5 kg) cow manure, 22 pounds (10 kg) poultry dung, 6½ pounds (3 kg) guano – or a mix of ¾ pound (750 g) wood ash, 2 pounds (1 kg) hoof/horn chips, 2 pounds (1 kg) cow pats, 2 handfuls kelp meal.

● Fill a jute sack with the ingredients and hang it inside a barrel. Let this ferment in the sun for about four weeks. Use diluted in the proportions 1:5 (½ gallon/2 liters liquid fertilizer to 2½ gallons/10 liters water).

Herbal brews

Loosely fill a 12½-gallon (50-liter) plastic barrel with coarsely chopped nettles or comfrey, or both, to halfway full. Fill with rainwater, cover, and leave to ferment for two to three weeks. Use diluted as 1:10 (4 cups/1 liter liquid to 2½ gallons/ 10 liters water).

---

water and fertilizer away from the tree. Only in the case of older, tall, standard trees can grass or lawn be allowed to grow over this area.

NB: "Green" fertilizer consisting of legumes or nasturtium is effective against woolly aphid.

Mulching

Place mulch on the soil under the tree. This will keep the soil moist and loose, and suppress the growth of weeds. Mulching may consist of grass cuttings, straw, and bark. Remove it before fall fertilizing; otherwise mice and other pests will invade the mulch.

Windfalls

Fruit lying on the ground should be collected regularly. If it is left to rot underneath the tree, it will attract pests and diseases. In particular, the codling moth likes to overwinter in windfall apples.

Watering

Young trees should be watered regularly the first year after planting. Later on, water only espalier fruit trees and trees grafted onto slow-growing stock during very dry periods. Lay a garden hose on the soil underneath the edge of the crown of the tree and let water flow gently for about 30 minutes or use a sprinkler.

Injuries

These can occur on the trunk or branches if you have pruned fairly vigorously or if entire branches have broken off (for example, through the action of storms, frost, hail, or if the fruit is abundant and very heavy) as well as through nibbling by grazing deer, etc. Such wounds are entry points for bacteria and fungi, and also often the cause of the dreaded fruit tree canker. Any wound that is larger than 1 in (2.5 cm) in diameter should be treated. Use a sharp knife to cut off the edges of the wound cleanly. Cut right down to healthy wood to remove cankers and frost damage wounds. Paint the open cuts with a wound-sealing substance. Very large wounds, for example, created by the breaking off of an entire branch or if wild animals have nibbled off a lot of bark, should be treated as follows:

● Mix two-thirds clay with one-third cow manure (without straw) to make a solid, moist paste.

● Smear a thick layer of the paste onto the wound. Tie a jute sack or some other coarse fabric over the wound. Keep it moist.

Suckers on a pear tree.

A mass of new shoots, the result of injury to the bottom of the stem.

Painting the trunk

Trees that will be standing in full sunlight during the winter months should have their stems painted. The constant alternating temperatures created by frost followed by milder weather will create tension in the bark, and cracks and tears will appear that can become a means of entry for germs, fungal spores, and pests.

A light-colored coating will help to prevent such damage. For painting the stem, use a calcium brew which can be bought ready-made or a special organic paint for tree trunks. **My tip:** If you have only one tree in your garden, you can stand a length of wood against the south- and east-facing sides of the tree during the winter as this will serve the same purpose as a protective coat of paint.

Suckers

These are shoots which sometimes grow up from the base of the tree trunk. Usually, the cause is an injury to the trunk at this point, for example, when mowing grass. The soil should be pushed away all around the trunk but do not dig down and risk damaging the roots. Then cut off these suckers with a sharp knife where they emerge. If you cut them off even a few inches (centimetres) above the ground, they will keep coming back and will interfere with the growth of the tree.

Shoots

Vertical shoots may appear en masse after rigorous pruning. They will drain the strength of the tree. They should be cut off flush with the branch during the first month of spring, except for the few that are required for rejuvenating.

Thinning out fruit

This will become necessary if a tree, particularly pear, peach, and certain apple varieties, produces too much fruit. Such thinning out can only be carried out on dwarf pyramid shaped trees. In the second month of summer, when the fruit is about the size of a walnut, take out about half the crop. Let only the largest fruits remain on the tree and in such a way that they are spaced at approximately 4-in (10-cm) intervals. This results in the remaining fruit growing larger and the bud formation for the following year, which is occurring at this time, will also be better. Never do this until after the first month of summer is over as around this time many fruit trees drop a lot of excess small, green fruit anyway.

93

Shaping fruit trees

If you let a fruit tree grow wild, it will soon display a dense, untidy crown that will produce very few, small fruits and in which fungal diseases will soon spread. As the branches become older and older, only a few weak shoots will be formed. Pruning a fruit tree is absolutely vital for its survival and well-being.

It must be said from the start that you cannot learn how to prune properly from a book. If you have several fruit trees in your garden, you would do well to take an evening course in fruit tree pruning during the winter. Fruit growing societies, gardening clubs, and various other groups, such as adult education, provide such courses. You can also always get advice from an expert at the nursery where you bought your trees. If you have only two or three trees, he or she will probably be prepared to prune them once or twice and show you the finer points of pruning.

Why prune?
A properly pruned fruit tree has an open crown in which all fruit is able to ripen properly and will receive enough light and sunshine. This is important for the ripening process and for the flavor of the fruit. In an open crown, wood that is able to bear fruit is formed along the entire branch not just at the tips. This

results in a greater yield and about the same amount every year. Properly pruned trees are also known to be more resistant to disease. Fungal diseases, in particular, do not stand a chance as the leaves dry off quickly after a rainfall and never provide the moist, warm micro-climate in the crown that encourages disease. Pruning a tree is, therefore, also a preventive measure for protecting the tree.

Can a tree be pruned at any age?
We have already discussed the planting cut. This is not enough, however, as a tree has to be cut or pruned in special ways at every age.
A training cut is necessary every year until the crown has attained its final shape and size. Until then you will still need to train branches and tie them up. During this period, main branches that have not yet developed properly can be replaced by new young shoots.

The maintenance cut serves to keep the crown in good shape. Only excess shoots are taken away from then on so that enough fruit-bearing wood can develop.
The rejuvenating cut should begin when no more fruit shoots appear on old wood. In the case of a small-growing tree this may be after ten years; in the case of a tall standard it may be after twenty years. After that, pruning is quite radical.
A thinning out cut becomes necessary for very old, uncared-for fruit trees that have not been pruned for many years and also for fruit species that are not normally given a training cut in the usual way. Here, too, radical cutting will be necessary to ensure that you obtain new fruit-bearing wood.

When to prune
The right time for pruning is late winter or early spring before the sap has started rising again. At this time, when there is no foliage on the tree, it is easy to see where corrective cuts should be carried out.
The summer pruning of young trees is done more often these days than it was in the past. It is carried out in addition to the winter cut and should be done during the second and third months of summer. Pruning in summer encourages growth of the crown, as superfluous shoots which are competing with the main branches can be cut away.

A rich harvest is the reward for the correct care of a fruit tree.

Pruning

Tools: You will need a good pair of secateurs, a branch cutter, a bow saw, and a pruning knife.

Glossary of technical terms
(illustration 1)
You will need to know a few technical terms in order to understand pruning properly. (See illustration 1.) Every fruit tree observes the following rules more or less:
● All shoots need as much light as possible so they tend to grow in the direction of most light.
● The bud that is highest will shoot most vigorously so no lateral branch should be longer than the central branch.
● Hardly any fruit-bearing wood grows on branches that grow vertically upwards; more grows on shoots on the long laterals.
● Fewer, but stronger, new shoots appear on severely pruned shoots.
● Branches that have been cut back less form many weaker, but still fruit-bearing, shoots.

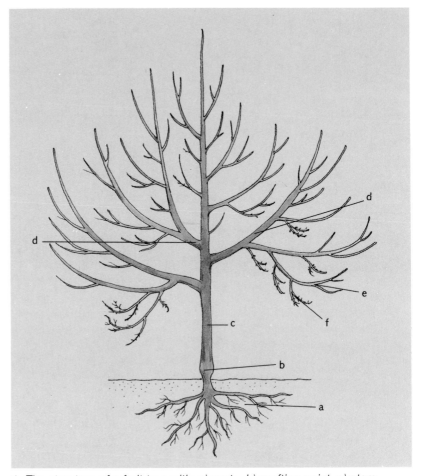

1 The structure of a fruit tree with: a) roots, b) grafting point, c) stem, d) main branches, e) fruit-bearing branches, and f) fruit-bearing shoots.

2 Prune the shoots below and new shoots will grow above.

3 Encouraging new shoots. A branch that has been tied horizontally will soon form short, new, fruit-bearing wood.

96

The formation of fruit-bearing wood
(illustration 2)
Branches that bear fruit over many years tend to hang down low, with the result that new, vigorous shoots appear on the highest point of the hanging branch. Three- to four-year-old fruit-bearing wood which points downward should, therefore, be cut off at the point where the new shoot appears. This shoot will then bear fruit and, following the natural law, will hang downward again. This sequence is a continuous process.

Encouraging the formation of shoots through tying
(illustration 3)
The young shoot should be tied horizontally so that it can bear fruit as soon as possible. First, short, fruit-bearing shoots, and then fruit, will appear on the upperside of a shoot. Be careful – if the shoot is tied too low, a vigorous shoot will only appear at the highest point. This means that the angle should be only a little less than 90 degrees. By contrast, illustration 3 shows a shoot that has been cut off, not tied up horizontally. It has not borne any fruit but does show several new young shoots and this can be just as important for training the crown.

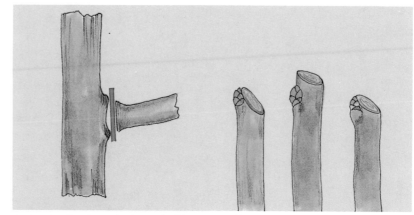

4 Cutting back to the branch. The quickest way for the wound to heal.

5 Cut above a bud. Left – too low, center – too high, right – correct.

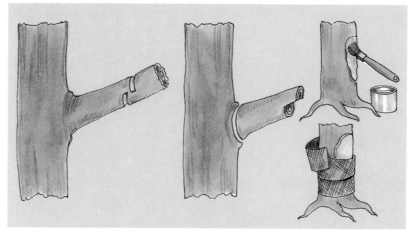

6 A large branch is sawn off in two stages. Right: treating small and large wounds.

Pruning back to the branch
(illustration 4)
All shoots, branches, and twigs that are growing too steeply upward should be cut back to the branch. The same goes for shoots that compete with others. The branch or shoot should be cut off with a sharp knife close to the stem so that the cut surface points slightly downward. This will prevent moisture penetrating the wood and discourage the spread of bacteria.

Cutting above a bud
(illustration 5)
In order to encourage a shoot to branch out, the shoot should be cut above a bud. This is particularly true for the planting and training cut that is supposed to create a regular-shaped crown. Only if the cut is made correctly above the bud will the shoot branch out properly.
The shoot should be cut off about ¼ in (5 mm) above a bud facing outward.

Cutting a branch
(illustration 6)
Occasionally, a branch will have to be cut off when thinning out and rejuvenating. Saw halfway into the branch from underneath about 8 in (20 cm) from the stem. Then saw into the branch from above, 2 in (5 cm) farther from the stem. The branch will break off. Saw off the stump where the branch emerged. A layer of callus will grow over the wound from this point. If you have sawn off a thick branch, the wound will have to be treated.

Pruning

A tree will require different kinds of pruning depending on its age. For all of the pruning measures mentioned below the following advice should be heeded. You must always prune very carefully and sensibly. A fruit tree need not be cut back severely every single winter. Often, small corrections will be quite sufficient. Have a good look at the tree and only prune whenever and wherever it is really necessary!

The training cut
(illustration 1)

After the fairly drastic planting cut, many new shoots will form, not all of which should be left to grow in the crown as it would soon become too dense. The training cut therefore serves to improve the shape of a crown so that it can benefit from light and air, and produce plenty of fruit-bearing wood. In the case of small-growing trees, a training cut will be necessary every winter for two to three years, and in the case of tall standard trees, up to eight years. For espaliers it may be necessary to carry out a training cut throughout the entire lifetime of the tree. First, cut out all competing shoots. These are shoots that are in competition with the three main branches and the extension of the stem. Cut them back to the branch from which they emerge. Where new shoots are growing too densely along the main branches, where they grow inward, and wherever too many shoots are growing on the upper sides of branches, they should be cut out at the point where they emerge. Each main branch should be let form a further three branches which fork. This can be done by shortening the central leader and the extensions of the main branches. The following general rule applies. If the

1 Remove competing shoots and shorten extensions of main branches.

new shoots are weak, cut them back radically; if the new shoots are strong, cut back lightly. The more drastically you cut back, the more plentifully the new shoots will grow. Shoots on branches that are not being trained as laterals should be tied horizontally so that they can produce new fruit-bearing shoots. On the central leader, also let vigorous shoots remain that are growing at an angle of about 45 degrees. Cut off branches that form an acute angle with the main branch as they will break off under the full weight of fruit. Cutting back the extensions of the main branches and stem is correct if all the buds shoot. Some of these will produce strong woody shoots but many will form fruit-bearing shoots.

The maintenance cut
(illustration 2)

When the crown has attained its proper shape and size, it should look as follows: a stem with a cen-

tral leader and several fruit-bearing branches spaced along it; three strong, main branches, each with three laterals that are spaced at least 2 ft (60 cm) from the stem; several fruit-bearing branches also growing from the lateral branches; short, fruit-bearing wood distributed all over the crown. This wood should be horizontal and keep producing new shoots. If the crown is shaped in this way, maintenance pruning will not be a big job. Every three years, the older fruit-bearing branches, which are beginning to hang down, should be removed so that new shoots can grow in their place. If young shoots have grown too densely on branches or masses of long shoots have formed, these should be thinned out so that sufficient light can penetrate the crown. If a proper maintenance cut has not been carried out regularly, a more drastic pruning will become necessary to thin out the crown.

For the thinning out cut, remove the following branches:
● branches that are growing at acute angles along the central leader
● branches on the upper side of the main branches, which have become too thick (so that new, young shoots can form)
● dried up or diseased branches
● branches that are growing too closely above each other and take light away from each other.
If the thinning out work looks like being very extensive, for example in the case of a tree that has not been cut back for a long time, it would be better to spread the work over two years so that the tree is not encouraged to produce too many new shoots. After this thinning out cut, plenty of long, lanky shoots will grow in any case and these should be cut off during the summer while they are still green.

2 Maintenance cut for thinning out, shortening and always making sure that the crown remains even.

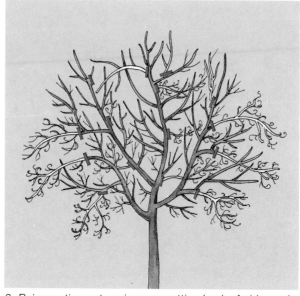

3 Rejuvenating cut: a vigorous cutting back of old wood to encourage the formation of new, young shoots.

The rejuvenating cut
(illustration 3)

When a tree finally becomes old, the yield will decrease noticeably. At this time it will often be well worth rejuvenating the tree. This is a job, however, that is best left to an expert as rather extensive pruning measures will have to be undertaken. The crown will have to be reduced by a third. This means that the central leader and the main branches should be cut back to the old wood. Depending on the size of the tree, this may be up to 10 ft (3 m). Make sure, while doing this, that the shape of the crown remains in balance. At least 20 in (50 cm) of all the lateral shoots growing on both the central leader and the main branches should be cut back to the branch. This will encourage the formation of new tips on the main branches, which will soon produce vigorous new shoots.
None of the lateral branches should be longer than these new tips which means that all lateral branches

should be cut well back into the old wood. The new crown should be opened up. About six to eight branches should remain, well distributed around the stem, and these should be properly pruned.
No shoots should be left growing on the upper sides of branches and everything that looks weak should be taken off the under sides. Fruit-bearing wood should remain. What

4 Summer cut to keep the crown light and airy.

is left should, if possible, be horizontal young shoots.
These very radical measures should only be inflicted upon a tree in a year after a poor fruit yield. It will bear a good harvest again during the following years.

The summer cut
(illustration 4)

A summer cut is generally carried out on young trees but it is also a good idea on a dwarf pyramid tree of any age. This means cutting away all superfluous shoots during the second and third months of summer because these shoots will compete with the main branches and the central leader. Also cut away long, lanky shoots that are growing too close together on the upper sides of branches and into the crown. During the summer, vigorous long shoots can be tied into a horizontal position so that they do not turn into main branches but, instead, become fruit-bearing branches.

Pests and diseases

Nature's own plant protection agents

If you are growing fruit in your own garden, you will obviously set great store by healthy, tasty fruit that should on no account be contaminated with the residue from toxic sprays. Prevention and the use of mechanical and biological plant protection agents will make it possible to do without toxic chemicals.

Biological plant protection means using the advantages and opportunities offered by nature. Your goal should always be to avoid upsetting the natural balance or to risk endangering any living species. Even where the biological equilibrium has already been interfered with, a small garden provides a great opportunity to recreate that natural balance with a little patience and knowledge. Unlike those involved in the mass production of food, you will not need to aim for as large a yield as possible or to produce visually perfect fruit.

This attitude is a lot easier in the private sphere. Prevention should always be the first rule before using any pest or disease control measures. During the last few decades, pest control in particular has done more damage than good. Not only were the pests themselves destroyed but, very often, useful insects that were their natural enemies were also wiped out. The fewer useful insects that survived, the more the pests multiplied.

The result was that spraying had to be carried out more and more often. In addition, many pests became resistant to insecticides. A vicious cycle was created that is not easy to break and requires a great deal of patience to rectify.

Prevention through care

Healthy, properly nourished, and well-cared-for trees are less susceptible to pests and diseases. The following points should always be observed.

The right position

Every variety of fruit has special requirements in relation to position. Several components play a part in this:
● the climate
● the altitude
● the position in relation to the house
● soil conditions.

Only where all of these preconditions are met can a fruit tree remain robust and healthy. When grown in the wrong position, it will be weak-

ened and thus become susceptible to pests and diseases.

My tip: It is better to abandon the idea of cultivating a particular type of fruit tree if it is not suitable for your garden. This will save you a lot of trouble and disappointment!

The right variety

The choice of the right variety is directly dependent on the position. For example, there are some fruit varieties that will still thrive at altitudes where other varieties could no longer cope. Some fruit varieties are also particularly susceptible to certain diseases or pests.

My tip: Local fruit varieties, of which there are literally thousands among apples and pears, are particularly robust and well adapted to the relevant climate.

The right cut

Pruning a fruit tree is essential but even here one should proceed with care and a clear goal in mind. A tree that has been thinned out properly will hardly ever become infested with fungal diseases as no moist, warm conditions can prevail in the crown. If, however, you cut the tree back too vigorously during one season, this may weaken it and make it susceptible to attack by pests.

My tip: Any radical pruning you intend to carry out is better done in stages over a period of two consecutive years.

The right spacing

In a small garden, the temptation to cram in as many trees as possible is great and they may end up being planted too close together. Trees that stand in a dense group are at risk from the rapid spread of pests and diseases.

These juicy pears of the variety "Tongern" were grown without recourse to chemical plant protection agents.

Avoiding a monoculture

If you plant several apple trees, for example, you should try to choose three or more varieties rather than just one. This will prevent the spread of diseases that are specific to certain varieties and will also ensure better pollination.

Care of the soil under the tree

Young trees require an open area of soil around their base. Grass or lawn would take away too much water and nourishment from the young tree. Small, low-growing trees will require bare soil underneath the crown for their entire lifespan. The soil here should always be mulched so that it remains "alive" and moist. The mulching material will rot in time and provide the soil with nutrients. The root system of a fully grown tall standard, on the other hand, is spread out far enough for the tree to manage without an area of bare soil around the base and therefore a tall standard can grow in an orchard full of grass or on a lawn. You should still avoid digging around the roots, however.

Fertilizing

Fruit trees need fertilizer but you should hold back on nitrogen. Nitrogen will encourage vigorous growth and large fruits but is not healthy in large quantities as the cells in the fruit tissues are then forced and end up being too soft,and therefore susceptible to attack by pests and diseases. It is more important to ensure that the tree has a well-balanced supply of nitrogen, phosphorus, and potassium in the right ratios.

Useful insects to combat pests

Useful insects are the gardener's most effective "troops" in the battle against all pests in fruit trees. If the useful insects are encouraged, or even introduced to trees, you can say goodbye to toxic sprays.

Ladybirds are great predators of aphids. Their larvae become active early in the spring. During its twenty-day larval stage, a ladybird can consume up to 400 aphids. The fully grown ladybird is equally as voracious.

Lacewings (Chrysopa vulgaris) are even more useful. Each lacewing larva can eliminate approximately 500 aphids, in addition to small caterpillars and the larvae of other species which suck the sap from leaves, before it enters the chrysalis stage after eighteen days. The fully grown insects live almost entirely on nectar which is why they can be coaxed to take up residence by planting many flowering plants in the garden or growing a flower meadow instead of a neatly cut lawn.

Pirate bugs are not beautiful to behold but they are extremely useful. They like to sit along the veins of leaves and at the base of stalks where they are sure to catch their main prey: spider mites.

Predatory mites (Phytoseiulus persimilis) are also specialists in preying on spider mites. Although they are tiny, they are extemely active. If you spray a tree with certain insecticides, such as tar oil winter wash, you will, unfortunately, end up exterminating the predatory mites and not the spider mites!

Hover flies look rather like wasps that have not grown properly but they do not sting. They are important for the pollination of fruit trees and, during their development, the larvae can devour up to 500 aphids each. If you plant plenty of umbelliferous plants between your fruit

Pests that may occur on all types of fruit

Aphids: Crumpled and rolled up leaves, honey dew formation, deformed fruit, masses of green or black larvae. Prevention: encourage useful insects. During the spring, put a sticky band on the trunk. Control: spray with plant soap solution or herbal brews.

Spider mites: The leaves display small, white spots, become brown, and drop off. Prevention: the right position; carefully balanced fertilizers; encourage and support useful insects. Control: during blossom time, spray with agents that do not harm useful insects.

Ermine moth: Masses of tiny caterpillars in white webs in the crown of the tree. Leaves will begin to drop if infestation is severe. Prevention: hardly possible. Control: cut off branches with webs and burn them. Collect by hand in the case of small trees.

Winter moths: Green caterpillars which eat the foliage until the tree is almost bare. Prevention: install a sticky ring in the fall. Control: biological methods are not possible. The tree will grow new leaf shoots next spring.

Fruit rot: Ring-shaped rotting marks on fruit with fungus formation. Prevention: thin out the crown properly. Collect all fallen rotten fruit, remove rotten fruit from tree during the winter. Control: biological sprays.

Leaf spot diseases: Small spots or holes in the leaves specific to each variety of fruit. Prevention: thin the crown out well, cut off severely infested branches and destroy them; avoid planting in the neighborhood of juniper as this species encourages the appearance of rust. Control: not possible.

trees, you will encourage hover flies to visit your garden.

Ichneumon flies lay their eggs in living aphids and in the larvae of whiteflies. The emerging larvae will devour their hosts from the inside out. Some ichneumon fly species have specializsed in preying on the dreaded ermine moth.

Spiders should be encouraged as they trap many harmful pests in their webs.

Earwigs, on the other hand, have been rather overrated. They are omnivorous and much prefer flower buds or fruit to eating aphids. In the spring, they do not emerge from the soil until the aphids have already taken over.

Useful insects to buy

A large number of useful insects can be purchased nowadays but they are intended mainly for commercial operations, large greenhouses, and conservatories. Lacewings and *Aphelinus* can be released outside providing the weather is warm enough. They should be attached to infested trees and the larvae will hatch after two days. *Bacillus thuringiensis* is a useful organism that can be used against harmful caterpillars by spraying it on. These organisms are often employed in commercial fruit growing.

Birds

Birds consume several times their own weight in insects annually, so they are extremely important for reducing pests in fruit cultivation. They will only breed where there is plenty of food and that means they will not spend time where insects are being controlled with chemicals.

Encouraging useful insects

The worst enemy of useful insects is people and their endeavors to get rid of pests quickly and thoroughly.

Even some biological sprays will kill off useful insects too. For this reason, a number of points should be observed so that useful insects can continue to live in fruit trees and multiply there.

● Nearly all useful insects overwinter as adult insects in the soil, under the bark of trees, in the casings of buds and other hiding places. Pests, on the other hand, usually overwinter as eggs or larvae. The standard winter spraying, for example with tar oil winter wash, will certainly kill off the useful insects, but only some of the pests as they are protected by their egg cases. If this spraying is discontinued, the useful insects will be present in large numbers at the same time as the pests hatch.

● Nearly all insecticides destroy both pests and useful insects. Pests, however, multiply much faster than useful insects, the reason being that pests live off the fruit trees (and other plants) but useful insects have become specialized to prey only on certain pests. If the pests are exterminated or even severely reduced, the useful insects are doomed to starvation.

● If infestation with pests is severe and you are using agents that do not kill the useful insects, you should ensure that not all pests are eliminated, but only about twothirds. The rest will not cause much damage and the useful insects will continue to find food.

Mechanical plant protection

Other measures can be undertaken to prevent infestation with pests so that spraying may not even be necessary.

Painting the stem or tree trunk
in winter with a readymade preparation will prevent the pests from establishing themselves in the scaly bark. Painting the bark

makes it smooth and it will not then be subject to cracking through the rapid alternation of mild and cold temperatures during the winter. It is a good idea to spray the solution into the bare crown of the tree also.

Sticky rings can be tied around the trunk (also around the support posts) in the fall to prevent the female winter moth from crawling up the tree to lay her eggs. The caterpillars are quite capable of eating the foliage of an entire tree until it is completely bare. Sticky rings also prevent ants from establishing colonies of aphids in the trees during the spring.

NB: In the case of young trees, the sticky ring will have to be replaced every three to four months; otherwise the ring will cut into the growing stem.

Sticky traps should be wrapped around the stems in the last month of spring. Larvae will collect here and will have to be removed regularly.

Pheromone traps are equipped with female sex hormones to attract the males. The male insects fly up and become stuck. You will be able to obtain these traps from garden centers. The traps themselves do not appear to be totally effective but at least they are a means of establishing which pests are attacking your fruit trees.

Fallen fruit should always be gathered up during the fall. Whatever is not used should be discarded on the compost heap. If you let the fruit remain under the tree, it provides ideal overwintering quarters for pests, bacteria, and fungus spores. Trees with a very rough, scaly bark should be scrubbed with a hard brush in the fall to prevent infestation by pests.

Pests and diseases of fruit with seeds (apples, pears, quinces)

Scab: Olive green, brown spots on leaves and fruit, the skin of the fruit cracks open and becomes scaly. Prevention: do not grow susceptible varieties; allow enough space between trees; thin out crowns properly. Control: biological sprays from mid-spring.

Mildew: White, powdery film on young leaves and flower buds. Prevention: keep the crown open. Control: cut off infested shoots and destroy them; cut out all infested shoots during the winter cut; spray with mare's tail brew.

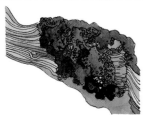

Fruit tree canker: Gnarled growths on the trunk and branches. Prevention: avoid wet, cold positions and overfertilizing with nitrogen; treat wounds immediately. Control: cut out cankers; cover up and seal wounds; disinfect all tools.

Codling moth: "Wormy" fruit, small red worms and tunnels inside the fruit. Prevention: install sticky worm trap rings in the first month of spring; protect useful insects. Control: not necessary.

Brown rot: Soft brown patches on the fruit, underneath which are small brown spots in the fruit flesh; fruit will not keep in storage. Prevention: avoid susceptible varieties; do not fertilize with too much nitrogen; avoid waterlogging. Control: not possible.

Fireblight: Shoots and flowers quickly wither and turn black; very infectious and dangerous. Prevention: not possible. Control: cut off infected shoots and destroy them; if necessary, cut down the tree.

What to do in the case of infestation

Even with the best care, pests or diseases may occur on such a scale that action has to be taken if one wishes to avoid losing the entire tree. Here, too, tried and tested methods can be adopted without resorting to toxins.

Mildew and Monilia

At the occurrence of these diseases during the spring, immediately cut off all affected shoots and destroy them (do not put them on the compost heap!). When carrying out a winter cut, make sure that every single affected shoot is removed along with any rotted fruit. Spraying with mare's tail brew is also very effective.

Mare's tail brew: add 2 pounds (1 kg) freshly cut mare's tail to 2½ gallons (10 liters) water. Bring to a boil, then cool and strain. Spray undiluted as a preventive or if plants are affected.

Biting and sucking insects

If there is an aphid infestation that is so severe that useful insects can no longer cope or if codling moths or other harmful insects threaten to take over, it is time to take action. In this case, a homemade brew may be used to combat the pests.

Nettle brew: Add 2 pounds (1 kg) of fresh nettle leaves to 2½ gallons (10 liters) water. Soak for 24 hours and then boil. Let cool, strain, and dilute in the proportions 1:4 (4 cups/1 liter of brew to 1 gallon/ 4 liters of water) and spray the tree.

Tansy brew: Put ½ pound (300 g) fresh tansy in 2½ gallons (10 liters) water. Bring to a boil, then cool and strain. Dilute with double the volume of water for spraying against aphids, ermine moth, and codling moth.

Diseases and pests of fruit with pits (cherries, plums, greengages, damsons, peaches, apricots)

Monilia on flowers and branches, particularly in cherry trees. Young shoots wither shortly after flowering and die. Prevention: hardly possible, infectious disease. Control: immediately cut off affected shoots and cut up to 8 in (20 cm) into the healthy wood, burn the shoots.

Resin bleeding: Copious secretion of resinous sap on all woody parts; the tree quickly dies. Prevention: not possible, infectious disease. Control: cut off affected shoots, cutting into the healthy wood, and burn the shoots.

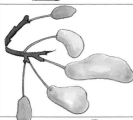

Pocket plums: Unnaturally long plums which are flat and brown under a powder-like film. Prevention: keep the crown open. Control: remove affected fruit constantly and destroy.

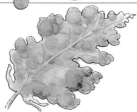

Peach leaf curl: During the spring this occurs in peach and apricot trees. Blistery leaves that are discolored whitish-green or reddish and dry up. Prevention: plant robust varieties; varieties with yellow fruit flesh are more susceptible. Control: destroy affected leaves and branches.

Wormy cherries and plums: Wormy fruit. Prevention: early varieties are less susceptible. Control: if infestation is severe spray with biological agents. NB: Avoid this if there are many bees about!

Plum pox virus: Various symptoms, such as severely cracked trunk, rubbery, inedible fruit, light-colored spots on leaves (does not affect cherries). A viral disease that is notifiable. Prevention: plant varieties that are resistant to it. Control: dig out the trees and burn them.

Soft soap solution: Dissolve ½ pound (300g) soft soap or plant soap in 2½ gallons (10 liters) hot water. Add a shot of mineral spirits as an adhesive and spray undiluted when cooled to control aphids and scale insects.

Pyrethrum preparations: Pyrethrum is an insecticide that is derived from the flowers of an African chrysanthemum. It works fast against all animal pests but is not entirely safe and should only be used if mechanical and gentle biological methods have failed. Use pyrethrum-containing agents only according to the manufacturer's directions and note any comments regarding the waiting time between its use and your consumption of the fruit.
Warning: Preparations containing pyrethrum also destroy useful insects! Always wear rubber gloves when handling these preparations. Pyrethrum must not be allowed to enter open wounds as it is a nerve toxin which may enter the bloodstream. Pyrethroids are artificially produced pyrethrum-like plant protection agents that are extremely toxic, very difficult to break down and should never be used in an organic garden.

Organic sprays to buy

Several organic sprays can be purchased. They can be used without any qualms but, just as when using chemical agents, the manufacturer's directions should be closely followed. When using these agents, also check whether they are safe for useful insects, bees, and fish.
Warning: Most of the organic plant protection agents are not without their risks either. Children and domestic pets should never come into contact with them.

The best way to grow superior fruit

Young fruit trees are usually grafted in tree nurseries. This is the only way to guarantee that the right variety and shape of tree are obtained. As a rule, grafting is not a technique for the layperson to carry out. However, regrafting new varieties on to a fully grown tree can offer the interested amateur gardener a host of opportunities.

How grafting is done

A fruit tree is grafted by growing a shoot of the desired variety on a chosen stock. Not only does this determine the variety of fruit but a large number of the characteristics of the future fruit tree can also be considerably influenced: its size, the height of the stem or trunk, its hardiness and response to soil types, etc.

The stock consists of the root and a section of stem or trunk measuring about 6 in (15 cm). Stocks are grown in tree nurseries from the seed of specific varieties of fruit through vegetative propagation (shoots, rhizomes, cuttings, etc.). The stocks, which grow first as simple shoots, are cut off about 6 in (15 cm) above the ground during the last month of summer. Depending on the stock, a tree will be tall or short, more or less hardy, or have a short or long life expectancy.

The scion is cut from a healthy tree that is known to yield well. Only one-year-old shoots which have short gaps between their buds are used. Scions of fruit trees with pits are cut in the last month of fall, and those with seeds in the second month of winter on the sun-facing side of the tree as the shoots should be fully mature on that side. A 8-10-in (20-25-cm) long piece of shoot with three to five buds is used for grafting. The shoot determines which variety of fruit the tree will bear.

The grafting of a young tree

By grafting, a scion of the desired variety is inserted into the stock. Where the two parts of the new fruit tree grow together, a thickened join is formed at the grafting point. The scion will carry on growing vigorously during the following year and is pruned the year after that, so that it starts to form lateral shoots. Young trees without lateral shoots are one year old, those with several lateral shoots are two-year-old grafted trees.

Grafting onto an adult tree

This measure, also called regrafting, can be carried out by an amateur gardener (see pp. 40-41). It is a possibility to consider if the yield of a particular tree is not satisfactory, if the variety is not suitable for the climate, or if several varieties of fruit are wanted from one tree.

Several varieties on one tree

It is entirely possible to graft scions of several different varieties on one tree (this is called a "family tree"). The most interesting situation is one in which a selection of varieties ripen at different times.

Advantages: You will not need another tree for pollinating as the blossom times will overlap. The harvest will extend over a longer period of time, yielding smaller amounts of fruit of different varieties.

Suitable varieties of fruit: In the case of apples, pears, sweet cherries, and plums particularly, it is recommended to combine an early, medium early and late variety on one tree.

NB: The shapes of growth should match. Slow-growing varieties grafted with vigorously growing varieties will not grow well. Spindly and drooping varieties side by side will result in an unattractive crown.

Examples: The following apple varieties go well together: "Klarapfel," "James Grieve," "Golden Delicious." With pears: "Frühe von Trévoux," "Gute Luise," "Tongern." With sweet cherry: "Frühe Meckenheimer," "Spitze Braune," "Schauenburger."

My tip: Plums and greengages can be grafted onto one tree.

Two varieties of apple on one tree.

Grafting

Whether you are grafting onto a young tree or onto an old one, you should practise the technique beforehand with a branch you have cut off, as a little skill is required to make the right cut.

Grafting a young tree
The grafting point
(illustration 1)
Every fruit tree that has been grafted in a tree nursery will have a grafting point just above the root. This should always sit above the soil; otherwise suckers will grow here that are difficult to remove. Where trunk-forming stocks are being used, for example, if a quince is required to obtain a tall stem through grafting it onto a hawthorn, you will find another grafting point just below the crown, which may become quite thick in old age.

Whip and tongue grafting
(illustration 2)
The best time for grafting a young tree is during the last month of spring. This is how a scion is grafted on to a stock in the tree nursery. The stock and the scion should have the same thickness, i.e. the same diameter.
● The stem of the stock should be cut diagonally with a sharp knife so that the cut surface is about 2 in (5 cm) long. A tongue should be cut out in the center of the sloping surface.
● The scion should be cut diagonally to the same length and also equipped with a tongue.
● When joining the two parts, the two cut surfaces are pushed together so that the lowest bud of the scion is opposite the cut surface. The tongues should fit together.
NB: The cambium layer, the layer between bark and wood of both

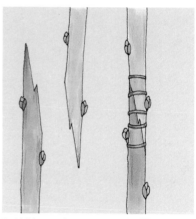

1 *A one-year-old tree after grafting.*

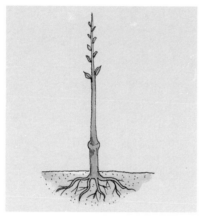

2 *Whip and tongue graft. The scion is set onto the rootstock.*

surfaces, should meet perfectly. This is vital if the two parts are to grow together. The tongues help the two parts to stay together and prevent them from slipping. The stock and the scion are tied together with a soft rubber band or raffia. Afterwards, coat the grafting join with tree wax. After six to eight weeks, the raffia should be removed so that it cannot cut into the wood.

Regrafting onto an adult tree
This is the name given to a procedure in which a young scion is grafted onto an adult tree.

In this case, the grafting head of the stock will always be a lot thicker than the scion. Among various different methods of grafting, the two most commonly used ones are as follows.

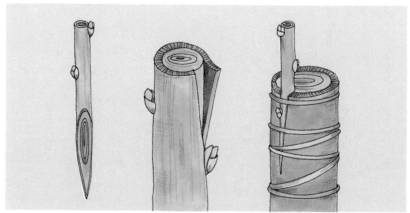

3 *Grafting behind the bark. The scion is pushed behind the bark after the latter has been peeled away.*

Grafting behind the bark
(illustration 3)

If you want to graft a new variety onto to a fully grown tree, the usual way is to graft behind the bark. This is a method of joining as much as possible of the cambium of the stock with the cambium of the scion in the best and simplest way. The cambium is the tissue responsible for letting the two parts grow together. The right time for this method of grafting is during the spring when the bark of a tree is easiest to loosen. Depending on the regional climatic conditions, this may be any time between the beginning of the second month and the end of the last month of spring.

● The upper part of the stock should be cut off straight with a sharp knife, taking care that the bark is not damaged.

● From the top edge of the stock, make a vertical cut, 2 in (5 cm) long, through the bark and into the cambium (but not into the wood!).

● Carefully open up the bark on one side of the cut. The scion, which should have been cut diagonally to the same length, should now be slipped under the bark and the bark closed up again around it.

● Tie up the bark and the scion

with raffia. The raffia should be wound in the same direction as the bark was laid across the scion. Finally, the entire grafting point should be sealed with tree wax.

Wedge grafting
(illustration 4)

This method of grafting is also suitable for grafting onto older trees. It should be carried out on mild days in the last month of winter or the first month of spring. Cut a wedge, which narrows at the bottom, into the top of the stock. The end of the scion should be cut into the same shape. The scion is then pushed into the wedge-shaped cut in the stock and tied up. The advantage is that wood is placed against wood so the scion sits very firmly on the stock. The only disadvantage is that this method should be practised beforehand as the wedge-shaped end of the scion must fit exactly into the wedge-shaped cut of the stock or the scion will not grow properly.

Care after grafting
(illustration 5)

With both grafting and regrafting, the raffia should be removed about six weeks later so that the thickening of the grafting point is not hin-

dered. Many new shoots usually grow out of the grafting point and they should be cut off as soon as possible to ensure that all the vital strength goes into the growth of the new scion. The scion should always be positioned so that it receives plenty of light.

Pruning

Before grafting onto a fully grown tree, the crown needs some special preparation. The branches that are to be used for the grafting process need to be radically shortened. For fruit with seeds this should be done in late winter, and in the case of fruit with pits, shortly before blossom time. The position where the cut was made and where, later on, the scion is grafted on is called the grafting point. It should have a diameter of less than 3¼ in (8 cm). Immediately before grafting, the grafting head should be shortened by another 4 in (10 cm) so that grafting can be undertaken on fresh wood.

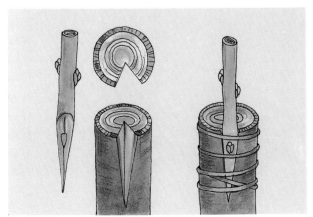

4 Wedge grafting. The properly cut scion is inserted into a wedge-shaped cut on the top of the stock.

5 After grafting, cut off all new shoots around the grafting point (with the exception of those on the scion).

Delicious fruit and its care

Splendid blossom and healthy fruit

In the spring fruit trees delight us with their wealth of blossom; later on the delicious fruit can be eaten. In order to enjoy fruit gardening to the utmost, it is important to know how to care for different species of fruit trees. The following pages give detailed tips on several of the most popular fruit trees. The following descriptions should help you to find the right fruit tree for your garden.

Glossary of keywords

The following pages give detailed instructions for care, with information on:

Name: First the common name, then the botanical one.

Flower: This gives data on the flowering time and appearance of the flower.

Fruit: Notes on the time of harvest and the appearance of the fruit.

Content: Information for people who like to know what they are eating.

Shape of tree: Important tips on the different shapes of trees and the most common stocks used for grafting.

Suitable for: Designs for your garden or balcony.

Position: What you should look out for when choosing the position for the fruit tree.

Soil: In what soil the species of fruit grows best and how the soil can be improved.

Pollination: Indicates whether the fruit tree requires another one for pollination.

Planting: Directions for proper planting.

Maintenance cut: Advice on the correct pruning of the tree.

Fertilizing: Tips on the right medium and suitable quantities.

Care: Tips for tree care all the year round.

Susceptible to: Among these are diseases that the tree is most commonly susceptible to.

Varieties: Recommended and popular varieties.

Harvest: How and when to harvest.

Use: Practical tips for the use of fruit.

Storage: The correct way to store different types of fruit.

My tip: Advice and tips resulting from the personal experience of the author.

Abundantly blossoming apple trees in a field of dandelions.

110

Bud stage ...

... and then, the beautiful apple blossom.

Apple
Malus domestica

Flower: Mid to late spring. The flower buds are deep pink; when open, in delicate pink and white clusters. Many late varieties have deeper pink flowers. They appear before the leaves.

Fruit: Harvest depending on the variety, from early spring to mid-fall. Apples come in many different shapes and colors: delicate green, yellow, green with red cheeks or streaks, brownish, dark red. They may be round or elongated, large or small, depending on the variety and condition of the tree.

A distinction is made between eating apples that can be eaten directly from the tree or after lengthy storage in a cellar, etc., or cooking apples which are used for preserving or apple juice.

Content: Fructose, vitamins A and C, as well as a few vitamins from the B-spectrum, also, fermentation substances, pectins (important for gelling), calcium, potassium, iron, and phosphorus.

Shape of tree: Tall standard trees will not yield fruit until about the age of ten years, semi-standards around seven years. If you purchase four- or five-year-old tall or semi-standard trees, it will be more expensive, but you will not have to wait so long for a harvest. Pyramid-shaped bushes that are grafted onto the usual stocks can grow up to 8 ft (2.5 m) tall, those grafted on slow-growing stocks will grow less than 5 ft (1.5 m) tall. They are planted when they are two-years-old, that is, a year after grafting. They will yield fruit for the first time by the second year, that is, at the age of four years.

Suitable for: Tall and semi-standard trees as solitary trees, pyramid-shaped bushes in small gardens, as hedges or espaliers, in large containers. Not suitable for

house wall espaliers as they are sensitive to too much warmth.

Position: Apple trees like to stand in a moist, cool, airy position. West- and east-facing sides of the garden, in very warm regions even on the north-facing side of a house. If planted in a position that is too dry and warm, the trees will remain small and be susceptible to pests and diseases.

Soil: Apple trees have shallow roots but still require a deep, humus-rich soil, preferably loamy. Sandy soils have to be improved as dry soil will cause the apple tree to have deformed growth.

Masses of tempting fruit growing on a well-cared-for apple tree.

Loosen up tough, heavy soil with sand. A pH factor of 5.5-6.5 is ideal.

Pollination: Non-self-pollinating. At least one other apple tree that flowers at the same time will be required in the immediate vicinity – better still, several others that will ensure good pollination. Find out, when purchasing, what the pollination requirements of the desired variety are. Possibly, a third tree will be required as a pollen donor.

Planting: Dig out a flat planting pit, no deeper than the roots of the young tree when spread out. Loosen the soil to a spade's depth at the bottom of the pit. Set the tree at a level that ensures the roots will end up close under the surface of the soil. The grafting point above the neck of the root should end up 4-6 in (10-15 cm) above the ground.

Maintenance cut: Cut off shoots that grow downward and are more than three-years-old. Vertical shoots and new shoots that grow outward can be left, only new shoots growing toward the inside should be cut back to the branch. Take out long, lanky shoots. The crown should be even and open so that the fruit can obtain plenty of sunshine.

Fertilizing: For young trees and pyramid-shaped bushes, place a 2-in (5-cm) thick layer of garden compost or well-rotted stable manure on the soil under the tree in early spring. If you cannot obtain either, use about ¼ pound per sq yd (100 g/m^2) of organic-mineral fertilizer.

NB: Do not give the trees too much nitrogen and do not apply lime without having first taken a soil sample. A trace element deficiency may be created if too much lime is supplied. From late spring, if there is a lot of developing fruit, water weekly with fermented plant brews. Older tall, standard trees should only be fertilized if there is visible evidence of nutrient deficiency.

Care: Keep the soil around the base of young trees free of all vegetation; older tall standards may be surrounded by grass or lawn. If the tree produces too much fruit, half of the fruit, particularly small fruit, should be removed from the tree during early summer. The remaining fruit will then become larger and the risk of brown rot becomes less. If there is an over-abundance of fruit, the branches will need supporting.

Susceptible to: Scab, mildew, fruit tree canker, brown rot, codling moth,

"Berlepsch" has a delicate, spicy flavor.

Juicy and crisp: "Schweizer Orangenapfel."

green apple aphid, ermine moth, winter moth, woolly aphid, apple sucker.

Varieties: Early: "Beauty of Bath," "Egremont Russet," "Stark Earliest," "Akane," "Discovery."

Summer apples: "Charles Ross," "Spartan," "James Grieve," "King of Pippins," "Cox's Orange Pippin," "Jonathan," "Elstar," "Jamba," "Worcester Pearmain," "Gala."

Late: "Berlepsch," "Gloster," "Golden Delicious," "Laxton's Superb," "Ontario," "Melrose," "Pomme Cloche," "Granny Smith."

Harvest: Summer apples and very early varieties should not be harvested until they are fully ripe which means that their seeds should be brown. Late varieties, apples for storing, should be picked before they are entirely ripe as they will keep better. Do not pick all the fruit at once but pick the ripe ones regularly. Grasp the entire apple with your hand when picking. If you use fingers only, you risk making dents that will later rot in storage. Many varieties of apple alternate between a year with a good harvest and one with a reduced yield.

Use: Late varieties for storage or also for drying. Early varieties and summer apples for immediate consumption, for preserving, for pies and tarts, for juice-making and fruit wine. Freeze cooked apples only as raw apples lose their flavor.

Storage: In a cool cellar with a humidity of at least 80%. Stored apples will remain fresh for a long time in polyethylene bags. Do not store them together with potatoes as the gas ethylene given off during ripening will cause the potatoes to germinate early and shrink.

My tip: Ask for native, older varieties that have been cultivated in tree nurseries on slow-growing stocks. They are particularly robust in the climate in which they were first raised decades ago and will hardly be at risk from diseases and pests. The fruit of these local varieties is also often very tasty.

A semi-standard apple tree in a large garden. Harvesting is easier than with a standard tree but the crop is no less abundant.

"President Drouard."

Pear
Pyrus communis

Flower: Middle to late spring; at risk from frost in altitudes with a harsh climate. Pure white flowers with red, later yellow, anthers, growing in clusters, appear before the leaves.

Fruit: Early varieties are ripe from late summer, the latest in mid-fall. They are elongated or rounded; large or small; green, yellow, brown, with red cheeks or yellow markings.

Content: Vitamin C and A, also some of the B-complex, plenty of fructose; depending on the variety, more or less pectin, potassium, calcium, iron, and phosphorus.

Shape of tree: Trees grown from seedlings turn into large tall standard trees with splendid, cone-shaped crowns. Full yield by the eighth to twelfth year. Pyramid-shaped bushes are grafted onto quince and grow up to 8 ft (2.5 m) tall. They yield fruit from their fourth year. Bush-shaped trees grow to 10 ft (3 m) tall, with a crown diameter of 13 ft (4 m).

Suitable for: Tall and semi-standard tree as a garden tree. Pyramid-shaped bushes as a hedge or single row espalier. Warmth-loving varieties as an espalier on a house wall.

Position: Plenty of warmth and sunshine. Late-ripening varieties will only thrive in a mild climate.

Suitable for a house espalier: "Red Williams Christ."

Delicately sharp: "Dr. Jules Guyot."

Trees grafted onto quince are not very hardy.

Soil: Tall and semi-standard trees with deep tap roots prefer loamy, nutrient-rich soil without waterlogging in which the roots can reach down to the water table. Trees grafted onto quince with shallow roots require humus-rich soil that need not be very deep.

Pollination: Non-self-pollinating. Requires pollen from a suitable donor variety. Some varieties are bad pollen donors, so it is best to plant three different varieties.

Planting: During mid to late fall in light soils; in early spring in heavy soils. Dig a planting pit that is at least two spades' deep and loosen it another spade's depth. Make sure the grafting point is above ground if the stock was grown from a seedling, and flush with the soil for quince stocks.

Maintenance cut: Cut off branches that are several years old and grow inward; also one-year-old shoots if the crown is becoming too dense. Regular cutting back only for espaliers.

Fertilizing: Only young trees during early spring, with about ¼ pound per sq yd (100 g/m²) organic-mineral fertilizer, manure, or garden compost.

Care: Mulch pyramid-shaped trees if conditions are very dry.

Susceptible to: scab, rust, fireblight, pear leaf midge.

Varieties: Early: "Louise Bonne de Jersey," "Packham's Triumph," "Williams Christ."

Medium: "Beurre Hardy," "Fertility Improved," "Josephine de Malines."

Late: "Concorde," "Onward," "Winter Nellis," "Gorham," "Doyenne du Commice," "Alexander Lucas," "Gräfin von Paris," "Madame Verté," "Bristol Cross," "Conference."

For a housewall espalier: "Frühe von Trévoux," "Gute Luise," "Williams Christ," "Alexander Lucas," "Gräfin von Paris," "Madame Verté." For pears for fruit wine and cooking (only tall standards) it is worth looking for local varieties.

Harvest: Harvest a few days before they are ripe. Most varieties will otherwise turn mealy. Pears for making fruit wine can be harvested as windfalls.

Use: Sweet pears can be eaten from the tree; pears for fruit wine making are inedible raw but will make a very good liqueur. Some old varieties are specially suitable for drying.

Storage: Should be consumed within a few days when ripe.

My tip: Do not plant ornamental juniper nearby as it harbors overwintering spores of pear rust.

Ripe in midsummer: "Schneiders Späte Knorpelkirsche."   "Büttners Rote Knorpel."

Sweet cherry
Prunus avium

Flower: Mid-spring before the leaves appear. Clusters of snow white flowers on 2-in (5-cm) long stalks.

Fruit: Ripens early to midsummer. Early varieties usually have soft, juicy fruit flesh. The later ripening cherries have firmer flesh. Colors range from light yellow with a red sun-facing side, to red yellow, fire red and dark red.

Content: Fructose, vitamins A and C, phosphorus, potassium, calcium.

Shape of tree: Stem to 26 ft (8 m) tall, diameter of crown up to 33 ft (10 m).

The pyramid-shaped bush is still rare but a rather large crown will develop on stocks like "Weiroot" or "Colt" on an approximately 32-in (80-cm) tall stem.

Suitable for: Solitary tree. Pyramid-shaped or bushy trees as open loose hedges.

Position: A position in full sunshine. Risk of frost damage in high altitudes.

Soil: Deep, loose, lime rich (pH factor 6-8).

Pollination: Non-self-pollinating. Requires another cherry tree that also needs to be of the right variety.

Planting: From mid-fall to early spring in a planting hole prepared with humus. Grafting point about 6 in (15 cm) above the soil.

Content: Vigorously cut back fruit-bearing shoots after the harvest to obtain a small crown.

Fertilizing: During late winter, ¼–⅓ pound per sq yd (100-150 g/m²) of organic-mineral fertilizer or, during the fall, well-rotted manure on the soil around the base. Enrich garden compost with lime.

Care: Plant nasturtiums under the tree to combat aphids.

Susceptible to: *Monilia*, canker, leaf spot, silver leaf, honey fungus, shot hole, winter moth.

Varieties: Early: "Early Rivers," "Noir de Guben," "Charmes," "Merton Glory."

Medium-early to late: "Compact Stella," "May Duke," "Van," "Napoleon Bigarreau," "Grosse Schwarze," "Sam," "Starking Hardy Giant."

Harvest: Pick for eating raw, for preserving and making juice – shake from the tree onto a cloth.

Use: Preserves, jam, juice, pies, tarts.

Storage: Use within three days.

My tip: To ensure pollination, hang a bucket of water and branches of blossoming wild cherry in your cherry tree.

Bitter cherry
Prunus cerasus

Flower: Mid- to late spring. Snow white blossom in clusters, minute leaves at the base of flowers. Hardier than sweet cherry.

Fruit: Ripens early to late summer. Light red, dark red to black red fruit with juice which may stain badly. Sharp taste.

Content: See sweet cherry.

Shape of tree: Smaller than sweet cherry. Tall standard, grafted beneath the crown, 5-6 ft (1.5-1.8m) tall. Bush-shaped trees with a stem height of 28-32 in (70-80 cm), dwarf trees only 20 in (50 cm).

Suitable for: Solitary, hedge, espalier on a house wall, large container.

Position: No great demands on climate. Requires a fully sunny to semi-shady position. Even the well-known "Schattenmorelle" does not like shade, in spite of the German name (*Schatten* = shade) as the name is actually derived from the French word *château.*

Soil: Undemanding but no heavy, cold soils with a high water table.

Pollination: Usually self-pollinating.

Planting: A spade's depth, with well-loosened soil at the bottom of the planting pit. Set tall standards as deep as they were in the tree nursery. Let the grafting point of bush trees remain several inches (centimetres) above the soil.

Maintenance cut: Bitter cherries like to form long, whip-like shoots that soon become bare. After harvesting, the fruit-bearing shoots should be cut back to the young shoots that have formed in the crown. Always thin out after the harvest in upright-growing varieties.

Fertilizing: Garden compost or manure on the soil under the tree.

Care: When the fruit is beginning to turn red, draw protective netting over the crown to prevent birds from eating the fruit.

Susceptible to: Canker, honey fungus, shot hole, silver leaf, cherry leaf roll virus, European rusty mottle virus, little cherry mycloplasma, cherry black fly.

Varieties: "Nabella," "Schattenmorelle," "Morellenfeuer," "Königin Hortense," "Schwäbische Weinweichsel" (tall standard only), "Heimanns Rubinweichsel," "Stevnsbaer."

Harvest: Do not harvest until the fruit is blackish-red; otherwise there will be no proper flavor.

Use: Juice, preserves.

Storage: Use right away.

My tip: If you have no garden, bitter cherries will grow well in a large container on a balcony or patio. They will not only yield fruit but also look very decorative.

Particularly popular: "Schattenmorelle."

Plums come in several different varieties.

Plums and damsons
Prunus domestica

Flower: Mid-spring. Small, white flowers with yellow anthers on thin stalks in clusters of two or three together. Flowers appear before the leaves.

Fruit: Ripe toward mid-summer to mid-fall. The type of plums referred to as damsons are egg-shaped with a pointed end. The dark blue skin has a light bloom on it and the firm fruit flesh is yellowish to orange, the pit flattened. Ordinary plums are larger, with rounded ends and the "seam" of the fruit clearly visible. The thicker skin, depending on the variety, may be dark blue, bluish-violet, or deep yellow. There is less bloom than on the damson. The yellow fruit flesh is generally difficult to remove from the roundish pit. The difference between a plum and a damson is not easy to describe. Damsons are mostly used for cooking. Many tree nurseries distinguish plums according to when they ripen (from early summer onward).

Content: The damson contains vitamins A and C, potassium, and plenty of fructose. Plums are sweeter.

Shape of tree: Medium-sized trees with round crowns that can also be grown as flat crowns. These are more practical for harvesting purposes as there are still no varieties with a short stem. Even on slow-growing stocks, they never grow less than 10 ft (3 m) tall. Grafting is carried out either on a vigorously growing stock that is suitable for dry, poor soils or onto the slower-growing "St. Julien" which prefers moist, nutrient-rich soils. Young trees with two-year-old crowns will bear fruit two years after planting.

Suitable for: A solitary tree in a small garden will provide shade for a garden seat, patio or composting station.

Position: Warm, sunny place. The fruit will not be quite as sweet in a shady position.

Soil: Nutrient-rich, humus-rich, moist soils. Some of the older varieties make very few demands at all. However, on no account should the soil be acidic so keep the pH factor at 6.5-7.

Pollination: The main domestic varieties are, as a rule, self-pollinating. Among less common varieties the situation is not quite clear. It is better to make sure that a pollen donor is provided. Blackthorn is suitable for this task if grown as an ornamental bush. In the case of a variety that is known to be non-self-

Yellow red "Victoria Plum."

Ready to pick.

pollinating, you can help matters by grafting a branch of another variety onto the tree.

Planting: Late fall. Do not make the planting hole deeper than the roots reach.

Maintenance cut: With a regularly yielding tree, only remove bare or hanging branches that are growing too densely together. New young shoots should be cut back by half in order to encourage a rejuvenation of the crown.

Fertilizing: Young trees with organic-mineral fertilizer, garden compost, or well-rotted manure in early spring. Only supply nutrients to adult trees if there are definite symptoms of nutrient deficiency (insufficient flower buds, chlorosis). Provide lime only after determining the pH factor of the soil.

Care: Both damsons and plums often bear more fruit than they can cope with. In the case of a very heavy yield, the branches will need propping up. Thin out the developing fruit of the yellow "Victoria Plum" after flowering or the plums will remain small and sour.

Susceptible to: Bacterial canker, honey fungus, shot hole, die back, brown rot, sawfly, plum pox virus, plum line pattern virus, necrotic ring spot virus, prune dwarf virus, bark split virus, spider mites, rust.

Varieties: Early: "Ariel," "Farleigh Damson," "Warwickshire Drooper," "Ontario" (yellow), "Ruth Gerstetter" (blue plum), "Magna Glauca."

Medium early to late: "Stanley" (particularly large), "Edwards," "Victoria," "Merryweather," "Pershore Purple," "Marjorie's Seedling."

Harvest: Only pick as many plums as you are able to eat raw. Let the rest remain on the tree until the stalk is slightly wrinkled, when they are ripest. Plums are sensitive to pressure and have to be very carefully picked to avoid bruising.

Use: Damsons are used for cooking. They can be frozen as they come from the tree. In the winter, you can make plum pies with them. Plums are not suitable for freezing but jam, sauce, preserves, and juice can be made with both types.

Storage: Use immediately.

My tip: If you love plums but have only a small family, have a plum tree grafted at the tree nursery so that early, medium-early, and late varieties grow on the same tree. This means you will be able to harvest a constant small supply of plums for three months.

Greengages require a really sunny position sheltered from wind.

Greengages
Prunus domestica

Many garden centers make no distinction between plums and greengages which can both be treated in much the same way.

Flower: During mid-spring before the leaves appear. Small, pure white flowers in clusters of two or three.

Fruit: Mid to late summer. Some varieties are the size of cherries, yellow in color and have red dots when fully ripe. Most greengages are smaller than plums, round and yellowish-green. Only the "Althans" variety is purple.

Content: Vitamin C and carotene.

Shape of tree: The trees do not grow very large, those with slow-growing rootstocks are only about 10 ft (3 m) tall. Crops appear at about six to eight years of age. As it is best to plant trees with a two-year-old crown, you will only need to wait for about four years for the first fruit. The fruit-bearing wood is short and very thin but grows densely.

Suitable for: A solitary tree in a small garden beside a house, beside a patio, also for a large container.

Position: Greengages only bear fruit in mild climates. They require a fully sunny position sheltered from the wind. Some of the smaller varieties are a little more robust and some varieties will even ripen in cool altitudes.

Soil: Not very demanding. The soil should be warm, nutrient-rich, and not too dry. Sandy soils are ideal as they are warm. However, do ensure that good humus formation takes place.

Pollination: As a rule, the large greengages are self-pollinating. Most of the small varieties are not, however. The non-self-pollinating "Graf Althans" greengage or the common domestic plum can be a pollen donor for the large greengage. "Graf Althans," on the other hand will require a very specific pollinator.

Planting: The best time is in the fall, in early spring only at cooler altitudes, as the young trees are sensitive to frost. Dig a planting hole to a depth of 20 in (50 cm) and loosen the soil underneath to a spade's depth. Improve light soils with bonemeal and compost. The grafting point should be 4 in (10 cm) above the surface of the soil.

Maintenance cut: Regular thinning out is required to ensure a good crop. Cut out any branches that are too dense or bare. Cut back young shoots by a half. A tree rejuvenated in this way

Sweet and juicy "Wilhelmine Späth."

Several greengage varieties will ripen at cool altitudes.

will produce more fruit.

Fertilizing: During the first few years, spread ¼ pound per sq yd (100 g/m²) organic-mineral fertilizer or a layer of garden compost on the soil under the tree during early spring. Later, only fertilize when symptoms of deficiency are visible and after soil analysis.

Care: Young trees should always be watered if the weather is very dry. The best way is to lay a garden hose on the soil and let the water trickle for about an hour. If the tree is carrying lots of heavy fruit, make sure the weaker branches are given some support or the tree may break. The green fruit can be thinned out in early summer in a tree that has been kept small by regular pruning. This will make the other fruit larger and tastier.

Susceptible to: Scab, bacterial canker, spider mites, and all the other pests and diseases mentioned under plums.

Varieties: "Nancy," "Cambridge Gage," "Early Transparent Gage," "Graf Althans Reneklode," "Oullins Golden Gage" (self-pollinating), "Wilhelmine Späth." As stated earlier, many garden centers or nurseries do not make a distinction between plums and greengages, selling them all as plums. Only specialist fruit tree nurseries will be able to offer the rarer greengages and give advice on them. Specialist nurseries do often run a mail-order service which may be of help.

Harvest: Pick greengages for preserving when they are not yet quite ripe as the flavor of the preserves or jelly will be stronger and slightly more acid. As greengages can be harvested in large quantities, the best method is to shake the tree over a large cloth spread out underneath. This makes it easier to pick up the fruit.

Use: For raw consumption, jelly, preserves, tarts, or the preparation of brandy or liqueur.

Storage: Process greengages immediately after picking them as they spoil very quickly.

My tip: Keep a single greengage tree in your garden as small as possible or the crop will be too large. Choosing a slow-growing stock is a step in the right direction and rigorous shortening of shoots during the winter will keep the crown small enough.

Peach blossom appears before the leaves.

A peach with red flesh: "Rekord aus Alfter."

Peach
Prunus persica

Flower: Early spring. White to dark pink flowers without stalks that emerge straight from the branches before the leaves.

Fruit: Ripens, depending on the variety, from midsummer to early fall. Late fruit with yellow flesh is tastier than the early ones with white flesh. Velvet skin.

Content: Plenty of carotene (particularly in the skin) and potassium.

Shape of tree: Tall bush with 32-40 in (80-100 cm) tall stem and open crown.

Suitable for: A solitary tree, wall espalier, large container.

Position: A risk-free crop can only be assured in mild, warm areas. Protect from late frosts as the flowers are very early.

Soil: Very demanding. Humus-rich, loose soil – best with deep gravel. Does not require a high water table. Varieties grafted onto plums will also thrive in heavy clay soil if it is not too cold.

Pollination: Generally self-pollinating.

Planting: Early to mid-spring. Loosen the soil and enrich with compost.

Maintenance cut: This produces the largest fruit on "true" fruit-bearing branches, about 20-in (50-cm) long young shoots with two flower buds and one wood bud. Shorten these shoots by a half. This will ensure the production of many fruit-bearing shoots during the following year. "False" shoots (only flower buds or only leaf buds) should be shortened to less than ⅜ in (1 cm) during flowering. Thin out well after the harvest.

Fertilizing: During early spring about ½ pound per sq yd (200 g/m^2) organic-mineral fertilizer. All year round with a layer of mulch, grass cuttings or compost.

Care: Keep the soil around the base free. The layer of mulch should not be let delay the warming up of the soil so loosen up this layer in sunny weather.

Susceptible to: red spider mites, aphids, scale insects, bacterial canker, brown rot, silver leaf, shot hole, peach mildew, honey fungus, peach leaf curl, chlorosis.

Varieties: "Amsden June," "South Haven," "Duke of York," "Peregrine," "Rochester," "Hayles Early."

Harvest: Pick with care.

Use: For raw consumption or preserving.

Storage: Fully ripe fruit will keep for about two days, semi-ripe fruit will keep longer but is not as tasty.

Apricot blossom is sensitive to frost.

A "Nancy" apricot.

Apricot
Prunus armeniaca

Flower: Early spring before the leaves appear. The almost stalkless flowers have a red calyx and delicate pink petals. They are very sensitive to frost.
Fruit: Crop from mid-summer. The dark yellow, slightly velvety, round fruit is easily removed from the large pit.
Content: Contains a particularly high amount of carotene and potassium.
Shape of tree: Semi-standard, pyramid, or small bush.
Suitable for: A solitary tree, best as an espalier on a south-facing wall.
Position: Warm, mild

areas. The tree itself is quite hardy but the blossom is easily destroyed by frost. A dry climate prevents fungal disease.
Soil: Loose, nutrient-rich, warm, not too dry.
Pollination: Self-pollinating. It often flowers so early that there are no bees about. An artist's paintbrush may be used to transfer pollen from one flower to another, thus ensuring a good harvest of fruit.
Planting: During mid-spring, in loose soil enriched with garden compost.
Maintenance cut: After harvesting, remove inward-growing and spindly old shoots.

Fertilizing: Every spring, before blossoming time, spread about ½ pound per sq yd (200 g/m²) organic-mineral fertilizer; in the fall spread a mulching layer of coarse compost under the tree.
Care: See peach.
Susceptible to: Red spider mites, scale insects, aphids, apricot die-back, rust, silver leaf.
Varieties: "Nancy," "Alfred," "Farmingdale," "New Large Early."
Harvest: Apricots are not sensitive to pressure but if they are picked when they are fully ripe, care should be taken.
Use: For eating raw, preserving, and drying.
Storage: Only for a few

days. Best fresh.
My tip: Apricots should be protected from rain as they are susceptible to fungal disease. The best place to plant them is against a house wall (south-facing) with overhanging eaves. However, care must then be taken to keep them well watered!

125

Beautiful quince blossom in late spring.

Pear-shaped "Bereczki" quince.

Quince
Cydonia oblonga

Flower: Late spring. Single, pink or bright red flowers appear on branches that already have leaves.

Fruit: Harvest from mid fall. Large, yellow, apple- or pear-shaped fruit with a velvety skin and very hard, coarse flesh, appearing particularly at the ends of young shoots.

Content: Tartaric acid, tannic acid, fructose, and vitamin C.

Shape of tree: A quince tree grows more like a bush than a tree. It is often grafted onto hawthorn to give it a straighter stem. This type of tree will often grow about 10 ft (3 m) tall, but there are also low-growing bush varieties and pyramid forms. A quince will produce the first proper harvest of fruit two to three years after planting.

Suitable for: A small garden; it looks attractive in an ornamental garden.

Position: Will only develop its full characteristic flavor in regions with a warm climate as the wood is not very hardy. Will require a sheltered, sunny or semi-shady position in a garden.

Soil: Thrives particularly well on light, warm soils with a pH value not over 7. Humus-rich, loamy soil is also suitable.

Pollination: Self-pollinating.

Planting: At the end of the first month of spring in a fairly shallow, well-loosened planting pit. The grafting point should be level with the soil.

Maintenance cut: Thin out only and do not shorten the young shoots as the fruits grow on their ends.

Fertilizing: Well-rotted garden compost or manure containing straw spread on the soil around the stem; other measures are not necessary.

Care: Not necessary.

Susceptible to: Codling moth, apple sawfly, aphids, red spider mites, apple mildew, brown rot.

Varieties: "Vranja," "Champion," "Constantinople," "Portugal," "Von Leskovac."

Harvest: Let fruits remain hanging on the tree until shortly before the first frosts.

Use: For jelly, wine, quince preserves. Not to be eaten raw. Rub the velvet off the skin before processing.

Storage: Should be processed as soon as possible or the flesh will turn brown.

My tip: In cool regions, protect the roots with straw mulch during the winter.

Long catkins, tiny flowers.

Walnuts ripening inside green skins.

Walnut
Juglans regia

Flower: During early spring, 4-in (10-cm) long male catkins and inconspicuous female flowers form on the same tree during the appearance of the first leaves.

Fruit: Harvest from the end of the first month of fall. The kernel is in a hard shell which, in turn, is covered with a tough, green skin. Depending on the variety, the fruit will be large or small, with a thin or thick shell.

Content: Lots of protein and fat.

Shape of tree: Up to 67 ft (20 m) tall; diameter of crown also up to 67 ft (20 m). The roots extend far beyond the edge of the crown so leave a space of 50 ft (15 m) from all other plants and from the house.

Suitable for: Large gardens.

Position: Sensitive to frost, so only in warm regions.

Soil: Loose, very deep, easy for roots to expand, warm and humus-rich. Very demanding.

Pollination: Self-pollinating.

Planting: Better than a seedling, buy a grafted (expensive) young tree. Dig a deep planting pit, loosen well, and dig right through deeper layers of clay.

Maintenance cut: Should not be pruned. Only remove broken or frost-damaged branches during late summer. Before that, the tree will "bleed" too much.

Fertilizing: Not necessary.

Care: Not necessary.

Susceptible to: Gall mites, honey fungus, late frosts.

Varieties: Recommended walnut varieties include "Excelsior of Taynton," "Leeds Castle," "Northdown Clawnut."

Harvest: Gather up nuts if they have fallen from the tree. By then, the green skins will have dried up and fallen off.

Use: In cake-making, for pickling, or eating raw.

Storage: Dry the nuts in the sun for a few days or in a warm place. They should keep until well past Christmas.

My tip: A walnut tree near the house will keep away flies.

127

The author, publishers, and the photographer Friedrich Strauss wish to thank the following for their support:

Author's notes
This book explains how to grow fruit trees organically. It includes instructions for the use of biological plant protection agents. Some measures of care should be taken when handling these substances: please follow manufacturers' directions meticulously. Keep children and domestic pets away when you are using these agents. Wear gloves when using agents containing pyrethrum. These substances should not be allowed to enter open wounds. Make sure you store all plant protection agents in such a way that they are inaccessible to children and domestic pets. Large fruit trees often tempt children and even adults to climb them. Serious accidents can then occur due to thin or rotten branches breaking. Always make sure you only harvest fruit using a safe ladder and make sure that children do not climb around in fruit trees.

Success with

Geraniums and Pelargoniums

ANDREAS RIEDMILLER

Series Editor:
LESLEY YOUNG

Contents

Contents

Introduction

It is the gardener's dream to gaze from a window at an idyllic view of lovely summer flowers in glowing colors. Try to imagine glorious blooms of red, pink and white - in a window box, on a balcony, or on a patio – and you will find you have conjured up a vision of luxuriantly blooming geraniums. For generations geraniums have been some of the most popular flowering plants for tubs and baskets. The gardener who looks after them, waters them diligently, and fusses over them, will have only one aim: to encourage them to continue to produce flowers endlessly. This guide will help you to buy and grow healthy plants that will later produce a mass of beautiful flowers.

One important point must be made right from the start. Few people are aware that the plant that most of us call "geranium" is, correctly speaking, a pelargonium. The real geranium, on the other hand, is actually a hardy garden shrub which looks quite different to a pelargonium. This guide will introduce you to the splendid range of colors and the enormous selection of pelargonium varieties and species with the help of over ninety color photographs and detailed individual descriptions. Among these are some new varieties of exotic wild, scented-leafed, fancy-leafed, and regal pelargoniums for indoors. Many of the beautiful photographs were specially taken by the author himself. You will be introduced to the sculpted leaves and orchid-like flowers of the wild and scented-leafed pelargoniums and to the vibrant colors of the regal pelargoniums. You will also learn new and often surprising facts about the universally popular balcony pelargoniums. Did you know, for example, that these popular flowers are really subtropical plants that originated in the dry, hot areas of South Africa? For this reason alone, their special requirements with respect to care must be observed. In this guide, Andreas Riedmiller provides a sound, basic knowledge of these plants in brief, easy-to-understand terms, and shares with the reader his gardening secrets so that your plants will flourish and flower more abundantly than ever.

Drawing on his own experience, he supplies detailed instructions on buying, care, and propagating. Color illustrations, with step-by-step explanations, supplement his excellent text. Advice on how to make your own potting compost, basic and regular feeding, and the use of the right plant containers backs up the mass of expert information. A section on problems, pests, and diseases will help to prevent such troubles and direct you toward the right treatment if difficulties do arise. If you wish to keep your beloved pelargoniums for more than one season, you will find advice on what to do in the chapter on overwintering, which covers various methods of nursing your pelargoniums through the dormant period. The chapter on propagating offers an alternative for those who wish to produce new plants for the following year, either from seeds or cuttings.

Note

In order to help you to find your way through this book more easily, each chapter has been divided into three sections, based on the position in which the pelargoniums will be kept, both indoors and outside:
- upright, hanging, and semi-pendent pelargoniums for balconies and patios;
- pelargoniums for indoors;
- geraniums for the garden.

The author

Andreas Riedmiller was born in 1952. He trained to be a gardener, specializing in the growing of flowering and ornamental plants, and then worked as a specialist adviser to garden centers for ten years before becoming the manager of a garden center. At present, he is a freelance photographer. The main emphasis of his work is now on ecological and biological topics and on landscape, nature, and plant photography. His publications include a guide to trees, and he has made numerous contributions to specialist and popular periodicals, books, and calendars.

Acknowledgments

The author and publishers wish to thank all those who contributed toward this volume, especially György Jankovics for his excellent color illustrations and the author's wife, Uschi Riedmiller, for all her help and cooperation in the compiling of the text. Special thanks go to Mrs Wiedemann of Geislingen-Aufhausen, to Mr Gibboni at the firm of Pelargonien Fischer, and to Mr Leinfelder at the Garden Research Center in Weihenstephan for permission to photograph rare and especially splendid varieties.

Prized flowering plants
Pelargoniums – here a hanging cascade variety – displaying their beauty in a sun-drenched garden.

All about geraniums and pelargoniums

Geraniums and pelargoniums are two completely different groups of plants whose names are used incorrectly and interchangeably all the time. This chapter will explain the differences between geraniums and pelargoniums and will give some interesting information on each group.

Naming and classification

When the first pelargoniums were brought by merchants from South Africa to Europe, around 1700, they were called *Geranium* and, even though the French botanist Charles-Louis l'Hertier de Brutelle eventually placed them among the pelargoniums in 1789, the popular but incorrect designation "geranium" has persisted in the English-speaking world to this day. Pelargoniums are among the most popular of all balcony and window box plants and are so simple to look after that it is easy to assume automatically that discovering the names of different varieties might be just as uncomplicated. Alas, this is not the case and it is for this reason that I wish to begin by explaining the names and terms so that you will find it a little easier to choose your plants. Although specialized pelargonium growers and plant nurseries or garden centers usually give the correct terms in their lists and catalogs, you will still often find them incorrectly described in florists and in markets, etc.

Pelargoniums

Whether their owners call them geraniums or pelargoniums, the plants that you see flowering in glorious shades of red on balconies, hanging luxuriantly from window boxes, or flourishing on patios, are really pelargoniums. Right from the start, in order to avoid confusion, I shall call these plants by their proper name – pelargonium – throughout this book.

Wild pelargoniums

One thing that you may not know is that the pelargoniums that we like to grow in our window boxes and on balconies and patios are nothing like the plants that arrived in Europe for the first time around 1700. Those plants that were introduced from the Cape in South Africa were wild plants with much smaller flowers, much smaller umbels, and, very often, smaller leaves too. Wild pelargoniums still grow in South Africa today, forming bushes up to 6½ ft (2 m) high. Today, wild pelargoniums are enjoying increasing popularity all over the world and are grown alongside hybridized pelargoniums. They are cultivated both as indoor pot plants and as summer plants outside. Their delicate flowers may sometimes resemble orchids, and the leaves of many species release a pleasant scent.

Scented-leafed pelargoniums are much sought after. Most are wild pelargoniums with scented leaves, but some are hybrid crosses of different scented-leafed species.

Hybrids

"Hybrid" is the correct term for a plant that has been created through crossing different species – sometimes called a "bastard cross." Except for the wild ones, all pelargoniums are hybrids, which makes them all the results of human interference. There are very many of these hybrids, which can be divided into five different groups.

My tip: You can recognize wild pelargoniums and hybrids by the way their botanical name is written: in the case of wild pelargoniums the genus name (the first name) is written with an uppercase (capital) letter and the species name has a lowercase (small) first letter. Hybrid names are written with uppercase letters for both names.

Zonal pelargoniums are hybrids that were created by crossing the *Pelargonium zonale* and the *Pelargonium inquinans*. They are also called "upright pelargoniums." The name zonal refers to the brownish ring (*zonale* = *girdle*) on the leaves.

Hanging pelargoniums (properly, *Pelargonium – Peltatum hybrids*) are the result of crossing *Pelargonium peltatum* and other wild pelargoniums. These are also called "ivy-leafed pelargoniums" or

Hanging pelargoniums, specially the cascade varieties, are most prolific, producing a mass of blooms.

"shield pelargoniums".

Semi-pendent pelargoniums

(properly, *Pelargonium – Zonale* x *Peltatum* hybrids) were created by crossing two hybrids: the zonal and hanging hybrids. They are also called semi-hanging or semi-peltate pelargoniums.

Fancy-leafed pelargoniums

belong, for the most part, among the zonal pelargoniums. However, some of them are also hanging hybrids. Mutations of their genetic composition have resulted in specially interesting leaf shapes and leaf markings. These pelargoniums are now being hybridized to perpetuate these characteristics, although they also possess beautiful flowers.

Regal pelargoniums (properly, *Pelargonium – Grandiflorum* hybrids) are derived from *Pelargonium cucullatum* and other wild species. They are also sometimes called "indoor pelargoniums".

The naming of pelargoniums

This is occasionally a confusing business. Over the years, all of the above-named hybrids have been the subject of hybridizing to produce hundreds of varieties of pelargoniums. It can prove very difficult for the amateur pelargonium grower to distinguish between plants which look very alike, specially in photographs, when new varieties seem to appear all the time.

The ancestors of all zonal pelargonium hybrids
Left: Pelargonium zonale. Right: Pelargonium inquinans.

How to distinguish pelargoniums from geraniums

Together with other genera, the two genera *Pelargonium* and *Geranium* belong to the family, or natural order, of plants called *Geraniaceae.* In addition to other characteristics, pelargoniums and geraniums may be distinguished quite easily by their flowers and fruits.

Pelargonium means "stork's bill" (Greek: *pelargos* = stork), which refers to the shape of the long fruits. The flowers may be divided into two symmetrical halves (zygomorph) and they have a nectary. *Geranium* means "crane's bill" (Greek: geranos = crane). This name also refers to the shape of the fruits, which are split and are a little shorter than those of the pelargonium. The flowers are regular, radial, and have no nectary.

However, a word of caution is due here: a new name does not necessarily signify a new hybrid. Some gardening catalogs may try to "freshen up" old favorites by giving them new, fanciful names every year.

My tip: Do not become confused if you come across yet another new term, namely pelargonium F$_1$ hybrids. "F" is the abbreviation for Latin *filia*, meaning daughter, and "F$_1$" designates the first daughter generation of a particular cross. F$_1$ hybrids are of special interest to the gardener, as they can be propagated from seed unlike all other pelargonium hybrids which can only be propagated from cuttings.

Geraniums

Geraniums are perennial, hardy shrubs that flower from late spring to early fall and are very undemanding. The parts of the plant above ground will die down every fall. Geraniums need no extra protection through the winter. In spring, they will put out new shoots.

Wild types: The wild varieties of geraniums are especially at home in the Pyrenées, the Caucasus Mountains, and Asia, where they still grow wild.

Hybrids: In gardens and garden centers you will usually find cultivated geranium hybrids, which can grow from 4 in (10 cm) to 40 in (1 m) in height, depending on the species. Their flower umbels are white, pink, red, violet, or blue.

Pelargoniums as medicinal plants

The South African peoples use the roots and other parts of pelargonium plants for medicinal purposes. The crushed stalks of one species serve as a remedy for headaches and as a perfume or body lotion, while other species yield leaves which can be dried and smoked like tobacco leaves. In southern Europe, some species of pelargonium, such as *Pelargonium radens* or *Pelargonium graveolens*, are grown for the subsequent extraction of geraniol (geranium oil), which is one of the basic substances used in perfume manufacturing. Other healing properties of the wild pelargonium are still largely unknown to the western world, and this plant may well yield other useful natural substances in the future.

Where to grow pelargoniums

As a rule, we tend to grow pelargoniums on patios, balconies, and indoors, whereas geraniums are only grown in the garden. How to choose the best site for each species or variety is explained in the following sections.

On patios and balconies
Most pelargoniums are kept in window boxes, on windowsills, on patios, or on balconies during the warm, frost-free months of the year. These are usually pelargonium hybrids of the zonal or hanging varieties.

Indoors
Regal, wild, scented-leafed, and fancy-leafed pelargoniums will flourish indoors and seem to thrive even in the dry atmosphere of centrally heated rooms. Regal pelargoniums, specially, are often considered to be true house plants because of these characteristics. During the warm part of the year, however, these plants are quite happy to be moved outside, where they will flourish in the sunshine.

In the garden
Geranium hybrids, as already mentioned, are hardy garden shrubs. They develop a widely spreading root system but will thrive equally well in large plant containers. *Pelargonium hybrids and fancy-leafed pelargoniums* can be planted in flower beds during the summer months. Because they are not hardy, however, they will not survive frosts and must be moved indoors before these occur. *Note:* Depending on their position, pelargoniums and geraniums require different kinds of care, so each chapter of this book is divided to take account of the three main sites.

Wild pelargoniums growing in a typical, arid position in South Africa.

Where to find geraniums and pelargoniums

Not all geraniums and pelargoniums are easy to obtain. Certain rare varieties seem only to be exchanged among specialist enthusiasts and are sought after as veritable treasures. The most usual source for the more common plants, however, will be garden centers or nurseries, etc.

Sources of supply
Nurseries: In nurseries, you may choose your pelargoniums from source, right out of the greenhouse. *Florists, gardening specialty stores,* and *garden centers,* also offer opportunities to buy these plants. During the planting season, you will also find a wide range of accessories in these places, such as potting compost, fertilizers, and plant containers. *Mail order nurseries* also offer pelargoniums in colorful, well-illustrated catalogs. You cannot go to choose your own plants when buying them this way but, on the other hand, you need not transport them yourself either.

Seeds or cuttings
F_1 hybrids and wild pelargoniums may be propagated from seeds but all other hybrids are propagated from cuttings only. You can obtain pelargonium seeds through gardening suppliers and acquire cuttings, perhaps from accommodating neighbors or friends, or even in garden centers, any time from the middle of winter until the middle of spring.

Fancy-leafed pelargoniums (here the silver-leafed variety, "Chelsea Gem") will thrive indoors or out in summer.

Buying geraniums and pelargoniums

Pelargoniums for patios and balconies

When to buy: You can buy pelargonium hybrid rooted cuttings from the middle of winter through to the middle of spring, as half-grown plants from early spring, and as full-grown plants from late spring.

Rooted cuttings should show compact growth, deep green foliage without any discoloration, and have numerous roots, which will protrude from the propagation pot. Rooted cuttings with yellowish leaves which straggle and look unhealthy should be avoided.

Half-grown plants are pelargoniums with one growing shoot, and are sold in pots of about 3½ in (9 cm) in diameter. These plants should show compact growth and have at least one bud that shows a little color or is in the process of opening.

Grown plants are sold in pots of 4¼ in (11 cm) in diameter. They will always have several shoots and their flower buds will be on the point of opening.

Healthy plants: Make sure that the plants display deep green foliage; this is a sign that they have been fed properly. Also take a look at the undersides of the leaves as this is where pests may lurk. Plants with fungal infestations, insects, or larvae, or decaying buds or roots should be avoided.

Withered flowers: If one of the flowers on an otherwise healthy plant happens to be withering, do

140

not let this put you off. When back home, just break off the stalk.

Pelargoniums for indoors
When to buy: Flowering regal pelargoniums, in pots with a diameter of 4¼ in (11 cm), are usually for sale nearly all year round. Scented-leafed pelargoniums and fancy-leafed pelargoniums, on the other hand, can usually only be obtained from spring onward into summer, at speciality stores. If you wish to buy one of these plants, you will often have to seek out a pelargonium nursery or specialized grower.
Healthy plants: When looking for regal, scented-leafed, or fancy-leafed pelargoniums, make sure the foliage is a deep green in color. Check whether the pelargoniums are infested with pests or diseases. Regal pelargoniums are fairly resistant to pests and white fly seems to be the only insect they are susceptible to, but they do appear to be extremely sensitive to waterlogging. Take a look at the saucer or tray in which the plant pot is standing. There should be no water in it.

My tip: Be especially critical if the pelargoniums you find for sale are placed near drafty entrances, under artificial light, or in rooms that are too dark. The plant will react to these situations with falling buds and yellowing leaves, and will recover very slowly.

Geraniums for the garden
When to buy: You can purchase geraniums from early spring to late mid-fall in shrub nurseries or garden centers.
Appearance: When you buy the plants, they should have finished shooting. They are usually sold in plastic containers with a diameter of 3½ in (9 cm).

Transporting plants and care before planting

The best methods of transporting plants are as follows:

Pelargoniums for the patio and balcony
Transport your pelargoniums standing upright in deep boxes or fruit crates.
If you are unable to plant the pelargoniums in their proper containers at home straightway, you should at least unpack them and stand them in a light, frost-free room, shed, or greenhouse. Water them if they require it and air the room often, as this will help to make them resistant to diseases. Do not remove the support sticks from hanging pelargoniums until several weeks after they have been planted in their new container, so that the plants are not accidentally broken.

Pelargoniums for indoors
If you buy flowering pelargoniums in winter, make sure that the plants are wrapped in thick wads of newspaper. Pelargoniums are very sensitive to frost and on no account should they be exposed to the cold winter air for any length of time. Pelargoniums intended for indoors need not be repotted immediately after purchase. The best position for them is a sunny windowsill.

Geraniums for the garden
As shrub geraniums are usually sold in plastic containers, they need not be planted immediately after purchase. Keep them in the garden, never indoors, so that the plants are not subjected to too much warmth and will not begin shooting too soon.

Geraniums add color to a wild garden (here Geranium meeboldi).

Planting and initial care

Geraniums and pelargoniums are versatile, decorative plants which have long been used to beautify the home and garden. The better you respond to their needs, the more they will flourish. If you pay careful attention to all their requirements right from the start, such as supplying the correct position, soil, nutrients, and containers, you will be well rewarded with a rich profusion of flowers.

Pelargoniums on patios and balconies

Pelargoniums provide an easy way of transforming your patio or balcony into a miniature paradise. When the last cold snap of late spring has passed, you can begin to put both home-grown plants and purchased pelargoniums outside. Now is the time to take young plants out of their propagating pots and plant them in their final pots. Providing you offer them all they require in the way of care – the right position, correct feeding, sufficient water, and a little attention – your new plants, cuttings, and overwintered favorites will respond with strong, healthy growth and a profusion of flowers.

The right position

Before planting, you must give some thought as to the future positioning of your plants. As they originated in a subtropical climate, pelargoniums need lots of sunlight and heat in order to grow properly. For this reason, the position you choose should be sunny or at least semi-sunny. Such conditions will be supplied by windowsills, patios, and balconies on the south, southwest or southeast sides of the house.

What the flowers and leaves of pelargoniums really love, of course, is a position in full sunlight. The roots, however, can react adversely to extreme heat. If the sunlight is very intense, therefore, and the plants are in thin-walled balcony boxes (for example, made of plastic), too high a temperature may occur among the roots and thus damage the plant. In order to avoid such problems, give your flower-boxes some protection by fastening a piece of wood along the side that is exposed to the sun. This will help to reduce the detrimental effects of heat on the roots somewhat, and also the soil will not dry out so easily.

Ready-mixed potting compost

General rule: Pelargoniums like medium-heavy soil (that is, a loose mixture of loam, peat, and sand) that is well aerated and rich in nutrients, and of a fine, crumbly consistency. This type of soil will crumble loosely in one's fingers, feel slightly moist, and have a pleasant, earthy smell. A pH of 6.5-7 is best.

Commercial potting composts: You will find a vast range of composts, with different names and of varying quality, in nurseries and garden centers. The differences between products can be very difficult for the layman to figure out. The main ingredient of all these commercial products is peat.

Cheap potting composts: Some of the cheaper composts consist of peat only. Such composts are not suitable for pelargoniums as the nutrients tend to get washed out of peat rather quickly in heavy rain. In addition, peat does not aid drainage and will make the compost either too wet or too dry. There is a great danger of the soil remaining wet for too long and pelargonium roots cannot stand being waterlogged. The darker kind of peat (sedge peat) is completely unsuitable for pelargoniums as it is too acid.

Standard potting compost: I recommend a standard potting compost for pelargoniums, with a loam content of at least 30%. The percentage of loam should always be indicated on the packaging of standard potting composts. This is more expensive than some other commercial composts but, due to its percentage of loam, it will retain nutrients much longer and ensure that the plants receive an adequate supply of water. Standard potting composts also contain a high per-

Pelargoniums will flourish in a sunny position and contribute color and vibrancy to their surroundings.

centage of nutrients, which means that you will not need to give your pelargoniums an initial feed of fertilizer, as you would when using other commercial composts.

Mixing your own potting compost

This is recommended if you already have some kind of soil at your disposal, whether it is humus or garden compost, or compost left over from the previous year.

Method 1 – using leftover compost as a base

If you have decided that you do not wish to, or cannot, overwinter your pelargonium plants but would like to grow pelargoniums next year, you might wish to try this.

Important: On no account should you reuse the soil of diseased plants – throw it away! Never overwinter sick plants!

Procedure: In late fall, cut off all the shoots above ground.
● Cover the plant containers with polyethylene, in order to retain

sufficient moisture in the soil.
● Place the plant containers in a frost-free position for the winter. The finer roots will have completely decayed by the following spring.
● Before planting the new pelargoniums in spring, empty the old flowerpots, remove the old rootstocks, then loosen the earth with your fingers. You should now have pure compost again. If there is not enough, you will be able to mix in bought, standard potting compost.
● This reused potting compost will need initial fertilizing.

Stay green: If you have a balcony or live in a town, you may be able to do your bit to protect the environment. As commercial potting composts consist mainly of peat, their use in gardening is leading to considerable detrimental pressure on our natural wetlands. For this reason, you should always be very aware of how you use purchased potting compost and try to conserve it whenever you can. Do not, however, keep any compost that has been in contact with diseased plants!

Method 2 – using humus as a base

Pure humus (the top, usually dark brown, layer of soil) or agricultural soil is too heavy for pelargoniums. *Procedure:* Mix equal amounts of humus with rotted-down leaf mold or, at a pinch, peat. In order to avoid the growth of weeds, try to eliminate all grass turfs and roots. This mixture of soil will need to be mixed again with a fertilizer.

Method 3 – using composting soil as a base

If you are lucky enough to be the owner of a compost heap, you should have exactly the right type of soil for your pelargoniums. Not only is garden compost full of nutrients, it also contains many micro-organisms that are capable of transforming organic substances into nutrients required by plants. *Procedure:* Simply pass the well-mixed compost through a wide-mesh sieve and then mix in a little lime. In this way, the nutrients that are abundantly present in the compost will be made accessible to the plant. Such compost will contain so many essential nutrients that you need not give your plants any initial fertilizer.

△ Zonal pelargoniums, variety "Casino."
▽ Zonal pelargonium "Kardinal" is suitable for flower beds too.

Feeding

Pelargoniums require the major nutrients of nitrogen (N), phosphorous (P), and potassium (K) for continuous growth and a profusion of flowers. In addition, they will also need small amounts of other substances (for example, magnesium, iron, sulphur, manganese, boron, copper, etc.). These are called trace elements. The simplest way to give nutrients to your pelargoniums is in doses of fertilizer. Fertilizers that contain all main nutrients are called compound fertilizers.

General rule: The correct initial fertilizer for pelargoniums is a compound fertilizer in a dry, granulated form, which is mixed with soil or compost.

Compound fertilizers

You can obtain compound fertilizers in a dry, granulated form (specially suitable for initial fertilizing) or as a liquid which is dissolved in water (specially recommended for the regular fertilizing of pelargoniums, see p. 22). There should be information about the nutrient content, the "N-P-K" ratio on the packaging. This may appear simply as a sequence of numbers, and indicates the percentages of each nutrient. For example: 15-11-15 means 15% nitrogen, 11% phosphorous, and 15% potassium. If this kind of triple ratio is given on the package, this will tell you that it is a compound fertilizer.

Compound fertilizers are not only distinguished by the form in which they are sold (bulk or liquid), but also by the way in which the main nutrients are bound to certain substances.

Inorganic (mineral) compound fertilizers: The best known representative of this type is a fertilizer which looks like small blue granules (such as lawn fertilizer). The nutrients and trace elements in inorganic fertilizers are bound to synthetic substances – for example, salts. In the case of bulk inorganic compound fertilizers, the nutrients are dissolved by moisture (for example, during watering or rainfall), while the nutrients are already dissolved in liquid, inorganic compound fertilizers. In both cases the plant can absorb the nutrients directly.

● Advantage: fertilizing action commences immediately.

● Disadvantage: too much moisture (for example, during long periods of wet weather) may cause the nutrients to be washed out rather quickly. This is something you must watch out for: if you use too much fertilizer, the soil may accumulate salts which may then burn the roots and leaves.

Organic-mineral compound fertilizers: These are fertilizers in which the nutrients nitrogen (N) and phosphorous (P) are bound to organic substances. (These can be animal products, such as horn meal, horn chips, bone meal, fish meal, dried blood, guano, and so on.) Potassium, on the other hand, is usually bound to inorganic substances. If you use one of these fertilizers on your pelargoniums, a very different process will be activated to the one that occurs with inorganic fertilizers. The plant is unable to absorb organically bound nutrients directly. The nutrients must first be broken down and transformed by soil-dwelling micro-organisms and bacteria. Incredible as it sounds, one handful of soil can harbor more of these micro-organisms than there are human beings living on this planet! During this transformation process, all the basic building materials needed by the plant for growth (for example, nitrogen, phosphorous, and so on) are released and can then be absorbed by the plant in the form of inorganic substances. This is called mineralization.

● Advantages: If you use a fertilizer with organic components, the activity of micro-organisms and bacteria in the soil is stimulated, more humus is created, and the soil will become more fertile. In addition, the soil will not become saturated with salts (as it can do with inorganic fertilizers) and the fertilizing effect will last longer. Organic-mineral fertilizers comprise natural, basic substances and are, therefore, environmentally friendly!

● Disadvantage: As the nutrients must be transformed before they become accessible to the plants, the fertilizing action cannot begin immediately.

Organic (biological) fertilizers: Purely organic fertilizers are very often not compound fertilizers. Usually they will lack the essential plant nutrient of potassium which occurs mainly in inorganic compounds. Gardening suppliers sell organic fertilizers in the form of horn meal, horn chips, bone meal, dried blood, guano, manure, and so on. Most of these fertilizers yield only one nutrient each; for example, horn chips provide nitrogen, bone meal provides phosphorous. Initial fertilizing should, therefore, include a mixture of different fertilizers containing different nutrients. These are sold as "bio-fertilizers" and can also be called compound fertilizers if they contain potassium too.

Initial fertilizing

General rule: Any soil in which you intend to plant pelargoniums – with the exception of garden compost and standard potting compost which already contain nutrients – should have a good bulk compound fertilizer mixed in with it.

The following are the two most useful methods of basic fertilizing:

Method 1 – basic fertilizing with organic minerals: There is a large range of ready-made organic-mineral compound fertilizers to choose from in garden centers. For a basic fertilizer, use a bulk compound fertilizer with a higher than usual percentage of nitrogen, as nitrogen encourages the growth of stalks and leaves and will strengthen your young plants. One alternative would be a bio-fertilizer (also a purely organic fertilizer mixture), but make sure to use a bulk fertilizer containing a high percentage of nitrogen.

● Use the proper dosage! The correct ratio of fertilizer to soil to be used is usually written on the packaging. If there is no indication, stick to an average value of a maximum of ⅓ cup (70 g) of organic-mineral fertilizer to 2½ gallons (10 liters) of soil. In a bio-fertilizer the nutrients are less concentrated than in ready-made organic-mineral or inorganic fertilizer mixes. This means that you will hardly ever run the risk of overfeeding your plants. Nevertheless, still make sure to consult the dosage directions on the packaging of bio-fertilizers.

● Distribute the fertilizer really thoroughly! Make sure the compound fertilizer is mixed in evenly with the soil. The best way to do this is to sprinkle the bulk compound fertilizer on to the soil and turn it over several times with a spade.

● Note how long the stock of nutrients will last. Organic-mineral compound fertilizers will supply the soil with about six weeks' worth of all essential nutrients, although this is only an approximate estimation. Note the date of application and then repeat the dose after six weeks, using a liquid compound fertilizer (with a higher phosphorous content which favors the develop-

ment of flowers) when you water.

Method 2 – controlled-release fertilizers as an alternative

Controlled-release fertilizers are inorganic compound fertilizers. They comprise small granules in which the nutrients are captured in a highly concentrated form. When the granules are moistened, they become permeable and continuously release a nutrient solution.

● Use the correct dose! Keep strictly to the quantities recommended on the packaging so that your plants do not suffer from a build-up of salts in the soil. If the quantities are not indicated, use the following guide: 1 tablespoon per plant or 5 tablespoons for a flower box about 32 in (80 cm) in length.

● Mix thoroughly! Stir the controlled-release fertilizer into the soil so that it is evenly distributed.

● Note how long the nutrient supply will last. Controlled-release fertilizers will provide plants with nutrients over a period of three to four months, and represent an alternative to organic-mineral fertilizing.

Important: It would be wrong to assume that the above method of fertilizing means that you need not be concerned with supplying nutrients to your plants for the next three months of the year. A period of heavy rain, for example, will cause nutrients to be released and washed out more quickly, so that the fertilizing process will be over sooner than planned and will usually stop rather suddenly. You will then notice that the foliage of your pelargoniums is beginning to turn yellow. If this happens, use an inorganic liquid fertilizer when watering or sprinkle a fast-working, bulk inorganic fertilizer (for example, the blue-granule type, obtainable at garden centers) onto the damp soil.

Plant containers

Pelargoniums may be planted in a variety of containers, for example flowerboxes on window ledges or balconies. Plastic boxes are very useful. They mostly come in two widths (6 in/15 cm and 8 in/20 cm), and varying lengths. They are not heavy, are easy to transport, and are strong and stable.

However, you need not be limited to boxes: pelargoniums will thrive happily in pots, basins, hanging baskets, amphorae, even in old sinks. On the whole, the material out of which the container is made should have no effect whatever on the growth of your plants, although you should make sure that the container does not contain oxidizing substances like copper, tin, or zinc, as these would have a detrimental, or even toxic, effect on your plants.

Choosing plant containers

● Pelargonium roots cannot tolerate waterlogging. Whatever type of container you choose, it must have drainage holes.

● Pelargoniums can develop into magnificent bushes of considerable width. Your containers should, therefore, be very stable so that they will not tip over at the first strong gust of wind.

● The pelargonium will need enough room to spread out its roots and develop properly. If you choose the wider type of balcony box (8 in/20 cm), your plants will reward you with an extra-abundant crop of flowers.

● Pelargoniums that are kept in boxes fixed to balcony railings should have suitable trays or other arrangements for catching drainage water and adjustable, strong balcony fixtures (those made of metal are best). Both of these items are obtainable from garden centers, etc.

● Hanging containers should be made of lightweight materials (for example, plastic); this makes them easier to transport and puts less of a strain on the fixtures.

● Only containers that are definitely frost-proof can be kept outside in the winter (for example, containers made of plastic). Clay pots are specially sensitive in freezing temperatures and may then crack or flake.

My tip: Containers that taper conically downward provide less surface area for frost attack and are, therefore, more frost-resistant.

Tips on preparing plant containers

New clay pots: New clay pots should be prepared for use by immersing them completely in water until you can no longer see any tiny air bubbles rising to the surface. This soaking will remove any production residue still adhering to the pot and will also prevent a very dry pot from depriving the soil of moisture by drawing it out.

How to use your plants artistically
Zonal and hanging pelargoniums in balcony boxes in combination with other summer flowers and in hanging baskets.

Used containers: Any residue of any kind should be rinsed off thoroughly. Use clean water for this purpose. Pots which have had diseased plants in them should be treated with disinfectant which, in turn, should be well rinsed.

Drainage holes: All pots will need workable drainage holes so that there will be no waterlogging. Do not forget to pierce the pre-marked holes in some new flower boxes.

Protecting the drainage holes: Before filling a flowerpot with soil, place a piece of broken pot, with the curved side up, over the drainage holes, to prevent the earth from clogging the holes. In the case of very large containers, it is a good idea to place an entire layer of pot shards or Hortag (a lightweight expanded clay aggregate) in the bottom of the pot.

Segregating layer: Over the top of the drainage layer, lay a piece of fabric which will prevent the soil from penetrating the drainage layer. This arrangement will help surplus water to drain away easily. Hortag stores moisture and will serve as a small water reservoir.

Filling in the compost: Now fill the pot with compost up to ¾ in (2 cm) below the top of the pot. To make things easier, stand all the pots close together to avoid spilling compost over the edges.

How to plant correctly

● Water the pelargoniums a few hours before planting them, so that their rootstocks will not be dry. Then line up the plants on your work table in the sequence of planting.

● To remove the plant from its pot, gently grasp the top of the rootstock between your second and third fingers (see illustration), turn the pot upside down and lightly tap the rim of the pot against the edge of the table. The pot can then

be removed quite easily, and without damaging the rootstock, by giving a slight twist. You should never remove the latticed netting used for propagating, through which the roots have grown.

● Make a depression in the soil and stand the rootstock in it so that the top edges of the roots are no deeper down than they were in the propagating pot.

● Using your hand, press the soil down all around the rootstock so that contact with the roots is ensured.

● Do not plant more than five pelargoniums in a box measuring 40 in (1 m) long.

● Make sure that hanging pelargoniums are planted leaning forward slightly.

● When all the pelargoniums have been planted, a gap of ¼ in (1 cm) must be left all around at the top of

Removing a plant from its pot
Grasp the rootstock between your second and third fingers, turn the pot upside down, and twist slightly with the other hand.

the box so that watering will not cause soil to be washed away.

Initial care

The newly planted pelargoniums should now be placed in their final position and watered gently so that the soil is not washed away. Check them over once more before leaving them:

● If leaves or flowers have snapped off during replanting or transportation to their new site, you should remove them now.

● If the pelargoniums are left standing under some kind of cover, they will be protected from rain and storms. Alternatively, you can buy polyethylene hoods to act as a protection against strong winds, rain and hail. These hoods are also very useful during long periods of incessant rain and will prevent constant wetness around the roots, which might cause them to decay.

Indoor pelargoniums

The best position
Regal, scented-leafed and fancy-leafed pelargoniums prefer direct sunlight, so you should place them near a south-facing window which can be shaded during periods of strong sunlight.

The right soil
Pelargoniums that are destined for indoors need not be repotted immediately after purchasing and will, therefore, not need new soil.

Initial fertilizing
This will be necessary as a basic fertilizing should always accompany repotting in new soil or compost.

Plant pots
Pelargoniums for indoors can

remain in the pot in which they were originally bought.

They should only be planted in a larger pot when the old one is too small. A pot is too small if the roots have used up all the soil and now fill the entire pot. This is not necessarily what has happened if you see roots hanging out of the drainage holes. If you think it is time for the plant to be repotted, remove it from its pot and check how much room the roots still have in the old pot. Plants kept indoors look particularly attractive in a decorative pot holder. There should be a gap of ⅗ in (1.5 cm) between the inner and outer pots as this creates better circulation of air around the plant pot. If you do place your indoor pelargoniums in pot holders, make sure, when you water them, that no surplus water remains in the bottom of the pot holder, which could cause the roots to decay.

Pelargoniums ("Feuercascade") in a hanging basket on an arbor.

Geraniums in the garden

The best position
Shrub geraniums prefer to be in a half-shady position, for example, between high grasses or other shrubs.

The right soil
As shrub geraniums favor a nutrient-rich soil, the best soil for them should contain humus or loam.

Initial fertilizing
Give each individual shrub geranium a handful of bio-fertilizer by sprinkling it into the soil when you plant. This will be sufficient to stimulate plant growth and produce lots of flowers.

Planting
You will nearly always buy shrub geraniums as container plants which can then be planted out at any time during the entire growing season. Occasionally, you may be able to obtain them as half-grown cuttings and then the right time to plant is early spring (shortly after the plant has begun to shoot) or in the fall (after the geranium has died back and the leaves and stalks have turned brown).

Method
● With a spade, dig a hole (about 12 by 12 in/30 by 30 cm) and mix the soil you have removed with a handful of bio-fertilizer.

● Fill up the hole again with half of the mixture.

● Carefully remove the shrub geranium from its container and use one hand to hold the top of the roots against the top of the soil because the geranium should not be planted any deeper in the soil than it was in its original container.

● With the other hand distribute the rest of the soil-fertilizer mixture around the rootstock and press it down lightly.

● Finally, water thoroughly so that the soil envelops the rootstock.

Initial care
If the weather is very dry after planting, you will need to water your shrub geranium occasionally. After two weeks, it should be established and further watering will not be necessary as the average amount of rain should generally be sufficient.

Successful care – simple but vital

Giving pelargoniums and geraniums the best care during the summer means, above all, supplying them with the proper amounts of water and nutrients. In addition, there are also other duties, such as removing withered leaves or flowers, shortening shoots that have grown too long, removing weeds, and taking preventive measures to avoid and combat pests and diseases.

Pelargoniums on balconies and patios

Now that you have planted your pelargoniums with loving care, you will be able to look forward to the day when they will develop a mass of brilliantly colored blooms. Very little care is required for this, as pelargoniums are easy to look after and will reward you for just a little care with a lavish display of bright flowers.

Watering

Pelargoniums love the sun and will not mind drying out completely very occasionally as they are able to store moisture in their fleshy stalks and leaves. In this way they are able to survive long dry periods in their country of origin without coming to any harm. Too much moisture, on the other hand, will quickly lead to rotting roots. Proper watering is extremely important for pelargoniums.

My tip: Pelargoniums in small containers will need watering more often than plants in window boxes.

When and how often to water

General rule: Do not water until the soil is really dry – but then do it thoroughly. A mere glance at the soil will not be sufficient; you will have to give the soil a prod with your finger to check whether it is still damp. If it is, it is probably better not to water.

On hot summer days the soil will dry out quickly and, for that reason, you should water the plants daily (in the case of small containers, perhaps even twice daily), preferably in the early evening and/or early in the morning, as less water will evaporate then than during the heat of the day.

On cool, rainy days check the soil thoroughly and, if damp, do not water, as continuous wetness can lead to root damage within six hours.

Occasionally, on rainy days, pelargoniums that are kept under a cover may be forgotten. You may simply have assumed that all the plants will be watered by the rain, without thinking about their position. Be sure to check all your pelargoniums, even during long periods of rain, and water them if necessary.

Distress signals: Zonal pelargoniums will display leaves that have dried up and hang limply when they are overdue for watering. Hanging pelargoniums will have pale, dried-up leaves, even though they are not withered.

My tip: When watering, remember that pelargoniums are stimulated to develop flowers by receiving lots of sunlight and plenty of heat but relatively little water.

What kind of water to use

Pelargoniums are not sensitive to hard water, so you can use regular main water as well as rainwater. *Exception:* If you have used a controlled-release fertilizer for the initial feed, you should then only use main water as rainwater will not activate the fertilization process.

How to water

Make sure the water is directed straight onto the soil without wetting the pelargonium's leaves in the process. This will require some care but will prevent an outbreak of fungal disease on the leaves.

Regal pelargonium
This pure white cultivar "Virginia" has especially large umbels.

Watering while you are away

Very often kind friends and neighbors are prepared to take on the task of watering plants while you are away on vacation. Make sure to leave exact instructions for the appropriate care of the pelargoniums on your windowsill, balcony, or patio. If there is nobody to help out, you may wish to try out one of various automatic or semi-automatic irrigation systems:

Irrigation system for brief periods of absence: For a short absence, containers of water, which will supply your plants with moisture via a woollen strand or a wick inserted into the soil, may be sufficient. Before going away you really should find out how long the water supply will last. In my experience, this method of supplying water cannot be controlled. A thick woollen strand will conduct too much water into the soil for pelargoniums, which will result in persistent wetness and lead to root damage. Before going away, test the thickness of strand needed to supply your plants with the right amount of water.

An alternative method is the use of clay cones (obtainable from gardening suppliers) which are inserted into the soil. These cones are connected to an adequate supply of water via a piece of twine, wool, or a wick. As the clay has a tendency to absorb a certain amount of moisture, it will soak up water through the line and pass it onto the soil.

Irrigation system for a lengthy absence: If you intend to go away for a longish period of time, a droplet irrigation system (obtainable from gardening suppliers) may serve well. This can also be purchased in kit form which you can set up yourself. Make sure you get all the necessary information on the working and safety of this installation and check that it works properly before you go away in order to avoid unpleasant surprises on your return.

Regular fertilizing

When planting, you should have given an initial feed of fertilizer containing nutrients that will be used up after about six weeks.

You will recognize the deficiency symptoms when the plant stops flowering so well and the leaves become smaller and yellowish. If you do nothing at this point, your pelargoniums will soon deteriorate and die. Do not let matters reach this point and remember to feed your pelargoniums regularly!

When and how to feed
General rule: Give your plants a liquid compound fertilizer in water once a week, and they will flourish.

It is a simple matter to calculate the correct dosage of liquid fertilizer – you need only follow the directions on the package. This should completely eliminate the chance of over- or underfeeding during regular fertilizing, and there will be no danger of the leaves burning through too much fertilizing

Compound fertilizers
Every compound fertilizer contains all the essential nutrients for plant growth (nitrogen, phosphorous, and potassium) along with trace elements . The effect of each nutrient on the plant is described in the table below.

The effects of nutrients

Nutrient	Positive effect	Negative effect if dosage too high	Source
nitrogen (N)	encourages growth of all green parts of plant (leaves, stalks, etc.)	oversized, bloated leaves, susceptibility to disease, fewer flowers, weak plant tissue, tendency for shoots to rot	in compound fertilizers, special fertilizers containing, nitrogen, horn products, horn chips, dried blood
phosphorous (P)	encourages development of flowers and seeds	dark green to blue green foliage	in compound fertilizers, "flower" fertilizers, guano, bone meal
potassium (K)	strengthens plant tissue, serves to toughen up and develop seeds	weak plant tissue, leaves that break easily, small seeds	in compound fertilizers, special potassium-rich fertilizers

Breaking off dead flowers
Break them off downward, close to the axil.

The plant will absorb nutrients according to the law of minimum content; that is, the absorption of all minerals is affected by whatever substance is missing. Therefore, a large amount of nitrogen cannot be absorbed by the plant if phosphorous is missing. For the gardener at home, this means that all nutrients must be given in a balanced ratio – and a compound fertilizer will always contain the right mixture. For regular feeding of pelargoniums you should use a compound fertilizer with a higher content of phosphorous as this promotes the development of lots of flowers. Compound fertilizers with a high phosphorous content are sold by gardening suppliers as "flowering" fertilizers. There are also other compound fertilizers among the "special" fertilizers, which are suitable for regular feeding. These fertilizers have been specially formulated to suit the requirements of a particular genus or group of plants.

Ask about these at your local garden center or nursery. The type made specially for balcony plants is ideal for feeding regularly to pelargoniums.

Single-nutrient fertilizer to treat symptoms of deficiency
In addition to the various types of compound fertilizer, there are some fertilizers that contain only one nutrient. These fertilizers should only be used if you notice symptoms of a deficiency in your pelargoniums, which can definitely be traced back to a lack of one particular nutrient.

Further care

Besides watering and feeding, pelargoniums will also need some tidying. This can be done quite easily at the same time as watering.
● Dried up or yellow leaves can be broken off at the axils. The same goes for withered flower stalks (illustration). This will help to prevent diseases from developing in the dead parts and the plants will also look tidier.
● Extra-long shoots (which occur quite often in zonal pelargoniums and stick out beyond the plant) can be cut off – a measure that will help the pelargonium to grow more compactly.
● Weeds in pots or balcony boxes should be pulled out as soon as possible as they will divert nutrients from the pelargoniums.
● Check your plants regularly for diseases or parasites.
Carefully turn over a leaf and look underneath it to see if there is any sign of pests. Often aphids or other harmful insects will be found on softer, younger shoots.
● During longer periods of wet weather, your pelargoniums may

begin to lose their beautiful appearance. Protect them against the rain with polyethylene hoods (obtainable from gardening suppliers). This will also prevent the roots from decaying and the nutrients from being washed out of the soil.

Indoor pelargoniums

Just like their outdoor relatives, pelargoniums that are kept indoors – such as regal, scented-leafed, wild, and fancy-leafed pelargoniums – need lots of light. They will thrive especially well in a bright window position, in direct sunlight, and with some means of ventilation. Fancy-leafed pelargoniums are the only ones that can tolerate semi-shady positions; however too much shade will cause them to lose their interesting leaf markings and the leaves will turn pure green. Dry indoor air will not harm your pelargoniums at all as the wild species which produced their ancestors live in very dry or desert-like regions and are used to drought. During the summer they will flourish outdoors in a position that is protected from too much rain.
Watering: Water all indoor pelargoniums sparingly. The soil should never be completely moist. The regal pelargonium will react most sensitively to too much water. If its soil becomes too moist, it will develop yellow leaves and the buds will die. If this should happen, let the soil dry out and the plant will recover again after a time.

Pelargonium odoratissimum.

"White Unique" (hybrid).

Pelargonium tomentosum.

Pelargonium quercifolium.

"Joy Lucile" (hybrid).

Pelargonium viscosissimum.

Pelargonium graveolens.

Pelargonium radens.

Pelargonium glutinosum.

Regular feeding: Regal and fancy-leafed pelargoniums should be given a liquid compound fertilizer once a week, containing a high percentage of phosphorous (for example, a "flowering" or "balcony" fertilizer). Make sure you follow the dosage directions on the packaging. Scented-leafed pelargoniums are usually a pure wild variety and should be fertilized only sparingly. They, too, should receive a liquid compound fertilizer with a high percentage of phosphorous, but only once every two weeks and only half the dose suggested on the packaging. If they are given too much fertilizer, these delicate plants will lose their original shape and their leaves and shoots will become unnaturally large. Stop feeding them just before the winter rest period (for fancy-leafed pelargoniums, early fall, for regal and scented-leafed pelargoniums, the second month of winter, so that the plants can rest. Do not start feeding them again until the early part of spring.

Flowers and old leaves should be snapped off and removed in the same way as with outdoor pelargoniums.

Repotting: The regal pelargonium, in particular, can develop into a vigorous bush which will need a new pot every year.

Scented-leafed and wild pelargonium leaves
A wealth of shapes, beautifully formed and usually with a pleasant scent which is released when the fine, scent-bearing hairs are touched.

● The proper time to repot is before the beginning of a new vegetation period (around early to mid-spring) or after the first flowering phase (around the second or third month of summer).
● For this purpose it is best to use a new clay pot which you have soaked well beforehand.
The new pot should always be ¾ in (2 cm) larger than the old one.
● The best potting compost is the standard kind, which you should mix with a little sand as the soil is already fertilized. If using a home-made compost, you may need to mix in a bulk organic-mineral compound fertilizer.

Checking growth: Vigorously growing pelargoniums should be cut back a little occasionally. Use a sharp knife or a pair of scissors to cut off the top shoots of the pelargonium. The dormant leaf buds in the remaining leaf axils will now start to develop into new shoots. This, in turn, will stimulate the plant to branch out and produce more compact growth. You can easily coax any cut-off shoots to begin rooting.

Preventive measures against pests: Pelargoniums kept indoors may occasionally become infested with white fly or red spider mites. A useful preventive measure consists of inserting a pest-control stick into each individual pot. Other pests or diseases are rarely seen on indoor plants.

Preventive measures against fungal disease: Do not position the plants too close together and air them well. Do not wet the leaves when watering. Be sparing with nitrogen-based fertilizers. Use disinfected tools to prune, in order to avoid transferring diseases to other plants.

Geraniums in the garden

Watering: As a rule, shrub geraniums in the garden will not need to be watered at all. These plants have a widely spreading root system which can absorb enough moisture from deeper levels of the soil. During long periods of drought and/or in sandy soils, however, the leaves of shrub geraniums may begin to go limp. Then is the time to water.

Regular feeding: If you have mature shrub geraniums, wait until early to mid-spring, when they begin to shoot again, before sprinkling a handful of bio-fertilizer around the plant and raking it lightly into the soil. You need not add inorganic fertilizer, as there are usually enough minerals in regular garden soil. This one feed should be enough for the whole summer.

Removing weeds: As soon as weeds start appearing around the shrub geranium, they should be removed so that they will not divert nutrients away from your plants. Small weeds can be pulled out by hand but larger ones with long roots need to be hoed out.

Aerating: Once or twice during the summer, the soil surface around the shrub geraniums should be gently hoed to aerate the soil. This procedure can be carried out in conjunction with the removal of weeds.

Supports and windbreaks: If tall geraniums happen to be positioned in windy places, they can easily tip over during the flowering period. Shrub supports, which can be obtained from garden centers, etc., will provide good stability and are recommended even for large shrubs.

Infestation by pests is unlikely, as shrub geraniums are very resistant.

Problems, pests, and diseases

Important: All plant-protection preparations, even biological ones, must be stored in a place that is inaccessible to children and pets. Only ever spray plants outside – never indoors!

NB: All plant-protection substances are kept in a locked cabinet at gardening suppliers and only ever handled by specially trained employees. Seek expert advice about the products you are using and, whenever possible, use biological forms of control.

Pelargoniums on patios and balconies

With proper care and handling, healthy plants should develop sufficient resistance to disease by themselves. While watering, remove any brown, dried-up leaves and old flower stalks in order to prevent decay. Occasionally, check the pelargoniums for infestation by pests. Aphids and other pests are often found on the undersides of leaves or on young, soft shoots. The control of aphids (see insect pests) is specially important as they are carriers of the dreaded blight, a bacterial disease (see bacterial diseases).

Indoor pelargoniums

Indoor pelargoniums are very robust. Occasionally they may become infested with red spider mites, aphids, or white fly (see pests). If the infestation is severe, you should use an insecticide, following the manufacturer's directions carefully.

Geraniums in the garden

Just like many other shrubs, geraniums can easily become infested with rust (see fungal diseases) during particularly wet years.

Mistakes in care

Odemas (illustration 1)
Symptoms: Cork-like growths on the undersides of leaves. These occur only on hanging pelargoniums. High humidity favors this condition. Widely varying amounts of water being received by the plant cause its cells to burst and develop into these cork-like masses.

Problems
1 *Odemas*
2 *Waterlogging or salt damage*
3 *Temperatures too low*

Prevention: Water regularly, but not too much. Great differences in the frequency and amount of watering are to be avoided. Try to give the same amount each time, not too much nor too little.
Remedy: Not possible. Odemas do not seem to harm the pelargoniums particularly, being merely unsightly.

Waterlogging or salt damage
(illustration 2)
Symptoms: Wilting, blue green foliage, and often brown, rotting root tips.
Prevention: Make sure there are sufficient drainage holes in your plant pots, water sparingly, and, if necessary, protect the plants from heavy rain.
Or: reduce feeding.
Remedy: If the plant is not affected too badly, repotting immediately will help. Remove the old soil by shaking it off, trim the root tips gently with scissors, and set the pelargonium in new soil.

Temperatures that are too low
(illustration 3)
Symptoms: Yellowish foliage with red leaf edges, especially on older leaves.
Prevention: Do not keep pelargoniums at temperatures of below 39° F (4° C).
Remedy: Raise the temperature and feed more. The discoloration should then disappear.

Pests

Red spider mites (illustration 1)
Symptoms: The leaves turn yellow and fine webs, filled with tiny reddish mites, appear between the leaf veins and the stalks.
Prevention: Regular care makes the plant more resistant. Avoid dry, warm air in rooms.
Control: Strong insecticides; if the infestation is severe, treatment is often unsatisfactory.

Aphids: (illustration 2)
Symptoms: These pests can be seen quite easily with the naked eye; very often they can be found on the undersides of leaves or on young shoots. The young leaves become twisted; light-colored

Fungal diseases

Pelargonium rust (illustration 1)
Symptoms: The undersides of leaves are covered with ring-shaped spore masses which release a dust when touched. Light yellow round spots appear on the uppersides of leaves.
Prevention: Regular aeration, taking care that the leaves do not become wet (for example, while watering or in rain).
Control: spray with a fungicide.

Decaying stalks (illustration 2)
Symptoms: The stalks turn black and then decay, starting at the top of the roots and moving upward.
Prevention: Avoid waterlogging. Temperatures should not drop below 59° F (15° C).
Control: Spraying with a fungicide.

Gray mold (illustration 3)
Symptoms: Expanses of gray mold on decaying leaves.
Prevention: Air well and do not set the plants too close together. Leaves should not remain wet overnight; it is better to water

your plants in the mornings.
Control: Spray with a fungicide.

Bacterial diseases

Bacterial blight (*Xanthomonas pelargonii*) (also bacterial stem rot)
Symptoms: First phase: small dot-shaped, light-colored spots on the leaves, which quickly become larger and develop into blackish-brown patches. Healthy leaves turn yellow and wither fast (illustration 1).

*Bacterial
diseases*
Bacterial blight
1 *First phase*
2 *Second
   phase*
3 *Third phase*

marks are visible on the leaves.
Prevention: Regular care makes the plants more resistant. Avoid dry, warm air in rooms. Nutrients (fertilizers) should be kept to a minimum; above all, avoid too much nitrogen as this will make the plant cells spongy and unnaturally large so that they tend to burst open. When this has happened, bacteria may enter.
Control: Biological methods are very effective; biological sprays made from a solution of nettles may help if applied several times. Otherwise, use commercially available insecticides.

White fly (illustration 3)
Symptoms: The leaves turn yellow and wither. When the leaves are touched, tiny white insects fly up. Regal pelargoniums in particular tend to become infested.
Prevention: see aphids.
Control: Use sticky, coated strips (bio-friendly greenhouse fly catchers) which lure insects with their bright color. Alternatively, try commonly available insecticides.

Fungal diseases
1 *Pelargonium
   rust*
2 *Rotting stalks*
3 *Gray mold*

Second phase: brown bacterial slime, which appears when the affected leaf-stalks are bent and broken (illustration 2). Third phase: blackish dry rot at the base of the stalk (illustration 3).
Prevention: When buying plants, make sure they are healthy. The bacteria can be transferred by pests, water or by touch. Tools and used pots which have come into contact with infested pelargoniums should be cleaned and disinfected before being reused.
Control: None. Destroy affected plants.

Overwintering

Pelargoniums that have lived on a patio or balcony all summer will need to be overwintered in a different way to those that bloom indoors. The overwintering of shrub geraniums is very different again. Each group has its own individual requirements, which are described below. If you have never tried overwintering your pelargoniums, you will be surprised at how easy it is.

Pelargoniums on patios and balconies

Most people find it difficult to part with pelargoniums that have produced veritable cascades of flowers throughout the summer and into the fall and, really, there is no reason why they should do so. Overwintering pelargoniums is not a very difficult business provided you have access to the right place. The advantages of this method are that properly overwintered plants will flower even better during the following year
and you will save on the cost of buying new pelargoniums.

My tip: If you are unable to overwinter pelargoniums in the traditional manner because of lack of space, there are space-saving overwintering methods,
or you can try cutting the top shoots off your pelargoniums in the fall, before getting rid of them
and rooting
these cuttings as a second generation of plants.

Which plants overwinter best?

● Only overwinter completely healthy, pest-free plants. Before making any other preparations, therefore, you should check that the general health of your pelargoniums is good. Examine the tops and undersides of leaves. Pelargoniums which show symptoms of bacterial diseases should be destroyed, so
that they cannot infect other plants.

● You can overwinter zonal and hanging pelargoniums but long, trailing plants can take up a lot of space and will need more care when being moved and during storage.
● Pelargoniums in individual pots are specially easy to overwinter, being easier to transport and store than plants in balcony boxes. When they begin to shoot again in the spring, they only need to be moved slightly apart so that they will obtain sufficient space and light for uninterrupted growth. Such overwintering will usually result in beautiful, compact growth.
● Pelargoniums can also be overwintered in a balcony box, often in combination with other plants.
NB: Annual plants (for example, lobelia or petunias) that are growing in the same box are not suitable for overwintering and will have to be removed. Daisies and fuchsias, on the other hand, can be treated and overwintered in the same way as pelargoniums. In their countries of origin, these shrubby plants are perennials, just as pelargoniums are, but they must be protected from freezing temperatures in less mild climates.

Suitable places for overwintering

General rule: The most suitable overwintering areas are bright and frost-free but not too warm. The most suitable of all is a small greenhouse but even light attics, light cellar rooms, or garages with access to sufficient daylight make good winter quarters for pelargoniums. Quite unsuitable places are warm cellar rooms, centrally heated rooms, or dark rooms. Pelargoniums that have been overwintered in small greenhouses will start flowering from the middle of spring onward because they have access to lots of light and are in appropriate cool temperatures. Plants that have overwintered in rooms with less light will produce flowers quite a bit later. However, do not be concerned: after six weeks outside, they will catch up in flowering and you will not be able to tell whether a particular pelargonium was overwintered in a greenhouse or on a windowsill. Give your pelargoniums as much light as possible during the whole period of overwintering and try to keep them close to a window.

My tip: If you have space on only one windowsill for a number of plants, you can buy a collapsible flower shelf made of steel to stand on the windowsill. This gadget has five shelves and can accommodate five filled flowerboxes or many pelargoniums in pots, and will also provide them with plenty of light. It is an excellent device for gardeners who have very little space or who live in apartments.

The rules of overwintering

Preparations
Preparations for overwintering should begin at the end of the summer. Reduce fertilizing from now on. The pelargoniums will gradually become ready for the approaching period of dormancy and will not put out any more new shoots. Examine the plants to see if they are healthy and suitable for overwintering. If everything is all right, it is time to decide where the best place for overwintering would be. There are many suitable places so almost everyone could manage to overwinter a few plants.

Protection from frosts
Depending on where you live, the first frosts may arrive as early as the beginning of fall. As pelargoniums cannot tolerate temperatures below freezing, you should find a frost-free place for them – for example, their future overwintering area. Whether you leave the pelargoniums there, or take them outside again into the warm fall sunlight, is up to you. From early fall onward, however, you must keep an eye on the local weather forecasts for frost warnings, so that you will be prepared ahead of time.

Care before dormancy
When the plants have been settled permanently in their cool, bright winter quarters, they must be tidied up thoroughly. Flowers and dead

Regal pelargoniums were popular in our grandparents' time.

leaves should be snapped off by hand. The over-wintering of hanging pelargoniums becomes a little easier if they are cut back a little with scissors. This will not harm the plant at all and will prevent the plant from becoming damaged when it is moved and during the rest period.

Dormancy
With less sunlight and cooler temperatures, the pelargoniums will now sink into a kind of hibernation phase, in which they will remain until the end of winter. Then, as the daylight hours increase noticeably, a new growth phase will begin and the plants will begin to send out new shoots.

Care during dormancy
The optimal overwintering temperature is about 39-50° F (4-10° C). Pelargoniums can tolerate

temperatures of 36-37° F (2-3° C) for short periods of time but if this goes on too long, their leaves will turn reddish. This, however, will return to normal again when the temperature rises. On no account should temperatures sink below 32° F (0° C) as pelargoniums cannot survive freezing.

● Water sparingly during this entire period (approximately once every two weeks). As the pelargoniums will now receive less sunlight than in the summer, they will also need less water. If you water too much, long, weak shoots will form, which are susceptible to disease and break off easily.

Cutting back after overwintering
Use a sharp knife, leaving three or four nodes above the woody brown stalks.

● Stop fertilizing as the plant should now be entering its dormant phase
● Occasionally break off dry leaves and old flower stalks.

● Regularly, check for pests and diseases. If there is any infestation, spray your pelargoniums with commercially available preparations.

Pruning after dormancy
The middle until the end of winter, at the latest, is the period during which you should cut back overwintered pelargoniums (see illustration). The right place to cut is always the green part of the stalk. Use a sharp knife or scissors and always let three or four leaf axils remain on the green stalk. It is from these leaf axils that new shoots will grow after pruning.
Important: Never cut into the woody part of a stalk as these parts of the plant rarely put out new shoots.

Repotting
I recommend planting pelargoniums in new compost after their third overwintering at the latest. When doing this, carefully loosen the plants, together with their complete rootstocks, tip them out of

their overwintering pots, and then remove as much soil as possible from the roots without damaging them. After that, plant your pelargoniums in standard potting compost.

New growth

In spring, as the daylight hours increase, temperatures will begin to rise. The pelargoniums will react to this with increased formation of

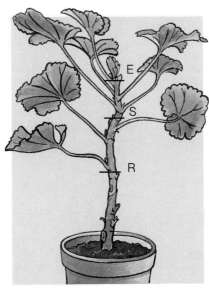

How to cut back
R: cutting back after overwintering; S: pruning; E: pinching out shoot tips

healthy, new shoots and leaves. A little care is now required in order to prepare the pelargoniums for their move outdoors:
● From the last month of winter onward, water more often.
● Every eight days, add a growth-promoting fertilizer (one with a larger percentage of nitrogen) to your watering can.
● If you have individual pelargoniums in pots, make sure they are

not standing too close together. The tips of their leaves should not touch each other. The plants need space in order to grow vigorously.
● The place in which the pelargoniums are kept should be aired often as this will make them more resistant to disease.
● If you pinch out the shoot tips or cut the shoots back a little, you will obtain bushy, compact pelargoniums.
This pinching out can be done by hand using your fingernails to take out the tips of the top shoots. This stimulates growth in the lower buds, which will soon put out more shoots. Cutting back means cutting off some of the particularly long shoots. These can then be used as cuttings.

My tip: Slow-growing pelargoniums should have their shoot tips pinched out. Fast-growing varieties, such as the hanging cascade pelargoniums, will respond to cutting back by ceasing to produce only a few long, trailing shoots and, instead, will branch out and grow more compactly.
At the end of dormancy: After the last cold snap in spring, put your pelargoniums outside.

Space-saving overwintering methods

The following are two fairly uncommon methods employed by some hobby gardeners. Be warned that not every pelargonium will survive this!

Overwintering in a plastic bag
● Water the pelargoniums well.
● Cut each plant back to about 6 in (15 cm).
● Carefully remove the plant, together with its rootstock and the surrounding soil, and put it in a plas-

tic bag. Freezer bags are especially suitable as they are quite tough.

● Tie the plastic bag up tightly so that no moisture can escape. This will prevent the pelargoniums from drying out.

● Use empty flower boxes (a box 40 in/1 m long will accommodate about seven to ten plants) to store the plants, or suspend them from a "washing line" stretched across or near a window.

Pinching out shoot tips
Pinch out the uppermost shoot tips with your fingernails.

● Check the moisture occasionally and add water if necessary.
● From the first month of spring onward, begin planting the pelargoniums in pots again.
● Overwintering temperatures should be 43-50 F° (6-10 C°). The plants will need lots of light!

Overwintering in paper
● Remove dead flowers and leaves and take the pelargoniums out of their containers.
● Leaves and stalks should be dry and the soil around the roots should be only slightly moist.
● Lightly shake some of the soil off the roots. Do not remove all of it!
● Wrap each pelargonium individually (roots, leaves, and flowers) in newspaper.
● Place these packages in a box and let them overwinter in a frost-free place in the cellar.

● At the beginning of the last month of winter, take these packages out of their winter quarters and cut back the shoots.
● Plant the pelargoniums in fresh standard potting compost and stand them in a warm room.
● As soon as new shoots become visible, give them as much light as possible!

Indoor pelargoniums
Overwintering in a warm room

In their subtropical countries of origin, pelargoniums do not have a period of dormancy and they will continue to flower all year round. This is why they may produce an odd flower even in winter if placed in the window of a warm room. If pelargoniums are kept in a warm room all winter, they must be fed and watered regularly.

Overwintering methods for obtaining lots of flowers

Fancy-leafed pelargoniums
These should be overwintered like pelargoniums on patios and balconies.

Scented-leafed and wild pelargoniums
Keep them near a window in a warm room until the end of winter, then stand them in a bright, cool room at an optimal temperature of 41° F (5° C). Keep them cool in this way for about four to six weeks but do not water or feed them during this time. It will be sufficient just to spray the leaves with water quite frequently. During this cool period, flower buds will form .
● After four to six weeks, put the

pelargoniums in a warm room again, in front of a window, but still do not water them. Carry on spraying them instead.
● From early spring onward, begin to water them carefully and feed them very sparingly, putting only half of the recommended dose of liquid fertilizer in the water.
● From the last month of spring onward, continue with normal care.

Regal pelargoniums
These plants will need a cool period of four to six weeks, just like the scented-leafed and wild pelargoniums. During this time, they should be watered sparingly. From early spring onward, water more and give a normal weekly dose of liquid fertilizer in water.

Geraniums in the garden

Every year in the fall, the parts above ground will die down and the plant will produce new shoots again in the spring.
In late fall, cut off the leaves and shoots that look brown approximately 8 in (20 cm) above the ground. Make sure you do not cut the above ground parts right down to the soil, enabling moisture from the soil to seep into the heart of the roots via the exposed cut surfaces, which would encourage decay. This rule applies to all garden shrubs. The robust geranium will not need any more care than this. Winter protection will not be needed. From early to mid-spring, the shrub will start shooting again. When the new shoots have reached a height of 2-4 in (5-10 cm), sprinkle a handful of bio-fertilizer around the plant, then work the fertilizer into the soil, so that it will dissolve better.

Propagating made easy

Generally speaking, very few gardeners use seed for propagating geraniums and pelargoniums. Which plants are most suited to this method and how to do it are both explained in this chapter. Propagating by means of cuttings is even easier and, like overwintering, makes it unnecessary for you to buy new plants the following year. It is also interesting and most enjoyable to propagate successfully.

Pelargoniums on patios and balconies

The right time to propagate

Pelargoniums can be propagated by using cuttings (vegetative) or from seeds (generative).
Propagating from cuttings is possible with all pelargoniums, but propagating from seed is only done with certain F_1 hybrids (see My tip, p. 8), wild pelargoniums, and shrub geraniums. Both methods of propagating are possible all year round.
If you wish to have pelargoniums that are carrying lots of buds by the end of the last cold snap in spring, you should follow the propagation schedules given below:
Propagating from seed: Sow the seeds from the middle of the first month of winter until the end of the second month at the very latest (method, see below).
Propagating from cuttings: Take shoots for cuttings at any time from late summer to the middle of the first month of spring at the very latest and plant them at once.

Propagating from seed

There are two methods of sowing seeds, in peat pellets or in seed trays, and each method requires different care. The germination and growth of young plants is equally successful using either method.

Method 1 – sowing seeds in peat pellets
You will need:
● a mini-propgator for use indoors, with a transparent cover (obtainable frome gardening suppliers at reasonable cost), or a plastic tray with a light-permeable plastic hood or glass plate;
● peat pellets (sold in garden centers);
● pelargonium seed;
● seeding compost (germ-free, special compost for seeds and cuttings, from garden centers, etc.);
● plastic or clay pots with a diameter of 4¼ in (11 cm);
● standard potting compost.

Procedure
● Place the dry, wheel-shaped peat pellets in the plastic tray of your mini-propagator and carefully pour tepid water over them.
● These peat discs will quickly swell to several times their previous size. Add more tepid water until no more is soaked up. Pour away any surplus water.
● Put one seed in each peat pellet and push it in with your finger to a depth of about ⅓ in (1 cm), so that the soil envelops it.
● Stand the plastic tray of seeds in a bright, warm position; the optimal place might be on a windowsill above a radiator.
● Place the plastic cover (or plate of glass) over the seed tray. Covering the seeds should promote the right kind of moist/warm atmosphere in the propagator. The seeds need a germination temperature of 64-68° F (18-20° C).

Development and care
A few days after planting the seeds, you will see the first delicate leaflets peeping out of the soil. *During the first fourteen days* after sowing, the tiny plants will need a lot of care and attention as they are very delicate and can be damaged quite easily.
● If condensation develops on the inside of the plastic cover, you will have to lift it off to air it in order to avoid the growth of mold. Many such mini-propagators have ventilation slits that can be opened and shut. If your propagator does not have these, simply place a small stick between the plastic tray and the cover. Whenever necessary, ventilate the propagator in this way for one or two hours each day.
● If the sunlight is very intense, it is a good idea to place some newspaper over the plastic cover in

Semi-pendent pelargonium "Schöne von Grenchen" will produce glowing red flowers even in semi-shade.

order to protect the pelargonium seedlings from burns.

● Use your fingers to check whether the peat pellets are still moist. You will probably have to add a little tepid water from time to time.

Three weeks after sowing the pelargoniums will be several inches (centimeters) high. Toughen up the young plants by removing the cover.

During the following weeks the pelargoniums will grow very quickly. When the leaves of the young plants begin to touch each other, they should be moved apart so that the plants can carry on growing without being restricted.

Five weeks after sowing the temperature should be lowered to 61° F (16° C) (the best thing to do is to place the pelargoniums in a bright, cool room) so that the plants can toughen up.

About ten weeks after sowing you will see little white rootlets growing out of the peat pellets. Now plant the young pelargoniums in a large plastic or clay pot with a diameter of 4¼ in (11 cm). This is the pot that the young plant will remain in until it is finally taken outside to be planted on a balcony or patio. When you plant the pelargonium in its final pot, it should be left in the old soil but you should add a little extra standard potting compost. Make sure the plant does not sit any deeper in the soil than it was before.

Sowing seeds

Pour tepid water onto the peat pellets and let them swell up. Using a folded sheet of paper, place one seed on each peat pellet, press it in to about ⅓ in (1 cm) deep, and cover it with soil.
After germination, the cover should be removed for ventilation if condensation develops.

Method 2 – sowing seed in special seeding compost

You will need:
● a mini-propagator for use indoors, with a transparent cover, or a plastic tray with a light-permeable plastic cover or glass plate;
● seeding compost;
● pelargonium seed (obtainable from garden centers, etc.);
● a dibble;
● peat propagation pots with a diameter of 2 in (6 cm). Made of pressed peat, these round or square pots, in various different sizes, are obtainable from garden centers, etc. The advantage of them is that the plants need not be removed from the pot as their roots will grow through the pot wall;
● plastic or clay pots with a diameter of 4¼ in (11 cm);
● standard potting compost.

Procedure

● Pour special seeding compost into the plastic tray, almost up to the edge. If necessary, crumble it a little to distribute it evenly.
● Carefully fill the tray with tepid water until the soil is thoroughly moistened.
● Sow the seeds in plots of 1 by 1 in (2.5 by 2.5 cm), using a folded piece of paper as an aid (see illustration). Lightly press the seeds into the soil with your finger (about ⅓ in/1 cm deep) and cover them with soil.
● Place the plastic tray in a bright, warm position, the best place would be a windowsill above a radiator.
● Now place the plastic cover (or plate of glass) over the seeding tray as the seeds will need moist, warm air to germinate at a temperature of 64-68° F (18-20° C).

Development and care

During the first three weeks after sowing the same care should be given as described for sowing in peat pellets.
When the little plants are big enough for their leaves to touch those of their neighbors, they must be pricked out so that they have more space in which to grow.
● Pricking out is quite simple: lift the tiny pelargoniums out of the soil carefully using a dibble (illustration right).
● If the roots are specially long, they can be pinched off with your fingernails (illustration right), which makes replanting easier.
● Put a little seeding compost in small peat pots (2⅓ in/6 cm), very carefully insert the young plants, and add as much soil as necessary

to fill up the pot.
● The seedlings should be planted right up to their leaves as more tiny roots will form above the existing roots.
● After all the seedlings have been pricked out, clean the plastic tray, which can now serve as a base for all the little pots.
● Stand the plantlets in the plastic tray and water them gently.
As growth increases, the pelargoniums should be moved apart so that the tips of the leaves do not touch.
Five weeks after sowing the temperature should be reduced to 61° F (16° C) (the best plan is to stand the pelargoniums in a bright, cool room), so that the plants can toughen up.

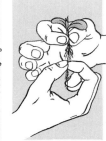

Pricking out
Loosen the seedling in the soil using the thin end of the dibble. Shorten the root tip.

Planting the seedling
Make a hole with the thick end of the dibble. Insert the seedling up to its leaves and press down lightly.

About ten weeks after sowing, the roots will have developed to the point where the plant will now require a larger pot. Do not remove the small peat pot but simply plant the young pelargonium, together with its pot and a little standard potting compost, in a plastic clay pot with a diameter of 4¼ in (11 cm). Make sure that the plants do not sit any deeper in the soil than they were before.

My tip: If done with care, both methods of sowing seed should result in the same time being taken for the plants to develop. You will find, however, that using peat pellets is less time-consuming as the seedlings do not need to be pricked out.

Propagating from cuttings

If you already grow pelargoniums, you will have the opportunity of taking cuttings from the mother plants for growing into new plants.

The best pelargonium cutting
● will be 3-4 in (just under 7-10 cm) long;
● will have at least one set of fully developed leaves;
● will have a stalk that is crisp, fresh and deep green. Do not take light green, young, soft shoots (they tend to decay when planted) nor older, brown, woody shoots as they will not root easily.

Propagating equipment
● a disinfected knife (so that no germs are transferred while taking the cutting);
● peat pellets (obtainable from garden centers, etc.) or peat propagating pots with a diameter of 2⅓ in (6 cm) (made of pressed peat, round or square, in various sizes and obtainable from garden

centers, etc.), the advantage being that the plants need not be removed from the pots as their roots will grow right through the wall;
● mini-propagator for use indoors, with a cover (available at reasonable cost in garden centers, etc.) or a plastic tray with a light-permeable plastic cover or glass plate;
● seeding compost (germ-free special compost for seeds and cuttings, made of peat, loam, and essential nutrients, obtainable from garden centers, etc.);
● plastic or clay pots with a diameter of 4¼ in (11 cm);
● standard potting compost (obtainable in garden centers, etc.).

Method
● A few hours before taking the cuttings, water the mother plants so that the cuttings are not limp, but strong and crisp.
● Look for suitable cuttings on the mother plant (description left) and, using a disinfected knife, cut them off approximately ¾ in (2 cm) below a set of leaves (illustration right). The cuttings should have stalks of about ¾ in (2 cm), so that they can be planted deep enough.
● Buds or flowers on cuttings should be removed, so that all the energy will go into the growth of the new plant.
● Plant the cuttings immediately after taking them from the mother plant – either in well-soaked peat pellets or in small peat propagating pots filled with seeding compost.
● Plant the cuttings at a depth of about ¾ in (2 cm) in the soil, press down gently, and water so that the soil envelops the unrooted cutting.
● Place the plantlets, in their peat pellets or peat propagating pots, in a plastic tray and cover this. The cuttings will thus live in an extremely humid environment and evaporation through their leaves will be reduced to a minimum. As the

shoots are still rootless at this point, and water absorption from below is not yet possible, it is vital to cover the plants during the first week.

Taking a cutting
Cut between two leaf axils with a sharp, disinfected knife. Break off the bud and stalk with your fingernails where the stalk grows from the main stem. Insert the cutting into a peat pellet and press down gently.

● Keep the cuttings in a very bright place (a window is best) at a room temperature of 64-68° F (18-20° C).

Development and care
A few days after planting, a callus (new plant tissue) will form on the cutting and, soon afterward, the first little roots will appear.

- If condensation appears inside the cover, you will have to air it or there is a risk of gray mold growing on the cuttings or on the soil.
- If the sunlight is extremely bright, lay a sheet of newspaper over the plastic cover, to protect the plants from burns.
- *After two weeks* you can remove the cover as the roots will have formed by now and will be supplying the plants with water from below.

Four weeks after planting you can expect to see many young roots growing out of the peat pots – a sign that your propagating efforts have been successful.

After another three to five weeks, plant the growing cuttings in plastic or clay pots with a diameter of 4¼ in (11 cm), adding a little standard potting compost. The pelargoniums should be left in their old soil. Propagating pots which are infiltrated with roots should never be removed as the rootstock would be destroyed in the process and the plant would receive an irreversible shock, affecting its growth. Make sure that the plants do not sit any deeper in the soil than they were before. The pelargoniums should remain in these peat pots until they are moved outside, onto a patio or balcony, for planting.

Care of the young plants

No matter which method of propagating you have chosen, planting the pelargonium in its final pot marks the transition from the infant stage to the youthful stage of the plant. From now on, care is the same for the former seedling as it is for the former cutting.

Place in a bright, cool position: At this point the pelargoniums should be kept in a place that is as light as possible (for example, a sunny windowsill or, ideally, a small greenhouse) and relatively cool (61° F/16° C).

Pinching out shoots: Two to four weeks after planting in their final pots, the pelargonium plants will have grown considerably. Now is the time to pinch out shoots, which means removing the top shoot tips with your fingernails. This should be done by the middle of the first month of spring. If you pinch the shoot tips out too late, flowering will be delayed.

Toughening up: By the end of the second month of spring your home-propagated pelargoniums will have developed fat buds. It is time to toughen them up now so that they can continue growing outside without suffering a temperature shock, which would affect their development. Ventilate the room frequently and keep it as cool as possible.

Check for pests: Check your plants occasionally for pests. Aphids should be controlled with the usual commercial products, as they may carry bacterial blight.

Avoid heat and cramped conditions: Zonal and hanging pelargoniums should not receive too much heat during the second and last months of spring and should not be placed too close together, or else their shoots may easily become long and weak.

Cultivating pelargoniums quickly

This method uses cuttings that are taken during the first two weeks of spring. You may utilize the cuttings that are created when you cut back the plant after dormancy.

- Use a plastic or clay pot with a diameter of 4¼ in (11 cm) and seeding compost.
- Plant three to four cuttings around the outer edge of the pot.
- After watering gently, draw a transparent polyethylene sheet over the pot and cuttings, so that no moisture can evaporate but the cuttings are not impeded in their growth.
- Stand the pelargoniums in a very bright place and encourage them to root at temperatures of 64-68° F (18-20° C).
- After two weeks, the polyethylene may be removed, as the cuttings will now have roots.
- Let the plants grow without pinching out shoot tips.
- During this phase, do not let the surrounding temperatures drop below 61° F (16° C).
- By the end of the spring you will have a splendid harvest of robust pelargoniums which should be on the point of flowering.

Indoor pelargoniums

Fancy-leafed pelargoniums

These pelargoniums can only be propagated from cuttings. The method to follow for propagating and aftercare of the fully grown plant should be the same as for pelargoniums kept outside. As fancy-leafed pelargoniums do not need to bloom at a certain time, they can be propagated at any time during the year. Propagating from seeds is not possible.

Regal pelargoniums

Regal pelargoniums can also only be propagated from cuttings. In addition, cuttings from these species do not always produce

Pelargoniums are a popular decorative plant for hotels and inns. Hanging varieties on an old wooden bridge.

roots readily either. It is best to dip the cut surface and stalk of the cuttings ¾ in (2 cm) deep in rooting powder (obtainable from garden centers, etc.). This will help them to form a callus.

If possible, take and grow cuttings from regal pelargoniums during the summer, as experience has shown they are less likely to root well during the winter season.

The method of propagating and aftercare is the same as for pelargoniums that grow outside.

Scented-leafed and wild pelargoniums

Propagating from seed

Wild pelargoniums can be propagated from seed. You will not, however, be able to obtain these from regular gardening suppliers and may have to try private growers instead. Contact can be established via small advertisements placed in plant magazines, etc.

Propagating from shoot tips

Scented-leafed and wild pelargoniums are usually propagated from cuttings as this is a fast and easy way to obtain robust, healthy plants.

The right time to take cuttings: Cuttings should be taken from the parent plant between the end of spring and late fall. Experience has shown that the best results are obtained during the summer months when there is maximum light and heat.

Suitable varieties: Note that not all scented-leafed and wild pelargoniums are equally easy to propagate.

Easily rooted species and varieties are: *Pelargonium tomentosum, Pelargonium capitatum, Pelargonium fragrans, Pelargonium papilonaceum*, and "Princess Anne."

Reluctant rooting species and varieties are: *Pelargonium gibbosum, Pelargonium cunanifolium*, and "Countess of Scarborough."

Propagating soil: For propagating, use compost that you have mixed yourself, consisting of one-third seeding compost, one-third sand and one-third Perlite, which is finely ground volcanic rock (obtainable from garden centers, etc.). This mixture will be highly water-permeable.

Plant containers: Plant the cuttings in previously well-soaked (p. 17) clay pots with a diameter of 2½ in (6 cm).

Important: Do not use peat for scented-leafed and wild pelargoniums, so that as little water as possible is retained around the sensitive roots. For this reason, the cuttings should not be planted in peat pellets nor in peat propagating pots.

Position: The cuttings should be watered sparingly and left to form roots at a minumum temperature of 64-68° F (18-20° C) on a sunny windowsill.

Development: The time it takes for scented-leafed and wild pelargoniums to develop will vary according to species. Watch the cuttings carefully. When they have grown, remove one from its pot and check to see how far the roots have developed.

Planting in the final pot: If the roots have reached the edge of the propagating pot, it is time to trans-fer the young plants to their final pots, which should be clay pots with a diameter of 4¼ in (11 cm). The lower third of each pot should be filled with Hortag or large pieces of broken pot and then filled with the compost mixture described above. This drainage layer will help surplus water to drain away.

Further care: Keep the young plants in a sunny, warm place. Take care that the roots are never left standing in water, as they will rot very easily. For scented-leafed and wild pelargoniums, a cool, dry period of four to six weeks will be required at the beginning of the second month of winter: the temperature should be 41° F (5° C), and the plants should not be watered, although you may spray them lightly. After this period, raise the temperature very gradually and give a little more water. These procedures will ensure a rich harvest of flowers.

Geraniums in the garden

Propagating from seed

Sow shrub geranium seed in seeding trays in the middle and third months of spring.

As the seeds of geraniums are much smaller than those of pelargoniums, it is not a good idea to plant them in peat pellets as it would be very difficult to place individual seeds in such beds.

The seed trays should be kept in a bright, warm place (64-68° F/ 18-20° C).

As soon as the seed has germinated and the plantlets are large enough, they should be pricked out and planted in small peat propagating pots. As soon as roots appear through the walls of the pots, the pots should be planted outside in flowerbeds.

Propagating by division

You may divide an older plant in the spring, while the shoots are still small. For this purpose dig the plant up and divide it, with a knife or spade, into several parts, which are then planted separately. This method is suitable for many garden shrubs.

The zonal pelargonium "Bern" will flourish all summer long, even in a flowerbed.

Baskets, pedestals, standards, and combinations with other plants

Imagine the effect of two pelargoniums, trained into the shape of pillars, standing on either side of a patio door or an arbor decorated with hanging baskets of pelargoniums. The possibilities for using these versatile plants for decoration are endless.

Pelargoniums on patios and balconies

Pelargoniums are very versatile plants – they will even grow downward – and they get along well with other plants. These features make possible a wide range of ornamental uses. Hanging baskets can be planted with hanging pelargoniums. Vigorously growing varieties can be trained into standards or grown on pedestals within a relatively short time, and pelargoniums can also be incorporated into the most magnificent color combinations when planted together with other colorful summer flowers.

Pelargoniums in hanging baskets

Around your house there may be protruding eaves, a roofed-over area, or an arbor where you can put up hanging baskets. When choosing such sites, however, do not forget that hanging baskets must be within easy reach for watering and general care.

Suitable plants

Use hanging pelargoniums for planting in baskets, preferably plants of the "cascade" varieties, which come in shades of wine red, brick red, lilac, and pink. They are specially suitable for baskets, for three reasons:

● They can cope in unfavorable positions, such as shady or drafty corners.
● They are "self-tidying," which means that the small petals roll up as they wither so that they are scarcely visible any longer. This is a definite advantage for baskets that hang high up and/or are difficult to reach.
● They flower very abundantly. The hanging varieties known as mini-cascades are unrivalled in the quantities of flowers produced.

My tip: If you have a basket that you want to fill with plants, when you buy your hanging pelargoniums, check to what length they are likely to grow. Mini-cascades will grow to 20 in (50 cm) at the most. Other cascade varieties can grow to a length of 5 ft (1.5 m).

Combinations with other flowering plants

If you do not wish to confine yourself to shades of red only for your hanging baskets, you may create symphonies of color by using other plants too. Hanging varieties of blue lobelia are popular basket plants, as are calceolaria – yellow; marguerite daisies – white and yellow; hanging verbena – pink; and brachycomes – sky blue.

Method

Plant containers: Plastic baskets with a removable dish underneath (obtainable at garden centers, etc. in all sizes) are very practical. They do not weigh much when empty and are easy to clean. Remember that the baskets will increase in weight as the plants grow and will need a device for hanging them up that can cope with the strain.
Planting: Plant no more than three hanging pelargoniums in a basket with a diameter of 10 in (25 cm) (for soil and planting methods, see pp. 12 and 18). Make sure a watering space of at least ¾ in (2 cm) is left at the top when planting, so that soil is not washed out every time you water the plants.

Tips on care

Care for pelargoniums in hanging baskets in the same way as for those in pots or flower boxes.
Watering: Mini-cascades tend to react rather sensitively to overwatering and cool temperatures during the first few weeks and will be inclined to develop root rot rather quickly. For this reason, make sure that no waterlogging occurs in the dish underneath, or even remove the dish if the position allows this. Sometimes pelargoniums in baskets are neglected when it comes to watering, because of their elevated position.

Pelargoniums in hanging baskets (here the cultivar "Galilee") should be fed frequently!

Do not forget them and remember that, even in heavy rain, basket plants will receive hardly any water if they are sheltered or under cover.

Feeding: Basket pelargoniums need feeding . The cascade varieties, in particular, should receive regular weekly doses of compound fertilizer in their water.

Cutting back: If the pelargoniums grow too long, you may cut them back at any time, using a sharp knife to cut to the desired length.

Overwintering

The overwintering of pelargoniums in baskets is the same as for pelargoniums in pots or boxes.

Standards

Training a standard is not as difficult as many people think and will take exactly a year. If you begin the growing of rooted cuttings in the spring, with consistent care you should be able to brighten up your balcony or patio with a fully grown standard by the following year. The best way is to start with several cuttings, of which only one, the strongest, will end up being trained as a standard.

Suitable pelargoniums

Zonal pelargoniums and hanging pelargoniums can be trained as standards. Zonal hybrids are easier to train.

Decorative underplanting

Low-growing annuals, such as alyssum, brachycomes, or *Sanvitalia*

procumbens, are very suitable for planting under standards. They bloom all summer long but will have to be renewed every year.

How to train standards

Start in early spring with a few robust cuttings that you have taken from overwintered plants and have rooted, or buy ready-rooted cuttings in a garden center.

Planting: As soon as the cuttings have rooted well, each individual cutting should be planted in a plastic or clay pot with a diameter of 4 in (11 cm).

Soil: Standard potting compost or a commercial potting compost which you should mix with basic fertilizer.

Regular feeding: Three weeks after planting, it will be time to give your plants some liquid compound fertilizer in water.

Encouraging upward growth: As the plant grows, the main stem will form side shoots and buds which you should pinch off immediately with your fingers so that all the growing energy goes into the height of the plant.

Final choices: During this growth phase, you will be able to decide which plant is especially suited to further cultivation. Plants should be chosen as standards if their main stem is specially straight, strong, and tall. Pelargoniums with crooked main stems are unsuitable, as are pelargoniums which obviously lag behind the others in their growth.

Repotting: In late spring the main stem should be about 20 in (50 cm) tall. Plant the pelargonium in a clay pot with a diameter of 7 in (18 cm).

Soil: standard potting compost or fertilized potting compost.

Tying to a support: After repotting, drive a 4-ft (1.2-m) long stick in beside the stem as a support for the plant and loosely tie the stem to it with raffia or twine. The tie is intended to give the stem support without constricting it.

Further care: Three weeks after repotting, start putting liquid compound fertilizer into the water once a week and continue to pinch out laterals and flower buds.

At a height of 30 in (75 cm): Carry on pinching out laterals and flower buds until the stem has reached this height (measured from the edge of the pot) but leave laterals and leaves above that height as they will form the head later on. The flower buds, however, should still be removed.

At a height of 40 in (1 m): At the end of the first month of summer and the beginning of the second month, the pelargonium should have attained a height of about 40 in (1 m). Now cut off the top of the main stem. Of the laterals that have grown out to over 30 in (75 cm), leave the topmost five or six as they will form branches for the future head. If possible, these laterals should be distributed evenly around the stem.

A tall, elegant standard
This specimen measures 8 ft 5 in (2.53 m). It was developed over a period of two years from four cuttings of a cascade variety.

Repotting: When the laterals have grown a little larger (about 2 in/ 5 cm), transfer the standard into its final pot, preferably a heavy clay pot, as this will give the pelargonium the required stability.
Soil: standard potting compost or a fertilized commercial potting compost.

This repotting procedure will probably require two people:
● Place the standard next to the new clay pot.
● Fill the new pot with soil up to about a level of 2 in (5 cm).
● At this point, you will need a helper to support the standard plant during the whole operation of repotting, so that it does not break.
● In order to extract the standard from its old pot unharmed, it will have to be laid on the ground. To do this, tip the pot slowly, without tearing off any roots or sections of roots. The support stick should be left in its position in the soil.
● Lift the standard upright by encircling the rootstock with both hands and then place it in the new pot.
● With your helper still supporting the standard, fill the pot with extra soil all around the rootstock. The soil should be pressed down firmly so that the plant stands up straight, but not so hard that it seems as if it had been cemented in!

Pinching tips out of laterals: when the laterals have grown to a length of about 10 in (25 cm), pinch out their shoot tips, so that they will branch out again. Soon a compact head will form with some first flowers which should no longer be pinched out.

Care during the first year
The standard has now reached its final shape. The following procedures should be carried out until overwintering begins:
Feeding: Put liquid compound fertilizer in the water once a week until the end of the summer. During the first month of fall feed only once every fortnight, then stop watering altogether so that the plant can enter its dormant phase.
Tidying: Continue to remove leaves and flower buds which form on the stem.
Support stick: Occasionally check the places where the stem has been tied to the support stick to make sure there is no constriction.

Overwintering
Before the first frosts appear, take the standard inside and place it in a bright, cool room. It should be overwintered like all other pelargoniums that have been outside.

When the pelargonium standard starts putting out shoots the following spring, you should pinch out the tips once more, by the second month of spring at the latest, in order to obtain a compact head. From the middle of the last month of spring onward, the pelargonium will bloom in full splendor. If you leave pinching out the shoot tips until later, you will delay flowering.

Tips on care during the second year
General care: Pelargonium standards should be cared for all year round just like all other pelargoniums on patios and balconies.

Cutting back: Long, protruding shoots which grow out of the head shape, should be cut off.

Support stick: During the second year, replace the support stick. The new one should be thicker (with a diameter of about ¾ in/2 cm) and extend right into the center of the standard head, so that the plant is given plenty of support as it grows.

Pedestals

Pelargoniums grown on pedestals will enhance the appearance of any patio, balcony, or bare corner.

Suitable plants
Both hanging and zonal pelargoniums are suitable for this purpose. Hanging plants are more suitable, however, as they generally grow much more vigorously.

Method
● In early spring, plant three rooted pelargonium cuttings in a clay pot with a diameter of at least 10 in (25 cm). The best pots are square, terracotta ones, as they offer great stability.
Soil: standard potting compost or simple commercial compost mixed with basic fertilizer.
● Drive a long stick into the middle of the pot of pelargoniums. All growing shoots should be tied loosely to this, using raffia or twine.
● Do not remove the laterals, but continue to cut them back until the second month of spring, so that, very gradually, they will grow into a compact cone shape.
● From the middle of the second month of spring onward, let the shoots grow and buds will soon begin to form.

Care
Pelargoniums grown on pedestals should be looked after exactly like pelargoniums in flower boxes or pots.

Combinations of pelargoniums and other summer annuals

Make a point of checking the arrangement for:
● colors that will blend in well to suit the surroundings in

which the arrangement is set;
● colors of flowers that go well together;
● large and small flowers to balance the arrangement;
● different kinds of leaves (color, shape, and size) which may enhance the general effect;
● plants that go together with respect to their growth and shape (for flower boxes, for example, it is preferable to plant hanging plants at the front and upright plants at the back).

Suitable plants
Choose sun-loving annuals that will bloom all summer long and will not grow too tall for a balcony box arrangement. They come in many beautiful shades, with large flowers (petunias, for example), delicate flowers (lobelia), hanging flowers (hanging verbena), or very upright flowers.

Tips on care
Mixed plantings containing pelargoniums should be cared for in the same way as pelargoniums in flower boxes or pots.
Cutting back accompanying plants: In wet years some summer flowers may outstrip the pelargoniums in their growth. Petunias and large daisies can become so large and overpowering that some cutting back will be needed. Petunias can stand rigorous pruning. With marguerite daisies, however, do not cut back to the woody parts!

Overwintering
Before overwintering begins, remove the summer annuals from the flower box as they will not survive the winter. Take this opportunity to move the pelargoniums to individual pots which, in turn, will stimulate more compact growth the following year.

A combination of various hanging pelargoniums growing on a pedestal.

Indoor pelargoniums

Pelargoniums kept indoors – the regal, fancy-leafed, and scented-leafed varieties – will not offer the same wide range of uses as the zonal or hanging hybrids on balconies and patios. Some varieties, however, can be trained into standards.

Suitable plants
Regal pelargoniums are quite suitable for training into standards. Among the scented-leafed and wild pelargoniums, to date only a few varieties are known to be suitable, these being the large-flowering pelargonium (*Pelargonium grandiflorum*), the cultivar "Princess Anne," and all scented-leafed hybrids.

Method
Indoor pelargoniums should be trained as standards in exactly the same way as zonal or hanging hybrids. However, you must also take into consideration the care requirements of the various species.

Geraniums in the garden

Shrub geraniums cannot be trained into special shapes. They do, however, blend well into arrangements of plants incorporating other shrubs. They come in colors that range through blue, white, and violet, as well as many shades of pink and red. They are grown as tall shrubs and also in the form of cushions.

Pelargoniums for patios and balconies

In this section you will be introduced to some popular varieties of zonal, hanging,
and semi-pendent pelargoniums. An indication of their appearance, characteristics, and care should help you when choosing plants.

Zonal pelargoniums

Zonal pelargoniums are hybrids (bastard crosses) whose parents were *Pelargonium zonale* (*zonale* = girdle) and *Pelargonium inquinans*. To date,
hundreds of different varieties have been bred. Depending on which parent is more dominant in a particular variety, a brownish "girdle" or ring marking can be seen on each leaf.

Appearance and similarities
All zonal pelargonium hybrids grow upright. Nearly all varieties have relatively large leaves and robust, slightly hairy shoots. The flowers grow on long stalks and consist of umbels with varying numbers of individual blooms. Some zonal pelargonium flowers are single but most are double.
Note: Single flowers means that the individual flower has five petals like its parents. Double flowers have more petals, as, through breeding, they have developed extra petals which have metamorphosed from the stamens and style. Zonal pelargoniums come in many colors: shades of glowing red, pink, and bright pink. Shades of salmon pink and pure white are fairly rare but can be used for unusual combinations of plants.

Zonal pelargoniums are specially suitable as:
● they can be arranged in combinations with other summer flowers;
● they can be trained into standards without a great deal of trouble;
● overwintering presents no great problems;
● they can be propagated easily from cuttings taken from shoot tips.

Hanging and semi-pendent pelargoniums

The hanging pelargoniums (*Pelargonium – Peltatum* hybrids) were created by crossing the wild *Pelargonium peltatum* (*pelta* = shield) with other wild species. The name refers to the leaves, which, in contrast with the softer, hairy leaves of zonal pelargoniums, are fleshy, thick and shield-shaped. The semi-pendent pelargoniums (*Pelargonium – Zonale* x *Peltatum* hybrids) are hybrids which were produced by crossing zonal and hanging pelargoniums. They are also known as semi-hanging or semi-peltates.

Appearance and similarities
In their South African homeland, hanging or semi-pendent pelargoniums may grow shoots up to 80 in (2 m) long. These shoots trail on the ground or climb, creeper-like, into higher bushes. The flowers of bred varieties are partly single, partly double. They come in glorious shades of red, pink, deep pink, and even white.

Cascade varieties
The cascade varieties are a special group, within the hanging pelargoniums, which was rediscovered a few years ago in France. Their outer appearance distinguishes them quite clearly from other
hanging pelargoniums, as their flowers look very similar to those of wild pelargoniums (see photo on inside front cover) with single, delicately shaped petals and small flowers. Their vigorous growth and abundance of flowers, however, is unrivaled among all other pelargoniums. Well-cared-for cascade varieties (for example, "Ville de Paris," No. 4, "Lachscascade," or "Feuercascade," No. 3) can form trailing shoots of up to 5 ft (1.5 m) in length, which are completely covered in flowers, while the mini-cascades (for example, "Lila Mini-Cascade" and "Rote Mini-Cascade") can grow up to 20 in (50 cm). Another advantage is that the cascade varieties are "self-tidying." When the flowers die, their petals wither and curl up so small that you can hardly see them. They do not fall. Anyone who has spent the summer sweeping up fallen red or pink petals under a large balcony, will appreciate what a boon this can be.

My tip: Overwintering the very long cascade varieties can be a little tedious. Instead, why not take cuttings in the fall and overwinter the young plants?

Pelargoniums for patios and balconies

Hanging and semi-pendent pelargoniums are specially suitable:
● as popular, easy-to-care-for plants for hanging baskets and flower boxes;
● in plant arrangements with upright summer-flowering plants, where they provide the ideal downward-growing element.

Tips on care

In brief, the following are the main requirements of pelargoniums on patios and balconies:
● a lot of sun;
● nutrient-rich soil;
● lots of nutrients;
● water, though not too much;
● no waterlogging;
● no frost.

My tip: The cascade varieties are less sensitive than the hanging or zonal pelargonium varieties.

A rustic balcony with the semi-pendent cultivar "Schöne von Grenchen" and the hanging pelargonium "Galilee."

Pelargoniums for patios and balconies

1 "Rio"

Flower: single. **Color:** light pink, becoming darker towards the center, with dark red markings. **Inflorescence:** umbel with 10-15 single flowers. **Leaf:** large, dark green with slightly wavy edges. **Growth:** upright, compact. **Note:** a recent variety with unusual flowers, blooms very abundantly, and is weather-resistant, suitable for indoors, balcony, or garden.

2 "Casino"

Flower: very large, double flower. **Color:** dark salmon pink, silvery undersides to petals. **Inflorescence:** large umbel with up to 20 individual flowers. **Leaf:** large, light green with a light brown "girdle" marking on the leaf, slightly wavy edges. **Growth:** upright, vigorous growth, branches well. **Note:** will thrive well indoors, on balconies and patios, and in the garden (also in flower beds).

3 "Champagne"

Flower: large, single flower. **Color:** light salmon pink with white center. **Inflorescence:** umbel with 10-20 single individual flowers, early flowering, abundant. **Leaf:** light green with light brown leaf ring, slightly lobed edges. **Growth:** upright, compact, branches well. **Note:** pretty variety which looks good against a darker background. Suitable for indoors, balconies, patios, and the garden.

4 "Fidelio"

Flower: large, double individual flowers. **Color:** pinkish-red. **Inflorescence:** umbel with 15-20 individual flowers. **Leaf:** large, deep green, faint light brown leaf ring. **Growth:** upright, vigorous growth. **Note:** very early-flowering variety, weather-hardy, suitable for indoors, balconies, patios, and garden (even in flower beds).

5 "Flirtpel"

Flower: large, semi-double individual flowers. **Color:** glowing pink, turning lighter toward the center, with fine dark red markings. **Inflorescence:** umbels with 10-15 individual flowers. **Leaf:** small, without markings, edges slightly lobed. **Growth:** upright, compact. **Note:** early-flowering balcony, container, and bedding pelargonium, needs lots of feeding.

6 "Kardinal"

Flower: very large, single individual flowers. **Color:** dark lilac, center of flower violet, orange, or scarlet. **Inflorescence:** very large umbels with 15-20 individual flowers. **Leaf:** large, dark green, faintly recognizable leaf ring, slightly lobed edge. **Growth:** upright, very vigorous growth. **Note:** suitable for indoors, balconies, patios, and the garden (in containers or flower beds), will tolerate semi-shady positions.

7 "Bolero"

Flower: large, double individual flowers. **Color:** glowing red. **Inflorescence:** umbels with 15-25 separate flowers. **Leaf:** dark green, slightly wavy edge. **Growth:** upright, branches quickly. **Note:** weather-resistant, early-flowering, for indoors, balconies, patios, and gardens.

8 "Cabaret"

Flower: large, semi-double individual flowers. **Color:** glowing salmon pink to orange red, silvery undersides to petals. **Inflorescence:** large umbels with 15-20 individual flowers. **Growth:** upright, branches very quickly. **Leaf:** dark green, lobed edge. **Note:** the withered petals do not fall off; suitable for indoors, balconies, patios, and gardens.

9 "Stadt Bern"

Flower: small, single flowers. **Color:** brilliant red. **Inflorescence:** umbels with 10-15 individual flowers. **Leaf:** small, dark green with black leaf ring. **Growth:** upright. **Note:** will tolerate semi-shade, suitable for indoors, balconies, patios, and gardens.

Zonal pelargoniums

1 *"Rio "*

2 *"Casino "*

3 *"Champagne "*

4 *"Fidelio "*

5 *"Flirtpel "*

6 *"Kardinal "*

7 *"Bolero "*

8 *"Cabaret "*

9 *"Stadt Bern "*

Pelargoniums for patios and balconies

1 "Amethyst"

Flower: large, semi-double individual flowers. **Color:** dark lilac with black markings in the center, the undersides of the petals are silvery. **Inflorescence:** umbels with 4-10 individual flowers. **Leaf:** dark green, fleshy, smooth on top, lobed edges. **Growth:** compact, short, hanging shoots. **Note:** very popular variety for balconies, containers, and mixed groups of plants, will stay compact even in a flower box.

2 "Solidor"

Flower: very large, semi-double, individual flowers. **Color:** light salmon pink with dark red eye. **Inflorescence:** umbels with 5-10 individual flowers, very abundantly flowering. **Leaf:** light green, fleshy, smooth uppersides, edges with pointed lobes. **Growth:** very weather-resistant, suitable for many uses (for example, containers, balcony boxes, etc).

3 "Feuercascade"

Flower: single. **Color:** fire red with fine, dark red markings. **Inflorescence:** umbels with 3-12 individual flowers. **Leaf:** small, dark green, edges with pointed lobes. **Growth:** hanging, very vigorously growing (up to 5 ft/1.5 m per year). **Note:** weather-resistant, "self-tidying," universally suitable for balconies, walls, baskets, large containers, requires lots of fertilizer. **NB:** often sold under the name of "Balkon Imperial."

4 "Ville de Paris"

Flower: single. **Color:** dark red markings on a lighter red background, which may grow a little paler in very sunny positions. **Inflorescence:** umbels with 2-8 individual flowers. **Leaf:** medium-sized, with smooth upperside, edges strongly lobed. **Growth:** hanging, very vigorously growing (up to 5 ft/1.5 m per year). **Note:** ancestor of all cascade varieties; suitable for all sites. **NB:** needs lots of feeding.

5 "Schöne von Grenchen"

Flower: large, semi-double, individual flowers. **Color:** warm, brilliant shade of red. **Inflorescence:** umbels with 3-10 individual flowers. **Leaf:** medium-sized to large, light green, lobed edges. **Growth:** semi-pendent (a cross between upright and hanging pelargoniums), compact growth. **Note:** well-known variety, weather-resistant, relatively resistant to diseases, easy to propagate, good for overwintering.

6 "Sugar Baby"

Flower: miniature to small individual flowers, double flowering. **Color:** light pink. **Inflorescence:** umbels with 4-10 individual flowers. **Leaf:** medium-sized, light green, fleshy, smooth, with 5 segments. **Growth:** hanging, medium vigorous growth. **Note:** attractive pot variety, also for baskets, basins, and individual planting, masses of buds; slightly sensitive to weather conditions.

7 "Mexikanerin"

Flower: very large, double flowers. **Color:** white with red edges and red markings in the centers. **Inflorescence:** umbels with 3-6 individual flowers. **Leaf:** medium-sized, lobed edges, faintly visible leaf ring. **Growth:** hanging. **Note:** early-flowering, will thrive in semi-shady position too; specially suitable for baskets and balcony boxes.

8 "Tavira"

Flower: large, double flowers with slightly wavy petals. **Color:** brilliant red. **Inflorescence:** umbels with 3-6 flowers. **Leaf:** medium-sized, lobed edges. **Growth:** hanging, vigorously growing. **Note:** very weather-resistant variety, suitable for balcony boxes, containers, and mixed groups of plants.

9 "Galilee"

Flower: medium-sized, semi-double flowers: **Color:** light pink becoming darker towards the center, with silvery undersides. **Inflorescence:** umbels with 2-6 individual flowers, profusely blooming. **Leaf:** small, dark green, fleshy, smooth upper side, edges very lobed. **Growth:** hanging, long shoots. **Note:** suitable for balcony boxes and containers, goes well with upright red pelargoniums, easy to overwinter.

Hanging and semi-pendent pelargoniums

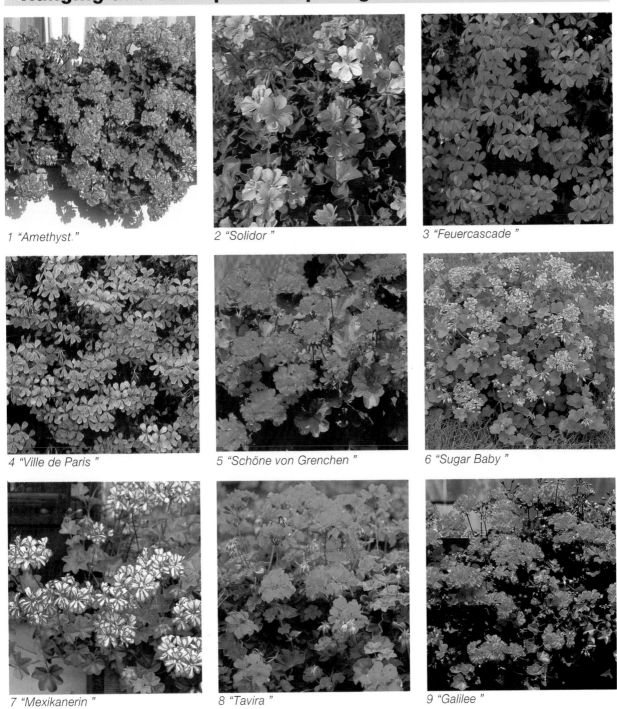

1 "Amethyst."

2 "Solidor"

3 "Feuercascade"

4 "Ville de Paris"

5 "Schöne von Grenchen"

6 "Sugar Baby"

7 "Mexikanerin"

8 "Tavira"

9 "Galilee"

179

Indoor pelargoniums

This section deals with varieties of pelargoniums that are especially easy to care for indoors.
● Scented-leafed and wild pelargoniums
with an unusual beauty of their own, which are presently being rediscovered by more and more pelargonium enthusiasts.
● Varieties of pelargoniums that were popular in our grandmothers' day.
● The charming fancy-leafed pelargoniums,
nearly all of which have flowers as well as leaves and which will thrive outdoors as well as indoors.

Scented-leafed and wild pelargoniums

Many scented-leafed pelargoniums are wild pelargoniums which exist in the same form in South Africa to this day. Some of them are even used in the manufacture of perfumes. Some scented-leafed pelargoniums, however, are hybrids, bred from crosses between various wild pelargoniums.

Appearance
Photographs of their leaves and flowers help to demonstrate just how varied the charming scented-leafed and wild pelargoniums can be.

Tips on care
Position: Light and airy; provide shade in the summer when the sunlight is very intense.
Watering: moderate.
Soil: water-permeable; for example, a mixture of standard potting compost with lots of sand.

Feeding: with liquid compound fertilizer in water; during the summer, half of the recommended dose every two weeks; stop feeding entirely during the second month of winter.
Overwintering: in the cool period (41° F/5° C) of four to six weeks during the second and third months of winter; do not water or feed during this period, only spray lightly.
Pests: white fly. Control.

Regal pelargoniums

Pelargonium grandiflorum hybrids were created by crossing *Pelargonium cucullatum* (still used today as a hedging plant in Cape Town) with other wild pelargoniums. Also called English or indoor pelargoniums.

Appearance
Regal pelargoniums are very compact-growing plants, which have flowers that tend to grow, most attractively, in the center of the plant, surrounded by leaves. The individual flowers are very large and grow in umbels. Their colors range from almost blackish-purple to briliant red and pastel shades of red to white.

Tips on care
Position: a light, airy windowsill; provide shade in the summer if the sun is very hot.
Watering: very sparingly.
Soil: very water-permeable and nutrient-rich, for example, a mixture of standard potting compost and sand.
Feeding: once a week in summer with "flowering" fertilizer in water; stop completely during the second

winter month.
Overwintering: as for scented-leafed and wild pelargoniums.
Pests: rare; white fly.

Fancy-leafed pelargoniums

Fancy-leafed pelargoniums are cultivars of zonal pelargoniums with specially interesting, colorful leaves. They were created by multiple crosses and mutations.

Appearance
Strikingly colored, variable-edged leaves. The flowers are usually smaller than those of other zonal hybrids and will only develop properly in a very sunny position.

Tips on care
Position: full sun.
Watering: sparingly, as for zonal pelargoniums.
Soil: water-permeable and nutrient-rich; for example, a mixture of standard potting compost and sand.
Feeding: once a week in summer with liquid compound fertilizer in water; stop completely in early fall.
Overwintering: as for zonal pelargoniums.
Pests: rare.

Scented-leafed pelargonium "Scarlet Pet"
This scented-leafed pelargonium is a cultivated hybrid with leaves that release the delicate aroma of oranges.

Indoor pelargoniums

1 Scarlet pelargonium
Pelargonium inquinans

Flower: single flowers, almost round. **Color:** intense scarlet (in exceptional cases also pale pink or even white flowers). **Inflorescence:** umbels with 5-30 individual flowers. **Leaf:** dark green, hairy upper sides, heart-shaped markings at base of stalk, lobed edges. **Growth:** upright, 40-80 in (1-2 m high). **Scent:** strong. ***Note:*** already cultivated in Britain by 1714.

2 Scented pelargonium
Pelargonium fragrans

Flower: single flowers with very delicate petals. **Color:** white with fine reddish lines. **Inflorescence:** umbels with 10-25 individual flowers. **Leaf:** tiny, heart-shaped leaflets on long stalks; leaves have lobed edges and are slightly wavy. **Growth:** delicate. **Scent:** when touched, strong smell of pine essence. ***Note:*** attractive indoor plant, easy to care for.

3 Myrrh-leafed pelargonium
Pelargonium myrrhifolium

Flower: very dainty. **Color:** delicate pink, upper petals have purple flamed stripes. **Inflorescence:** umbels with 2-6 individual flowers. **Leaf:** fine, feathery, hairy. **Growth:** shrub-like, up to 16 in high (40 cm). ***Note:*** will flower nearly all year round, loves sandy soil.

4 Almond-scented pelargonium
Pelargonium blandfordianum

Flower: single, delicate flowers, ½ in-¾ in (1-2 cm). **Color:** white, red style and stigma, upper petals have dark pink markings. **Inflorescence:** umbels with 2-4 individual flowers. **Leaf:** delicate, feathery, shiny gray green. **Growth:** dainty. **Scent:** pleasant smell of almonds; the scent may vary at times to smell more like sage or wormwood. ***Note:*** very suitable for indoors.

5 "Els"
(Pelargonium – Stellar hybrid)

Flower: star-shaped, up to 10 fine, pointed petals arranged in a circle. **Color:** dark salmon pink. **Inflorescence:** umbels with 3-10 individual flowers. **Leaf:** star-shaped, soft hairs. **Growth:** remains small. **Scent:** strong. ***Note:*** this scented-leafed pelargonium belongs to the group of stellar hybrids which possess star-shaped leaves and flowers and are specially suitable for indoors.

6 Wood-sorrel-leafed pelargonium
Pelargonium acetosum

Flower: fine, delicate, narrow petals. **Color:** salmon pink to white. **Inflorescence:** umbels with 2-7 individual flowers. **Leaf:** upside-down, oval, blue green, fleshy, very lobed edges, and slightly tinged with red. **Growth:** bushy, well-branched, small shrub, up to 2 ft (60 cm) high, sparse foliage. **Scent:** faint. ***Note:*** very suitable for indoors.

7 "Prince of Orange"
(hybrid)

Flower: single flower, up to just over 1 in (3 cm). **Color:** light pink with fine, dark red markings. **Inflorescence:** umbel with 1-2 flowers. **Leaf:** small, slightly curled and slashed edges. **Growth:** upright, up to 12 in (30 cm) high. **Scent:** smell of oranges. ***Note:*** a pleasantly scented hybrid that is easy to propagate.

8 Gout pelargonium
Pelargonium gibbosum

Flower: fine, slightly recurved, small petals on long stalks. **Color:** ocher yellow to greenish-yellow. Inflorescence: umbels with 6-14 flowers. **Leaf:** blue green, divided, very fleshy. **Growth:** climbing, swollen nodes on the stalks (hence the name!), up to 80 in (2 m) high. **Scent:** flowers smell strongly of musk at night. ***Note:*** the scent is released after sunset to attract moths for pollination.

9 "Scarlet Pet"
(hybrid)

Flower: dainty. **Color:** brilliant red. **Inflorescence:** umbels with 3-8 flowers. **Leaf:** medium-sized, dark green, slit edges. **Growth:** vigorously growing, hairy stems. **Scent:** smells of balm and oranges. ***Note:*** a fast-growing, profusely flowering pelargonium hybrid that is easy to propagate.

Scented-leaved and wild pelargoniums

1 *Pelargonium inquinans*

2 *Pelargonium fragrans*

3 *Pelargonium myrrhifolium*

4 *Pelargonium blandfordianum*

5 *"Els"*

6 *Pelargonium acetosum*

7 *"Prince of Orange"*

8 *Pelargonium gibbosum*

9 *"Scarlet Pet"*

Indoor pelargoniums

1 "Jupiter"

Flower: large, single, individual flowers. **Color:** shades of lilac, stronger dark lilac markings, clearly visible patch of the same color on the two upper petals.
Inflorescence: umbels with 4-10 individual flowers. **Leaf:** medium-sized, almost round, serrated edges. **Growth:** fairly vigorous, upright. **Note:** ideal pelargonium for indoors.

2 "Mickey"

Flower: medium-sized, single. **Color:** mainly violet; the two upper petals have an extensive blackish-purple marking and the three lower petals a blackish-purple dot. **Inflorescence:** umbels with 4-8 individual flowers. **Leaf:** five segments, finely serrated edge.
Flower: medium-fast-growing.
Note: an unusual variety, branches well.

3 "Mikado"

Flower: large, wavy petals, edges of petals turning out. **Color:** dark salmon pink with a dark red patch on each petal. **Inflorescence:** dense umbels with 6-8 individual flowers. **Leaf:** heart-shaped with 3-5 segments and clearly serrated edges. **Growth:** medium-fast-growing, the flowers are close above the leaves. **Note:** flowers very profusely.

4 "Muttertag"

Flower: large, almost round petals, arranged in a circle.
Color: orange red with dark red markings on the two upper petals and white ones on the three lower petals, all finely edged in white.
Inflorescence: umbels with 2-6 individual flowers. **Leaf:** small, lobed, with serrated edges.
Growth: medium-fast-growing.
Note: very striking markings on flowers.

5 "Jasmin"

Flower: large individual flowers, petals slightly wavy towards the edges. **Color:** pure white with fine purple violet markings on the two upper petals. **Inflorescence:** loose umbels with 2-6 individual flowers. **Leaf:** heart-shaped and round with a serrated edge. **Growth:** fast-growing. **Note:** flowers profusely.

6 "Frühlingsgruss"

Flower: large individual flowers with a slightly wavy edge.
Color: delicate pink with a large purple-red marking on the two upper petals, while the three lower petals have fine purple rays.
Inflorescence: umbels with 4-8 individual flowers. **Leaf:** 5 segments with very serrated edges. **Growth:** medium-fast-growing. **Note:** flowers profusely.

7 "Silvia"

Flower: slightly wavy petals. **Color:** brilliant red with dark red markings on the two upper petals.
Inflorescence: loose umbels with 4-6 individual flowers. **Leaf:** heart-shaped with serrated edge.
Growth: medium-fast-growing.
Note: do not place in strong sunlight!

8 "Göttweig"

Flower: very large single flowers, petals slightly wavy.
Color: salmon pink, upper petals tinged dark red with dark veins, lighter center. **Inflorescence:** loose umbels with 2-6 individual flowers. **Leaf:** large, slightly lobed, 3-4 segments, dentate. **Growth:** fast-growing. **Note:** flowers profusely.

9 "Valentin"

Flower: large single flowers with almost round, smooth petals, which are arranged in a circle.
Color: brilliant violet with dark violet markings on the two upper petals, lighter center.
Inflorescence: loose umbels with 2-4 individual flowers. **Leaf:** large, divided into 3 segments, serrated edges. **Growth:** fast-growing.
Note: flowers profusely.

Regal pelargoniums

1 "Jupiter"

2 "Mickey"

3 "Mikado"

4 "Muttertag"

5 "Jasmin"

6 "Frühlingsgruss"

7 "Silvia"

8 "Göttweig"

9 "Valentin"

Indoor pelargoniums

1 "Pink Golden Harry Hieouver"

Flower: single, medium-sized. **Color:** salmon pink. **Inflorescence:** umbels with with 5-15 individual flowers. **Shape of leaf:** very large, slightly lobed, hairy. **Color of leaf:** light green basic color, partly golden yellow, wide leaf ring turning lighter toward the outer edge. **Growth:** upright, fast-growing. *Note:* suitable for all positions.

2 "The Czar"

Flower: single. **Color of flower:** carmine red. **Inflorescence:** umbels with 7-10 individual flowers. **Shape of leaf:** medium-sized, slightly lobed. **Color of leaf:** basic light green, dark brown, very broad leaf ring. **Growth:** upright, medium-fast-growing. *Note:* suitable for all positions.

3 "The Boar"

Flower: single. **Color of flower:** salmon pink. **Inflorescence:** 5-10 individual flowers. **Shape of leaf:** almost round, slightly lobed. **Color of leaf:** light green, brownish-black center, colored along veins. **Growth:** upright, fast-growing, but delicate. *Note:* suitable for indoors.

4 "Masterpiece"

Flower: small, semi-double. **Color of flower:** light orange. **Inflorescence:** umbels with 5-10 individual flowers. **Shape of leaf:** large, slightly lobed. **Color of leaf:** dark green center, blackish leaf ring very visible, outer edge creamy white with traces of red. **Growth:** upright, fast-growing. *Note:* suitable for all positions, easy to propagate.

5 "Miss Burdett-Coutts"

Flower: single. **Color:** light red. **Inflorescence:** umbels with 5-10 individual flowers. **Shape of leaf:** very small, lobed. **Color of leaf:** multi-colored, green center, dark brown leaf ring, wine red overlying color, rippled, narrow white edge. **Growth:** upright, slow-growing. *Note:* very suitable for indoors.

6 "Dolly Vardon"

Flower: single. **Color:** light red. **Inflorescence:** umbels with 7-15 individual flowers. **Shape of leaf:** small leaf, slightly lobed edge. **Color of leaf:** multi-colored, dark green center, almost black leaf ring, bright red overlay, rippled, narrow, cream outer edge. **Growth:** medium-fast-growing. *Note:* very suitable for indoors.

7 "Bird Dancer"

Flower: single, star-shaped. **Color:** salmon pink with irregular white circles. **Inflorescence:** umbels with 5-10 individual flowers. **Shape of leaf:** small, star-shaped, tapering leaf segments. **Color of leaf:** dark green, blackish-brown ring, green tips. **Growth:** small flowers, compact growth. *Note:* very suitable for indoors, stellar hybrid (= star-shaped leaves or star-shaped flowers).

8 "Madame Salleron"

Exception: no flowers are formed. **Shape of leaf:** small to medium-sized leaves, almost completely round, upper side slightly convex, slightly wavy edges. **Color of leaf:** grayish-green basic color, white edge of varying widths, no leaf ring visible. **Growth:** upright, medium-fast-growing. *Note:* popular variety for decorating graves, known since 1877.

9 "Freak of Nature"

Exception: no flowers are formed. **Shape of leaf:** medium-sized leaves, edges wavy and holed, lobed. **Color of leaf:** light cream center, extending more or less to the edges, edges green. **Growth:** upright, fast-growing. *Note:* difficult to propagate because of its chlorophyll deficiency.

Fancy-leafed pelargoniums

1 *"Pink Golden Harry Hieouver "*

2 *"The Czar "*

3 *"The Boar "*

4 *"Masterpiece "*

5 *"Miss Burdett-Coutts "*

6 *"Dolly Vardon "*

7 *"Bird Dancer "*

8 *"Madame Salleron "*

9 *"Freak of Nature "*

Geraniums in the garden

Geraniums are hardy shrubs which are sometimes called "stork's bill" although *Geranium* really means "crane's bill".

Geraniums are used in plantings of mixed shrubs, rock gardens, in wild gardens, and in wild flower gardens. Low-growing species are useful for their ground-covering properties and for covering large expanses between shrubs that grow taller. These undemanding plants flower from late spring to late summer and love chalky, nutrient-rich soils which may also include a little clay. You can buy them in large plastic containers at garden centers and nurseries, etc. from early spring to late fall. Plants bought in spring should have already put out all their shoots. They will flower during the first year after planting. In the fall, when the parts of the plant above ground have turned brown, cut off the stalks about 8 in (20 cm) above the soil. Do not cut them back too early, as they turn a lovely shade of red in the fall. Winter protection will not be necessary. The simplest method of propagating is division of the rootstock in the spring. Propagating with seed is possible but time-comsuming.

A wild garden with a harmoniously balanced plant community, comprising geraniums, grasses, Aruncus, and saxifrage.

Geraniums in the garden

Tall crane's bill
Geranium macrorrhizum
Flower: pink, "Spessart" is blue violet, "Ingversson" deep pink.
Flowering time: late spring to late summer. **Growth:** up to 40 in (1 m), large bushes.

Caucasian crane's bill
Geranium platypetalum
Flower: large flowers, light violet with beautiful markings.
Flowering time: early to late summer. **Growth:** up to 32 in (80 cm), vigorous growth.

Dalmatian crane's bill
Geranium dalmaticum
Flower: pink, "Album" is pure white.
Flowering time: early to late summer. **Growth:** up to 4 in (10 cm), large cushions.

French crane's bill
Geranium endressi
Flower: bright pure pink.
Flowering time: late spring to early fall. **Growth:** up to 1 ft (30 cm) large bushes.

Dwarf crane's bill
Geranium subcaulescens
Flower: carmine red with darker centre. **Flowering time:** early to midsummer. **Growth:** creeps.

Bloody crane's bill
Geranium sanguineum
Flower: reddish-violet. **Flowering time:** early summer to early fall. **Growth:** up to 1 ft (30 cm), ground-covering.

Meebold's crane's bill
Geranium meeboldii
Flower: blue violet with wine-red markings. **Flowering time:** early summer to early fall. **Growth:** up to 1 ft (30 cm), large bushes.

△ The Armenian crane's bill (Geranium psylosteum) flowers in midsummer.
▽ The flowers of Geranium grandiflorum may be 1½ in (4 cm) across.

NOTES

Success with

Your
Garden Pond

PETER STADELMANN

Series Editor:
LESLEY YOUNG

Contents

Lysichithum americanum and Primula growing along the course of a stream.

Bulrushes.

A sunbathing frog.

Introduction

Where is the best place to sit and dream in a garden? There can hardly be a more idyllic spot than beside a garden pond, where water lilies unfold their delicate colors, graceful dragonflies hover on the breeze like miniature helicopters, and butterflies flutter over the water plants, while down below gleaming goldfish twist and turn, pond skaters hunt for insects, the gentle croaking of a toad can be heard from the marshy depths, and a frog sunbathes on a lily pad.

Such a peaceful scene can be created fairly easily in almost any garden and just how to do it is explained by pond expert Peter Stadelmann in this full-color guide. His clear, detailed instructions will enable any garden owner to design and build their very own pond – be it an ornamental pond with lilies and goldfish, or a wild pond where nature is more or less allowed a free rein. The author offers easy-to-follow instructions for the creation of a pond, from the planning and design stage and digging out of the pit, right through to choosing and planting water plants around the edge of the finished pond. Full-color step-by-step illustrations demonstrate how to use specific materials for building the pond and show what is needed to create a decorative backdrop. The author has produced a wealth of ideas and inspiration for designing an attractive surround, again with step-by-step illustrations, and there are also extensive suggestions for the planting of suitable marginal and water plants in and around your pond. How to care for a garden pond all the year round is covered in detail, in particular, the measures required for overwintering a pond containing fish. This guide gives advice on which fish will feel particularly at home in a garden pond and how to look after them. If you wish to play host to a large number of wild visitors, like frogs, newts, and other amphibians, you will find many tips here on how to provide an ideal environment for such creatures by providing the right food and shelter. This includes the creation of a wild marshy area which has the added attraction of providing a splendid display of flowering and green marsh plants. One chapter is entirely devoted to the particularly attractive idea of creating a running stream, which makes an ideal biological filter and also provides a habitat for plants and animals. Fascinating color photographs of exceptionally lovely ornamental and wild ponds, as well as photographs of the most beautiful pond plants, fish, and other creatures, are sure to inspire the reader to turn their dream of a pond into a reality that can be enjoyed all year round.

The author

Peter Stadelmann is a zoo supplier and also a specialist in the planning, designing, building, and stocking of garden ponds.

Warning

Various electrical gadgets and their uses are described in this book. If you are intending to use any of these devices, remember that electrical work of any kind should only be carried out by a qualified electrician. This includes the installation of any kind of electrical gadget as well as laying electrical cables. Make sure that your pond has been made safe for yourself and others; this is especially important if there are small children or pets in your household or if the pond is situated in a part of the garden that is not fenced off.

We highly recommend taking out insurance to cover any activities associated with the pond. Every garden pond owner should ensure that no water (either on the surface or underground) is able to penetrate a neighboring garden. This means regularly checking the water pipes and changing the water in the pond or emptying it in the proper manner.

A garden pond beside a patio
This miniature Eden of water and luxuriant plants invites you to sit and dream.

Forward planning is essential

Even though you are just longing to get started on the physical work, your new pond will turn out far more successfully if you plan it carefully beforehand. The finished pond will be made to measure and any additions, such as a running stream or a marginal marshy area, can be designed in from the very start. One of your chief planning aids will be nothing more sophisticated than a garden hose.

Nature pond or ornamental pond?

If your aim is a pond filled with frogs, newts, and other amphibians living together peacefully with colorful goldfish and gleaming koi amid a beautiful display of exotic water lilies by a fountain, you are doomed to disappointment. It is just not possible to combine these three ambitions in one single pond. You will only gain the maximum benefit and pleasure from your pond if you take into consideration the very different basic requirements of individual plants and creatures. This is not very difficult. If your aim is an ornamental pond containing goldfish, koi, and other fish, but you also want to coax plenty of wild visitors to take up residence, make sure you plan and build your pond and its surroundings in a way that will meet the requirements of all these creatures. This means that:
● Ornamental fish, which require clear, oxygenated water,
will need a larger area of water surface than other creatures.
● Visitors to your garden pond will appreciate an additional habitat in the shape of a marshland or mar-

ginal area beside the pond or a stream.
On no account should goldfish be introduced *if you want to create a wild pond* which will offer the optimal living conditions for amphibians, dragonflies, and countless tiny water creatures, like diving beetles, pond skaters, or water fleas. Other fish, like sticklebacks or *Leucaspius delineatus*, are better suited to the life cycle of a nature pond. Some nature pond enthusiasts are of the opinion that no fish at all should be allowed in a wild pond. My own opinion is that a small stock of fish can be kept in a pond that is more than 160 sq ft (15 sq m) in area. My advice is to observe how life develops in your nature pond, check in specialist literature regarding the requirements of those creatures that have established themselves in the pond and then decide on the issue of fish
A wild or nature pond is an individual biotope which should remain undisturbed, if possible. Only a minimum of care will be required and any work should be carried out with some thought.
Both types of pond have one thing in common: they can accommodate

beautiful water plants. The selection of flowering and green water plants is so large that nearly all your preferences can be met in either an ornamental or nature pond.

The size of your pond

Right from the start, you should give some thought to the approximate size of the finished pond and check carefully whether the position you have chosen is suitable for the installation of a pond.
The area of water: It would be almost impossible to give a minimum recommended area.
The basic rule must be that the larger the pond is, the less sensitive it will be to interference. However, let me stress that even a small garden pond, which is all that is generally feasible in most gardens due to lack of space, will still work perfectly well if you design and build it properly and look after it well. You should hardly have any problems with a roundish pond that has an area of about 64 sq ft (6 sq m) – 120 by 80 in (3 by 2 m). This size is appropriate for ornamental and nature ponds. For any pond with an area of less than 64 sq ft (6 sq m), the possibilities of designing it in an attractive way, stocking it with fish, or providing a habitat for other pondlife are fairly restricted.
Depth of the water: One section of the pond – an area of about 11 sq ft (1 sq m) – needs to be at least 28 in (70 cm) deep.
This area of deeper water is essential for fish and other creatures, particularly for overwintering.
NB: If you wish to insert a layer of soil or gravel at the bottom of the pond, the pit will have to be dug 8-12 in (20-30 cm) deeper, so that the necessary depth of water can still be attained later on!
The shape: This has no bearing on

An attractive geometric layout of pond and plants.

the life processes within the pond. Basically, you can choose whatever shape you wish providing it is suitable for the available insulating material.

My tip: A pond can nearly always be built, even in the smallest of gardens. If you have very little space, you may still be able to build a terraced pond, which will enable many beautiful water plants to flourish.

The ideal position

If you are keen on watching pondlife and enjoy growing water plants, it is probably a good idea to choose a position close to a patio or much frequented corner where you often sit. You will, however, have to take into consideration certain factors that are prerequisites for the existence of a healthy, flourishing community of pond creatures and plants.

Take a long garden hose and lay it out at the chosen site in the shape of the pond you are intending to build. Then take a good look at your design with the following points in mind:

Length of exposure to sunlight: light, warmth and, of course, shade are important factors for the growth of plants.

- Note the number of hours during which the site you have chosen will be in shade.
- Ideal: shade during the midday period; exposure to sunlight during the rest of the day.
- The pond must have a minumum of eight hours' exposure to sunlight per day.
- If the chosen position is in intense sunlight all day long, you will have to erect shade providers (hedges, tall-growing edge, or bank plants).

Weather influence: The pond should be protected on the side exposed to the prevailing wind (specially if this is to the north or northwest).

The installation of some kind of protection against weather must be designed close to the pond if the wall of a building or other existing plantings do not already offer protection. Good weather protection devices are:

- an earth wall, which can be built with the soil excavated from the pond basin;
- a dense planting, approximately 16-20 in (40-50 cm) tall, around the edge of the pond.

NB: Weather protection can also have a favorable effect on the mini-climate (the climatic conditions in the immediate vicinity) that will develop around the pond. This is important for the growth of the plants and for the living conditions of wildlife in and around the pond.

Trees: If possible, a pond should not be built immediately under trees. If too many leaves and conifer needles are let drop into the water during the fall, they may alter the quality of the water to a point where it begins to endanger the well-being of water plants and pondlife. At a sufficient distance from the pond, however, trees may become welcome providers of shade.

The curious mating display of the azure damselfly (Coenagrion puella).

The frog is a popular visitor to a garden pond.

Soil suitability: A trial trench will give you some idea of the prevailing conditions and tell you whether you will be able to dig down deep enough in the chosen position to provide a depth of at least 28 in (70 cm).

If you come across large pieces of rock or stone, the problem can be solved with the help of some protective material.

● If the subsoil is very rocky, it would be better to construct a pond with a raised water level.

Main conduits, pipes, etc.: Make sure there are no electrical cables or water or drainage pipes near the pit that you dig for the pond. Either your own building plans or the relevant planning office will be able to give you information on the course of main supply lines.

My tip: The installation of a garden pond does not normally require planning permission. What you are required to do, however, is to include safety provisions for the protection of children and to make sure that water is not able to penetrate a neighboring property.

Room for extending the pond: In my experience you would not be the first gardener who, after completing the construction of a pond, suddenly decided that an area of marshland or a running stream was the one thing they needed to complete their design, and then found there was not enough room for your plans. This is why I recommend giving some thought to this possibility right from the start, so that there will be room, later on, for an attractive extension.

NB: You may also need room for a soakaway which can accommodate pondwater if the water level rises to overflowing level during periods of heavy rain.

Water and electricity

Usually, the pond will have to be supplied with water and electricity from the house. Check before you start whether this is feasible.

Fresh water supply: The simplest solution is to have a sufficiently long, sturdy garden hose to supply water from the house to the pond, laid at about a spade's depth underground.

Electricity and oxygen supply: You will require two PVC pipes for this purpose, with a diameter of about 1 in (2.5 cm) (obtainable from builders' merchants or electrical suppliers). These pipes will accommodate electrical cables and an air hose from an air pump.

The pipes should be buried at a spade's depth and so that they run slightly downhill from your house. This means laying the pipe a few inches (centimeters) deeper at the pond end, so that any moisture in the pipe will run away from the house.

My tip: There are a number of possibilities for conducting electricity to your pond or for installing electrical output units near the pond. The best plan is to obtain advice from a professional electrician.

Warning: Remember that all electrical installations should only be carried out by an expert! I would warn any layperson against installing their own cables or against any do-it-yourself connection of electrical devices. Liability for accidents arising from the use of electricity rests with the person who carried out the work. If you use electrical gadgets in your pond, which would probably be the case in an ornamental pond or a running stream, please read and take note of the safety advice in the section on "helpful gadgets".

Insulation materials

It is best to decide during the planning phase which insulation material you intend to use in your pond. The most frequently used materials nowadays are PVC lining material or ready-molded ponds. However, instead, you may wish to use clay as an insulation layer in a nature pond. If you have not already made your decision on this, it might be a good idea to read through the instructions for carrying out the work in the following chapter, so that you have some idea of what is involved. Any mistakes will probably prove expensive to correct and may also spoil your enjoyment of the finished result.

From my own experience, I can offer the following advice:

The easiest materials to work with are various types of pond insulation material. Even those of you who have not had much experience with do-it-yourself projects will find it easy to handle. Using this PVC lining, ponds of any size or shape can be constructed with ease. Using *ready-molded ponds* is equally problem-free; fiber-glass molded ponds can be obtained in a wide range of sizes and shapes.

Clay will involve more work and some skill. I would not recommend insulating a pond with roofing felt or fiber-glass reinforced polyester resin. From my own experience of using them in garden ponds, these materials have not proved themselves to be very durable.

You will need the help of an expert if you decide to use *concrete.*

Constructing a garden pond

Now that the planning phase is over and you have decided on the optimum position, shape and size of your garden pond, it is time to get to work. The more meticulous you are in the laying out and construction at this stage, the less planning or alteration will have to be done later on and the better the plants, fish, and other creatures will do in your garden pond.

Initial considerations

No matter what insulation material you have decided to use, the following advice will be important for anyone constructing a garden pond.

Excavation work
Do not be too eager to get started and think seriously whether you really want to dig the pit yourself with a spade or shovel. The work involved in excavating a large pit should not be underestimated. I have known even dedicated amateurs, who would think nothing of building anything from a raised bed in the garden to a homemade dresser, lose all their enthusiasm for a garden pond because the excavation work turned out to be such a backbreaking slog. You can imagine some of the possible consequences of such unaccustomed physical exertion on an unfit person. Blisters on your hands might be the least of your troubles and it is definitely worth avoiding overdoing things and ending up with back problems. Remember, the larger the pond, the greater the quantities of earth that have to be moved. From my own experience, I would suggest the following:

● If you dig out a pond by yourself, only work as long as you really feel up to it at any one session – even if it takes days until the desired size of pit has been excavated. That way, aches and pains can be kept within reasonable bounds.
● Why not invite friends around for a "digging party?" In a large group, working together (with something sustaining and delicious to eat and drink afterwards), this rough work will be done much more quickly and it will be more fun too. The finer work, like smoothing the shape of the pond, is best done alone as too many cooks will spoil the broth in this situation!
● The simplest, but also the most expensive, solution is to rent a small excavator from a construction company. However, access for the excavator would be a prerequisite for this alternative.

The pond profile
This is the shape of the pond. What kind of pond profile to use should be decided on before excavating the pit. In the case of a ready-molded pond, of course, the profile will be predetermined. With all other

materials, you can decide on the depth of the pond and the course of the bank.
The ideal pond profile: The shape is comparable to a soup plate. This will make reinforcing the soil around the edges of the pond unnecessary. The flat banks of the pond will offer plenty of room for decorative marginal and shallow-water plants.
Wide, flat/shallow edges: This will cut down the risk of accidents involving children and will make it easier for any animals that have

accidentallly fallen into the pond to climb out again. This is also a good way to construct a marginal area.

Steep banks: A pond should not have steep banks all the way round. Should it be impossible, on account of the position of the pond – perhaps against the wall of a raised patio – to install a dish-shaped profile all the way round the pond, the steep bank will have to be reinforced with the help of a drystone wall or with

rounded lengths of wood that are buried vertically along the edge.

Plant terraces: These will provide lots of space for planting baskets but their construction will require additional work. They are not absolutely necessary. Any bank can be planted with luxuriant vegetation using special verge matting or – in the case of a pond lined with PVC – latticed bricks or stones that are stuck to the PVC liner. Some ready-molded ponds also incorporate a section of plant terraces.

Marginal area (marshy bed): This is an ideal habitat for many animals and plants. Do consider it during your planning stage.

Digging out the pit

You will probably have to store the excavated soil on your lawn. In order to protect the lawn, find three large polyethylene sheets to hold the grass turfs, topsoil, and excavated earth. Spread out the sheets some distance away from the pond building site.

A waterfall enriches the water with oxygen.

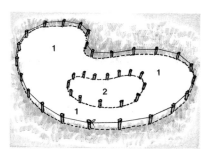

Laying out the shape of the pond
Using twine and small wooden pegs, lay out the shape of the pond (1), and also mark out the deep-water area (2).

Method
● First lay out the shape of the pond with the help of small wooden pegs and some twine. Do not forget to mark out the different zones or areas, i.e. shallow- and deep-water zones (see illustration above).
● Make spade's-width-sized incisions in the turf, slice the flat turfs off, lift them with a garden fork, and stack them on the sheet.
● Remove the topsoil and subsoil and heap it separately on large sheets.

My tip: If possible, do not transport the excavated soil away immediately. It might come in useful for constructing a stream course, a waterfall, or for an earth bank.

Adjusting the water level

In order to prevent your pond running dry later on, like a tipped soup plate, you must make sure the edges of the pond are level.
Method: In the case of a small pond, it will usually be sufficient if you lay a plank, edge upward, across the edges of the pond and check with a spirit level to see

whether the edges are horizontal. This can be corrected by removing more soil or heaping some back. In the case of a larger pond, take a hose level (made out of a garden hose, see illustration right):
● Stick a small transparent PVC tube into the opening at each end of the hose.
● Fill the hose with water. The hose level functions according to the principle of communicating vessels, which means that the water levels in both transparent end tubes will always be at the same height.
● Lay the hose in the excavated pit. Tie one end of the hose to a post so that you can move around with the other end in your hand. Walk around the edge of the pond and, if necessary, mark out the future edge of the pond with wooden pegs.
● The edge of the pond can be corrected by extra digging or by replacing soil.

How to install a PVC liner

According to many experts, and in my own experience, special PVC lining material is best for the construction of a garden pond.

The right kind of lining material
Only use specially made garden-pond PVC liner for insulating your pond.
Good pond insulation material is made by various manufacturers and is obtainable from gardening suppliers.
A guarantee should be given when you buy a good insulating material and, in the case of reputable manufacturers, this guarantee should last for many years. The guarantee should certify that the sheet is:
● UV-resistant (resistant to ultra-violet rays in sunlight);

● resistant to pressure from roots;
● tear-proof;
● heat- and frost-resistant:
● non-degradable;
● naturally, the manufacturers should also guarantee that the PVC does not contain substances nor release substances that are harmful to animals or plants.

My tip: Many manufacturers print their company's name on the sheeting, so that the source of the insulation material is available if there is cause for complaint.

The thickness of the lining material should not be less than 0.6 mm; a thickness of 0.8-1.0 mm is highly recommended.
The usual colors of commercially available material are anthracite, black, grayish-olive, olive green, or earth color, so that the garden pond will look natural and not take on the appearance of a swimming pool.
Totally unsuitable: the kind of tough polyethylene sheeting used in the foundations of houses. This is not UV-resistant and contains "softeners," which are released on exposure to sunlight and which quickly make the material brittle and leaky. In the worst types of this sheeting,

Adjusting the projected water level
You can check whether the edge of the pond (and the future surface level of the water) is horizontal using a water hose level.

the released substances have proved so harmful to animals and plants that the liner has had to be removed from the pond.

How much material is required?

The example calculation below will help you to work out how much insulation material you are going to need, when you insert your own relevant measurements.

Insulation material for ponds can be obtained in various sizes and can be bought by the yard (meter) in rolls of different widths.The standard size will usually be sufficient for *small ponds*. This will save you having to glue or heat-weld lengths of insulation material together. It is a good idea to do a rough calculation of the requirements for insulation material for a small pond before you start digging out the pit. Often, minor changes in the projected length or width of the pond will enable you to manage with commercially available sizes of PVC liner. Lay out your garden hose in the desired shape of the garden pond. Measure the length and width as shown in the illustration (right) and use the measurement for the planned depth of the pond. Do not forget to add the necessary extra insulation for the edges of the pond (see calculation below).

In the case of larger ponds, welding together lengths of insulation material will be unavoidable. You can do this yourself or ask a manufacturer to deliver ready-welded insulation material direct to you. The advantage of this is that the manufacturer will provide a guarantee for the durability of the welded seams (which he would not do if you join them together yourself). You will, of course, incur an additional cost for labor and transport.

My tip: If you are intending to con-

struct a marginal area too, calculate the additional insulation material required as you would for the pond.

Joining lengths of insulation material

There are three ways of joining lengths of insulating material:
● welding the lengths together with an expanding adhesive, using the cold-welding technique. These substances can be obtained from specialized gardening suppliers;
● sticking them together using tape or liquid joiner (obtainable from specialized gardening suppliers);
● hot welding – this method is really only suitable for an expert as a layperson would find it difficult to obtain an absolutely watertight seam.

Warning: Expanding adhesives and other adhesives have to be used with great care as they can be hazardous to health if used in the wrong way! Make sure to observe the following advice:
● follow all instructions exactly;.
● never carry out any work in a closed room;
● wear protective gloves;
● use safety goggles;
● keep naked flames or lit cigarettes well out of the way;

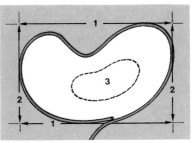

How to work out the quantity of lining material needed
The following measurements will be needed to calculate the amount of lining material needed:
1. The maximum length of the pond;
2. The maximum width;
3. The maximum depth of the deep-water zone.

● the remains of expanding and other adhesives should be disposed of with special waste, not poured down the drain or thrown into your garbage can.

How to glue or weld

It is extremely important to make sure that the areas to be joined are completely free of dirt or dust.
● Lay the lengths of insulation material on a bench or plank so that they overlap by about 2 in (5 cm).

How to work out the required amount of insulation material

A sample calculation for a pond with a water surface area of 64 sq ft (6 sq m) and a deep-water area with a depth of 28 in (70 cm).

Maximum length of pond + 2 x the depth of water (28 in/70 cm) + for edging = length of material along the edge	120 in (3.00 m) 56 in (1.40 m) 40 in (1.00 m) 216 in (5.40 m)	Maximum width of pond + 2 x depth of water (28 in/70 cm) + for edging = length of material along edge	80 in (2.00 m) 56 in (1.40 m) 40 in (1.00 m) 176 in (4.40 m)

Thus, you will need insulation material measuring 216 x 176 in (5.40 x 4.40 m).

Three important steps when laying the pond lining

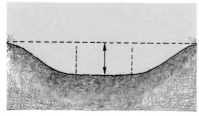

Dig out the pit
It is important to have a pit that measures at least 40 in (1 m) and a deepwater zone of at least 28 in (70 cm).

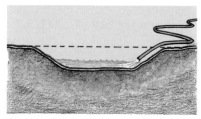

Laying the lining material
First remove any sharp objects from the pit. Next, line the pit with a layer of material that will protect the lining. Then lay out the PVC lining and immediately run water into the pond – very slowly.

Securing the lining to the edges
Around the edges, draw the lining across stones or rounded sections of wood (cover the stones with a protective layer of material). Bury the lining in the earth so that the edges of the lining are directed upward.

● With a brush, paint the adhesive onto both edges of the insulation material.
● Press down hard on the glued joins with a rubber roller, then weigh down each section with a sandbag for about five to ten minutes.

How to line the pond with the insulating material

After you have dug a pit for the pond and adjusted the edges, you may continue as follows.

Preparations: Make sure to remove all sharp objects from the pit (such as nails, stones, or buried builders' rubble). Any sharp-edged, large, buried rocks should be worked with a hammer and chisel until they are fairly rounded and smooth.

Protective layer: Avoid any damage to the insulation layer from below by first lining the pit with a protective layer of material (obtainable from builders' merchants). If the subsoil is rocky or very stony or simply very hard, first insert a layer of sand in the pit, then lay the protective material over it.

Inserting the insulation layer: The larger the pond, the heavier the insulation material will be – so a couple of strong helpers are highly recommended!
● In the case of small ponds, you can spread out the insulation material beside the pit and then drag it over the pit so that it overlaps the pit by about 12 in (30 cm) on all sides.
● For larger ponds, it is advisable to place the folded material in the center of the pit, then gradually unfold it toward the edges. Again, it should overlap all around the edges of the pit.

Filling in with water: Immediately after laying down the insulation material, very slowly fill the pond with water, until it is three-quarters full. The water will press the material down into the pit. While the water is rising, you will still be able to get rid

of folds and wrinkles in the material, or adjust them so that they will be less visible. Folds and wrinkles will not adversely affect the durability of the insulation material.

Corrections to the profile of the pond: For small adjustments, merely lift the insulation material at the edge and use sand or soil to correct the mistake. If major corrections become necessary, you will have to lower the level of water by means of a pump.

Reinforcing the bank: Places around the edge of the pond, in particular those which will later be trodden on a great deal, will require reinforcing with stones or lengths of rounded or squared wood.

Securing the insulation material along the edges of the pond: No matter how you decide to construct the edge of the pond, you will have to secure the insulation material to the edges so that no fine channels of water can form which will deprive the pond of water through capillary action.
● The insulation material should be covered by soil to a depth of about 4-6 in (10-15 cm) around the edges.
● The best way to do this is to draw the material over stones covered with some of the protective layer material or across rounded or squared lengths of wood.
● Place the ends of the material in the soil in such a way that the pull is upwards.

Solving problems

What should you do if your garden is situated on a slope or if the subsoil is so hard that only a pneumatic drill will be able to penetrate to any depth? There are quite simple solutions to both these problems.

A pond lined with insulation material on a slope

The most important point to consider with a pond on a slope is that the soil must not start slipping. The slope must be securely reinforced by means of L-shaped builders' blocks (obtainable from builders' merchants), as shown in the illustrations on the right. Two possible ways of reinforcing the pond on the valley side are also shown on the right.

A lined pond with a raised water level

This method is very suitable for terrain with extremely hard subsoil and for those people who are not so keen on digging. If the deep-water area is planned at, say, 32 in (80 cm), you will only have to dig out this area to a depth of 16 in (40 cm).

Method

● Peg out the outline of the pond pit, making sure to indicate the area of deep water as well as the shallow part.

● Bury vertical lengths of rounded wood along the pond edge so that they protrude 40 cm (16 in) above the ground.

● Dig out the deep-water area to a depth of 40 cm (16 in).

● Place the excavated soil behind the rounded lengths of wood to reinforce them.

● Insert the insulation material. Nail the edges of the insulation material to the wood and then bury it in the earth bank so that the edges of the material are pointing upward.

● If the earth bank is going to be walked on later, reinforce the relevant section by means of a drystone wall.

● Plant the earth wall or bank with the kind of plants that will form a good rooting system to consolidate the bank.

A pond in front of a patio wall

If you wish to be able to view the pond from your patio, you will need to build it right beside the patio wall. Very often, a steep bank will be created that will require reinforcing with a drystone wall.

Method

● After digging the pit for your pond, you will have to build a foundation for the drystone wall. This can be laid in concrete or you may obtain ready-made foundation stones from your local builders' merchant.

● The drystone wall is erected by placing the bricks together without mortar! If necessary, fill any cracks or uneven sections between the bricks with soil.

● It will be absolutely necessary to insert a protective layer of material between the drystone wall and the layer of insulation material. The same goes for the patio paving stones, which may lie on top of the insulation material around the edge of the pond.

A patio pond

Some gardens are so small that there would be no room for a lawn or flower bed if you wanted to install a pond. However, the owners of such gardens can still consider the possibility of constructing a pond on the patio. You will need lengths of squared wood and insulation material.

Method

● You can obtain squared wood of different lengths in builders' yards. Some types of wood are prepared in such a way that they only need to be slotted together in the desired position.

● Drill holes vertically into the joins with a ⅜-in (10-mm) wood drill.

Building a pond on a slope; reinforcing the slope and valley sides

Dig out the slope
Dig out the slope to a depth of about 28 in (70 cm).

Reinforce the slope side
Secure the soil to stop it from slipping by using L-shaped stones. Lay the lining, weigh it down with lattice bricks or stones, and, using silicon adhesive, glue it to the L-shaped stones.

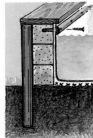

Securing the valley side
Left: Sections of rounded wood are sunk into a foundation of ready-made concrete. Wrap the lining around a small rounded piece of wood and nail it to the large section of wood.
Right: Bury the rounded wood at least 16 in (40 cm) deep. Construct a drystone wall and secure the lining to it with the help of a wooden batten, screws, and countersunk screws. Lay a plank loosely across the top.

209

● Then hammer in bolts (obtainable from hardware stores). If the pond is situated on soil, the bolts must be long enough to be firmly anchored in the soil beneath the wood.

● If the pond is built on patio paving stones, the bolts need only reach down as far as the paving stones without penetrating them.

NB: Some lumber merchants stock ready-made kits for constructing patio ponds of certain sizes, for example, 86 in (2.15 m) long, 50 in (1.25 m) wide and 24 in (60 cm) deep. When clad with insulation material, these ponds will hold about 435 gallons (1,600 liters) of water.

Important: The joined lengths of wood will have to withstand a considerable pressure of water. Make sure, therefore, that the joins are strong and secure. Obtain advice when buying the wood about suitable reinforcement materials.

A patio pond is very easy to look after. All you need to do is replenish evaporated water and remove withered parts of plants.

The edge of the pond should be surrounded with low-growing water plants such as miniature water lilies, pickerel weed (*Pontederia cordata*), lobelia, water lettuce (*Pistia stratiotes*), or water plantain (*Alisma plantago*). Watercress, chives, and monkey flower (*Mimulus*) will flourish in shallow bowls around the edge. Do not put any soil on the bottom of the pond. The plants should be placed in the pond in baskets.

Fish can only be introduced if you equip your patio pond with the technical accessories of a large cold-water aquarium.

How to install a ready-made pond

The selection of commercially available ready-molded ponds is quite large. Good manufacturers will also guarantee that the material is harmless to animals and plants and, in addition, UV-resistant, non-degradable, frost-resistant, and shock-proof.

The range of different shapes should cater for almost every conceivable wish, from rectangular to oval to L-shaped and kidney-shaped ponds – there should be something to suit every taste.

A division into different sections is particularly useful in larger ponds. These are equipped with several planting terraces and deep- and shallow-water areas. Some ready-made ponds even have a so-called biotope edge, which is a special bay-like section for planting edging plants.

The size of ready-made ponds ranges from small ponds with a capacity of about 27 gallons (100 liters) to really large ones that are divided into sections and can hold several thousand gallons (liters).

Installing a molded pond is really quite simple, except that you need to be more exact in digging out the pit than with the insulated type. The more curved the edges of the pond are, the more difficult installation will turn out to be. A ready-made pond must be installed evenly or the water will be tilted in the basin. This is visually unattractive as well as making the pond liable to overflow at one side.

Installing large ready-made ponds that are designed in sections is not quite as easy as the installation of a single basin.

Making the pond pit

● Peg out the outline of the prospective pond. This will be easier if the manufacturer has supplied a template of the pond. If not, stand the molded pond on the proposed site and draw around the shape with a stick. Then add about 6 in (15 cm) all the way round. This is the margin you will need for washing soil around the edge of the pond.

My tip: Molded ponds are very stable but it will still be necessary to remove stones, roots, and other sharp objects from the pit.

● First dig out the pit for the deepest part of the pond. It should be 6 in (15 cm) wider and 2-4 in (5-10 cm) deeper than the actual molded pond.

● Cover the floor of the pit with a 2-4-in (5-10-cm) thick layer of sand. The sand should be shaken down by tapping it with the flat blade of a spade so that it forms an even surface.

● Now dig out the rest of the pegged-out area and cover it with a layer of sand.

● Insert the molded pond and adjust the top edge so that it is completely horizontal. Two planks and a spirit level will be useful for this operation.

How to wash in soil: The hollow spaces round the pond and any remaining hollow spaces underneath must be filled with soil or sand washed in with water. This will prevent the pond from sinking or tilting later on.

● First fill the spaces around the deepest part of the basin with sand and press the sand down with the end of a plank.

● Then – very important! – fill the deepest section with water (let it run in very slowly).

● Let the water run slowly over the sand so that it becomes evenly distributed.

Kingcups (Caltha palustris)
These are the heralds of spring among pond plants. Their golden yellow flowers begin to appear in mid-spring.

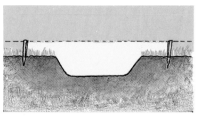 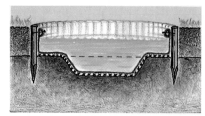

Building a pond with a raised water surface
Left: Lay out the shape of the pond and mark out the deep-water zone.
Right: Bury rounded sections of wood in an upright position around the edge of the pond so that they protrude about 16 in (40 cm) from the ground. Pile up the soil excavated from the pit behind the wood. Line the pond with a protective layer and PVC liner. Nail the edges of the liner to the wood.

● After that, wash soil or sand into the remaining hollow spaces, while letting water run slowly into the pond, gradually adding soil and water, if necessary.

A clay-lined pond

Some nature pond enthusiasts prefer clay for lining a pond. It can usually be obtained from builders' merchants but may be difficult to find in some areas.
Method: The pit for the pond must be lined with a layer of clay approximately 12 in (30 cm) thick.
● First, distribute the crumbly-dry clay evenly in the pit and then wet it.
● Lightly knead it with your feet or a trowel.
● The idea is to build up a layer of clay that is as evenly distributed as possible and about 12 in (30 cm) thick.
● Next, add a 4-in (10-cm) thick layer of coarse sand. This will prevent pond creatures from churning up the clay later on and making the water cloudy.
● Finally, slowly fill the pond with water. To begin with, some of the water may drain away but this should soon cease as the cracks and fissures will rapidly close up.

● You will need slightly less clay if you insert unfired brick rubble (obtainable from a builder or brickworks) as a base under the clay.

My tip: Pliable clay bricks are available and can be worked like Plasticine. They are fitted together by means of toothed edges and then the joins are covered with a special substance or pressed together.

A run-off

If the water level rises due to heavy rainfall and the pond water runs over the edge, many garden owners let the overflow run away into the garden. This avoids the construction of a water run-off and in many cases it will be sufficient. Sometimes, however, the ground cannot cope with the volume of surplus water, so that the surroundings remain very wet for a long time or the water may run into a neighboring garden (which could cause damage and give your neighbors grounds for complaint). In cases like this, a soak-away will have to be built to carry surplus water into deeper levels of soil before it can spill over the edge of the pond and flood the garden.

For this, you will need a composting basket and enough fist-sized stones to fill the basket.
Method
● Dig a hole deep enough to accommmodate the wire basket.
● Line the walls of the basket (not the floor!) with PVC liner and fill the basket with the stones.
● A connection between the pond and the soak-away is formed by means of a section of gutter or a PVC pipe.
● If you need to walk across the soak-away, cover it with wooden boards.

My tip: As a rule, the simple soak-away described above will be adequate. If problems continue to occur, very often only a proper drain into the main sewer will help. In such cases, it will be necessary to consult a sewer or drainage expert.

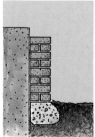 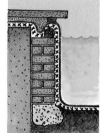

A pond beside a patio wall
Left: Build a drystone wall on a foundation against the patio wall.
Right: Lay a rounded section of wood on the drystone wall. Install the protective layer and the PVC liner. Insert a layer of sand between the liner and the patio paving-stones. Glue the stones to the liner with silicon adhesive.

Safety precautions for the protection of children

Any body of water, along with the creatures living in it, attracts children like a magnet. It is not possible to explain to small children that they may drown in a garden pond. If you really do not wish to delay the construction of a garden pond until your children are older and more sensible, you will need to provide safety barriers around the pond. Flat banks alone will not be sufficient as a safety precaution. You should secure the pond all the way around but must definitely make safe any kind of steep bank.

A protective grid in the pond

A protective grid is a very practical and almost invisible solution. Plants can grow through the grid and any fish living in the pond will not feel in the least disturbed by it. It can be removed again quite easily later on.

Method
● You will require a frame, with wire mesh (obtainable in hardware stores) nailed to it, which is as wide and long as the surface of the water.
● The mesh should not be wider than 2½-2¾ in (6-7 cm), and must be rust-proof (get advice from your dealer).
● The grid can be supported on stacked bricks.
● Stack the bricks in such a way that the grid lies about 4 in (10 cm) horizontally below the surface of the water. Make sure it cannot tip up if a weight is applied on one side!

My tip: Any uneven places between the bricks and the bottom of the pond can be smoothed out with silicon adhesive.

Protective fencing
Fences simply invite children to climb them, so they are not quite as safe as a grid in the pond. If you do decide on a protective fence, however, you can do a few things to make it more difficult for human monkeys to scale it.

A fence around the dry edge of the pond (in grass or a flowerbed)
● A wooden fence that is at least 24 in (60 cm) high is very suitable. It should have slats that run vertically. You may purchase sections of ready-made fencing with slats from wood merchants.
● The top ends of the slats should be rounded!
Warning: A cross lattice fence is completely unsuitable as the rather sharp tops of the slats may injury children badly, while the cross lattice itself is just another invitation to climb. Finally, some children may decide to poke their heads through the diamond-shaped holes of the lattice and then find themselves unable to extract them again.
● When buying the fence or the materials to build one, make sure that the substance used to treat the wood does not contain harmful additives which might be washed out by rain and end up in the pond.

I recommend materials that are marked as being environmentally safe.
● If you are going to treat the wood of the fence yourself, do not use substances that will kill plants or harm fish if they leak into the pond.
● Let the fence act as a support for luxuriantly growing plants like scarlet runner beans, mint, lemon balm, nasturtium, or nettles. This will also discourage children from climbing it.

For a marginal area
The best solution here is a chicken-wire fence.
● For posts, use angle irons of the desired height that have been cemented into large flowerpots.
● Bury the pots in the subsoil.
● Fix plastic-coated chicken wire to the posts.
Warning: The width of the mesh should be 4 in (10 cm) so that birds can fly through it. Small-mesh fencing wire near a pond can become a lethal trap for birds. Use reed-like plants such as bulrushes or grasses to mask the fence.

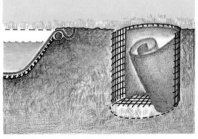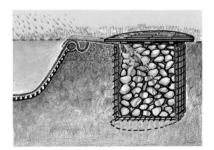

Building a soak-away
Left: Bury a composting wire-mesh basket. Line the walls (not the floor) with PVC liner.
Right: Fill the pit with large stones. Lay a gulley, lined with PVC liner, from the pond to the pit. Cover the pit with boards.

A goldfish pond with a wooden footbridge, harmoniously blended into a colorful, flowering rockery.

My tip: Build a small play pond for your children. A very shallow plastic molded pond can be buried in the ground and a large pile of sand beside it, for building castles, will be an invitation to paddle and play and will probably distract small children from the more dangerous attraction of the garden pond. Tiny children should not play unsupervised near water, no matter how shallow!

Liability for accidents

Most garden owners will be very aware of the safety of their own children. Many, however, will not be so aware of the fact that certain safety precautions must be taken to ensure the safety of other persons (strangers, visitors, etc). Comprehensive information on legal liability cannot be given within the constraints of this small book but the garden-pond owner should be alert to the question of health and safety precautions.

What you should know: If the garden pond is within a fenced-off area of garden, the garden-pond owner may assume that no unauthorized persons will intrude onto their land. However, if this does happen, and there is an accident, the injured intruder might wish to sue the pond owner and it would be wise to consult a solicitor as to where you would stand. If the garden pond is situated in an unfenced-off front garden, the garden pond owner must take all reasonable precautions to preserve a third party from accidents.

214

Warning: If there is any risk of children or adults falling into a garden pond which has not been secured properly in a front garden, you should take steps to put this right. In law, extremely high demands are very often made on an individual's duty to provide safety for others. I highly recommend taking out special insurance with reference to the garden pond. When doing this, you should give a detailed and exact description of the position of the pond and any safety devices provided, and obtain written confirmation from the insurance company that these measures are adequate and any remaining risk is covered by the insurance policy.

Safety precautions for animals

Small mammals, like hedgehogs, mice, and pets, frequently fall into a pond. Steep banks and overly smooth edging material, like PVC liner or molded ponds, can become veritable death traps if the animal cannot find anything to hold onto when trying to climb out. There are several simple measures that will enable animals to escape from a pond.
● Build a hedgehog ladder or install a gently sloping plank.
● Fix a few thick branches to the edge of the pond so that they jut out into the water but do not tip in.
● Lay out a "bathing mat," made of hemp or a similar material, along the edge of the pond so that the mat can be half-buried along the edge or under the grass turfs. Weigh the mat down in the pond with stones. Plant creeping-Jenny (*Lysimachia nummularia*) on both sides of the mat so that it grows over the mat and, in time, you will hardly be able to see it.

Designing interesting surroundings

When the pond itself has been built and filled with water, it is time to think about designing a decorative surrounding. This is not the only way to make your pond look attractive, however. A marginal area, a fountain, bridge, stepping stones, even lighting are further ways to enhance your pond. Choose something that will not only make your pond beautiful but will be practical or sensible for the particular site.

A marginal area

In the wild, the marshy marginal area around a pond is a biologically delimited part of the shallow zone, with its own plant and animal life. In a natural pond, the shallow-water zone ranges very gradually from a depth of about 10 in (25 cm) to 0 in (0 cm) where it becomes a wet, marshy area.

In order to create a similar marginal area beside a garden pond, the pond would have to be very large (over 161 sq ft/15 sq m). However, even with a small garden pond you will be able to imitate nature to a certain degree by creating a marshy area on the edge. This will provide a habitat for marginal plants and many animals will find shelter and food here.

The ideal solution is a marginal area for ornamental ponds that contain goldfish and other ornamental fish. As already mentioned on page 6, you cannot expect to find very many pond visitors, such as frogs, toads, and newts in that kind of pond. The needs of ornamental fish and the other pond creatures vary far too much. A marginal area that is not too small may help to balance these differences a little. However, please remember that a combination of an ornamental pond and a marginal area is not the same as a nature pond.

How to create a marginal area
If you have made your pond with lining material, the marginal area can be created in the same way as the pond. In the case of a *ready-made molded pond*, you may still use insulation material or install a specially formed basin right beside the pond (36 by 24 in/90 by 60 cm; depth 10 in/25 cm). This basin is designed in such a way that it will always be supplied with water from the pond.

Please note the following points:
● The larger the marshy area, the better it will fulfill the requirements as a habitat for wildlife. An area of about 10½-21½ sq ft (1-2 sq m) is about right (depth 8-10 in/20-25 cm).

A marginal area with a soil bottom
Line the area with PVC liner. Pile up stones between the pond and the marginal area and glue them to the liner. Fill the hollow with soil.

● The border between the pond and the marginal area should lie partially under the water's surface so that a water supply from the pond is maintained.
● Stack the stones between the pond and the marginal area in such a way that small caves are formed which will serve as shelter for animals. Fix them with silicon adhesive. Also glue the stones to the insulation material beneath.
● It will not harm the plants very much if the marginal area dries out briefly on the odd occasion. If there is a longer period of drought, however, an ornamental pond will have to be topped up anyway.

A marginal area with baskets
Insulate with PVC liner. Glue the stones between the pond and the marginal area to the liner. Put the plants in planting baskets.

● A sand-clay mixture is suitable for the bottom of the pond. This will provide a lime-containing soil, which is what many marginal plants require. You can choose from a large number of plants for **stocking your marginal area.**
● The plants can be planted directly into the bottom if all plants have the same requirements.
● Put any plants with special requirements in baskets, i.e. if your marginal area contains lime-rich soil, plants that require acid or lime-poor soil will have to be placed in baskets – or vice versa.

My tip: Plants that grow luxuriantly should always be set in planting baskets and the baskets themselves sunk into the soil. This will prevent the weaker plants from being smothered.

Designing the edge of the pond

Designing the edge of the pond is a matter of taste. Some people like a pond they can walk right round;, others prefer an edging that is planted. A combination is probably most practical for either an ornamental or nature pond. If part of the edge can be walked on, you will be able to observe any pondlife from close up and the pond will be accessible to any measures of care you might have to undertake. The other part, where you cannot walk, will be left completely undisturbed for plants and animals.

An edge that can be walked on
There is a large choice of materials and designs.
Paving stones, like those used for paths or patios, will need a hard base.
● The steeper the edge of the pond, the harder and more stable

Paving stones along a flat bank
Reinforce the edge with stones, cover the stones with protective material, then draw the liner over them, directing the edges of the liner upward. Put a layer of sand on top.

the base will have to be. If you have a steep bank, a drystone wall should be constructed,
otherwise the bank may
begin to give way or sink over a period of time if you walk on it.
● Lattice bricks are best for the drystone wall but you can use ordinary red bricks or medium-sized stones.
● In the case of low banks, large stones (or squared pieces of wood) will be sufficient as a base (see illustration above).
Important: Do not place stones immediately on top of any insulation material! Insert a layer of sand, about 2 in (5 cm) thick, between the insulation and the stones. To prevent the sand from seeping into the pond, create a barrier of silicon adhesive between the stones and the insulation.
Natural stones (obtainable in builders' merchants) look particularly attractive around a pond. Here, too, a stable base will be necessary. The most suitable types are a drystone wall or large stones and squared pieces of wood.
Wood is a very popular material for designing the edge of a pond.
● Bury rounded pieces of wood standing upright (nail the insulation

material to the wood) and arrange paving stones, natural stones or a gravel layer behind them.

● Try building a wooden footbridge resting on rounded pieces of wood.

● Secure the edge of the pond with squared wood (see illustration right).

Important: Any wood that you use near or in a pond must not be treated with substances that are harmful to animals or plants. Toxic substances used for treating wood, or other harmful substances, could be washed out by the pondwater or by rain to poison the pond. Do not use old railraod ties; they have usually been painted with large quantities of anti-woodworm agent, herbicide, etc.

A edge that is not intended to be walked on

Plants and stones are both useful for decorating the edge of a pond.

Verge matting is an ideal solution if you want an invisible transition from pond plants to edge plants. In addition, they will cover the insulation material or ready-made pond walls between the surface of the water and the edge of the pond. Various manufacturers produce verge matting made of coconut fiber or woven plastic. The mat is filled with suitable soil and planted. The soil will

not be able to slip into the pond and the roots of the plants will have plenty of support. Verge matting with planting pockets is particularly useful. The pockets can be filled with soil, so that even steep banks can be effortlessly planted.

Important: The matting is secured with special hooks but they should never, either in the pond or around the edge, be poked through the insulation material. Always affix the hooks outside the insulation material. The matting can be weighed down with gravel.

A small marshy ditch along the edge of the pond.

● Dig out soil to a width of 12-16 in (30-40 cm) at the edge of the pond and at the same level as the surface of the water.

● Lay the insulation material over the ditch you have dug, then draw it over some rounded pieces of wood, and let the edges of the material stand up vertically (to stop moisture seeping away into the garden).

● Lay stones along the edge of the pond (right beside the water). If necessary, glue heavy stones to the insulation material with silicon adhesive so that they are unable to tip over into the pond.

● Fill the marshy ditch with soil and plant marginal plants in it.

A stone wall along the edge of the pond is a simple and very attractive

Edging made of squared wooden sections

Lay a protective layer, then the liner over the bottom sections of squared wood. Lay the top sections on top and glue them to the liner. To secure the joints, drill through the wood and drive in bolts.

feature. In the case of an insulated pond, lightweight stones should be glued to the material with silicon adhesive to prevent them from slipping.

A lawn or flower bed may reach right to the edge of the pond.

● If you have not already done so when you dug the pit for the pond, now remove a width of grass turf to a depth of about 2¾ in (7 cm) or remove soil from a flower bed.

● Draw the insulation rnaterial across the edge of the pond so that it overlaps by about 12 in (30 cm) (make sure the edges of the material stand up vertically).

● Lay the turf you removed earlier (or flower bed soil) on the insulation layer. The grass turfs will soon grow together again.

● In the area on top of the insulation layer, a moist zone will now be created in which shrubs can flourish. This area should not be confused with a proper marginal area which will always be supplied with pond water by virtue of its design. The plants that grow here will not cope with constant waterlogging, unlike marginal plants.

Paving stones and a drystone wall providing a path along a steep bank

Pile up stones, filling the cracks with soil (do not use mortar). Lay a protective covering between the wall and the liner. Install a layer of sand, then apply a thick layer of silicon adhesive between the paving stones and the liner.

*A pond edge
with verge
matting and
plants*

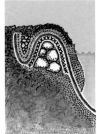

Pull a protective layer and then PVC liner over stones at the edge. Bury the liner so that a gulley is formed which will be filled with gravel. Lay the verge matting in such a way that it is secured by the gravel or secure the verge matting behind the liner with special hooks sunk into the soil. Do not drive the hooks through the liner. Fill the matting with soil and insert the plants.

A waterfall

A waterfall beside your pond will offer several advantages, for example:
● The water flowing down will become enriched with oxygen and will supply the pond with extra oxygen.
● The gentle trickling sound of the water may neutralize traffic noise – at any rate, the trickling of water is much more pleasant than the roar of traffic.
● If you wish to combine the waterfall with a running stream, the waterfall can form the mouth of the stream.

How to build a waterfall
You can build a waterfall at the same time as you dig out the pit for a pond. You
will need pond insulation material, three paving stones, a few roof tiles, silicon adhesive, and soil (a mixture of sand and clay in a ratio of 1:3 or 1:4).
● The height and width of the waterfall will depend on the size of the paving stones.
● Pile up the soil you have excavated into a mound, making it high enough to embed the three paving stones in it.
● Cut a step into the mound.

● On the side facing the pond, cover the mound up to the top with insulation material and then draw this over a rounded piece of wood at the top.
● Bury all the edges of the insulation material in the soil so that they point upward.

My tip: If the insulation material you have used to line the pond is not long enough, connect the material you are going to use for the mound by welding it so that no water can seep through it.

● Arrange roofing tiles on the step in the mound in such a way that the paving stones can be laid on top, angled slightly downward.
● Lay the paving stones on top and secure them with silicon adhesive.
● The water used for the fall should be pondwater: a garden hose should be inserted into the pond, connected to a water pump and then laid up to the top of the mound.
● Cover the hose and the insulation material with stones.
● Plant colorful summer flowers (day lily, calendula, marsh marigold, or grasses) on the mound. It is also ideal for a small rockery.

My tip: You will be able to make a waterfall even quicker if you spread out a piece of insulation material at the edge of the pond (weld it to the pond insulation layer) and pile up some stones on it. Lay the garden hose between the stones so that it points upward. This will give the effect of a spring.

More ambitious waterfalls
There are endless ways of making waterfalls.
Stones in many sizes, shapes, and colors can be arranged to form steps for the water to flow down.
A series of steps can be made out of a varied range of small basins (made of plastic or ceramic) which can be obtained from specialized gardening suppliers.
NB: The more elaborate your waterfall, and the heavier the material, the more stable the base will need to be. A loosely piled up mound will not be solid enough to support heavy stone steps or ceramic basins.
● For this you will have to bury a framework of upright, rounded pieces of wood or, even better, build a step-like solid drystone wall.
● The mound is then piled on top of this base and the path of the waterfall secured with pond insulation material.
● Heavy stone steps and basins should be secured with cement (never with lime-based mortar).

My tip: Make sure the slope (or the individual steps) of the waterfall is not too steep. In a nature pond, or even in an ornamental pond containing fish, it is not exactly beneficial to pondlife to have water gushing down with great force and a lot of noise onto the surface of the pond.

Various types of fountains

In addition to a waterfall, there are other ways of introducing moving water into your pond. From a water spout to a regular fountain, devices for spraying water are available from gardening suppliers in the most imaginative variations. It is, however, quite easy to overdo things. If water is bubbling, squirting, and trickling in every nook and cranny of your pond, the plants will not flourish so well and the fish will not like it much either. Visitors, like frogs and newts, may even "emigrate."
Stick to these three basic rules:
● A small pond should have only a small waterfall.
● At most, a nature pond will only tolerate a gently bubbling fountain or a spring stone at the edge of the pond (see illustration right).
● Large fountains should not be installed in ponds that contain fish and water lilies. If you really do want a fountain among water lilies, make sure the water does not trickle down onto the lily pads.

Water spouts, spring stones and small fountains

A large selection is available from gardening suppliers, installation is usually quite a simple matter and there will be something for every taste and purse. If you have a pond with plants and pondlife, the running water should not be switched on all the time. The best idea is to switch it on only when you are actually spending time at the pondside. A practical solution is to connect a small fountain to the main supply for additional fresh water. The alternative is to run the fountain with pondwater and a small water pump.
Water spouts are available in various different materials – from plastic to ceramic to sculpted sandstone – shaped like frogs, garden gnomes, or cherubs.
● A water spout should be placed on the edge of the pond in a way that will prevent it from tipping into the pond.
● Protect the insulation layer by inserting a piece of suitable material between the layer and the water spout.
● If the figure is very heavy, a dry-stone wall should be built under-

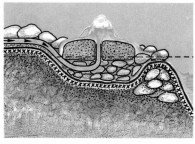

A spring stone
Dig a shallow pit at the edge of the pond and line it with protective material and PVC pond liner. Fill the hollow with stones and set the spring stone on top. Thread the water hose through the hole in the spring stone.

neath it or it can stand on rounded pieces of wood buried vertically.
Spring stones are often boulders with a chiseled hole. They can be obtained in different sizes, made of natural or synthetic stone.
● They may be set in shallow water or in a separate basin beside the pond so that the water can run into the pond can be obtained from gardening suppliers.
● Kits, which include a spring stone, a basin (insulation material or squared wood), and stones for filling the basin,
Small fountains can be placed in the pond, fixed to a lattice brick and fed by a water pump. They are less overpowering than a large fountain; water falling from a minimal height will not disturb pondlife so much.

A large fountain
A large fountain has no business in a nature pond. Do not try it in an ornamental pond with fish and water lilies either. If you really do long for both a pond and a large fountain, my advice is to install the fountain in a separate basin. Too large a fountain can actually cause damage to a pond!

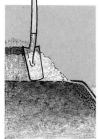
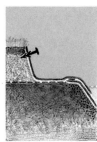

Building a simple waterfall
Pile up a mound at the edge of the pond and dig out a step. Cover the entire mound to the top with PVC liner, making sure the liner is as wide as the waterfall. Anchor the liner in the soil or draw it across rounded wood sections at the top. Glue the liner to the edge of the pond. Tilt the first paving stone at an angle on several roofing tiles and secure it with silicon adhesive. Fill the spaces with sand. The other paving stones should be laid on in steps and glued to each other with silicon adhesive. Connect the water hose.

Cross-sections of tree trunks used as stepping stones.

The constant hard splashing down of water from a high fountain causes great stress for fish, which have extremely sensitive organs along their sides for registering pressure waves. Such incoming signals are then passed onto the brain. This could be compared to the effect of a person being constantly tickled without being able to escape from their tormentor. The fish will eventually die of massive over-stimulation.

The leaves and flowers of water lilies will probably not be damaged by drops of water falling on them but if they are constantly wet, they will be unable to extract vital gases from the air and will deteriorate and die after a short time.

The pondwater is constantly pushed through minute openings in the fountain's jet and is swirled about so fiercely that micro-organisms living in the water begin to die. The result is that the biological balance in the pond is quite severely disturbed.

NB: You may find complete fountain building kits in gardening suppliers, complete with insulation material, pump shaft, pump, fountain attachments and a cover for the pump shaft.

My tip: Foam bubblers should always be installed in a separate basin. If they are put in a garden pond containing wildlife, the water will begin to smell rotten after a very short time. This is caused by algae rapidly multiplying in the vicinity of the bubbling device. The algae can usually only be eradicated with the help of harmful chemicals.

Footbridges, stepping stones and lights

These decorative elements really belong to a more sophisticated type of garden pond design. They will involve a great deal of time and work and are quite expensive too.

Footbridges made of wood, natural sandstone, or concrete can be obtained in almost all sizes from gardening suppliers, wood merchants, and some builders' yards. The degree of difficulty involved in their installation will depend largely on the size and weight of the bridge. A solid foundation (made of concrete or wood) will usually be necessary.

Stepping stones will make it possible to walk across the pond. They are very practical in the case of large ponds as they will make routine care in or around the pond a great deal easier. The stepping stones should be placed on solid concrete pillars. I advise getting help from an expert when it comes to installing these.

My tip: Builders' yards can usually provide U-shaped stones (from 16 in/40 cm upward) which make excellent bases for stepping stones. Fix the stepping stone to the base with silicon adhesive. Be very careful with the U-shaped stones, however, as they have rather sharp edges, so laying a couple of layers of insulation material between the base and the stepping stone, to act as padding, is a good idea.

Lights beside, or even in, the pond will create a magical atmosphere on warm summer evenings. You may even find floating, globe-shaped lamps on the market, which can be anchored to the bottom of the pond. An underwater cable forms a connection to the mains.

NB: Remember that all electrical installations should be carried out by an expert!

Plants around your pond

Growing plants around the garden pond will help to create a natural look. The plants should be green and in flower from spring to fall, and this is quite possible if you choose the right plants. The amount of time you will need to spend on caring for the plants will be minimal during the summer months, so you will still have time to enjoy the pond.

Soil for the pond and planting baskets

Nature pond enthusiasts will probably decide from the start to install a proper layer of soil at the bottom of the garden pond. In the case of an ornamental pond, however, which will usually contain fish such as goldfish or koi, a layer of soil would soon become churned up so that you would be unable to see the pondlife anymore. Planting baskets are more practical for this situation. Whether you choose to use planting soil in baskets or a layer of soil at the bottom of the pond, the decisive factor for the well-being of plants and pond creatures will always be the constituents of the soil mixture. A badly composed mixture can considerably interfere with life in a pond.

Basic rules for the right soil

● The soil mixture should be poor in nutrients.

● Most garden soils or humus made with compost are too rich in nutrients. These soils may cause algae to flourish or even create an imbalance in the chemical content of the water.

● Fertilized soils will introduce substances to the pond that also encourage the formation of algae.

● A layer of pure gravel is not the ideal solution either as debris will become lodged in it and biologial decomposition processes will be activated in the tiny pockets between the pieces of gravel. The nutrients thus liberated remain concentrated in the gravel layer to begin with and are then released into the water as welcome food for algae and other single-cell lifeforms. Overproduction of algae, cloudy water, and even layers of slime on the surface of the water will be the result.

Good soil for the pond

● A clay and sand mixture in a ratio of 1:3 or 1:4, which is one part clay, three or four parts river sand (from a builders' yard, grains up to $\frac{1}{16}$ in/2 mm in size).

● Special pond soil is also available, but do check the pH factor. If possible, the soil should not contain any fertilizer; if fertilizing becomes necessary, target individual plants; do not dose the entire soil.

● You will need to empty the water from the pond with a pump before putting in the soil layer. This should be at least 4 in (10 cm) thick, although it may be thicker in some places.

● First install the plants in this layer, then slowly fill the pond with water again.

Plant soil in an ornamental pond: If you are intending to keep fish in your pond, I recommend placing soil only in the marshy area. Any plants you set in the pond should be in baskets, then the water will remain clear even if you introduce fish that like to dig around at the bottom. A sand and clay mixture will be ideal for the marshy area and for the planting baskets.

● Mix aquarium soil (obtainable from aquarium suppliers) with builders' sand (sand containing clay) in a ratio of 1:3.

● Instead of builders' sand, you could use aquarium or birdcage sand (pet shop suppliers).

● A little crushed charcoal will offer protection against decay.

● This mixture will not tend to rise to the surface once it is under water. There is no need to weigh it down with gravel.

● Waterplant soil is special soil for ponds (obtainable from gardening suppliers). Ask an expert at the garden center what kind of fertilizer to use.

NB: The sand and clay mixture described above will be suitable for all plants which require soil containing lime. Never add peat to the planting soil!

Several kinds of marginal plants will have **special requirements** with respect to soil. If they require soil lacking lime (a peaty soil), add a little peat to the sand and clay mixture described above, using an average mixing ratio of 1:1:1, although for certain plants, like golden club

Water fringe (Nymphoides peltata) flowers all year round.

(*Orontium aquaticum*) and *Pontederia cordata*, the ratio should be 3:3:1.

Important: As peat may affect pond-water detrimentally, these plants should only be grown in a marshy area. They can be planted in latticed baskets together with other plants which require soil containing lime.

A choice of plants

The selection of possible garden-pond plants is so vast that they cannot all be described in this book. As the plants live in different depths of water in the wild, these requirements will have to be considered when choosing plants. When looking for plants for your pond, there are four basic types:

● marginal plants;
● surface plants;
● submerged, oxygenating plants;
● floating plants.

It is important for all areas of the pond to contain plants, which means that each of the four groups of plants should be represented as this is vital for the quality of the water and for the creatures that live in or around the pond (such as dragonflies or frogs).

NB: Only a few species are described for each of the four groups.

Marginal plants (for marshy areas): Only the roots and lower parts of the plants are submerged in water. They are planted in the shallow area of the pond, in a stream, in a marshy area, or in very moist soil at the edge of the pond.

Amphibious bistort (Polygonum amphibium) flourishes both in marginal areas and in deeper water.

Surface plants: These plants root in the soil. Their leaves and flowers are set on long stalks and float on the surface of the water. In a garden pond they should be planted in areas that are deeper than 16 in (40 cm).

Submerged, oxygenating plants: These have leaves that remain underwater and only very exceptionally protrude above the surface. Many species root in the soil at the bottom of the pond but some float freely in the water. Most of them need plenty of light. Submerged plants should not be omitted in a garden pond as they are extremely important for the quality of the water: they produce lots of oxygen and also utilize waste products from fish, which, in turn, deprives algae of nutrients, helping to keep the growth of algae in check. Some species, like rigid hornwort (*Ceratophyllum demersum*), Canadian pondweed (*Elodea canadensis*), and water milfoil (*Myriophyllum*), grow very vigorously, so you should not plant too many of these species, to prevent the pond from becoming overgrown. In the case of smaller ponds, thin out the plants occasionally during the summer months.

Floating plants are plants with more or less defined roots, which float freely on the surface of the water. They can be installed in all areas of the pond. The only thing to watch out for is that the entire surface of the pond does not become overgrown, so install few plants and thin them out during the summer.

What to watch for when making a choice: Plants should be installed in all areas of the pond but make sure that at least a third of the surface is kept free.

● To begin with, do not use too many plants or they will grow all over each other.

● Some marginal plants require soil that is poor in lime (peaty soil). Plan on placing these plants in a marshy area, not in the pond itself.

● Take note of the flowering time of the plants and choose plants to provide flowers from early spring through to the last warm days of fall.

● Two, or even three, plants can be placed together in a basket. The plants should have the same requirements regarding soil and position.

My tip: The following examples explain which plants can be planted together in a planting basket:

● common flag (*Iris pseudacorus*), bog bean (*Menyanthes trifoliata*), and water forget-me-not (*Myosotis palustris*);

● purple loosestrife (*Lythrum salicaria*), water mint (*Mentha aquatica*), and amphibious bistort (*Polygonum amphibium*);

● flowering rush (*Butomus umbellatus*), *Pontederia cordata*, and water crowfoot (*Ranunuculus aquatilis*);

● branched bur-reed (*Sparganium erectum*), mare's tail (*Hippuris vulgaris*), and pond weed (*Potamogeton*).

Buying plants

Sometimes garden enthusiasts are gripped by a kind of madness when they go to choose plants for their garden ponds, being totally overcome by the range and the splendor of the colors. Usually, however, this can be resisted by the use of a pencil and paper. Make a planting plan and write down what is to grow where. This will take the pressure off your purse and your pond will not

Attractive marginal plants

These plants require soil containing lime.

Brooklime (*Veronica beccabunga*) For water up to depths of 6 in (15 cm), in a marshy area, or edge of a stream; blue flowers from late spring to early fall. In the fall, cut it back radically. It will not tolerate peat; if in a stream, place some limestones in the water.

Purple loosestrife (*Lythrum salicaria*) (see photos, inside front and back cover) For water up to depths of 6 in (15 cm), marginal zones, marshy areas, and in streams. Flowers from midsummer to the first month of fall; blood-red inflorescences, usually more than 4 in (10 cm) tall. Do not place it with reeds or other fast-growing plants.

Water plantain (*Alisma plantago*) For shallow water (up to 6 in/ 15 cm above the rootstock). Flowers from early summer to the middle of fall; small flowers, white, rarely pink to reddish. In fall, cut it back to just above the rootstock; after one or two years divide the rootstock and replant.

Monkey Flower (*Mimulus* species) For marginal areas of marshy ground. Flowers constantly from early summer until the first month of fall; the flowers are various colors (yellow, pink, blue-violet).

Yellow loosestrife (*Lysimachia vulgaris*) For water of depths up to 2 in (5 cm); along the edges of streams. Flowers from early summer until late summer; the flowers are brilliant yellow. Tends to grow vigorously, so needs to be thinned out in summer and cut back in the fall.

Lobelia cardinalis For water of depths up to 6 in (15 cm), or in a marshy area. Flowers from late summer until mid-fall; glowing red flowers. Do not let it become overgrown by other plants. If the pond is very unsheltered, overwinter the plants in a cellar.

Arrowhead (*Sagittaria sagittifolia*) For water of depths from 6-16 in (15-40 cm), edges of streams. Flowers from early summer until midsummer; flowers white to reddish. Only the rootstock is hardy. Remove the remainder of the plant in the fall. An important competitor with algae for nutrients!

Creeping-Jenny (*Lysimachia nummularia*) Will grow anywhere. Flowers from late spring until midsummer; flowers yellow, about ½ in (1.5 cm). Easy to propagate; place a piece of stalk (with two leaves) in water and it will form roots.

Marsh marigold or **kingcup** *Caltha palustris* For water of depths up to 6 in (15 cm); marginal areas, marshy areas, stream edges (the roots must be in water). Golden yellow flowers from mid-spring until early summer. In shallow water, cut back four-fifths of the plant in the fall. In other positions, leave withered foliage until spring.

Water forget-me-not (*Myosotis palustris*) Marshy areas, edges of streams. Flowers from late spring until early summer and from late summer until early fall. Flowers are light blue to pale pink. In the fall, cut back all parts of the plant protruding into the water to prevent decay and cut the other parts of the plant down to 2 in (5 cm) in the spring.

Mare's tail (*Hippuris vulgaris*) For water up to depths of 8-20 in (20-50 cm). Flowers from late spring to late summer. Will not tolerate peat; thin out regularly.

suffocate under masses of flourishing plants. Be warned, most garden pond plants tend to be quite small when they are bought! However, in a very short time they will develop into splendid plants which require plenty of room. If they do not have enough room to start with, they will become sickly and die.

Where to buy garden-pond plants

You can obtain plants for your garden pond in garden centers and nurseries. Healthy, disease-resistant water plants and marginal plants have been bred and raised by specialists over many generations of plants. These cultivars will grow and flourish in a garden pond without any problems.

Do not stock your pond with plants obtained from the wild, that is, from their natural habitats. The rarity and survival of water plants and marginal plants have become matters of great concern in the last few years on account of the draining and drying out of so many of the wetlands of the world, and a safe future for the plants has only been secured in a very few areas. Many wild plants are now protected by law, so you could be breaking the law by removing them. Please also remember that every garden pond that has been properly installed and maintained is a small but active contribution towards nature conservation.

The following are *good sources* for purchasing plants, with selections large enough to meet all your wishes:
- aquarium suppliers and specialist garden centers;
- specialist water garden nurseries which will often send plants by mail order;
- mail-order companies.

My tip: Some water plant nurseries or garden centers have a selection of ready-made combinations of water plants, which they have put together for the initial planting of small ponds. When ordering these, all you need to do is give them the size of your garden pond and any special preferences you may have.

Tips on buying healthy plants

Take a careful look at the plants when you buy them or, in the case of mail order, when you open the package immediately it arrives. Healthy plants are identifiable by their roots.

● The roots must be white – bluish-black or brown root tips can indicate decaying plants.
● The rootstock, together with its "heart," which will later produce leaf shoots, should be large and healthy.
● Tubers or bulbs should feel firm.
● The rootstock should smell of fresh earth – on no account should it smell rotten. Exception: water lilies stink dreadfully as very often part of the rootstock has in fact died and decomposed. This is a completely normal state of affairs for water lilies and is in no way detrimental to their well-being.

My tip: If the plants are on sale in small plastic containers – which often happens nowadays – ask the salesperson to open the container so that you can take a good look at the roots.

Planting your purchases

When to plant: The best time to plant is during the growth phase when plants will be supplied with all the right conditions for growing well. This is during the period from mid-spring to early fall. The careful gardener will always wait until the last cold snap of the last month of

The correct way to plant water lilies
Remove all decayed parts and shorten the hair roots. Place the rhizome horizontally (not vertically!) in the basket. Carefully cover the rhizome with a sand and clay mixture (ratio 1:3). Gently press down the mixture. A layer of gravel is not absolutely necessary.

spring has definitely passed.
Important: Garden-pond plants should be planted as soon as possible after purchase, as storing them for a while is not good for them. If you cannot plant them immediately, you will have to water them well (container plants) or set them in a bathtub full of water. Dried-out pond plants are extremely difficult to revive.

Warning: Some water plants and marginal plants can prove harmful to human health, particularly if they are consumed by small children. If you are not an expert on plants, I recommend asking about this at the time of purchase.

Marginal plants with special soil requirements

These plants require soil that contains little lime; the best soil is a clay-sand-peat mixture.
The most suitable ratio for this mixture should be indicated on a label tied to each plant.

Lysichithum americanum
For water up to 12 in (30 cm) deep. Brilliant yellow flowers from early spring to early summer. In regions with hard winters, over-winter plants in a cellar or somewhere similar; soil mixture 1:1:1.
Golden club (*Orontium aquaticum*)
For water up to 12 in (30 cm) deep; marshy area; needs sheltered position. Flowers from late spring to early summer. Flowers

brilliant yellow, protruding up to 4 in (10 cm) above the water's surface. In regions with harsh winters, overwinter the plant in frost-free conditions. Soil mixture 3:3:1.
Pontederia cordata
For water up to 8 in (20 cm) deep; marshy area. Flowers from mid-summer to early fall; blue inflorescences. Proliferates vigorously; cut back radically in the fall. Soil mixture 3:3:1.
Cotton grass (*Eriophorum* spp.)
For the edges of marshy areas; very moist soil; should not stand in water. Flowers from late spring to late summer; seed heads are woolly, white. Soil mixture 1:1:1.

Surface and floating plants

In a small pond, which can also accommodate water lilies, vigorously proliferating floating plants should be installed sparingly. Make sure to thin them out often so that they do not take over the entire pond.

Pondweed (*Potamogeton* spp.) Surface plant. Grows anywhere in a pond. Flowers from late spring to late summer. Inconspicuous inflorescences. Thin out regularly; remove almost completely in the fall. Competes with algae for nutrients; provides spawning places for fish.

Water fringe (*Nymphoides peltata syn Villarsia nymphoides*) Surface plant. For water up to 20 in (50 cm) deep. Brilliant yellow flowers from early summer to early fall; flowers protrude a little above the water's surface. Remove nine-tenths of it in the fall or the pond will become completely overgrown. Ideal environment for fish spawn and young fish.

Frog-bit (*Hydrocharis morsus-ranae*) Free-floating plant with surface rosettes. Will grow anywhere in the pond. White flowers from early summer to late summer. Cannot tolerate lime.

Water soldier (*Stratiotes aloides*) Floating plant. Will grow anywhere in a pond. Flowers from early to late summer; white flowers with yellow anthers. Flourishes in nutrient-rich water, free of lime, but will cope with some lime.

Water lettuce (*Pistia stratiotes*) Floating plant. Will grow anywhere in a pond. No flowers. Leaves shaped like shells, set in rosettes.

Submerged, oxygenating plants

Although some of these underwater plants, like *Elodea, Ceratophyllum* (hornwort), and *Myriophyllum* (water milfoil), proliferate wildly and may fill up the pond, they should still be present (just do not plant too many!). They produce large quantities of oxygen and utilize the waste products of fish, which, in turn, deprives algae of nutrients. They are also ideal hiding places for young fish.

Water milfoil (*Myriophyllum* spp.) For water up to 20 in (50 cm) deep. Flowers from midsummer to early fall; pale pink inflorescence protrudes about 6 in (15 cm) above the water's surface. Water requirements depend on the water in which they naturally occur (ask at the garden center, etc.)

Rigid hornwort (*Ceratophyllum demersum*) Floats freely in the water. Does not flower. Forms tangles of plants that may be up to 40 in (1 m) across. Remove nine-tenths in the fall. Will not cope with peat. Competes with algae for nutrients.

Duckweed (*Lemna minor*) Will grow anywhere in a pond. Does not flower. Fish out quantities of it regularly during the summer and remove nine-tenths in the fall. Competes with algae for nutrients.

Canadian pondweed (*Elodea canadensis*) Grows anywhere in a pond. Rarely flowers in Europe. If lime is added to the water, it proliferates explosively! Remove nine-tenths in the fall. Competes with algae for nutrients.

Preparing the plants

Before planting, a few measures are necessary, for example, cutting back the rootstock.

For these procedures you will need a sharp knife. Pruning clippers are not suitable as they squash and bruise the plants, which can lead to disintegration of the tissues and decay. The following points are very important:

● Remove all damaged or broken roots.

● Shorten long, straggling roots to a rounded ball.

● Carefully cut out decaying parts of the tuber or rootstock. Sprinkle a little charcoal powder on the cut surface to prevent decay.

● Remove damaged or bent leaves.

NB: Floating and submerged plants should be laid loosely in the water; marginal and surface plants should be planted in planting baskets, verge matting or in pockets in the same, or directly into the soil.

Fertilizing

Many gardeners believe fertilizing will provide a good start for pond plants and will not harm them. My advice is that, apart from water lilies, you should not fertilize pond plants as fertilizer will merely support the formation of algae. Only add fertilizer to the soil in which water lilies are planted – they will then flower better. Use only a special aquarium or water plant fertilizer (and follow the directions!). Regular plant fertilizers are no good as they may harm pondlife. In particular, they have a deleterious effect on the sensitive mucous membranes and respiratory organs of fish.

If you use ready-fertilized, water-plant soil, wait for two or three weeks before you put the fish in the pond, and change half of the water every week to eliminate any surplus fertilizer that is dissolved in the pondwater.

A glorious palette of colors for an ornamental pond.

Plants for an ornamental pond

*1. Nymphaea hybrid "Escarboucle,"
a splendid carmine red water lily
with ruby red anthers and an orange
yellow base. For a depth of 24-32 in
(60-80 cm) of water.*

*2. Nymphaea hybrid "Direktor
Moore," a water lily with flowers that
are 4¾ in (12 cm) across and large
green pads. Must be overwintered in
a frost-free position. For water
12-16 in (30-40 cm) deep.*

*3. Nymphaea hybrid "Rosenymphe,"
a profusely flowering water lily with
reddish-green leaves. The flowers
turn white as they fade.*

*For water 12-28 in (30-70 cm) deep.
4. Nymphaea hybrid "Moorei," a
water lily with delicately scented
flowers. For water 24-40 in
(60-100 cm) deep.*

*5. The yellow water lily (Nuphar
lutea) should be cared for in the
same way as other water lilies. For
water up to 16 in (40 cm) deep.*

*6. Nymphaea hybrid "Laydekeri pur-
purata," a profusely flowering dwarf
water lily whose foliage is brownish-
red when it emerges from the water
and then turns green on the surface.
For water from 12-16 in (30-40 cm)
deep.*

*7. Iris sibirica hybrid, one of the
many colorful cultivars of the yellow
iris. For water that is a maximum of
8 in (20 cm) deep.*

*8. The water hyacinth (Eichhornia
crassipes) will only flower if the
water temperature rises above 68°F
(20°C). It will grow anywhere in the
pond. Overwinter only in an
aquarium.*

*9. Common flag (Iris pseudacorus),
one of the most beautiful marginal
plants, which only occurs rarely in
the wild in a few areas (protected
plant). For water up to 8 in (20 cm)
deep.*

Green and flowering garden-pond plants. The available selection is huge.

Plants for a nature pond or an ornamental pond

1. Branched bur-reed (Sparganium erectum), a hardy marginal plant which will also grow in deeper water. The seed capsules resemble hedgehogs in shape and appearance. For water up to 40 in (1 m) deep.

2. Hemp agrimony (Eupatorium cannabium), a vigorously growing plant for the moist marginal area. Thin it out occasionally during the summer.

3. Bog bean (Menyanthes trifoliata) will not tolerate lime; mix peat with the planting soil. Ideal for a marginal area or along a stream. Water up to 8 in (20 cm) deep.

4. Water crowfoot (Ranunculus aquatilis) is a toxic plant! It grows vigorously; thin out when necessary. A competitor with algae for nutrients. A good hiding place for small fry.

5. Flowering rush (Butomus umbellatus) should only be set in planting baskets in an ornamental pond as it has a widely spreading root system. For water up to 10 in (25 cm) deep; must always stand in water.

6. Water chestnut (Trapa natans) forms rosettes that float on the surface; turns red in the fall. The mother plant will die off in the fall; the fruits drop down and, in the spring, form new shoots.

7. Common bladderwort (Utricularia vulgaris), an underwater plant whose flowers protrude 6-8 in (15-20 cm) above the water's surface. The leaves are covered in numerous bladder-like tubes which serve to catch small water insects. Thrives best in water containing little lime and few nutrients.

Using planting baskets

If you do not want a real nature pond with a proper soil bottom which will manage for long periods of time without any special care, I can recommend placing your plants in planting baskets.

The growth of vigorously proliferating plants will be kept within bounds by these baskets and, in the fall, when cutting back is required, they are easily lifted out of the pond.

Special lattice baskets for water plants can be obtained from gardening suppliers in various sizes and shapes. Plants in baskets will receive an adequate supply of oxygen to their roots as the water moves gently through them.

My tip: Oval-shaped lattice baskets are ideal for the longish rootstocks (rhizomes) of water lilies.

Ordinary flowerpots are **unsuitable for waterplants**, as are plastic buckets with holes or PVC containers. The plant roots would not receive enough oxygen in these containers.

How to plant in lattice baskets

● Line the basket with a special thin planting material (obtainable from gardening suppliers, etc.) or with very thin foam rubber sheets (1/32-1/16 in/1-2 mm thick and decay-proof).

● Fill two-thirds of the basket with planting soil. Leave enough room so that the roots will not be bent upward when the plant is inserted.

● The roots, tubers or rootstocks should be inserted in such a way that the tiny first shoots of the leaves point upward.

Important: The rootstocks of water lilies must be laid horizontally in the soil.

● Now fill the rest of the basket with soil, making sure the shoots are still showing.

● Press the soil down gently and moisten it. The best idea is to stand it in a bathtub into which water can be poured very slowly, thereby moistening the soil from below.

● Covering the surface of the soil with gravel is not necessary if you use the soil recommended.

Placing the planting baskets in the pond

In the case of small ponds, the baskets can be put straight into the filled pond. If you do not wish to climb into the water in case the bottom will be churned up or because it is simply too cold, lay a beam across the pond and sink the baskets with the help of two long metal hooks.

Important: If you set the baskets in an empty pond, you cannot wait too long before letting in water, otherwise the plants will dry up. Fill the pond very slowly!

With the exception of water-lily baskets, all baskets can be placed in their final positions from the start. If you have an insulated pond, the baskets can be placed in the desired positions with the help of lattice bricks or stones which have been previously stuck to the insulation material with silicon adhesive.

Water-lily baskets should be moved several times as this will make the water lilies flower earlier and produce lots of blossom. Proceed in the following way with all water-lily baskets:

● In the spring, place the water-lily basket in shallow water.

● Lift the floating leaves up a little above the surface, then push the basket into deeper water until the leaves are barely submerged.

● Repeat the process, until the basket ends up in the desired position in deep water.

My tip: If, for some reason, you are unable to carry out this step-by-step procedure of gradually pushing the baskets into deep water, stack up as many roof tiles as possible in the desired final position to place the basket in a simulated shallow-water zone. Then lower the basket gradually, by taking away the tiles one at a time, until the basket is at the desired depth.

Verge matting

Verge matting made of natural fibers or plastic makes ideal plant containers for steep banks.

Verge matting with integral planting pockets is the most practical form.

How to plant in the matting

● Anchor the matting with special fixtures, special nails, or bolts intended for use in soil (obtainable from gardening suppliers) beyond the edge of the insulation material at the edge of the pond.

● Fill the pockets with plant soil.

● Insert the plants from above through the mesh. The mesh can be pulled apart slightly to let the roots pass through without damaging them. Even plants with a compact rootstock can be planted in this way.

My tip: The verge matting should only be let protrude a little way into the water of an ornamental pond. The interior of these mats will develop its own biological climate, which might create problems with algae in a pond stocked with fish.

Helpful gadgets

You cannot just let nature take its course in a small pond. In particular, ornamental ponds containing fish will need some care and equipment in order to meet the requirements of both fish and plants. Pondlife will only flourish without problems if you have the means to make sure there is a plentiful supply of oxygen and as little as possible in the way of waste products.

Technical devices

You will rarely need technical devices for a nature pond without a waterfall or stream. Life in such a pond is intended to develop and flourish undisturbed and to be self-regulating. In small nature ponds, however, there may be occasional disruptions, which will make the installation of an air pump necessary in order to supply the water with oxygen.

A water pump is indispensable if you wish a small waterfall or a stream to flow into your pond

An ornamental pond which is intended to provide a home for goldfish or koi and plants will hardly manage without some technological help. If you want to provide a healthy environment for your pondlife all year round, you will have to take control at certain times. Always keep two important points in mind:

● The pond requires an adequate supply of oxygen. It will be necessary to supply oxygen with the help of an air or water pump or with an oxygenator.

Important: The critical months, during which you will have to keep a sharp eye on the oxygen content of the water, are the last month of winter and the middle of the summer. Toward the end of winter, the water will begin to warm up slowly under the ice, while in the midsummer months it is heated up far more than usual due to the weather. Both times may see a drop in the oxygen supply as warm water absorbs and stores less oxygen than cooler water.

● The pond must not be allowed to become overloaded with waste products, so a good filter will be necessary.

My tip: If possible, equip your pond with a stream of water. This will provide the best and most natural filter and oxygen provider.
As long as the stream is flowing, you will not need technical gadgets for oxygenating or filtering.

Devices to aid overwintering (for example, ice-preventers combined with an oxygen supply) are important for both nature ponds and ornamental ponds. Even at times when a sheet of ice has formed on the surface, gases created through decay must still be able to exit through an ice-free spot in the pond, so that the overwintering pondlife is not harmed.
You will require a well-functioning *pump for running fountains* or a stream, and for changing the water.
The technical equipment needed for a garden pond is usually easy to run and all gadgets are obtainable from gardening suppliers.

Accidents involving electrical equipment

Pumps and filters are run on electricity and everyone knows that electricity and water do not really mix, so, if the combination is handled carelessly, fatal accidents may occur. Safety must be made top priority during the installation of any electrical equipment or cables around or in a pond!
Take careful note of the following safety recommendations:
● Electrical installations should only be carried out by an expert!
● When you purchase equipment, make sure that it carries a guarantee of reliability.
● Use cables that are sufficiently long – never use extension leads!
● Turn off the power and always remove the plug from the outlet before removing an electrical gadget from the pond!
● Repairs should only be carried out by an expert. If you carry out repairs yourself, or even make alterations to the device, you will be personally liable for any damage or accidents.
● Never remove a device from the pond by hauling it out by its cable.

My tip: Devices that are equipped with a handle or grip can be extracted from, or inserted into, the pond by means of a long piece of strong, bent wire or by a chain attached to the device, which is then anchored somewhere along the edge of the pond.

● A circuit breaker will provide additional protection. If there is a fault in the gadget or damage to the cable, this will immediately break

A small pond with red water lilies, water fringe, and colorful flowering plants around the edge.

the flow of the current. If you do not already have one, have a circuit breaker built into your fuse housing. If this is not possible, have the circuit breaker inserted between the electrical source and the gadget.

Power supply
The routes of electrical lines running from the house or the position of electrical connections near the pond should be carefully considered when you plan your pond and should be installed during the pond-building phase.

Important: The best plan is to lay the cables through an underground PVC pipe. It is important to make sure that the underground cables will not be accidentally dug up by someone else in the garden, such as anyone who comes to do

any form of work or repairs on your property. If you do not use a PVC pipe, use only rodent-resistant cables (specially designed for underground) and, again, never use extension leads! It is all too easy for extension leads to become disconnected, while rats and mice can cause unbelievable amounts of damage to wires and cables, making them both dangerous to use and expensive to replace.

Low-voltage electricity

Low-voltage (24 volt) electricity provides a high degree of protection against electric shocks or worse. Special water pumps and filters can be obtained from gardening suppliers, which are designed for use with low-voltage electricity. In order to use these devices, you will need a low-voltage transformer which should be installed inside the house.

My tip: Lights installed in or around the pond will run on 12 volts and can be run off an automobile battery.

Gadgets running on low-voltage electricity provide more protection but also use up more current than ordinary 240-volt equipment, as the transformer uses additional current. The transformer will often use as much current again as the pump itself.

Water pumps

You will need an electrical connection outlet for a water pump.
Use: Water pumps can be used for several different purposes.
● For agitating the water. By moving the water around, the pond is supplied with oxygen and a balance of temperature is attained between the sun-warmed upper levels of water and the colder, lower levels.
● For emptying the pond and for changing the water.
● For powering a running stream.
● For powering a waterfall, or fountain, etc.
● For filtering.
The right pump: There is a large selection of available pumps, so it is very important for a layperson to seek specialist advice (ask at your garden center). Note the following points:

● Underwater or immersion pumps are the most useful and can be used for all the above-mentioned purposes. They are oil-cooled pumps that are hermetically sealed against water or set in artificial resin.
● They should be mounted on a lattice brick or fixed to a special pump mount in the pond.
Important: The pump should come supplied with proper instructions and state that it is suitable for operation under water. It should carry a relevant safety symbol.
Output of the pump: Pumps with an output of 547 gallons (2,000 liters) per hour should be quite sufficient for the above-mentioned purposes. The height of water moved (measured from the surface) can be up to 80 in (2 m). When buying the pump, indicate how you are intending to use it as a good salesperson will always give you the right advice.

My tip: Fountain pumps with an output of more than 2,735 gallons (10,000 liters) per hour and able to move water 120 in (3 m) high are neither sensible nor necessary for a small garden pond. They are better for a fountain running in a separate basin.

Care of a pump: With regular servicing, a good underwater or immersion pump should run without problems for many years. Have your oil-cooled pump serviced by the manufacturer once a year (your retailer should take it in for servicing). If servicing is not carried out regularly, even the best pump can develop leaks around the seals so that oil escapes and pollutes the water. If the pump should run dry, only let an expert repair it! Pumps encased in artificial resin need practically no servicing.

Tips on use: To prevent plant debris from clogging the filter intake holes, the pump should not just be mounted on a lattice brick or fixed to a pump mount, but the intake holes should also be protected by an intake basket, a filter (filled with coarse nylon fiber waste), a plastic cage, or a grid sieve (all obtainable from aquarium or gardening suppliers).
Pumps not recommended: Air-cooled pumps should never be run under water. They should be installed in a frost-resistant pump shaft beside the pond. Some aquarium pumps, or even washing machine pumps, are totally unsuitable as they are not safe enough.

My tip: A solar pond pump is now available, which runs on solar energy with an output of 27 gallons (100 liters) per hour under a clear sky. This is a new development which has probably not quite reached perfection yet but is definitely a step in the right direction.

Air pumps

If laying an electrical cable becomes necessary, the best

An oxygenator
An oxygen-providing device that will enrich water with oxygen all year round. It will continue to function during the winter, even under a covering of ice.

method is to lay an underground PVC pipe and pull the electrical cable or the air line belonging to the air pump through it. The air line must be long enough to reach the deep-water zone if necessary. It should not be bent.
Use: These pumps provide a good service in both summer and winter.

● For supplying additional oxygen to the water: the pump blows air (and with it oxygen) into the pond and creates a revolution of the water at the same time to maintain the temperature balance between the water layers.

● For running a foam rubber or ceramic pot filter.

The right pump: You can choose between two types of pump:

● Ordinary air pumps are not resistant to splashes of water. They may only be suspended in a completely dry position (inside the house, or cellar), never outside.

● Splash-resistant air pumps (this must be stated in the instructions!) can be installed outside; this goes for garden pond air pumps too.

Tips on use: The ordinary pump must not be let get damp, as it will then oxidize and this will cause it to become faulty. To prevent condensation (specially in winter) from running back toward the pump, it is worth installing a non-return valve (obtainable from aquarium suppliers or garden centers) between the pump and the stream stone (see column right). Please read thoroughly any directions that come with a garden pond air pump as they will contain important information on setting it up and looking after it.

Impellers for an air pump

Impellers are connected to the air hose of the air pump to help with the oxygen supply and the movement of the water. Several different kinds of impeller can be obtained

from gardening or aquarium suppliers.

Plastic and silicon dioxide impellers are cheap but rapidly become clogged up, so that they need to be cleaned and exchanged very often.

Ceramic impellers are a little more expensive than plastic and silicon dioxide ones, but more advantageous. They create a particularly fine "pearling" of the stream of air, which means an improved oxygen supply. They take much longer to become clogged. Impellers which have become clogged up can be baked over a gas flame (remove all plastic parts first!).

"Pearling" hose: This is a porous hose which can be connected to the air hose at any desired length. The fine pores create a kind of "oxygen curtain" which is particularly favorable for the circulation of the water. It will not clog up very quickly.

Oxygenators that are not run on electricity

These devices can be obtained from gardening suppliers under various names. They are particularly practical for gardens without a supply of electricity.

Use: for additional oxygen supply in summer and winter. These devices will even function under a covering of ice.

How to use them: The oxygenator consists of a ceramic container with fine pores, which, in turn, contains a plastic container with a tiny catalyst. Some devices come equipped with several catalysts. (Do not lose the catalysts!) The device is filled with hydrogen peroxide. Read the directions carefully!

Warning: Be careful when filling these! Hydrogen peroxide has cor-

Garden pond filter
Left: ceramic pot filter.
Right: foam rubber filter.
Both gadgets are run on an air pump.

rosive properties. Store in a place that is out of reach of children and animals!

Position: Stand the device in an accessible position in the pond.

Refilling: Hydrogen peroxide disintegrates to produce water and oxygen – the higher the temperature, the faster it will break down. When the contents are used up, the device will rise to the surface and will have to be refilled – in summer this will be approximately every six to eight weeks; in winter every three months.

Filters

A good filter is important in a garden pond stocked with fish as otherwise the water will become polluted with waste matter.

My tip: Use a special garden pond filter. Aquarium filters are too small.

Electric filter

Various types of garden pond filter can be obtained which are driven by a circulating pump.

Use: very easy to run, using very little electricity (from 10 watts). They can carry out several tasks at the same time in a pond:

A nature pond in the fall when the plants are preparing for winter.

Winter dormancy; the pond will come to life again in spring.

- filtering;
- water circulation, during which the water is enriched with oxygen;
- running fountains or similar, for example, a small jet or water spout;
- ideal as a pre-filter (filled with small clay pipes) for powering a running stream.

Care: Apart from occasional cleaning out or changing the filter, these types of filters need practically no servicing.

Foam-rubber filters

The foam-rubber filter material will hold onto all kinds of debris, so the water is filtered mechanically. In addition, there is a small-scale biological filtering effect, as micro-bacteria colonize the pores of the foam rubber and, in time, break down organic debris.

Use: This filter is run on an air pump. It will keep 2½ cu yd (2 cu m) of pond water clean for one week (1¼ cu yd/1 cu m = 273 gallons/1,000 liters). If you wish, several filters can be combined. Two filters will be quite sufficient for a pond that is about 64 sq ft (6 sq m) and contains about 820-1,090 gallons (3,000-4,000 liters) of water.

Care: Wash out the foam rubber once a week in tepid water (without any cleaners).

Ceramic pot filter

The filling material consists of lots of small clay pipes and foam rubber. It cleans the water mechanically, just like the foam rubber filter, and partly biologically too.

Use: It is run on an air pump, just like the foam rubber filter, and is used and handled in the same way.

Care: Wash out the pipes and the foam rubber in tepid water (no cleaners!) or fill with new clay pipes.

Overwintering

During a hard winter it will often be necessary to make sure that there is an ice-free patch in the ice cover on your ornamental or nature pond. There are two practical devices to help with this.

An ice-preventer: which consists of special polystyrene parts. As it is not only very inexpensive but very simple to use (no electricity), I can highly recommend it as a reliable aid during the winter. The instructions are very easy to understand.

Pond heater: The name is rather misleading as the gadget does not actually heat the pond, but merely keeps a hole free of ice, at low wattage. You will need a supply of electricity. The device is switched on when the temperature drops below zero; when the thaw sets in, you can unplug it.

Important: Never use an aquarium heater with an extension cable in a pond!

My tip: If your pond heater should get frozen up because you have forgotten to put the plug in the outlet, never try to hack it out with an ice pick. You would frighten the fish and, in addition, you might damage the cable, the cork float, or even the heater itself, which might short-circuit the device.

How to care for your pond

During the summer, a pond does not create much work. Checking the water and looking after the plants does not take long. In the fall, however, you should take some time to prepare the pond thoroughly for the approaching winter, so that fish and other pond creatures will survive the winter well and the plants will flower again the following spring.

Water

The degree to which plants and pond creatures feel at home in your pond will depend largely on the quality of the water. The decisive factors for this are the acidity (pH factor) and the nitrite and nitrate content. It is necessary to be aware of these values, so that you can intervene if it becomes necessary. For **ornamental ponds**, a regular check of the water is necessary so that, in an emergency, fast action can be taken.

In a nature pond which contains no, or few, fish, checking will only become necessary in the case of disturbances (like too much weed growth).

Measuring the water values

The pH factor and the nitrite and nitrate contents can be measured with simple, inexpensive procedures. The values obtained – the water values – will give you information as to whether intervention is required. Indicators (reagents), indicator strips, and other agents can be obtained from gardening suppliers. Exact, easy-to-understand directions are supplied.

Acidity of the water

The degree of acidity of the water is expressed by the pH factor:
- a neutral reaction is indicated by a value of 7;
- values from 0 to 6.9 indicate that the water is acid;
- values from 7.1 to 14 indicate that the water is alkaline.

The right pH factor: pH values from 6.5 to 8.5 (slightly acid to slightly alkaline) are good for fish. Values below pH 6 may endanger your stock of fish.

The pH factor will fluctuate: During the course of a day, the pH factor may fluctuate slightly through the influence of the weather or through the presence of plants. These short-term fluctuations are normal and will not harm the fish.

Measuring the pH factor: During the warm part of the year you should make routine checks, with one measurement being particularly important:
- In the summer, after a heavy shower of rain, acid rain may detrimentally affect the pH factor.

● In the fall, if leaf fall is heavy, large quantities of dead leaves may end up in the pond in a very short time. The rapid onset of decomposition may quickly reduce the pH factor to values around 5 – these are lethal values for most fish.

Regulating the pH factor: You will have to intervene if the pH factor deviates from values that are comfortable for fish.

● If the pH factor is too low: slowly change one-third of the water, and repeat if necessary.

● If the pH factor is too high: suspend a sack of garden peat in the pond until the desired value is attained. Check regularly as the pH value should not drop too low.

The nitrite and nitrate content

A constant process of change takes place in a pond. The organic waste produced by creatures and plants – for example, plant debris, excrement, remains of fish food – are decomposed by bacteria. This creates nitrites that are harmful to fish, which are then changed into nitrates which are harmless for fish. The process uses up oxygen in the water. As long as plenty of oxygen is available, and there is not too much waste matter in the water, this process will function without a hitch. The nitrite and nitrate contents will remain low and will not affect the well-being of the fish.

If the nitrite and nitrate contents become too high: The more waste matter that accumulates in the water, the greater the danger of nutrient over-enrichment and lack of oxygen. Too much nitrite is formed and also too much nitrate, which binds a lot of the oxygen in the water. The consequences are that:

● Too many nutrients lead to increased growth of algae.

● A high nitrite content will lead to symptoms of poisoning in fish.

● Due to a lack of oxygen, the fish rise to the surface gasping for air (emergency respiration).

Prevention (important in an ornamental pond!)

For this reason, it is very necessary to:

● change one-third of the water every three weeks;

● feed the fish properly.

In an emergency: change the water and add an oxygenator (read the directions carefully).

My tip: The best prevention is to employ a running stream as a biological filter.

Hardness of the water

The calcium and magnesium content of the water will determine the degree of hardness.

The various degrees of hardness of water are determined as follows: 5-10 degrees Clark = soft water; 10-21 degrees Clark = medium hard water; 22-38 degrees Clark = hard water.

Suitable hardness: medium hard, although many species of fish will cope with harder water. American main water generally has the right degree of hardness. You can discover the degree of hardness of your main water by approaching your local water utility or measuring it yourself with the relevant reagents.

Carbonate hardness is important for measuring water hardness. This indicates the amount of carbonates, which are compounds of calcium and magnesium with carbonic acid. The degree of carbonate hardness will determine how easy it will be to offset the fluctuations of the pH values, which would become extreme without the carbonate hardness and would have a lethal effect on many organisms. Carbonate hardness is part of the total hardness and is determined separately (reagents can be obtained from aquarium suppliers).

The right water

Main water is usually suitable for garden ponds. In some regions, however, main water may contain a high amount of nitrates because residues from artificial fertilizers used in agriculture have seeped into the groundwater. Later on, pond plants will absorb these products but there may be increased algae growth to begin with. In the case of water that is polluted with nitrates to a high degree, it is recommended that you add a suitable agent. (Ask at your garden center.)

My tip: In some households, main water runs through an ion-exchanger so that the pipes do not become furred up with calcium deposits. In this case, the water will have to be extracted from the main before it reaches the ion-exchanger because the exchanger demineralizes the water, which may kill the fish.

Rainwater that has been collected outside can be used quite safely in your pond. If the rain runs through a roof gutter, however, you should wait for some time after long periods of dry weather, until the rain has washed away most of the accumulated dirt from the roof.

Exotic flowers and vivid green leaves
Water lilies, water soldier (Stratiotes aloides), and Pontederia cordata (in the background).

Filling and changing the water

As a rule, let fresh water run in very slowly. Connect a spray attachment to your hose. The fine spray will drive out any chlorine. Too much chlorine can lead to acid burns on the fishes' gills.

My tip: If you have one, check your water meter before and after the first filling of your pond. This will tell you the capacity of your pond. This value will dictate the number of fish you can install in the pond.

Emptying the pond: For this, you will need a water pump, to which you should attach a long hose. Make sure to equip the suction opening of the pump with a suction filter or it will become clogged with plant debris.
Changing the water in an ornamental pond: Change one-third of the water every three weeks, if possible. Add water treatment agents after the complete change of water following the fall cut-back of plants.

Changing the water in a nature pond: Only do this in an emergency. If the water level has dropped sharply and no rain is expected within the forseeable future, let water run in very slowly.

What to do with the water from your pond

A huge quantity of water is involved in the changing of pondwater, certainly with a complete emptying and refilling. There are two ways of removing a large volume of water from a pond without too much fuss.
Let it soak away in the garden: If you use a water pump with an output of 273 gallons (1,000 liters) per hour, the volume of water moved

Pontederia will require a soil consisting of a clay, sand, and peat mixture.

when emptying a small pond (about 820-1,090 gallons/3,000-4,000 liters) will soak away very easily in a normal, porous soil (lawn or flower bed) without creating a flood. Watch the pond constantly during the removal of the water so that you can intervene if it does not soak away quickly enough. The water must not be let penetrate your neighbors' gardens. Always let the water soak away a good bit before the boundary of your land. There should be no problems when removing only part of the water in your pond.
Using an outlet into the sewer: There is often the opportunity to conduct the water into the end of a downpipe from your roof gutter (house or garage). There is usually a water drain or gully at this point and sometimes you can push the hose into the downpipe or drain.

Responsibility for water damage
This is a very important point as far as you are concerned. If there is any damage, the conventional rule is that the person who built the pond and laid the water inlet or drainage line (whether this is the owner of the plot or a tenant) is the one who is liable. If a damaged water pipe or improper emptying of the pond leads to flooding of a neighbor's land, the responsible person pays the cost of the damage.

My tip: Check the water pipe regularly to make sure it is in order and, whenever you empty the pond, make sure no water is flowing onto a neighbor's land.

Cotton grass (Eriophorum), an ideal plant for the marginal area of the pond.

Controlling algae without the use of toxic substances

Algae do have a place in a pond. Without them the pond would be biologically dead. They fulfill important functions, such as supplying food for water snails and micro-organsims, and provide protection and a hiding place for fish. The algae should not, however, be let gain the upperhand.

The cause of excessive growth of algae is an accumulation of nutrients in the pond, caused by the decomposition of plants, animals, food, and excrement, as well as the addition of fertilizers.

Measures against excessive growth of algae

To keep algae growth within limits you must implement all of the measures mentioned below. One measure alone will not lead to success.

Plants: Employ marginal and water plants. They remove nutrients from the water, which will deprive the algae of their main source of food. Plants like *Elodea*, *Potamogeton*, or *Myriophyllum* (water milfoil) should be included when stocking your pond but do not plant too many.

As the growth of algae will increase with rising temperatures, shade-providing plants, like water lilies, *Nymphoides peltata* (water fringe), and other surface plants, will be useful aids in keeping the temperature of the water down.

Fish: Algae-eating fish, like grass carp (*Ctenopharyngodon idella*), silver carp (*Hypophthalmichthys molitrix*), and bitterling (*Rhodeus sericeus*), can be used to keep algae in check.

Water snails: If you introduce a few to your pond, they should not get out of hand as long as you do not feed the fish so much that remains of food sink to the bottom to provide extra food for the snails.

Care during the summer

The pond and pond plants will require only minimal care during the summer months; in the fall, when you are making preparations for overwintering, more is involved in the way of care.

Ornamental ponds: Regular checks, changing water, routine checking of water values, and a bit of care for the plants are all that is necessary.

Plants which proliferate vigorously will do so almost explosively in the spring, providing there are plenty of available nutrients. This may lead to the pond becoming overgrown, so that slow-growing plants, which do not flower until the fall, are smothered. Another thing that may happen is that the nutrient supply required by the fast-growing plants is suddenly used up, which will make the plants die off rather rapidly. The debris will then decompose very quickly and this can often lead to a biological collapse of the pond within a few days. Fast-growing plants should, therefore, be thinned out regularly during the summer.

● Cut off troublsome growth as close as possible to the source with a pruning knife or rose clippers.

● Floating plants which have spread too widely can be fished out by hand or with a hand net.

Nature ponds: Only replenish water that has evaporated and, if necessary, thin out wildly proliferating plants. If the temperature of the water rises above 68°F (20°C), I urgently recommend supplying extra oxygen.

When building and caring for the pond, the following points should be borne in mind:

● Design your pond in such a way that remains of lawn fertilizer are not washed into the pond every time it rains.

● Routinely check the pH factor of the water and, if necessary, regulate it.

● Supply sufficient air. The more air that is pumped into the pond with an air pump, the more carbon dioxide is pushed out and the cooler the water will become.

● Carefully remove existing algae (long clumps and cotton wool-like formations).

● A running stream is recommended as a biological filter.

Unsuitable measures: I would strongly advise against using chemical agents to control algae growth. These contain toxins that provide only temporary relief in removing algae, which will quickly grow back again.

Overwintering of the pond

When the temperature of the water falls below 54°F (12°C) in the fall, the leaves will change color and start falling, and it is now time to carry out several measures to ensure that both fish and plants survive the winter safely.

Preparing an ornamental pond for winter

The most important signal for the start of fall care is the temperature of the water. When it drops below 54°F (12°C), most fish will stop feeding.

Removing some of the pond water: You will have to remove a good two-thirds of the pond water before you can begin your preparations for the winter.

Catching the fish: As soon as the

water has been removed, take out the fish and any amphibians (frogs and newts, etc.). These creatures are easy to catch in shallow water with the help of a net or even with your hand if you are gentle.

Be careful: the sensitive mucous membranes of fish must not be injured. Immediately place the fish (not the amphibians, which would drown!) in a large, water-filled container (a bathtub or aquarium). The water should be provided with plenty of oxygen (use an air pump). Cover the container with a cloth as the fish might otherwise leap out because they have been scared by the catching procedure. Do not use a hard cover, which might injure the fish if they leap against it.

NB: Release the amphibians in a secure, damp, sheltered position near the pond.

Clearing out the pond: Decaying processes during the winter rest period might seriously lower the quality of the water. For this reason, everything that might decay during the winter should be removed from the pond.

● Stand all planting baskets by the edge of the pond. This will make it easier to work in the pond.

● The bottom sludge, which contains decomposed plant matter and other debris, should be completely removed if possible.

● The algae along the edge of the pond should be scrubbed off with a brush.

● Cut back all vigorously proliferating plants by four-fifths; they will start shooting again in the spring.

● Some plants (like water lilies), which have roots that grow as rhizomes, bulbs, or tubers, will need special care.

● Please note the tips on care for individual species.

Filling the pond again: After completing all the work, the pond can

be filled with fresh water. The water should be treated with a suitable agent (obtainable from aquarium suppliers).

Preparing the pond for overwintering

Change one-third of the water. The best way is to let the pond run over slowly. Only very large nature ponds, with a surface area of more than 538 sq ft (50 sq m) should be left without any preparation for the winter. In the case of a small nature pond, more care will be necessary; otherwise it would silt up or even dry up within a few years' time.

Care of water lilies

The rhizome of the water lily is constantly growing at the tip and decaying somewhere else. It will, therefore, always smell rather strongly of rotten eggs. When the water lily root is submerged in the pond, however, you cannot smell it and it does not affect the beauty or health of the plant.

Care: Water lilies (and all other plants with rhizomes) must be transplanted in the fall.

● Cut back the rhizome by a third and remove all decaying parts with a sharp knife.

● Remove leaves, flowers, and stalks. Do not cut off any embryonic leaves or flowers that are already present in the fall. The young leaves are rolled up and shaped like arrowheads.

● Plant the rhizome again, in a larger planting basket if necessary.

● Hardy species can be planted in the deepest part of the pond.

● More sensitive species should be overwintered in a frost-free position, covered with dead leaves, preferably in a cool cellar. Check the rootstocks occasionally, as decaying parts should be removed.

Propagating: Water lilies are easy to propagate in the fall. Divide the rhizome between the buds (where shoots will grow) with a sharp knife. The buds are shield-shaped, usually triangular, and about the size of a fingernail. Set the divided rhizome pieces in planting baskets.

Care of bulbous or tuber-like roots
The bulbous or tuber-like swellings of the root system must not be damaged as the rootstock would then quickly decay and the plant will die.
Care: In the case of perennials, remove only the leaves in the fall, then carefully remove the young tubers and set them in a planting

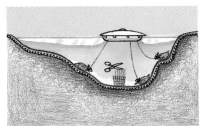

After preparing the pond and the other plants, place the baskets of water lilies in the deepest part of the pond and insert a device for keeping a hole in the ice.

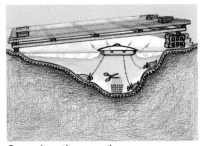

Covering the pond
Lay the air pump hose in a medium-deep part of the pond. Stand a lattice brick at the northern edge of the pond. Arrange wooden rafters in a grid pattern and lay a transparent corrugated plastic sheet over them.

basket. In the case of annuals, like *Sagittaria sagittifolia* (arrowhead), the mother plant, which dies in the fall, is removed and the young tubers are planted.

Overwintering fish in a pond

If your fish are to overwinter in a pond, measures must be taken to ensure that the fish survive the winter safely. Even if you were to adopt only one of the measures described below, this would benefit the fish and the entire pond. The best results will be obtained, however, if you combine several of the measures or even use all of them.
NB: All overwintering measures will also benefit pond visitors that overwinter in the water (such as dragon-fly larvae, snails, and frogs).
Warning: If the deep-water zone is less than 28 in (70 cm) deep, you should overwinter the fish in an aquarium. In order to find out how to do this, you must consult a book on aquariums or seek advice from an aquarium expert.

Covering the pond
In my experience, the ideal overwintering measure is to cover the pond with transparent material. This will help to utilize the sun's warmth, just as in a cold frame or greenhouse.
The time for covering up is before the leaves begin to fall from the trees. This will prevent the wind from depositing large quantities of leaves in the pond.
Covering material: glass, plexiglass, or corrugated plastic. Corrugated, transparent plastic is very stable and tough and can be rolled up when not in use (saving storage space during the summer). It can be obtained from builders' merchants in various widths (up to 15 ft/4.5 m).

Method (see illustration left)
● Place the covering over the pond at an angle so that rainwater will run off the upper side and condensation can run off the under side, and so that a slight but vital amount of ventilation is assured.
● The slope of the covering should face south.
● Weigh down the edges of the covering with lattice bricks.
● In regions that experience frequent falls of slushy snow, support widths of corrugated plastic that are longer than 8 ft 4 in (2.5 m) with lengths of wood (1 by 2 in/24 by 48 mm). Arrange the lengths of wood like a grid, spacing them 24-32 in (60-80 cm) apart.
Care: Sweep off thick layers of wet, slushy snow. Powdery snow can be left, as it is an excellent additional insulator which will considerably hinder ice formation on top of the pond.

Keeping a hole free of ice
If you can keep part of the surface of the pond free of ice all winter, by using a pond heater or ice-preventer, you will ensure an adequate supply of oxygen.

An oxygen supply during the winter
If you have a covered pond containing few fish, you need not necessarily add oxygen (although it is better if you do). However, you will have to provide additional oxygen if:
● a covered pond is stocked with lots of overwintering fish;
● the pond is not covered.
Air pump: Blowing in air will provide the pond with necessary oxygen and will hinder constant freezing up.

• Lay the air hose in a medium deep part of the pond. If air is blown in at the deepest part, a rather strong current would be created in the pond. This would be stressful for the fish and they would tend to lose condition.

My tip: Hang the air pump up in a heated room so that warmer air is pumped into the pond. Again, this will hinder rapid freezing over of the pond.

Oxygenator: This can provide up to three months' supply of oxygen under the ice, but it will not keep a hole open in the ice as an air pump will.

What you should not do!
Never hammer a hole in the ice cover. You will only succeed in disturbing the dormancy of fish and other pond creatures. It would probably frighten them so much that they would start swimming around in a panic and might injure themselves badly. Never throw polystyrene, twigs, bundles of straw, or automobile tires into the pond to prevent freezing up. This would do more harm than good.

Pond care in the spring

If you have prepared your pond properly for the winter, just a few measures will be necessary in spring to prepare it for the summer.
• Check the reinforcement of the banks and secure loose stones or paving stones.
• Check the drainage and make sure it is not clogged with decomposing leaves.
• Check all gadgets to make sure they are functioning properly.
• Resume use of the filter or stream.
• Lower the water lilies gradually, at intervals of one week.
• Test the water and, if necessary, regulate.
• In the first month of spring, add plants if required.
• When the temperature of the water rises above 50°F (10°C), start feeding the fish that have overwintered in the pond.
• Do not put fish that overwintered in an aquarium back into the pond until the difference in temperature between the aquarium and the pond water is only a few degrees. Reintroduce the fish into shallow water!

Problems can appear in spring if you neglected to care for the pond in the fall. It is quite likely that not all of the pondlife will have survived if your pond was not properly prepared for winter. If you have been negligent, by early spring the oxygen content of the water will be so low that you really must take measures, during the last month of winter and in early spring, to prevent the biological collapse of the pond and damage to the fish.

Danger signal! You must act quickly if the fish come up to the surface to gasp for air as they may end up freezing to the still existing ice cover. Take the following action:

• Immediately blow in oxygen and thaw the ice at the relevant place with a stream of water.
• Let fresh water into the pond very slowly!
• Remove the ice cover. It will be lifted up by the rising water level, so it can easily be broken and lifted off.
• Afterward, let more water run in and, by letting the pond run over, gradually exchange the water in the pond.
• Fish out any sludge that rises to the surface, using a net.
• On no account feed the fish, even if they are swimming around at the top. As soon as the oxygen situation has normalized, they will return to the deeper regions of the pond until the temperature of the water rises.

How to indentify and control problems

Symptoms	Possible causes	Remedy
The water is transparent but amber-colored. New leaves of plants are slightly reddish (for example, the submerged leaves of arrowhead).	The nitrite and nitrate contents are too high; the pH value is too low, probably below 6; too much humic acid caused by too much peat; large quantities of dead leaves in the water.	Slow change of water; for three days running, change one-third of the water; check the nitrite and nitrate contents and the pH factor; if the nitrite content is too high, use a water-improving agent. Remove peat and dead leaves.
The water is transparent but amber-colored, rising bubbles do not burst immediately at the surface. If oxygen is added, foam forms. The fish are swimming at the surface, gasping for air and "swaying." The plants are losing leaves; the water lilies are no longer flowering properly.	The pond is overloaded with harmful substances; dying plants, algae, and excrement are being broken down by bacteria as not enough movement is taking place in the deeper levels of the water; oxygen-poor deep-water zone where the plants are short of oxygen around their roots.	Vigorous airing is required (air pump); thin out plants; remove algae; change one-third of the water; fish out decomposed leaf remains lying on the surface using a wide-mesh net.
The water is the color of white coffee; all levels of the water are cloudy. The plants are growing well. The goldfish are well, but all other fish are dying.	Too many carp-like fish churning the bottom up because they are getting too much food; the carbon dioxide content of the water is too high (oxygen for fish is sufficient). Possibly, sand or humus has got into the pond.	Clean out filters and the course of a stream; almost complete change of water; vigorous airing to get rid of excessive carbon dioxide; use an oxygenator.
The water is bright green. The plants are growing well. The fish are thriving.	Explosive proliferation of *Volvox* spp. (a single-cell organism containing chlorophyll).	Silver carp eat *Volvox*, or use an oxygenator. Introduce fresh water mussels. *NB:* Chemical water-cleaning agents may cause biological collapse.
The water is clear in the morning, but becomes milky and cloudy toward the evening in the upper levels. The plants are thriving. The fish are having trouble breathing, swim close to the surface, and gasp for air.	Explosive proliferation of micro-organisms.	Do not change the water; vigorous airing required. In minor cases, lowering the pH factor with peat may help; otherwise use a chemical water-cleaning agent (follow the directions meticulously). *Warning:* These agents are toxic. Store them in a safe place as they must be kept away from children and pets!

The stream – a biological filter

The best and most natural filter for a pond is a slow-flowing stream which rises near the pond or somewhere in the vicinity and then runs into the pond. It also creates additional habitats for many green and flowering plants and numerous animals. Even if you have only a small pond, it is no great problem to install a stream to provide clean water for the pond.

The functions of a stream

As a biological filter: A stream that has been properly designed and constructed, with plenty of plants on its banks, has a cleansing effect on an ornamental or nature pond and improves the living conditions for animals and plants. Waste particles are captured in it, and the bacteria living in the stream break down such organic waste into nutrients that can be used immediately by plants. When the stream is full of running water, from spring to the fall, it will admirably fulfil its purpose as a biological filter.

As a habitat, it is a magnet for many animals. Frogs, toads, newts, dragonflies, and butterflies will find plenty of food in and around the stream, along with suitable places for breeding. As these visitors would find it hard to survive over long periods of time in an ornamental pond stocked with goldfish, the stream is a good way to invite them to make a home in your garden.

Planning the course of the stream

The course of a stream will have to be planned and built just as carefully as a pond if it is to fulfil its function.

Calculating the length of the stream: The stream must be of a certain length in order to act as a biological filter. The required length will depend on the volume of water in your pond.

Equipment for constructing a stream

a long garden hose;
PVC lining or ready-molded sections;
silicon adhesive or other welding substances;
gravel (¼-⅜-in/5-7-mm-sized-pieces);
quartz gravel or similar;
material for constructing a small waterfall;
a stream pump;
plants;
planting baskets.

General rule

When calculating the length of the stream, estimate 5 ft (1.5 m) per cubic yard (meter) (273 gallons/1,000 liters) of water. A pond with a surface measuring 64 sq ft (6 sq m) will contain about 5 ¼ cu yd (4 cu m) (1,090 gallons/4,000 liters) of water, so the stream should be 20 ft (6 m) long.

The width and depth of the stream: The best measuring device is a spade. The bed of the stream should be one spade's depth (about 10 in/25 cm) and two spades' width (about 20 in/50 cm).

Course: Do not be perturbed by the required length of the stream. In most gardens a stream measuring 20 ft (6 m) in length (or longer) is easy to accommodate. For example, you can lead the stream right around the pond, along a fence or in S-bends around trees. Work out the future course of the stream by laying out a long garden hose.

Insulating materials: there are several possibilities.
● PVC pond lining is excellent.
● Ready-made parts, made of fiber glass or natural sandstone, or basin-like shapes, which are basins linked together to form a stream.
● I would advise against all other materials, like clay or concrete, as they create far too much work.

The gradient: If you use PVC pond lining material or pre-molded basins, you will have to provide a gradient. The natural sandstone basins can be slotted into each other in such a way that they create a gradient.

How to build the course

The following directions apply to the building of a stream using PVC lining material. The information given here is also applicable to artificial basins.

A stream with kingcups (marsh marigolds) and a mass of Primula.

Constructing a gradient

The gradient is very important when laying the bed of the stream as the water is pumped from the pond into the beginning of the stream and will have to flow slowly downhill, along the course of the stream, and back into the pond without any additional means of power supply.

The right gradient: A gradient of 10 in (25 cm) for a distance of 10 ft (3 m) or 20 in (50 cm) for a length of 20 ft (6 m) is quite adequate.
If the water is intended to flow into the pond via a small waterfall, raise the beginning of the stream farther, so that there is enough gradient at the end of the route to create a waterfall.

Earthworks: Before you begin to move any earth, you should lay out the course of the stream using a rope and some small wooden pegs.

● In most gardens, the only way to create the necessary gradient is to build a mound. The earth you have dug out for building the pond is ideal for this purpose.

● If a natural gradient already exists (if your garden is on a slope), digging a trench along the course will direct the flow of the stream.

Building the bed of the stream: On the mound or slope, dig the bed of the stream to one spade's depth.

Installing a waterfall: My advice is to install a small waterfall at the mouth of the stream. The enormous quantities of bacteria that will colonize the stream and perform valuable filtering services, will also create a surplus of carbon dioxide in the water.

If this water, now saturated with carbon dioxide, were let flow back into the pond, it would lead to excessive growth of algae. A small waterfall installed at the end of the stream will drive out any surplus carbon dioxide and supply the water with oxygen.

My tip: If you really do not want a waterfall, lay a few stones the size of tennis balls in the stream; they will provide plenty of turbulence so that enough oxygen is mixed with the water.

Securing the banks: This is advisable, particularly if the subsoil is fairly soft and at bends in the stream where the soil will tend to be washed away. You can build a bank with the earth dug out of the stream bed. The banks can be secured with:
● stones;
● large boulders;
● vertically buried lengths of rounded wood.

How to insulate the stream with PVC lining
The lining should be laid in the same way as described for the pond.
Measuring the lining material: Again, the best aid is your garden hose.
● Measure the width by first laying

Building the course of a stream
Line the bed with PVC pond liner. Reinforce the banks with stones. Fill the bed with filling material (gravel). Lay a few stones (the size of tennis balls) in the bed of the stream.

the hose across the stream bed.
● Measure the piece of hose with a measuring tape.
● Very important: add 12 in (30 cm) of lining material along the edges on both sides, just as you did for the pond.
● Now measure the length of the stream with the help of your hose. Add another 40 in (1 m) at the end, so that you may be sure the length of lining material will be sufficient.
Joining the lengths of lining material: If you are prepared to add a little to the cost of purchase, you may be able to leave the joining of the lengths of PVC lining to the manufacturer. If you wish to do it yourself, make sure, when it comes to welding the lengths together, that you follow the directions meticulously, specially any recommended safety precautions.
Joining the lining of the stream bed to the pond lining material: At the mouth of the stream, the stream lining will have to be joined to the pond lining with great care. No water should be let leak away as this would cause the pond to lose considerable amounts of water. There is no need to do any joining at the beginning of the stream's course.

Filling material and reinforcing the banks
Before securing the lining material at the edges of the stream, you must install the filling material on the bed of the stream. This is the first step toward turning the stream into a filter. The filling material provides the same function as a mechanical filter by trapping particles of debris as they are carried downstream by the water. This additional biological effect of the stream should have begun about two weeks after the stream begins to flow. Bacteria colonize the filling

Placing plants in the stream
Set the plants in narrow, rectangular baskets. Bury them in the gravel, alternating them, as close to the bank as possible.

material and then break down the trapped organic debris in such a way that it can be used as nutrients by the plants.
Suitable filling materials:
● gravel (grains of ¼-⅜ in/5-7 mm);
● quartz pebbles.
Warning: Do not use limestone gravel. If water runs through limestone gravel, this may, in the long run, have a detrimental effect on the pH factor by driving it up too high.
Sources: You can obtain cleaned filling material from garden suppliers, which can be used at once. If you buy material from builders' merchants, you will have to wash it yourself before use.
Quantity: You will need about 55 pounds (25 kg) of filling material per yard (meter) of the stream's length. The stream bed is filled up in such a way that the top edges of planting baskets will later be submerged in the filling material.
Trial run: Before burying the lining material at the edges of the stream, do a trial run by letting water run down the stream.
● With the help of a pump and a connecting hose, run water into the stream.
● Observe the rate of flow. The stream should flow slowly. If it flows too fast, it will lose part of the filtering effect.
● By making the bed of the stream

deeper, you can speed up the flow; by making the bed more shallow, you can slow it down.

● Now is the time to make any necessary corrections to the edges of the stream.

Fixing the lining material to the edges of the stream: There must be no capillary action along the edges of the stream. The lining material should be laid over the stones or rounded wood sections used for securing the banks, then buried along the edge so that the ends of the material are pointing upward. You can place plants along the edges of the stream or let a lawn grow over them.

Installation of a water pump

The water supply of the stream is ensured by means of a water pump.
Position: It should be set up as far as possible from the pond end of the stream. The length of hose from the pump to the beginning of the stream should be as short as possible. If the pump were to be situated too close to the mouth of the stream, it would suck in the already-filtered stream water and very little of the dirty pond water would end up in the stream.

The output of the pump: The stream should flow very slowly. The faster it flows, the less filtering will take place. For this reason, stream pumps with an output of between 98 gallons (360 liters) at 6 watts and 55 gallons (200 liters) at 19 watts are quite sufficient.
The low-voltage pumps described are also very suitable for powering the stream.

Unsuitable pumps: With their huge output, fountain pumps would churn the stream up so much that the filtering effect would be lost and the filling material would be washed

into the stream. The stream would also rise and overflow, so that the pond would soon be empty.

Plants along the stream

The stream would not be complete as a biological filter if there were no plants in it. The substances broken down by bacteria in the water have to be utilized by plants in the stream; otherwise there would be an excess of nutrients in the pond, which would create an increased growth of algae. If your stream is to be a perfect biological filter, you cannot be stingy with plants.

Suitable plants: Many attractive marginal plants are suitable for a stream too. Choose fast-growing, medium-tall plants that can tolerate regular cutting back of leaves near the roots. Suitable stream plants

are water crowfoot, irises, cotton grass, lemon balm, water mint, forget-me-not, dwarf bulrushes, rushes, sedges, branched bur-reed, creeping-Jenny, and arrowhead.

Planting: Good planting soil is provided by a soil mixture that is poor in nutrients (sand and clay in equal parts).

● Set the plants in narrow, rectangular planting baskets (obtainable from garden centers).

● Sink the baskets into the filling material in the stream as close to the banks as possible and alternate them, so that two baskets are never opposite each other.
This arrangement will ensure that the water does not flow straight down the middle of the stream but has to meander around each basket, which extends its path and slows down the rate of flow.

Plants for your stream

Brooklime (*Veronica beccabunga*) 8-12 in (20-30 cm) tall, prostrate growth. Blue flowers from late spring until early fall.
Purple loosestrife (*Lythrum salicaria*) (see photos, inside front cover and back cover)
Up to 48 in (1.20 m) tall, flowers from mid summer until early fall, blood red, usually over 4 in (10 cm) long.
Yellow loosestrife (*Lysimachia vulgaris*)
Up to 5 ft (1.5 m) tall. Brilliant yellow flowers from early until late summer. Thin out in the summer; cut back radically in the fall.
Sweet flag (*Acorus calamus*)
Up to 32 in (80 cm) tall. Only flowers occasionally in temperate climates, from early to midsummer. Flowers small and greenish.

Arrowhead (*Sagittaria sagittifolia*)
Arrow-shaped leaves. Flowers from early to midsummer, rarely later; white to reddish on a robust stalk. Only the bulb-like root clump overwinters, the rest of the plant dies (remove in the fall).
Marsh marigold or kingcup (*Caltha palustris*)

Forms cushions that are usually 8 in (20 cm), rarely 20 in (50 cm) tall. Yellow flowers from mid-spring to early summer. Important: do not remove the dead foliage until the spring.
Water mint (*Mentha aquatica*)
Grows up to 24 in (60 cm) above the surface of the water; the 1¼-in (3-cm) leaves smell of peppermint when rubbed. Lilac to violet flowers from mid- to late summer. Remove the plants as far as possible in the fall.

Overwintering the stream

In summer the stream will require no special care. If necessary, you can thin out the plants occasionally if they proliferate too much.

My tip: During the warmer part of the year, if possible, do not ever switch off the pump that runs the stream, or, if you do, not for any length of time, as the stream would then no longer function well as a biological filter. In as short a time as two or three hours, the bacteria would die through lack of oxygen.

In the fall, when you are preparing your pond for winter, the stream should be turned off.
● Turn off the pump and remove it from the pond.
● Cut back the plants and thin them out.
● Place the fish in the pond or in a cold-water aquarium.
Early in spring, clean the stream out before starting it again, as decaying matter will have accumulated on the bottom during the course of the winter.
● Rinse the filling material on the bottom of the stream bed with a vigorous stream of water from a hose.
● After cleaning the stream, pump one-third of the water out of the pond and then let fresh water run in slowly. This means that a large amount of the dirty, cloudy water will immediately be removed from the pond.
● Connect up the stream pump and pump water into the stream.
● If necessary, change another third of the pond water.

An ornamental pond with goldfish
A pond like this is an ideal environment for the most popular pond fish, the goldfish, which can be obtained in many colorful varieties.

Fish and other inhabitants of a garden pond

Gleaming goldfish, colourful koi, or less-exotic native fish will bring life to your pond. With the right selection of fish and proper food and care, you should have many years' pleasure from your fish. In addition, if you are able to provide the right habitat for them, a few visitors may also turn up and even make themselves at home, like frogs, newts, toads, dragonflies, butterflies, and other fascinating creatures.

Tips on buying fish

The best place to buy fish for your garden pond is at an aquarium supplier.
Goldfish and koi, the most popular garden-pond fish, are regularly for sale in garden centers or aquarium suppliers, or they may be able to obtain them for you.
Other fish, like *Leucaspius delineatus* or *Phoxinus phoxinus* (minnow), are more difficult to get hold of. Ask your local aquarium supplier if he or she can find you healthy, suitable fish. Never go to catch fish in the wild. Many indigenous fish are protected by law. In addition, wild specimens usually have a hard time getting used to conditions in a garden pond.
Some basic points to watch out for when buying fish:
● Find out first about the requirements of the fish you wish to keep (ask an aquarium supplier or consult a good book on keeping freshwater fish).
● If other pond owners offer you fish, do not just look at the fish but also take a look at the pond where they live – the symptoms of a "sick pond."
● Fish for consumption and bait fish do not belong in a garden pond. Fish used for bait are usually infested with disease.

Tips on choosing fish

The number, size and lifestyle of the fish will be important factors when you are choosing fish, particularly if you are putting together a community of different species.

How many fish to have?
You will find tables of recommended fish stocks. These communities of fish should thrive in a well-cared-for ornamental pond. You should, however, restrict yourself to only a few fish in a nature pond.

Fascinating fish which will feel right at home in a well-cared-for garden pond.

Fish for your garden pond

1. Three-spined stickleback
(Gasterosteus aculeatus). The male's under side turns brilliant red (see photo) at spawning time. This fish has three spines which it can raise in front of its dorsal fin. Predatory, so do not introduce more than two couples to your pond. Acclimatizing is a little difficult for this species. Will eat anything it can swallow!

2. Goldfish (Carassius auratus). The most popular of all pond fish. There are many breeding varieties, which differ in color and the shape of their bodies and fins. Keep them as a shoal. Excellent biological filtering is necessary. Omnivorous, will eat animals or plants, and like commercial fishfood. Reproduction is problem-free in a garden pond.

3. Minnow (Phoxinus phoxinus). The male displays a red belly and edges to its lips during spawning time (see photo). Keep as a shoal. Very suitable for small ponds. Eats insects, their larvae and small crustaceans. Protected species in the wild!

4. Leucaspius delineatus. Keep in small shoals. Does not like water containing lime. Eats insects, their larvae, small crustaceans, submerged algae.

5. Golden orfe, a variety bred from the orfe (Leuciscus idus). Keep in a small shoal. Good insect eater. Eats everything, mainly flying insects (crane flies).

6. Bitterling (Rhodeus sericeus). Introduce at least four to six specimens. Eats insect larvae (mosquito and midge larvae), likes commercial fishfood. Needs freshwater shellfish for its reproductive cycle. The wild European species are protected.

The lifestyles of fish

Fish are divided into two groups, depending on their habits – predatory and non-predatory fish. Both groups can live together in one pond, but in a small pond you will have to keep an eye on the numbers of fish and maintain the correct ratio (see tables right).

Predatory fish: Introduce them only in pairs (and keep only a few pairs).

Non-predatory fish: introduce a small shoal. The shoal will provide protection against enemies. Only if a fish is too slow or too sick to swim with the shoal will it fall prey to the predatory fish.

Shoals of fish in a garden pond

Introduce at least ten specimens of one species. For example, if you introduce too few orfe, they will remain shy and stay in the deeper water all the time. If you want lots of different species of fish, you should restrict yourself to one shoal of orfe and introduce only a few other species.

Leucaspius delineatus and rudd (*Scardinius erythrophthalmus*) will feel quite comfortable in a shoal of orfe; koi (Japanese carp) will enjoy swimming with a shoal too (see table right, non-predatory fish).

Useful fish

When choosing fish you should not forget those species that are extremely useful in a pond on account of their food intake.

Algae eaters: Algae-eating fish will keep the growth of algae in your pond in check. I know of three different algae-eating species, each of which specializes by eating different types of algae:

● the grass carp (*Ctenopharyngodon idella*) eats all species of filamentous algae;

● the silver carp

(*Hypophthalmichthys molitrix*) eats submerged algae;

● the bitterling (*Rhodeus sericeus*) eats blue algae.

NB: If, temporarily, there is not enough algae in the pond to satisfy these fish, they will also eat commercially produced fish food.

Insect eaters: Insects are an important source of food for some fish, which keeps the numbers of insects in and around the pond in check.

● Golden orfe live mainly on flying insects. Their favorite food is mosquitos and crane flies.

● Gudgeon (*Gobio gobio*) eat dragonfly larvae and diving beetle larvae.

● *Leucaspius delineatus* lives on flying insects and particles of algae.

Feeding fish

Feeding the fish is just as much fun for adults as it is for children but you can quickly overdo things. Incorrect feeding may lead to disturbances in the natural balance of the pond, so you should observe several important rules and also explain to your children how to feed the fish correctly.

Suitable food: Commercially produced fish food (flakes or feeding sticks), which is specially prepared for garden-pond fish, can be obtained from aquarium suppliers. Species of fish which prefer animal food can be offered live food occasionally. This can be fresh, freeze-dried, or deep frozen, and is also obtainable from aquarium suppliers.

Harmful food: stale bread and kitchen refuse of any kind. If you give the fish live food, do not give them *Tubifex* spp. (worms) as they are carriers of dangerous diseases.

Fish stocks
Non-predatory and predatory fish

Size of pond: 64 sq ft (6 sq m)

Species	Number	Details
golden orfe	10	non-predatory, insect eater;
stickleback	4	predatory, territorial;
grass carp	3	non-predatory, algae eater;
gudgeon	2	predatory;
bitterling	4	non-predatory, tends young;
Leucaspius delineatus	5	non-predatory, insect and algae eater;
pumpkinseed fish	8	predatory, interesting mating habits.

Fish stocks
Non-predatory fish

Size of pond: 64 sq ft (6 sq m)

Species	Number	Details
golden orfe	20	insect eater (flying insects);
grass carp	4	algae eater (filamentous algae);
silver carp	2	algae eater (submerged algae);
goldfish	4	no problems reproducing;
gudgeon	2	eats dragonfly larvae and larvae of diving beetles;
bitterling	4	interesting care of young;
koi	3	colorful ornamental fish.

A properly built and well-established garden pond offers food and shelter to many other animals.

Visitors in and around a garden pond

1. **Dragonfly** larvae live entirely in water during their very long period of development. When they emerge to metamorphose, the nymphs crawl up the stem of a plant and unfold their wings as splendid dragonflies.

2. **Great diving beetle** (Dytiscus marginalis). A diving beetle which can also fly very well. It sticks the back of its body out of the water at short intervals to take in oxygen.

3. **Smooth newt** (Trituris vulgaris). Prefers areas of ponds that are full of plants and weed. Will also live in streams. Lives on insects, earthworms, and small water creatures. Overwinters on land.

4. **Common frog** (Rana temporaria). Likes living in company; can often be seen sunbathing. Lives on insects, worms, snails, and small invertebrates. Overwinters in the pond.

5. **The pond skater** (Gerris lacustris) lives on the surface of the water. It moves in a jerky, staggered way when hunting its prey – small insects that have fallen into the water. Overwinters on land.

6. **Common backswimmer** or **water boatman** (Notonecta glauca). Swims on its back; flies very well. Lives on small water creatures and fish fry. Overwinters in the pond.

7. **Swan mussel** (Anodonta cygnaea). The largest European freshwater pond mussel. Lives on tiny creatures which it filters out of the water. It provides a spawning place and nursery for bitterling. Overwinters in the pond.

8. **Common toad** (Bufo bufo). The most common species of toad. Overwinters on land.

Feeding the fish: You can feed them several times a day, but only offer as much food as they will eat immediately. The food should never end up sinking to the bottom of the pond.

● Give the food slowly and in small quantities, so that you can see if the fish really eat it all.

● Never give them extra food. Even if you have forgotten to feed them for two or three days, the fish will not starve to death. The pond contains plenty of food.

Important: As soon as the temperature of the water drops below 54°F (12°C), you will have to stop feeding.

Refusal to feed: If the fish sometimes refuse to take the food, do not worry. They have probably stuffed themselves on food that occurs naturally in their pond (insects, plants). However, note how long they refuse to take fish food. Refusal to eat can be a symptom of disease!

Sick fish

Fish will rarely become ill in a well-cared-for pond. However, organisms that cause disease can be brought to the pond by newly bought fish, or by birds or insects that have also visited an infested pond in your neighborhood.

Fungi and parasites
About 90% of all diseases in garden-pond fish are due to fungi or parasites.

Symptoms: Fungal infections are characterized by cotton-wool-like layers on the body or fins. Parasites show as whitish, spotted, rice-grain-like attachments or cloudy-looking skin; the fish can be seen rubbing against plant stalks and showing oddly uncoordinated movements and will refuse to feed.

Treatment: You should be able to obtain the right medication from aquarium suppliers or a veterinarian, who will be pleased to advise you if you describe the symptoms you have observed as exactly as possible.

Care of sick fish: The fish should always be treated in the pond. A sick fish may have already infected others without your knowledge, so the entire pond has to be treated. Naturally, dead fish should be removed at once.

How to treat fish: Before putting the medication into the water, change half of the water.

● Treat the fresh water carefully; treatment agents can be obtained from aquarium suppliers.

● Make sure additional oxygen is provided with the help of an air pump or an oxygenator.

● Check that the filter is in good working order.

● Do not feed the fish for a week.

● When using medication, stick to the directions given.

Following treatment:

● Do not immediately change the water. Wait for about two weeks, then change a maximum of one-third of the water three times at intervals of one week.

● Prepare the fresh water with only half of the recommended dose of medication (read the directions).

Warning: Never put cooking salt or lime into the pond! These old home remedies will endanger life in the whole pond.

Making visitors welcome

The garden pond and marginal area will provide food and shelter for many animals. However, you can do a little more for these visitors to your pond if you make the vicinity compatible with the lifestyle of amphibians (frogs, newts, and toads), birds and insects. A few simple measures will help.

Dead twigs: Pile up large and small branches and twigs near the bank, with dead leaves, grass cuttings, and compost on top. This will provide a hiding place for frogs, newts, and toads, which only spend part of their time in the water during their reproductive cycle. Here they will find rich pickings in the way of earthworms and insects.
Hedgehogs will also be grateful for a home in a pile of dead twigs and leaves.

Stones and rotting pieces of wood: If left near a pond or in a quiet spot in the garden, these will attract visitors to your garden pond.

Bird bath: What would a garden be without birds? Choose a clear space for the bird bath. There should be no shrubs or bushes in the immediate vicinity of it because when birds are drinking or bathing, they become so preoccupied that they often relax their natural watchfulness and may easily fall prey to a cat lurking in the nearby bushes.

Protection of amphibians: You can obtain detailed information on the protection of toads and other amphibians from local nature protection groups or books on the care and protection of amphibians.

NOTES

Success with

Hanging Baskets
and
Trailing Plants

MARTIN WEIMAR

Series Editor:
LESLEY YOUNG

Foreword

Many people love the idea of a hanging garden on their balcony or patio and it is not at all difficult to design and create an overhead display of flowers and scented herbs in a favorite corner or above a garden seat. In this useful guide, Martin Weimar shows you how to transform your balcony or patio with the help of hanging baskets, boxes, and other interesting plant containers.

There are lots of practical tips on securing the containers and on ways of grouping plants in them, as well as advice on the right way to water your plants and on overwintering them. Full-color step-by-step illustrations show the correct way to do all that is necessary to create a lovely, year-round display. The section on design suggests attractive ways of grouping plants and the instructions given are easy for a novice gardener to follow. The book is divided into sections on sun-loving, semi-shade-loving and shade-loving plants to enable you to choose the right plants for each site.

Contents

The herbs in this basket smell delicious in the sunshine.

Petunias.

Patience-plants.

The author
Martin Weimar is a gardener and flower artist who has contributed to numerous art exhibitions. For many years he has given courses on designing with plants and has written several successful guides on this subject.

The photographer
Jürgen Stork has worked as a freelance photographer since 1982, mainly in the areas of fashion, advertising and nature. He has contributed photographs to many periodicals and to many of the titles in the "Success with" gardening series.

The illustrator
Renate Holzner lives in Regensburg and works as a freelance illustrator and graphic designer. Her wide range extends from line drawings to photo-realistic computer graphics. Among her regular clients are many well-known publishing companies.

Hanging flowers

There is no reason why flowering plants should remain firmly rooted in the ground. With a little help from you your plants can conquer the heights on airy balconies and patios.

Photo above: Patience-plants are decorative in shady places.
Photo left: Rudbeckia, lobelia, ivy, and patience-plant waiting to be planted in baskets.

Hanging flowers

Cascades of flowers on different levels

Many people would love to accommodate more and more plants on a balcony or patio that is already packed with luxuriant greenery but are not sure where to fit them in. Do not despair: there is more room – above your head – and this guide will show you a multitude of possibilities for adding to your plant collection. You can design attractive arrangements in hanging baskets or even plant them in your own individually designed plant containers. If you choose the right plants and care for them properly, your overhead garden will turn into a feast for the eye and can even provide food for the table.

The Hanging Gardens of Babylon

One of the seven wonders of the ancient world was the legendary garden that Semiramis, Queen of Babylon, is supposed to have created some 3,000 years ago. She built the famous Hanging Gardens of Babylon, so the story goes, to remind her of the beautiful mountainous area that she came from. The gardens were built on a slope, in many step-like terraces, one above the other.
You could design a hanging garden of your own on a balcony

or patio, for example with a plant stair (photo, right) or by using a table covered in flowering plants.

Beauty for every season

Annual plants are ideal for planting in a hanging garden. During the course of a single year, these plants will grow and flourish and will often bloom continuously throughout a whole season. In addition, with annuals, the trouble of overwintering is avoided. Each season different plant groupings can be put together to take full advantage of their flowering times.
Spring flowers, like pansies, forget-me-nots, primroses, or wallflowers, are ideal for an early, frost-hardy arrangement.
Summer flowers, like petunias, pelargoniums, or lobelias can be planted after the last cold snap of late spring. They make an attractive eye-catching feature during the summer months. When fall arrives, they can be removed or, depending on the type of plant, overwintered in frost-free conditions.

Fall plants like *Erica*, chrysanthemums or asters will cope with a few degrees of frost. Many spring-flowering plants are offered for sale as early as the previous fall. With the correct care during the winter, they will remain hardy and

present a continuous display from fall until late spring.

Perennial planting

A hanging garden of perennials can be maintained for many years. This will, of course, require a certain amount of attention to correct care and overwintering. Many hardy perennials will flower for only a short while but will continue to look good for the rest of the time because of their attractive green foliage.

Planning ahead

You will be able to enjoy your planting arrangements without any real problems if you consider some important points before you begin.
● Observe the light and climatic conditions at the chosen site and choose plants that will thrive in these conditions.
● Use suitable containers and make sure they are adequately secured.
● When placing containers in certain positions, think of plant care and access etc.
Plants that are difficult to reach generally end up being given less care.
● Make sure nothing is dangling down in your way or hinders access to areas used often, for example a seat. Always hang the

A flowering staircase.

Fruit and vegetables ready to pick.

containers in such a way that you will be unable to injure yourself on them and so that neither the plants nor your furniture can get damaged.
● Choose plants with the most suitable shapes of growth for the intended position.
● When securing heavy containers in their position, think about weight distribution and any legal responsibility you may have.

Designing with plants

You can increase the effect of individual plants if you remember a few rules of good design when combining them.
A clever
selection and the arrangement of plants according to their shapes of growth are particularly important points when planting a hanging garden.

Shapes of growth

You can grow plants so that cascades of flowers and foliage burst out of the containers. Look for plants with very different shapes of growth.
● Creeping or rhizome-forming plants like convolvulus (*Convolvulus sabatius*), *Scaevola*, ground ivy (*Glechoma hederacea*), strawberry plants, *Chlorophytum comosum,* and ivy are ideal for making decorative hanging curtains.
● Plants that grow in the shape of large cushions, like *Portulaca*, *Dorotheanthus bellidiformis,* and *Gazania* work best if they are planted close to the edge of the container. Here they will form an attractive link between the plants that grow upward and those that hang downward.
● Plants that are bushy and pendulous, for example hanging fuchsias, hanging pelargoniums, or hanging begonias, will send a wealth of blooms upward as well as downward.
● Some climbing and trailing plants, such as *Rhodochiton atrosanguineus* or nasturtium, will not require climbing aids and will grow easily over the middle and upper sections of an arrangement.
● Plants with upright growth, like kitchen herbs, are ideal for the upper level.

Planting for the best display

The level at which plants are to be grown will also determine your choice of shape and attitude of growth.
Hanging containers *at eye-level* look very effective with a combination of different shapes of growth. The upper, middle and lower parts of the planting will all be easy to see.
Plants placed *below eye-level* look best with upright, cushion-forming and bushy, overhanging plants. However, only the upper parts of the plants and those hanging over the edge of the container will be visible to the onlooker.
Containers placed *above eye-level* do not require any plants that send their flowers upward. Here, all shapes of growth can be used provided they look decorative from below.
Balcony railings, banisters, plant tables, and plant stairs can all be equipped with different shapes of growth depending on the local conditions and climate.

267

Hanging flowers

Buying plants

Nurseries, garden centers, and markets offer a wide selection of seasonal plants as well as ready-to-plant, flowering young plants. Your decision will depend not only on the price – young plants are cheaper – but also on the way you intend to plant them. Vegetables are obtainable as young plants only. Growing your own plants from seed is recommended if you wish to cultivate rarities in your hanging garden and they are not available as seedlings. A few seed mail-order firms offer special seed mixtures for hanging gardens.

The right soil

You can use the same pre-fertilized plant compost for hanging containers that you would for balcony boxes and can obtain the various different types of compost in the trade. Garden soil is too heavy for use in containers and has a tendency to become compacted very easily. A good, light soil with a high capacity for storing water can be obtained by mixing 3 parts of garden soil with 3 parts of well-rotted, sifted garden compost and 2 parts each of peat or sand. Alternatively, mix garden soil and purchased flower compost in a ratio of 1:1.

Positioning the plants

Depending on the site and conditions, you can arrange plants to one side to make a splendid display, or in the round. Garden centers offer a wide range of containers for variations on both of these basic concepts.

Hanging baskets

One of the most ideal containers for planting an attractive all-round arrangement is a large-mesh, stable basket made of painted wire, with chains for hanging it up. Such planting containers have been used very successfully for years in many countries. A profusion of flowers pours from every opening, as both the walls and the bottom of the basket are planted through. Nowadays these baskets can be obtained almost anywhere in a range of sizes and colors, semi-spherical or with a flattened bottom. Planting them successfully requires a little skill, however.

Alternative: If you do not own a ready-made basket, you can use a large-mesh bicycle basket made of painted wire or something similar.

Accessories: Wire baskets require strong, ornamental hooks or brackets for securing them to a house wall.

These baskets can also be obtained in the form of semi-spherical bowls for securing to a wall.

Chains, wires and ropes

Builders' suppliers, hardware stores, rope makers and ship's chandlers can all provide useful supports for securing hanging plants.

Chains can be found in various sizes. They are distinguished by their type and capacity for carrying weight. Circular steel-link chains are very strong and are suitable for securing heavyweight plant containers. Ornamental chains are only suitable for very light containers.

My tip: The best plan is to have chains cut to the right length at the time of purchase. Thick chain links, in particular, cannot be cut or taken apart without using bolt cutters or a hacksaw.

Petunias in brilliant colors. These classic balcony flowers are always charming.

Wire can be obtained on a roll in various thicknesses. Galvanized or green plastic-coated tying wire is particularly suitable. Tying wire of the sort used for making garlands or wreaths is too weak. **Galvanized** wire ropes are obtainable in different gauges. They are distinguished by their weight-carrying capacity. They will need to be equipped with rope clamps for hanging them up. They can be cut with sharp pliers or wire cutters.

Warning: The ends of lengths of cut wire are sharp and can cause injuries.

Plastic-coated ropes and straps are also suitable for hanging up containers. Fixing and securing them is relatively uncomplicated and they are very strong and durable. They are also obtainable in bright colors to give a plant arrangement that extra something, but do consider whether this could clash with the colors of the flowers in the basket.

Planting baskets

If you look around any garden center or residential street you will be amazed by the luxuriantly flowering hanging baskets used for decorating balconies and patios. You can easily make your own beautiful hanging baskets if you follow a few rules.

Equipment

The following accessories are required:

a basket with a chain inserts to keep the compost in the basket and cover the lining (see below). Traditionally, sphagnum moss was used but moss from your own lawn or loose coconut fiber matting from a florist or garden center is better for ecological reasons. Cardboard, textile, or foam inserts can be obtained from garden centers. Some of these are biodegradable, recyclable products.

NB: Loose lining material is not a substitute for compost. You should use lining material of the correct thickness for lining the walls of the basket so that your plants have as much compost as possible to hold nutrients and water;

polyethlene to keep moisture in and prevent water from running out unhindered;

plants – for a basket with a diameter of 14 in (35 cm), depending on the size of the plants, about 10-15 plants depending on how large they grow and their habit of growth. Ideas for suitable plants are given throughout this book in the relevant sections.

1 A basket with insert and lining.

2 Cover only the bottom with the lining.

3 Carefully thread the plants through the wall.

4 Wrap moss around the neck of the root.

Using young plants

Advantages: They are less expensive. The small rootstocks are easy to insert through the mesh of the wire.
Disadvantages: It will take longer from planting to flowering. There is a smaller selection of these in garden centers and nurseries than of ready-grown, mature plants.

Using mature plants

Advantages: A large selection of plants is available. The plants flower sooner.
Disadvantages: They are more expensive and have larger rootstocks. A few special tips will help with planting:
● Pull the wire mesh apart a little so that there is more room to insert the plants.
● Cut the wire open using wire cutters.
● Larger plants can be carefully divided if several of them are growing in one pot.

Preparing the basket

(illustrations 1 and 2)
You can prepare the basket in two different ways.

1 First, completely cover the inside of the basket with a prepared insert (see illustration 1), moss or coconut fiber, then lay in the liner. The insert will hide the liner and prevent the compost from falling through the planting holes. Planting will require some deftness as each plant has to be pushed through narrow holes made in the two layers.

2 The neck of the root of each plant is surrounded with moss or coconut fiber after the plant has been inserted. No liner is used to line the inside of the basket before you start, but it is added gradually as you insert the plants. The disadvantage with this method is that the compost may dry out faster.

My tip: Cover the floor of the basket with coconut fiber or moss and liner, covering the

5 An attractive wall bracket will complement a hanging basket.

inside to a height of about 2 in (5 cm) (see illustration 2). This "dish" will hold water and also prevent it from running through and dripping away when watering. Do not make any holes in the insert and start planting above it. You can also insert a saucer or something similar in a very flat basket.

Special ways of planting

(illustrations 3 and 4)
There are two possibilities.

1 Carefully wrap the plant quite tightly in foil or cellophane, taking care not to damage any part of the plant, and insert it through the basket mesh shoots-first, from the inside to the outside (see illustration 3).

2 Insert it rootstock-

first from the outside inward.

How to plant

Hang the basket up at chest height, then prepare it as above. Remove the plants from their pots. Water dry plants first.
Planting should always be done from the bottom upward; i.e. plant the floor of the basket first.
● Cut a slit in the insert for each plant.
● Push the plant through the mesh and insert it to the beginning of the stalk. Close the opening around the neck of the root (see illustration 4). Distribute half of the plants in this way at the bottom of the basket.
● Sprinkle compost between the roots and press down. Repeat the procedure at the top and water.
Design tip (see illustration 5): When the basket has been freshly planted, it will look untidy. This will sort itself out after a few days when the shoot tips and leaves begin to turn toward the light.

271

Hanging flowers

Containers can be found in many shapes and styles.

Plant containers

You can obtain plant containers in many different materials.

Ceramic containers: Plants look particularly good in earth-colored or terracotta hanging containers. Unglazed containers promote the growth of roots as the walls of the vessel are porous; this also means, however, that water will evaporate more quickly and the compost will dry out faster. As some such containers are not frost-proof, it is best to check this point before purchase. Colorful glazed containers are an additional decoration for your plant collections. Their great weight makes large ceramic containers very stable. Hanging containers should be safely secured because of their weight.

Stoneware containers: Stoneware boxes are available everywhere in garden centers. They are tip-proof, frost-proof, and let the roots breathe.

Plastic containers: They are ideal for hanging plants because of their light weight and because they do not break easily. They retain moisture in the compost as their walls are not porous. They tend to be rather unattractive but the sides are soon covered up by hanging plants.

Wooden boxes, willow baskets: Containers made of natural materials, like wooden boxes, fruit crates, or willow baskets, make attractive plant containers which harmonize with the plants. Their durability is, however, rather limited because of constant moisture from watering. The life of wooden containers can be extended by applying a protective coat of paint or plant-friendly wood preserver. Another possibility is to line the inside with polyethylene sheeting (do not forget to make holes to let water run away!). The same goes for baskets made out of any natural materials. The baskets should be checked frequently as both the floor and handles may rot away.

Semi-spherical-shaped containers for planting against a wall: These containers, made of terracotta or plastic, are very suitable as an ornament on a wall and will not take up much space. Baskets of the same shape can also be obtained.

NB: Every container will require a drainage hole so that rainwater or regular water is not stored inside the containers to waterlog the plants.

Holders for single pots: Potholders made of wire are also obtainable for single pots.

Complying with the law

If you own your house, you should be able to use your balcony or patio in whatever way you wish. If you own or are living in an apartment which has a balcony, you must make sure that nothing you do infringes upon the rights of, nor endangers or inconveniences, your landlord, other tenants, or the general public. As a rule, with the exception of the outside façade, a tenant may secure plant containers to balcony railings or on a patio and install plants in them, provided this is done safely.

NB: Check the weight-carrying capacity of the balcony.

A few important points should be considered if you are a tenant:

● Before securing boxes to the outside of balcony railings, check whether your tenancy agreement expressly permits this, otherwise the landlord may prohibit such use. If you own your apartment, there may also be rules of usage governing the installation of plant containers on the property.

● Make sure you secure the plant containers in such a fashion that even a storm will not tear them from their anchoring. Use balcony box fixtures with a safety lip.

● Only use chains, ropes, hooks, and dowels with sufficient carrying capacity for holding up hanging containers and baskets. The weight will increase

Environmentally friendly containers made of recycled material.

dramatically when the plants are being watered. As a guide, use the weight data in the design section.

● Suspend hanging containers or baskets only from galvanized chains or wires or plastic-coated ropes. Untreated chains or wires may rust under the influence of moisture (watering, rain) and come away. Ropes made of natural fiber may rot and break.

● Check all fixtures at regular intervals.

● Make sure that water dripping down does not damage the façade or run onto a neighboring property or onto the street below. Always stand a bowl under plants you are watering.

● Only ever spray plants with protective agents when there is no wind. Always make sure that spray mist cannot drift onto a neighboring balcony.

Making and securing your own containers

You can easily make your own original hanging flower bed or vegetable garden without a great deal of technical expertise.

Hanging plant bed

(illustrations 1 and 2)

A base for a hanging bed that can then be covered, according to your taste, with containers and plants is easily and quickly assembled without a great deal of technical knowledge and using parts obtainable from most builders' merchants. You will only require tools for securing it to the ceiling. When purchasing parts, you should make sure that they all have the correct carrying capacity (after watering, the bed will weigh about 40 pounds/18 kg). Also make sure that the parts fit together before you begin.

Equipment

● 1 metal grid, as used for scraping shoes or for covering cellar window pits. Grids like this can be obtained in various different sizes. If you intend using a fruit crate as a plant container, one measuring 16 by 24 in (40 by 60 cm) will be large enough.

● 4 circular steel-link chains (length 40 in/100 cm each) with a carrying capacity of at least 40 pounds (18 kg). Have the pieces of chain cut to size when you purchase them.
● 4 S-hooks for attaching the chains securely to the metal grid.
● 1 adjustable chain link with thread (see illustration 5) to gather the four chains together at the top.
● 1 block and tackle for lowering and raising the plants for watering.

My tip:
Galvanized or painted parts will last longer.

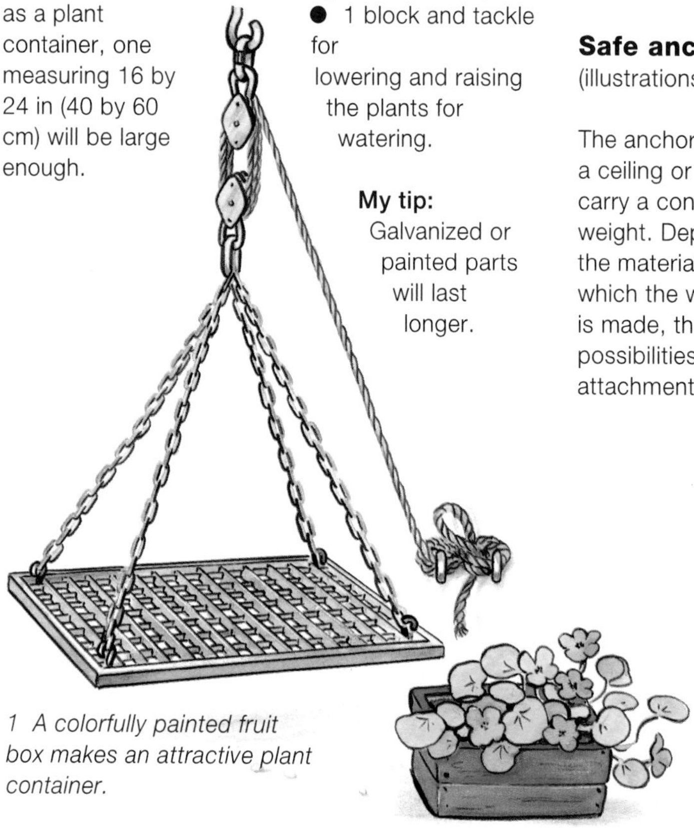

Assembling the hanging bed

● Attach a chain to each corner of the metal grid using an S-hook.
● Gather the four chains together at the top by means of an adjustable link.
● Attach the block and tackle to the ceiling and fix the rope.
● Suspend the hanging bed from the block and tackle.

Safe anchorage

(illustrations 3-6)

The anchoring point on a ceiling or wall has to carry a considerable weight. Depending on the materials from which the wall or ceiling is made, the possibilities for securing attachments may vary.

1 A colorfully painted fruit box makes an attractive plant container.

2 An S-hook attaches a chain to the metal grid.

3 Balcony box fixture with safety lip.

4 Rope clamps secure the ends of the rope.

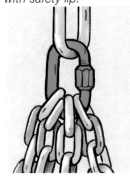

5 Adjustable chain link with screw fixture.

● Always use plastic-coated dowels to install fixtures in brick or rendered walls or ceilings (see illustration 6). They can be obtained in various sizes. Use a drill to bore a hole of the correct thickness and length for the dowel (always use a masonry bit), insert the dowel in the hole (if necessary gently tap it in with a hammer), and screw the hook into the dowel. Before drilling, make sure there are no electric cables underneath. If you are not used to handling a drill, it is better to let a professional do the job as you could be in danger of injuring yourself!

● If you are making a hole in a massive wooden beam, use a screw-in hook. In the case of open balconies (or on an arbor, etc.), wrap a chain or plastic-coated rope around the beam and attach the plant container to this. Take extra care with wooden ceilings or walls as the carrying capacity of panels is very low and a screw-in hook will only be adequate for a very lightweight plant container. It would be better to bore right through the wood and insert a dowel in the concrete or stone behind it.

● Wall fixtures, like ornamental hooks and brackets, should always be supported at the bottom and secured with further screws.

● Fixtures with safety lips can be obtained for balcony boxes (see illustration 3). These will prevent the box from tipping off.

Various other aids will also help to secure hanging containers. *S-shaped hooks* can be used to connect a chain attached to the container and the actual chain used for suspension. They are also useful for other joins. They come in many different sizes. *Rope clamps* (see illustration 4) can be used to fix the ends of wires and plastic-coated ropes. They can be obtained for different gauges of rope. *Adjustable chain links* (see illustration 5) are single chain links that can be opened on one side and closed again. They are excellent for gathering several chains together.

6 A dowel holds the hook securely in the ceiling.

Stylish ideas

With a little basic knowledge about gardening and a lot of imagination, a beautiful display of plants can be created in almost any position. Check through the suggestions in the following pages.

Photo above: Gazania displays its full beauty in sunlight.
Photo left: With the right aids, such as polyethylene, coconut fiber, and the correct tools, it is not difficult to design an attractive hanging basket.

277

Stylish ideas

The right position is most important

Before buying your plants, you should take a very good look at the position in which you are intending to grow them. Whether they thrive will not depend entirely on water and nutrients but also on the light and the prevailing climatic conditions they will be asked to live in. Different plants have different requirements with respect to light, temperature, wind, and rain. To make the choice of plants for your intended position easier, the following design ideas for groups of plants have been arranged for plants that prefer sunny, semi-shady, and shady positions. The special requirements of free-hanging planting arrangements have also been taken into consideration. The exposed nature of the planting containers means that it is sometimes easier to care for some sun-loving plants in semi-shady conditions and that they will grow even more luxuriantly there. Before deciding, you should make sure that you know which conditions prevail on your balcony, patio, etc.
● Which direction does the position face?
● Is there a roof or awning over the intended position or do trees or a house wall protect the position from direct sunlight?
● What are wind and rain conditions like?

Plants for sunny positions

Spring planting
pansies (*Viola wittrockiana* hybrids)
English daisies (*Bellis perennis*)
bulbous plants such as tulips (*Tulipa*)
narcissi (*Narcissus*)
crocuses (*Crocus*)

Summer planting
Gazania hybrids
Livingstone daisies (*Dorotheanthus bellidiformis*)
portulaca (*Portulaca*)
Swan River daisies (*Brachycome iberidifolia*)
pelargoniums (*Pelargonium*)
petunias (*Petunia* hybrids) ☠
fleabane (*Erigeron karvinskianus*)
Scaevola saligna

Fall planting
violets (*Viola cornuta* hybrids)
heath (*Erica herbacea*)
chrysanthemums (*Dendranthema grandiflorum* hybrids)
ivy (*Hedera helix*) ☠

A sunny position

South-facing balconies, patios, or roof gardens are typically the sunniest positions, which also means that there is a lot of heat during the day in the summer and, depending on the position, the air may not move much. Sensitive plants may burn here. In all cases, you will have to water a great deal. If you are not sure whether you will always be able to water frequently, you should go for a particularly robust selection of plants or consider the installation of semi-automatic or automatic irrigation.
Positions that face southeast or southwest should be less vulnerable to such extreme conditions. The same goes for a situation where a tree, a house wall opposite, or a roof protects the plants from too much sunlight. The position is classified as shady if the balcony is facing south but has a roof or something similar which keeps the sun off completely. This fact should be reflected in your choice of plants.
Look at the chosen site at various times during the day as conditions may alter as the sun moves round.

A herb basket above the table releases its spicy scent.

Stylish ideas

An exotic blend of colors

This is where plants from hot, dry climatic zones meet up. All the plants in this basket enjoy plenty of heat and lots of sunshine and can also manage on little water – ideal for a sunny position. They will not mind if they do not receive water regularly on schedule as they either have a built-in water reservoir or a special talent for using up the precious liquid frugally. In their countries of origin they have evolved to cope with long periods of drought.

Plants for a wire basket with a diameter of 14 in (35 cm):
5 gazania (*Gazania* hybrids)
3 Livingstone daisies (*Dorotheanthus bellidiformis*)
4 portulaca (*Portulaca*)
2 convolvulus (*Convolvulus sabatius*)
Total weight of the group: 22 pounds (10 kg).

Planting and care

All plants can be bought from the last month of spring onward. You can increase the number of different colors in your arrangement if you use varieties that come in a range of colors. *Gazania*, *Dorotheanthus* and *Portulaca* are usually planted several to a pot in nurseries and often produce several different colors in one pot. Prepare the wire basket and insert the plants.
Plant a *Convolvulus sabatius* at both the front and the back of the bottom of the basket. Its long, trailing shoots will look best growing freely downward. Toward the top of the basket alternate *Gazania, Dorotheanthus* and *Portulaca*.
Water the basket well (place a bowl underneath!) and keep it as evenly moist as possible. Fertilize weekly. Cut out any dead and faded flowers and foliage as this will encourage the formation of new flowers. These plants react sensitively to continuous rain and waterlogging. During longer periods of wet weather, it is a good

Terracotta wall container.

Terracotta hanging container.

idea to protect the arrangement from too much moisture by hanging the basket underneath an overhanging roof.

For people who are away from home all day

The glowing, colorful flowers of these plants are open only during the day and when the sun is shining. If you are not at home all day, you should probably choose plants whose flowers are open all the time.

Choice of colors

Plants originating from regions with plenty of sunshine are often very brightly colored. If you like strong colors, you can combine them with complementary colors. If you feel this would create too much of a garish splash, you can also use a combination of quieter shades or tones.

Design tip

The plants used here will also suit smaller containers with very little compost in them. They are ideal for summertime plantings in ceramic hanging containers or half-bowl-shaped containers made of terracotta.

Compact and full of color.

Stylish ideas

An aromatic herb basket

Plants with highly scented flowers or leaves are always a pleasure for the senses. Honey melon sage, lemon thyme, and curry plant provide a real feast of wonderful aromas. As these plants are usually to be found growing on the ground, it is generally necessary to bend down to enjoy the full impact of their scent as you crush their leaves and flower heads in your fingers. However, if you plant various scented plants in a hanging basket and suspend this at nose level, the plants will release their pleasant perfume at just the right height. If you suspend the basket using a block and tackle, you can even go a step further and vary the level at which the plants hang.

In addition, an airy position like this is the ideal place to grow kitchen herbs with superb flavors. It will make things even easier still if you hang the basket right beside an outdoor table on your

Most herbs have very delicate flowers.

Pocket amphora.

balcony or patio, then you can pick the herbs fresh to eat with your meal. Depending on the plants chosen, such a combination of plants can prove quite robust if subjected to short-term periods of drought.

Plants for a wire basket with a diameter of 14 in (35 cm):
2 honey melon sage (*Salvia elegans*)
1 sage (*Salvia officinalis* "Tricolor")
1 golden sage (*Salvia officinalis* "Aurea")
1 scented-leafed pelargonium with an aroma of nutmeg and white/green variegated leaves (*Pelargonium fragrans* "Variegata")
1 scented-leafed pelargonium with a fruit scent and red leaves
1 curry plant (*Helichrysum italicum*)
1 hyssop with pink flowers (*Hyssopus officinalis*)
2 large quaking grass (*Briza maxima*)
2 lemon thyme (*Thymus x citriodorus*)
These plants are not commonly available everywhere but you should be able to purchase them through specialty mail-order nurseries.

An alternative collection
If you want to grow your own herb garden in a hurry, you can fall back on the usual kitchen herbs, for example basil (*Ocimum basilicum*),

marjoram (*Majorana hortensis*), dill (*Antheum graveolens*), or parsley (*Petroselinum crispum*). These herbs not only smell nice but can also be used to give flavor in cooking.
My tip: Hanging baskets can even be transformed into vegetable gardens if they are planted all the way around with young vegetable plants. Total weight of the arrangement: 18 pounds (8 kg).

Planting and care
Plant after the last frosts in the last month of spring. Prepare the basket.
Honey melon sage needs the most room so plant one of these to the right and left of the bottom of the basket wall. Between these, at the front and back, plant lemon thyme which grows in cushions. Distribute the other herbs all over the basket.
Fill up all the empty spaces between the plants with compost. Press the compost down and water the basket well. Fertilize

regularly. If you have the space available, you can overwinter this arrangement in a frost-free room during the winter months as all these plants are perennials. Cut the plants back before overwintering them.

My tip: Honey melon sage (*Salvia elegans*) has a profusion of foliage and requires lots of water. If you are unable to water regularly, it would be better to choose a plant that does not mind a bit of dryness or else hang the basket in a semi-shady position.

The following plants require *less water* than most:
sage (*Salvia officinalis*), rosemary (*Rosmarinus officinalis*)
lavender (*Lavandula angustifolia*)
oregano (*Origanum vulgare*)
marjoram (*Majorana hortensis*)
sedum (*Sedum reflexum*)
various species of

thyme (*Thymus*)
lavender-cotton (*Santolina chamaecyparissus*)
winter savory (*Satureja montana*)

Tip on containers
Ceramic pocket amphorae present an attractive possibility for overhanging plantings. You can plant herbs or even strawberry plants in the pockets. These containers are also sold under the name of strawberry pots in garden centres.

Be aware that the larger strawberry barrels do become very heavy when planted up. They can become impossible to move or lift, so you must decide where you wish to place the pot or barrel before you plant it up.

Stylish ideas

Strawberry fair

By growing the right varieties of strawberries and giving a little extra care, you can be certain of a rich harvest of fruit over several months. The lovely white flowers also make an attractive feature. The strawberry plants ensure their own propagation by producing long runners which form tiny new strawberry plants. These young plants look very pretty when they produce flowers at the ends of the runners, followed by fruit. A rustic tub barrel made of light oak looks superb when full of strawberry plants.

Plants for a container with a diameter of 12 in (30 cm):
1-5 strawberry plants (*Fragaria*)
The best plants for this arrangement are hanging or climbing strawberries which will be available in garden centers from the last month of spring into the first month of summer. These types flower and produce fruit all summer long. They are sold as large container plants or as small young plants. The number of plants you will require for a planting in a wooden container will depend on the size of the individual plants. If you cannot find any plants to buy during these months, you will certainly be able to obtain them during the last month of summer which is the best planting time for garden strawberries.

An alternative suggestion

The small Alpine strawberries make a dainty ornament as well as producing tasty fruit. If you wish to grow the fruit only as a visual delight, you can also use the "fake" strawberry (*Duchesnea indica*). This grows vigorously; its fruits are the same size as wild strawberries but have no flavor. The flowers are yellow.

Total weight of the planting: 37 pounds (17 kg). Make sure the attachment is particularly strong and secure as this container is a considerable weight.

Planting and care

Before planting, check whether the container is equipped with drainage holes.

Place a drainage layer in the bottom of the container, for example clay pellets (Hortag), to a level of about 2 in (5 cm) and then cover this layer with permeable fabric. This drainage layer will not only protect your plants from the effects of waterlogging but will also reduce the overall weight of the planting. If you want to reduce the weight even more, you can double the thickness of the drainage layer.

Fill the remainder of the container with compost and plant the strawberry plants. Press the compost down so that the rootstocks are well covered with compost on all sides and then water well. If the runners of the strawberry plants become too long, they can be trimmed.

Fertilize strawberries in the same way as herbs and vegetables. Depending on the variety, strawberries are particularly susceptible to mildew if the humidity is high and temperatures are constantly changing.

To build up the plants' immunity, and as a preventive, we recommend watering your plants regularly during the growth period with mare's tail brew, nettle brew, comfrey brew, or yarrow brew, all of which contain silicic acid.

You will receive years of pleasure from this arrangement if you position it in a sheltered spot outside or overwinter it indoors at no more than 41°F (5°C).

Securing containers

If the wooden container has no means of attachment, drill three holes at equal intervals in the top of one of its walls and insert S-hooks.

Make sure the distance between the holes and the top edge of the container is great enough to prevent the wood from giving way. Hang a circular-link steel chain from each hole. Gather the three chains together at the top with an S-hook or an adjustable chain link.

Wooden barrel.

Tip on containers

Do-it-yourself enthusiasts may wish to transform an old wooden barrel into a strawberry barrel. A particularly attractive effect is created if the strawberry plants do not just cascade out of the top of the barrel but also out of additional holes that can be sawn into the walls of the barrel.

Strawberries make an attractive arrangement.

Stylish ideas

A semi-shady position

These sites are characterized by receiving plenty of light but without constant, aggressive, intense rays from the sun. Burning noontime sunlight should generally be avoided. On the other hand, this sort of position does not mean that the plants are sitting in deep shadow. Semi-shady positions are generally east- or west-facing. An east-facing balcony receives softer morning sunlight. A west-facing balcony receives rays from the afternoon and evening sun but, being the side more exposed to weather, it may often be battered by storms and rain. Your hanging containers should, therefore, be very well secured in west-facing positions. In all cases, the prevailing conditions on site should be considered. Even south-facing balconies in full sunlight, or shady north-facing ones, may become semi-shady if, for example, a tree blocks out the sunlight or a neighboring house wall reflects the sun's rays.

Choosing plants

A semi-shady position is ideal for hanging plants as the relatively small amount of compost in the containers will not dry out so fast. On the other hand, sun-loving plants will thrive here just as much as in a sunny position.

Plants for semi-shady positions

Spring planting
forget-me-nots (*Myosotis sylvatica*)
pansies (*Viola wittrockiana* hybrids)
double daisies (*Bellis perennis*)
primulas (*Primula vulgaris* hybrids)

Summer planting
black-eyed Susan (*Thunbergia alata*)
morning glory (*Ipomoea*) ☠
climbing nasturtium (*Tropaeolum peregrinum*)
nasturtium (*Tropaeolum majus*)
Lotus berthelotii
pelargonium (*Pelargonium*)
lobelia (*Lobelia erinus*)
begonia (*Begonia semperflorens* hybrid) ☠
tuber begonia (*Begonia – tuber begonia hybrids*) ☠
Calceolaria integrifolia

Fall planting
heather (*Calluna vulgaris*)
fall asters (*Aster*), various species

As you can see from these lists, with simple care you can take full advantage of a suitable position to grow a wide range of plants. Plants that form lots of leaves in a very short time do particularly well in a semi-shady position. Among these are a wide selection of climbing plants.

Symbols used in the gardening trade

Purchased plants often have labels attached to them. These labels bear symbols giving the requirements of the plant with respect to position and light.

○ **sun:** This plant requires, or can cope with, full sunlight and heat, even at noon. A completely sunny, south-facing position will be necessary for the production of plenty of flowers.

◑ **semi-shade:** This plant requires a bright position without intense midday sunlight. Morning and evening sunlight, i.e. east- and west-facing positions, are ideal for this plant. Even light shade is suitable for growing this sort of plant.

● **shade:** This plant can cope with, or prefers, shade.

This hanging basket provides an attractive visual screen.

287

Stylish ideas

A colorful flower swing

Traditional balcony flowers in glowing colors create a wonderful effect from a distance. The hanging varieties are also excellent for trailing over a balcony railing. Using an interesting or original container, you can place these easily cared-for, continuous-flowering plants in a free-hanging position.

Plants for a box 28 in (70 cm) long:
1 hanging pelargonium (*Pelargonium peltatum* hybrids)
1 *Bidens ferufolia*
5 nasturtiums (*Tropaeolum majus*)
1 *Scaevola saligna*
Total weight of the planting: 44 pounds (20 kg)

Planting and care

Scaevola saligna, *Bidens ferufolia* and hanging perlargoniums can be bought as ready-to-plant plants from the last month of spring onward in nurseries and garden centers. Nasturtiums can be obtained in the form of young plants or you can grow them yourself from seed. Fill a third of the box with compost. Place the pelargonium on the left, the *Bidens* and the *Scaevola* in the center, and the nasturtiums on the right. Fill the box with compost, press down, and water well. Nasturtiums will flower more profusely and produce fewer leaves if you do not fertilize them too often. In order that the other plants will receive an adequate amount of fertilizer, use controlled-release fertilizer or fertilizer sticks in a targeted way around their root systems . In this way you can avoid the use of liquid fertilizer. Regularly remove dead flowers and leaves. If the nasturtiums threaten to smother the other plants, cut them back a little.

Securing the container

Balcony railings: You can attach the box of plants to the railings with special fixtures.

Free-hanging: If you wish to suspend the balcony box from the ceiling, you will require an overbox (paint it to protect it from rotting) which you can build yourself with a bit of experience or have a carpenter make for you. Make sure it has an attachment which you can easily make yourself.

● Stand the balcony box in a rather wider box made of heavy wood. Allow a gap of 1¼ in (3 cm) between the inner and outer boxes so that the inner one can be removed easily.

● Make sure that both the inner and outer boxes are equipped with drainage holes.

● Stand the box on narrow wooden battens so that excess water can run away unhindered.

● Take two narrow-gauge iron pipes, which correspond in length to the width of the overbox, and pass them underneath each end of the overbox; insert chains through these pipes and suspend the box from the chains (see photo below).

My tip: If you wish to grow perennial plants, insert a layer of polystyrene between the two boxes as protection against the cold.

Color tip

If you enjoy the pink shades of pelargoniums during the summer, you can have the same colors again in the fall by planting winter heather.

Heath in a pot.

Flower box attachment.

A free-hanging balcony box on chains.

Stylish ideas

This cascade of flowers forms an attractive visual screen.

Visual screens

This basket is enveloped in luxuriantly growing plants that will produce long shoots and dense foliage in the shortest period of time. It is simply overflowing with eye-catching nasturtiums and various varieties of *Asarina barclaiana*. The latter are distant relatives of the snapdragon and are generally grown as climbing plants.

Nasturtiums.

If no climbing aids are present, the long, trailing shoots will hang down over the edge of the container. This basket provides a dense visual screen and an eye-catching decoration all in one.

Plants for a wire basket with a diameter of 16 in (40 cm):
3 climbing nasturtiums (*Tropaeolum peregrinum*)
2 nasturtiums (*Tropaeolum majus*)
2 hanging pelargoniums (*Pelargonium peltatum* hybrids)
1 ground ivy with white and green variegated leaves (*Glechoma hederacea* "Variegata")
2 *Asarina barclaiana*
2 *Asarina scandens*
1 *Rhodochiton atrosanguineus*
1 convolvulus (*Convolvulus sabatius*)
3 coleus (*Coleus blumei* hybrids)
Total weight of the planting: 40 pounds (18 kg).

Planting and care

The right time to plant is after the last frosts, about the middle of the last month of spring. You can purchase the plants in nurseries and garden centers or grow them yourself from seed during the middle of the second month of spring. Prepare the basket and plant it.
All the plants, with the exception of pelargoniums and

coleus, can be distributed evenly on the base and walls of the basket. Only the colorful coleus and pelargoniums should be placed in the upper portion and on the surface of the basket. When planting, make sure that the spaces between the rootstocks are completely filled with compost.
Water the basket well; after three weeks use a liquid flower fertilizer once weekly.
If one of the plants begins to dominate the arrangement, cut back its shoots. You can break up this arrangement before the first frosts in the fall. Plant the pelargoniums, convolvulus, and coleus in individual pots and overwinter them in a frost-free position.

My tip: To help the climbing plants to produce a more bushy appearance after planting them in the basket, pinch out the tips of the first shoots. This will encourage the formation of plenty of lateral shoots.

Morning glory sown from seed.

Design tip

If you want to cover a wall or the railing of a balcony or patio with greenery but do not have enough room on the ground or floor for a large plant container, you can hang a basket of climbing plants near a trellis or balcony railing. Carefully tie the long shoots from the basket to the railing. The plants in the basket will then climb all over the trellis or railing throughout the summer. When positioning the basket, remember that after its climbing shoots are entwined around a support, you will no longer be able move the basket about. This means hanging it up in such a way that it is easy to reach for watering.

An alternative planting

To obtain a cheap planting for your hanging basket, after the last frosts in late spring, sow morning glory (*Ipomoea*) seed or scarlet runner beans (*Phaseolus coccineus*) directly into a basket filled with compost or into a ceramic hanging container. Keep the compost evenly moist during germination. After about ten days, the plants will begin to germinate and, throughout the entire summer, will grow all over the container. The *Ipomoea* has brilliant blue flowers and the bean flowers are an intense scarlet as their name suggests.

291

Stylish ideas

A hanging vegetable garden

You can plant a vegetable garden in a very small space in this way. The basic construction is simple and you can put it together from parts that can be found in any builder's merchant. The actual plant container is made from a painted fruit box that can easily be purchased at a weekly market or in a greengrocery. Naturally, if you do not wish to grow vegetables, this hanging garden can be filled with flowering plants instead.

Plants for an orange box of the dimensions 24 by 16 in (60 by 40 cm):
1 cherry tomato plant
1 red cabbage
3 lettuce plants (choose varieties with different leaf colors and shapes)
1 gourd
red basil plants
Total weight of the planting (inc. the metal grid): 35 pounds (16 kg).

Securing the container

This hanging bed requires a basic construction comprising four chains and an attached metal grid. It will be easier to care for the plants if it can be lowered for watering. A block and tackle arrangement should be installed for this purpose.

Planting and care

You can start to plant after the last frost at the end of spring. You will find a large selection of young vegetable plants in garden centers at this time. Use a fruit box, preferably with high sides, as this will ensure a large volume of compost for the plants. Give the box a coat of paint before planting as this will make your arrangement more attractive. Let the paint dry properly and then line the inside of the box with polythene sheeting. Cut several holes in the bottom of the sheet so that excess water can run out. Before planting, fill the box with compost and insert the plants. Place the red cabbage at the front so that it inclines forward, plant the tomato on the left, and then place the other young plants between them.

You can sow lettuce seeds in the gaps and harvest them before the other vegetables have grown very big. The lettuces will germinate quickly and produce salad leaves. In addition, they will later produce pretty, creamy-white, star-shaped flowers that look enchanting among the other plants. After three weeks, fertilize the vegetable garden weekly. Check for pests regularly.

My tip: Cherry tomatoes do not have to be tied to sticks. They produce very attractive yellow flowers and their miniature, brilliant red fruits are quite eye-catching as well as delicious.

Positioning

If you place this arrangement beside an outside table, you can pick fresh tomatoes straight from the plant to eat with your meal. Cress is also ideal for this method of growing or you could even sow a whole boxful of lettuces. Naturally, this kind of hanging bed can also be filled with herbs.

Water melon.

Eggplant.

Design tip
Vegetables can produce a very attractive effect. The creamy-colored flowers of lettuce can be very ornamental.
These flowers are formed when the lettuce "bolts" and the flower head shoots up.
Water melons and eggplants also make interesting and delicious additions to your hanging vegetable garden.

Line the inside of the box with polyethylene.

A painted fruit box makes a good container.

Stylish ideas

A shady position

A shady site requires just as careful a choice of plants as a sunny one. North-facing positions are perpetually in the shade as direct sunlight will never reach them. However, even a square courtyard or a planting position directly under a tree with dense foliage will create very shady spots. Because there is less sunlight in shady positions, the plants placed there and the surface of the compost in the container tend to lose less water through evaporation. This means that moisture is retained for longer in the compost. One advantage of this is that the plants do not need to be watered so often. On the other hand, there is a disadvantage if the plants become waterlogged as this may cause damage to the roots. Although there is a smaller selection of plants that feel at home in a shady position, with a little careful thought you can still have a profusion of summery flowers on your north-facing balcony. You can also resort to short-term decoration by using plants that can be replaced with others when they have finished flowering. This sort of short-term use is best achieved by standing the plant in its pot inside the hanging container. This will enable you to exchange it for another easily and quickly.

Plants for shady positions

Spring planting
forget-me-nots (*Myosotis sylvatica*)
primulas (*Primula vulgaris* hybrids)
spring anemones (*Anemone blanda*) ☠

Summer planting
tuber begonias (*Begonia* – tuber begonia hybrids) ☠
ivy (*Hedera helix*) ☠
Tradescantia
Chlorophytum comosum
Mimulus luteus
fuchsias (*Fuchsia* hybrids)
patience-plants (*Impatiens walleriana*)

Fall planting
heather (*Erica heracea*)
heather (*Calluna vulgaris*)
fall asters (*Aster*), various species
forget-me-nots (*Myosotis sylvatica*)
Gaultheria procumbens
chrysanthemums (*Dendranthema grandiflorum* hybrids)

My tip: Have fun experimenting with a selection of plants as many plants are very adaptable. Some sun-loving plants will still produce flowers in the shade although they do not develop quite so profusely.

Reaching for the light

Sunlight is vital for plants so they tend always to grow toward the source of light and will produce most flowers in sunny conditions. The part of the plant that is farthest from light tends to become bare and often becomes unsightly. Positions that are not built up and obtain light from all sides are, therefore, ideal for the creation of attractive, all-round plantings. In order to encourage this ideal all-round growth in unfavorable conditions, for example on a cramped balcony that is roofed over, one method is to paint the walls etc. white. You should not continually turn an arrangement to expose all sides of it to the light. This creates great stress for the plant and hinders its growth.

A profusion of plants can be grown even in a shady position.

Stylish ideas

Baskets of begonias and fuchsias

This elegant basket arrangement, containing hanging begonias in shades of pink and apricot amid variegated green and white foliage, will bring clusters of flowering color to even the shadiest nook. The small-flowering fuchsias are ideal for shady positions. Although they are true children of the sun, mint, scented-leafed pelargoniums, and ground ivy with its aromatic foliage will quickly become accustomed to a shady position.

Plants for a wire basket with a diameter of 14 in (35 cm):
2 hanging begonias (*Begonia* – tuber begonia hybrids)
3 hanging fuchsias (*Fuchsia magellanica*)
1 *Rhodochiton atrosanguineus*
3 ground ivy (*Glechoma hederacea* "Variegata")
2 pineapple mint (*Mentha suaveolens* "Variegata")
2 *Chlorophytum comosum*
2 scented-leafed pelargoniums with a scent of peppermint (*Pelargonium tomentosum*)
Total weight of the planting: 26 pounds (12 kg).

Planting and care

Plant after the last frosts at the end of spring. The plants for this pretty combination can be bought at garden centers and nurseries or from mail-order firms. This arrangement will take its overall balance from a subtle combination of different shapes of growth. The graceful curtain of foliage and downward-trailing shoots have their stable base in the compact, bushy plants at the top of the basket. Prepare the wire basket and install the plants. In the lower and middle levels of the basket, plant ground ivy and *Rhodochiton atrosanguineus* alternated with scented-leafed pelargoniums and hanging fuchsias. Distribute the remaining plants at the top near the sides of the basket and over the surface. Water the plants well and begin fertilizing three weeks later. Pick out dead flower heads and leaves. The more vigorously growing plants, like mint and pelargonium, should be lightly cut back from time to time if they start crowding the other plants.

My tip: Mint can be obtained in many different varieties. Not only do the many types of mint have differently scented leaves but they also grow vigorously and have interesting, attractive foliage. You can also use them as herbs in cooking. If you cannot find any pineapple mint in garden centers but still wish to have variegated green and white decorative foliage, try planting *Plectranthus*, which is easier to obtain, or simply use an ivy (*Hedera*) with variegated leaves.

Color

Hanging begonias come in many different colors, from deep red and glowing yellow to delicate pink and white, and with double and single blooms. All pastel shades go well with the variegated green and white leaves of ground ivy and pineapple mint. A particularly enchanting effect can be obtained with a combination of apricot and pink or by mixing different shades of pink. You could design your basket entirely in shades of one color if you add white tuber begonias and fuchsias to the white and green foliage. If in doubt, you should go for fewer colors in a combination and plant flowers of each color in one or two larger groups.

A profusion of fuchsias

Fuchsias are wonderfully adaptable plants to use in designing baskets and hanging containers. The hanging fuchsias are best for this mode of

Pineapple mint.

planting. The colors, sizes, and shapes of the flowers of the hanging varieties are just as varied as those of the upright-growing varieties, for example "La Campanella" (white/violet), "Elfriede Ott" (salmon/pink), or "Annabel" (white).

The scented-leafed pelargoniums spread an aroma of peppermint.

Stylish ideas

Bellflowers and grasses

Experiment by planting unusual plants in an unusual container. For example, here a small selection of woodland plants have been grown in a section of guttering as an interesting and novel hanging box that is perfect for a shady patio or balcony. All the plants shown here are perennials and the arrangement can be kept outside during the winter.

Plants for a section of guttering with a length of 28 in (70 cm):
2 large selfheal (*Prunella grandiflora*)
3 yellow corydalis (*Corydalis lutea*)
1 giant bellflower (*Campanula latifolia*)
1 barrenwort or bishop's hat (*Epimedium x rubrum*)
2 tufted hairgrass (*Deschampsia cespitosa*)
1 periwinkle with green/white leaves (*Vinca major* "Variegata")
Total weight of the planting: 18 pounds (8 kg).

This guttering container can be filled with woodland plants.

Making the plant container
The container consists of one section of roof guttering, with two end pieces to close both ends of the gutter and chains for suspending it. The best solution is to let a plumber or expert handy person put it together for you.

Guttering comes in several different widths and the measurements do not refer to the diameter of the gutter itself but to the width of the metal/plastic/PVC etc. before it is bent into a gutter shape.

Wall attachment.

The best gutters for this purpose are those made of metal or stout PVC that are about 13¼ in (33 cm) wide before shaping. They will hold more compost and the plants will do better. Avoid waterlogging by drilling several holes in the bottom of the gutter. The finished bed will be suspended on chains, so holes for these have to be made at both ends, front and back, about ¾ in (2 cm) below the upper edge, using a drill. Insert an S-hook in each hole to which you can attach the chains.

An alternative method

Wire ropes can be used instead of chains. Push a piece of wire through a hole drilled in the guttering from the outside, draw it along the inside wall of the guttering, and push it out through another hole drilled at the other end. Repeat this along the other side of the guttering.

My tip: The most attractive gutters are those made of galvanized metal that will not rust. Copper gutters are only suitable for planting if they have been coated with bitumen on the inside. Plastic and PVC gutters are also obtainable in the construction trade. They are not as attractive as the metal ones but can be painted any color you like. They have the advantage of being less heavy when planted up but do remember to use a robust plastic gutter.

Planting and care

Hardy perennials can be bought all year round in garden centers and nurseries. The best time to plant is during the first two months of spring, which gives the plants time to acclimatize well before the fall so that they can face the winter months with a well-developed root system.

A particularly interesting effect is obtained with this kind of arrangement if you distribute tall and low-growing plants unevenly along the gutter, for example by creating a focal point at the right end with taller plants. Place a few low-growing plants between the tall ones. They will form a link to the left end of the arrangement and the low-growing species of plants.

From the middle of spring until the end of summer, use liquid fertilizer every two weeks. Make sure the arrangement is kept moist during the winter. Do not cut the plants back until the following spring. The seed heads of the grasses and the trailing shoots of periwinkle will look most decorative throughout the winter. If one of the plants should die during the winter, you may wish to plant pansies or forget-me-nots in the gaps.

Fixing a wall attachment

The usual roof gutter fixtures (obtainable in the construction trade) can be used to transform a gutter into a wall garden.

This attachment can be fixed to the wall with dowels and screws.

Containers

Galvanized metal buckets look good next to a plant container made out of a gutter. The handle of the bucket can be used for suspending it. The best idea is to plant the entire arrangement of plants in a plastic bucket with holes in its base and then insert this into the metal bucket. This will enable excess water to run out of the compost and into the metal bucket which should be emptied daily, if possible, to prevent waterlogging.

Bucket with insert.

Stylish ideas

A romantic flower table

This decorative plant arrangement is perfect for the summer. It has uncomplicated, continuously flowering hanging plants.

Plants for a bowl with a diameter of 24 in (60 cm):
6 patience-plants (*Impatiens walleriana*)
4 hanging fuchsias (*Fuchsia* hybrids)
1 large ivy for a hanging container and 3 small ivies with different colored foliage (*Hedera helix*)
2 *Tradescantia* of different species or varieties

Planting and care
Tradescantia and ivy are available in garden centers all year round and at reasonable prices. Patience-plants and fuchsias can be bought from the last month of spring onward. Before planting, make sure that the plant container has drainage holes at the bottom. Cover the bottom of the bowl with a thin layer of compost. Place the green/white

Tradescantia and the large ivy to the left, hanging over the edge of the bowl and, on the right, plant the other *Tradescantia*. Place the fuchsias and the smaller ivy plants at the front and back between the first two groups of plants. The center of the bowl should be filled with compost to form a small mound where the patience-plants should be planted.
Regularly remove dead flower heads and leaves. Cut the ivy and *Tradescantia* back if they start to grow all over the flowering plants.
Do not place the bowl directly on the surface of the table. Slip short battens of wood under the bowl so that the drainage holes do not

become blocked. *Tradescantia* and ivy can be planted individually in containers in the fall and then used as robust indoor plants even in dark positions within a room.

My tip: Ivy plants are often placed several to a pot by gardeners. You can carefully divide their rootstocks and plant them separately.

Design tip
A certain degree of artistic flair can be achieved with this arrangement if the edge of the bowl is left visible in several places. When the arrangement is established, the edge of the bowl should be clipped free to expose it in certain places every so often.

Containers
You can create an elegant effect with this kind of arrangement if you use containers with flat edges. You will also achieve a luxuriant overall effect if you choose a terracotta urn as a container.

Securing pots
There are various ways of securing pots to a balcony railing. (see illustration 3, p. 17, for an example)
Decorative baskets and ordinary pots obtained from garden centers are ideal for holding replaceable plants or for short-term decoration.
● Bicycle baskets are also suitable for this purpose.

Two decorative wire pot holders.

This cascade of flowers covers everything except the legs of the table.

Successful care

What could be finer than to sit on your balcony or patio contemplating a firework display of colorful flowers high above your head? It can all be achieved by using plants in baskets and hanging containers. To ensure that your efforts are well rewarded and will give pleasure for as long as possible, however, it is worth establishing a regular program of good care. The advice given in the following pages will help you to do this.

Photo above: Petunias are popular balcony plants.
Photo left: Spray bottle, ceramic cones, and watering can are important aids for watering. Liquid fertilizer, fertilizer sticks, and granules supply the plants with nutrients.

Successful care

Fertilizing

Plants in containers have to make do with a minimum of compost and are still expected to provide a long-lasting profusion of flowers and vigorous growth. As the nutrients contained in the compost are generally used up after a very short time, you should definitely start fertilizing two to three weeks after planting.

Types of fertilizer

Fertilizer is obtainable in solid and liquid forms, for watering or sprinkling on. It is easy to measure doses of liquid fertilizer into water. Controlled-release fertilizers are also practical. They are offered in granule form to be mixed into the compost or sprinkled onto it later. They will then release nutrients at an even rate over a period of 10-12 weeks. Overfertilizing and the resultant damage to the plants is impossible if controlled-release fertilizer is used properly as, by its very nature, it releases nutrients slowly. The same goes for fertilizer sticks. These should be completely inserted into the compost around the rootstock. The number of sticks to use will depend on the diameter of the container and the number of plants. Fertilizer sticks and controlled-release fertilizer are also ideal if you are combining plants which have varying

requirements for nutrients. Use a compound fertilizer for flowering plants. Fertilizer intended for leafy plants, on the other hand, will only encourage the formation of foliage.

Fertilizer for edible plants

If herbs and vegetables are intended only as ornaments, they can be fertilized in the same way as other plants. If, however, they are intended for consumption, the plants should be supplied with nutrients in a different fashion. Growth-promoting fermented herbal brews can be used all summer long. With this form of mild, organic fertilizing, the nitrate content of vegetables and lettuce is much lower than if you use mineral fertilizers. You can also mix a small handful of hoof/horn chips into the compost. Biological fertilizers based on molasses are also obtainable from garden centers.

Tips on fertilizing

Please note the following points.
● Continuous rain will wash nutrients out of the compost. This is why plants often look yellowish and unhealthy after sustained periods of rainy weather. Giving them additional doses of fertilizer will usually help them to recover rapidly. Use

liquid fertilizer twice weekly, diluted in water and according to the manufacturer's recommended dosage. You can also give the additional benefit of leaf fertilizer. Spray the plants with water containing this fertilizer. The nutrients are then absorbed through the surfaces of the leaves.
NB: Never fertilize plants in full sunlight as this will cause burns on the leaves. The best time is in the evening as the plants will then have time to absorb the fertilizer during the night.
● Dry planting arrangements should be watered with fresh water first and then fertilized, otherwise the roots may suffer burns.
● Granules or water containing fertilizer should not be allowed to come into contact with the leaves (if they do, rinse them off immediately).
● It is better to fertilize plants more often and less plentifully than seldom but in huge doses!
● Plants that are to be overwintered should not be fertilized from the first fall month to let their shoots ripen before they are moved into their winter quarters.
● You can place liquid fertilizer in a reservoir if the plants are being semi-automatically irrigated.

Spider plants (Chlorophytum comosum) produce long, decorative plantlets. These plants are undemanding but will develop particularly well if they are fertilized regularly during their growth phase.

Watering systems

1 A spray attachment on a pole will help you to water high containers.

To ensure that your hanging garden will thrive and grow vigorously, it will be necessary to water regularly. Both the plants and the hanging containers will lose water through evaporation all the way round and they will require regular and plentiful watering. There are several very different systems of watering that will ensure an adequate and manageable system. You should always make a point of avoiding damage caused by water dripping from hanging containers.

of these materials do not draw water away from plants so the total amount of water given remains available to sustain the plants in their growth.

Watering by hand
(illustrations 1 and 3)

Watering cans: The simplest method is watering with a can with a spray attachment. If the plant containers are hanging up high, you should have taken this into consideration when planning beforehand and have a set of steps handy. These, in turn,

will require additional space for storage.
A spray stick attachment (see illustration 1): This spray-head attachment on a long stiff pipe can be attached to a garden hose. Even containers that have been secured way above your head can be watered comfortably from ground level using this method.

A pump can (see illustration 3): Special watering vessels with a pump attachment for watering hanging containers are now available in many garden centers. A hand pump conducts water via a pipe up to the hanging container.

Watering plant containers

You can prevent excessive water evaporation through the walls of the containers if you use plastic, stoneware, or glazed ceramic containers. Unlike unglazed, porous clay pots, vessels made

2 Ceramic cones and a container of water will replace daily watering for several days.

Semi-automatic watering
(illustration 2)

Irrigation systems that are reasonably priced and easy to install are able to supply water automatically to plants for several days at a time.

Various different types are available in the specialist trade.

Ceramic cones (see illustration 2): Watering is carried out by means of a cone with a thin hose attached to it, the end of which is completely immersed in a container full of water. The cone should be inserted into the compost right to its top. Use two cones for large containers. For boxes of plants, use one at intervals of every 6-8 in (15-20 cm). The surface of the water in the feeder vessel must be lower than the top of the cone. Positioning the reservoir higher or lower will affect the amount of water conducted to the plant container. Light-impermeable material for the reservoir will discourage the formation of algae.

Water reservoirs: Flower boxes can be obtained with built-in water reservoirs. The compost sucks water up through a wick leading to a tank in the double floor of the container. The reservoir is replenished via a refill pipe.

3 A pump can for very high containers.

Fully automatic irrigation
(illustration 4)

You will hardly need to bother with hand-watering at all any more if you install a fully automatic irrigation system. Even long absences will present no problems. The installation is quite involved but the cost and the effort will be rewarded with considerable easing of regular work and an even, superb growth of plants. In these systems water conduction comes from the main supply through a valve and an in-built pressure control. The water is distributed through thin plastic hoses. The amount of water and the rhythm of watering is controlled by varying mechanisms. Some systems are even computer-controlled.

Water supply: There are two systems for regulating this.

1 A ceramic "feeler" is inserted into the compost for each irrigation circuit. If the compost begins to lack moisture, the "feeler" emits an electronic impulse that opens a valve to provide more water. When the compost is moist enough, the "feeler" activates the closing of the valve.

2 Regulation via a time clock ensures that water is supplied at regular intervals.

Disadvantage: The supply of water is not controlled by the requirements of the plants and changes in the weather as is the case with a ceramic "feeler."

NB: Check the function of semi-automatic or fully automatic irrigation systems regularly to avoid unpleasant surprises. Occasionally, problems may occur. In all cases, a newly installed system should be closely observed over a certain period of time, just as a trial run.

4 Automatic irrigation will care for the plants while you are away from home.

Pests, diseases, and mistakes in care

While watering, you should regularly take time to do a thorough check of your plants, especially the leaves and shoot tips, in order to spot trouble as soon as possible. Only quick action can prevent pests and diseases from spreading and endangering neighboring plants. Mistakes in care can also be the cause of an occurrence of disease and pests. For example, plants that are placed in a position that is not suitable for their requirements, are watered the wrong way, or are not receiving sufficient nutrients will all be weakened and this will make them particularly susceptible to disease or attack by pests.

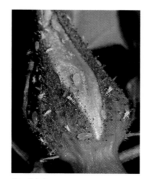

Aphids

Symptoms: Aphids (greenish or brownish-black) suck the sap out of buds, young leaves, and shoots, causing sticky, rolled up or crinkled leaves. Ants often follow as they utilize the sticky honeydew produced by the aphids for feeding their young.
Cause: Moist, warm weather and/or weakened plants. If humidity drops again, the aphid attack often subsides. Severe infestation can also occur if plants are overfertilized.
Remedy: Prevention through species-targeted care. Use plant protection agents when plants are infested.

Spider mites

Symptoms: The undersides of leaves are coated in fine web-like structures; light-colored dots on leaves.

Spider mites.

Cause: Dry, warm, stagnant air and/or weakening of the plant through mistakes in care.
Remedy: Plant protection agents. Prevent with good circulation of air. In advanced stages, web-like structures appear in the leaf axils.

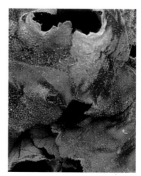

Powdery mildew

Symptoms: A flour-like film on the top and undersides of leaves as well as on stalks and flower buds. Withering of leaves in advanced stages.
Cause: Temperature fluctuations as well as constantly wet leaves during cool, wet weather.
Remedy: Do not wet the leaves when watering. Protect the planting arrangement from rain. Prevent by using plant-fortifying agents.
Affected parts can be carefully cut off and destroyed.
Subsequently, thoroughly clean tools and your hands to avoid spreading the fungus.

Sunburn

Overfertilizing

Dryness

Nutrient deficiency

Symptoms: Reddish-brown or grayish-silver discoloration of the leaves which does not always appear on the whole plant but usually only on the parts of the plant that face the sun. It is easy to confuse the symptoms with those of spider mite infestation.
Cause: Exposure to intense sunlight, ozone burns (particularly on medium-warm days), or frost damage during light night frosts.
Remedy: Prevent through the choice of a position suitable for the species. Newly purchased plants or overwintered plants have to be acclimatized gradually. Protect plants from night frost.
There is no protection against ozone damage.

Symptoms: Individual parts of shoot tips, buds, flowers, or leaves turn brown and start to develop mold. They do not dry up and do not drop off either. The greater part of the plant is not affected by the problem.
Cause: Overfertilizing. In particular, sensitive plants are most affected, for example those with variegated green and white foliage or soft leaves or herbs. Regular doses of fertilizer that are exactly right for nutrient-hungry plants will cause this reaction in more sensitive plants.
Remedy: Immediately cease regular fertilizing. Cut off affected parts.

Symptoms: Clearly discernible parts of individual leaves become discolored yellowish-brown and dry up.

Nutrient deficiency.

Cause: Lack of water in plants that can normally cope with little water (e.g. pelargoniums).
Remedy: Water more frequently. Cut back parts that have become unattractive. Water and fertilize regularly.

Symptoms: Yellow discoloration of older leaves. The plant becomes bare lower down and looks unhealthy and yellowish. Particularly noticeable after drenching rain showers and in summer plants that grow very fast, like petunias.
Cause: Nutrient deficiency through lack of proper fertilizing, particularly in plants that require lots of food. Heavy rain that washes nutrients out of the soil will also cause symptoms of deficiency.
Remedy: Spray the plant with leaf fertilizer in the evenings or in dull weather.
Then fertilize once weekly.

Successful care

Plant protection

Prevention is the best form of plant protection. Avoiding mistakes in care
means that you can eliminate most types of disease. If pests or diseases do appear, check first of all whether the affected plants are provided with the best conditions of growth for their species.
Note the following points.
- Choose the right position.
- Use the right kind of fertilizer and apply the correct dosage. Too much fertilizer can make a plant just as susceptible to disease as nutrient deficiency.
- On hot summer days, water your hanging plants, for example those in baskets, at least twice and do it plentifully, the best times being mornings and evenings. Remember that groups of plants will also dry out on cloudy days with strong winds. Plants placed right up against a house wall or under balconies and overhanging roofs will often not receive any rainwater.
- Water the plants very thoroughly. If the arrangement has dried out, water it several times in succession.

Mechanical methods

The simplest method of preventing infestation by pests is to collect the pests by hand, spray the leaves with a strong stream of water, or cut off affected parts of the plant.

Biological measures

A number of biological methods can be used for pests.
- If the infestation is not severe, or even as a preventive, you can use brews, fermented brews, or plant extracts. If an infestation has become severe, however, such remedies may not prove satisfactory. Furthermore, they should not be used too often as the plant may become damaged through a reaction to the brews. Plant extracts can be bought in garden centers.
- A well-tried home remedy that you can easily prepare yourself is a soap solution mixed with mineral spirits. Insects that eat the leaves or suck the sap of plants, like aphids and spider mites, can often be successfully controlled with this. Dissolve 1 tablespoon of soft soap in 4 cups (1 liter) of tepid water and add 1 tablespoon of mineral spirits. Spray the colonies of pests with the solution several times at intervals of a few days.
- Garlic brew works well against fungal infections. Crush 1 clove of garlic and pour 4 cups (1 liter) of boiling water over it. Let it cool, strain, and then spray undiluted.
- Preparations that are made out of paraffin or oil. They are non-toxic and do not, therefore, act as a nerve toxin on pests but, instead, clog up their breathing ducts with a film of oil. These preparations should not be used too often or they will also clog up the minute transpiration slits of the plants being treated.
- Pyrethrum extracts are derived from the flowers of an African chrysanthemum. They act as a nerve toxin on pests.
Warning: Although preparations containing pyrethrum are made from plant extracts, they are toxic to humans and animals as well if they enter the bloodstream. Do not use these agents if you have an open wound. Always wear gloves when handling these preparations and never inhale the spray mist. Do not use them in the close vicinity of aviaries, beehives, ponds, rivers, or aquariums and keep them away from children and pets.

Chemical agents

These really should be your very last resort when all other methods have failed or an infestation occurs in epidemic proportions. In fact it is often better to replace the affected plants instead of using chemical agents which require so many accompanying precautions.

● Never use highly toxic agents.

● Follow the rules for dosage and use stated on the packaging and also observe the suggested spraying intervals.

● Wear rubber gloves and do not eat, drink, or smoke while spraying. Do not inhale the spray mist.

● Only spray on windless days so that the agent cannot drift on to a neighbor's property.

● Never spray in sunlight as this may cause the plants to burn. It is better to spray in the mornings, evenings or when the sky is overcast.

● Always keep plant protection agents in the original packaging. Never, ever store them together with foodstuffs or within reach of children or domestic pets.

● Remains of spray solutions should not be kept as they quickly become ineffective. They should be put into sensitive waste disposal, not poured down the drains (check with your local council).

Healthy Gazania plant.

Healthy rootstock.

Sick rootstock.

Roots

All plants will develop well if they are watered and fertilized properly according to the requirements of their species. Disturbances in their growth pattern may occur if they receive too much or too little water. In both cases, the plant will wilt and become limp. A quick glance at the root system may help you to determine the cause.

Correct watering: With regular amounts of the right quantity of water for the particular species, a light-colored, felty root system (see central photo) is a recognizable sign of a healthy plant. The roots are intact and the transportation of water and nutrients from the bottom upward takes place without any problems.

Incorrect watering: The roots of the plant will become damaged if there is waterlogging or water is provided irregularly. They will first turn brown, then black and begin to rot (see bottom photo). The parts of the plant above the soil will begin to wilt and die because they cannot obtain water. The symptoms are very similar in plants that have suffered either drying out or waterlogging.

Watering and care

A beautifully proportioned hanging garden can transform any area. Throughout the year you can change the look and atmosphere simply through your choice of planting arrangements. However, an arangement that starts off looking beautiful can become a nightmare if the care you give is inadequate or inappropriate.

Plants that are difficult or uncomfortable to reach often end up being neglected so that they are not watered or looked after properly. The result is infestation with pests, disease, or, at the very least, lack of proper growth.

The importance of planning

When planning and designing you should ensure that there will be easy access to your hanging garden. This does not mean that you must always keep a tall ladder standing beside a hanging container that is out of easy reach. With the help of easily installed block and tackle equipment or pulleys that can be purchased from a builder's merchant, this kind of arrangement can be raised and then lowered to the right height for you to care for the plants easily.

1 Always place a bowl underneath when watering.

Water damage
(illustration 1)

Excess water will simply drip downward, particularly from hanging baskets.
● Place the arrangement in a position where the water can run away properly and will not damage anything underneath it. The ideal place is above a stone-flagged area with cracks between the individual slabs. On no account should excess water be allowed to run onto a neighboring balcony or patio.
● When watering, stand a bowl underneath to catch the water running through (see illustration 1). Placing an old cloth inside the bowl will prevent the running water from splashing over the edges.
● Water that runs through should not be allowed to drip onto plants underneath. Such constant showers from above would soon damage them.

2 Complete immersion is a relief for dry plants.

Emergency watering
(illustration 2)

Another way of watering hanging plants is to immerse them. This is recommended if the compost in the pot has dried out to the point where it will no longer absorb water during ordinary watering.

To do this, lower the hanging container or remove it from its hook and immerse it in a bath of water until no more air bubbles are seen to rise to the surface of the water. You may have to hold the pot down at first.

When carrying out this procedure, make sure that the shoots do not end up lying in the water or are damaged, or made dirty. The best way to avoid this is to hang the shoots carefully over the edge of the bath of water.

Rope and pulley
(illustration 3)

Pulleys are practical aids for lowering large, heavy plant containers. They can be purchased in the construction trade, from builders' merchants or in ship's chandlers specializing in sailing accessories. They are distinguished by the thickness of the rope and their carrying capacity. Simple or double rope pulleys are ideal for hanging containers or baskets that are not very heavy. Some pulleys are fixed with a screw at the top which means that the entire device can be screwed quite easily into a wooden beam. Others are made for attaching sideways, for example to a house wall. If you use a number of pulleys, you

3 The pulley guides the rope.

can run the rope over quite a distance and in different directions. This makes sense if fixing the rope close to the container is impossible, for example if your garden seat is right beside it. Even if it is conducted across several pulleys, the rope should still move evenly, without sagging. Use a hook firmly fixed in a handy position for tying up the end of the rope. It is possible to buy a kit that comes complete with all essential parts for a practical installation of ropes and pulleys.

Block and tackle
(illustration 4)

In the case of heavy hanging containers, free-hanging balcony boxes (see p. 30) or baskets, you may wish to install a block and tackle between the ceiling and the container.
With the help of this device you can lift and lower heavy weights very easily. A reasonably priced block and tackle from a builder's merchant, with a lifting capacity of 440 pounds (200 kg) will be quite sufficient for your purposes. Some means of securing it, in the form of a hook, for example, should be installed in order to fix the rope at the desired height.
Do make sure the apparatus is securely fixed and can lift the weight you propose to hang from it. If you are not a good handy-person, it might be a good idea to have the pulley or block and tackle installed by a professional.

4 A block and tackle make it easy to lower the plants into a comfortable position for you to reach.

Successful care

Caring for your plants

The correct care depends on the requirements of the species of plant. Always check your plants when carrying out daily watering in order to spot pests or diseases in their early stages so that you can immediately take measures against them. Less-involved measures of care, such as removing dead flower heads, tying up, or cutting back, will increase growth and willingness to flower among your plants. Plants are living organisms with a strong urge to survive. With the right care and in the optimal position, they will flower endlessly except during natural, seasonal rest periods or if there has been some kind of growth disturbance.

Removing dead flower heads

It is the natural function of plants to produce flowers and, later on, seeds. The formation of seed, however, also brings about the fading and withering of the flower as its natural purpose has now been fulfilled. By regularly removing dead flower heads, you will prevent the formation of seeds and encourage the production of more flowers. Also, no dead petals will be left to drop down onto other parts of the plant where they will start to decay, thus providing a fertile bed for diseases. If the flower

has a long stalk, remove the stalk along with the dead flower head. The trigger for seed formation in many balcony plants often comes in the form of great heat and long periods of drought. In their countries of origin, these plants would only flower during a wet period. When the dry period begins, flowering ceases.

Cutting back

Dead parts of the plant should be cut off with scissors and destroyed as they can become veritable "nurseries" for diseases of all kinds. Cut back shoots that are too long and also plants that threaten to smother their neighbors or rampage all over the container. Many plants become bushier when they are cut back in a systematic fashion. This is a useful exercise if only one meager shoot is present. After carrying out plant protection measures, cutting back can encourage plants, that have become weakened through attack by disease or pests, to produce new shoots. A rejuvenating cut encourages flower formation after the first crop of flowers.

Replacing plants

Plants are easy to replace, for example as the flowering season changes, if they are placed in

individual pots. Individual plants that have become unsightly amid a group of hanging plants can be carefully dug out with a trowel. Fresh compost and a new plant can be inserted in the hole. Follow the same procedure for dying plants in baskets. Cut off dead plants in the sides and base of the basket at the neck of the root. These bare patches will soon be covered over by neighboring plants. You can freshen up the used compost in long-term plant groups if you loosen the surface around the rootstocks and sprinkle fresh compost here.

Overwintering

Outside: Hardy groups of plants can be overwintered outside with a few careful precautions. Remember that, whether full or empty, containers that remain outside must be frost-proof. Ceramic containers will often crack in winter, particularly if the compost in them is moist and begins to expand during freezing weather. Plastic containers should not crack when frozen. They should be kept either in a frost-free room or, if you do not have such a space, under a roofed-over area outside. Cover containers with plants in them with brushwood or something similar and water them on frost-free days. Remove hanging containers and place them in

Begonias and fuchsias will flourish if they are given good care.

suitable winter quarters. Hardy plants removed from baskets should be planted in pots in the fall.

Overwintering in frost-free conditions: Groups of plants that are expected to be sensitive to cold should be cut back before taking them inside to be overwintered in a position that is as bright and cool (but frost-free)

as possible. A cool conservatory is ideal. Many plants will even flower here during the winter. During the coldest time of year, water them sparingly but do not let them dry out.

Protection against early or late frosts

A hanging planting arrangement with plants that are sensitive to frost is easy to protect from light frosts in the spring or fall if it is moved to a frost-free position overnight or covered over and wrapped up all around in polyethylene or something similar.

NOTES

Acknowledgments

The author Martin Weimar and the publishers wish to thank Claudia Worner, florist and gardener, for her help in the taking of these photographs. Thanks also go to Angelika Sage, who offered the use of her balcony and patio for photography.

This edition published 1996
by Landoll, Inc.
By arrangement with
Merehurst Limited
Ferry House, 51-57 Lacy Road,
Putney, London SW15 1PR

A candlelit dinner on the patio

What could be nicer on a summer's evening than to dine outdoors on a patio where the warm evening air is filled with the enchanting scent of star balm (*Zaluzianskya capensis*) and tobacco flowering (*Nicotiana suaveolens*). In this hanging garden these two have been combined with ivy. The best way to grow these plants is from seed during the second month of spring and then to plant them in hanging containers after the late frosts in the last month of spring. If you wish, you can add *Nicotiana sylvestris* (left in the photo) which also has a lovely evening fragrance.

An enchanted evening setting with candles and scented plants.

Success with

Herbs

CHRISTINE RECHT

Series Editor:
LESLEY YOUNG

Contents

A roundel with herbs and flowers is the centerpiece in an ornamental garden.

Contents

Butterflies love herbs.

Attractive flowering chives.

Paprika – a hot and spicy decoration.

Introduction

For centuries people have been fascinated by herb lore and the secrets of herbal remedies. Herbs are such rewarding plants. Through their spicy taste and wonderful aroma, they give food that special flavor, improve the digestion, help you to enjoy better health, and are a sheer visual delight for any plant enthusiast, with their attractive green leaves and delicate flowers. As anyone who regularly uses herbal teas knows, they are an excellent pick-me-up when you are feeling tired and their regular use can make you feel fitter and more relaxed. There is nothing like the pleasure you get from harvesting home-grown plants and then using them to prepare delicious meals. You do not even need to own a garden. A balcony or even a windowsill will serve equally well for growing most species of herbs. In return for only a little effort and attention, you will be able to enjoy the results of your own organic herb garden.

This colorful guide will tell you all the important things you should know about herb gardening. The instructions and advice offered by author and herb expert Christine Recht are easy for anyone to follow. Even those readers who have hardly done any gardening, or even none at all, will soon find themselves looking forward to a bountiful harvest of herbs. Whether you decide to raise herbs on a windowsill, a balcony or in the garden, you will find plenty of useful advice here to lead you through the herbal year, starting with buying, sowing, and care, seeds and cuttings, choosing the best position, supplying light and warmth, and the right soil, and, finally, harvesting your herbs. Even if you are a complete novice, the step-by-step color illustrations will help you to acquire the necessary gardening know-how, and will simplify the various stages of sowing, germination, repotting, watering, and further care. Ignoring the restrictions of the traditional herb bed or flower pot, the author will delight you with numerous original ideas for various ways of planting or combining herbs: in raised or pyramid beds in the garden, in your own herb-growing box, or in a terraced arrangement for the balcony or patio. Tips on the biological control of pests and diseases are included, as well as advice on propagating your own herbs. At the climax of the herbal year, there is advice on how to harvest your crop and how best to preserve the herbs so that they will retain their aroma and delicious flavors. There is plenty of advice on preserving (drying, freezing, and pickling), as well as on the best herbs to use for different dishes. Lovely color photographs, most of which were specially taken for this guide, will whet your appetite and provide you with the incentive to start your own herb garden. Individual instructions on the care of the most popular herbs used in cooking make it all so much easier, and there are excellent color photographs of every plant described to make identification simple.

The author

Christine Recht, who works as a co-editor on several specialist gardening periodicals, is also the author of a number of books on plants and gardening. Everything she describes in this guide has been tried and tested on her balcony or in her own garden.

Acknowledgments

The author and publishers wish to thank all those who have contributed towards this volume, especially Karin Skogstad and the other plant photographers for their exceptionally beautiful color photographs, and Ushie Dorner for her excellent, informative illustrations.

NB: Herbs are good for you, there is no doubt about that, but too much of any good thing can be detrimental, especially when you are using herbal teas for healing purposes. We strongly recommend that you consult your doctor first if you intend to use herbs for medicinal purposes over an extended period of time. Please take note of all the points headed "NB" or "Warning" given throughout the descriptions of herbs. These notes will tell you if there are any restrictions or possible allergies to be considered before you use a particular herb.

Home-grown herbs
You do not need to have a garden – herbs will flourish on a balcony or windowsill.

Where to grow herbs

Fresh herbs can be the making of an excellent meal and you do not need to own a garden to have a constant supply of fresh herbs at your disposal. You can grow herbs in any sunny, warm spot, on a balcony or patio, or in a small back yard. You can even cultivate home-grown herbs indoors in pots on a windowsill. The following chapter will give you a few ideas on just where to look for a space to grow your own herbs.

Herbs on a balcony or patio

Herbs are not demanding plants at all and they are even more resilient than many balcony pot plants. They will flourish in tubs and pots, although it must be admitted that some herbs may not grow quite as tall or as well in small containers as they would in a herb bed in the garden. Their wonderful aroma, however, will pervade a balcony or patio just as pleasingly as if they were planted in a traditonal herb garden. Almost any home nowadays, whether in the town or in the country, will have either a patio or a balcony. Indeed, some balconies in large modern apartment blocks are almost the size of a patio or terrace, while other urban buildings even boast a roof garden. You can have a herb garden virtually anywhere. You will be amazed at just how many different herbs can be grown in a very small space and what an abundant harvest they will provide – given the proper care of course.

The right position

A south-facing position is absolutely ideal for herbs that love to grow in full sunlight. Herbs that prefer a semi-shady habitat should be positioned where they will not be exposed to sunlight all day long – perhaps in the shadow of other, larger plants, or in a corner that is shaded from the midday sun.
West- and east-facing positions are quite suitable for most herbs used in cooking. Warmth-loving herbs should be placed right up against a wall that is exposed to the sun for several hours a day. Even when the sun is no longer shining directly onto the balcony or patio, the wall will still give off retained heat.
A north-facing position is most unsuitable for herbs. About the only species you can grow successfully here are cress and maybe chives. Sun-loving herbs will not thrive in such a site.
Windy balconies and patios in exposed positions, or those higher than five floors up, are not ideal. Never hang boxes of herbs on the railings as they will not thrive in draughts. A better position to choose is on the inside of a balcony wall or, better still, on the balcony up against the house wall. Balconies or patios on the lower floors of tall buildings situated **on busy roads** with a lot of traffic are particularly unsuitable for growing herbs. These sensitive plants will absorb the pollutants from exhaust fumes in the air and they should not be eaten!

Watch the weight of your containers!

When gardening on balconies and elevated patios etc., the weight of the containers and boxes you use is a very important consideration. The individual plants may not weigh much but the total weight of the containers plus soil should never be underestimated, while this weight may increase by up to half as much again when they have been thoroughly watered! *The approximate extra weight* is probably somewhere around 550 pounds (250 kg) per square metre or square yard, not including the weight of any kind of plant stand or plant saucers. If you have any doubts, ask a structural engineer or building surveyor, or check the building plans.

Plant containers for your balcony or patio

The range of plant containers on the market is so vast that you are sure to find something suitable for your patio or balcony. Just in case you do not, however, this section also contains ideas for making your own containers.

Flowerpots

Nearly all herbs will flourish in flower pots.
Size: Make sure that herbs with

Sun-warmed steps are an ideal place for all herbs. They will thrive particularly well in clay pots.

large rootstocks or long tap roots are planted in sufficiently large, deep pots.

Flat-rooted varieties, like thyme or parsley, can be grown in shallow basins. The rule of thumb is, the larger the pot, the better the plant will thrive. You really cannot expect a herb to grow very much in a pot with a diameter of 4¾ in (12 cm) – the pot should be at least 8 in (20 cm) wide.

Clay pots: These are, on the whole, much better for growing herbs than plastic pots. Most herbs prefer to

be in fairly dry soil. The porous walls of fired clay pots allow moisture to evaporate steadily.

Plastic pots: Water will generally evaporate upward, so these are more suitable for moisture-loving herbs like parsley and chives.

Positioning: If you intend to grow a number of different herbs, individual pots will take up a lot of space. There are a few ways to make the most of your space:

● Stand the pots in terraced rows. For example, one row of pots on a garden bench and a second row

below. The sun-loving ones should be set higher than the herbs that prefer a semi-shady position.

● This principle can be used to set up wall shelves.

● You can erect a "herb ladder" (with three steps) on one of the shorter walls of your balcony. Such a device can quite easily be built using a few strong planks.

● The outside ledge of a sunny window overlooking a balcony is another good place for herbs in pots. You can combine your herb pots with flowering plants in pots.

*A wooden box
on castors*

*Measure and cut the wood for the bottom and sides with dovetailed or
overlapping joints and make a ledge with mitered corners. Drill drainage
holes in the bottom. Fit the sides together, then glue them to the bottom so
that they protrude a little but cannot interfere with the castors. Glue the
ledges to the top edge of the side walls and screw them down. Coat the
inside of the box with silicon-based paint.*

Herb boxes

A herb box will really save space on
your balcony and you can grow
several different kinds of herbs
here.

Size: The most important consideration is to build the boxes large
enough and deep enough to provide room for the roots of several
plants. A box that is 2 ft (60 cm)
long and 16 in (40 cm) deep should
accommodate at least five plants.

Materials: Wooden boxes are
attractive but there is nothing wrong
with well-designed boxes made of
plastic. Although small plastic pots
are not a good idea for herbs, using
large plastic tubs can be an advantage as water will not evaporate
quite so quickly because of the
large surface area of soil. Avoid
containers made of concrete as
they are much too heavy for balconies.

Positions: Plant boxes can be
bought in all shapes and sizes for
growing large container plants and
balcony flowers. Think what shape
of box might be most useful for your
purposes: triangular boxes will fit
neatly into a corner; small hexago-
nal boxes can be fitted together as
a group; while round containers
take up more room. Regular flower
boxes, the kind used for balcony
flowers, are very useful for smaller
herbs. They can be hung on a balcony railing or placed on a window
ledge or on plant stands (obtainable
from garden centers).

*How to make your own wooden
boxes* (see the illustration above)
Note the following points:

● Hardwood (oak or beech) will
last much longer than softwood (fir
or pine).

● Dovetail the joints or screw them
together using angle irons or brass
screws. Nails will rust too quickly.

● Make sure you drill drainage
holes in the floor of the box and
stand the box on small pegs or
blocks of wood so that air can
circulate underneath it. A wooden
bottom that is wet most of the time
will rot away very quickly.

● Coat the inside of the box with a
substance that is not harmful to
plants, for example, silicon paint
(sold in hardware stores). If you
decide to line the box with metal
foil, cover only the sides. Water
must be able to drain away at the
bottom as herbs are sensitive to
waterlogging.

My tip: Standing the herb box on a
base with wheels, or screwing furniture casters to the four corners, can
prove useful. This idea is particularly
practical in spring and fall, when
you will find it easy to trundle the
box around effortlessly, following
the path of the sun across your balcony or patio.

A lean-to greenhouse

Small, lean-to greenhouses in
various sizes can be obtained from
garden suppliers. Make sure there
is adequate ventilation, however, as
sunny days can result in heat building up behind the glass so that conditions may become too hot even
for warmth-loving herbs. In the
spring, you can start growing your
herbs in this little greenhouse, along
with your balcony plants. If the
greenhouse is situated against a
south-facing wall, you will have to
provide some kind of shade. A
bamboo roller shade or a fabric
curtain may be sufficient.

Hanging baskets or containers

Containers made of all kinds of
materials, such as clay, wood, and
plastic, or even wire or wicker baskets may be used as hanging containers. Baskets should be lined on
the inside with aluminum foil, which
should have enough holes pierced
in it to let water drain out. Make
sure hanging containers are not
positioned in a draught. This may
harm the plants and, in very windy
conditions, may even lead to accidents.

NB: The device from which the container is hung must be safely secured.

A herb barrel

This type of container is an
extremely practical, as well as simple, solution. It can be positioned
anywhere. Your herbs will have
plenty of room in which to grow
downward, while being confined to

a very small horizontal space. Barrels for growing strawberries can be bought at garden centers, etc. They are made of plastic or clay, with holes or small protruding pockets all over the sides.

How to make your own herb barrel:
You will need a small plastic barrel:

● Cut a number of holes in the wall of the barrel at staggered intervals, making them approximately 6 in (15 cm) across.

● Drill several drainage holes in the bottom of the barrel, using a ⅛-in (approx. 6-mm) wood drill.

● Place a large cardboard tube in the center of the barrel and fill the tube with coarse gravel. This will provide an adequate supply of moisture later on.

● Fill the barrel with gravel to a level of about 8 in (20 cm).

● Use a mixture of soil and compost to fill up the rest of the barrel.

● The following trick can be used to prevent the soil and plants from falling out of the holes. Cut up pieces of cotton or hessian fabric or pieces of old stockings or pantyhose. The pieces should be slightly larger than the holes in the barrel. Cut small holes in the center of these scraps of fabric, through which the roots of the herb cutting can be pulled.

● Plant the herb cuttings from the bottom of the barrel upward, pushing each cutting through from the outside into the barrel, then press the fabric scrap against the inside wall of the barrel and fill the barrel with soil.

● The cardboard tube should be kept vertical. After planting, a plastic pot without a bottom should be placed on top of the tube, through which the plants can be regularly watered. The cardboard will disintegrate and a core of gravel will remain, through which you will be able to water your herbs for years.

How to build a herb barrel

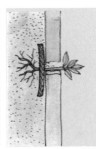

Cut holes in the side of a plastic barrel, put in a layer of gravel, insert a cardboard tube in the center, and fill it with more gravel. Plant from the bottom upward. Push the roots of the cuttings through the holes in the barrel. Use the fabric scraps to hold the roots on the inside of the barrel. Fill the barrel with soil.

My tip: The soil or compost will decompose in time as the roots grow through it. It will no longer fall out of the holes and the tedious procedure with bits of fabric will no longer be necessary whenever you replace a plant.

Special tips for ground-level patios

Many houses or first-floor apartments have a patio that does not have a balustrade or railings. None the less, such patios offer the same possibilities for growing herbs as a balcony.

Make sure your herbs receive the amount of sunlight that is essential

A box without a bottom
Place breeze blocks together, or screw together large pieces of squared wood using angle irons.

for their growth. Remember that other groups of plants, whether in beds or as a windbreak, etc., may create quite a bit of shade. If your patio is sheltered by an arbor covered by a creeper or an awning, the herbs should be positioned at the front where there is plenty of light. If your patio is well exposed to the sun, the best position is right up against the wall of the house.

Boxes without bases
This type of box could be a permanent bed for herbs. You will be able to grow many different kinds of herbs here and to cover them up with a polyethylene tunnel in spring and fall, as you would an early sowing bed. This will give you an opportunity to harvest herbs very early and also to continue picking them very late in the year.

Position: Place the box in a permanent position. It must be filled with plenty of soil, so it would be a difficult task to move it to another location. The ideal position would be at the edge of a patio, but not on a paved area. This avoids any problems with water drainage. If you are already planning the use of such a box when you build your patio, you can leave out a section of paving stones.

You can, of course, still place the box on a paved area, as long as the water can drain away easily.

Build your own herb box
You will have to build your own box without a bottom, as they are not generally for sale in garden suppliers.
● The box should not be higher than 20 in (50 cm), as the pressure of the soil when full would then be too great.
● Suitable materials: squared lumber or wooden railroad ties which should be fixed at the corners with angle irons, or thick boards that are screwed to pieces of squared wood at each corner.
Note: Railroad ties and other wood treated with certain types of wood preservative contain substances that are toxic to plants. You will have to place tough polyethylene sheets against the inside walls before you fill the box with soil. Raw wood will have to be painted with a plant-friendly preservative (obtainable in garden centers), as the wood will rot away very quickly without any kind of protection.
● Other possibilities: Build a box out of bricks or breeze blocks by simply placing them together. The breeze blocks can even be filled with soil, thus providing extra planting space.
Important: If the box is standing on the patio, you will have to provide some kind of drainage facility. Boxes made of wood can be equipped with drainage holes by sawing out small sections along the bottom edges at intervals of 8 in (20 cm). You will need to use a proper masonry drill to make drainage holes in the sides of a stone-built box.

Fragrance and color
Lavender bushes provide scent and color. Plant them among large container plants on a balcony.

● Pour a 4-in (10-cm) layer of gravel into the finished box, cover the gravel with a sheet of interfacing fabric or polythene, with slits in it, and pour compost on top.

My tip: Patios or terraces usually slope slightly downward away from the house so that excess water will run off them. Before building a box, check your patio with a spirit level to make sure this slope (a maximum of 2%) has been incorporated. If it has not, do not make holes in the side of the box nearer to the house.

A herb staircase
A kind of staircase or terrace can be built on both sides of steps leading from a patio down to a garden. This will provide lots of room in which to stand several pots and shallow basins full of fragrant growing herbs. The following points should be observed:
● The top step should be twice as wide as the other steps. This will provide space for large pots.
● The steps should be very stable, as they will have to bear a considerable weight.
● Position these steps in such a way that all the levels receive plenty of sunlight. Therefore, do not position them facing south, as one side of the plants would then be in perpetual shade. It is preferable to build the steps in an east-west direction and stand the most sunloving plants at the south end.

Herbs around the patio
You can plant herbs in among the ornamental plants around your patio. Generally speaking, a terrace will be slightly elevated, and the rubble and other material underneath it will be permeable and the soil fairly dry. If you have a rock garden too, the Mediterranean herbs, such as oregano, thyme, marjoram, rosemary, and sage, will

feel completely at home. The rocks will retain heat from the sun and then release it during the night, which makes this kind of site ideal for herbs. Other herbs can be planted between shrubs and summer flowers. Just make sure that any combinations of plants have similar requirements with respect to nutrients and watering.

Herbs in the garden

There are far more possibilities for planting herbs in the garden than anywhere else. Even the tiniest garden plot, which would not accommodate a vegetable bed, will still have room for a herb roundel in the center of a lawn. Besides the traditional herb garden, there is a whole range of other decorative options.

A herb mound
A mound, planted all over with herbs and edged with low-growing summer flowers, is a very useful as well as an eye-catching feature.
How to design your mound:
● Using a length of twine, a stick, and a few small pegs, draw a round on your lawn and then remove the turf from inside the circle.

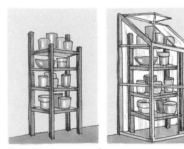

A balcony greenhouse
In the spring and fall a simple set of shelves can be transformed into a greenhouse. A small lean-to greenhouse can be bought from garden suppliers.

● Loosen the earth to a spade's depth.

● Build a dry-stone wall, out of rocks or chunks of sandstone, to a height of 20 in (50 cm) all around the round. Merely lay the stones on top of each other; do not use mortar. Fill the gaps with soil and plant rock garden plants in these spaces.

● Inside the round, spread a layer of gravel, about 4 in (10 cm) thick, for drainage purposes, then cover this with a mixture of soil, sand, and compost, right to the upper edge of the stone wall and then carry on building a small mound of soil in the center.

● The largest herbs, which need most sun, should be planted on the summit of the mound; the other herbs can be distributed down the slopes, depending on their need for sunlight.

A herb spiral

A further development of the idea of a herb mound is a herb spiral. This arrangement will cater for the various sun or shade requirements of different herbs.

Method (see illustration below):

● Build a spiral dry wall (like a rising snail shell) out of fragments of stones, rocks, or bricks. The top should not be any higher than 80 cm (32 in).

Building a herb spiral

● Fill the inside first with gravel then with a mixture of soil, compost and sand.

● The topmost layer should be composed of fairly poor soil, and this is where all the sun-loving herbs should be planted.

● At the base of the spiral, use richer soil, containing more compost, for those herbs that need more nutrients.

My tip: You could even build a miniature pond at the lower end of the spiral. A plastic, molded pond or even a plastic bathtub would be sufficient to provide a home for water cress or water mint.

A round bed (roundel)

A round bed is the simplest solution for a herb bed, for example, in the center of the lawn.

Method:

● Draw a round, as described above, and remove the turf.

● Loosen the soil and fill up the round with a mixture of soil, compost and sand.

● Low-flowering plants will form an attractive border around the edge of the bed.

A raised bed

A raised bed should be situated on the ground, not on a concrete or

stone-paved patio surface.

Method:

● Build a square box out of thick boards or planks, new railroad ties, or bricks. It should be at least 40 in high (1 m). Anchor it well (build a foundation or drive some boards into the soil), as the walls will have to take the strain of a large volume of soil.

● Thoroughly loosen the soil underneath and all around the raised bed, so that water can drain away easily.

● Finally, fill the raised bed. The bottom layer – about 16 in (40 cm) thick – should consist of twigs and other biodegradable substances: first, thicker ones that have been broken up into small pieces, followed by thinner twigs, also broken up, then grass cuttings or similar material that is well decomposed. On top of this, place a layer of soil and, finally, a 8-in (20-cm) thick layer of a mixture of garden soil, compost and sand.

● The raised bed will settle a little over the years as the lower layer rots away (creating a lot of heat which benefits the herbs). This means that you will have to top up the bed with a little soil and compost every year.

● You may plant lots of different herbs quite close together as their roots will find it quite easy to spread downward in the loose soil. Depending on your own preference, around the edge you can plant a ring of hanging flowers or vegetables that grow downwards.

A pyramid bed

A pyramid bed is built in a similar way to a raised bed. The pyramid consists of three boxes of different widths, all without bottoms, and all about 16 in (40 cm) high.

Method:

● Thoroughly loosen the earth in the vicinity of the bed.

Build a spiral-shaped dry-stone wall out of broken quarry stones or bricks (no higher than 32 in/80 cm). Fill in with nutrient-rich soil at the bottom and poorer soil at the top. Make a small pond at the foot. Plant sun-loving herbs at the top and nutrient-loving herbs at the bottom.

A pyramid bed and a raised bed

Build a box out of thick planks (left) or bricks (right) about 40 in (1 m) high. Protect it from rodents with fine-mesh wire. To make a pyramid herb bed, place a smaller box on a raised bed (center). Herbs may be planted close together and hanging plants or vegetables can be placed around the edge (cucumbers, strawberries, etc.).

● Place the largest box in the desired position and fill it up with woody refuse and soil, just like a raised bed.
● On top of this, place the second, medium-sized box, fill it up, then place the third and smallest box on top, and again fill it with soil.

My tip: The three tiers of the pyramid shape will provide various types of herbs with all they need: fill the lowest box with nutrient-rich soil for those herbs that require this and fill the topmost box with less nutrient-rich soil, containing plenty of lime for the sun-loving herbs.

A herb border around the lawn
Herbs will also thrive in flower beds all around the lawn, particularly if you choose herbs that have the same kind of requirements (water, fertilizer, and light) as the neighboring shrubs. When planting, check that your herbs will have plenty of room to expand as they will grow a lot during the summer.

The traditional herb bed
The simplest solution, of course, is to plant your herbs in the garden. One square yard (approx. 1 sq m)

will be quite sufficient for all the herbs you are likely to want. Make sure that the soil is loose, not too rich and, if necessary, add sand or fine gravel to a very loamy soil. A low box-tree border makes a particularly decorative feature.

Herbs in your back yard

Over recent years, there has been an increasing trend towards transforming small, paved back yards with greenery. So, why not find a space to plant a herb bed? One thing the yard will need is plenty of sun and, as the ground is usually covered with concrete or paving stones, the bed will have to be a raised one. This takes us back to the same kind of arrangements that are required on a balcony or patio, for example, a herb barrel or even a raised bed or a pyramid bed.

Flower boxes outside a window

A whole range of herbs will find sufficient room to grow in a flower box. The herbs will thrive in plenty of sun and fresh air, so you can place the

box in front of a window if:
● the window is no higher than five floors up (any higher will tend to be too windy);
● the outside window ledge is wide enough;
● you can fix the flower box to the ledge in such a way that the box hangs below the ledge.
Warning: The box must be secured properly so that there is no risk of it falling down!

My tip: Transparent protective hoods can be bought for the boxes. They will protect your plants from strong winds or heavy rain.

Herbs on the windowsill

Another good idea is to grow herbs on a windowsill inside the house. They will not flourish quite as well here as outside, of course, and most of them will never develop the full aroma of herbs grown outside. Nevertheless, there are a number of plants that can be grown quite easily on a windowsill. The best candidates are the annual herbs. This means that you will have to replace them with new plants after they have been harvested.
Suitable plants: Basil, chervil, cress, lemon balm, parsley, salad burnet, thyme, and chives.
Which window: Herbs will grow best in east- or west-facing windows. A south-facing window is not suitable as it will get much too hot in summer. A north window is unsuitable and the plants will not thrive.
Important: Herbs on windowsills will have to be watered more often than those outside as they will dry out fast in the arid atmosphere of a room, particularly in the summer when indoor air is much drier than the air outside. Misting with soft water is also essential.

1. Green basil.

2. Red basil.

3. Curly basil.

4. Chervil.

5. Oregano.

6. Tarragon.

The photographs show:

1. Basil: the green variety has a stronger aroma and flavor.
2. Basil: the red varieties are very decorative.
3. Basil: this variety, called "Green Ruffles," is still quite rare.
4. Chervil: will grow fast, even in pots.
5. Oregano: requires plenty of room to grow.
6. Tarragon: will grow fast if the shoot tips are pinched out regularly.

My tip: On warm days move your windowsill herbs onto the window ledge outside. Sunshine and fresh air will help to improve the aroma and flavor. Make sure the pots and boxes are secure so that they cannot fall down into the street!

Plant containers for your windowsill

Flowerpots are the best containers for herbs on a windowsill. Clay pots are better than plastic ones, even if you have to water them more often. Waterlogging and "cold feet" are lethal for nearly all herbs. If you stand the flowerpots in decorative pot holders, you should make a point of checking them an hour after watering to see if the outer pot is full of water – if so, it should be poured away.

Plant troughs are an attractive alternative to individual pots. Terracotta troughs, for example, may accommodate a number of herb pots; fill the spaces with Hortag or peat to absorb any moisture that escapes through the drainage holes and then release it

1. Parsley.

2. Lemon balm.

3. Peppermint.

4. Marjoram.

5. Rosemary.

6. Sage.

back to the plants as the soil around the roots dries out. In this way there is no waterlogging and you need not water so often. Another advantage is that the moisture absorbed by the filling material will evaporate and pass humidity from the air to the herbs' leaves, which suits them very well.

A window shelf
A shelf suspended within a window frame will guarantee the maximum amount of light for the herbs placed there. However, this device is only really suitable for small pots and lightweight plants.

Method:
● Hang several narrow shelves on doubled, very strong nylon rope or on thick wire.
● Prop them up underneath with a narrow strip of wood.
● Fix two strong hooks securely to the top of the window embrasure and suspend the shelf from these.
Warning: This type of shelf is only suitable for windows that cannot be opened or tipped.

The photographs show:
1. Parsley: the smooth-leafed variety has a stronger flavor.
2. Lemon balm: in a pot this will grow very tall and spread out.
3. Peppermint: will release a delicate fragrance.
4. Marjoram: is very sensitive to cold.
5. Rosemary: for use in cooking or as an ornamental shrub.
6. Sage: for flavoring and for herbal remedies. The multi-colored varieties are very decorative.

The right kind of soil

The right kind of soil is particularly important for the well-being of herbs, especially if you are growing them in plant containers. Even though most herbs are quite undemanding, they still require certain nutrients. Unlike garden soil, the soil of plant containers is not naturally replenished with nutrients after the original ones have been used up by the plants.

Soil in plant containers

Outdoors, in garden soil, nutrients are replaced almost automatically and millions of micro-organisms and earthworms are constantly working the soil. Herbs, which are never very demanding in respect to fertilizers, will flourish for years in garden soil.

Plant containers are a different matter: too much fertilizing is not good for herbs and the soil in pots will probably become "exhausted" after about a year. This means that you will have to make sure, right from the start, that your herbs have sufficient quantities of the right kind of nutrients in the limited space of the plant pot. You will have to change the soil every year and the old soil will only be fit for adding to well-fertilized flower compost for your balcony plants.

Commercially available compost

Ordinary flowering-plant potting compost: Generally, this is not at all suitable for herbs. Only lovage, chives, tarragon, and borage will thrive in a mixture of flowering-plant potting compost, sand, and ordinary compost. Flowering-plant potting compost contains too much fertilizer and most herbs like only small amounts of fertilizer. Some will not thrive at all in soil that is too well-fertilized, while others will grow tall but will lose their aroma and flavor.

Peat composts: Inquire at your garden center for the right type of commercially produced compost for growing herbs. This will be low in fertilizer and will simulate the poorer types of soils that many herbs are happiest in. Herbs tend to need soils containing large amounts of sand, gravel and lime.

Standard potting compost: This compost consists of loamy soil, peat, and polystyrene granules or another aerating material. It is reasonably suitable for cultivating herbs but even this type of compost should first be mixed with additional sand or peat compost, or both, depending on the requirements of the herb in question.

Peat: Peat contains no nutrients at all, but has good water-retaining properties. Nothing will grow in pure peat. Herbs that like very poor soil will grow quite happily in a mixture of equal parts of peat and sand or very fine gravel and peat compost.

Soils that cost nothing

You can always use garden soil for your attempts at herb gardening in plant containers, although such soils will have to be prepared a little. If you have ever tried to grow a plant in a pot of garden soil, you will have found that the soil turns into a rock-hard lump in no time at all.

Make sure that the soil you use is not full of fertilizer, pesticides, or other harmful substances. If it is not from your own garden, check with the owner of the land when you ask for permission to take the soil and be very cautious about soil taken from an arable field or somewhere similar.

Garden soil: You can probably obtain small quantities of this from friends who have a garden or even from a helpful local plant nursery. Make sure you know what type of soil you are dealing with:

- Sandy garden soil need not have any more sand added to it but will probably need a little peat and Perlite to help it to retain nutrients and water.
- Humus-rich garden soil from flower beds is ideal and should be loose and crumbly. It should be loosened up with sand or peat and a little compost.
- Loamy garden soil is only suitable for herb gardening if it is mixed with equal amounts of sand or peat, or with compost.

Soil taken from mole hills: This is very suitable, as it is free of all weed seeds. It will not, however, contain many nutrients as moles throw it up from fairly deep levels in the soil. Depending on the type of soil involved, it will be sandy or loamy. If it is going to be used to grow herbs, it will have to be prepared beforehand, just like garden soil. It will need mixing with a controlled-release fertilizer and more compost than garden soil, which already contains lots of nutrients.

The right mixture

The best mixture of soil for herb gardening will depend largely on the requirements of the particular herb, which, in turn, will depend a lot on the origins and natural habitat of the herb's ancestors. Never forget that herbs are really wild plants! They will thrive best in soil that is very similar to the soil in the places where they grow naturally. Which mixture is best for which herbs is explained.

Basically, there are three different types of soil, which are obtained by varying the mixtures.

Very poor soil: Mix ⅓ peat-based compost with ⅓ sand and ⅓ compost. If you need to add lime, which is vital for some herbs, you should calculate for about 1 teaspoon per flowerpot.

Semi-poor soil: Mix ⅔ peat-rich compost or garden soil with ⅓ compost and a little extra peat or sand (one handful for a flowerpot with a diameter of 8 in (20 cm).

Nutrient-rich soil: Mix ⅓ garden soil or peat-based compost with ⅔ compost. Sand and peat should only be added if the garden soil is very loamy.

How to mix: All the components of these soils should be mixed together thoroughly.

The very decorative hyssop makes a tasty addition to vegetarian dishes.

Rue is too large to grow on balconies but is attractive in a garden.

The right soil for your herbs

Poor soil	Semi-poor soil	Nutrient-rich soil
cress	basil	bay leaf
lemon balm	chervil	borage
marjoram	chives	lovage
oregano	dill	nasturtium
rosemary	mint	tarragon
sage	parsley	
thyme	salad burnet	
	summer savory	

The best time to mix the different ingredients is when they are dry. Only the peat should be moistened beforehand.

● Place the ingredients on a large plastic sheet or in a large container.
● Break up any large lumps by hand and, if possible, run the sand through a sieve.
● Mix it well together with a small trowel or by hand and then fill the pots and boxes.
● After watering, the soil will settle a little, so always keep a small amount of the mixture on hand for topping up later on.

How to make soil less heavy

Large containers and boxes can become extremely heavy when they are filled with soil so it is an advantage to have containers that are filled with material that is as light as possible, particularly on a balcony where plants need to be moved about, or if they have to be brought indoors for the winter. You can make the containers less heavy by mixing polystyrene granules, Hortag or Perlite with the soil, instead of sand or peat. Hortag, however, will tend to soak up lots of water, which can make it heavy again.

Warning: If there is any risk of the wind toppling the boxes or contain-ers over, they should not be made too light. Large plants, like rose-mary or a bay tree, will need to stand firmly in a heavier soil base.

Soil in small beds

It goes without saying that a few buckets of mole-hill soil or a sack of peat-based compost will not be adequate for a raised bed or a herb spiral. If you have no garden soil at all at your disposal, you will have to purchase some. The best value for money is real topsoil which has been mixed with compost to obtain a suitable soil for a particular herb (see table above).

Topsoil: This can be obtained from some builders' merchants and occasionally from large nurseries and garden centers. About ⅓-½ cu yd (1-2 cubic meters) should be sufficient to build a herb mound or raised bed.

Never buy topsoil over the telephone; always check the soil on the spot. Often soil derived from the excavation of deep layers is sold as topsoil. This deep-level soil contains no nutrients, is often full of clay, and is totally unsuitable for growing herbs. Always try to obtain real topsoil.

Mixtures for a herb bed

A raised bed, herb mound, and pyramid bed have certain require-ments, as described in the section on herbs in plant containers.

Very poor soil: Topsoil (or garden soil) should be mixed with equal parts of sand and compost.

Semi-poor soil: Mix ⅔ topsoil with ⅓ compost and then add approxi-mately five buckets of sand to every ⅓ cu yd (cubic meter) of the mixture.

Nutrient-rich soil: Mix topsoil with compost. If the topsoil is very com-pact, add some sand.

How to mix: Make sure all ingredi-ents are dry before mixing.

● Break down any hard lumps; remove stones and pieces of wood from the compost and topsoil.
● Place the ingredients together on a clean surface and mix well.

Different types of soil in one bed

With care, it is possible to arrange this. If you are planting very differ-ent kinds of herbs together, it will be absolutely necessary.

Here are two further tips for making herb mounds and barrels:

● Pour the nutrient-rich soil into a large hole in the herb mound, then plant the herbs that thrive best on that type of soil.
● In a herb barrel: Plant the herbs that prefer poorer soil in the pock-ets in the side of the barrel. Pour in a layer (8 in/20 cm thick) of nutrient-rich soil right at the top and plant the herbs that require more nutri-ents in this.

Compost

As herbs are grown for human consumption, they should be fed with organic-based nutrients. Mineral fertilizers usually contain too much nitrogen. Compost is an ideal nutritional base for all herbs, even for those which prefer poor soil. If you cannot obtain compost or make it yourself, other organic fertilizers can be used.

As compost is the cheapest and most natural source of nutrients for herbs, it is better to try to buy compost before exploring other avenues.

Where to buy compost

● Some nurseries and garden centers occasionally sell their own compost by the bucketful.

● Some municipal or parish councils own composting facilities and will sell smallish quantities at reasonable prices.

● You can also buy small quantities of commercially produced compost through gardening suppliers. Some firms sell special herb compost that is actually made out of composted herbs.

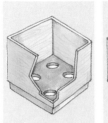

Drainage facilities for boxes
Drill a sufficient number of holes. Fill the bottom with a layer of gravel and spread a sheet of interfacing fabric over it. Fold the fabric up around the edges, then fill in with soil.

How to make your own compost

Making compost in your own garden is a simple affair. However, even if you are one of the growing army of balcony gardeners, making your own compost need not be a difficult or even smelly business.

For a balcony or patio garden: you will need a composting sack. This can be stored away unobtrusively in a corner, which should be warm.

● Fill the composting sack with alternating layers of organic kitchen waste, dead flowers, etc. If you are able to add a handful of bio-composter flakes or compost accelerator per 2½-gallon (10-liter) content in the sack, so much the better – the waste material will decompose even faster.

● If you have a working fireplace in your home, you can even add two or three shovelfuls of wood ash to your sack of waste.

● In six to nine months the waste will have been transformed into nutrient-rich compost which will only take up a quarter to half of the original volume in the sack.

In the garden: Here, you can set up a compost silo or barrel. These containers should be filled with waste, etc. in the same way as described above for a composting sack. The composting tub should not be placed in a position that is completely exposed to sunlight and, during long periods of drought, it should be watered occasionally.

Drainage

Supplying the soil with all the best ingredients and creating the ideal mixture will all be in vain if the pot or container becomes waterlogged as the soil will then become dense and airless, nutrients and oxygen

will no longer be accessible to the roots, and the plant will die. This is why proper drainage beneath the soil is so important for the health of your herbs. If you are using ***flowerpots***, a piece of broken pot placed over the drainage hole of the pot will be sufficient; alternatively, fill the bottom of the pot with a ¾-in (2-cm) thick layer of gravel or fragments of broken brick. This way the drainage hole cannot get clogged up.

Boxes or containers must be equipped with a sufficient number of drainage holes – one only will not do. Cover the bottom of the container with a 2-4-in (5-10-cm) layer of fine gravel, fragments of brick, Hortag, or polystyrene granules. Cover this with a sheet of interfacing fabric to prevent the soil from being washed into the drainage layer; fold the fabric upward around the edges (see illustration below).

Raised beds, herb pyramids and boxes without bottoms will require even more elaborate drainage facilities:

● Loosen up the soil to one spade's depth around a raised bed, pyramid, or box.

● Fill in coarse gravel or brick fragments.

● On top of this, add a layer of broken twigs.

Important: Good drainage will ensure that water can easily run away, even during heavy rainfalls. If drainage facilities are inadequate, water will run out of the sides of the beds.

Growing herbs from seeds and seedlings

Deciding whether to grow your herbs from seed or to buy young plants will depend, on the one hand, on how much space you have for cultivating herbs and, on the other hand, whether you are growing annual, biennial, or perennial herbs. Annuals and biennials can quite easily be grown on a windowsill. It is better to buy perennial herbs as young plants.

The right seed

A wide range of herb seed is available on the market. Very small amounts will be sufficient for balconies, patios and small beds, such as a herb mound or raised bed.

Fresh seed: The seeds of a large number of herbs will only germinate if they are very fresh, which means from the last harvest. Good seed suppliers will print a "best-before" date on the seed package. A good guarantee for viable seed is when they are sealed in a plastic envelope.

Germination time

You should have some idea of the time it will take for the seeds to germinate so that you will not lose patience and give up watering the soil. Usually, herb seeds will germinate two to four times as fast indoors as they would outdoors (see table).

Sowing seed on a windowsill

The earlier in the year you sow the seed, the sooner you will be able to harvest your herbs. If you start sowing seed intended for a windowsill at the end of the winter, you will have strong, healthy young plants by the middle of the last month of spring, which can then be planted outside.

Germinating aids

All seeds germinate better in humid air. The same kind of moist, warm climate that is found in a greenhouse can be created under the transparent plastic cover of a mini-propagator or under a polyethylene cover and this will encourage germination. You must remember to air the seed tray several times a day as soon as the first tiny leaflets have appeared, to prevent the formation of mould. There is a range of different containers and other aids to germination on the market, which will ensure the right type of mini-climate for the germination of your seeds.

Mini-propagators consist of a flat plastic tray with a removable, transparent cover. Two or three different "temperature zones" can be created in these very efficient miniature greenhouses.

Heating elements of various types can be installed underneath mini-propagators or seed trays and pots to ensure a constant soil temperature. This is particularly important if the room is not heated at all or if the temperature falls at night.

Peat pellets (obtainable at garden centers) will swell up to several times their original size when soaked in water. They contain everything the seeds need for germination.

Place the pellets side by side in a plastic tray or, even better, in a mini-propagator. You can even use an ordinary plate to germinate seeds but the peat pellets must be kept very moist.

Peat propagating pots are used for pricking out seedlings, the advantage being that the rooted plantlets will not have to be removed from their pots when you put them in their final position. The plants will be able to carry on growing very well in these as the pressed peat disintegrates in moist soil and the roots can grow quite easily through the wall of the pot.

Germination times for herb seeds (in days)

Herbs	Indoors	Outside
basil	4	7
borage	4	14
chervil	7	14
chives	5	14
cress	2	4
lemon balm	7	28
lovage	11	21
marjoram	3	7
mint	7	28
nasturtium	7	21
oregano	10	28
parsley	9	29
rosemary	14	30
sage	5	12
salad burnet	4	14
summer savory	5	14
tarragon	3	8
thyme	5	10

A window shelf is the ideal position for herbs as they will receive plenty of light.

How to create the right climate

There are several quite simple methods of creating a suitable greenhouse climate for propagating herbs.

● Pour some soil into a large jar that is wider at the bottom than at the top. After sowing the seeds, place another jar upside-down over the open top of the first jar.

● Sow the seeds in small, flat boxes which have been lined beforehand with polyethylene, and place a plate of glass on top of the box.

● Large seeds that have been sown in flowerpots (for example, nasturtium or borage seed) should be covered with a transparent, plastic freezer bag which can be supported by two crossed wires. The bag is tied down around the top edge of the pot.

How to sow

Soil for germinating: The soil should be as "poor" as possible for the germination of herb seed. Special soils for herbs are available from gardening suppliers. They are usually mixed with additional sand.

Moist air is needed for germinating
Place a jar over the germinating pot or pull a plastic bag over two crossed pieces of wire and tie it down firmly.

An alternative: Mix a peat-based compost or pure peat with a little sand and approximately 10% herb compost (sold by gardening suppliers). This soil should be poured to a depth of two fingers' width into seed trays or mini-propagators, or up to the edge in pots.

Sowing outdoors: Seeds should be sprinkled thinly onto the soil. The closer the seeds are sown, the less well the seedlings will thrive as they will be in competition with each other.

Exceptions: Cress, chervil, and chives – these herb seeds should be sown densely.

Note: Before sowing herb seeds, you need to find out first whether they germinate in the light or in the dark – usually this will be indicated on the seed package.

● Light-germinating seeds will only germinate in bright light, so they should not be covered with soil. Sprinkle them on top of the soil and then cover them with a sheet of white paper.

● Dark-germinating seeds should be lightly pressed into the soil or be covered with a thin layer of soil that is four times as thick as the thickness of the seed. For example, $\frac{1}{16}$-in (1-mm) thick seeds should be covered with $\frac{1}{4}$ in (4 mm) of soil.

Keeping the seeds moist and thinning out

Once sown, the seeds will require some care.

Keep them moist: No seed will germinate without water. Water will awaken the germ and help the seed to activate all the substances that let a tiny seed grow into a large plant. As soon as you have sown the seeds in the soil, moisten the soil with a misting bottle but never with a watering can. The soil should be kept moist until the shoot pushes up out of it. Do not lose patience as the seedlings will die if the soil dries out.

Thinning out
When you can hold a seedling between two fingers, pull out as many as necessary until the remaining plants are spaced out. If you sowed the seed thinly in the beginning, you may not even need to do any thinning out. Now remove the plastic or polyethylene cover as the plant will require plenty of fresh air for further growth. If the seedlings remain under cover for too long, they will grow leggy and weak. On no account leave them to stand in a draft, for example by a window that is open. Carry on watering the seedlings regularly but do not drown them as they are still very sensitive.

Pricking out

As soon as the seedlings are 2-3 in (5-7 cm) tall, they should be pricked out. This means transplanting them into peat propagating pots or small flower-pots. Depending on the herb in question, they should be planted singly or in groups.

How to prick out

The soil in the new pots should be "poor;" peat-based compost mixed with a little regular compost and sand is best.

● Carefully lift the plantlets out of the soil with a dibble.

● Insert the dibble into the new soil and push it sideways a little, thus creating a hole for the new plantlet.

● Water gently so that the soil is packed closely around the rootlets.

● After a few days, stand the plants in a slightly cooler position so that they can toughen up gradually. On warm days, stand the pricked-out seedlings on your balcony – but do not place them in direct sunlight or expose them to drafts!

● Toward the end of the spring (if sown in late winter), the young plants can be replanted in larger pots containing soil that is suitable for the particular species.

Light- and dark-germinating seeds

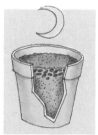

The seeds of light-germinating plants are placed on top of the soil, pressed down gently and then covered with a piece of paper (left). Dark-germinating seeds should be pushed down to a depth that is four times their own thickness. Mist the seeds – do not water – to keep them moist until they germinate.

Taking the young plants outside

In general, most herbs should not be taken outside until there is no risk of frost. Usually this is about the end of the third month of spring. Even if they are hardy species, young plants are very vulnerable to frosts. If you have raised your young plants in peat propagating pots, they can be planted while still in these pots in larger flower pots, in boxes or outside in a bed. If the young plants are in clay or plastic pots, take them out, together with their rootstocks, and replant them.

The young herbs should not be planted any higher or lower in the ground or container than they were in their previous pots. A thorough watering is important, so that the old soil is mixed well with the new soil in the pot or bed.

Sowing in a bed

Remove all weeds and large stones and break up any large lumps of earth in the place where you are intending to sow your seed. The tiny herb seeds will require fine, crumbly soil.

When to sow: Do not sow any seeds until the earth has warmed up, preferably at the end of the third month of spring.

Early sowing: You can push the sowing time back to around the middle of the second month of spring if you cover the flower bed with a polyethylene sheet with slits in it. The earth will warm up quicker underneath the sheet. Let the sheet remain over the seeds until all danger of frost is over. The slits will let the sheet expand and make room for the plants.

Sowing the seed: Sowing outside is really no different from sowing seed in a box on a windowsill, although you can, of course, sow a lot more seed in a bed than in the

Thinning and pricking out

Seedlings growing very close together should be thinned out so that they do not compete with each other. When they are 2-3 in (5-7 cm) tall, transfer them to peat propagating pots using a dibble. The rootstock, together with the peat propagating pot, will later be planted in a prepared plant pot. The peat pot will disintegrate in time.

limited area of a seed tray. You will save space if you avoid sowing the seed in rows and, instead, sow in large patches, rounds, or along the edge of a flower bed. Remember to consider the spacing requirements of the grown plants (see p. 22) and sow sparingly, so that you need not do any thinning out later on.

My tip: Slugs and snails will swarm all over these young seedlings and devour every one, so it is a good idea to cover the seed with a thin layer of bran. The seedlings can grow through this bran layer but the slugs and snails will avoid crawling over it. Even in a raised bed or a box, the seedlings will not be safe from hungry slugs and snails. Protect them by fixing a protruding strip of metal along the edge of the box.

Care of seeds sown outside

Even outside, the seeds will need some care.

Keep them moist: Check regularly to make sure the soil has not dried out. Soil will stay moist longer if it is covered with polyethylene or something similar. As soon as the little seedlings appear, you can remove the covering. Now carry on watering, using your own judgment. The risk of drowning the delicate

seedlings in a bed outside is not as great as it is for those in pots.
Thinning out: Thin out all the seedlings of herbs that will grow tall and spread out.

Important: Leave the strongest, healthiest-looking plants to carry on growing.

My tip: If you sow seed in late summer (parsley, for example, will prefer this), you can take some of the young plants you have thinned out and put them in a pot on the kitchen windowsill.

Good seedlings
Compact, bushy seedlings (left) will thrive better than seedlings with long, lanky shoots lacking branches (right).

Herbs grown from seeds in a suitably warm position.

Growing herbs from seedlings

If you only want one or two herbs, it is worth buying a couple of seedlings, which are young, ready-grown plants, particularly if they are perennial herbs. It would take several years before you could harvest leaves from a rosemary bush grown from seed.

Tips on buying
Buy a medium-sized plant so that you can use the herb straightaway.
Sources: Seedlings are usually quite inexpensive – only the rarer varieties will cost a little more.
● The best place to buy herb seedlings is in a plant nursery which also sells vegetable seedlings.
● You can often find good offers at fruit and vegetable markets during the spring.

● Mail-order firms offer a large range of robust herbs as young plants.
Not recommended: Herb seedlings sold in the vegetable section of supermarkets. These are usually forced plants which are intended for immediate consumption. They will generally not survive an attempt at planting them in a bed outside.
Healthy seedlings
look compact and bushy.
They should have a well-developed rootstock. Young plants of perennial herbs should branch out well.
Toughening up seedlings: If the herb seedlings were kept in a greenhouse until brought out for selling, and were accustomed to a constant moist, warm climate without direct sunlight, you will not be able to plant them outside straightaway. If these young plants are

subjected to day and night temperature fluctuations and bright sunlight without an acclimatizing interim period beforehand, they will suffer from shock which will stop them from growing. They may even suffer burns from exposure to the sun. For this reason, stand the little plants in a semi-cool, sheltered place for a few days, where the sun will shine on them only in the morning or evening. After that, you can move them to their final position.

Repotting the seedlings
The pots in which seedlings are sold are generally rather small so the young plants will need repotting.
In pots and boxes: Place enough soil on top of a drainage layer to ensure that the rootstock of the plant is level with the top edge of the pot, then fill up the pot with soil.
Planting outside: Each young plant should be planted in a hole that corresponds to the size of its rootstock, so that the plant ends up no higher or lower than it was in its propagating pot. Gently press the seedling down after planting and water thoroughly.

Watering seedlings
Watering is extremely important during the first three weeks after planting. The roots of the young plant should be in close contact with the surrounding soil so that they can anchor themselves properly and develop fine rootlets for absorbing nutrients. During this phase of development, all herbs, even those which normally enjoy a dry position, will need a regular supply of water. Many herbs will not be able to stand a dry environment until they have grown properly – you will be able to tell when this new stage has been reached when they start forming new shoots.

Caring for herbs

Nearly all herbs are indigenous to southern Europe. Their healing properties and spicy aroma develop best in full sunlight and in a sheltered, warm position. It is not at all difficult, however, to create better conditions in an unfavorable environment. If your herbs are cared for properly, they will thrive here just as well as in a sunny Mediterranean climate.

The right climate on balconies and patios

The climate on a balcony, patio, or in a small front garden is not necessarily identical to the climate found elsewhere in your area. The combination of temperature, sun, and wind in a particular and limited area is referred to as a micro-climate. On a sheltered balcony this micro-climate may be almost Mediterranean, that is, corresponding to the average climate of Mediterranean countries, even if you live in the northern part of your country or in a mountainous area. It is worth taking a good look at the place where you intend to grow your herbs.

Light: In the spring and fall, when the sun is low in the sky (and the angle of sunlight is oblique), the sun's rays may penetrate a balcony, patio or yard more than they do in the middle of summer, but this will only be for short periods of time. When the sun is high in the sky during the summer months, it may not shine on parts of the balcony that are set farther back but the parts that are illuminated will benefit for longer periods of time. Furthermore, when the sun shines at an oblique angle in the spring or fall, neighboring trees or buildings will provide more shade than in the middle of the summer. Remember these points when deciding on the best position for your herbs.

Temperature: Naturally, this will depend on the general climate and the season. Nevertheless, a spot that is sheltered from the wind is generally several degrees warmer than an unsheltered one. Cities, with their constant "dome" of haze, consisting of dust and exhaust fumes, are generally considerably warmer than the fresher air of the countryside. Walls and stones in a rock garden store heat during the day and release it during the night.

Wind: Windy positions are not good for herbs. Wind will cool the air and the soil, and the soil will dry out much faster.

Air pollution: Most herbs do not seem to mind a little air pollution. However, do remember that herbs that are to be used in cooking should be protected from polluted air. The lower floors of apartment buildings near busy roads or beside a garage should all be avoided when planting herbs.

How to improve a micro-climate

A position that does not seem ideal for growing herbs can easily be turned into a better one with a few well-tested tricks:

More warmth: You can use the following tips to provide your herbs with as much warmth as possible, so they will develop their aromatic properties to the full.

● Heat will be retained by a white wall, by heat-absorbing stones, dark tiles, or a concrete floor.

● Warm water will release heat in the evening and during the night. Paint the inside of an old washtub black and fill it with water. The herbs should be positioned all around it, at the same height as the surface of the water.

● Covers made of glass will capture a lot of heat. If you do not have a small greenhouse for your balcony or patio, you can make do with a plate of glass – part of an old window pane, for example – positioned at an angle, facing south, in front of a box of herbs.

Important: Remove the glass on hot days as it will then absorb too much heat.

● Covers made of polyethylene sheeting will provide the same effect as glass. Stretch transparent polyethylene over a frame and stand it at an angle above the herbs.

More light: Sufficient light is even more important than heat for all herbs. Do not position your herbs behind a solid balcony railing as it would then be too dark for them. It is a good idea to place pots and boxes in a raised position, so that your herbs have the benefit of plenty of light all day long.

● Fix castors to your herb boxes so that you can roll the boxes across the balcony during the spring and fall, following the path of the sun.

● Wooden walls and walls with a very rough rendered finish will absorb a lot of light. A piece of wood painted white or a piece of plywood covered in aluminum foil will reflect light.

You will have to remove the foil-covered board when the sun is shining directly on to it, however, as the herbs might get burned.

Protection from wind: Herbs are sensitive to drafts and wind.

● A shatter-proof sheet of glass, fixed on the weather-exposed side of the balcony or patio, will keep the wind off them.

Warning: Stick a few silhouettes of birds onto the glass so that birds will not crash into it and injure or kill themselves.

● A trellis with climbing plants is also good protection against wind and weather. You could plant vegetables against this, such as scarlet runner beans, cherry tomatoes, and cucumbers.

Shade: There is often too little shade on a patio or balcony.

● Observe which parts of the balcony or patio are in the shade for hours at a time and keep these spots for herbs that do not like strong sunlight.

● Vulnerable, young plants can be protected from strong midday sunlight by hanging cardboard cones on sticks above them (see illustration, p. 28) or by propping up a plank to create shade.

Cooling: Occasionally, this will be required too. The most important way to lower the temperature is by providing shade.

● On very hot days you can protect sensitive herbs with a parasol.

● If a south-facing wall is too hot, grow climbing plants on it.

● Watering in the mornings and evenings will cool the herbs. Water will cool the soil and evaporating water will cool the air all around the plants.

How to water herbs

If you have ever been told that herbs should not be watered, forget it. This may be true for herbs growing in gardens during wet summers, as herbs really do not need a lot of water, but herbs in large containers or boxes will all have to be watered regularly.

Indoors, the soil in pots should never be let dry out completely. Indoor air is very dry so the plant has no way of absorbing water from the air through its leaves as it would do outside.

● Check every day to see if the soil is still moist – prodding the soil with a finger will tell you.

My tip: If you happen to have forgotten to water and the soil is as dry as a bone, the water will run right through it without reaching the roots. Stand the plant pot in a container of water for about ten minutes to soak the soil thoroughly.

On a balcony or patio, herbs should be watered regularly but not too much.

● Water should never be allowed to stand in pot holders or dishes under the pots.

● During hot spells, water in the mornings or evenings, never around midday.

● On cool, rainy days, you will hardly need to water at all.

● Perennial, woody herbs must not be let dry out. They will not show signs of drying out until it is almost too late but, when they have dried out, no amount of watering will save them.

● Herbs with soft, juicy leaves, like basil, borage, or salad burnet, will wilt very quickly if they get too dry but will recover again after they have been watered.

In the garden: You will only need to water if it has been very hot and dry

for several days. Other factors will also determine whether the herbs need watering:

● Many herbs grow in very poor soil which will let rainwater and additional water run away too quickly.

● If the herbs are growing very close together or with other plants, they will provide shade for the soil with their leaves. The soil will not dry out so quickly as with free-standing plants.

Watering in winter

Some of the perennial herbs should remain outside in large containers or boxes during the winter. They should be watered sparingly in frost-free weather. Most plants do not freeze to death in their pots, they simply die of thirst. Herbs that are planted outside in beds will not need additional water.

The right kind of water

Rainwater is much better for watering than main water, which usually contains too much lime and is generally much too cold. If you cannot collect rainwater, let the water stand for a day in your watering can so that it can warm up a little.

Feeding herbs

Adopt a very restrained attitude about fertilizing herbs. Most herbs will make do just with some compost mixed in with the soil and a dose of herbal infusion now and again. Only use organic fertilizer. It is better for the herbs and for you.

Mineral fertilizer contains too much nitrogen for herbs. Some herbs will flourish on it and grow very large but they will taste rather insipid. Certain herbs will actually stop growing if they are given too much nitrogen.

Colorful summer flowers will help to turn your herb balcony into a paradise.

A single exception: A large bay tree will need about 2 teaspoons (5 g) of mineral fertilizer every four weeks.

Important: Even if you use organic fertilizers, you must be careful that you do not give your herbs too much nitrogen.

Buying biological fertilizers

Most organic or biological fertilizers are basically controlled-release fertilizers, which means they are released very slowly in the soil and will not overfeed the plants.

Horn chips contain a lot of nitrogen. For herbs which prefer a poorer soil, 1 tablespoon of horn chips per 4 cups (1 liter) of soil will be more than sufficient.

Mixtures of horn, dried blood and bone meal are organic compound fertilizers. They contain phosphorous, potassium and small amounts of nitrogen. Mix in 2 tablespoons of soil per 4 cups (1 liter) of soil.

Special compound fertilizers for pot plants can be obtained from garden centers. They are organic compound fertilizers with a small proportion of nitrogen. This kind of fertilizer will contain additional natural micro-organisms which keep the soil viable for much longer in pots and large containers.

There are a few **other kinds of fertilizer** which can also be given to your herbs during their growth period. These are only really necessary if the young plants do not seem to be growing properly or for herbs that grow very fast and need a lot of nutrients. Liquid organic fertilizers that are suitable for herbs can be obtained through the gardening trade; for example, guano and other proprietary fertilizers (usually, the amount suggested for pot plants should be halved for herbs).

You can create more light through the use of aluminum foil
Cover a piece of chipboard with aluminum foil; the foil will then reflect more sunlight.

Other substances
Crushed rock etc. (e.g. Perlite) is, strictly speaking, not a fertilizer but its minute particles are able to absorb water and nutrients and it therefore serves as a store. Crushed rock is added to very sandy soils to stop them drying out quickly. *Lime* is absolutely vital for quite a number of herbs. If you need to add lime, use lime derived from algae, which will not harm the roots. It should be mixed with the soil before planting (1 tablespoon per 4 cups/1 liter).

Making your own fertilizer
Some good fertilizers can be made at home.
Garden compost is probably the very best fertilizer for herbs.
Nettle brew: Give your herbs one dose of this concoction in the spring when they need nutrients and the young plants are growing well, and then repeat the procedure once more in the middle of the summer.
The recipe
● Fill a bucket with freshly cut, chopped stinging nettles and add water.

● Let this mixture stand in the sun for a week and stir it often.
● Dilute the concoction as 1 part nettle brew to 2½ gallons (10 liters) of water and use it for watering your herbs.

My tip: You can prepare the above concoction with bought, dried nettles. Use 7 ounces (200 g) of dried nettle leaves to 2½ gallons (10 liters) of water.

Comfrey brew can be prepared using the same recipe as for the fresh nettle brew. You may find comfrey growing along the verges of country lanes or in meadows during the summer months.
Animal manure is totally unsuitable for all herbs!

Cutting back to rejuvenate herbs

What to do when you are ready to cut the leaves and shoots at harvest time is described in the chapter on harvesting and preserving. Quite independently of this, however, it is sometimes necessary to rejuvenate some herbs by cutting them back.
Thyme, sage, rosemary, and bay should be cut back into shape in the early fall. If you neglect to do this, the plants will begin to look bare from the center outward and will produce only a few shoots the following year.
Method: Cut out all long, protruding shoots and shorten the others so that you obtain a compact, bushy shape.
The following herbs should be cut right back to the ground before winter: lovage, oregano, lemon balm, mint, and tarragon. You may dry the cut-off shoots and leaves for use during the winter.

Pests and diseases

Herbs are basically wild plants and, therefore, fairly resistant to pests and diseases. You should experience hardly any problems in the garden. If they are grown in pots or containers, however, they may become infested with greenfly or blackfly, spider mites, and scale insects.
Warning: Do not use any insecticides on these pests! The substances contained in such products are toxic. If herbs in pots, large containers or boxes are severely infested with pests, there is only one thing you can do: throw them all in the bin and buy new plants. Large perennials (such as rosemary and bay) can be saved.

Prevention is the best protection
On balconies and patios the problem may often be that there are too many plants and a muggy climate, both favoring infestation by pests, bacteria and fungi. Do not plant your herbs too close together and make sure they have enough fresh air. Avoid drafts, which encourage aphids.

Shading
An umbrella or cardboard cones on sticks can be used to protect sensitive young plants from the strong midday sun.

Avoid waterlogging
Place a broken piece of pot over the drainage hole (left). Never let water stand in saucers (right).

Weak plants are more likely to be attacked by pests than strong, healthy ones. Soil that is too wet or contains too much or too little fertilizer will weaken your herbs. The plants most at risk are those that have been forced on too quickly. Their cell walls are relatively thin and therefore more accessible to insects that like to suck their juices. Strong plants with thick cell walls are avoided by insects.

Fungal disease will often spread via the soil, especially if the soil is very dense and hard as well as exhausted. Make sure to repot your herbs in new soil every year.

Scale insects will become established if evergreen herbs, such as bay and rosemary, are overwintered in surroundings that are too warm.

Combinations of plants may cause problems but these can easily be avoided. Lovage, for example, will interfere with other plants because it produces secretions from its roots and leaves. The neighboring plants will not thrive and will become vulnerable to attack by diseases and pests. Balcony plants that are vulnerable to pests, such as petunias, should not be used as neighbors for herbs as they cannot be protected.

My tip: Nasturtiums seem to divert blackfly from other plants.

Controlling pests
Check the plants every day so that you will notice any early symptoms of infestation.

First aid: Cut off infested shoots and destroy them or remove the pests with a small stick or your fingers. A good dousing with clear water will often chase away the vanguard of an insect colony. If the plant is still very small, hang it head down in a bucket of water for about two hours. (Lay two sticks across the rim of the bucket and suspend the pot from them.)

Tansy tea is a good remedy for fighting off pests and also a good guard against fungal diseases.

Recipe: 1 cup (30 g) of dried tansy leaves and flowers (can be bought) or ⅔ cup (20 g) of fresh tansy (found along verges and paths during the middle of summer). Add 5½ quarts (5 liters) boiling water, let it draw for fifteen minutes and strain. After it has cooled, dilute it with water, in one part tansy brew to three parts water, and spray your plants with the liquid. (Do not forget the undersides of the leaves.)

Wormwood tea has the same effect as tansy tea and should be prepared in the same way. Unlike tansy, it is used undiluted.

Warning: Tansy and wormwood teas taste bitter, so wash your plants down with clear water two or three hours after treating them. Tiny *yellow strips* covered in a special sticky substance can be pushed into the plant pot.

Disadvantage: They will also trap useful insects.

Preparations for emergencies
If your plants are severely infested with harmful insects, you should destroy the annual and biennial plants. Naturally, of course, you will not wish to get rid of a well-grown bay or rosemary, thyme or oregano. This is an opportunity to employ non-toxic insecticides. After this kind of treatment, however, you should not eat any parts of your herbs for several weeks.

Pyrethrum is a natural insecticide which will also kill useful insects. It is effective for only a few hours.

Other biological preparations are available which will not harm most useful insects. Ask about these at your garden center or nursery – but only use these preparations in an emergency!

Warning: Read all directions very carefully and keep to the waiting period recommended before you use the herbs again!

Cutting back and rejuvenating

In the fall, some herbs should be cut back to just above the ground (left). Thyme and sage should be cut back by about a third (center). In the case of perennial herbs, when cutting back to rejuvenate, cut the long, lanky shoots so that the plant will grow more compact and bushy (right).

Harvesting and preserving herbs

Even if you have very limited space in which to grow your own herbs, you will still be able to harvest quite large amounts and preserve them for the winter. If you do not wish to go without the flavor and aroma of your own herbs during the winter months, you should work out carefully what quantities of each herb you are likely to need. Even if you can only preserve small amounts, it will be well worth the effort.

How to harvest herbs

While the herbs are still very young, they should be left alone. When they have lots of leaves, however, you can start harvesting them.

Care when harvesting

Herbs should be handled very gently when harvesting. This goes for harvesting fresh herbs and certainly when harvesting herbs for drying and preserving for winter use. Leaves and shoots should be cut off with a sharp knife or scissors. Do not leave the herbs lying around after you have cut them – use them immediately.

Tips on harvesting

● Never cut off all the shoots. *Exception:* cress and chervil, which will not grow any more afterward anyway.
● Always cut chives halfway down the stalks, no farther.
● Basil, summer savory, and marjoram should be cut about 4 in (10 cm) above the ground, then they will grow up again quite fast, and branch out.
● Only ever cut the tips of shoots with young leaves on large herbs like tarragon, borage, lovage, or mint. New shoots and new leaves will form below the cut tops.
● If you regularly cut a few shoots of perennials like oregano, lemon balm, or mint right down to the ground, they will continue to produce new shoots with young, tasty leaves.
● Never cut more than a third of the length of a shoot of sage, thyme, or rosemary.

The right time to harvest herbs

In the case of herbs you intend to use in cooking, you will obviously want to cut them immediately before using them.
Herbs for preserving should be harvested when the herbs have attained their optimal aroma and flavor. Watch your herbs closely, as picking them at the correct time will make all the difference in their contribution to various dishes.

A few tips

● Harvest marjoram, thyme, summer savory, and oregano for preserving just before and during their flowering times.
● Preserve the young, juicy leaves of tarragon, lovage, mint, borage, chives, parsley, and lemon balm.
● You can wait until fall to harvest sage, bay leaves, and rosemary for preserving.
The right time of day to harvest herbs is when the aroma of the plants is at its most intense. For all herbs with a strong flavor and aroma, that time is midday. Herbs with juicy leaves should be harvested earlier in the day: any dew should have evaporated but the plant should not be limp with heat.

Preparing herbs for preserving

● Make sure all parts of the plant are undamaged.
● Shake the herbs well to dislodge any insects or other creatures that have made a home in them.

A beautiful herb in a large container
A large, well-grown rosemary bush is very decorative in a big container. You can harvest rosemary sprigs all year round.

Fresh herbs taste particularly good – but it is also worth preserving some for the winter months.

● If you have herbs with large leaves, check underneath the leaves too, as pests love to settle there.

● If your herbs are growing in a position that is exposed to polluted air, you will have to wash them thoroughly before use.

Drying herbs

This is the oldest and simplest method of preserving herbs for the winter.

Air-drying: You can do this by tying several shoots into a bunch with an elastic band and hanging the bunch in a warm, shady place. Do not hang them up in the kitchen as the air will be too humid and may contain minute particles of cooking oil used in frying. When the herbs are so dry that they rustle, they can be broken into small pieces and stored in screw-top jars. If you are drying individual leaves, do it on a clean cloth in a warm, shady position.

In the oven: You may dry herbs in the oven if there is no suitable place to air-dry them. Even if the herbs have had to be washed because of a high degree of air pollution outside, this method of drying can still be used.

Lay the herbs on a rack covered in aluminum foil and dry them at a temperature of 122° F (50° C). The door of the oven should be left slightly ajar.

A drying machine: This will make drying an easy matter. The times and temperatures can be controlled and drying takes place automatically. Make sure the herbs do not become too dry.

Important: All dried herbs should retain their green color. Dried herbs that are gray or brown have been dried in temperatures that were too high, or for too long – they will have lost most of their flavor and aroma.

Freezing herbs

Most herbs can be preserved in the freezer without problems. Freeze very small portions, then you will always have the quantities you need for a particular dish. Mixed herbs can be frozen too.

Using the ice-cube tray is a good way of freezing small portions. The herbs should be chopped very finely and fast-frozen with a tiny amount of water in the ice-cube tray. Later, take out the "herb cubes" and pack them in labeled bags for using in the winter.

Freezing herbs in bags is the quickest way. Pack the herbs – stalks, leaves, and all – in freezer bags and fast-freeze them, then take them out of the freezer and break them up by hand while they are still in the bag. These little pieces can then either be left in the bag or, even better, packed in small freezer boxes. As the herbs were broken up in a frozen state, the pieces will not stick together and can be extracted quite easily in quantities of your choice.

My tip: Deep-frozen herbs can be put straight into the food you are preparing. For salad dressings, however, add the herbs twenty minutes before serving so that their flavor can permeate the dressing properly.

Pickling herbs in oil and vinegar

If you decide to pickle your herbs in vinegar or oil, you are not really preserving the herbs themselves but rather their flavor and aroma as the liquid will rapidly absorb the flavor of the herb. This is useful for flavoring salads and many other dishes. You can pickle herbs individually or as mixed herbs.

The herbs should always be washed before pickling. Choose particularly decorative sprigs, as bottles of herb vinegar and herb oil are nice to look at too.

Pickling herbs in vinegar: Push the herbs (stalks and leaves) into a bottle made of light-colored glass. Then fill up the bottle with a good quality wine or apple cider vinegar. The vinegar should not be too immature, otherwise a deposit may form between the herbs. Stand the bottle on a sunny windowsill for two weeks, by which time the vinegar will have absorbed the flavor of the herb. Now you may take the herbs out. If you leave them in the vinegar, you will have to keep filling up the bottle as you use the vinegar because any parts of the herb that stick up out of the liquid will soon become very unappetizing to look at.

Pickling in oil: Chop the herb up a little, as the oil will then absorb the flavor better. Place the herb in a dark-colored glass bottle and fill it with oil. This herb oil should be left to stand in a warm place for four weeks. Olive oil will not become rancid but other oils will have to be used up quickly.

Salting herbs

A number of herbs may be preserved in salt, especially lovage and parsley. The leaves and stalks should be washed clean and then coarsely chopped. Using a wide, dark glass jar or a stoneware jar with a lid, fill this with alternate layers of salt and herbs in a ratio of 1:5 and force down the layers with the handle of a wooden spoon. These salted herbs will keep for up to two years.

Important: This mixture is very salty. Use additional salt very cautiously.

Herbs in the kitchen

Which herb goes best with which dish?

Roasts: lovage, sage, thyme, bay leaf, rosemary.
Egg dishes: basil, borage, dill, cress, chives, salad burnet.
Refreshing drinks: lemon balm, mint.
Fines herbes: chives, parsley, tarragon, chervil, basil
Fish: tarragon, bay leaves, sage, dill.
Poultry: tarragon, rosemary, sage, thyme.
Green sauce: chervil, parsley, chives, salad burnet, dill, borage, lemon balm.
Cucumber: borage, dill, dill seed, bay leaves.
Cheese: borage, parsley, chives.
Potatoes: summer savory, marjoram, sage, bay leaves, parsley, thyme.
Cabbage: bay leaves.
Lamb cutlets: rosemary, sage, mint.
Carrots: parsley.
Pasta: basil, oregano, thyme, rosemary, sage.
Pizza: oregano, thyme, sage.
Salads: basil, borage, dill, tarragon, chervil, cress, lemon balm, parsley, chives, nasturtium leaves, salad burnet.
Sweet dishes: borage flowers, muscatel sage, peppermint.
Soups: parsley, chives, chervil, dill, oregano.
Teas: lemon balm, sage, rosemary, peppermint, thyme.
Tomatoes: basil, dill, parsley, chives, marjoram, oregano, salad burnet.
Venison: bay leaves, sage, thyme.
Cold meats: lovage, parsley, chives.

The healing properties of herbs

If you wish to use herbs for healing purposes, you absolutely must look up as much information as possible regarding the exact dosage and uses in a good book on herbal remedies.
Warning: Using too large a quantity or using certain herbs continually over long periods of time may result in undesirable side effects and could damage your health.
Basil: calming; anti-spasmodic for stomach and intestines; diuretic.
Bay leaves: improves digestion.
Borage: for strengthening the heart; as a tonic; good for rheumatic pains.
Chervil: cleanses the blood.
Cress: good for tiredness in the spring.
Dill: good for flatulence and upset stomachs.
Lemon balm: soothing.
Lovage: diuretic; improves digestion; helps against flatulence.
Marjoram: soothes the nerves; helps to alleviate cramp; good for digestive problems and colds; good for digesting greasy foods.
Mint: good for digestive and intestinal problems.
Oregano: expectorant; soothes the nerves; good for colic.
Parsley: diuretic; good for strengthening the heart.
Rosemary: improves the circulation; soothes the nerves.
Sage: anti-inflammatory; use to make tea for gargling.
Summer savory: beneficial to the digestion; good for coughs and accumulations of phlegm.
Tarragon: diuretic; improves digestion.
Thyme: expectorant; good for stomach cramps.

Sow dill seed in several places as it is sure to germinate in one of them.

Propagating and overwintering

If your herb gardening efforts were crowned with success all through the summer, you will probably want to take the next step and continue cultivating your own herbs during the following year. There are various ways of doing this. You can use seeds harvested from your own herbs or take cuttings. You can overwinter your perennial herbs, either indoors or outside.

Propagating herbs

Round off your success as a herb gardener by propagating your own herbs. There are several good reasons for doing this:

● The annual and biennial herbs have to be sown again every year. Herbs grown from seeds produced by your own plants will demonstrate your obvious success as a herb gardener and save you money.

● Perennial herbs will deteriorate a little in their old age, particularly if they are grown in pots. Propagating will ensure that you always have strong, young plants.

How to collect herb seed

In the temperate zone of the northern hemisphere not all herbs will produce seeds. Real "southerners" like basil, thyme, and sage do not have enough time for their seed to ripen as their growing season is too short.

Herbs that produce seeds

Cress, chervil, and borage produce seeds that can be harvested. This means that one or two plants should be left untouched to grow to their full size and produce flowers. Annual herbs will produce flowers and seeds in the same year in which they were sown; the biennials will not produce seed until the second year. Perennial herbs will flower every year but it is preferable to propagate these by another method.

Harvesting the seeds: Do not wait until the seeds become ripe on their stalks and start dropping off.

Method

● Cut the stalk, together with the seed head, before the seeds are ripe. The seed pods should not yet have opened and the seeds themselves should be dark-colored.

● Hang the seeds (on their stalks with their heads down) in a shady spot above a clean cloth or piece of paper.

● When the seeds are ripe, they will fall onto the cloth or paper. Gently blow on them to get rid of dead leaves and bits of seed husk.

Harvesting seed
Hang the seed heads upside down so that the ripe seeds will drop onto a cloth. Store the seeds in paper packages in a screw-top jar.

Storing the seeds: The most important thing is to make sure that the seeds are completely dry or they will turn moldy.
● To be quite sure, dry them again on a plate in front of a radiator or, briefly (maximum of ten minutes), in a pre-warmed oven at 122ºF (50ºC).
● Store the seeds in a cool, dark place in a clean, dry, screw-top jar.
Important: Check occasionally to see whether the seeds have been attacked by insects, etc. Throw away any infested seeds.

Propagating from cuttings

Sage, rosemary, thyme, and bay should be propagated from cuttings.
Taking cuttings: During the second and third months of summer, use a sharp knife to cut off 4-in (10-cm) long shoots which have grown that year. The cut should be made underneath a set of leaves. The leaves above the cut should be removed.
Rooting your cuttings: Insert several cuttings in a small pot filled with a mixture of peat or peat-based compost and sand. If you place the cuttings near the edge of the pot, so that the cut surfaces of the shoots touch the wall of the pot, they will root better.
To prevent the cuttings from drying out quickly (as they do not yet have roots), tie a transparent plastic bag over the pot (support the bag with two crossed wires). As soon as the cutting has formed roots (the appearance of new shoots and leaves is an indicator), remove the bag.
Further care: Once the cutting has formed proper roots, it should be planted in a larger pot with soil that contains more nutrients. Cut off the shoot tips on two or three occasions so that the young plant will branch out well.

Layered shoots
This involves a special kind of shoot that can be used, for example, to propagate sage.
Method: Bend a long woody shoot downward so that it touches the soil and secure it with a hairpin, a piece of wire, or a stone. As soon as roots have formed, separate the shoot from the parent plant and plant the young sage plant in a new pot.

Propagating by division

Lovage, lemon balm, oregano, and chives can be propagated by dividing the rootstock.
This should preferably
be done in the fall or spring when there are few shoots on the plant.
Method:
● When the plant has developed a large rootstock (after two or three years), remove it from the soil – after soaking it well.
● Use a sharp knife or garden shears to cut up the rootstock into three or four separate pieces, taking care not to damage the hair roots.
● Shoots with leaves should be cut back by about a half.
● The new sections should be planted immediately in pots or in the garden, but only as deep as they were before.
● In the spring, the pots containing these new root sections should be kept in the shade until new shoots have formed, then place them in suitable positions.
● In the fall, move them indoors and overwinter them in a north-facing window.

Propagating from stolons (underground shoots)

Tarragon, mint, and lemon balm form underground shoots (stolons)

Propagating from cuttings
Using a sharp knife, cut off slightly woody shoots that have grown the same year. Place them around the edge of a pot containing a sand and soil mixture. Plant them close to the edge as they will root better there.

that come up to develop tiny new plants. They will only form properly if the plant has enough room to spread out.
Method: If you notice that the parent plant has produced a new little plant somewhere nearby, cut it off, together with the long piece of root attached to it, and plant it in a pot or in another position in the garden. The part of the plant that is above

ground should be cut back a little so the roots do not have to cope initially with nourishing a lot of foliage.

My tip: Whichever method you choose for propagating your herbs, never place the young plants in strong sunlight but keep them in a warm, shady place until they have grown properly.

Overwintering

Perennial herbs will give years of pleasure to a herb gardener but they will only flourish, however, if a rest period is observed during the winter. If you move thyme, rosemary, sage, or oregano into the house for the winter, and then continue to harvest sprigs and leaves, you will end up disappointed. If the plant is well looked after, it may continue to form new shoots and leaves for a while but very soon its reserves will be exhausted. By the spring it will have lost all its energy and will look sickly or die.

Overwintering outside
Oregano, parsley, lemon balm, mint, lovage, and tarragon can quite easily overwinter outside, provided they are given some protection against frost.
If they are planted in the garden, they will not even need much protection. A thick layer of dead leaves will do quite well.
If they are kept outside *in pots and boxes*, there is always a risk of them drying out, particularly if the rootstocks are frozen for days on end. To prevent this from happening, stand the herb pots in a sheltered position and wrap plastic bubble pack or thick wads of newspaper around the pots. Boxes on balconies or patios will need some kind of winter protection too, like a

Propagating by division
Many herbs can be propagated by dividing them (chives, for example). Cut off part of the foliage and carefully divide the rootstock.

layer of dead leaves or conifer branches. Only water on frost-free days, but do it regularly.

Overwintering indoors
Potted bay, rosemary, and sage should be moved into winter quarters just like pelargoniums or large container plants. The plants may remain outside until frosts of 23°F (-5°C) are forecast. These plants should never be stored in a dark cellar or room. They will need a light, cool, frost-free place. Temperatures should not rise above 59°F (15°C). Water the plants sparingly during the winter months although the soil should not be let dry out. As soon as the weather starts getting warmer, move the plants outside again. This may be as early as the first or second month of spring as the plants can cope with temperatures as low as 23°F (-5°C) providing there is no frost.

Tips on overwintering
All perennial herbs that have been cut back can be placed in a dark place: lovage, tarragon, oregano, lemon balm, and mint. If you have no sheltered place to overwinter herbs outside, stand the pots in a cool position until the last month of

winter. Do not water them during this period. From the middle of the last winter month onward, the herbs should be taken to a lighter, warmer position and watered lightly, but regularly. This will soon start them shooting again. All young plants which originated as cuttings or divided rootstocks, should be kept in a light position. They should be treated like indoor plants and regular watering and misting will be necessary. Do not use leaves from these young plants, no matter how great the temptation.

Harvesting in winter
This can be done under certain conditions. For a supply of fresh herbs in winter, use plants that you have taken into the house and which were sown or planted especially for this purpose during the summer. Parsley and chives can be removed from the garden bed in the fall and planted in pots indoors; the same goes for summer savory, basil, and marjoram. They should be looked after like herbs on your windowsill. Do not be disappointed, however, if these windowsill herbs do not develop quite such a good flavor and aroma as those that have grown outside. Cress and chervil can be sown in pots on the windowsill throughout the winter.

Herbs for use in cooking

The following pages will tell you all the essentials of growing and caring for herbs. You will also find plenty of information on the flavors of different herbs and their use in cooking.

Explanation of keywords

The first name is the common English name, followed by the botanical name in Latin. The word "appearance" will be followed by a description of the characteristics of that particular herb. The ideal use in cooking will be given, depending on the flavor. Practical tips on treating seeds and cuttings are given under "growing." The right mixture of soil is very important for successful herb gardening. "Position" describes where the plant will thrive – on a balcony, windowsill or in the garden. This is followed by important advice on light and temperature for the various herbs. The right amount of watering and fertilizer are also very important. "Harvest" refers to the best time for picking each herb. The best method for propagating each herb will be given. You will also find out what to do with your herbs in the winter and which methods of preserving to use. "NB" or "warning" will alert you to times when you should not use a particular herb.

Explanation of symbols

 The herb will prefer a light, sunny position.

 The herb should be positioned in a bright place but not exposed to sunlight all day long; semi-shade.

 Annual herb. If it is sown in the spring, it will die in the fall.

 Biennial herb. Will flower and bear seed in the second year after sowing, then die.

 Perennial herb. Will have a long life if cared for properly.

A beautiful wild herb
An early-flowering species of wild thyme which prefers growing on chalky soil (Thymus praecox arcticus).

358

Basil will grow better in a pot than in the garden.

Various red varieties of basil are obtainable.

Basil

Ocimum basilicum

"King of herbs"

Appearance: square stalks with oval, slightly concave leaves, depending on the variety: emerald green (stronger flavor and aroma), or reddish-brown (very decorative). Small-leafed varieties (height: 6-10 in/15-25 cm) are better suited to a position on a windowsill or balcony and are particularly aromatic. The larger-leafed varieties (height: up to 20 in/50 cm) are more robust and better suited to growing in the garden. From early summer onward, whitish to pink flowers appear at the tips of the shoots.

Flavor: peppery-sweet, very aromatic, will mask the flavors of other herbs used with it.

Use: add fresh leaves to tomatoes, salads, eggs, pesto sauce, Mediterranean dishes, fish, and cheese. Do not cook the basil with the dish.

Growing: annual. Light-germinating seed, do not cover the seeds with soil. When the seedlings are about 4 in (10 cm) high, replant them in clumps in pots or boxes.

Soil: ½ part peat-based compost, ¼ sand, ¼ regular compost.

Position: in pots and boxes on balconies, patios and on window sills, in the garden only during hot summers.

Light: sunny, bright.

Temperature: the seeds will not germinate until night-time temperatures are above 50°F (10°C). During cooler summers, place in a warm position on a balcony or on a window ledge.

Watering: never let the soil dry out. Water daily during hot periods.

Fertilizer: a little organic controlled-release fertilizer mixed in with the soil; four weeks after planting, fertilize with nettle brew.

Harvest: young leaves. Cut off shoot tips, this will encourage the plant to branch out; harvest all summer.

Propagating: buy seeds; they will not ripen in a temperate climate.

Winter: sow a second batch of basil seeds at the end of the summer for harvesting from the windowsill. Flavor and aroma will not be as strong.

Preserving: pickle in vinegar or oil or freeze.

My tip: A pot of basil on your windowsill during the summer will drive away flies.

Summer savory needs plenty of warmth and sunlight on a balcony.

The flower of summer savory is quite beautiful.

Summer savory
Satureja hortensis

Also: bean herb

Appearance: branching, woody stalks (up to 12 in/30 cm high) with narrow, dark green leaves. From the second month of summer onward, pink to pale lilac flowers form in the leaf axils.

Flavor: intensely aromatic, peppery, stronger than the winter variety.

Use: leaves or whole stalks with leaves in bean dishes or used with other grains, potato soup, stews, fatty meats, sausages.stuffings. Appetizer; helps digestion. Should be cooked with the dish.

Growing: annual. Light-germinating seed. Sow in a mini-propagator or on a windowsill. When the seedlings have reached a height of 2 in (5cm), prick them out in large pots (three plants to a pot with a diameter of 4¾ in/ 12 cm). From the middle of spring onward, savory can be moved out into the garden. Do not let the young plants dry out before they are fully grown, nor let them become too wet. Later, it will not matter so much if the soil is very dry.

Soil: ½ peat-based compost, ¼ compost, ¼ sand, a little lime.

Position: in pots, tubs and boxes on balconies and patios, in flower boxes in front of a window, on a windowsill in winter. In the garden.

Light: a sunny position.

Temperature: requires a lot of warmth.

Watering: keep moist only, can tolerate dry soil.

Fertilizer: will impair the flavor.

Harvesting: savory will release its full aroma most while it is flowering and around midday in the sun. Cut the shoots about 4 in (10 cm) above the ground, then the plant will carry on growing and branching out.

Propagating: from seeds; they will not ripen in temperate climates.

Winter: If you sow more seed after midsummer to late summer, you will have an adequate additional supply of fresh herbs for the winter. You can plant several seedlings in a fairly large pot and stand it on the kitchen windowsill. The shoots will not carry on growing after being cut.

Preserving: drying or freezing.

My tip: Freeze some savory together with green beans.

The brilliant blue flowers of borage are very decorative and much loved by bees.

Borage
Borago officinalis

"Herb of gladness"

Appearance: very hairy stalks with large, light green, hairy leaves. Brilliant blue flowers at the shoot tips. A decorative ornamental plant, much frequented by honey bees and bumble bees. Will grow up to 40 in (1 m) in the garden, a little smaller in pots.

Flavor: slightly acid, fresh, slight taste of cucumber.

Use: young leaves for flavoring salads, egg dishes, cheese dishes, for pickling cucumbers (gherkins), used as garnish for Pimms. Do not cook, use fresh only.

Growing: annual. Dark-germinating seed. Sow it straight into the soil. Large seeds which can be sown exactly where you want them to grow. Outside from the end of the second month of spring onward, a little earlier in pots. Seedlings are hard to transplant because of their long tap root. In the garden they should be planted at intervals of 16 in (40 cm), and only one or two plants per pot. If borage plants are grown too close together, they will tend to become infested with mildew or aphids.

Soil: ½ peat-based compost or garden soil, ½ compost.

Position: in large pots and deep boxes on balconies and patios, as underplanting under tall plants in large containers, outside in a flower bed. Needs plenty of space.

Light: bright, sunny.

Temperature: needs plenty of warmth for optimal growth but will also germinate in cool weather.

Watering: daily in hot weather.

Fertilizer: compost or organic fertilizer given as controlled-release fertilizer, mixed in the soil. Fertilize every four weeks with nettle or comfrey brew.

Harvest: do not harvest before the plant has developed strong stalks. If you harvest too early, the plant will become weak. The topmost young leaves and leaves growing out of leaf axils have the best flavor.

Propagating: from seed.

Winter: sow a few more seeds in one or two pots at the end of the summer, then you can keep the plants on your windowsill until the middle of winter.

Preserving: freezing is possible but it will lose most of its flavor. The flower can be candied.

362

Dill

Anethum graveolens

Appearance: stalks up to 40 in (1 m) high with a profusion of extremely feathery leaves.

Flavor: leaves, fresh, spicy flavor, very aromatic. Seeds taste a little like caraway.

Use: leaves for green salads, cucumber or potato salads, sauces, mayonnaise, and fish. Do not cook. Use seeds for pickling gherkins.

Growing: annual. Dark-germinating seed. Sow seeds in the soil from second month of spring onward. Never let it dry out. Replanting only possible when plants are very small because of the long tap root. Dill is temperamental and will not always germinate!

Soil: ½ compost, ¼ garden soil, ¼ sand.

Position: in deep pots and boxes on a balcony or patio in a draft-free position.

Light: needs plenty of sun but keep the base of the plant in the shade – do this by sowing it between other herbs or mulching.

Temperature: needs plenty of warmth; stand in a sheltered position during a cool summer.

Watering: the soil should never be let dry out. Waterlogging should always be avoided.

Fertilizer: not necessary.

Harvest: the green leaves can be harvested constantly. Stalks can also be used. Use young plants from thinning out for cooking. Harvest seeds from the end of the summer into early fall.

Propagating: from seeds. The seeds will remain viable for four years.

Winter: sow again at the end of the summer in a large pot. Some varieties are more robust than others and will thrive on a windowsill even if the light is not very good. (Check with your garden center.) Take pots indoors before the first frosts and stand them in a very light place.

Preserving: seed heads and leaves can be pickled in vinegar. Dry the seeds. Leaves survive better if frozen.

Warning: People with kidney complaints should not use dill!

My tip: Sow dill everywhere between your other herbs. This will ensure the best chance of some of it germinating in at least one place.

Dill seeds are excellent for any kind of pickling.

Tarragon will always flourish, even in cool summers or inhospitable elevated regions.

French tarragon
Artemisia dracunculus

Appearance: heavily branching stalks with narrow, longish, deep green leaves. Greenish panicles appear on the shoot tips from early summer onward. Will grow up to 5 ft (1.5 m) in garden beds, smaller in pots.
Flavor: bitter-sweet, slightly spicy.
Use: leaves in salads, with fish, poultry, soups, *fines herbes*. Do not cook.
Growing: perennial. Dark-germinating seed.

Two varieties: Russian tarragon is not quite as spicy but very robust. It is sown in pots on windowsills and when the seedlings are well rooted they should be moved to large plant containers or outside into the garden. French or true tarragon is more aromatic but is also more sensitive to cold temperatures. It can only be propagated by means of stolons. A tarragon plant may last up to four years outside, then it will gradually become bare from below.
Soil: ½ garden soil, ½ compost.
Position: in large pots and plant boxes on balconies and patios, out-side in a bed in a sheltered position, even among shrubs.
Light: rather demanding. The best place is beside a light-colored wall which will reflect sunlight.
Temperature: will grow well even during cooler summers in less-sympathetic climatic conditions.
Watering: requires a lot of watering during dry periods but watch out for waterlogging in pots.
Fertilizer: a little organic fertilizer and 1 tablespoon of crushed rock (Perlite) mixed with the soil. Fertilize with nettle or comfrey brew every four weeks.
Harvesting: leaves, constantly.

Propagating: Russian tarragon from seed. French or true tarragon from stolons.
Winter: cut back to ground level in the fall. During cold winters, supply winter protection by covering with conifer branches or a layer of dead leaves. Take the pot plants indoors for the winter and harvest the leaves until the plant is used up. Sow new seed in spring. You can plant stolons from French tarragon in small pots during early fall and overwinter them on a bright windowsill. Do not harvest until the spring!
Preserving: pickle in vinegar or freeze.

The glowing colors of nasturtiums amid dark foliage.

The flower buds can be used like capers.

Nasturtium

Tropaeolum majus,
T. nanum

Appearance: there are two varieties. *T. majus* has shoots that grow up to 40 in (1 m) long, *T. nanum* grows like a bush. Round blue green leaves grow on juicy stalks, the flowers are very large, have a spur, and are light yellow to deep red.

Flavor: like cress, but not as peppery.

Use: leaves finely chopped in salads or with soft cheese. The flowers are used as edible decorations. Use flower buds as capers. Do not cook with the dish.

Growing: annual. Dark-germinating seed. The large seeds should be planted individually ¾ in (2 cm) deep in the soil. Place the large seeds far enough apart! If you want this plant to flower as early as the middle of spring, sow them in pots on a windowsill. Do not sow them outside until the very last frosts have passed. If the shoots grow too long, they can be cut back. The plant will continue flowering until the first frosts arrive.

Soil: ½ flower compost or garden soil, ½ compost.

Position: in flower boxes as decorative flowering plants, in front of a window, as an edging along a bed in the garden and on a patio, as underplanting for plants in large containers. Not an indoor plant.

Light: nasturtium will only flower in a very sunlit position.

Temperature: not very sensitive, will grow and thrive even during cool summers and in unsympathetic climatic conditions.

Watering: in balcony boxes, regularly, as with all other balcony plants. Outside in the garden, water only during dry periods.

Fertilizer: not necessary.

Harvesting: fresh, young leaves, flowers, flower buds.

Propagating: from seed, which can be collected from your own plants.

Winter: seeds that have been dormant in a bed outside will germinate the following year.

Preserving: buds in salt or in vinegar, leaves and flowers in vinegar.

Important: Aphids love nasturtiums above all other plants. This preference can act as a protection against these pests for other balcony plants. If a few leaves are infested with aphids, try to put up with it but total infestation will require destroying all the nasturtium leaves.

Chervil is a delicacy for the connoisseur.

The young leaves taste best.

Chervil
Anthriscus cerefolium

Appearance: light green, soft, feathery leaves on a stalk that branches profusely lower down but less higher up. May grow as tall as 2 ft (60 cm) in a bed. It produces a tall white umbel from late spring onward.

Flavor: spicy-sweet, like aniseed, but milder.

Use: young leaves in soups (chervil soup), salads, *fines herbes*. Be careful when mixing chervil and lemon juice, as it may rapidly become too acid. Do not cook with the dish.

Growing: annual. Dark-germinating seed. Seeds of smooth-leafed or curly-leafed chervil are obtainable from garden centers. Both are equally flavorful and aromatic. Sow seed fairly densely at the end of the first month of spring or the beginning of the second month, in shallow bowls, boxes, or straight into a bed. A week later, the first seedlings will appear in a pot, but allow two weeks for seed to germinate in a bed. Chervil can be cut after six weeks. If cut too young, it will not grow again. If you sow further batches of seed at intervals of two weeks, you can harvest fresh chervil all the year round. Use fresh soil for every new sowing in pots or boxes.

Soil: ⅔ peat-based compost or garden soil, ⅓ sand.

Position: in boxes and shallow bowls on balconies, patios and windowsills. In rows in a bed.

Light: chervil will thrive best in a semi-shady position. It does not like strong sunlight apart from during the first two months of spring.

Temperature: not particularly sensitive. Can be sown out in the first month of spring.

Watering: keep moist constantly or the foliage will turn red and the plant will flower before you can harvest any leaves. The flavor and aroma will be lost slightly at flowering time.

Fertilizer: not necessary.

Harvesting: young leaves before the plant starts flowering.

Propagating: from seed. Let a few chervil plants grow in the garden and produce seed. These will give a good harvest for the following year.

Winter: chervil can be grown on a windowsill like cress.

Preserving: freeze.

366

Cress is easy to grow on a windowsill all year round.

Cress
Lepidium sativum

Appearance: light green, variable, feathered, small leaves on tough stalks. The base leaves are small and oval, which is the form in which cress is mostly used. If you let cress continue to grow, small white flowers will appear at the ends of the shoots.

Flavor: like radish, hot and fresh.

Use: in salads, with cottage cheese, eggs, and on sandwiches. Tends to mask the flavors of other herbs. Do not cook.

Growing: annual. Light-germinating seed. The seeds germinate after two to three days. If you sow cress seed every eight days, you will have a constant supply. Outside, in a bed, cress is also suitable as groundcover in beds that are to be planted later on. Cress is not suitable for growing among other plants as the presence of its sharp mustard oil will interfere with the growth of other plants.

Soil: not a priority, as cress is harvested very young. Sand, peat, and flower compost are equally suitable but cress will also grow well on sheets of moist kitchen paper towel or on wet cotton wool.

Position: in a semi-shady position in a bed, in shallow bowls, boxes, flat plates on a balcony and on a kitchen windowsill.

Light: semi-shade, preferably a north-facing window rather than a south-facing one.

Temperature: not really important as the seed will germinate outside from the first month of spring onward and also in a heated room.

Watering: keep seeds and plants moist.

Fertilizer: not necessary.

Harvesting: only very young plantlets up to a height of 4-6 in (10-15 cm).

Propagating: from seed.

Winter: will grow well on a windowsill all winter long. A good provider of vitamin C during the winter season.

Preserving: not possible, and not necessary either, as cress can be grown all year round on a windowsill.

My tip: During hot summers, cress will develop a flavor that is too hot and bitter if sown outside. The right place for a summer crop is in a semi-shady position on a balcony or on a windowsill.

367

Lovage flowers from midsummer onward.

Use the very tasty leaves sparingly.

Lovage
Levisticum officinale

Appearance: square stalks bearing tough, serrated leaves. Outside in a flower bed it will grow to a height of 5 ft (1.5 m) with a bushy shape. The shoots are a reddish color in the spring. From the middle of summer onward, yellowish-green panicles appear on the tips of the shoots.

Flavor: strong spicy taste, a little like celery.

Use: leaves and stalks in soups, ragouts, stews, and salads, also with cold meats. Use sparingly, as the taste is strong. Can be used fresh or cooked.

Growing: perennial. It is not worth trying to grow lovage from seed. The seeds will only germinate if they were produced the previous fall and even then only about 40% germinate. As one single plant is sufficient for one family, it is preferable to buy a ready-grown young plant.

Soil: ⅓ garden soil or peat-based compost, ⅔ compost.

Position: in large, flat plant containers on balconies or patios, and only in a shrubbery if planted in the garden as this plant requires more fertilizing than most herbs.

Light: sunny or semi-shady.

Temperature: not sensitive to cold, can be put ouside as early as the second month of spring, provided the place chosen is sheltered.

Watering: plenty, daily on hot days.

Fertilizer: if no compost is available, use a handful of organic controlled-release fertilizer (horn chips) mixed in the soil. Use nettle or comfrey brew every four weeks. Plant pot herbs in fresh soil every year.

Harvesting: fresh leaves from the last month of spring right through to the first month of winter.

Propagating: divide a young lovage plant in its second spring.

Winter: cut the stalks off for the winter. Lovage can overwinter quite happily outside in a bed. Pot herbs should be kept in a cool room just like plants in large containers. Lovage needs a rest period in winter. If you stand it in a bright position in early spring, and water it regularly, you will soon be able to harvest the first young leaves.

Preserving: dry, freeze or salt.

Warning: Pregnant women should not eat lovage!

Do not use the berries of the bay tree.

Older trees may occasionally produce flowers.

Bay
Laurus nobilis

Sweet bay, bay laurel

Appearance: vigorously growing shrub with woody branches and longish, leathery, evergreen leaves. Older plants will flower in late spring. The flowers are small, white, and sweet-smelling. The black berries are not used.

Flavor: the very spicy, fresh leaves are slightly bitter.

Use: leaves in soups, fish and meat dishes, with potatoes, venison marinades, for pickling gherkins, sauerkraut.

Growing: perennial. Propagate only from cuttings.

Soil: ½ garden soil, ½ compost.

Position: as a large container plant on balconies and patios; young plants can be kept indoors during the winter, in a room that is not too warm.

Light: bright during the summer but not in the sun all day long.

Temperature: can survive temperatures as low as 14°F (-10°C) for short periods of time.

Watering: twice a week. If the leaves wither and dry up, the plant will die.

Harvesting: constantly, fresh leaves.

Propagating: bay is propagated only from cuttings, which grow very slowly. Do not pick any leaves during the first few years as the plant needs them for photosynthesis. If the bush is large enough, it can be pruned into a pyramid shape or trained as a standard.

Winter: overwinter in a bright room up to 59°F (15°C), and water every four weeks.

Preserving: dry leaves in bunches or individually. If the leaves become brown, the flavor and aroma will be lost.

Important: during the summer, spray the leaves occasionally with a vigorous stream of water from a hose, to get rid of aphids. The plant may become vulnerable to attack by scale insects in its winter quarters. Check regularly, and pick off any insects.

Warning: Bay may trigger allergic reactions!

My tip: When you have pruned the shrub in the fall, tie any cut-off branches in a bunch and dry them in a shady place. They look very decorative as part of a herb bouquet in the kitchen.

The curious spherical sepals are typical of marjoram.

A young shoot with a strong, spicy flavor.

Marjoram

Majorana hortensis
(syn. *Origanum majorana*)

Appearance: reddish, square stalks with finely haired, oval leaflets. From June onward, the shoot tips bear white or pale lilac flowers between green sepals. Will grow quite bushy if looked after well and can reach a height of 20 in (50 cm) – so it will need plenty of room.
Flavor: strong and spicy.
Use: leaves or twiglets with meat dishes, potatoes (fried or roasted), tomatoes, eggplants, zucchini, stews. Should not be added to the dish until ten minutes before the end of cooking. Does not go with most other herbs and spices.
Growing: annual in a temperate climate. Light-germinating seeds. Two varieties: French marjoram is quite robust. German marjoram is more sensitive but will grow faster. Both varieties are suitable for growing on a balcony or patio. For planting in a bed or in a less-temperate climate, French marjoram is preferable. Growing from seed is only worthwhile if you use a great deal of the plant. It is simpler to buy one or two young plants.
Soil: ½ humus-rich soil, ½ sand, a little lime.
Position: in boxes or large pots on a balcony or patio, in a flower box in front of a south-facing window or in a rock garden. Place it on a sunny windowsill during the winter.
Light: bright, sunny.
Temperature: very sensitive to cold. Should not be put out in a bed until the end of spring and should be taken back indoors before the first frosts in the fall.
Watering: do not let young plants dry out. Well-grown plants may be left to stand in dry conditions for a while.
Fertilizer: not necessary.
Harvesting: the young shoot tips, the spherical green sepals of the flowers can also be used. The flavor and aroma of marjoram are at their most intense early in the morning or late in the afternoon.
Propagating: from seed; seed will not ripen properly in temperate climates.
Winter: one or two strong plants can be placed in a light window during the fall. You can continue harvesting the leaves but the shoots will not grow any more.

Crushing the leaves in a mortar will release lemon balm's strong flavor.

Lemon balm

Melissa officinalis

Melissa

Appearance: light green, dentate, oval leaves on square stalks. Small pink or white flowers appear in the leaf axils in midsummer. Can grow up to 40 in (1 m) high in a bed.

Flavor: fresh lemon taste, slightly bitter-sweet.

Use: in salads, with tomatoes, herb sauces, mayonnaise, fish, rice, in punches, and as a herbal tea. Use fresh and only cook very briefly in dishes. The flavor will be stronger if the leaves are crushed.

Growing: perennial. The best method is to buy seedlings as one plant is sufficient for one family.

Soil: ⅓ garden soil, ⅓ compost, ⅓ sand.

Position: in large pots or boxes on balconies and patios, in a flower box in front of a window, indoors in a light but not too warm place. In a bed where it will not interfere with other plants.

Light: requires full sunlight, indoors in a south-facing window.

Temperature: not sensitive to cold; if cut back, it will overwinter quite happily in a flower bed. In a pot it can be moved outside from the second month of spring onward.

Watering: do not let young plants dry out. Older plants can tolerate dry conditions.

Fertilizer: use nettle brew once in late spring and again in midsummer.

Harvesting: young, light green leaves from early spring to late fall.

Propagating: a large plant can be propagated in spring by dividing the rootstock.

Winter: can comfortably overwinter in a flower bed; during mild winters, it may start shooting as early as the last month of winter. If it is planted in pots, it should be taken indoors as soon as forecasts predict sub-zero temperatures. Depending on the size of the plant, it can be kept in a cool, light room and will retain its leaves. Large plants should be rigorously cut back and overwintered in a cool, dark room. At the beginning of spring, stand it in a light position and water regularly. The plant will start shooting very quickly.

Preserving: dry or freeze.

My tip: Stand your lemon balm on a balcony or patio and it will give off a delicate scent of lemons.

371

An aroma of the Mediterranean in your kitchen.

A profusion of delicate pink oregano flowers.

Oregano
Origanum vulgare

Appearance: many small, finely haired, grayish-green leaves on long, hard, reddish stalks up to 28 in (70 cm) long. Pinkish clusters of flowers from midsummer onward.

Flavor: sharply spicy.

Use: in all Mediterranean dishes, pizzas, cheese, meat, cold sausage, and as a herbal tea. Should be cooked with the dish.

Growing: perennial. Dark-germinating seeds. Can be started by planting from seed on a windowsill. From late spring onward, it can be moved outside. It is a lot simpler to buy young plants as they will develop much faster.

Soil: ½ peat-based compost, ¼ compost, ¼ sand, a little lime.

Position: in large pots, shallow bowls, on balconies and patios, in a flower box outside a south-facing window, in a bed or rockery. Oregano needs plenty of space – a large wooden box or large shallow containers or urns are better than pots. It needs a place where it can spread out if planted in a garden.

Light: full sunshine.

Temperature: will flourish even during cool summers but its flavor will not be quite as strong. Will need some kind of winter protection in regions with rough weather.

Watering: tend to keep it fairly dry.

Harvesting: leaves and shoot tips with flowers. Occasionally cut off some of the long shoots and dry them. New shoots are formed from the roots and will have very strongly flavored young leaves.

Propagating: the rootstock can be divided after the plant is two years old.

Winter: oregano should be cut down to the ground in the fall and overwintered with a covering of dead leaves. Pots and boxes on a balcony should be protected from long periods of frost. If conditions are really bad, overwinter the pot in the cellar or some other cool, dark place.

Preserving: dry or freeze.

Warning: do not use oregano when pregnant!

My tip: At the end of summer/beginning of fall, split off a section of roots with young shoots and plant it in a pot. In the middle of fall, it can be placed on the kitchen windowsill and can be harvested a few weeks later.

Parsley will flourish in large pots. Plant both curly-leaed and smooth-leved varieties.

Parsley
Petroselinum crispum

Appearance: the square stalks bear curly or feathery leaves. In its second year, it will bear a greenish-yellow umbel on a long stalk.
Flavor: spicy, slightly bitter.
Use: smooth-leaved parsley has a stronger flavor than the curly variety, which, in turn, is more decorative. Use the leaves for salads, potatoes, vegetables, sauces, and with soft cheese. Do not cook in the dish, add it when the dish is done.
Growing: biennial. Dark-germinating seeds. Parsley should be sown in early spring in a pot or box on a windowsill and then, in the middle of spring, when the plants are stronger, it can be moved outside. Sow seed in a bed in late summer, then you will be able to harvest the herb the following spring. It will not taste good during its second year when the flowers form. You will have to sow new seed every year.
Soil: ½ garden soil or peat-based compost, ½ compost.
Position: in deep pots or boxes on a balcony or patio, in a flower box in front of a window. If sown in a flower bed, choose a different position every year.
Light: semi-shade but in a light position if placed on a windowsill during the winter.
Temperature: will flourish even during cool summers.
Watering: do not let the soil dry out in a pot.
Fertilizer: no mineral fertilizer, no animal material fertilizer; use controlled-release fertilizer in a pot with plenty of organic fertilizer.
Harvesting: do not pick the herb until plenty of vigorous leaves have formed. After that, it will grow better the more often that you cut it.
Propagating: from seed, which can be harvested again every second year.
Winter: may overwinter outside in a bed. If planted in a pot, it will not survive a winter outside. During the cold season of the year, bring some of the stronger plants in from outside and plant in a pot which should be placed on the kitchen windowsill for use as a freshly picked herb.
Preserving: dry, freeze, salt.
Warning: the seeds are poisonous!

Mint is very versatile in cooking.

The pink flower spikes appear in high summer.

Peppermint
Mentha piperita

Appearance: dark green or reddish leaves with dentate edges on long, square stalks. In mid- to late summer, pink spikes form at the shoot tips.
Flavor: cool and distinctively refreshing taste, stong aroma.
Use: leaves for mint tea, summer drinks, liqueur, potatoes, lamb dishes, salad dressings. Use fresh or cook with the dish.
Growing: perennial. Sowing seed is not worth the effort; it is preferable

to buy a young plant. Interesting varieties for balcony gardeners: orange mint, apple mint, pinapple mint, and spicy mint. If you like mint with lamb, as the British do, you should use curly mint which has a milder flavor. Water mint, which also grows wild, has a particularly delicate flavor and aroma. Young spearmint plants can be bought; this tends to have a sharper taste.
Soil: ½ garden soil or peat-based compost, ½ compost.
Position: on a balcony or patio in a large pot or large shallow plant container. Can be planted with balcony flowers in a

balcony box. If planted in a bed, it should be limited, as it is very invasive. One way to stop it spreading is to plant it in a bottomless bucket.
Light: sunny, semi-shady.
Temperature: the flavor and aroma will be stronger in hot summers than in cool ones. Not very sensitive to frost.
Watering: do not let young plants dry out. Older plants should only be watered in periods of drought.
Fertilizer: not necessary.
Harvesting: shoot tips with young leaves (better taste). Occasionally cut a number of shoots down to the ground (you can dry these), so that new

shoots will then form.
Propagating: from stolons.
Winter: cut back radically. Give some winter protection if the plants are in an exposed bed. If in pots, mint should be overwintered in a cool, dark cellar.
Preserving: dry or freeze.
Warning: the digestive system of nursing babies and toddlers will not cope very well with mint!

My tip: The rarer varieties can generally only be obtained as stolons. With the prior permission of the owner, dig up a few stolons with young shoots and plant them in a small flower pot.

The young leaves of salad burnet taste nutty.

The spherical, red flowers appear from early summer onward.

Salad burnet
Sanguisorba minor

Appearance: the small, dentate leaves grow in dense rosettes on long stalks. From early summer onward, reddish-green flowers appear.
Flavor: fresh, nutty, slightly like cucumber.
Use: young leaves in salads, egg dishes, sauces, and dressings. Use raw.
Growing: perennial. Dark-germinating seeds. Sow in the pots or boxes in which they are to be kept from the second month of spring onward, or in a flower bed. As soon as the seedlings are large enough to be grasped between two fingers, thin them out. If they are left too close together, they will not thrive. Leave spaces of 8 in (20 cm) between plants in a bed. Only one plant should be allowed per pot with a diameter of 4¾ in (12 cm). Always leave the strongest of three to four seedlings.
Soil: ⅔ garden soil or peat-based compost, ⅓ sand with a little lime.
Position: in deep pots or boxes on a balcony or patio; in a window during the winter. The stalks will lean well over the edge of the pot. This makes the plant suitable for edging a bed or for a corner of a herb box or raised bed.
Light: light and sunny, particularly during the winter if it is kept on a windowsill.
Temperature: not sensitive to cold, will grow equally well in cool summers and in beds up to the onset of the first frosts. Harvest until the first snowfall.
Watering: tends to prefer dry conditions. If the leaves look limp, the plant will quickly recover after a good dousing.
Fertilizer: not necessary.
Harvesting: constantly, fresh, light green leaflets.
Propagating: seed will self-sow in a bed.
Winter: if you wish to continue harvesting through the winter, sow more seed in a pot in late summer and then take the young plants in their pots inside in mid-fall.
Preserving: freeze, but it is preferable to continue harvesting during winter.
Important: cut off the flowers as this will encourage more leaves to form. It will also prevent the plant from going to seed in a bed. Salad burnet is often invasive.

My tip: Sow some salad burnet seed under a standard plant in a large container as this will prevent the moisture in the soil from evaporating.

The leaves on young rosemary shoots are still quite soft.

The flowers provide some of the first nectar for bees in early spring.

Rosemary
Rosmarinus officinalis

Appearance: up to 40 in (1 m) tall, woody shrub with blue green, long, narrow leaves with whitish undersides. From early spring onward, the plant has blue flowers.

Flavor: spicy-bitter, with a very strong aroma.

Use: in Mediterranean dishes, roasts, light meats, pasta, tomatoes, vegetables. Should be cooked in the dish. Aids the digestive processes.

Growing: perennial. Rosemary can be sown but it will grow very slowly. You might have to wait up to three years before you can harvest the leaves. It is preferable to buy young plants.

Soil: ½ garden soil or peat-based compost, ¼ compost, ¼ sand or fine gravel, a little lime. The plant does not like packed soil.

Position: in a large container on a balcony or patio. In a flower bed. Can be planted in a pot and moved into the house during the winter.

Light: very light, lots of sun.

Temperature: the warmer, the better for the full development of the flavor and aroma.

Rosemary will cope with temperatures as low as 23°F (-5°C), but take it inside if the temperatures drop any lower.

Watering: keep it moist.

Fertilizer: not necessary.

Harvesting: constantly, fresh shoots. Do not, however, go wild when cutting off shoots as the plant may then stop producing them. Cut off shoots in a way that gives the whole plant a good shape. During the winter, use fewer shoots as the plant will not start shooting again until late winter/early spring.

Propagating: cuttings can be taken from young plants by the second year. Plants that are older than five years will not produce so many shoots, so make sure you have follow-on plants.

Winter: overwinter inside but stand the plants outside on warmer, frost-free days, in sunlight.

Preserving: not necessary as leaves and shoots can be harvested even in winter.

NB: Rosemary is very stimulating so do not put rosemary sprigs in your bath before bedtime as you will not sleep so well!

My tip: If you do not like chewing the rather tough leaves during your meal, you can put rosemary in a herb mill or cook the whole sprig and remove it before serving.

Young sage leaves have a milder taste.

Pretty and also edible: garden sage "Tricolor."

Sage
Salvia officinalis

Appearance: very woody, slightly straggly, evergreen shrub (12-20 in/30-50 cm tall), with silvery, hairy, blue green, oval leaves. Blue or violet flowers appear on long stalks during the second and third months of summer.

Flavor: strongly spicy, slightly bitter.

Use: leaves, sparingly, with ham, Mediterranean stews, fried in butter to go with pasta. Should always be cooked in the dish. Very beneficial as a herbal tea for gargling.

Growing: perennial. Dark-germinating seeds. Can be grown from seed, on a windowsill from the second month of spring, in a bed from the last month of spring. When the seedlings are 4-6 in (10-15 cm) high, plant three or four together in a large pot in the bed where they are to grow.

Soil: ½ garden soil, ¼ compost, ¼ sand, a little lime.

Position: in pots and boxes on a balcony or patio. In a flower box hanging from a south-facing balcony or in a bed in a sunny position. Stand the pots outside during the summer as the flavor and aroma will develop better in sunlight.

Light: very light; even in winter it should be placed on a sunny windowsill.

Temperature: the warmer, the better.

Watering: tends to prefer dry conditions.

Fertilizer: not necessary.

Harvesting: the small leaves of young plants are particularly suitable for flavoring food as their flavor has not become too strong. As you will only need to use it sparingly, sage will grow well. It can be cut back in late summer and the leaves can be dried. The plant will form new shoots before winter.

Propagating: from shoots that are pegged to the soil (layering) so they can form roots.

Winter: can be left outside in a bed. If temperatures drop to below 14°F (-10°C), cover the plants with dead leaves or, temporarily, with plastic bubble pack or similar. If the plants are in pots, only take them inside in freezing temperatures.

Preserving: dry.

My tip: try the variety called muscatel sage (*Salvia sclarea*). It is used mainly in sweet dishes. Some of the ornamental varieties of sage and meadow sage are not suitable for flavoring food.

Chives can be harvested all year round.

A mild taste of garlic: knolau.

Chives
Allium schoenoprasum

Appearance: thin, green, hollow tubes grow out of tiny bulbs in thick clumps. From the second month of summer, pink, false umbels appear on the ends of tougher stalks.

Flavor: strongly of onions.

Use: in salads, soups, with cottage cheese, eggs, potatoes, pancakes, and in sandwiches. Do not cook.

Growing: perennial. Sow straight into a flower bed from the second month of spring. Sow densely, as you will want a thick bunch of chives to grow. Do not harvest the thin green stalk-shaped leaves too soon as the plant will die. Faster results are obtained if you buy one or two rootstocks in the spring. If you use a lot of chives, keep resowing seed as pot plants, in particular, become exhausted rather quickly.

Soil: ½ garden soil, ½ compost, a little lime.

Position: in pots on balconies, patios, and in windows; in a flower box or outside a north-facing window. In a bed.

Light: sun, semi-shade.

Temperature: cooler rather than warm.

Watering: keep moist, but no waterlogging.

Fertilizer: if you have no compost, use organic fertilizer. Fertilize with nettle brew.

Harvesting: the best method is always to cut only half of the "stalks," then take the remaining half after they have grown again.

Propagating: by dividing the rootstock in spring or fall.

Winter: no protection needed in a flower bed. If in pots, stand them in a dry, cool place.

Preserving: freeze or, better still, harvest fresh from a pot on the windowsill.

My tip: If you are growing chives outside, you can prepare them for a move to a windowsill in the following way: take the tiny bulbs out of the soil in the fall and let them dry for four to six weeks. Brief exposure to freezing temperatures will not harm them. The chives will grow well in a pot on a windowsill. When the plant is exhausted, put it back in the garden.

NB: You can obtain a cross between garlic and chives. The leaves are flat and the taste is milder than that of garlic. It is very tasty in salads or in sandwiches.

Summer thyme for your balcony.

Delicate pink flowers in summer.

Thyme
Thymus vulgaris

Appearance: very woody, small shrub with narrow, gray green, hardy leaves. Produces a mass of pinkish flowers from early summer onward.

Flavor: very spicy with a strong aroma, slightly bitter.

Use: leaves, flowers and shoots in meat dishes, pasta, stews, potatoes, and with venison. Should be cooked with the dish and will aid digestion.

Growing: perennial. Thyme can be grown from seed indoors. The seedlings will grow fairly slowly, spread out in all directions while the stalks are still soft and hang over the edge of the pot. If you keep bending them back into the pot, they will form a cushion. A simpler method is to buy young plants. You can start harvesting right away. Outside, in a bed, thyme may appear to have difficulties getting established but, when it is, it will grow very fast. Most varieties of thyme are well suited to growing outside and can withstand freezing temperatures.

Soil: ½ garden soil or peat-based compost, ¼ compost, ¼ sand and a little lime.

Position: in pots, boxes, and shallow bowls on a balcony or patio, in a flower box outside a window, in a garden bed or in a rockery.

Light: plenty of sunshine.

Temperature: the best flavor and aroma will develop on hot days.

Watering: dry rather than moist.

Fertilizer: not necessary.

Harvesting: constantly.

Propagating: from slightly woody cuttings in the second and last months of summer.

Winter: in early fall cut the shrub back by about two-thirds, then it will branch out more the following year. Dry the parts you have cut off and make them into a herb bouquet to hang in your kitchen.

Preserving: dry or freeze.

My tip: Try to obtain some wild thyme (*Thymus praecox arcticus*) for your garden. It has a more delicate flavor than garden thyme.

Making the most of your houseplants

Houseplants are beautiful and exotic aliens in our homes and offices. In order to stay healthy, they require only one thing – to be given similar conditions to those in which they live in their countries of origin.

Written by **Gisela Keil**

Position

The care of houseplants begins with choosing the right position. This section will tell you what is important, how to make the light, air, and temperature just right, and how you can control pests or diseases without resorting to toxic agents.

Watering

All houseplants require the right amounts of water and humidity. In order to care for them properly, you must understand how important water is for plants. Very few of them will be happy with regular floods, constant waterlogging, or cold, hard main water.

Fertilizing

Nourishment is vital for your houseplants! Most fertilizers include nearly all of the nutrients required by plants. Individual requirements do vary, however, and the range of fertilizers is vast. Here you will find useful advice to guide you through the array of fertilizers and to help you to choose and use the right ones.

Repotting

All houseplants need "healthy feet" if they are to thrive and flourish. There is lots to learn about soil, composts and plant containers as well as the practicalities of repotting. In addition, there are important tips on hydroponics and on a fairly recent alternative, using clay granule compost.

First aid for indoor plants

If you act fast in times of trouble, you may be able to save most plants. Mistakes in care produce unmistakable symptoms but many can soon be remedied.

Introduction and Contents

It is not surprising that houseplants are now more popular than ever before. They are able to bring a little magic to your home or office, giving even the most sober and boring room a touch of greenery or a hint of color and scent, or creating an exotic mood. Many people like to keep houseplants but very few really know what they need in the way of vital care. Often bought on the spur of the moment, many plants soon lose first their beauty, then their lives. This is when you need help – and here it is! This useful guide covers the care of houseplants right down to the basics. It is concise, informative and essentially practical. In this book the author offers advice that will ensure success for beginners or more experienced houseplant owners – whether at home or in the office. Just open the book at the relevant place and follow the instructions! In this guide you will discover what it is that houseplants really need in order to thrive and produce healthy foliage and beautiful flowers – the right position in a room, the right amount of watering and fertilizing, and repotting at the right time. In addition, there are tables giving tips on care for 100 of the most popular flowering and green houseplants. Excellent color photographs will help you to identify plants and to choose your favorites.

A weekend supply of water! Cotton wicks conduct moisture to the pots.

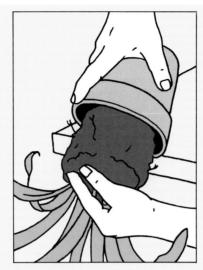

Repotting tip: *Tap the upside-down pot against the edge of the table to loosen the roots.*

The author

Gisela Keil is a student of education and psychology and of German, English and comparative literature. An author of gardening books for many years, she has been an enthusiastic houseplant keeper for twenty years, and also spends much time in her wild garden and on promoting "green" gardening methods.

The photographers

Ulrike Schneiders trained as a photographer at the Bavarian Institute for Photography and also worked with her father, Toni Schneiders. She has worked professionally for calendar and art publishers since 1978, with a special emphasis on flowers, landscapes, and still life. The majority of the photographs in this guide were taken by her. The other photographs were taken by other well-known plant photographers.

The illustrator

After studying at the Academy of Art in Budapest, György Jankovics attended the Academy of Art in Hamburg. He then trained as a technical artist and subsequently worked for several well-known publishing companies. For many years he has been an acclaimed illustrator of books on animals and plants.

The requirements of houseplants vary as much as their appearance. Light, temperature, and humidity can all be measured indoors and, if necessary, adapted to suit the requirements of individual plants.

388

Position

The secret of success with houseplants lies in the choice of the right position. When choosing a position for your plants, look for a spot that will provide, as far as possible, the same conditions in respect of light, air, and temperature that they would enjoy in their country of origin. When you have done this, all other care is mere child's play!

Position

What are houseplants?

Nature did not invent houseplants as there are no closed rooms in the wild. It was people who first began, thousands of years ago, to bring plants of all kinds into their living areas. But what is the attraction of such plants?

● Houseplants nearly all originate from tropical or subtropical regions.

● They are not usually hardy or frost-resistant and would not survive outside in temperate climates.

● They are dependent on being grown in containers indoors.

● They enchant us with the beauty of their leaves and flowers or with their interesting shapes.

● Nearly all of them are in leaf all year round.

● Many houseplants are no longer pure species, as in nature, but have been developed from hybrids, etc. Generally, the following goals have been sought: longer flowering times; larger, more intensely colored, multi-colored, or double flowers; better chances of survival indoors; and a decreased susceptibility to pests and diseases.

Masters of adaptation

Like all other plants, the plants that we keep indoors have resulted from millions of years of specialization in growing in certain climates and positions and have developed a multitude of techniques to enable them to survive. Over time, they have adapted so well to the prevailing conditions in their places of origin that these special characteristics have become part of their genetic programming. Among the more relevant conditions for maintaining healthy growth, the most important are the timing and amount of warmth, water, humidity, and nutrients.

Appearance and shape of growth: The overall shape of plants, be it the shape and size of their leaves, the characteristics of their flowers and roots, or their upright, climbing, prostrate or pendulous growth, is one way in which plants have adapted to their position in the wild, with the sole aim of surviving and reproducing.

Growth cycle: This also evolved through the adaptation of plants to the conditions of their original climate. Few species will form buds and flowers if you do not observe their preferred phases of growth and rest.

● Growth periods are usually restricted to times of maximum warmth, allied to plenty of light and moisture. This is when plants form shoots and produce flowers.

● Rest phases usually occur in times of drought or in the cooler, darker time of year when growth ceases. In the case of bulbous or tuberous plants, this is the time when the leaves will turn yellow and the plants will die back, storing nutrients in their underground organs.

My tip: In temperate climates, most houseplants have a rest phase during the winter, as do most native plants.

Where this is not the case, the individual needs of plants must be taken into consideration, for example, a cooler, shadier position, little water, no fertilizer – all at the right time! Plants from tropical rain forests have no natural rest phase. They are, however, forced to undergo a rest phase in temperate climates where there is a decrease of light in the winter. Try to give them as bright a position as possible during this time and water them sparingly.

The country of origin is a decisive factor

Tropical plants come from very varying climatic zones.

● Rain forest plants (like maidenhair fern, *Adiantum tenerum*) are used to heavy rainfall without dry periods, high humidity, and cool nights. When kept indoors, they will not like full sunlight or dry air and do not require a rest phase.

● Plants from savannahs and steppes (like *Pentas lanceolata*) have adapted to alternating rainy and dry seasons. They will require a rest phase corresponding to a natural dry season.

● Plants from tropical mountain forests (like *Camellia*) like very bright light with lots of rain, mist, and cool temperatures. When kept indoors, tropical mountain plants will require a combination of plenty of light, high humidity, and cool temperatures.

● Plants from desert regions, like cacti, can cope with any amount of sunlight, high temperatures, and drought. Indoors, they will require plenty of light all year round. During the winter, they must have cool temperatures and dry conditions; otherwise they will not produce any flowers.

Subtropical plants have adapted to hot summers and mild winters. Representatives from regions that receive summer rain need a rest period during the winter and to be placed in a cool, dry position. Plants from regions that receive rain in winter need light, warmth, and plenty of water during the winter.

How plants live

The roots supply water and nutrients and anchor the plant firmly in the soil. Many roots are also able to store the starch produced by the plant or to retain it in enlarged organs, like rhizomes, tubers, or bulbs, until needed.

Depending on the plant, the shoots can be leafy-green or brown and woody. They contain vascular tissue which conducts water and nutrients from the roots to the leaves of the plants.

The leaves are equivalent to the lung and the digestive organs of humans. Most of the respiration, the photosynthesis, and the processing of nutrients takes place in the leaves (see illustration right).

The flowers are only a transitional phase for the plant, indicating its readiness for reproduction.

Care of plants

Houseplants can be divided into two groups: flowering plants and plants with attractive foliage. The following pages will tell you how plants in these two groups should be cared for.

The metabolic processes of plants by day

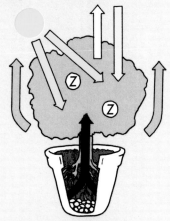

1. Photosynthesis: This process is only possible because of the green pigment called chlorophyll which is contained in the leaves. Sunlight causes the plant to absorb carbon dioxide (CO_2) from the air and, with the help of water, transforms this gas into carbohydrates (sugar). During the process, the plant releases oxygen (O) to the air.

2. Assimilation: Together with nutrients, the carbohydrates are transformed into the basic building elements of plants and then conducted to the growth zones of the plant or held in storage organs.

3. Respiration (see right-hand column): Respiration and photosynthesis occur simultaneously during the day.

4. Transpiration (see right-hand column): Under the influence of sunlight and the sun's warmth, plants release more moisture (H_2O) through evaporation during the daytime than at night.

The metabolic processes of plants by night

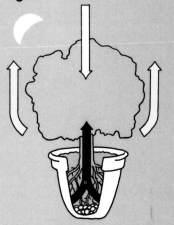

1. Respiration: Through their pores, the leaves absorb oxygen (O) from the air and also release carbon dioxide (CO_2). Carbohydrates stored during the day are partly released again during this process.

2. Transpiration: Like many other living things, plants "perspire" when the temperature rises by releasing moisture through their leaves. This creates a certain moisture deficiency and a strong suction effect from below, which enables the roots to suck up the necessary amount of moisture. If more moisture is evaporated through the leaves than the roots are able to replenish, the plant will become limp.

Another advantage is that transpiration also helps the plant to cool its leaves.

When temperatures drop at night, the plant transpires less. When the weather is dull and cool, watering should be cut down.

Position

*A beginners' orchid:
Phalaenopsis.*

Flowering time

If you wish, you can
surround yourself with
flowering plants all year
round, although this is only
possible with species that
flower at different times,
one after the other. The
length of plants' flowering
times can vary just as
much as the time each
flower lasts. Some plants
have flowers that last for
just one day; others last
for weeks.

African violets.

*Easter cactus is also
suitable for hanging
containers.*

The flower

Flowering plants are the
most popular houseplants,
even though the flowers
appear for a relatively
short time. When the
flower buds start forming,
the plant is reaching
maturity. All its energies
now go into fertilization so
that it can produce fruits
or seeds. Plants invest an
inordinate amount of
energy in this process.

My tip: If you want to
keep flowers blooming for
as long as possible, you
should cut off any dead
heads as soon as you can
to prevent the plant using
up energy unnecessarily.

A bulbous plant: Amaryllis.

Orchids

Orchids will generally only
produce flowers if great
attention is given to their
natural growth cycles.

Late winter/spring: The
amount of light and water
should be increased at the
beginning of the growth
phase.

Early spring/summer:
Water and fertilize
regularly. This is the
growth phase.

Late summer/fall: Lower
the temperature by at least
39-43° F (4-6° C) at night,
water less, but give plenty
of light. This is the time of
bud formation.

Fall/winter: Rest and
flowering times. Give more
light but not very much
water.

Cacti

There are countless
species of cacti, many of
which have quite different
requirements.

Desert cacti
like a
bright position all year
round.

● full sunlight in the
summer, fresh air, and
plenty of water as well as
sparse amounts of fertilizer
containing very little
nitrogen;

● in the fall, bright, but no
sunlight; at 41-54° F (5-
12° C), do not water any
more;

● in the spring, cautiously
begin watering again.

Exceptions: The warmth-
loving disco and melon
cacti which can overwinter
in heated rooms.

The bromeliad Aechmea.

In spite of its delicate flowers, the blue passion flower (Passiflora caerulea) is quite robust and will produce shoots up to 40 in (1 m) long in one year. It is overwintered like a large container plant: in a bright, cool position

Care at a glance

Name	Flowering time	Light	Watering	Humidity	Fertilizing	Further tips on care
● *Adenium* ☠ desert rose	4-8	☀	💧		every 2 weeks; 3-8 cactus fertilizer	compost, hydroculture; O: around 59° F/15° C, cool, dry.
Aechmea (bromeliad)	5-10 flowers once!	○	💧	💨	every 2 weeks: 3-8	compost, hydroculture, some epiphytic; O: 64-77° F/18-25° C.
Aeschynanthus	5-8	○	💧	💨	every 2 weeks: 3-8 low doses	compost, hydroculture; hanging plant; O: 68-77° F/20-25° C (for 4 weeks at 59° F/15° C).
Anthurium scherzerianum hybrid flamingo flower	all year	○	💧	💨	weekly: 3-9 low doses	compost, hydroculture; O: 68-77° F/20-25° C, light, humid.
Aphelandra squarrosa saffron spike, zebra plant	6-10	○	💧	💨	every 2 weeks: 3-8	compost, hydroculture; O: 68-79° F/20-26° C.
● *Begonia elatior* hybrid flowering begonia	all year	○	💧		every 2 weeks	one year only! O: 64-75° F/18-24° C.
Brunfelsia ☠	1-8	○ – ◑	💧	💨	every 2 weeks: 3-9	compost, hydroculture; O: 11-1 at 50-54° F/10-12° C.
● *Cactaceae* genera/species of desert cacti	3-9	☀ – ○	💧		every 2 weeks: 4-10	mineral compost, cactus fertilizer O: 41-50° F/5-10° C, bright, dry.
Camellia	10-3	○	💧	💨	every 2 weeks: 4-7 azalea fertilizer	compost only; O: 43-50° F/6-10° C, bright, well-ventilated.
Catharanthus roseus ☠ Madagascar evergreen	5-10	○	💧		every 2 weeks: 3-8	compost only; O: around 59° F/15° C, bright.
● *Chrysanthemum indicum* hybrids pot chrysanthemum	all year	○	💧		weekly: 3-10	compost, all year round; not over 64° F/18° C.
Clerodendrum	3-10	○	💧	💨	weekly: 3-8	compost, hydroculture; hanging plant; O: 12-2 at 54° F/12° C, bright, then warmer.
Clivia miniata ☠	2-5	○	💧		every 2 weeks: 3-7	compost, hydroculture; O: 10-2 at 46-50° F/8-10° C, almost dry.
Columnea	depends on species	○ – ◑	💧	💨	weekly: 3-8 low doses	compost, hydroculture; hanging plant; O: 30-40 days at 59° F/15° C, encourages flowers.
Cyclamen persicum cyclamen	9-4	○ – ◑	💧		before and during flowering: weekly	compost only; O: 59° F/15° C, airy.
Cymbidium (orchids)	9-2	☀ – ○	💧	💨	every 4 weeks: 3-9 orchid fertilizer	Orchid compost; 5-6 warm in daytime, night-time: 61° F/16° C; O: daytime 68° F/20° C, night 61° F/16° C.
Dipladenia ☠	5-10	○	💧	💨	weekly: 3-8	compost only; climbing plant; O: 59-75° F/15-24° C, bright, humid.
Epiphyllum hybrids (leaf cacti)	5-7	○ – ◑	💧	💨	every 2 weeks: 3-8 cactus fertilizer	compost only; also hanging plant; O: 54-59° F/12-15° C, drier.
● *Euphorbia milii* ☠ crown of thorns	10-3	☀ – ○	💧		every 2 weeks: 3-8 cactus fertilizer	compost, hydroculture; O: 59-75° F/15-24° C, bright.
Euphorbia pulcherrima poinsettia	11-2	○	💧		weekly: 6-10	compost, hydroculture; O: up to 68° F/20° C.
● *Exacum affine* Arabian violet, Persian violet	7-9	○	💧		every 2 weeks: 5-8	annual or biennial
Gardenia	7-10	○	💧	💨	weekly: 3-8 low doses	compost, hydroculture; O: 59-64° F/15-18° C, bright, humid.
Hibiscus rosa-sinensis	3-10	☀ – ○	💧	💨	weekly: 3-8	compost, hydroculture; O: around 59° F/15° C bright, humid.
Hippeastrum hybrids ☠ amaryllis	1-4	○	💧		weekly: 3-8	from 8, hardly any water; to 12 at 59° F/15° C. when no foliage, pot bulb, warm, bright.

The symbols: ● the plant is easy to care for, suitable for beginners and offices. ☠ Warning: plants or parts of them are toxic.
Light ☀ = full sunlight, south-facing window; ○ = bright, east- or west-facing window; ◑ = semi-shade, north-facing window; ● = shade, small north-facing windows.

Name	Flowering time	Light	Watering	Humidity	Fertilizing	Further tips on care
Hoya wax plant	5-10	☀–○	medium		every 2 weeks: 3-8 low doses	compost, hydroculture; hanging, climbing plant; O: 59-64° F/15-18° C, bright.
Hydrangea macrophylla	3-7	○–◐	medium		every 2 weeks: 5-8 azalea fertilizer	compost only; O: 39-46° F/4-8° C, dark, loss of leaves.
● *Hypocyrta*	8-3	○	sparingly		every 2 weeks: 3-8	compost only; hanging plant; O: 54-59° F/12-15° C, almost dry.
● *Impatiens* patience-plant	nearly all year round	○–◐	medium		weekly: 3-9	compost, hydroculture; also hanging plant; O: 64-77° F/18-25° C, bright.
Jasminum jasmine	6-9	○	medium		every 2 weeks: 5-8	compost only; climbing plant; O: below 50° F/10° C, bright.
● *Kalanchoë blossfeldiana* flaming Katy	2-5	☀–○	sparingly		every 4 weeks: 3-8 cactus fertilizer	compost, hydroculture; O: 61-77° F/16-25° C, bright
Kalanchoë manginii	2-3	○	sparingly		every 4 weeks: 3-8 cactus fertilizer	compost only; hanging plant; O: 50-57° F/10-14° C, drier.
Medinilla magnifica	4-7	○	medium	medium/high	weekly: 3-8	compost only; O: for 2 months at 61° F/16° C, otherwise always above 68° F/20° C !, moist and warm.
Miltonia, pansy orchid	6-11	○	medium	medium/high	every 3 weeks: 3-7 orchid fertilizer	orchid compost; O: daytime around 68° F/20° C, night 59-64° F/15-18° C, humid air.
Paphiopedilum hybrids slipper orchids	depends on variety	◐	medium	medium/high	every 3 weeks: 4-9 orchid fertilizer	orchid compost; 9: 2-3 weeks cool at night, daytime, sunny, O: 68-75° F/20-24° C.
Passiflora passion flower	6-9	☀–○	medium	medium/high	weekly: 3-8	compost, hydroculture; climbing plant; O: around 59° F/15° C, bright, airy.
● *Pelargonium grandiflorum* hybrids	all year round	☀–○	medium		weekly: 3-8	compost only; O: 50-59° F/10-15° C, airy.
Pentas lanceolata	9-1	○	medium		every 2 weeks: 3-8 low doses	compost only; O: 54-59° F/12-15° C.
Phalaenopsis hybrids	all year round	○	medium	medium/high	every 2 weeks: 5-8 orchid fertilizer	compost, hydroculture; O: daytime 68-75° F/20-24° C, cooler at night; fall 4-6 weeks at 61° F/16° C.
Rhipsalidopsis hybrids	3-5	○–◐	medium	medium/high	every 4 weeks: 5-8 cactus fertilizer	compost only; also in hanging baskets; O: 8 weeks at 50° F/10° C, otherwise 64-77° F/18-25° C.
Rhododendron indoor azalea	11-4	○–◐	medium	medium/high	every 2 weeks: 5-8 azalea fertilizer	compost only; O: from 10 about 41-50° F/5-10° C; buds appear at about 64° F/18° C.
● *Saintpaulia ionantha* hybrids African violet	all year round	○–◐	medium		weekly: 3-8 low doses	compost, hydroculture; O: 64-77° F/18-25° C, bright, humid air.
Schlumbergera hybrids	12-3	○–◐	medium	medium/high	every 2 weeks: 3-8 cactus fertilizer	compost only; also in hanging baskets; O: 64-72° F/18-22° C, bright.
Senecio cruentus hybrids cineraria	3-4	○	medium	medium/high	weekly: 2-4	annual
Sinningia hybrids gloxinia	3-8	○	medium	medium/high	weekly: 3-8	after flowering, wait for leaves to retract. O: the tuber in a dry place at 59° F/15° C.
Stephanotis floribunda	6-9	○	medium	medium/high	weekly: 3-8	compost, hydroculture; climbing plant; O: 54-57° F/12-14° C, warmer when buds begin to form.
Streptocarpus Cape primrose	5-9	○–◐	medium	medium/high	every 2 weeks: 3-8	compost, hydroculture; O: 64-75° F/18-24° C, bright, humid air.
Tillandsia (bromeliads)	depends on species	○	spray	medium/high	every 2 weeks: 5-8 low doses	tied to branches, epiphytic; O: grey species 50-59° F/10-15° C, green ones 68-79° F/20-26° C.
Zantedeschia	3-7	☀–○	medium		weekly: 8-flowering	compost, hydroculture; after flowering, keep dry for 2 whole months. Repot, then water more.

Watering: = water a lot; = medium watering, keep the plant constantly moist; = water sparingly, allow compost to dry off.
Humidity: = medium or high humidity. Roman numerals = months. O = overwintering.

Position

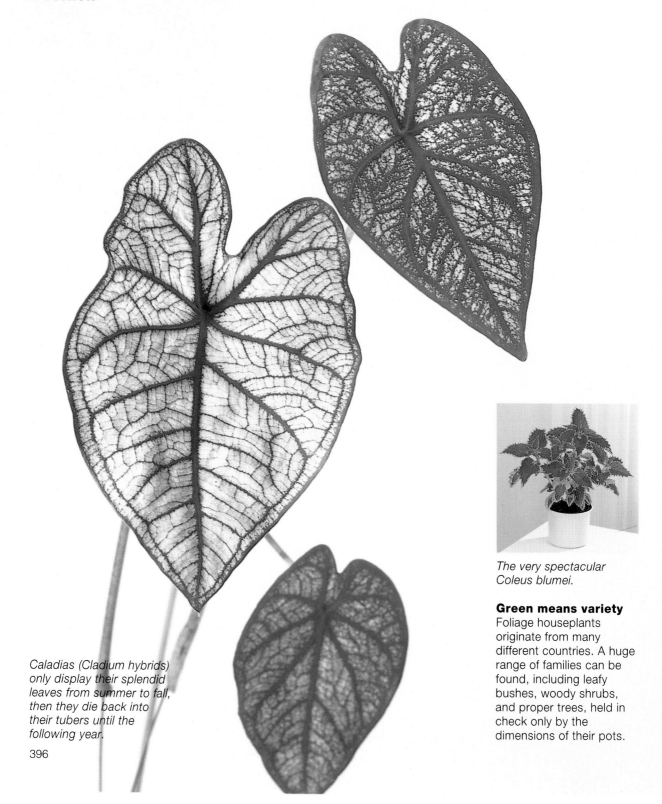

Caladias (Cladium hybrids) only display their splendid leaves from summer to fall, then they die back into their tubers until the following year.

The very spectacular Coleus blumei.

Green means variety
Foliage houseplants originate from many different countries. A huge range of families can be found, including leafy bushes, woody shrubs, and proper trees, held in check only by the dimensions of their pots.

Shades of green: Maranta.

water through evaporation. They will always need plenty of humid air. ***Leathery, tough leaves*** are a feature of plants that can cope with plenty of light (but not sunlight) and which will survive a temporary shortage of water.

The ribbed fern.

A spreading Washingtonia.

There are upright, prostrate, climbing, and hanging species, with large or small, soft or tough, single colored, or multi-colored leaves. Naturally, such individuality calls for very different requirements as to care. Many of the plants' needs can be guessed at by looking at their leaves.

What the leaves tell us
Fleshy leaves usually indicate that the plant is able to store moisture and can cope with a temporary lack of water and plenty of sun.

Variegated leaves (white- or yellow-patterned foliage) contain less chlorophyll than green species and should be placed in brighter (but never sunny!) positions.

Large, soft leaves should never be left in the sun or they will lose too much

The variegated leaves of Epipremnum pinnatum.

Indoor ferns
These are among the oldest plants in the world and they do not reproduce through flowers but through spores. Nearly all indoor ferns are natives of tropical rain forests, with evergreen fronds and similar requirements for care:
● no bright sunlight!
● keep warm from below; never allow cold drafts!
● high humidity. This is the reason most ferns do not thrive in the dry air of centrally heated rooms;
● soft, lukewarm water;
● a constant rate of moisture in the soil;
● no waterlogging.

Palms
These leafy beauties generally grow very slowly. A distinction is made between feathery palms with deeply indented fronds, like *Chamaedorea elegans*, and fan palms with more rounded leaves, like the *Washingtonia* species.

The requirements for care are as follows:
● very bright position but never in bright sunlight;
● humid air; the tips of the leaves go brown in dry air;
● medium moist soil, but no waterlogging. Never water the "heart" of the palm, as it decays very easily;
● use tall, narrow pots when repotting.

Care at a glance

Name	Light	Watering	Humidity	Fertilizing	Further tips on care
Adiantum maidenhair fern	◯ – ◑	💧	spray	every 2 weeks: 3-9 low doses	compost, hydroculture: O: as in summer, never below 64° F/18° C.
● *Aeonium* (succulent)	☀	💧		every 2 weeks: 5-8 cactus fertilizer	compost only; O: almost dry, 50-61° F/10-16° C.
Ananas decorative pineapple (bromeliad)	☀ – ◯	💧		every 2 weeks: 5-8	compost, hydroculture: soft water! O: 64-77° F/18-25° C.
Araucaria heterophylla Norfolk Island pine	◯	💧	spray	every 2 weeks: 3-8 low doses	compost, hydroculture; soft water! O: 41-59° F/5-15° C, a little drier.
● *Asparagus* ornamental asparagus ☠	◯	💧		weekly: 3-8	compost, hydroculture; O: never below 54° F/12° C, dry.
● *Aspidistra elatior*	◯ – ●	💧		every 2 weeks: 3-8	compost, hydroculture; O: never under 50° F/10° C, a little drier.
Asplenium nidus bird's nest fern	◯ – ◑	💧	spray	every 2 weeks: 3-9	compost, hydroculture, also epiphytic; O: 61-77° F/16-25° C; soft water!
Begonia foliage begonia	◯	💧	spray	every 2 weeks: 3-9	compost, hydroculture; soft water! O: 61-77° F/16-25° C.
Caladium	◯ – ◑	💧	spray	weekly: 3-7	compost, hydroculture; O: tubers dry at 64° F/18° C.
Calathea	◯ – ◑	💧	spray	every 2 weeks: 3-8	compost, hydroculture; O: 61-72° F/16-22° C.
● *Chlorophytum comosum* spider plant, St Bernard's lily	◯ – ◑	💧	spray	weekly: 3-8	compost, hydroculture, also hanging plant; O: 50-72° F/10-22° C.
● *Cissus*	◯ – ◑	💧		weekly: 3-8	compost, hydroculture, climbing, hanging plant; O: 61-75° F/16-24° C.
Cocos nucifera coconut palm	◯	💧	spray	weekly: 4-9 low doses	compost, hydroculture; O: 64-75 ° F/18-24° C.
Codiaeum ☠	◯	💧	spray	weekly: 3-8 low doses	compost, hydroculture; O: 61-75° F/16-24° C.
● *Coleus blumei* hybrids	☀	💧		every 2 weeks: 3-8	compost, hydroculture O: 55-75° F/13-24° C.
Cordyline fruticosa	◯	💧	spray	every 2 weeks: 3-8	compost, hydroculture; O: 61-75° F/16-24° C.
● *Crassula aborescens* (succulent)	☀ – ◯	💧		every 4 weeks: 5-8	compost, hydroculture; O: around 50° F/10° C, dry.
● *Cyperus*	◯	💧	spray	every 2 weeks: 1-8	compost, hydroculture; O: 59-75° F/15-24° C.
Dieffenbachia ☠	◯ – ◑	💧	spray	weekly: 3-8 low doses	compost, hydroculture; O: 61-75° F/16-24° C.
● *Dracaena* dragon plant, ribbon plant	◯ – ◑	💧	spray	every 2 weeks: 3-8	compost, hydroculture; O: 64-77° F/18-25° C.
● *Echeveria* (succulent)	☀	💧		every 2 weeks: 5-8 cactus fertilizer	compost only; O: 55-61° F/13-16° C, a little drier.
● *Epipremnum pinnatum*	◯ – ●	💧		weekly: 3-8	compost, hydroculture; hanging plant; O: 61-75° F/16-24° C.
Fatshedera lizei ☠	☀ – ◯	💧	spray	every 2 weeks: 3-8	compost, hydroculture; O: 50-64° F/10-18° C, a little drier.
● *Ficus* rubber tree, *Ficus benjamina* and others	◯	💧	spray	every 2 weeks: 3-8	compost, hydroculture; some species are hanging plants; O: 64-59° F/18-25° C.

The symbols: ● the plant is easy to care for, suitable for beginners and offices. ☠ Warning: plants or parts of them are toxic.
Light ☀ = full sunlight, south-facing window; ◯ = bright, east- or west-facing window; ◑ = semi-shade, north-facing window; ● = shade, small north-facing windows..

Name	Light	Watering	Humidity	Fertilizing	Further tips on care
Fittonia verschaffeltii	○–●	(medium)	(humidity)	every 2 weeks: 4-10	compost, hydroculture; O: 64-77° F/18-25° C.
Hedera ivy ☠	○–◐	(medium)	(humidity)	weekly: 2-8 low doses	compost, hydroculture; climbing and hanging plant; O: not below 59° F/15° C.
Howeia	○–◐	(medium)	(humidity)	weekly: 3-9 low doses	compost, hydroculture; O: 64-77° F/18-25° C.
Maranta	○	(medium)	(humidity)	every 2 weeks: 4-8 low doses	compost, hydroculture; O: 64-75° F/18-24° C, a little drier.
● *Monstera deliciosa* Swiss cheese plant	○	(medium)	(humidity)	every 2 weeks: 3-8 low doses	compost, and hydroculture; climbing plant; O: 64-72° F/18-22° C, humid air.
Myrtus communis myrtle	☀–○	(medium)	(humidity)	weekly: 3-8	compost only; O: 43-50° F/6-10° C, bright, dry.
Nephrolepis exaltata ladder fern	○–◐	(medium)	(humidity)	every 2 weeks: 3-9 low doses	compost, hydroculture; O: 64-77° F/18-25° C, humid air.
● *Pachypodium* Madagascar palm ☠	☀	(sparingly)		every 4 weeks: 5-8 cactus fertilizer	compost, hydroculture; O: 64-77° F/18-25° C.
● *Pelargonium* foliage and scented pelargoniums	☀–○	(sparingly)		weekly: 3-8	compost only; O: 50-54° F/10-12° C, bright and dry.
Peperomia dwarf pepper	○	(medium)	(humidity)	every 3 weeks: 4-9	compost, hydroculture, some species are also suitable for hanging baskets; O: 59-72° F/15-22° C.
● *Philodendron* philodendron	○–◐	(medium)	(humidity)	every 2 weeks: 3-8	compost, hydroculture; some climbing; O: 64-79° F/18-26° C.
Platycerium staghorn fern	○–◐	(medium)	(humidity)	every 2 weeks: 3-9	compost or epiphytic; also hanging plant; O: 64-77° F/18-25° C.
● *Pogonatherum paniceum* indoor bamboo	○	(medium)	(humidity)	every 3 weeks: 3-8	compost only: O: 59-75° F/15-24° C.
● *Radermachera sinica*	○	(medium)	(humidity)	every 3 weeks: 3-8	compost only; O: around 59° F/15° C.
● *Rhoicissus capensis*	○–◐	(sparingly)		every 2 weeks: 5-8	compost, hydroculture; climbing plant; O: 50-61° F/10-16° C.
● *Sansevieria trifasciata* mother-in-law's tongue	☀–◐	(sparingly)		every 3 weeks: 3-8	compost, hydroculture; O: 59-75° F/15-24° C.
● *Saxifraga stolonifera* saxifrage	○–◐	(sparingly)		weekly: 3-8	compost, hydroculture; hanging plant; O: 59-75° F/15-24° C.
● *Schefflera*	○–◐	(medium)	(humidity)	every 2 weeks: 3-8	compost, hydroculture; O: 61-75° F/16-24° C.
● *Sedum*	☀–○	(sparingly)		every 4 weeks: 4-8 cactus fertilizer	compost only, some species are also suitable for hanging baskets; O: 41-50° F/5-10° C.
Sparmannia africana African hemp	○	(medium)	(humidity)	weekly: 3-8	compost, hydroculture; O: 50-59° F/10-15° C, a little drier,
● *Tetrastigma voinierianum*	○–●	(medium)		weekly: 3-8	compost only, climbing plant; O: 50-75° F/10-24° C.
● *Tolmiea menziesii* youth on age	○–◐	(medium)		every 2 weeks: 3-8	compost only, also for hanging baskets; O: 41-50° F/5-10° C.
● *Tradescantia*	○	(medium)		every 2 weeks: 3-8	compost, hydroculture; hanging plant; O: 50-75° F/10-24° C.
● *Yucca*	☀–○	(medium)		every 3 weeks: 3-8	compost, hydroculture; O: 41-50° F/5-10° C, a litle drier.

Watering: (icon) = water a lot; (icon) = medium watering, keep the plant constantly moist; (icon) = water sparingly, allow compost to dry off.
Humidity: (icon) = medium or high humidity. Roman numerals = months. O = overwintering..

Position

The vital requirements of plants

Houseplants will thrive and flourish if their basic requirements are adequately met. This means supplying everything they need to live, at the right time and in the right amounts. The requirements for growth are:

- water;
- air and humidity;
- nutrients;
- temperature, i.e. warmth and coolness at the right times;
- light.

My tip: Houseplants will do best if all these factors are combined correctly. Stick to the following general rules.

Water

- Water supports the metabolic processes of plants. Plants comprise 90% water, which evaporates through tiny openings that are usually situated on the undersides of the leaves. This creates a lack of moisture in the plant, which, in turn, creates a suction effect and causes the plant to draw water up through its roots.
- Water carries dissolved nutrients, gathered through the roots from the soil.
- Water not only conducts nutrients to the plant, it also washes out the waste products of metabolic processes.
- Water helps the plant to cope with high temperatures. When it is very hot, the water evaporates and this provides an auto-cooling system for the plant. Without this facility, the plant would die in intense sunlight.
- Water keeps the plant tissues firm. If there is a lack of water, the cells become flabby. We can recognize this by the limp and faded appearance of the plant.

General rules

1. Never water too much, as waterlogging will rapidly lead to decaying roots and thus prevent nutrients from reaching the plant.
2. When temperatures are low or humidity is high, water less as the plant is losing less water through evaporation than when the air is dry.
3. If temperatures are high and the air is dry, water more and frequently as the plant loses water through evaporation.

Air

Plants require air to breathe and to stay healthy.

Stagnant air, which is created when plants are left standing too close together, or intense sunlight which penetrates a south-facing window (heat accumulation), will soon render plants susceptible to infestation by pests.

The plants also take in moisture with the air. The requirements of tropical plants are often above 60% humidity.

General rules

1. Plant care also involves airing the plant and providing humid air.
2. The higher the temperature is in a room, the more humidity is required by the plants.
3. Drafts are harmful to all houseplants. Particularly in winter, protect your plants from drafts whenever you air the room!
4. Stale air or air laden with harmful substances (for example, cigarette smoke) is bad for plants and may cause leaves, flowers, and buds to drop off.

Nourishment

As a rule, nutrients are delivered to the plant through the soil or compost or by fertilizers.

A distinction is made between the main nutrients and trace elements.

Individual houseplants have very different nutritional requirements. Some just seem to gobble up nutrients, while others use only very small amounts (for example, cacti and orchids). The size of the plant also determines the amount of fertilizer it needs. Large, fast-growing plants will require more nutrients than young plants.

General rules

1. Always fertilize whenever there is more light, warmth, or increased watering during the main growth phase.
2. Never fertilize during times of dormancy, when it is cool, there is less light, and watering is at a minimum.
3. Typical symptoms of a lack of nutrients can be alleviated very fast with the use of liquid fertilizers or with leaf fertilizer that is sprayed on.
4. Even regular fertilizing will not replace necessary repotting.
5. Houseplants that are grown in hydroculture or an alternative medium, like clay pellets (Hortag), will require special fertilizers that are intended for use with this kind of medium.

Epiphytes – like this nest fern – colonize trees and require semi-shade as well as high humidity.

Temperature

Plants slow their metabolic rate when temperatures drop, while warmth causes an increase in growth as well as encouraging the absorption of nutrients.

With respect to temperature, most houseplants have similar requirements to humans, which is somewhere between 61-72° F/16-22° C – but, in keeping with prevailing conditions in their countries of origin, they generally prefer lower temperatures at night. Orchids, in particular, require a drop in temperature at night in order to produce flowers.

One factor which nearly always has a harmful effect on tropical plants is a low temperature near the ground. During the winter, and in transition from one season to another, the temperature around a plant container may often sink faster than the room temperature if the plant is positioned on a cold, badly insulated windowsill or placed in front of a drafty balcony door. In such cases, the plant should be moved to another position or you should provide some kind of insulation, like polystyrene sheets or cork mats.

General rules

1. A rest phase always requires a drop in temperature! The plants should hardly be watered at all and should not be fertilized.
2. Beware of cold around the base of the plant! Tropical plants are particularly sensitive, as are all plants grown in hydroculture as they are not protected from the cold by soil.
3. Cold floors/windowsills, etc., combined with waterlogging, are lethal for all houseplants.

Position

The effect of light

All parts of plants that grow above ground reach toward the light, especially flowers and leaves. It is quite different for the underground parts of plants – roots always grow away from the light.

My tip: After they have developed buds, do not turn plants that are positioned on a windowsill.

Light and plant care

Light is measured in lux. When you buy a houseplant, you will often find it accompanied by a little card or tag with instant information represented by small care symbols. Usually, these include the light requirements of the plant, perhaps with the following symbols:

-☼- = full sunlight. A position in a south-facing window or outside. The light intensity factor is above 2000 lux.

○ = bright. An east- or west-facing window, as well as southeast and southwest positions with sunlight shining in for several hours of the day but no intense midday sun. On average, 1500-2000 lux.

◐ = semi-shady. Unshaded, north-facing windows as well as northwest and northeast positions which never receive direct sunlight but are not obscured by any objects. On average, 1000 lux.

● = shady. Small or shaded north-, northwest- and northeast-facing positions as well as positions inside a room up to 2 m (80 in) away from the window. Light intensity factor below 1000 lux.

My tip: These factors may deviate considerably upward or downward. You can measure the conditions at your window with a luxmeter, which functions like a light meter and is obtainable fom specialty suppliers.

Is the light OK?

Plants soon show whether they are happy or not with the existing light conditions. Light is such an important part of their lives that it has a direct effect on their shape and appearance. On average, it is important for plants to receive twelve to sixteen hours of light per day. If it receives the **correct amount of light**, a plant will grow compact and dense.

● The shoots will be robust, the spaces between branches and leaves small.

● The flowers will be numerous and a good color.

● Colored or variegated (white- or yellow-patterned) leaves will be particularly well marked.

If there is **not enough light**, the plants will only grow toward the source of light.

● Their shoots will grow lanky (particularly if the plant is kept warm and watered regularly), which makes it become "leggy" so that the spaces between branches and leaves will greatly increase.

● The leaves will look untypical and be small and yellowish; colored or variegated foliage turns green.

● Flowers are hardly ever produced.

If there is **too much light**, plants respond rather like we do – they suffer sunburn. At first the plant goes limp, then yellow; later, brown spots appear on the leaves.

South-facing windows

This position will receive full sunlight from morning to afternoon.

● During the winter, when there is much less light, this is a good position for all plants which prefer light or semi-shade at other times of the year.

● Be careful in the summer! From the first month of spring right through to fall, it will become so hot here that only sun-loving plants, like cacti, succulents, and large container plants, can cope.

Tips for plants in a south-facing window

● You can use a south-facing window for plants all year round if you do not place them directly in the window but, instead, near the window, so that they are not exposed to the rays of the sun.

● You can stand all light-loving plants on a south-facing windowsill as long as you provide shade on sunny days, both in summer and in the winter. For example, half close the shutters or shades, or place paper or shading foil between the glass and the plants.

● Alternative: During the winter, move plants from an east/west-facing window to this position. From the first month of spring, move them back to their less-exposed window seats.

● From spring to fall, it is the turn of the "sun worshippers." Later, they can be moved to cool, bright winter quarters to enjoy their rest period.

Generally speaking, during the summer you should move all plants as far away from the windowpane as possible so that they cannot get burned.

● In addition, water and air them daily so that no accumulation of heat takes place behind the windowpane.

East- and west-facing windows

East-facing positions receive soft morning light and west-facing positions the mellow evening light. Both windows enable plants to avoid the intense burning sunlight of midday but they will still receive enough light for most of your houseplants to thrive there – for example, most foliage plants, particularly those with colored or variegated leaves, and numerous flowering plants, even orchids.

Tips for plants in east- or west-facing windows

● In the case of southeast- or southwest-facing positions, provide shade at midday to filter out the harmful rays of the sun.

● During the winter, move plants from a north-facing window to one of these positions so that they will receive enough light.

North-facing windows

This position receives the least amount of light and is not suitable for most plants. Nevertheless, a wonderful assortment of plants can be kept here, particularly if the room is always kept at the same pleasant temperature all year round. You can grow all tropical rain forest plants here, most of which are characterized by attractive leaf shapes and markings – for example, *Maranta* plants, ferns, and *Araceae*, like *Philodendron*, *Dieffenbachia*, and *Alocasia*.

Tips for plants in north-facing windows

● Colored- or variegated-leafed plants may suffer from lack of light during the winter. If they start to lose their markings and turn green, it is a good idea to move the plants to an east- or west-facing window or make temporary use of a plant lamp to alleviate the problem.

● Drafty, north-facing windows must be insulated as tropical rain

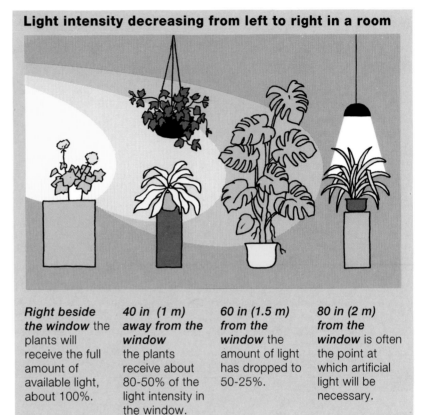

Light intensity decreasing from left to right in a room

Right beside the window the plants will receive the full amount of available light, about 100%.

40 in (1 m) away from the window the plants receive about 80-50% of the light intensity in the window.

60 in (1.5 m) from the window the amount of light has dropped to 50-25%.

80 in (2 m) from the window is often the point at which artificial light will be necessary.

forest plants are particularly sensitive to "cold feet." Root rot and falling leaves are often the consequence.

● If the plants are placed on a cold windowsill made of stone during the winter, they should be insulated through the use of warming mats, polystyrene sheets, or humidifier dishes.

What reduces the intensity of light?

The amount of light in a room can be reduced by various factors:

● the size of the window;

● curtains – even light-colored shades will considerably reduce the amount of light penetrating the room;

● the position of the room;

● the immediate surroundings of the building; a large tree growing in front of a window will cast a large shadow;

● the seasons; plants receive more light in the summer than in the winter.

403

Position

When houseplants need help

The wrong position and mistakes in care are the main causes of infestation by pests or disease.

Evil number one: Much suffering is caused when houseplants are in positions where they cannot thrive.
Prevention: Make a point of considering the light and temperature requirements, as well as the growth and rest phases, of the plant!

Evil number two: Most plants are watered too much. If their roots stand in water for long periods of time, they will no longer be able to breathe and will begin to rot. As a result, the plant can no longer absorb water or nutrients in sufficient amounts and will gradually starve to death.
Prevention: Water regularly but sparingly.

Evil number three: If houseplants receive too many or too few nutrients, they will rapidly fall prey to pests like aphids, spider mites, or scale insects.
Prevention: Fertilize regularly but sparingly!

Evil number four: Overwintering in a position that is too warm, with arid air, encourages infestation by thrips, spider mites, and white fly.
Prevention: Let the temperature drop in winter and make sure that warm rooms contain enough humidity!

Evil number five: Stale, polluted air or air that is too humid encourages the formation of fungal disease.
Prevention: Air the room regularly; do not place the plants too close together and do not spray or water the leaves.

Aphids
Symptoms: green or blackish-brown insects on young shoots, buds or leaves; sticky, deformed leaves.
Remedy: lacewings (*Chrysopa vulgaris*), gall midges, agents containing pyrethrum, tobacco brew.

Sooty mold
Symptoms: a sticky, black layer on leaves. Mold that grows on the sticky secretions of aphids.
Remedy: remove very badly affected leaves; wash off mildly affected leaves with lukewarm water.

White fly
Symptoms: approximately ⅛-in (3-mm) long white flies with wings shaped like roof tiles, which fly up immediately the plant is touched. Their larvae are yellowish-green. Flies and larvae sit on the under sides of the leaves and suck the sap of the plant, depositing sticky honeydew which, in turn, encourages infestation with sooty mold. The leaves become spotted with yellow marks and eventually wilt. Infestation is encouraged by warm, dry air.
Remedy: spray with warm water or use ichneumon flies, sticky fly catcher cards or agents containing pyrethrum. Prevent by providing high humidity.

Thrips

Symptoms: 1/16th-in
(1-mm) long, fringed-wing
insects, striped yellow and
black. They suck the sap
of leaves and flowers. The
first signs are whitish dots
all over the leaves, along
with tiny black spots of
excrement. Later, when
infestation is very heavy,
the under sides of the
leaves turn silvery-white.

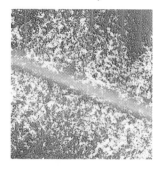

Infestation is encouraged
by dry, warm air.
Remedy:
spray the plant
with lukewarm water or
use sticky fly catcher
cards or agents containing
pyrethrum. Prevent by
providing high humidity.

Spider mites

Houseplants are often
attacked by the common
red spider mite.
Symptoms: the red mites,
which are related to
spiders, are so minute
that they are difficult to
see with the naked eye.
Signs of infestation: the
upper sides of the leaves
show tiny whitish spots.
As infestation progresses,
the dots merge to form
larger marks and
gossamer-fine webs
appear on the under sides
of the leaves and in the
leaf axils.
Remedy:
fast action is
required! Spray the plant
frequently with lukewarm
water. Employ robber
mites *(Amblyseius)*, a
plant sauna or special
preparations for use
against spider mites.
Prevent by providing high
humidity and correct care.
Spider mites are typical
parasites on weakened
plants.

Scale insects

There are several different
species, all of which are
difficult to control.
Symptoms: brown scales,
which are immobile
mature adults. The
younger insects are lighter
and more mobile. These
pests attack the shoots
and leaves, and suck the
sap from the main veins
on the under sides of
leaves. They also secrete
a very sticky honeydew
which rapidly encourages
infestation with sooty
mold .
Remedy:
fast action is
required! Scratch off the
scale insects or paint
them with a solution of
detergent and mineral
spirits. Hard-leafed plants
can be sprayed with tar oil
but soft-leafed plants will
not respond well to this.
My tip: Infestation by the
closely related mealy bug
produces very similar
symptoms, although these
pests can be distinguished
by the appearance of
cotton-wool-like shapes
instead of scales. Use the
same remedies as for
scale insects!

Mildew

Fungal disease.
Symptoms: genuine
mildew manifests itself as
a whitish-gray, flour-like
film on the upper sides
and under sides of the
leaves as well as on
shoots, flowers and
seeds. False mildew only
appears on the under
sides of leaves. The
fungus penetrates the
plant and spreads inside
it.
Remedy:
infested plant
parts should be removed
and destroyed. Lecithin
preparations or chemical
fungicides can be used.
My tip: Some plants are
particularly susceptible to
infestation by mildew,
such as hydrangea,
Kalanchoë, African violets,
Rhoicissus capensis, and
roses.

Position

Protection and first aid

Houseplants will thrive and grow into robust specimens if they are given the right position and cared for properly. If there are occasional problems, the important thing is to deal with them as early on as possible.

Regular plant checks are part of a proper program of care and are not an arduous task. During regular watering, take a look at your plants. Look closely at the shoot tips and buds as well the upper and under sides of the leaves.

What to do when problems arise: Houseplants can become infested with pests and fungal, viral, and bacterial diseases.

There are remedies to use against pests and fungal infections. The earlier you discover the problem, the better your chances of successful control.

Unfortunately, bacterial and viral diseases are a different matter as there are no real cures. Fortunately, plants are very rarely attacked by them. If they should occur, however, the correct procedure is to destroy the infested plant immediately but do not put the plant on a compost heap as this may cause the problem to spread to other plants.

My tip: Isolate any houseplants that have become infested with pests or fungal diseases so that the problem cannot spread to other plants. If the plant is badly affected, you should consider whether the cost and time involved in employing toxic agents are really warranted, or whether it would be better to replace the plant with a new one.

Alternative methods of control

Plant sauna

High humidity is a good remedy for spider mites. Water the plant well, then cover it with a transparent plastic bag tied around the pot to create an air-tight "bubble." Leave the plant like this for a few days. Warning: Soft-leafed plants may begin to decay.

Bio friendly fly catchers

These sticky cards are a useful way of controlling white fly, *Liriomyza*, *Sciaridae*, and thrips. Push the cards into the soil. The pests are attracted by the bright color and then become stuck to the substance with which the card is coated.

Useful insects

The eggs of insects that prey on pests are stuck on little cards which can be hung among the leaves of the affected plant until they hatch.

Alternative sprays

Fill a plant misting bottle with the agent and spray the plant. Repeat at intervals of several days.

Mechanical control

The earlier you discover an infestation, the less damage will have been done so that matters can often be put right easily. For example, by:
● cutting off infested or diseased parts of the plant;
● scraping off or spraying the pests;
● submerging the above-ground parts of the plant in a lukewarm detergent solution.

Biological measures

(see table, left)

Useful insects, which are the natural enemies of the pests, can be employed. Their eggs, which are attached to leaves or to a small piece of card, can be obtained from garden centers. They are hung among the leaves of the plant and become effective as soon as the larvae emerge from the eggs (which means there is a slight delay).
● for aphids, use damsel flies and predatory gall midges;
● for white fly, use ichneumon flies;
● for spider mites, use robber mites *(Amblyseius)*;
● for mealy bugs, use Australian ladybirds *(Cryptolaemus montrouzieri)*
● use nematodes against *Sciaridae.*

Sticky yellow cards attract white fly, *Lyriomyza, Sciaridae*, thrips, and other insects with their bright color. The insects then stick fast to the substance that coats the cards.

Agents containing pyrethrum are sprayed on the affected plants. This substance is effective against all biting, sucking insects, in particular, white fly, and aphids. These biological agents are derived from the flowers of a

Take care when using plant protection agents!

● Do not use highly toxic agents.
● Follow the directions for use and dosage meticulously. Keep to the prescribed intervals for spraying, so that succeeding generations of the pest are destroyed at the same time.
● To protect the environment, do not use any sprays containing CFCs.
● Only use the spray outside.
● Wear gloves and a mask to avoid inhaling the spray.
● Never eat, drink, or smoke while handling plant protection agents.
● Always store plant protection agents in their original packaging, out of reach of children and pets, and locked away.
● Do not store remains of any agents. The effectiveness of these preparations dissipates rapidly. Do not discard any surplus in ordinary household refuse but take it to a special collection point for environmentally sensitive waste.

species of chrysanthemum and are not harmful to bees.

Never employ an agent containing pyrethrum if you have an open cut or wound, as the substance may enter your bloodstream and cause poisoning. Never use it in a room containing an aquarium!

Agents containing oil, for example, paraffin or tar oil, will clog up the tracheae of insects so that they suffocate. These agents are particularly good against mealy bugs, scale insects, and spider mites but, just like sprays that make leaves shine, they are only tolerated by hard-leafed plants.

Agents containing lecithin are sprayed on the leaves to combat fungi that cause mildew.

Detergent-spirit solutions are easy to make up and are particularly successful against mealy bugs and scale insects.

Dissolve 1 tablespoon soft soap in 4 cups (1 liter) tepid water and then add 1 tablespoon mineral spirits. Spray the plant with the solution or dab it onto infested patches.

Tobacco brew is a good remedy for scale insects.

Remove the tobacco from about two cigarettes and soak it in 1 pint (500 ml) water for about eight hours, then strain it. This undiluted solution can be sprayed straight onto the plants.

Warning: This solution is highly toxic! Use it only on robust plants! Keep it away from children and pets!

Chemical agents

Use these only if all other methods have failed.
● Insecticides kill insects and may be sprayed, poured, or sprinkled on the soil or compost, or pushed into the compost in the form of small sticks.
● Acaricides destroy mites.
● Fungicides are effective against fungal infections.

Water is essential for plants. Houseplants receive water through spraying or watering. If you happen to forget occasionally, a good soak will help.

Watering

It is an unfortunate truth that most houseplants do not die of thirst but are watered to death. The following pages will explain the right way to water houseplants. Arid, centrally heated rooms also require some attention!

Watering

In their natural state, plants receive all the moisture they need from rain, dew, mist, or snow and have spent thousands of years adapting to the water supply that is available where they grow. Most plants draw up the greater part of the moisture they require through their roots: some even live on dew which they absorb through their leaf scales (e.g. *Tillandsia*).

In the artificial environment of a room, plants require proper care that will, as far as possible, replicate the conditions they are used to in the wild. Watering is a vital part of good care. In order to water properly, you must take various factors into consideration, giving each plant:
● the right kind of water;
● at the right time;
● in the right quantities.

Hard or soft water

The quality of the water used is more important than many people know. Every indoor gardener should give some thought to the kind of main water they have before buying any plant to take home. It is important to know that the water will not be too hard and does not, therefore, have a high lime content. Few plants can cope with very hard water for a long time.

How to assess the hardness of your main water: The hardness of the water is measured in degrees Clark and depends on the content of certain mineral salts which are dissolved in it, foremost among them being magnesium and calcium compounds. These substances are needed in small quantities by most plants. If they are present in too great a concentration, however, they may hinder the absorption of nutrients and interfere with the metabolic processes of the plant.

Water hardness

Very soft water up to 3.19 deg. Clark	Not suitable for watering plants when pure. Can be mixed with harder main water to make it less soft.
Soft water 3.20-10 deg. Clark	Best for watering.
Medium-hard water 11-20 deg. Clark	Too hard for many plants. ● Many plants can still manage on 11-13 degrees Clark if the water has been left to stand overnight. This causes some of the lime to be removed (in the form of a residue) and the water becomes slightly softer. ● At 13-20 degrees Clark, boil the water and let it cool. Large quantities of lime will be removed in the form of lime deposits in the container used for boiling and the water becomes softer.
Hard water 21-38 deg. Clark Very hard water above 38 deg. Clark	Definitely needs softening. The best way is to obtain softening agents from garden centers or use filter watering cans which are able to produce specially soft water for watering plants.

What makes the water hard? The total hardness of water comprises the carbonate hardness (CH) and the non-carbonate hardness (NCH).
● Carbonate hardness (CH) is the main element of the total hardness and is decisive for the care of plants. It is also called temporary hardness as it can be altered relatively simply and quickly by boiling the main water. The carbonate hardness in water used for watering houseplants should, if possible, not exceed 10 CH as, otherwise, the soil or compost in which the plant is growing will become increasingly alkaline, which means that the pH factor will rise. In turn, this means that the plant will have difficulty in absorbing some of the nutrients and trace elements. In spite of plenty of fertilizing, the plant will suffer from mineral deficiency (chlorosis), the leaves will turn yellow, and only the veins will remain green.
● Non-carbonate hardness (NCH) cannot be removed by boiling the water and is, therefore, called permanent hardness. It is based on sulphate compounds of calcium and magnesium, and is usually unimportant in respect of plant care.

How to measure the hardness of your main water

Main water may show considerable regional variations in hardness. You can find out about your own particular values by inquiring at your regional or local water authority.

If, however, you wish to make a test yourself, you can acquire reagents from an aquarium supplier to determine either the total hardness or just the carbonate hardness. There is also an old gardening trick for roughly determining the hardness of water. If chalky rings appear on the leaves of sclerophyllous plants that you have sprayed with water, then the water is medium hard or very hard and should definitely be softened.

Be careful with very soft or distilled water!

Neither very soft water (below 3.19 degrees Clark) nor distilled water should be used for watering plants. The nutrients that are lacking in the water cannot be replaced by fertilizer. Water from ion exchange devices that are regenerated with salt should never be used for watering plants either as this would be harmful for them. Desalinated water obtained by these methods can, however, be mixed with main water to make it softer.

My tip: In most households there will often be a supply of water that can be used for plants because it contains little lime and may even contain some valuable nutrients, for example, cooled water left over from boiling potatoes or water used for cooking green vegetables.

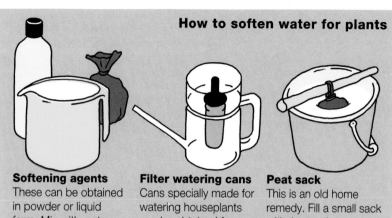

How to soften water for plants

Softening agents
These can be obtained in powder or liquid form. Mix with water and leave to stand for six to twelve hours so that the lime can accumulate at the bottom of the vessel. Then either pass the liquid through a coffee filter or pour off the softened water, leaving the residue behind.
My tip: This is very useful for anyone needing lots of water.

Filter watering cans
Cans specially made for watering houseplants can be obtained from garden centers. The filter cartridge, which contains ion exchange substances, will have to be changed regularly. This filter softens the water and filters out harmful substances.
My tip: This is practical if only small amounts of water are required.

Peat sack
This is an old home remedy. Fill a small sack with 1 pound (500 g) dry peat and suspend it overnight in a bucket containing 2½ gallons (10 liters) water. Change the peat after it has been used three times.
My tip: Only use this method if you have no other alternative as the overextraction of peat is a threat to the natural environment.

Main water or rainwater?

As a rule, *main water* is harder than rainwater and, in many cases, also contains chlorine. It will often have to be treated before it can be used for watering plants.

Rainwater is not available to every indoor gardener and the quality of some rainwater is not always very good. Depending on where you live, you may not be able to collect rain water. People living in country areas or in an environment that is unpolluted should be able to collect it without problems. If you live in an area that is polluted by industrial fumes or other air-pollutants, you may not wish to use rainwater for your precious plants. Nevertheless, most of the time it is plant-friendly, soft, and at the right temperature. However, do remember the following rules:

Watering

● Do not collect rainwater until it has been raining for a half hour to an hour and the majority of dirt particles and other harmful substances have been washed from the air.

● If you suspect your rainwater may be too acid, you can obtain test strips and indicators for checking the pH factor from garden centers or at aquarium retailers.

The degree of acidity (pH factor)
The degree of acidity is measured in pH values on a scale from 0–14; the value 7 indicates a neutral reaction.

● The ideal pH value for water for houseplants is around 5.5 to 6. Most plants do best at these pH values.

● If the pH value is below 5, the water will be too acid for most plants and should not be used for watering.

● A pH value of more than 7.5 can be lowered by softening the water.

What can be done about harmful substances in the water?
Both main water and rainwater may contain substances that are harmful to plants.
In rainwater, **heavy metal compounds** containing cadmium, copper, and lead are toxins which can interfere with the metabolism of plants.

● Remedy: special filters for treating water.
The filter cartridges containing special ion exchangers have to be changed regularly and can be taken back to the retailer for recycling.

Houseplants that require soft water

● flamingo plant, *Anthurium*
● zebra plant, *Aphelandra*
● begonia
● camellia
● *Dieffenbachia*
● *Dipladenia*
● *Dizygotheca*
● *Fittonia*
● gardenia
● hydrangea
● *Ixora*
● jasmine, *Jasminum*
● South Sea myrtle, *Leptospermum*
● *Maranta*
● *Medinilla*
● myrtle, *Myrtus*
● *Pentas*
● indoor azalea, *Rhododendron*
as well as indoor ferns and palms, bromeliads, and orchids.

Chlorine and substances forming chlorine compounds interfere with the growth of plants and affect their health. Water used for plants should contain no more than 50 mg per 4 cups (1 liter).

● Remedy: Let water stand overnight as the chlorine will then disperse. Information about the chlorine content of main water can also be obtained from your local water utility.

The right tools
Many houseplants cannot cope with water or moisture on their leaves and flowers. With very few exceptions, it is best to water the compost or soil. The following implements are best suited for this purpose.
Watering cans with long, narrow spouts, as the compost can be reached directly, even through bushy plants.

My tip: Watering cans with a spray device are unsuitable for houseplants as, although they make the water soft, they distribute it too widely.

Filter watering cans with ion exchangers are particularly practical but do be careful when buying one as there are two kinds: those that prepare water for the household (as for coffee, tea, and electric steam irons) and those that are specially designed to produce softened water for houseplants.
Pumping cans, with a long, curved spout, are eminently suitable for watering hanging baskets and hanging arrangements. The water is pumped up from the bottle-shaped can and out through the spout by pressure.

My tip: Look after your watering can! Limestone, bacteria, and other residue may be deposited in a watering can. I recommend cleaning the can thoroughly, including the inside, once a week under running water.

Use only soft water for orchids and definitely avoid waterlogging. Provide high humidity!

Technique

When to water
- If you can no longer feel any moisture when you push your finger ¾ in (1-2 cm) into the soil.
- If tapping a clay pot yields a high-pitched tone. If the soil is well moistened right through, the tapping will sound muffled.
- It is absolutely essential if the soil has shrunk away from the edges of the pot and the plant is looking limp.

My tip: You have given your plant too much water if clay pots are constantly moist or are coated with a layer of green algae on the outside. Moisture meters are very useful (see illustration 3). They are pushed into the soil in the pot.

1. Watering – from above or below?
a) Constant watering from below carries water and nutrients upward.
b) Vigorous watering from the top will distribute water and nutrients evenly in the pot.

2. Special watering methods
a) Water the funnels of bromeliads.
b) When giving plants a "bath," keep them submerged until no more air bubbles rise up. Then let the plant drip dry.

414

Watering methods
Watering from below (see illustration 1a) is recommended for plants with sensitive tubers, stalks, or leaves, like cyclamen, African violets, or gloxinia. Let water accumulate in the saucer under the pot for no longer than a half hour, after which any surplus should be poured away so that the roots do not decay.

The disadvantage of this method is that nutrients are transported upward, along with the water, so that they are no longer available to the finer roots at the bottom of the pot but tend to accumulate on the surface of the soil which becomes crusty and full of salts.

Watering from the top (see illustration 1b) is recommended for most houseplants. Always pour the water directly onto the soil, not on to the plant. The soil will become well moistened and nutrients contained in the water will be distributed evenly from the top downward so that the finest roots are able to absorb them.

Epiphytic bromeliads should be watered by tipping the water *straight into their funnels* (see illustration 2a) as they have special cells at the funnel bottom for absorbing water.

Submerging (see illustration 2b) is the best method for epiphytes and orchids as this lets the water-permeable compost absorb the moisture properly. Submerging is also ideal for plants in hanging baskets or ferns in lattice baskets. It is also a good first-aid measure for plants whose rootstocks have completely dried out.

The ten golden rules of watering
1. Always consider any special *requirements that different species may have.* Find out whether each particular species needs lots of water or very little.
2. *During their growth phase* and at flowering time (usually in spring and summer) water plentifully and often.
3. *During their rest phase* (in the fall and particularly in winter), reduce the amounts of water gradually and later water only as much as is needed to prevent the rootstock from drying out.
4. You will need to *water more often if plants are in:*
- dry, warm rooms;
- bright, sunny positions;
- clay pots;
- small pots that have become filled with matted roots so that the plants have hardly any compost left to store water.
5. *Water plants less often:*
- in cool rooms with high humidity;
- in positions with little light;
- in plastic pots;
- in pots with sufficient compost around the roots as the compost will be able to hold moisture.
6. *Use only tepid water.* Cold water makes it more difficult for the plant to absorb nutrients, hinders growth, and can lead to root decay.
7. *Never pour water on the leaves and flowers* as this may cause spots on the leaves and fungal infections.
8. *Never water plants in full sunlight.* Drops of water can act like magnifying glasses and cause burns on the leaves.
9. *Do not water plants in the same place every time* as this will create little channels in the pot, through which the water will run straight down without letting the

rootstock soak up moisture.

10. **Be careful with saucers or pot holders** underneath the plant pot as it is often impossible to see if surplus water has accumulated in them. Waterlogging drives air out of the compost and then the roots will be unable to absorb water or nutrients. The result is root decay, which will eventually lead to the death of the entire plant. In principle, check the saucer or pot holder about a half hour after watering.

Automatic watering

A range of devices is obtainable from garden centers for use by those people who are unable to water regularly or might have to be away from home for long periods of time. Ask for advice about these at your garden center, however, as some systems are only suitable for

3. Moisture meters are useful watering aids for beginners.

4. Automatic watering systems

a) Insert clay pegs into the soil and place their water pipes in a container filled with water.

b) Absorbent fabric is able to supply water to several plants (in clay pots) at the same. A tilted draining board is excellent.

short-term, weekend use, while others will supply water to your plants over a period of several weeks. Some good methods are described below.

Clay pegs (see illustration 4a) are filled with water and inserted in the compost. Moisture is supplied at a constant rate through the clay. As the moisture is released, it is also replenished through a pipe leading from a storage container. A 2½-gallon (10-liter) bucket can supply a plant with water for up to a month at a time.

Absorbent fabrics (see illustration 4b) can supply water to several plants at once. Fill a sink to serve as a reservoir. The mat should reach from the sink to the draining board but should not hang over the edge of the draining board as this will cause water to drip onto the floor. Plants in clay pots will soak up water from the drenched fabric, which means that they can regulate their own water supply.

Water-absorbent wicks (see illustration 4c), made, for example, of cotton or fiberglass, can be pushed deep into the compost or threaded on a large darning needle and pulled up from below and out through the top. The other end of the wick should be placed in a

c) Cotton wicks are inserted deep in the soil; the other end is weighted down with a stone in a bucket of water.

bucket of water and weighted down with a stone so that it cannot slip out.

NB: The water level in the bucket must be higher than the plant pots so that the system will function properly. The wicks should not be allowed to hang down in loops; otherwise the water will drip off them before ever reaching the flowerpot.

Watering

Such a window position can become a death trap for ferns on account of hot, dry, centrally heated air during the winter.

Why do plants need humidity?
Country of origin: Many houseplants originate from tropical regions and are accustomed to naturally high humidity, particularly:
● plants from tropical rain forests, which live in an atmosphere of steaming heat and a humidity of up to 90% all year round;
● plants from tropical mountain forests, which have adapted to intensely bright light, cool temperatures, mists, and very high humidity.

Plants from more arid regions, for example, cacti and succulents from desert regions, or subtropical plants from dry areas, which are often equipped with water storage organs and other measures to protect themselves against water loss through evaporation, can be kept as houseplants, even at low humidity.

Moisture: Nearly all plants are able to maintain the right balance in their water supply by absorbing water and then letting it evaporate. This happens by means of tiny pores which open mainly in the daytime in order to absorb

carbon dioxide from the air. During this process, they also release oxygen and moisture from their cells.

Too much moisture: If the air is completely saturated with moisture (a state of affairs that rarely occurs in their natural environment), the plant can no longer release water through evaporation and the result is that water and nutrients are no longer absorbed. The consequences are as follows:

● There is a temporary cessation of growth.
● The plants become susceptible to attack by fungal diseases.

Too little moisture: Dry air and high temperatures speed up evaporation. Even with frequent watering, the roots can no longer balance the loss of water in the leaves quickly enough and the following happens:
● The leaf tips turn brown.
● The leaves dry out.
● The flowers and buds drop off.

When plants drip: Do not be surprised if philodendrons, *Dieffenbachia,* or other houseplants produce tiny droplets even though you have not watered or sprayed them. This is not a symptom of disease but a simple reaction in the plant which has been unable to evaporate as much as it needs to in the position it has been given and needs to get rid of some water. It will secrete more moisture, thus enabling its roots to absorb larger amounts of water.

The right amount of humidity

More humidity is required by:
● plants with large, soft leaves, like *Ensete* and *Sparmannia*;
● plants with delicate, thin leaves, like *Caladium* and maidenhair fern (*Adiantum*);
● epiphytic plants, like many orchids, bromeliads and *Tillandsia*;
● ferns.

Less humidity is required by:
● plants with leathery, tough leaves like the rubber tree (*Ficus*) and *Monstera deliciosa*;
● plants with reduced leaves or needles, like *Cupressus macrocarpa*;
● cacti;
● succulents, like *Aeonium*.

What is humidity?
One of the most important factors of proper plant care is "relative humidity," which indicates, as a percentage, how much water the air contains compared to complete saturation (100%) at equal temperatures.
Humidity can be measured quite easily with a hygrometer, obtainable from specialty gardening suppliers.
Values for plant care:
● below 50% = low humidity;
● 50–60% = medium humidity;
● above 60% = high humidity.
The prevailing humidity levels are around 60–90% in the tropical countries of origin of many houseplants, so you should maintain a medium level of humidity

in a room where plants are kept.
Humidity and warmth: The higher the temperature, the more water vapour the air can absorb. If the amount of water remains the same and the temperature rises, the air actually becomes drier. When this happens, the plants lose more water through evaporation so that they then require twice as much moisture.

Winter
By far the most difficult time for houseplants is winter. This is when they usually have to cope with a position on a windowsill above a radiator and various other unpleasant conditions. Many die, for one of several possible reasons.
The air in a room is particularly dry in winter (often humidity levels are at 15–40%). The minimum acceptable level of humidity for most flowering and foliage plants is about 50%.
During the winter, the air is particularly cool and dry. This means that when you air the room, dry air streams in and robs the existing air of further moisture.
NB: During the winter, the climate in the room needs to be enriched with moisture to ensure the well-being of the plants.

Technique

Humidity through spraying

Using a misting bottle will not raise the humidity in the entire room but it can still be useful.

Indirect spraying (see illustration 2a) creates a short-term supply of moisture all around the plant. This is recommended for plants with hairy leaves that cannot stand direct misting and for others whose leaves and flowers tend to become spotty or whose buds might begin to rot.

Never spray directly onto:
begonias, *Calceolaria* hybrids, *Codiaeum*, *Dieffenbachia*, *Fatsia*, *Fatshedera lizei*, *Amaryllis* (*Hippeastrum* hybrids), *Mimosa*, *Peperomia*, African violets (*Saintpaulia ionantha* hybrids), gloxinias, (*Sinningia* hybrids), or *Streptocarpus.*

Direct spraying (see illustration 2b) provides direct moisture and imitates the natural formation of dew drops, which is required by

1. A bottle garden with its own mini-climate
An ideal home for plants in dry indoor air. Insert a drainage layer of Hortag and use small plants!

Tillandsia and other epiphytes like *Platycerium.*

NB: Use soft water, adjust the misting bottle to a fine setting, do not spray the flowers, and preferably spray in the mornings and not in direct sunlight.

Trays on the windowsill

The worst plight is experienced by houseplants that are placed on windowsills during the winter months and are constantly plagued by hot air rising up from the radiators beneath. Some simple measures can be taken to improve the living conditions of such plants.

Use an evaporator tray (see illustration 3). Large dishes with a grid insert are available from garden centers. They are placed on the windowsill, filled with water and the grid is inserted. The plants do not come into direct contact with the water but are surrounded by evaporating moisture.

● Advantage: You can accommodate several plants in such a tray.

● Alternative: The same result can be achieved by using any large, flat dishes filled first with clay pellets, pebbles, or gravel and then with water. Arrange the plants so that they do not suffer from "wet feet."

Make narrow windowsills wider, for example, by laying wooden boards on the windowsills. The hot, dry air rising up from the radiators is deflected by this device and will no longer flow past the leaves of the plants on the sill.

Install a wide plant basin: This method is usually the most successful. A plant basin of whatever dimensions you choose can be used like a window box.

● Choose a basin that is wide enough to cover the entire area of

2. Create humid air through spraying
a) Spraying above the plant will supply indirect humidity.
b) Tillandsia and other epiphytes should be sprayed directly.

the windowsill and radiator.

● Stand plastic bowls or dishes inside the basin or line the basin with foil or something similar to make it watertight. Then insert a layer of clay pellets or pebbles, pour in water, and stand the plants on the pebbles.

● Alternatively, you can insert a layer of clay pellets or peat in the basin and then bed the plants in this up to the tops of the pots.

NB: These plants should be planted in closed pots (without a drainage hole) so that they are not permanently exposed to moisture from below.

My tip: Evaporator dishes need constant attention and the regular addition of water. Clean them out once a week as lime, bacteria, and algae tend to become deposited in them.

Moisture for individual pots

● Place clay granules or fine bark mulch between individual plant pots and pot holders (see illustration 4a) and keep this moist.

● Stand individual pots on a small, upturned dish or balance them on four, halved corks in a larger dish filled with water (see illustration 4b). The moisture will evaporate upward, flowing past the plant itself.

My tip: The smaller the evaporation tray, the more often it will need filling with water.

Electric humidifiers

These devices raise the humidity all around the plant and guarantee that humidity levels are raised in the entire room. Humidifiers work on various principles:

Misters, which cause water to be sprayed in the finest drops through centrifugal force.

Evaporators heat the water until it turns to water vapor.

Condensing devices blow or suck air through a moist filter. They are very cheap to run but require a regular filter change.

Further tips for raising humidity

If you do not wish to keep an electric humidifier running constantly, you can employ several methods at once in a room as most of the methods described below will only raise the humidity in the immediate vicinity of the plant.

Mechanical humidifiers: Hang these on your radiator in winter and refill them with water every day.
Evaporator dishes serve the same purpose for open fireplaces, boilers, etc.
Aquariums, which have a constant movement of water due to a filter

pump, will also make a small contribution toward raising the humidity in a room.
Spring stones set amid plants are gaining in popularity as they are extremely attractive and create a pleasant atmosphere in a room.

3. Trays for the windowsill
This is ideal for providing several plants with humid air. Lay a grid in the tray and pour in water to just below the grid.

A large number of plants, or several large plants, have more soil and roots and can therefore store much more moisture than a few plants in small pots. If you have several plants, or large ones, it is worth grouping them together. The water that is evaporated will benefit them all in the form of humidity.

Moisture-producing places, like bathrooms and kitchens, are more suitable for moisture-loving plants than offices with a very dry atmosphere. At the same time, you have to remember that such places are aired frequently and longer. Protect plants in an office from cold air and drafts.

In summer, fresh outdoor air is ideal for stabilizing houseplants during the warm season of the year. Particularly during, and immediately after, a rain shower, the air will be laden with moisture. At such times, stand your houseplants at an open window or on a balcony or patio.

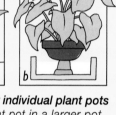

4. Humidity for individual plant pots
a) Bed the plant pot in a larger pot filled with peat or clay granules.
b) Stand the plant on an upside-down pot in a large dish filled with water.

The delicate maidenhair fern (top left) requires different fertilizing to the robust Gerbera or Tillandsia (a bromeliad). A wide range of nutrients, in various forms, is available from garden centers, etc.

Fertilizing

Although plants are the only living things that are able to utilize sunlight directly for their own growth, they are still unable to live on light and air alone. Houseplants will not thrive without the right amounts of plant nutrients.

Fertilizing

Nutrients

A well-balanced supply of nutrients will ensure that plants thrive and produce flowers. At the same time, nutrients will help to make the plants resistant to pests and diseases. Most plants absorb nutrients, together with water, through their fine roots but even the leaves are able to absorb small quantities of nutrients. The most unusual plants in this respect are bromeliads, *Tillandsia,* or orchids, which live and grow on trees and have specially adapted devices inside their funnel-shaped leaf shafts to absorb water and nutrients. Water should be delivered directly into their funnels (see illustration 2a) and they should be fertilized in the same way.

Every plant will require fairly large amounts of the *main nutrients* (macro-nutrients, see table). Among these are nitrogen (N), phosphorous (P), potassium (K), calcium (Ca), magnesium (Mg), and sulphur (S).

The trace elements (micro-nutrients) are necessary for the healthy growth of the plant and are just as important as the main nutrients but are absorbed in much smaller quantities. Among these are iron (Fe), copper (Cu), manganese (Mn), molybdenum (Mo), zinc (Zn), chlorine (Cl), and boron (B).

Nutrient balance: Houseplants must be fertilized as essential nutrients are generally only present in restricted amounts in potting compost and are used up fairly quickly. The most important thing to remember is that nutrients have to be combined in the proper proportions when fertilizing houseplants. Over- or under-dosing with a particular nutrient may leave the plant unable to absorb other nutrients, even if they are present in a plentiful supply. For example, if there is too much or too little calcium in the water or compost, the plants will be unable to absorb other nutrients.

Compound fertilizer

Good compound fertilizers contain the main nutrients and many trace elements in proportions that are plant-friendly and well balanced.

● Compound fertilizer can be obtained in almost any form, liquid, pulverized, or solid, as granules, in tablet form, or as small sticks or cones.
● It may contain organic components or synthetic substances ("artificial fertilizer").
● It comes in various grades, containing varying amounts of certain elements, so that nitrogen, phosphorous, or potassium is emphasized, depending on the requirements of the plant. This is very important because each of these elements is responsible in different ways for supporting the growth and well-being of the plant (see table, right).
● You can also obtain fertilizers in different concentrations: concentrated, high-percentage fertilizers, and light, low-percentage ones.
● Depending on their effect, a distinction is made between fast-working, compound fertilizers and controlled-release fertilizers.

Be sure to read what is written on the packaging! Compound fertilizers are easier to handle if you know exactly what they contain. Many manufacturers indicate the proportions of the main nutrients in percentages on the packaging. The sequence is always the same – N (nitrogen), P (phosphorous), K (potassium) – and is usually indicated in figures, for example:
● 8/6/12 (or 8:6:12) which means that this fertilizer consists of 8% nitrogen, 6% phosphorous (to be more exact, P_2O_2 = water-soluble phosphate), and 12% potassium (actually K_2O) = water-soluble potassium oxide) and is, therefore, a compound fertilizer with an emphasis on potassium.
● 7/3/6 indicates a light fertilizer with an emphasis on nitrogen, containing 7% nitrogen, 3% phosphate, and 6% potassium oxide.

Buying tip: The prices of compound fertilizers vary considerably due to the varying concentrations of nutrients. You will have to use more of the light fertilizers than the concentrated ones in order to obtain the same fertilizing results. They are usually cheaper but are also used up more quickly.

The main nutrients and their effect

Nutrients	The right dose	Overdosing	Lack of nutrients	First aid for symptoms of nutrient deficiency
nitrogen (N)	encourages the growth of leaves, shoots, and roots	lanky growth, spongy tissue, susceptibility to aphids and fungi	older leaves turn yellowish, deformed growth	hornmeal, dried blood, compound fertilizers with an emphasis on nitrogen
phosphorous (P)	encourages the formation of flowers and ripe seed	metabolic disturbances, lack of iron, impaired formation of roots	red brown discoloration of leaves, leaves grow sharply upright, weak flowering, hardly any seed	bonemeal, guano, liquid superphosphate, compound fertilizers with an emphasis on phosphorous
potassium (K)	encourages firm tissue and the formation of roots	impedes growth, lack of magnesium and calcium	older leaves become discolored and brownish around the edges, then die	potassium compound, guano, wood ash, compound fertilizers with potassium emphasis
magnesium (Mg)	encourages the formation of chlorophyll and firm tissue	encourages susceptibility to infestation with aphids and spider mites, possibly lack of potassium	older leaves turn yellow, the veins remain green	magnesium lime, algae lime, wood ash
calcium (Ca)	encourages growth of roots and regulates the growth of shoots	leads to lack of phosphorous and reduced growth of roots	buds die off	calcium carbonate, algae lime, guano
sulphur (S)	encourages metabolic processes	results in dwarfism	the youngest leaves turn yellow. Rare!	instead of fertilizing, change the compost

Organic fertilizers

More and more manufacturers are producing houseplant fertilizers based on natural (animal or vegetable) substances. Organic fertilizing is ideal for establishing a harmonious, long-term programme of care for your plants.

If, however, an acute lack of nutrients is diagnosed, you should use a synthetic "artificial" fertilizer, as the nutrients bound in such salts are immediately available for absorption by the plant.

In these fertilizers, the nutrients are bound to synthetic salts which dissolve easily and can be used at once by the plant. A lack of nutrients is thus easily remedied but the danger of overfertilizing is then also greater as the plants have no other option but to absorb these "instant meals." Too much nitrogen, for example, will cause the cells to swell and become spongy. This will make the plant susceptible to diseases and pests.

Another problem is that the compost in the plant pot may become saturated with salts. The micro-organisms in the compost will then find it increasingly difficult to survive and your plants will suffer accordingly because the micro-organisms are no longer fulfilling their function. A healthy environment in a plant pot really is a matter of the delicate balance of so many important factors.

423

Fertilizing

The right fertilizer

Green plant fertilizer should be used for foliage plants. These compound fertilizers, which have an emphasis on nitrogen, can be obtained in liquid form or as tablets, small sticks or cones. Liquid fertilizer is immediately effective; the solid forms are usually controlled-release fertilizers with an effective range of four to six weeks.

Flowering fertilizer should be used for flowering plants. The proportion of nitrogen is less in these fertilizers but phosphorous and potassium are present in larger proportions.

Orchid fertilizer should be used for orchids and bromeliads as well as for other plants that react sensitively to mineral salts. These fertilizers contain far fewer mineral salts and can be mixed with water for watering or sprayed on the leaves.

Cactus fertilizer should be used for cacti from dry desert regions, as well as for succulents. It is poor in nitrogen and calcium but is quite rich in phosphorous and potassium.

Ericaceous (rhododendron) fertilizer or fertilizer for marsh plants should be used for azaleas, heaths, and hortensias, which all require an acid soil and fertilizers that are low in mineral salts.

Leaf fertilizers should be well diluted and sprayed onto the leaves. They are particularly recommended as a remedy for damaged roots. Many preparations that can be sprayed on also contain vitamins and trace elements which will encourage growth. Indoor gardeners are advised to use leaf fertilizing as a special treatment in addition to regular fertilizing. It is particularly recommended for balancing the lack of a single nutrient. If a deficiency of iron is diagnosed, iron preparations will provide fast relief.

NB: This fertilizer is not suitable for very hairy leaves.

Special fertilizers should be used for plants grown in hydroculture or special granules.

in the flowerpot means that soil organisms often do not flourish well; indeed, many commercial composts have a very low count of soil organisms. However, some very effective organic fertilizers are now on sale, intended for pot plants and enriched with additional micro-organisms. These powdered fertilizers are mixed with the potting compost when the plants are potted, then regularly sprinkled on the compost and mixed in with a small stick. Always water thoroughly!

The danger of overfertilizing and creating an accumulation of salts is hardly possible with this kind of fertilizing and repotting is required less often.

Organic-mineral fertilizers endeavour to combine the advantages of both processes. These are fast-working, mineral fertilizers for houseplants, which are mixed with organic components such as humic acid or guano.

Fertilize according to the requirements of the plants!

In order to feed your houseplants properly and according to their individual needs, you will need some knowledge of the requirements of the different species. Just like humans, plants have different likes and dislikes.

"Big eaters" are plants that use up their nutrient supply very quickly and must be fertilized weekly during their main growth phase. Among these are:

● foliage plants that produce masses of leaves in a very short time, such as *Caladium* or *Sparmannia*;

The plant is now only able to obtain nutrients from the artificial fertilizer, on which it increasingly depends. If mistakes are made in fertilizing, weakened plants will quickly succumb to diseases or pests.

My tip: Make sure you read the manufacturer's directions for dosing with mineral fertilizers and find out about the individual needs of the plants (whether they require large or small amounts of nutrients, see right) so that they are not overfed. It is better to fertilize too little than too much!

Organic fertilizers provide plants with a "wholefood" menu consisting of animal or vegetable products. First, however, these have to be broken down by organisms in the soil and converted into nutrients that are accessible to the plant, which means they take much longer to be effective. The restricted space

Desert cacti will only display their enchanting flowers after overwintering in a bright, cool position. Special cactus fertilizer is recommended.

● flowering plants that are expected to produce masses of flowers, like *Gloriosa rothschildiana*, hibiscus (*Hibiscus rosa-sinensis*), or passion flower (*Passiflora*).

"Small eaters" often require nutrients in fairly low doses and no more frequently than every three to four weeks. When using solid compound fertilizers, give the plants only half of the recommended dose or, if it is liquid fertilizer, use double the amount of water. Among these types are:

● foliage plants that produce few or small leaves, like *Beaucarnea recurvata*, *Ceropegia woodii*, *Cupressus macrocarpa*, *Fittonia verschaffeltii*, *Peperomia*, *Sansevieria*, *Senecio rowleyanus*, and *Yucca*;

● cacti (with the exception of leaf cacti);

● succulents;

● orchids;

● ferns;

● many species of palm.

Nutrition specialists:
The horticultural trade has introduced commercial compound fertilizers for cacti, succulents, orchids, bromeliads, and azaleas, which are exactly suited to the requirements of these particular plants.

Plants in special mediums, like clay pellets or other granules, should only be fed with fertilizers that have been specially designed for them.

Fertilizing

The ten golden rules of fertilizing

1. Only fertilize plants during their growth phase. For most plants this means that you should begin fertilizing cautiously at the beginning to middle of the first month of spring. As daylight increases, the new shoots will begin to grow. Gradually increase the supply of nutrients and then, from early fall onward, reduce it again.

2. Plants that flower throughout the winter (like cyclamen or camellias) have different growth cycles and should be fertilized in different ways before and after flowering (see table "Flowering plants," as well as table "Foliage plants").

3. Plants with definite rest phases (like passion flower, *Passiflora*), during which the plant should hardly be watered at all and should be kept in a dark, cool position, should not be fertilized either. Plants with a medium rest phase (like *Spatiphyllum*), which are grown in a bright, warm position, should be fertilized every four weeks during winter but in very sparing doses.

4. Never fertilize a dry rootstock as the nutrient salts may burn the fine roots. Always water the plant before fertilizing.

5. Freshly repotted plants should not be fertilized for at least six weeks. The nutrients in the new compost should last until then.

6. Do not fertilize sick plants.

7. To begin with, do not fertilize young, small plants with few roots and later do so sparingly every four weeks.

8. The amount of fertilizer will depend on the nutrient requirements of the plant and on its size. Large plants need more food than small ones.

9. If in doubt, fertilize often in small amounts rather than seldom in large doses.

10. When using mineral compound fertilizers, read the instructions on the packaging carefully. Use only half of the recommended dose or use a special fertilizer for cacti, succulents, orchids, palms, ferns, and bromeliads.

What to do if the plant has been overfertilized

Depending on the main nutrient in the fertilizer, various symptoms may appear if too much is given (see table). The danger of overfertilizing is much greater with mineral compound fertilizers. There are a few symptoms to watch out for.

● If white salt deposits and crusts appear on the outside of clay pots or on the surface of the compost.

● If the leaves of the plants wilt or become deformed and you feel sure you have not made mistakes in watering and there is no indication of pests.

● If the leaves produce brown spots and blackish-brown burns along their edges.

Prevention: Plants that are several years old and can cope with repotting should be planted in fresh compost every year.

First aid: If you are sure your houseplants have received too much fertilizer and are already showing symptoms of damage, you can save them by taking the plant out of the pot and submerging the rootstock in water for about fifteen minutes. This will dissolve and wash out the surplus salts. Soak the pot too and scrub off any salt deposits with a brush. Then let the rootstock drip dry and replant the plant in the clean pot with fresh compost.

How to fertilize in hydro-culture

A supply of nutrients is particularly important when using this form of culture as the plant is exclusively fed by the fertilizer provided and does not receive any other nutrients from soil or compost. Two types of fertilizer have been found to be successful.

Nutrient solutions, which can be mixed with water. Read the directions for dosage on the packaging very carefully!

Fertilizer batteries containing ion exchangers can be fastened beneath the inner culture pot. They are particularly useful because they remove calcium, chlorine, and other harmful substances from the water over a period of four to six months.

The advantages are:
● You will not need to fertilize for long periods of time.
● Overfertilizing is impossible with this method.
● You can use main water for watering – in fact this is necessary as the salts dissolved in it are required for the working of the ion exchange process.

My tip: This is the ideal way to supply nutrients to houseplants in an office and to foliage plants owned by people who are out at work all day.

Replenishing nutrients
● If you use a nutrient solution, you will have to renew the entire amount after about six to eight weeks and also rinse the plant well.
● If you use fertilizer batteries, you should renew the water at the same time as you change the batteries, which is every four to six months; also rinse the plant well.
● How to rinse plants in hydroculture: Leave the plants in their container but remove this from the pot holder. Spray slightly warm water over the clay pellets and the pot for about five to ten minutes so that everything is well rinsed off. While waiting, clean the pot holder thoroughly.
● Let the plant drip dry, insert the water level indicator, put everything back into the pot holder, and fill the main container with fresh water containing a nutrient solution or a new fertilizer battery.

How to apply fertilizer correctly

Type of fertilizer	Use	Effect
liquid fertilizer	mix with water	fast
powder, crystals	dissolve in water	fast
foaming tablets	dissolve in water	fast
sticks, cones	push into the compost	controlled-release fertilizer: the nutrients are released over a period of about 4-6 months
slow-dissolving granules	mix with the compost when planting	controlled-release fertilizer: the nutrients are released over a period of 4-6 months
leaf sprays	spray on leaves (not on hairy leaves!)	fast

Alternative plant fortifiers
These substances, which are derived from plants, are not considered to be primary sources of nutrients but are rich in trace elements, vitamins, hormones, enzymes, and other substances which encourage growth. They help to strengthen the plant and encourage its development and resistance to disease.
Marine algae extract is derived from brown algae and sprayed onto the leaves in a very diluted form, just like leaf fertilizer. Use this substance if your plant is weakened due to lack of proper care or disease. It will fortify the plant's resistance on a broad basis.
When diluted, *mare's tail extract* can be sprayed on the leaves or given in water when watering the plant in the normal way. Treatment with this solution will strengthen the cells of the plant and act as a prevention against fungal disease.
Valerian extract can also be used for watering or spraying. It promotes the well-being of soil organisms and encourages better flower formation.
Camomile tea: Add 4 cups (1 liter) boiling water to ⅓ cup (10 g) dried camomile flowers. Let this cool and strain it. Dilute as 3 parts water to 1 part tea and use to water the plant. This will encourage growth and resistance to disease.

427

If things are not going well inside the plant pot, the plant will not be able to grow properly.

Repotting

Even in a pot, roots never stop growing in their constant search for new sources of nutrients. The compost soon gets used up and the pot becomes too tight. Repotting is necessary for the healthy development of your houseplants.

Repotting

Repotting is a necessary part of plant care

People often ask why it is not sufficient for the roots to have enough soil to sit in and to be nourished with fertilizer. In actual fact, plants can be cared for in this manner in hydroculture, while growing plants in granules also
works well. Even then, however, you still have to change the water or pot every so often.

Repotting so that the plant can grow: In the wild, whether it is a dwarf moss or a tree, every plant maintains a state of balance in respect of growth. This means that the root system has grown to exactly the point where it can best supply the above-ground parts with nutrients and water. There is a balance between what goes on above ground and below ground.
With plants that are grown in pots, the roots are unable to develop freely as they would in the wild, in accordance with their genetic programing. Not enough space or not enough soil containing nutrients will both hamper the growth of roots. Fewer roots means that less plant material can be supplied with what it requires to grow and so the growth of the above-soil parts of plants in containers is much slower.

Repotting rule 1: If you want your plants to grow larger and bushier, you should repot them once a year and give them a larger pot with fresh compost each time .

When to repot

A glance at your plant, the soil and the pot will give you some idea.
1. When the young leaves of new shoots remain small.
2. If the plant does not seem to grow properly or fails to flower.
3. If, when removed from the pot, the rootstock appears to have used up all the soil and the roots are densely matted.
4. If the roots are growing out of the drainage hole in the pot.
5. If root tips are peeking out of the soil at the top of the pot.
6. If the roots look ill – are blackish, spongy, or smell bad – or have died.
7. If the roots look matted or are growing in a round at the bottom of the pot because they are searching for more space.
8. If white sediment is forming on clay pots.
9. If clay pots are covered in green algae or if moss is growing on the compost. Both are indicators of overwatering, waterlogging, or of compost that has become hard and dense.
10. If the plant has been standing in surplus water for a long time.

My tip: The ideal time for repotting is always at the beginning of the new growth phase. For most plants, this is the first month of spring. This moment will be signaled by the formation of new shoots. Never repot a plant during flowering time or during its rest phase!

Repotting rule 2: If the plant has reached the point where you do not wish it to grow any larger, repot it only every two to three years. Renew the soil but keep the same size of pot.

My tip: Some plants are reliable bloomers even if their root space is restricted, for example, amaryllis (*Hippeastrum* hybrids) and *Clivia miniata*.

Repotting to provide a renewed supply of nutrients: Plants do not just absorb water and nutrients through their roots; they also secrete metabolic waste matter, an accumulation of which can impede growth. In the wild, these substances are partially recycled by micro-organisms in the soil. In a flowerpot, this process can only function in a very limited way and, over time, the waste matter accumulates in the confined space of the pot.
In addition, it is not only plant-friendly substances that are introduced to the pot when watering. Substances that are harmful to plants, or salts that bind mineral nutrients, will gradually become deposited in the potting medium. This encourages the soil to become richer in lime and salts so that the plant is no longer able to absorb nutrients properly and becomes weakened in growth and resistance.

Repotting rule 3: Growing a plant in a pot eventually causes the compost to be used up. This has to be renewed at least every two to three years.

Soil

Plants grow and thrive in the wild where they are part of the natural cycle of birth and death. Just as they derive nutrients and water from the soil, they also return their waste products to it and are later converted into nutrient bases for new life when they die.

These regular cycles are interrupted in the case of houseplants as the plants derive nutrients and water from the soil in a one-sided process. The indoor gardener is the one who has to make sure the supply continues.

Garden soil: Never use pure garden soil for your houseplants. The quality of such soil varies and, for this reason, it may be too light or too heavy for growing plants in pots, or may contain too many or too few nutrients. Garden soil also often contains the seeds of weeds or germs that cause disease. If used at all, garden soil should be only one component of a soil mixture.

My tip: Garden soil should always be used after it has been sieved and sterilized in your oven at a temperature of 400 °F (200 °C) for 30 minutes.

Garden compost should likewise be only one component of a soil mixture as pure compost contains too many nutrients. Garden compost should also be sieved before being used in a potting compost mixture (see table). Never use semi-mature compost. It must be completely mature and free of fermenting substances.

The right soil/compost

Plant groups	Recommended ready-made potting composts	Recipes for your own mixtures
Most houseplants, also: ● leaf cacti ● ferns ● bromeliads ● palms ● camellias	● standard potting compost ● bark compost ● peat-free and other potting composts containing little peat	2 parts garden soil; 1 part ripe compost, leaf mould compost or bark compost; 1 part fine Hortag or pumice sand; a little hornmeal and crushed lava meal
cacti, succulents	cactus compost	3 parts pumice grit; 1 part quartz sand or lava grit; 1 part ripe compost, leaf mold compost or bark compost
azaleas, hortensias, camellias, heaths	ericaceous (rhododendron) compost	1 part ripe compost, leaf mold or bark compost; 1 part garden soil; 2 parts hygromulch or wood fiber
orchids as well as epiphytic bromeliads and ferns	orchid composts	1 part crumbled cork; 1 part pine bark; 1 part polystyrene flakes; ½ part ripe compost; ½ part charcoal; ½ teaspoon (2 g) calcium carbonate per 4 cups (1 liter) of mixture
palms palm ferns	palm composts or standard potting compost	1 part ripe compost; 1 part hygromulch or wood fiber 1 part sand; ½ part polystyrene flakes; ½ part loam

Repotting

Hortag is the ideal, easy-care compost for plants in an office as they only need watering and fertilizing at long intervals.

Potting compost

Basically, this is any medium used for growing plants in pots. Potting compost is always a mixture of different substances and may even contain no proper soil at all. It can be mixed at home or bought ready-mixed and packed.

NB: There is a large range of ready-made mixtures of varying quality and at very different prices. Do not be stingy! Choose only high quality ready-made compost for your houseplants to give them a good start and help them to flourish. Potting compost endeavors to provide the plants with the best possible medium for growing and flourishing in the unnatural conditions of an indoor environment. It has to have very special qualities. The ideal compost should be:

Loose and permeable so that the roots can breathe and develop properly and so that there is no waterlogging which would drive the oxygen out of the compost. This would cause the roots to decay. Able to **store water,** so that the compost does not dry out too fast, as water is needed to help the plant to absorb nutrients and also to transport them.

Good compost is **structurally stable**, which means that it does not rot down too fast, remains loose for a long time, and does not become dense. It should also provide a firm footing for the roots. Fast-rotting substances have the disadvantage that they release additional nutrients during this process. On the other hand, structurally stable composts guarantee an even distribution and release of nutrients.

It stores nutrients, which means that the nutrients remain bound in the compost so that they are at the disposal of the plant when it needs them. Sand, for example, cannot hold nutrients so they are washed away with the water.

It should be free of diseases and weeds so that the plant will remain healthy and not have any competition for nutrients.

It should be slightly acid – between 5-6.5 in the pH range. The acidity factor is one of the most important properties of the compost and the action of micro-organisms in the compost is directly dependent on this, as is how well the plants will be able to absorb nutrients. The pH value of the compost also determines how well the plants will grow.

The most important components of good compost

● Peat or peat substitutes are able to bind water and air, are poor in nutrients, and structurally stable. They keep compost loose for longer.

● Loam stores nutrients and water particularly well and releases it in favorable doses to the plants. In addition, its mineral components are released very slowly, so it is structurally stable.

● Sand makes compost water-permeable and prevents waterlogging.

● Polystyrene flakes and similar materials prevent waterlogging and keep the compost mixture porous.

● Hortag and other clay granules are structurally stable and poor in nutrients. They are able to store water and air very well and to release them on demand.

Suitable compost

If you wish, you can mix your own potting compost (see table).

The effort is definitely worthwhile for garden owners who usually have a supply of garden soil or garden compost anyway. The majority of houseplants will manage very well in standard potting composts but there is a small group with some special requirements.

Standard compost is suitable for most flowering and foliage houseplants. It is universally usable and consists of 60-80% sedge peat and 40-20% clay or loam, including fast-working and controlled-release fertilizers and trace elements.

Flower compost is a term that is used to refer to a range of composts of varying degrees of quality.

Peat-based composts consist mainly of sedge peat with added lime and nutrients. They can be used for very leafy plants but should be used with restraint in order to curb the exploitation of natural wetlands and peat bogs.

Special composts for cacti and succulents are water-permeable as well as poor in nitrogen and organic matter. NB: Leaf cacti should be grown in ordinary flower potting composts.

Ericaceous (rhododendron) composts possess a very low pH factor of 4.5-5.5 and contain large amounts of peat.

Orchid composts should be poor in nutrients and air- and water-permeable. They comprise coarse peat fiber, bark, polystyrene flakes, charcoal, and mineral substances like pumice gravel, lava, or Perlite. Their pH factor is usually around 5-6.

Epiphyte planting medium is made out of chopped marsh moss, *Osmunda* fern roots, and coarse peat fiber. You can also use orchid composts for epiphytes.

Clay granules are tiny clay beads of various sizes, which can store water, let air penetrate, and are structurally stable. Their main task is to provide a firm hold for the roots of the plants.

Hortag pellets are specially made for hydroculture.

My tip: Do not use seeding compost or compost when pricking out young plants for repotting houseplants. Neither of these composts contains any fertilizer, or hardly any, and therefore they are only suitable for sowing or propagation.

Technique

The ten golden rules of repotting

1. Never repot plants during flowering time or their rest phase.
2. Never repot plants with a completely dried-out rootstock; always give them some water beforehand.
3. Damaged or sick (blackish or spongy) roots should be cut off.
4. Carefully remove old soil or compost from the surface, sides, and below the rootstock.
5. Do not damage the very finest roots!
6. Fine roots that have formed a densely matted mass can be cut off or trimmed.
7. Any injured fleshy roots should be dusted with charcoal powder so that no disease-inducing germs can penetrate the plant.
8. Use only thoroughly cleaned containers (soak clay pots in water).

1. The best way to pot a plant
A pot sherd is placed over the drainage hole and a drainage layer of Hortag provides the right amount of moisture inside the pot.

2. How to remove a plant from its pot

a) Water the plant well two hours earlier. This will help to loosen the roots from the pot.
b) Lay the palm of your hand on the surface of the soil and hold the plant between two fingers.
c) Turn your hand and the plant upside down and tap the pot against the edge of a table so that the rootstock is loosened inside the pot.

9. After repotting, water the plant thoroughly.
10. Do not fertilize a plant that has been repotted for at least six to eight weeks.

How to repot small plants
● Water the plant two hours before repotting so that the rootstock is well moistened (see illustration 2a).
● Lay the palm of your hand on the surface of the soil in such a way that the plant protrudes between two of your fingers (see illustration 2b).
● Holding the plant and pot, turn your hand upside down and carefully tap the edge of the pot against a table top to loosen the rootstock (see illustration 2c).
● Never use force to remove the pot as too many roots could tear. If the rootstock is really stuck inside the pot, it is preferable to break a clay pot carefully with a hammer (see illustration 4a). Plastic pots will require cutting open with robust household scissors.

Repotting large plants
● Water the plant well a few hours before repotting (see illustration 3a).
● Loosen the roots from the walls of the pot with a long knife (see illustration 3b).
● Lay the pot on its side and carefully pull the plant out of the pot. If the roots are still stuck at the bottom of the pot, tap the pot with a piece of wood while turning the pot at the same time. Hold the plant with the other hand (see illustration 3c).

The right way to repot
Prepare the container. Only use thoroughly clean pots for replanting. The new pot should be about 1¼-1¾ in (3-4 cm)larger than the old one. Clay pots should be completely submerged in water for one or two hours so that they can soak up water and will not draw moisture from the potting compost later on. Lime deposits can be scrubbed off old pots using vinegar diluted in water. Alternative: Soaking the pots for three days in peat water will also dissolve the salts.

Trimming the rootstock

The very fine roots are responsible for supplying the plant with water and nutrients, so they should only be cut back if it is absolutely necessary, for example, if:

● the rootstock has developed a densely matted mass of roots. Using scissors, cut off the matted parts around the outside of the rootstock;

● the roots look blackish or glassy and smell bad; usually this means they have decayed. All of these roots need removing but do not cut off any light, beige-colored, healthy roots.

My tip: If trimming the roots involves cutting the thicker ones, you should dust the latter with charcoal powder so that no germs can invade the tissue.

Remove old soil: Algae, moss, and old compost should be crumbled off. With a small stick, carefully remove old soil from the sides and bottom without damaging the fine roots.

Planting: Cover the drainage hole in the pot with a piece of broken pot; insert a 1¼-2-in (3-5-cm) thick drainage layer of Hortag, clay granules, or gravel in the bottom of larg-

3. How to remove large plants from their pots
a) Water the plant well about an hour earlier.
b) Loosen the roots from the sides of the pot using a strong knife.
c) Use a chunk of wood to tap the side of the pot and loosen the remaining roots.

er pots. Add new compost so that the plant will be sitting at the same height in the new pot as it did before in the old one (see illustration 4b).

Fill the pot and press the compost down lightly, leaving a space of about ¾ in (2 cm) for watering (see illustration 4c).

Aftercare: Place the plant in a bright position with warmth from below – but never in full sunlight! Stand the pot in a dish or pot holder and water the plant well. After about a half hour, pour away any surplus water. Do not fertilize for about six to eight weeks, at the earliest.

Repotting in the same sized pot

If your houseplant has already attained a considerable height and circumference and you cannot give it a larger pot, you should still repot it. There are two alternative methods.

Renew the topmost layer of compost: Using a small stick or spoon, remove the top layer of compost from the pot without damaging the roots. Then refill the pot with new compost.

Cut the rootstock back: Remove the plant from the pot and trim the rootstock slightly all round so that it is smaller. Now you can easily repot the plant with fresh compost in the same, cleaned pot.

NB: Not all plants respond well to this method. If you do not wish to run the risk of losing your plant, I recommend propagating new plants from cuttings or by air layering.

4. Repotting the easy way

a) If the roots are stuck, the last resort is to break a clay pot with a hammer.
b) Insert a drainage layer on top of the pot sherd and set the plant in the pot at the same height as before.
c) Pour in soil and press it down lightly. Leave a ¾-in (2-cm) space for watering.

435

Repotting

Peat

When choosing potting compost, you can make a contribution toward protecting the environment. Before you buy, read the packaging to find out the contents of the mixture. This information should be clearly visible, although some potting composts are still offered for sale without any indication of their contents. Choose potting composts:

● that clearly list the contents and components of the compost;

● that are, if possible, free of peat or contain little peat. More and more manufacturers are beginning to offer composts containing less peat. The peat is then replaced with other substances, for example, bark humus, hydromulch, and, increasingly, wood fiber whose properties are very similar to those of peat. These composts contain fast-working starter fertilizer. The work of long-term fertilizers is taken over by the organic nutrients contained in the compost or by the addition of controlled-release fertilizers.

There is a wide selection of products for sale in garden centers, many of which are suitable for houseplants. Look for commercial potting compost, sold under various brand names, that contains no peat or potting composts that contain very little peat (no more than 40%).

Plant containers

Containers in many shapes and sizes, and made of many different kinds of material, are available for houseplants.

Standard pots all have a drainage hole (or several) to get rid of surplus water. Their size is measured across the diameter at the top. This will also correspond to the height of the pot.

Flat pots (azalea pots) are wider than they are high and are designed for plants whose roots spread sideways.

Narrow, tall pots (palm pots) are ideal for plants whose roots tend to grow downward.

Bowls and plant basins provide an opportunity of combining several different kinds of plants in a group. The following points should be noted.

● The larger the container, the more important it is to have a drainage layer that is at least 2 in (5 cm) thick so that the roots are not left standing in water after generous watering.

● Only combine species of plants that have the same requirements with respect to water, compost, nutrients, light, and temperature. If you do this skillfully, you will soon notice an interesting side effect: the plants tend to do better in groups than singly.

Hanging containers and baskets provide space for several plants if there is no more space on surfaces in the room. These containers are closed at the bottom so that no water can drip out.

NB: Provide the hanging plant with a thick layer of drainage material or place the plant in a special pot so that the hanging container functions as a pot holder. In this case, cover the bottom of the hanging container with a 2-in (5-cm) layer of Hortag granules, as it is difficult to see into a hanging container to check for surplus water.

Lattice baskets provide an environment close to their natural state for epiphytes like ferns or bromeliads.

NB: Watering requires some care and thought as the water tends to run right through. The best method is to submerge this kind of plant in water .

Closed terrariums, glass cases, or bottle gardens provide the plant communities inside them with an ideal climate for growth and leave them unaffected by the arid air in a room. The water absorbed is then released by the plants through evaporation, condenses on the glass walls and runs back down to the bottom. These plants will hardly require watering. Plant homes of this type are ideal for offices. They are neat, attractive and make few demands with respect to care.

My tip: Clay pots require more care than plastic pots.

● New clay pots should be cleaned thoroughly before planting to remove any lime deposits, algae, or germs. Lime can be removed quite easily with vinegar in water. Rinse well and soak in clean water afterwards.

Ferns in an aquarium – an attractive idea which also provides the plants with the necessary humidity.

Technique

1. Changing over from soil to hydroculture

better than flowering plants.
● Plants with many fine roots find it harder to adapt.
● The best chances of success can be expected in the case of young plants with robust, thick roots, like the flamingo flower (*Anthurium*), *Chlorophytum*, *Hoya*, and *Schefflera*.

a) Water the plant and carefully remove it from its pot.
b) Carefully remove the soil from the roots by hand.
c) Rinse the roots with tepid water until all soil has been removed.

Using clay granules

Clay granules are manufactured by different processes for use in pure hydroculture as well as for combined soil and granule culture.

Hortag (clay granules) can be obtained from garden centers in various different sizes. These are the most common granules used in hydroculture in which plants are grown with their bare roots suspended in Hortag and nutrient solution.

Alternative planting granules make possible a combined cultivation using soil and granules. This involves removing the plant from its pot and simply placing the rootstock still in its soil in the new clay granules.

The advantages of clay granules

● The plant is rarely attacked by pests or disease-inducing organisms that linger in soil as there is no suitable milieu for them.
● They are particularly plant-friendly as their pH value is between 6 and 6.5.
● They are air-permeable, do not become dense and hard, and cannot rot.
● They provide the plant with optimal amounts of oxygen, water, and nutrients.
● Mistakes in watering are almost impossible as a water level indicator in hydroculture, and moisture meters in the case of other plant granules, will indicate when they need more water.
● Plants cultivated in this fashion are ideal for offices. The water supply will usually last for about one to two weeks, so they will not need watering very often. Fertilizing is a similar matter: special long-lasting fertilizers ensure that you only need to fertilize every four to six months in hydroculture, and every two months in the case of other plant granules.

Before changing to hydroculture

Changing from soil cultivation to hydroculture is possible – but not with all plants and there is always a risk involved. Before making the attempt, you should realize that such a change brings an initial shock for the plant as it is suddenly forced to adapt its entire root activity and nutritional needs to hydroculture.
● Sickly or weak plants will rarely survive the ordeal.
● Older plants also rarely cope with the change.
● Not every plant is suited to hydroculture (see tables).
Leafy plants cope

2. Setting the plant in an alternative medium
Rinse the medium well and let it soak up water. Set the plant rootstock, with its soil, in the new medium, no deeper than previously. Insert a moisture meter in the rootstock.

Changing over to hydroculture

Essential tools
- a container;
- water level meter;
- a pot holder;
- Hortag, which should be thoroughly rinsed before use and allowed to soak up water.

Water the plant and carefully remove it from its pot (see illustration 1a). Do not damage the roots; if necessary, break the pot or cut it open.

Carefully remove loose soil (see illustration 1b): You may gently pull the rootstock apart to remove as much soil as possible.

Rinse off any remaining soil (see illustration 1c) with lukewarm, soft, running water. If possible, let the roots soak overnight. The soil must be completely removed from the roots or they will begin to decay in hydroculture.

Only cut off bent, diseased or decayed parts of roots.

Insert Hortag into the culture container.

NB: The granules should be well rinsed and soaked before use. The container can be any size. Insert a 1¼-2 in (3-5 cm) layer of Hortag in the bottom.

Hold the plant in the container so that it sits no deeper than before. Spread out the roots and let the Hortag slide in gently.

Shake the container gently so that the Hortag is dispersed properly. On no account press the Hortag down.

Insert the water level indicator and stand the plant in a pot holder.

Pour in clear, hand-warm water, but not so much that the roots are left standing in water.

NB: Place a transparent plastic hood over the plant and seal it well. This ensures that high humidity is maintained. If the inside of the bag develops condensation, you should air it daily for about fifteen minutes. The position chosen should be bright (but not sunny) and the plant should be kept warm from below. A warming mat placed under the plant is excellent. As soon as the plant produces new shoots, you can remove the hood and begin to add low doses of special nutrient solution.

Repotting in hydroculture

Houseplants grown in hydroculture quickly develop a dense root system. If you place them in large containers, you will not need to repot them every year. It is time to repot when the roots have filled the container.

- Remove the plant from its container and gently remove the Hortag (see illustration 3a).
- Clean the new container thoroughly, rinse it and let it soak.
- Insert a 1¼-2-in (3-5-cm) layer of Hortag and set the plant at the same depth as before (illustration 3b).
- Carefully distribute the granules around the plant and shake the container a little so that they are distributed more evenly (see illustration 3c).
- Insert the water level indicator and pour in the nutrient solution (see illustration 3d).

Repotting in alternative clay granules

With this type of culture (see illustration 2), the plant, its rootstock, and soil are simply replanted in the new clay medium. According to the manufacturers, this is possible with all plants. The best time for repotting is early spring to fall.

Fill a third of a closed container with well-rinsed granules. Place the plant, together with its soil and rootstock, in the container and fill it up with more granules. Insert the moisture meter into the root area and pour in water containing the special liquid fertilizer.

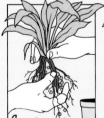  

3. Repotting in hydroculture:
a) Lift the plant from the container and remove old Hortag granules.
b) Fill a new container to a depth of 1¼-2 in (3-5 cm) with new Hortag.
c) Set the plant in the container and fill the container with Hortag all the way round.
d) Insert the water level indicator and pour in water mixed with a suitable nutrient solution.

Flowering plants in a south-facing summer window

Plants that will thrive in a sunny window during the summer are the sun-worshippers, like desert cacti and succulents – plants that are able to store water in their stems or fleshy leaves and can cope with lots of sunlight.

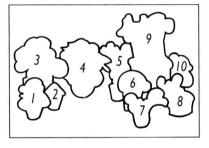

Plants in a south-facing window
(from left to right):
1. Kalanchoë blossfeldiana
2. Echeveria
3. Bougainvillea glabra
4. blue passionflower (Passiflora caerulea)
5. Dipladenia hybrid
6. Sonerila margaritacea
7. Kalanchoë blossfeldiana
8. Desert cactus (Opuntia micro-dasys) (left), Echinocactus grusonii (front right), Cereus jamacaru (back)
9. lemon tree (Citrus limon)
10. Hibiscus rosa-sinensis

NOTES

Mistakes in care will often result in problem
or disease. However, if you apply first ai
quickly, you can generally restore your plant
to health

Sun burn.

Iron deficiency.

Completely dry.

Brown spots on the leaves

Irregular spots on slightly wavy leaves indicate burns. Immediately remove the plant from direct sunlight.

My tip: A bad sunburn can also cause large, silvery, clearly defined spots on the leaves.

Brown leaf tips and edges

These are unmistakable signs of arid air. Increase the humidity immediately. Several courses of action are possible.

Falling leaves

This is caused by too little light or not enough nutrients. The plant may also be suffering from damage to the roots (for example, waterlogging) so that it is no longer able to sustain its parts above ground. The plant must be removed from its pot. Cut off any decayed roots and plant it in fresh potting compost. Depending on the extent of the damage, the plant may have a chance of surviving.

Yellow leaves with green veins

This plant is suffering from lack of iron. This can be most quickly remedied by using a preparation containing iron, which is sprayed onto the leaves. Water the plant with soft water only. Iron deficiency usually occurs if the water contains too much lime. This forms compounds with the iron so that the plant no longer has access to it.

My tip: Similar symptoms appear with a lack of magnesium. In that case, the areas around the veins remain green.

Limp leaves and shoots

The plant is suffering from lack of water and it is high time to water it. Usually, the rootstock is so dried out that it can no longer absorb water. The only thing that will save the plant now is a long soak.

Rolled-up leaves

This plant is trying to cut down on water loss through evaporation by curling up its leaves. The reasons may be manifold. For example, a position in too much sunlight, arid air or too little water. Put things right immediately.

Falling leaves.

First aid

A recipe for success
Even sickly houseplants will became strong and healthy again if they are allowed to spend time outside in the summer. Place them on your balcony or patio – but only after careful acclimatization in the shade.

Campanula isophylla can tolerate water that contains lime and should be placed in a bright position outside during the summer.

Introduction

In many cultures roses symbolize perfect beauty, and what gardener would be really content without at least one rose in their garden? This full-color guide to rose growing is tailored for the complete beginner but will also offer new ideas to experienced rose lovers. In this book, author Halina Heitz, herself a passionate rose gardener, explains all the most important facts you need to know to ensure problem-free roses that will flower profusely from summer right through into fall. A veritable kaleidoscope of roses is introduced here, including attractive, sweetly scented, and, above all, robust bedding roses, tea roses, climbing roses, bush roses, old-fashioned rose varieties, and English roses, together with ground-cover roses and miniature roses. There is also basic advice on the practical care of roses: planting, pruning, propagating, and grafting. Step-by-step illustrations are used to demonstrate the correct way to do these simple tasks and make them easy enough for anyone to follow. The chapter on diseases and pests provides useful full-color leaf checklists which will quickly help you to identify what is wrong with your roses and eliminate the need to spend ages hunting in other books. In addition to all the gardener's lore, you will also find plenty of ideas and suggestions for planting and positioning roses so that they are shown off to their best advantage, whether in a bed or large container, against a house or garden wall, in an archway or grown as a charming standard rose. In addition, recipes that use roses as ingredients in tea and punch are included, as well as ideas for health and beauty preparations.

Contents

Miniature rose "Bluenette."

Delicate perfection – "Eden Rose 85."

An enchanting combination of plants – roses and blue larkspur.

Author's Notes

The author
Halina Heitz has written several books on gardening, covering subjects such as palms, orchids and houseplants. For fifteen years, she was editor in chief of a well-known gardening magazine and is a passionate rose grower in her spare time.

Acknowlegments
The author and publishers would like to thank the Federal German rose raisers and rose tree nurseries for their invaluable information and recommendations on varieties; Eckard Riedel, garden architect and head of the gardening department of the council of the town of Lahr in Germany, for his interesting ideas on design; Bernard Mondo, head of the Roserie at the Bagatelle Park, Paris, for his help in classifying roses; also Jürgen Stork and the other plant photographers for their beautiful photographs; and, finally, Ushie Dorner for her very informative illustrations. Special thanks go to garden director Josef Raff, President of the VDR.

NB: Please read the Author's Note in order that your enjoyment of this fascinating hobby may not be spoiled.

Beautiful blooms on thorny stems

What are Floribunda and Polyantha roses, what are dormant buds, and what is a grafting point? A short description of the botany of roses will answer all such basic questions and will quickly give you a simple overview of the life cycle of this splendid ornamental plant.

What is a rose?

The botanical name of the rose is *Rosa*. It is included in the family of *Rosaceae* and is actually closely related to apple and cherry trees, *Potentilla*, hawthorn (*Crataegus*) and *Geum*. Nobody really knows how many species of rose there are. There might be 175, or even 400, as the rose is naturally inclined to producing hybrids, which means that one species of rose will cross quite happily with others without any help from humans. Each species includes countless varieties. It is estimated that there are currently more than 20,000 varieties. Roses are included among trees and shrubs as they produce soft, leafy shoots during the summer, which become hard and woody in the fall. Even when viewed quite soberly, without any poetic license, the rose can be counted among the most beautiful, resilient and versatile flowering plants we have.

A brief anatomy of roses

Like most other plants, roses consist of roots, shoots, leaves, and flowers. Each part of the plant has its own task to fulfill.

The roots support the rose stems or bush and serve to absorb water and nutrients. At first the roots grow very long, then they branch out, and, with increasing age, become several yards (meters) long and as tough as steel cables.

The crown (or grafting point in a grafted plant) is the thick lump at the neck of the root, at the union of the stock and the scion, which should always be covered with soil, particularly during the winter.

The shoots include all the parts of the rose that grow above ground, both the new, young shoots and the older, woody shoots. In the case of grafted roses, the main shoots grow out of the grafting point, branch out during the summer (annual shoots), and produce a wealth of leaves, from the axils of which numerous flowers appear and grow more profusely every year.

The buds are evenly distributed along the shoot above an imaginary horizontal line. The upper buds are generally fat, look ready to burst and usually produce shoots. The lower buds remain like tiny dots and are therefore called dormant buds. They will form reserve buds for the following year.

The thorns are fairly densely distributed along the shoots and branches, and, in some species, even on the under sides of the leaf veins and on the hips.

They may be fine, bristly or tough, and are colored red, green, brown, or pale yellow. If they are removed from the plant, the epidermis of the shoot will not be damaged; all that remains will be an oval mark. Most roses have thorns, although some are only sparsely equipped, while a very few have no thorns at all.

The leaves grow alternately along the shoot and consist of three, five, seven, nine or 15 individual small leaves. The stalk of the leaf is constructed in such a way that the leaf is fairly mobile and is, therefore, protected from the effects of the weather. The leaves help with the transpiration of water and are among the most important organs of the plant for absorbing nourishment. They are like miniature factories which extract carbon dioxide from the air and produce organic substances, such as starch and sugar, with the help of light, water, and chlorophyll.

The enchantment of a rose arch
A doorway to a magic land may open in any garden as in this rose garden at the Beutig in Baden-Baden, Germany. In the foreground is the white climbing rose "Venusta Pendula."

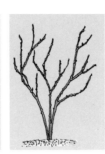

Shapes of growth

1. Bedding or tea roses can grow up to 16-40 in (40-100 cm) tall. Bedding roses produce several umbel or panicle-like inflorescences; tea roses usually have individual flowers on long stalks.
2. Bush roses spread and grow up to 40-120 in (1-3 m) tall.
3. Standard roses are bedding, tea, or climbing roses that have been grafted onto a stock. They will grow to heights of 2, 3 or 5 ft (60, 90 or 140 cm).
4. Climbing roses produce 5-20-ft (1.5-6-m) long shoots, depending on the variety.

While there are hardly any variations in the shape of the leaves, they can be distinguished according to surface consistency, color, and the shape of the edges. There are shiny, matt, leathery, delicate, smooth, wrinkled, light, medium and dark green, bronze and copper-colored leaves. The red coloring of the young shoots depends on the species of rose and is thought to be a protection against sunlight. Particularly during the spring, roses store anthozyane (a plant pigment) which protects the plant from being burned by the aggressive spring sunlight.

The flower is the botanical feature which serves to identify the individual species or variety of rose. It consists of green sepals and petals, male stamens with filaments, and the female part (gynaecium) with the style and stigma.

The number of petals varies considerably. Single flowers have less than eight petals, semi-double have eight to 20, double flowers 21-29, and some many-petaled doubles have 30-40 or even as many as 70 or more. The petals can be round,

oval, heart-shaped, or wedge-shaped, with wavy or fringed edges.

The shapes of flowers arise from the number of petals. You can find deep-cup, open-cup or shallow-cup flowers, pompons, flat flowers, rosette-shaped, star-shaped, and carnation-like flowers.

The colors of flowers range from white, via all shades of yellow, pink, and red to bluish and violet. Pure blue or black roses do not yet exist. Most roses are one single color, but there are some in two colors, several colors, or stripes and even specimens showing only a hint of another color.

The shape of the flower bud depends on the number of petals and may be egg-shaped, spherical, pointed, slim, or urn-shaped.

The fruits of the rose are called hips and, depending on the age and size of the rose and its species, there may be 12-50 hard little pods which contain seeds. Hips come in many shapes: spherical, flattened spherical, pear- or egg-shaped, spindle- or bottle-shaped, and are colored red, orange, green, brownish-red, or blackish-red. Inside, the

hips are packed with bristly hairs, known to many country children as "itching powder" when a hip is broken open and the contents emptied down a playmate's collar!

Many roses produce extremely beautiful hips which make an attractive feature in the garden. The fruits of some roses are renowned for their extremely high content of vitamin C. About 3½ ounces (100 g) of fresh hips from *Rosa haematodes*, for example, can contain four times as much vitamin C as an orange! In the case of *Rosa rugosa*, the same amount can be obtained from 940 mg; from *Rosa villosa* 920 mg; from *Rosa moyesii* 850 mg. The hips of cultivated garden roses, on the other hand, contain only meager amounts of vitamins.

The life cycle of the rose

The vegetative phase of the rose begins with the shoots. These appear after the winter rest period, growing from the buds that remained dormant and undamaged throughout the winter. The shoot grows and is initially nourished by nutrients stored in the plant. As soon as the leaves have unfolded, photosynthesis begins to take place in order to supply the plant with nutrients. During this process, carbohydrates (sugars) are made with the help of water and light, and carbon dioxide drawn from the air. The nutrients produced in the leaves are transported throughout the inner part of the shoots to all parts of the plant where new tissue is being formed, which is mainly in the shoot and root tips, in the tissue responsible for the thicker growth of the shoots (cambium), and in the parts of the shoots and roots that have already turned woody, where the nutrients are stored. Extracting nutrients from the soil is an equally important process. The very fine, hair-like roots absorb water containing dissolved nutrients and, if required to do so, will absorb a systemic insecticide in the same way. This mixture is then transported through the shoots to the leaves where water is constantly evaporated (through transpiration).

The soil must be well aerated and warm for this process to take place naturally. Other important factors are sufficient moisture in the soil and plenty of nutrients.

My tip: Always keep an eye on the foliage of roses. Lots of healthy-looking leaves are a prerequisite for the good growth of wood and a profusion of flowers. Roses which have produced leaves by the third month of spring will flower earlier.

Grafted roses

Most of the roses grown in gardens are grafted plants. Grafting roses offers two advantages:
1. New varieties can be propagated quickly.
2. An attractive, but naturally weak-growing variety is made stronger through grafting.

In grafting a budding shoot (or scion) from a chosen variety is grafted onto the neck of the root (the stock) of a particularly robust and healthy species of rose (e.g. *Rosa canina* "Intermis," *Rosa canina* "Pfänders," *Rosa* "Laxa," *Rosa multiflora* and others).

The scion will fuse with the stock and carry on growing. Shoots will grow and the stock and roots will supply the new plant with moisture and nutrients. The grafting point is the most sensitive part of the plant and should, therefore, be covered with up to 2 in (5 cm) of soil.

Different shapes of growth

Obviously, most people who plant roses would like to know beforehand how a particular variety will develop later on – whether it will climb, hang down, creep along the ground, remain low, grow tall, spread out, or remain compact. It is often impossible to tell by looking at a bare plant in a nursery what it will look like when it has grown, as plants that are offered for sale have usually been pruned back. Pictures of flowers on packages or tags do not convey much either. The lovely blooms they show could belong to 12-in (30-cm) high dwarf roses or to 2-ft (2-m) high bush roses. Depending on their shape of growth, roses are divided into seven different groups (see table below).

Distinguishing roses according to their history

In most catalogs, different varieties of rose are often not only distinguished according to their shape of growth, but sometimes according to their historical origins.

Very old or old-fashioned rose varieties: Strictly speaking, a rose is classed among the old species or varieties if the class it belongs to was known to exist before 1867, the year in which the first hybrid tea rose "La France" was introduced. Among the most important groups are Gallica, Damask, Portland, Alba, Centifolia (cabbage) roses, Moss, China, Bourbon, Noisette, tea, and hybrid perpetual roses. The latter represent the link between the old and modern roses.

Modern roses: This is the name given to the varieties and hybrids which were bred from these groups.

English roses: These are modern roses created by the British rose cultivator David Austin who managed to combine the charm and scent of old roses with the abundance of flowers and vitality of modern roses.

Roses grouped according to their shape of growth

Bedding roses, depending on the variety, will grow from 16 to 40 in (40 to 100 cm) tall and bear numerous single, semi-double, and double flowers on umbel or panicle-like inflorescences. They are also known as Polyantha or Floribunda roses because of their profusion of flowers.

Tea roses, also known as hybrid teas, grow to about the same height as bedding roses. The main difference between the two kinds is that the flowers of tea roses usually grow singly on long stems, have a particularly handsome appearance, and are often scented.

Bush roses are 3-10 ft (1-3 m) tall bushes which will flower once or several times during the summer, depending on the variety.

Climbing and rambling roses, depending on their origins, may grow 5-10 ft (1.5-6 m) long. Both once-flowering and repeat-flowering varieties are available.

Dwarf roses, as a rule, attain a maximum height of 12 in (30 cm) and produce numerous clusters of flowers with small blooms. They are also called miniature roses.

Standard roses and cascade roses do not grow naturally in these shapes but have been created by grafting bedding, tea, or climbing roses onto wild stock. May grow up to 24 in (60 cm), 32 in (90 cm) or even 5 ft (1.5 m) tall.

Ground-cover roses creep or form hanging, arching shapes. They rarely grow higher than 32 in (80 cm) but may form shoots up to 6 ft (2 m) long. Some grow upright and, because of their delicate appearance, are often planted between shrubs.

Flower shapes

The appearance and the number of petals give the flower its typical shape. The individual petals may differ considerably: round, elliptical, heart-shaped, wedge-shaped, some with wavy edges, some with smooth edges.

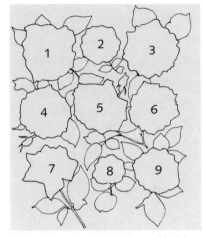

1. A many-petaled variety with 30-70 petals.
2. A double to semi-double flower with 10-12 petals.
3. Flowers with a shallow cup.
4. A flattish flower shape with short, regularly arranged petals.
5. A double flower with more than 20 petals.
6. A single flower with less than eight petals.
7. A classical hybrid tea shape.
8. A globular shape, in which the petals form a sphere.
9. A quartered flower.

Scent

Without doubt, one of the most attractive features of the rose is its beautiful scent. As a rule, dark-colored roses are more strongly scented than light-colored ones and roses with numerous, substantial petals have a stronger scent than those with simpler petals. Red and pink roses mostly produce the typical scent of roses, while yellow and white ones may have a scent reminiscent of nasturtiums, violets, lemons, or irises, and orange roses may smell of fruit, irises, violets, or clover. Other roses smell of ferns, moss, oranges, laurel, honey, wine, lily-of-the-valley, pepper, parsley, or even of linseed oil, like *Rosa foetida*, the Austrian briar rose. A heavier soil will generally engender a stronger scent in roses than a light soil. Roses that have been treated with fertilizer do not develop such a strong scent.

The legendary oil of rose, prized since antiquity, is obtained through distillation or enfleurage. Out of all the presently known roses, there are really only two species that are now of major importance for oil extraction.

● *Rosa damascena* "Trigintipetala" produces the finest and most expensive rose oil of southeastern Europe, also called attar of roses.

● *Rosa centifolia*, the cabbage or Provence rose, is cultivated predominantly in the region of Grasse in southern France and produces rose oil for the perfume industry. Rose oil is an orangey-green color. Thirty roses are required to produce one drop of rose oil and at least 6,000 pounds (3,000 kg) of flowers are needed to distil 2 pounds (1 kg) of rose oil! The oil has a special place in herbal medicine and in the cosmetics industry and is also used to make potpourri.

Blue or black roses

The creation of a blue or black rose is a long-held ambition of rose cultivators all over the world but, unfortunately, one that is doomed never to be fulfilled. A blue pigment has actually been found in roses, but it is always bound to a red pigment so that the best one can obtain is a more or less exciting shade of lilac. The crucial factor for blue flowers, the purple pigment delphidin, does not occur in the *Rosaceae* family. One report from the nineteenth century stated that the Arabs grew blue roses the color of lapis-lazuli but this later turned out to be a piece of gardeners' trickery. Still, there are a few so-called "blue" roses among the enormous selection of species and varieties. Their colors are variously described as lavender, lilac, violet, mauve, or purple. Examples include "Shocking Blue," "Big Purple," "Veilchenblau," "Mainzer Fastnacht," "Charles de Gaulle," "Blue Perfume," and "Nil Bleu." Equally, the dream of a genuine black rose has never been fulfilled, which is probably just as well as funereal black really would not suit the rose. The well-known British rose expert Jack Harkness is of the opinion that nature refuses to cooperate with the raisers who seek such dark colors because very dark-colored flowers would be ignored by insects and this, in turn, would endanger the survival of the species. Therefore, let us simply enjoy what nature does allow, such as dark red roses whose flowers remind one of old Burgundy wine, e.g. "Tatjana," "Bakarole," "The Squire," "Black Lady," "Mildred Scheel," "Burgund," and "Papa Meilland."

455

Roses are true sun-lovers

Roses love a sunny position. If cared for properly, they may flower for up to 20 years in the right spot. Choose the variety and position for planting in with great care. Always make sure the plants are of good quality as, in the long term, it will pay off.

Considerations before buying

There is no doubt that if a rose is planted in the best position, you should have few problems and will derive much pleasure from it. Before planting, check the chosen position for its suitability. The type of soil and the prevailing climate will have a greater influence on the growth, formation of flowers, and health of a rose than is generally appreciated. Those of you who have had to dig up a rose because it just did not seem to be thriving, produced few flowers, and was practically never free of black spot, will know how very difficult and tedious this job can be. Rose roots grow very deep.

The ideal position for a rose

Roses need light, air, and sunshine. They will thrive in any nutrient-rich, well-aerated, and water-permeable soil, but why are these factors so important?

Light and sunshine are absolutely indispensable for the development of flowers. Roses need a minimum of five to six hours of sunshine daily. *Air* – not a draft, but a gentle, warm breeze moving through the foliage – will protect the rose from diseases.

Nutrients should be present in the correct ratios for a plant which grows and blooms so luxuriantly.

Water-permeability is extremely important as roses have deep roots. A layer of impermeable clay or stone underground will obstruct drainage and create problems with the growth of roots.

The following positions are unsuitable:

● positions that have densely packed soil, particularly underground (e.g. the gardens of newly built houses);
● shady positions;
● extremely hot positions. Even though roses are sun-lovers, they like their "feet" to be shady and cool. Heat accumulation along a house wall has a particularly negative effect on rose plants. The roses will fade more quickly and the colors will deteriorate; in some varieties the petals may become burned;

● positions where there is considerable pressure from the roots of other plants;
● in the corners of walls or thickets of shrubs where air cannot circulate;
● positions where the wind is able to whip trailing branches about and dry them out; as well as drafty, cold positions;
● beds in a hollow. Cold air is heavier than warm air and sinks. In winter this may create frost pockets;
● an extremely acid peaty soil or sandy soil. Do rhododendrons, azaleas, heaths, and blueberries grow particularly well in your garden? If so, it is not advisable to plant roses.

Exhausted soil

Never plant new roses in soil in which roses have already been grown for several years. The new plants would soon begin to deteriorate because the soil has become "rose tired." It is believed that the cause of this is an imbalance in the minerals and trace elements in the soil, which has been created through a one-sided absorption of nutrients or through imbalanced fertilizing. In addition, it is assumed that toxic waste products from the old roses' roots remain in the soil and then interfere with the growth of the new roses. Sometimes the soil is also infested with eelworms.

My tip: If you still wish to plant roses in the same place that roses grew before, you will have to dig out the soil to at least a depth of 24 in (60 cm) and replace the "rose-tired" soil with fresh, vital soil from another part of the garden. The exhausted soil should be tipped onto the compost heap. If you add *Tagetes* and *Calendula* to the compost heap, you will find that secretions produced by both of these members of the Compositae family will kill eelworms.

The best soil for roses

The wonderful thing about roses is that they can actually manage to grow on most types of garden soil. None the less, some rough guidelines may be useful.

The ideal soil profile (which means a section cut through the various soil layers), consists of the following levels, according to the famous Swiss rose grower Dietrich Woessner:

- a permeable bottom layer of gravel, pebbles, or sand, through which water can run as through a sieve;
- an in-between layer consisting of a mixture of fine particles of rock, silt, and clay;
- a thin layer of humus and clay particles;
- a richer layer, 24-32 in (60-80 cm) thick, of loamy and humus-rich agricultural or garden soil. The best type of all is a neutral, fertile loess.

The acid content of the soil is expressed by means of pH values. For roses this should be between pH 6.4 and 7.5, which means that the plants will thrive in a slightly acid, neutral to slightly alkaline soil. In my experience, however, roses will also grow quite adequately in soils with a pH value of 8 or even a little over, as long as the other locational factors are good.

A balanced supply of nutrients means that the main nutrients of nitrogen (N), phosphorous (P), and potassium (K) are present in sufficient quantities. A soil sample will determine this. For this purpose, six to eight spadefuls of soil are dug out at different points in the position where the roses are to be planted. Take a handful from each of these portions, mix them all together and send a 1-lb (500-kg) sample of the mixture to a soil analysis expert in a strong plastic bag (ask about this at your local garden center).

Glass globes will provide a dramatic contrast to the color of the roses.

457

Looking for roses of quality

Plants of the very best quality (left) should have three shoots; roses of lesser quality should have two strong, healthy shoots.

You can also obtain do-it-yourself soil analysis kits which are easy to use at home.

Preparing the soil

You should start to prepare the soil at least three months before planting so that it can settle and mature. Dig the soil over to a depth of 24 in (60 cm). Then loosen the bottom layer of soil with a garden fork and enrich it with organic material (e.g. well-rotted compost or chopped up grass turfs). The soil consistency may vary considerably from one part of the garden to another as no two soils are exactly alike. The best way to get to know your garden soil is to test it with your hand. You will soon discover how its structure can be improved. The main types of soil are:

● Clay-rich soil. This soil is heavy, feels sticky, and can be formed into a lump. The addition of compost or sand will make it looser.
● Loamy soil is of a crumbly consistency and falls apart easily. If the sand content is very high, the humus content can be increased by mixing in compost. Flakes of various water-retaining materials can be worked in.
● Sandy loam feels grainy and can be formed into a ball more easily. It will generally not need any additional compost etc.
● Acid soil should be improved by mixing in lime.
● Alkaline soils can be improved by working in peat.

A selection of tried and tested roses

(* = flower once; all other varieties are repeat-flowering)

Tea roses
"Carina" – silver pink, 28 in (70 cm)
"Duftwolke" – coral red, 28 in (70 cm)
"Evening Star" –
pure white, 28 in (70 cm)
"Gloria Dei" –
creamy yellow/with a hint of pink along the edge, 28 in (70 cm)
"Piroschka" –
pink, 20 in (50 cm)

Bush roses
"Centenaire de Lourdes" –
rich pink, 64 in (1.8 m)
"Dirigent" – blood red, 80 in (2 m)
"Lichtkönigin Lucia" –
lemon yellow, 60 in (1.5 m)
"Marguerite Hilling" – carmine pink, 80 in (2 m)
"Mozart" – pink/white center, 60 in (1.5 m)
"Robusta" – red, 80 in (2 m)
"Scharlachglut"* – scarlet, 100 in (2.5 m)

"Schneewittchen" –
pure white, 48 in (1.2 m)

Bedding roses
"Bella Rosa" – pink, 20 in (50 cm)
"Bonica 82" – pink, 28 in (70 cm), spreading
"Friesia" – yellow, 28 in (70 cm)
"Ludwigshafen am Rhein" – light red, 28 in (70 cm)
"Märchenland" –
salmon pink, 40 in (1 m)
"Manou Meilland" –
dark pink, 28 in (70 cm)
"Margaret Merrill" – white/breath of pink, 28 in (70 cm)
"Nina Weibull" – carmine red, 28 in (70 cm)
"Queen Elizabeth" – silver pink, 40 in (1 m)
"The Fairy" –
pink, 28 in (70 cm), spreading
"Tornado" – fiery red, 24 in (60 cm)

Climbing roses
"Flammentanz"* –
blood red, 160 in (4 m)

"Golden Showers" –
lemon yellow, 100 in (2.5 m)
"Ilse Krohn Superior" – white, 120 in (3 m)
"New Dawn" – delicate pink, 140 in (3.5 m)
"Parade" – dark pink, 160 in (4 m)
"Rosarium Uetersen" – dark salmon pink, 120 in (3 m)
"Sympathy" – dark red, 160 in (4 m)

Ground-cover roses
"Heideröslein Nozomi"* – delicate pink, 12 in (30 cm) tall, 20 in (50 cm) wide
"Palmengarten Frankfurt" –
carmine red, 28 in (70 cm) tall, 40 in (1 m) wide
"Repandia"* – pink, 16 in (40 cm) tall, 120 in (3 m) wide
"Rote Max Graf"* – red, 20 in (50 cm) tall, 120 in (3 m) wide
"Snow Ballet" – pure white, 20 in (50 cm) tall, 40 in (1 m) wide
"The Fairy" –
pink, 28 in (70 cm) tall, 40 in (1 m) wide

My tip: While preparing the soil, use this opportunity to remove all weeds with tenacious root systems, like field bindweed *Convolvulus arvensis, Ranunculus repens* (creeping buttercup) and dandelion (*Taraxacum officinale*). This will save a lot of tedious weeding between the rose bushes later on. Leave all small stones in the soil as they will help to aerate it.

Where to buy roses
Roses are among the most popular flowering plants and are therefore almost always included in the standard selection of plants sold by garden suppliers. Good sources are:
● Rose cultivators and mail order firms where you can order from a catalog or buy direct. These firms will obviously have the largest selections (for addresses, ask at your local garden center).
● Tree nurseries which also sell other shrubs usually have a large selection of roses and will also know about local soil conditions, etc.
● Garden centers, whose selection generally represents a cross-section of the best-known varieties.
● Garden mail order firms, whose fall catalogs generally include a wide selection of roses (ask at your local garden center for names and addresses).

Choosing varieties
Like all woody plants, roses are planted at the time of their dormant growth period (the exception being container roses). This means that they have to be bought when they are not flowering, have been pruned back, and all look more or less the same. As the flower is the main reason for buying the plant, it is necessary to be clear beforehand about varieties, colors of flowers, and other criteria such as the shape of growth, hardiness, and common health problems.

How roses are offered for sale

1. As a plant with bare roots, the most usual way.
2. As a container plant. The selection is somewhat restricted.
3. Prepacked in bags, boxes or cartons. The roots are enveloped in moisture-retaining material.

A selection of tried and tested varieties
If you are not sure what you want and have no great experience with roses, it is best to fall back on the sort of list that is compiled by experienced rose growers. The best thing to do in these circumstances is to visit a reputable rose-growing nursery and discuss your requirements with a trained member of staff. If you can tell them as much as possible about the position in which you intend to plant your roses, the kind of soil you have, and what your prevailing weather conditions are, etc., they should be able to suggest a suitable selection of plants for you to choose from. If you are unable to visit a nursery, the next best thing is to send off for some catalogs from nurseries recommended to you by your local garden center. Such catalogs are usually very informative and the choice of plants on offer is usually wide. There is the further advantage that plants from such a source will be healthy and strong so you can get them off to a good start. If you buy plants from supermarkets, traders' stalls, or other less-specialist outlets, then you may be unlucky as to quality. Certainly, you are unlikely to receive any reliable advice from non-specialist retailers or their staff.

Looking for quality when you buy
Roses of the best quality should display at least three well-matured branches, of which at least two should be growing out of the grafting point; the third may grow out of the stem above the grafting point.
Roses of slightly lesser quality should display at least two branches which must both grow out of the grafting point. Things are slightly different if you are looking at standard plants. The prerequisite for the best quality standard roses is shoots with two buds. When buying standards of slightly lesser quality, you should look for one bud. In addition, the height of the standard plant should also be considered. For cascade or weeping types, look for a height of about 56 in (140 cm); for ordinary standards, look for plants making a height of 36 in (90 cm); and for miniatures, choose plants with stems of about 16 in (40 cm).

How roses are sold

There is a traditional way of selling roses and three more modern methods.

● Plants with bare roots are most frequently offered for sale just as the tree nusery staff have dug them up. They can be bought individually or in bundles of five or ten. Occasionally, the shoots are treated with a coating of wax to prevent them from drying out through evaporation.

● Plants in plastic bags, boxes, or cartons. These are prepacked rose plants whose roots are wrapped in moss or some other moist packing material.

● Rose plants with a rootstock that is ready for planting.

● Container plants.

These roses stand in plastic pots and are also sold when they are in flower. However, not all roses can be obtained in containers, only the most popular varieties.

When to order and purchase?

This will depend mainly on the planting time. In most regions, fall is considered to be the ideal time. In very cold regions or if you have very heavy soil, it would be advisable to plant roses during the first or second months of spring. Container roses can be bought and placed outdoors all year round except when temperatures are freezing, but they will grow better if they are planted during fall or spring.

When buying roses from a catalog, the following points should be considered.

As a rule, order the plants as early as possible and always in writing! If

A scented rose from New Zealand
"Big Purple" is a new 32-in (80-cm) tall tea rose cultivar with large buds and many-petaled flowers.

you have noted the names of some favorites during the summer months and find them advertised in your catalog, then send off for them right away. The dispatching of plants is usually done by rose tree nurseries during the middle of the second month of fall, following the sequence in which orders were received. If you have placed your order early, the plants should be on your doorstep at the ideal time, sometime in the third month of fall. If you would prefer to plant roses in the spring, you can place your order from the first month of winter onward. Delivery will be from the first month of spring in frost-free weather.

Standard roses will usually be sent a few days later than other roses during the fall, as they require longer to prepare.

If you go to pick up the plants yourself, you will be able to buy your roses at short notice without a long wait for delivery time. In the case of rarer varieties, check first to make sure that they are in stock.

Container roses are available all the year round but the selection will probably be at its largest at the typical rose-planting times of the year, in the fall and spring.

What to watch out for when purchasing roses

A healthy well-grown plant is the first step toward success. A good quality rose should have the following appearance:

● It should have green shoots and a smooth bark.

● The wood should be well matured, and the shoots should feel firm when squeezed.

● The plant should have strong roots.

● Prepacked roses may dry out if they have been left to lie around for too long. Check to see whether the shoots look fresh and green.

My tip: When purchasing container roses, ask if you can look at an example of a plant removed from its pot. You will be able to tell the quality of the container plant by its well-developed rootstock.

Choosing roses

Rose gardens are like shop windows. The most beautiful rose displays, exhibiting the greatest number of varieties, can be found in:

● rose gardens (information can be obtained from your local rose growers' society, or local tourist office);

● parks and public gardens;

● gardens of historic houses, etc.;

● at garden and flower exhibitions;

● show gardens of rose nurseries.

My tip: If you go to Europe on vacation, keep an eye out for special roses! Many varieties which you might discover in Britain, Germany, Switzerland, or France will also thrive in the US and can be ordered from a good rose tree nursery when you get home again, although it may be sold there under a different variety name. If you are a member of a gardening club or rose growing club, you may be able to view roses in private gardens.

Rose catalogs are sent out every year by the big rose tree nurseries. They usually come with photographs in full color, a detailed description of the variety, and valuable tips from experts on how to grow them successfully. Sometimes a small handling charge is made but this is always well worth the expense as every brochure is like a small reference book and the charge is often refunded when a purchase is made.

Roses, herbaceous plants and shrubs

Mixed borders are the kind of garden bed that reflects all that is best about the summer months – roses, herbaceous plants, and shrubs. Although the rose is considered by many to be the queen of flowers, it is still very willing to share its space with other plants such as *Campanula*, larkspur (*Delphinium*), catnip, and sage. The small-flowered, modern rose cultivars are especially suited to unusual combinations. Their flowers are like scented dots of color in an impressionist painting.

The planting of colorful "English" beds is popular all over Europe and is an idea frequently employed by garden designers such as the famous garden architect Eckard Riedel. However, if you wish to combine shrubs and herbaceous plants with roses, you will have to plan your bed very carefully. Only then will the flower bed do you justice.

Like a painting by Monet
Small-flowered Floribunda roses in shades of pink harmonize beautifully with flowering herbaceous plants and shrubs in the same range of color or in pastel shades.

462

Designing a rose bed

Roses will enrich any garden provided that they are positioned in a knowledgeable way. This means not just planting things in any old place without thinking about it first! A few basic principles of good design must be taken into account.

● Never plant tea roses or bedding roses individually. A group of three to ten specimens looks much better.

● Never plant roses together with woody shrubs which will grow higher than the roses and deprive them of light or prevent you from caring for the roses properly. Make sure the root systems of shrubs will not impede the growth of the roses.

● Avoid the close proximity of plants which produce very bright summer colors.

● Instead, use low-growing, sun-loving shrubs with less conspicuous colors, or flower and leaf colors which harmonize well.

● Surround roses with a framework of plants like box, lavender, or cushions of herbaceous plants in suitable colors.

● Choose backgrounds made of tranquil conifers, green ivy, blue-violet *Clematis*, etc.

My tip: There is a current trend for planting small-flowered, delicate-looking roses in a bed full of shrubs and herbaceous plants. This can look very effective.

Roses for different purposes

Roses can be used in a very versatile way in gardens and on patios and balconies because of their varying shapes of growth and their wide range of colors.

Bedding and tea roses can be used as a group in small and large beds, together with herbaceous plants, for borders along paths, and for use as cut flowers.

Climbing roses can be used as a decoration on house walls, as solitary plants, as climbers along fences, walls, over statues, arbors, pillars, espaliers and as a background for herbaceous plants and low-growing shrubs.

Once-flowering bush roses can be used as solitary plants to help to anchor banks and slopes, to provide winter food for birds (hips), as part of a natural hedgerow, or for opening up a nature garden.

Bush roses which bloom several times a year can be used as solitary plants in open, flowering hedges, as a background for shrubs or herbaceous plants, and together with low-growing shrubs or deciduous or coniferous trees.

Miniature roses can be used in borders, for planting in cemeteries, for balcony boxes, containers, or troughs, and in a rockery.

Cascades or standard roses can be used as solitary plants in a classical, symmetrical garden design.

Ground-cover roses can be used to anchor banks and shrubberies, for troughs, and in a rockery.

Should roses be given an underplanting?

Underplanting should only be done if the roses are well spaced out. The best companion plants to choose are low-growing shrubs and herbaceous plants which can be used as underplanting for climbing roses or bush roses which have become bare below.

Do not underplant roses with bulbs if at possible. Jobs like digging holes and moving soil will disturb the bulbs and the roses' thorns will interfere when you dig up the bulbs.

Exception: Flowering bulbs which have been left to go wild can live under very hardy, older roses or under roses in milder regions, which do not need to be protected in winter by banking up soil.

Making the most of color in planting combinations

With white roses: plants with green, silver gray, and blue gray foliage as well as plants with blue and white flowers.

Examples: box, *Dianthus plumarius* "Diamant," fat hen (*Sedum spurium* "Album superbum"), common lady's mantle (*Alchemilla vulgaris*), *Campanula lactiflora*, snow-in-summer (*Cerastium*), wormwood (*Artemisia*), *Santolina*, *Gypsophila*, sneezewort (*Achillea ptarmica*), *Stachys lanata* "Silver Carpet."

With red roses: for red shades with a tinge of yellow, try plants with blue gray, silver gray, green, brownish-violet, and yellowish-green foliage. For red shades with a tinge of blue, the ideal flower colors are blue. For red shades with a tinge of yellow, try flowers that are orange or golden yellow.

Examples: fat hen (*Sedum album* "Coral Carpet"), *Sedum floriferum* "Weihenstephaner Gold," *Campanula portenschlagiana*, catnip, lavender and larkspur (*Delphinium*).

With yellow roses: with roses in warm shades of yellow try plants with blue, violet, brown red, or orange flowers, or plants with silvery or golden yellow foliage.

Examples: catnip (*Nepeta*), lavender, *Helichrysum*, thyme (*Thymus rotundifolius*), and *Stachys lanata*.

With pink roses: plants with blue green, silvery, or green foliage, as well as inflorescences in shades of violet, purple, or blue violet.

Examples: fat hen (*Sedum album* "Coral Carpet"), lady's mantle (*Alchemilla vulgaris*), *Campanula*, *Polygonum affine* "Superbum," thyme, (*Thymus pseudolanugenosus, Thymus serphyllum* "Coccineus").

Suggested combination 1
Floribunda rose "Sankt Florian" with larkspur (Delphinium belladonna "Völkerfrieden"), Achillea filipendula "Sonnengold," tickseed (Coreopsis verticillata "Grandiflora"), and sage (Salvia officinalis "Berggarten").

Suggested combination 2
Floribunda rose "Boys' Brigade" with Gypsophila paniculata "Schneeflocke," Potentilla "Goldteppich" or sage (Salvia nemorosa "Ostfriedland"). If you like, you could add a blue element, e.g. Campanula persicifolia "Grandiflora Alba."

Suggested combination 3
Ground-cover rose "The Fairy" with larkspur (Delphinium x cultorum "Sternenhimmel"), catnip (Nepeta faassenii), Capanula carpatica "Chewton Joy," Stachys lanata and lady's mantle (Alchemilla mollis).

Suggested combination 4
Bedding rose "Esther Ofarim" with larkspur (Delphinium x cultorum "Sternenhimmel"), lavender (Lavandula angustifolia "Munstead"), golden rod (Solidago hybrid "Leraft") and phlox (Phlox paniculata "Schneehase").

The most beautiful roses

A selection for your garden

If you have developed an enthusiasm for planting roses, on the following pages you will find illustrations and descriptions of splendid varieties picked from the most popular groups of roses. Choosing will not be easy as they are all beautiful, charming, and worth a place in your garden.

The range and possible choice of roses is so enormous that one would need many books filled with photographs and descriptive text to introduce all the many varieties that are for sale today. The following cross-section is intended merely to give you an idea of the great variety of flower colors and shapes. We have taken our selection from the roses most often recommended by raisers – tried and tested varieties selected with the benefit of many years' experience.

Note: Most modern varieties bloom more than once in their flowering season. Roses which flower only once but do so profusely are included. If you wish to use the following illustrations as a guide to choice, you should be aware that you may find variations in color and shape of flower which can be caused by varying climate or soil.

The sequence of our selection
● Bedding roses.
● Tea roses or hybrid tea roses.
● Bush roses.
● Climbing roses.
● Old-fashioned and English roses.

● Ground-cover and miniature roses.

You will find characteristic features listed for every group, plus indications as to their most suitable use and brief details about each individual rose, conveying essential information on growth, height, color of flowers, scent, and other interesting features. With some groups of roses there are additional recommendations on variety, e.g. scented flowers or those with particularly attractive hips.

Special recommendations
By means of a questionnaire, a survey was carried out among rose growers, which asked them to make recommendations of particular varieties for certain purposes. Some of the results are given below.

Roses for planting on steep slopes: The most suitable are bush roses which are not too high and ground-cover roses.
Examples: "Fair Play," "Fiona," "Fleurette," "Heidekind," "Heidekönigin," "Hermann Schmidt," "Immensee," "Max Graf," "Palmengarten Frankfurt," "Red Meidiland," "Red Yesterday,"

"Repandia," "Repens Meidiland," "Rote Max Graf," "Sommerwind," "Super Dorothy," "Super Excelsa," "Swany."

Roses for screening
Examples: "Bischofsstadt Paderborn," "Castella," "Ferdy," "Feuerwerk," "IGA 83 München," "Lichtkönigin Lucia," "Queen Elizabeth," "Robusta," *Rosa rugosa* and hybrids, "Rosika," "Royal Show," "Schneewittchen," "Shalom."

Roses with few thorns are found mainly among the greenhouse roses which are used for cut flowers
Examples: "Bonica 82," "Karl Höchst," "Kronpinzessin Viktoria" (no thorns), "Madame Sancy de Parabière," "Montana," "Sutter's Gold."

Roses for flower arrangers
Examples: "Alliance," "Berolina," "Bonica 82," "Carina," "Carmen," "Corso," "Desirée," "Diadem," "Flamingo," "Kardinal," "Konrad Henkel," "Kristall," "Lady Rose," "Landora," "Mabella," "Majolica," "Marlies," "Monica," "Pascali," "Prominent," "Queen Elizabeth," "Rouge Meilland," "Rumba," "Sutter's Gold," "Tatjana," "The Fairy," "Träumerei," "Uwe Seeler."

Roses that are resistant to traffic exhaust fumes (for planting along busy roads)
Examples: "Alba Meidiland," "Anne Cocker," "Bonica 82," "Centenaire de Lourdes," "Dagmar Hastrup," "Fanal," "Flammentanz," "Max Graf," "New Dawn," "Red Meidiland," *Rosa nitida*, *Rosa rugosa* hybrids, "Sarabande," "Swany," "The Fairy."

Cascades of flowers
The much-loved, but not very resistant, "Dorothy Perkins" is now available without a susceptibility to mildew under the name "Super Dorothy."

Most beautiful in groups

Bedding roses

Depending on the variety, bedding roses can grow from 16 to 40 in (40 to 100 cm) tall and will produce numerous single, semi-double, or double flowers with umbel-like or panicle-like inflorescences. They are also called Polyantha or Floribunda roses because of their profusion of flowers. They are used in beds, together with shrubs, in borders along paths, and as cut flowers.

"Traumerei" growing in a box-edged border.

Scented bedding roses
White: "Margaret Merrill"
Yellow: "Arthur Bell," "Friesia"
Red: "Duftwolke," "Ludwigshafen am Rhein," "Prominent," "Traumerei"
Pink: "Elysium," "Manou Meilland," "Pariser Charme"

"Apricot Nectar" blooms well into the fall and has 4-in (10-cm) wide, large double flowers. This bushy-growing Floribunda rose has dark green foliage and grows up to 32 in (90 cm) tall. It has a wonderful scent.

"Lilli Marleen" is considered to be one of the most beautiful dark red Floribunda roses. Its open, double, cup-shaped flowers are about 3 in (8 cm) across. This rose flowers profusely, grows bushy and will grow up to 24 in (60 cm) tall. Its foliage is bright green and resistant to disease.

"Friesia" belongs among the top class yellow roses and is often used in mixed borders together with shrubs. It grows up to 26 in (65 cm) tall, upright and bushy, and has fresh green, shiny leaves. The deep yellow, semi-double flowers do not lose their color, are strongly scented and fade neatly. Particularly hardy.

"Bella Rosa", a Kordes cultivar from the 1980s, enchants with its giant umbels of double flowers in glowing pink. The petals unfold from rounded buds and release a scent of wild roses. This variety has won countless gold medals. It grows up to 24 in (60 cm) tall and sports fresh, green, shiny foliage. Its compact, bushy growth makes it an outstanding bedding rose.

"Märchenland" is notable out for its extraordinary resistance to disease. The flowers of this variety, which grows up to 40 in (100 cm) tall, are salmon pink, large and semi-double, the leaves are medium green, matt, and leathery. This rose grows strongly and spreads. Suitable as a small bush rose.

"Lavaglut" produces rounded, black red buds which turn into double, blood red, very rain-resistant flowers. It grows up to 24 in (60 cm) tall and spreads. The foliage is dark green and shiny.

The aristocrats among roses

Tea roses and hybrid teas

These roses are particularly enchanting on account of their generally strongly scented flowers which are large and handsome and usually grow individually on long stems. Tea roses or hybrid teas grow, on average, from 20 to 40 in (50 to 100 cm) tall, are bushy and very upright, and look particularly attractive in small, exclusive groups or in the company of shrubs with silvery green foliage. Of all the groups of roses, they provide the most elegant cut flowers. We recommend pinching out the lateral buds early on in order to obtain large single flowers for cutting. The range of colors extends from white through cream, champagne, pink, salmon pink, orange and red to such unusual colors as blue violet, burgundy or black red.

Tea roses in two colors
"Caribia," "Circus Knie," "Die Welt," "Königin der Rosen," "Las Vegas," "Monica," "Neue Revue," "Piccadilly," "Rebecca," "Wimi."

Black red tea roses
"Bakarole," "Black Lady," "Burgund," "Erotika," "Ingrid Bergmann," "Oklahoma," "Papa Meilland."

Blue and violet varieties
"Big Purple," "Blue River," "Charles de Gaulle," "Mainzer Fastnacht."

"Susan Hampshire:" The parents of this 32-36-in (80-90-cm) tall, strongly scented hybrid tea rose are the pink to salmon pink variety "Monique," the carmine pink, large flowered "Symphonie" and the famous "Maria Callas" – also known as "Miss All-American Beauty." This very successful cultivar from the famous French rose-growing family of Meilland was first introduced in 1974 and produces densely packed, deep pink flowers from outstandingly large buds. The foliage is a fresh green shade and grows robustly. When planted in a bed, they look best and most elegant in small groups, perhaps framed by box.

"Mildred Scheel:" A deliciously scented rose with large, black red buds which gradually open into velvety red, double flowers. This strongly growing hybrid tea rose, also known by the name "Deep Secret," branches out well and forms very tough stems with matt, dark green leaves. It grows to 28 in (70 cm) tall.

"Evening Star," which was created from the hybrid tea rose "White Masterpiece" and the Floribunda rose "Saratoga," displays 4-in (10-cm) wide double flowers in umbels on long, branching stems, and enjoys particularly good health for a white variety. This 40-in (1-m) tall hybrid tea, with its dark green, shiny foliage, grows well, and has a strong scent.

"Konrad Adenauer:" This 24 in (60-cm) tall hybrid tea, with its clear, velvety dark red, strongly scented blooms, is a creation by the well-known German rose raiser Mathias Tantau. It grows bushy, branches well and possesses extremely healthy, light green foliage.

"Chicago Peace" has double flowers in two colors, consisting of 50-60 petals, and grown on very strong stems. The foliage is deep green and the plant spreads. It can grow up to 28 in (70 cm) tall.

"Charles de Gaulle:" The variety "Mainzer Fastnacht" gave this hybrid tea its attractive lilac shade, and the delicious scent originates from "Prelude." This is a vital, strongly growing 24 in (60 cm) tall rose from France with tough, resistant foliage.

"Gloria Dei" is the most frequently bought and most prize-winning rose in the world. This 40-in (1-m) tall, strong-growing hybrid tea has giant, 6-in (15-cm) wide, many-petaled, yellowish-pink blooms and shiny green foliage. It is considered a symbol of joy and peace and is often sold under such names. It was named on the very day, in 1945, when peace was proclaimed in Europe.

Bush roses

Bush roses grow up to 40-80 in (1-
2 m) tall and, depending on the
species or variety, flower once or
several times. While the once-
flowering roses (seen growing wild
or in parks) are often used for
stabilizing slopes and embankments, as part of a natural
hedgerow, for producing a crop of
rosehips, and for interspersing
among other plants in an organic or
rustic garden, gardeners also like to
use the modern cultivars, which
bloom often (ornamental bush
roses) as solitary plants or as effective backgrounds for shrubs or
herbaceous plants. Bush roses that
only flower once still possess all the
charm of wild or botanical roses
and are becoming ever more popular as design elements in the planning of natural-looking gardens.
NB: Do not give everlasting flowering roses a spring pruning. It will be
quite sufficient to clear out the
dead, old, or withered wood.

Solitary roses for small gardens
"Angela," "Blossomtime,"
"Centenaire de Lourdes," "Kordes
Brillant," "Märchenland,"
"Mountbatten," "Rosika,"
"Schneewittchen," "Yesterday."

Attractive rosehips
Rosa canina, *Rosa moyesii*, *Rosa
pendulina* "Bourgogne," *Rosa rubiginosa*, *Rosa rugosa*, *Rosa swegin-
zowii* "Macrocarpa,"
"Scharlachglut."

Once-flowering bush roses
"Conrad Ferdinand Meyer,"
"Dornröschen," "Frühlingsgold,"
"Hansa," "Maigold," "Marguerite
Hilling," "Pink Grootendorst," "Red
Nelly," *Rosa nitida*, "Scharlachglut."

"Lichtkönigin Lucia" is a profusely
flowering, long-lived, outstandingly
robust and healthy bush rose. The
lemon yellow, about 3-in (8-cm)
wide double flowers grow partly
singly, partly in clusters of several
flowers, and are slightly scented.
This rose grows at a medium rate,
is upright, and can reach up to 40-
80 in (1-2 m) tall. The leaves are
dark green and shiny.

"Westerland" appears to the
observer rather like a flickering
burning bush when it is in full
bloom. The large, open, double
flowers have a strong scent and
appear right up until the first frost.
The foliage is dense and deep
green. This rose grows quickly, is
spreading, and can attain a height
of 60-80 in (1.5-2 m).

"Centenaire de Lourdes" is a French
variety with handsome, open, double, glowing pink flowers of about 3
in (8 cm) in diameter. The foliage is
shiny green and healthy, growth
being a little lanky. Height: about
40 in (1 m). It is also sold as a
Floribunda rose.

"Golden Wings" will even grow in
positions that are a little shady, will
attain a height of about 60 in
(1.5 m), and bears 5-in (12-cm)
wide, sulphur yellow, single flowers
throughout the entire summer.
Particularly conspicuous are the
orange red stamens which look like
gold threads. The leaves are light
green and matt. This *Rosa spinosissima* variety is very hardy but tends
to produce suckers from its roots.

"Schneewittchen" is one of the most popular pure white bush roses. It is very dainty in appearance and grows to only about 40 in (1 m) in height. Its 3-in (8-cm) wide, double flowers grow densely together, appear until the first frost, and stand out beautifully from the shiny green foliage. This rose is sometimes sold under the name of "Iceberg."

"Bischofsstadt Paderborn" is a medium-fast-growing rose, can be grown in smaller gardens, and is often planted as a hedge. This rose produces a fine display of semi-double, cup-shaped flowers in a particularly glowing shade of red. It grows to a maximum height of 60 in (1.5 m). The leaves are red at the shooting stage and turn medium green later on.

Rosa moyesii: Whether pink, red, or white, roses of the *Rosa moyesii* group always provide an eye-catching feature, even though they flower only once profusely and then display only an occasional flower here and there. At flowering time, the ordinary *Rosa moyesii* is simply smothered in blood red, single flowers which later develop into glowing red rosehips. The white "Nevada" flowers equally as

profusely. The pink variety, "Marguerite Hilling," is just as beautiful. It creates a real firework display of colors as early as the last month of spring, and will flower a little again in the fall. Height: up to 80 in (2 m). Foliage: matt green, dense.

473

Tall roses with masses of flowers

Climbing roses

This group of roses produces splendid drifts of flowers and can attain a height of up to 20 ft (6 m). Climbing roses spread their enchantment over everything: house walls, embankments, stone walls, fences, statues, pillars, and espaliers. Both once-flowering and continual-flowering types, with or without scent, are available. Climbing roses that have been grafted onto standards are particularly popular as their flowers appear to cascade down like a waterfall.

In principle, climbing roses are not suited to growing on very exposed south-facing walls as they are in danger of getting burned by the sun, the colors of the flowers may bleach out, and there is an increased susceptibility to attack by spider mites. As long as the base of the plant is kept shady and plenty of water is provided, however, some robust varieties may manage in such a position and not suffer from fading colors.

Robust climbing roses
"Colonia," "Compassion," "Dortmund," "Flammentanz," "Ilse Krohn Superior," "New Dawn," "Parade," "Super Dorothy," "Super Excelsa," "Sympathy."

Scented climbing roses
"Casino," Compassion," "Coral Dawn," "Goldfassade," "Ilse Krohn Superior," "Lawinia," "Morning Jewel," "New Dawn," "Parade," "Rosanna," "Sympathie," "White Cockade."

"Sympathie" is a perpetual-flowering rose with large, very double, velvety red flowers. It grows fast, produces robust shoots and is therefore ideal for training against house walls or over arbors or arches. The flowers do not lose their color and will emit a pleasant scent of wild roses. Height: 10-14 ft (3-4 m). Foliage: deep green and shiny.

"White Cockade" is a handsome, creamy white climbing rose with 4 in (10-cm) wide, handsomely formed double flowers which have a strong scent. This rose grows fast and forms shoots up to over 8 ft (2.5 m) long. The medium green leaves are shiny.

"Golden Showers" forms flowers which are under 5 in (12 cm) across, semi-double, light golden yellow which turns lemon yellow as they fade and are grown singly or in clusters at the ends of shoots. The leaves are medium green and shiny. Strictly speaking, it is not a genuine climbing rose but rather a bush rose with shoots which grow 7-10 ft (2-3 m) long.

"Flammentanz" was created out of a *Rosa rubiginosa* hybrid and *Rosa kordesii* and is an improvement on the old "Paul's Scarlett Climber" which was once commonly grown all over Europe. This once-flowering rose grows in a spreading pyramid shape, has lots of foliage, and is very hardy in frosty conditions. The flowers are glowing red, medium large, and double. Height: 14-16 ft (4-5 m). Foliage: matt, dark green.

"Dortmund" has been popular for more than 30 years. Its blood red, single flowers, which hang in luxuriant umbels from strong shoots up to 10 ft (3 m) long, seem to glow because of the white "eye" in the center. The leaves are small and shiny. This plant is particularly effective as a freestanding bush rose.

"Intervilles" is a luxuriantly flowering climbing rose which can be utilized in different ways. It can be used to cover the trunks of old trees and will make a splendid display scrambling over espaliers or arbor beams, or turning fences into a fiery sea of flowers. "Intervilles" was introduced by Robichon in 1968. It flowers more than profusely and right through until the first frosts, displaying glowing, semi-double flowers. Height: 8-12 ft (2.50-3.50 m). The foliage is green and healthy. Other, equally profusely flowering climbing roses include "Blaze Superior," "Flammentanz," "Parkdirektor Riggers," "Rote Flamme," "Santana," and "Sympathie."

Old-fashioned and English roses

These two groups have something in common even although they were created a century apart. They possess all the charm and poetry of the roses we admire in old paintings and tapestries. The main difference between the two groups is that the modern English roses flower more often, a trait rarely found in the old-fashioned species and varieties. Twenty years ago the British rose grower David Austin realized that nostalgia for old roses could help to bring about a spectacular come-back for the old *gallica, damascena,* and *centifolia* roses with their subtle colors, magnificent scent, and beautiful double flowers. He incorporated these old-fashioned roses in his hybridizing work and came up with some astonishing results: roses that look like ancient roses but enjoy all the advantages of modern roses – robust good health, weather hardiness, and continual flowering. In addition, he was able to extend the range of colors by several nuances which did not hitherto exist: apricot yellow, golden yellow, and salmon pink.

At the present time, some 40 different English roses are available on the market. Most of them do not grow a great deal during the first two to three years, but then make up for it. They do not grow quite as tall as their ancestors and are thus extremely suitable for modern gardens which are, unfortunately, becoming smaller and smaller.

"Gros Chou de Hollande" is also referred to as a Bourbon rose or a *centifolia* in rose catalogs, probably because this very old rose is difficult to categorize. It is well worth growing for its large rose red flowers with an alluring scent. Height: just under 80 in (2 m). Once-flowering.

"Charles de Mills" is an enchanting *gallica* rose with conspicuous dense, many-petaled, scented, burgundy red flowers, 3 in (8 cm) across. This upright, fast growing bush can attain a height of 60 in (1.5 m). Once-flowering.

"Madame Isaac Pereire," a Bourbon rose dating back to 1881, grows more than 2 m (80 in) tall, and produces very double, scented flowers in a lovely shade of purple pink. This fast-growing plant forms shoots that are well armored with thorns and has large leaves. It will require some protection during the winter.

"Leda," a damask rose, was created before 1827. It is also known by the name "Painted Damask" and is sometimes seen to flower more than once. The buds are reddish-brown on the outside. The milky white petals are edged with carmine, densely packed in globular, double flowers, and have a wonderful scent. Height: up to 60 in (1.5 m). Deep green, large, elliptical leaves. Hardy in frosts.

"The Squire," with its carmine red flowers, is considered to be one of the most beautiful of the English roses. The very large, many-petaled flowers possess a delectable scent. The colors do not fade in the heat and the petals bear up well in heavy showers. The foliage is dark green. Height: 48 in (1.2 m).

"Königin von Dänemark", also known by the names "Belle Courtisane" or "Naissance de Venus," flowers once only but in profligate splendor. In good years for roses the branches hang down almost to the ground due to the weight of the blooms. This rose is the offspring of *Rosa alba*, probably crossed with a damask rose in 1816. "Königin von Danemark" grows robustly and open and may be up to 6 ft (1.8 m) tall. The shoots are strong and frost-resistant; the foliage dark, almost blue green. The densely packed, many-petaled flowers, first carmine pink, later much paler, emit a scent of wild roses.

"Charles Austin," an English rose, comes in a rather rare shade that goes very well with the colors of old roses. The very large, apricot-colored, double flowers smell of fruit. This plant grows robustly, is bushy, and can attain a height of 5 ft (1.5 m).

Small, low-growing, and versatile

Ground-cover and miniature roses

The ground-cover roses produce shoots up to 10 ft (3 m) long, generally do not grow higher than 32 in (80 cm), creep, grow prostrate or very arched, and rapidly form luxuriant carpets of flowers. Important: do not plant them too close together, otherwise they will force each other to shoot upward by their third year because of a lack of space and will then lose their

"The Fairy" grows spreading, compact, and slightly overhanging.

attractive low-growing habit. Miniature roses flower equally profusely and will also remain low, at a maximum of 14 in (35 cm) in height. In contrast to ground-cover roses, they grow very slowly, so they are very suitable for planting in roomy balcony boxes or tubs.

"The Fairy" produces masses of small flower umbels with double flowers in a very light shade of pink. The delicate shoots branch profusely and soon spread out. This is a robust, healthy rose with small, shiny leaves, which grows to about 28 in (70 cm) tall. Suitable both as ground cover or as a very small bush rose.

"Swany" is a 16-in (40-cm) high, small bush rose with swan white, 1½-2⅓-in (4-6-cm) wide, beautiful double flowers. It grows well and spreads out its long, prostrate or arched branches. Spacing between plants should be 40 in (1 m). The foliage is dark-green and shiny. Very attractive in a front garden and as a cascade on stone walls or gentle slopes.

"Fairy Dance" develops into a carpet during its first year and displays a mass of flower clusters with small, dark red individual flowers. During the second year the branches begin to hang down and will grow to 20-24 in (50-60 cm) long, with shiny foliage.

"Lutin," a charming miniature rose from France, grows no more than 10-12 in (25-30 cm) tall, and flourishes in pots. Its light pink flowers are many-petaled and scented. Also known as "Rosa Gem."

"Orange Meillandina" was introduced in 1980 by Meilland and is eminently suitable for pots and balcony boxes but also looks good as an edging around a border. This 12-16-in (30-40-cm) high miniature rose displays 1¾ in (4-cm) wide, large, signal red, double flowers and is noted for its healthy, medium green, slightly shiny leaves. It also comes as pink "Lady Meillandina" and salmon pink "Pink Meillandina."

"Baby Maskerade" stands out on account of its unusual, attractive coloring. The open, double flowers are orange yellow with copper red edges. This miniature rose grows upright and bushy, has matt green, thick foliage, and is resistant to diseases and pests. Height: 16-20 in (40-50 cm).

Lots of tender care – and pruning

Roses are not always easy to look after. They require attention and care but you will then be rewarded with a splendid display of flowers which often last all summer long. Looking after roses is a relaxing hobby and one of the best ways of countering stress.

Tools for the rose gardener

With the exception of a special fork for digging, most of the tools needed are the ordinary ones used in the garden:

- a spade and garden fork for preparing the soil;
- a claw-rake for scraping away banked-up earth and for loosening the soil;
- a two-tined rose fork for loosening the ground where plants are close together. This is the best tool for minimizing damage to the roots of the roses;
- well-sharpened secateurs;
- branch cutters with long handles, which can cut through thick branches up to about 2 in (4.5 cm) in diameter;
- a knife for digging out weeds;
- a watering can or garden hose;.
- spraying gear for use with pest control agents and plant care agents;
- a grafting knife;
- gardening gloves for protection against thorns.

The ideal planting time

Roses with bare roots can be planted in the fall or spring, while container roses can even be planted in the summer. The second and third months of fall are considered the best time for planting roses in most regions. In regions with rougher weather or where the soil is heavy, it is preferable to plant from the first to second month of spring. Planting methods vary in only one detail: if the roses are planted in the fall, the shoots should not be cut back until the spring or else they may freeze during the winter. The most important consideration is that the soil should be frost-free, fairly dry, and should have been loosened or prepared.

Planting roses

Never, ever add any kind of mineral fertilizer to the soil at the first planting. Fertilizing should not be done until six to eight weeks later, when the rose plant has developed a sufficient number of fine hair-like roots.

Planting roses in containers

Low-growing Floribunda roses, miniature roses and slow-growing ground-cover roses are most suitable. The container should be equipped with drainage holes and be at least 20 in (50 cm) deep and equally wide so that the rose will have enough soil to develop a proper root system. A larger container would be even better. Before filling the container with compost, place a 2-in (5-cm) thick drainage layer of gravel, sand, Hortag, or coarse polystyrene flakes in the bottom of the container. The compost should be bought ready-mixed or composed of loamy garden soil mixed with a little peat and sand.

Roses for large containers and boxes: "Alba Meidiland," "Baby Maskerade," "Bassino," "Bonica 82," "Friesia," "Guletta," "Heinzelmännchen," "Ingrid Weibull," "La Sevillana," "Nozomi," "Red Yesterday," "Rosmarin 89," "Schneewittchen," "Swany," "Vatertag," "Zwergkönig 78."

Watering

Roses should only be watered until they have developed a proper root system. Always water according to the principle of better once very well than three times superficially. After two to three years you will no longer need to water your roses (except during unusually dry periods, in very dry positions or in sandy soil). Before watering, loosen the soil around the stem a little and then water the root area abundantly. **Warning:** Do not wet the leaves when watering as this will promote the formation of sooty mold. Also avoid wetting the leaves of your roses with the lawn sprinkler.

"Raubritter" only flowers once in high summer but then it displays an almost profligate splendor of blooms.

Hoeing

In the spring, after taking away any winter protection from your roses and removing the banked-up soil, it is time to hoe the surface of the soil all around the roses. This will enable air, warmth, and moisture to penetrate the deeper layers of the soil. You should also hoe before and after every watering, as well as after thundery downpours and, of course, whenever weeds start growing. We recommend using a two-tined rose fork for dense plantings of roses, as this will make the job a lot easier without damaging the roots. Hoeing is also very beneficial in late fall.

You will not need to hoe so often if you use mulch.

Mulching

Mulching means laying finely chopped organic material at the plant's "feet." This is quite an easy job to carry out if you have free-standing bush roses. Mulching will smother the growth of weeds, keep the soil moist, and encourage the development of beneficial micro-organisms in the soil, which produce humus and thus provide the plants with additional nutrients. It will not, however, replace fertilizing! Suitable materials: dried lawn clippings, chopped straw, and well-rotted manure. The ideal mixture is one consisting of both coarse and fine particles. The best time to start mulching is in the spring after removing the banked-up soil, hoeing, and fertilizing. In the fall, you can work this material, which by now will have decomposed, into the soil you use to bank up the roses.

Planting

Planting roses with bare roots

Remove any packing materials from the roses. If the plants have been delivered during a period of frosty weather, they should be left to thaw out slowly in a cool room.

1. Water the roses a few hours before planting them; the grafting point (the thick "lump" beneath the branches) should be immersed in the water.

2. Cutting back: remove all damaged roots to avoid danger of decay and shorten any long ones to about 8 in (20 cm). Cutting back the roots makes planting easier and encourages the formation of the fine roots that absorb water. Simultaneously, prune above-ground shoots – not too much if you are planting in the fall, more if planting in spring. This cuts down on surfaces that will lose water through evaporation and the rose will retain more strength for the formation of new roots.

3. Dig a hole deep and wide enough to accommodate the roots comfortably and to enable the grafting point to end up about 2 in (5 cm) below the surface of the soil. If the roots appear to grow mainly in one direction, do not dig a round hole but make it oval. Hold the rose plant in the hole and spread out the roots on a small hillock of soil.

4. Add a mixture of soil and compost until the hole is filled loosely. Then press the compost down firmly (or carefully tread it down), until a neat gulley for watering is obtained.

5. Water this depression several times with plenty of water which will help to wash the soil close to the roots.

6. When the water has drained away, shovel in the rest of the soil and check the position of the grafting point once again.

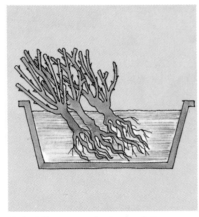

1. Let the rose plants soak for several hours before planting.

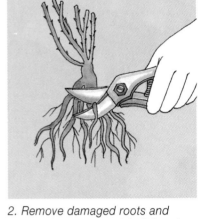

2. Remove damaged roots and shorten long ones to 8 in (20 cm).

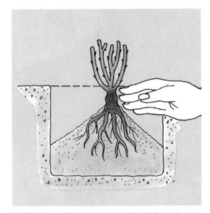

3. The grafting point should end up about 2 in (5 cm) below the surface.

4. Fill the hole with planting compost and gently press it down.

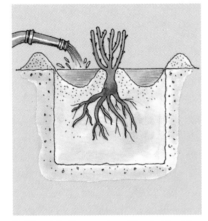

5. Provide the roots with plenty of water.

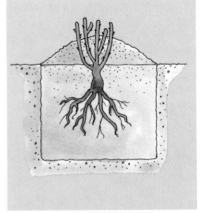

6. Pile up loose soil to protect the shoots from frost and sun.

Surround the shoots with a "mole-hill" of banked-up soil to protect the rose from frost, sun, and wind.
NB: Plant waxed roses in the same way.

My tip: Plants which arrive when the soil is frozen or covered in snow should be put in a bucket of damp sand or soil and placed in a frost-free place (e.g. a cellar or shed). As soon as the soil is frost- and snow-free, you can plant out the roses.

Planting roses in containers
Water the plant thoroughly. Make the hole for planting large enough so that a hand's width of space is left all around the inside of the container. Remove the plastic cover or pot from the plant but do not prune the plant.
Loosen the surface of the rootstock a little. Stand the rose in the hole so that the top of the rootstock is level with the surface of the soil. Fill up the spaces with a soil and compost mixture. Press the compost down well and water the plant thoroughly.

Planting standard roses
Around 95% of standard roses are sold with bare roots, the rest having well-developed root systems in containers. The method of planting will depend on the type of standard you have purchased. In any case, the support post should be driven into the planting hole beforehand. After that, place the rose plant next to it, leaving a space of about 2-3¾ in (5-8 cm). After planting, pressing down, and watering, tie the rose to the support post with figure-of-eight-shaped loops. Protect the stem from pressure at the tie by inserting a piece of rubber or sacking.

My tip: It is a good idea to have treated the support post some weeks beforehand with a plant-

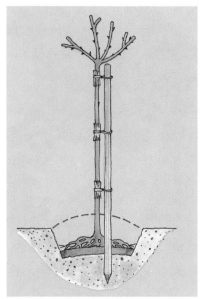

7. *Drive in a support stake before planting a standard rose.*

friendly wood preservative. Plastic sticks are particularly durable (available from garden centers).

Planting climbing roses
Both the size of the hole for planting and the cutting back of the plant are done in the same way as for the usual planting method.
If you intend to grow the rose on a wall espalier, dig the planting hole 8 in (20 cm) away from the wall so that the roots will not run the risk of drying out. Lay the roots in the hole at an angle so that the above-ground shoots bend toward the ties. The grafting point should still be 2 in (5 cm) below the surface of the ground. Shovel in the soil-compost mixture, press it down and water the plant thoroughly. Water often during the first year.

If you cannot plant the rose immediately
In this case, you should heel the roots into the soil in the garden.

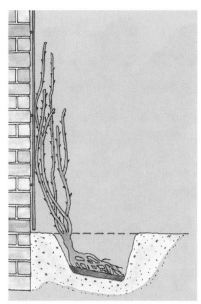

8. *Climbing roses should be planted leaning toward their support.*

Choose a shady, sheltered spot and dig a slanted hole, lay the rose in it, cover it with soil, then water well. Roses in containers should be placed in the shade and watered.

Spacing between plants
● Bedding and tea roses: 7-10 plants per 10.75 sq ft (1 sq m).
● Miniature roses: 10-12 plants per 10.75 sq ft (1 sq m).
● Ground-cover roses: 1 plant per 10.75 sq ft (1 sq m).
● Climbing roses: require a wall surface area of 160 sq ft (15 sq m). For espaliers, a distance of 10 ft (3 m) should be left between plants.
● Standard and cascade roses: a distance of several yards (meters) should be left for appearance's sake.
● Bush roses: will require 16-75 sq ft (1.5-7 sq m) for optimal development, depending on the species and the variety.

Climbing, supporting, and espaliers

Climbing roses can produce shoots up to 20 ft (6 m) long. As they do not possess any tendrils or other organs for clinging, they have to be given help and support. The classic rose arches, made of fired zinc, for use freestanding or for leaning against a wall, can be bought from garden centers. Various arches can also be placed together to form pavilions, double arches, and arcaded walks. In addition, there are numerous other possibilities, e.g. rose arches made of hard PVC or other plastics, cascade rose supports, support fences and espalier kits for driving into the ground, T-espaliers, and pyramids. There is always the alternative of building your own individual rose espalier or frame out of treated wooden battens.

Fertilizing

Plants which grow as fast and flower as abundantly as roses should be very well supplied with nutrients. This is done by fertilizing and is all the more important if the roses have been growing in the same place for some time. Freshly planted roses should not be fertilized until they have been established for a while.

Like all other plants, roses need nitrogen (N) for growing leaves, phosphorous (P) for producing flowers, and potassium (K) for ripening wood. They also need calcium and silicon to strengthen their tissues as well as iron and magnesium for synthesizing chlorophyll.

Head in the sun, feet in the shade
Herbaceous plants and shrubs planted beforehand will prevent the soil from drying out too quickly.

Which type of fertilizer to use

It does not matter much in what form the rose receives these nutrients. There are different types of fertilizer to choose from.

Organic fertilizer, like ripe garden compost, nettle brew, or other plant brews, horn or bonemeal, or well-rotted manure, promotes the development of useful micro-organisms in the soil and thus encourages the formation of humus. However, such materials often contain too much nitrogen and cannot be regulated properly. As it often takes months until they are broken down sufficiently to be available to the plants, they can be spread on the soil in the fall/winter.

Mineral fertilizers, also called NPK fertilizers, are immediately available for the plant's use. These are applied in the spring when they are required for shoot formation and the growth of leaves (apply in the amount of 2½-3 ounces/70-80 g per 10.75 sq ft (1 sq m).

Organic-mineral fertilizer is also applied in spring (about 4¼-5¼ ounces/120-150 g per 10.75 sq ft/1 sq m)

Further notes on fertilizing: The ideal situation is if it rains after fertilizing. In dry weather, plenty of watering will be required or the fertilizer may "burn" the roses.

If you apply organic-mineral fertilizer to your roses after the beginning of the last month of summer, the roses will remain for far too long in their vegetative phase and this will prevent the shoots from becoming woody and hard, which is extremely important for the hardiness and health of the plant. It is preferable, during the first month of fall, to work 1-1¼ ounces/30-50 g per 10.75 sq ft (1 sq m) of magnesium sulphate loosely into the soil around the roses. This will encourage the wood to form properly before the winter.

My tip: I always combine organic and mineral fertilizing. During the spring I work one handful of mineral or organic fertilizer per plant into the banked-up soil. At the first sign of flowering, the roses should receive another equal dose. After that I observe a strict fertilizer rest period. In late fall I apply well-rotted compost to my plants.

Indicator plants

Indicator plants are generally referred to as weeds and only germinate in particular soil conditions. However, they are not 100% reliable as they sometimes invade untypical terrain.

● Indicators for nutrient-rich soil that is good for roses: scarlet pimpernel (*Anagallis arvensis*), dog's mercury (*Mercurialis perennis*), stinging nettle (*Urtica*), chamomile (*Matricaria chamomilla*), speedwell (species of *Veronica*), fumitory (*Fumaria officinalis*), wild radish (*Raphanus raphanistrum*), and tufted vetch (*Vicia cracca*).

● Places where the following grow naturally are unsuitable for roses: corn mint (*Mentha arvensis*), mare's tail (*Hippuris vulgaris*), and coltsfoot (*Tussilago farfara*).

Pruning roses

The effect of pruning
Roses flower on the young wood, i.e. on shoots which emerge from buds in the spring. The fattest buds sit right at the ends of the shoots. They start developing first, forming leaves and later flowers. The smaller buds farther down remain dormant and will not start to develop until later on. This means that the more you cut back, the longer you will have to wait for buds. On the other hand, cutting back does encourage the formation of new shoots. Cutting back also promotes long life, a willingness to flower, and the health of the rose plant.
The main pruning of roses is done in the spring, after removing the banked-up soil.

Repeat-flowering roses should also be pruned regularly during the summer. When the first flowering is over, you should remove the remains of the flowers but not the healthy-looking buds below them (the best one is the thickest bud in the leaf axil of the second leaf under the inflorescence). This encourages a second flowering.
Once-flowering roses should not be cut back after flowering as they will often produce attractive rose hips.

Some tips on pruning
Crushed or torn shoots, as well as parts that have not been cut off cleanly, can be a source of invasion by all manner of diseases. For this reason you should only use the very sharpest scissors and secateurs. Make sure that the cut part of the plant is not dirty. If the cut branch or shoot is thicker than a pencil, it is advisable to paint over it with a tree sealant. Diseased or infested shoots should be cut back to healthy wood. Healthy wood is recognizable

Remove all suckers
Suckers grow from the stock below the grafting point. Remove some of the soil and, if possible, cut off the sucker as close to the root as possible.

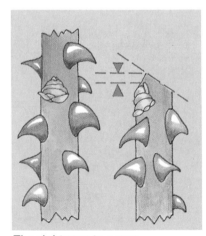

The right way to prune
Cut off the shoot ⅛-¼ in (3-5 mm) above an outward-facing bud.

by its white pith; diseased wood has brown pith.

The planting cut
Shorten the above-ground shoots when planting or moving plants. Cutting back in this way reduces the surface area that is exposed to evaporation and lets the plant retain more strength for the formation of new, fine, water-absorbing roots. When planting in the fall, cut back sparingly, but in the spring cut back radically, leaving only a few buds on the outsides of the stems.

The maintenance cut
This should take place during the first or second month of spring when the buds begin to swell. (If you wish, you can start cutting back long, lanky shoots in the fall.) In principle:
● It is best to cut too little than too much. Radical cutting back always results in fewer flowers.
● Let thick shoots remain longer; weak or thin ones can be cut back farther.
● Old, diseased, dried up, crossing, or dense wood should be removed.
● Only cut away the faded flowers of continual-flowering varieties (see left column).

My tip: Minor injuries cannot be avoided when cutting roses, in spite of the protection of gloves. Disinfect open wounds immediately with a suitable remedy from your first aid kit. If you deal with roses on a frequent basis, you should make sure you are protected by an injection against tetanus.

Continual-flowering bush roses
(see illustrations 1 and 2)
Frozen, withered, or dense wood and shoots which grow sideways should be thinned out. Lightly cut

back shoots from the previous year and, if necessary, cut back thin shoots to three or four buds.

Exception: Do not cut once-flowering roses. Only very old wood which bore hardly any flowers the year before should be removed. This will rejuvenate the plant.

Continual-flowering climbing roses

(see illustrations 3 and 4)
Old, withered wood can be cut back to just above the ground. Shoots which grow diagonally should be removed. New, strong lateral shoots should be cut back to two to five buds. Overhanging shoots should be tidied and tied back.

Exception: With once-flowering roses, pruning should take place immediately after flowering so that the young shoots can grow strong before the fall. Flowering shoots branching off from healthy main shoots can be cut back to three to four buds. Old wood should be removed just as with continual-flowering climbing roses.

Bedding and tea roses

(see illustrations 5 and 6)
Shorten the shoots by about a third. Cutting more radically will produce longer-stemmed flowers for use as cut flowers. If this is what you want, you should cut back weak-growing varieties to 4-6 in (10-15 cm) and medium-growing varieties to 6-10 in (15-25 cm).

Standard roses

(see illustrations 7 and 8)
Cut back shoots to about 6-8 in (15-20 cm) so that a beautiful round crown is produced. Later, pinch out the new leaves to about three leaves so that the crown becomes bushy.

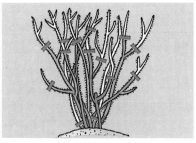

1. Dead wood which is densely packed should be cut out.

2. Shoots from the previous year should be shortened.

3. New lateral shoots should be shortened to two to five buds.

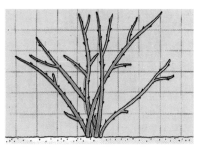

4. Dead wood and crossing shoots must also be removed.

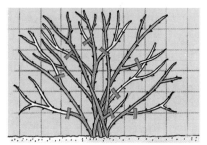

5. Shorten shoots by about a third and remove crossing shoots.

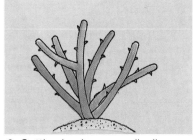

6. Cutting back more radically produces long-stemmed flowers.

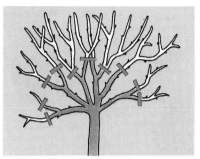

7. Pruning standard roses: cut back the shoots to 6-8 in (15-20 cm).

8. Later, shorten the shoots to three leaves per shoot.

487

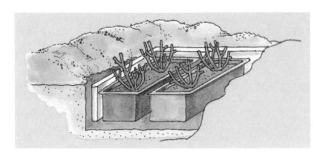

Balcony roses overwintering in an earth pit
Dig a large pit. Line it with polystyrene sheeting. Stand the rose boxes in the pit and cover them with leaves and brushwood.

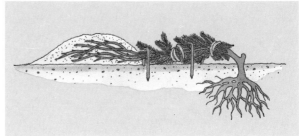

Overwintering young standard roses
Bend the rose downward. Protect the stems with conifer branches and fix them to the ground with pieces of wire. Cover the crown with soil.

Protection in the winter

Most roses (apart from wild roses which, without exception, are all hardy) are grateful for winter protection. Before beginning to bank up the soil and wrap your roses up in the last month of fall, remove all the fallen leaves from the ground (in which, for example, the spores of sooty mold like to overwinter). Any leaves still left on the shoots should be cut off. Then bank up the soil around the stem of the rose plant to a height of about 8-12 in (20-30 cm). Suitable mediums are compost, well-rotted manure or soil. On no account use peat as it absorbs water and would work like an icepack when the temperature drops below freezing!

Tea roses should also be given protective packing using material such as conifer branches which will shield them from aggressive winter sun and drying winds.

Climbing roses should also receive extra protection by tying layers of fine conifer branches over them. Climbing roses on posts, etc, should be enveloped in brushwood, straw or sacking. Tie up the shoots beforehand!

Standard roses are particularly at risk as their grafting point is situated immediately below the crown. Younger standards (see illustration above) are best loosened from their support, carefully bent over toward the ground (if necessary, loosen the roots a little) and then fixed in position with crossed sticks. The crown (remove the leaves because of the risk of decay!) should be covered with soil. In the case of older specimens which can no longer be bent over, envelop the plant from the crown right down to below the grafting point in conifer branches, sacking, or straw. Do not use plastic sheeting!

Balcony roses should not be left outside in winter as the small amount of soil in the container will not be sufficient to protect the roots from the cold. They should be overwintered in a frost-free room (cellar, garage, shed, attic) or sunk in a flower bed. For this purpose, dig a sufficiently large pit and line it with polystyrene sheets or thick cardboard. The roses should be pruned first, then placed in the pit still in their tubs, and covered with straw, thin twigs, dry leaves, and/or conifer branches (see illustration left). The soil removed from the pit should be banked up all around the edge of the covering to secure it, but not on the covering itself! In the spring, the tubs are retrieved from their winter quarters and placed in a bright, but not sunny position so that they can begin shooting. If night frosts are forecast, take them inside again!

Removing the winter protection

Toward the end of the first month of spring, the conifer branches can be removed but do not remove the banked-up earth until no more late frosts are expected, generally around the second month of spring. Standard roses should not be straightened up again immediately, but should be left lying for several days after removing the covering. They can then be carefully straightened up, the loosened roots should be firmly pressed down and the standard stem tied back to the support post with figure-of-eight-shaped loops.

A charming two-colored rose
When planted in a group, this compact and low-growing tea rose "Caribia" produces the effect of a sea of flame.

Romantic climbing roses

This house in Tuscany looks as if it has been uninhabited for a long time. The roof tiles are crumbling, the rendering is cracked, the drapes are closed. In winter it must look quite forbidding. In the last month of spring, however, these old roses transform the ancient walls into Sleeping Beauty's castle with their abundance of flowers! Only climbing roses are able to achieve such an attractive wall covering with their long shoots. This rose might be "Paul's Scarlett Climber" which forms 20-ft (6-m) long shoots thickly beset with faintly scented, scarlet clusters of flowers. This variety of climbing rose has been planted throughout Europe since 1916 and is still very popular. It stands up to wind and weather with vigor and displays its timeless beauty, just like the old house itself.

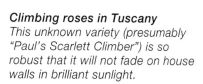

Climbing roses in Tuscany
This unknown variety (presumably "Paul's Scarlett Climber") is so robust that it will not fade on house walls in brilliant sunlight.

Prevention is better than cure

Ladybirds form a first defence against aphids but are not always able to dominate these pests and then it becomes necessary to spray the roses. If the right type of protection is used in the right position, the rose will usually be resistant to all attackers.

Just as there are no humans who never, ever catch a cold, there are no absolutely resistant roses. This is because of the multitude of environmental factors which affect the rose in any given position. Some varieties thrive particularly well in a certain area but will barely survive in another environment. Some enjoy excellent health for many years and then suddenly become sickly as if they had exhausted all their strength. It is not always possible to find out the causes of poor health. Still, several things can be done to protect your plants from harm.

Precautionary measures

First of all, if you are not quite certain that you are able to offer your roses the very best growing conditions, you should settle for robust roses.
These roses have been tested under adverse conditions and will put up with a great deal. Further measures which may help to render the use of plant protection agents unnecessary or at least minimize their necessity, are:

● the right variety for the right position;
● good preparation of the soil;
● balanced fertilizing, which should cease at the correct time;
● correct care (pruning, working the soil, winter protection);
● careful observation;
● planting accompanying plants whose emanations tend to ward off pests and fungi, e.g. nasturtiums, garlic, lavender, marjoram, *Tagetes*, wormwood, ornamental chives, and onions;
● the avoidance of monocultures (too many roses or *Rosaceae* in one position).

Warning: In the case of gardens of newly built houses, do remember that the soil may have become densely compacted and hard deeper down because of the action of caterpillar vehicles, excavators, etc. Roses which are planted on top of this will rarely thrive and will tend to look sickly as normal water percolation has been considerably disrupted and the roots will become diseased.

Soil samples: Before planting, bore several holes 20 in (50 cm) deep in the position where you intend to plant, and fill them with water. If this has not drained away within an hour, the subsoil will have to be loosened up and improved or drained.

Method: Dig a 24-in (60-cm) deep trench along the entire length of the flower bed. In this, lay a plastic pipe with plenty of perforations in such a way that it leads downward away from the bed. (If this is not possible, the standard method of loosening the soil will have to be employed.) Fill the trench with 2 in (5 cm) of gravel. Afterward, the roses can be planted or replanted. If the roses have just been dug up, cut off any decayed roots and shorten the shoots. If more than half of the roots are damaged, the roses should be replaced with new ones.

Controlling pests and diseases

In principle, the sooner methods of controlling pests and diseases are implemented, the more effective they are and the less the healthy development of the rose will suffer. Pests and diseases can be controlled in various ways:

Chemically: with insecticides, fungicides, and other substances which ward off harmful pests.

Biologically: with plant and mineral plant-care agents and fortifying agents (oils and essences, plant extracts, algae preparations). Also with useful insects.

Mechanically: by collecting beetles, caterpillars, infested leaves, etc. by hand and by cutting out diseased shoots and webs. By scratching off and spraying down infested parts of plants.

Warning: All plant protection agents should be kept out of reach of children and pets.

Employing useful insects

If you find masses of ladybirds crawling about on your roses, it is a sure sign that aphids are present. Aphids draw ladybirds as a delicious banquet draws a gourmet. If you are lucky, their appetite will be sufficient to wipe out the aphids. Very often, however, they cannot cope with the sheer numbers and then spraying becomes necessary. What kills aphids, unfortunately, also kills ladybirds.

Recipes for plant-fortifying agents

The following three plant brews have been used very successfully on roses by organic gardeners.

Mare's tail brew: Soak 7 ounces (200 g) dried leaves (obtainable from herbalists) in 2½ gallons (10 liters) water for 24 hours. Boil for an hour. Leave to cool and strain. Dilute it as 1 part brew to 10 parts water and drench the roses every two weeks with this concoction to fortify their tissues and as a prevention against fungal infections. Mare's tail can also be obtained as an extract from garden suppliers.

Garlic brew: Chop up 10 cloves of garlic and boil them with 3¾ pints (2 liters) water. Let cool and dilute with ten times the amount of water. Spray the roses weekly with the brew. Do not forget to spray the soil beneath! Also spray if the rose is diseased. Garlic contains fungicides and antibacterial sulphur compounds which are still effective even when extremely diluted.

Fermented nettle brew: Allow 2 pounds (1 kg) fresh nettle leaves or 7 ounces (200 g) dried leaves (from health food stores and herbalists) to ferment in 2½ gallons (10 liters) rainwater for two weeks.

What can be read in the appearance of leaves

Damage caused by the climate and mistakes in care

Frost damage: wavy, blistery leaves with spots and brown edges. The cause is late frosts. Leaves which are still growing are particularly at risk.

Sunbun: these spots are caused by watering the leaves in full sunlight. The drops of water act as tiny magnifying glasses. Not a fungal disease!

Waterlogging, also automobile fumes and herbicides, will cause this damage in which the leaves display large yellow patches spreading from the stalk of the leaf.

Dryness: leaves which turn yellow in irregular patches and suddenly drop off indicate that the soil has dried out.

Acid burns are caused if some of the grains of mineral fertilizer land on wet leaves. Young shoots are particularly at risk.

What to do

Damage to the leaves causes the rose to lose vital surface area that is required for the assimilation of sunlight. Damaged leaves – with the shoot if necessary – should be removed to encourage the formation of new leaves. In the case of waterlogging, the plant should be dug up and the hole carefully drained. Diseased roots and crown should be cut back carefully and the rose – even if it is the middle of the growth phase – should be replanted. If the weather is extremely dry, water the plant once, very thoroughly and plentifully, then loosen the wet soil.

Symptoms of deficiency

Nitrogen deficiency: The symptoms are sickly-looking shoots, slender, pale green leaves which drop off early and, occasionally, lots of little reddish dots.

Potassium deficiency: The young leaves shine reddish-brown, the older ones have brown edges, the leaves remain small. Often occurs on sandy soil.

Phosphorous deficiency: Young, dark green leaves with purple spots on the undersides and early fall of leaves are symptoms of this problem.

Chlorosis (pale leaves): The absorption of iron needed for the synthesis of chlorophyll is hindered by a high content of calcium compounds in the soil, waterlogging and damage to the wood. Only the veins in the leaves remain green.

Magnesium deficiency: The leaves display yellowish-red, dead areas in the center of the leaf. Older leaves fall off first. The synthesis of sunlight by chlorophyll is impaired.

What to do
If there is a deficiency in the most important plant nutrients like nitrogen, phosphorous, and potassium, rapid relief should be provided by using a fast-working mineral fertilizer or a special rose fertilizer which, as a rule, will also contain the necessary trace elements. If magnesium is missing, magnesium sulphate can be worked into the soil. If chlorosis is displayed, fertilizing the leaves with iron chelates or plant tonics will help. If chlorosis was caused by damage to the wood, the yellowing shoots should be cut back to healthy wood, and then nitrogen-based fertilizer should be given – but only until the first month of summer.

Stir daily until the brew has stopped producing foam.
Dilute as 1 part brew with 10 parts rainwater. Combat the smell of fermentation by adding valerian flower tincture to the brew.

The correct way to spray
Roses, and particularly their young shoots and leaves, often react very sensitively to chemical plant protection agents. The following points need some consideration:
● Any insecticide or fungicide should be suitable for roses, so ask an expert for advice.
● The doses should be correct. One way to be sure is to use dosing devices which enable the gardener to measure out even the smallest quantities.
● Any brew used for spraying should be distributed as a fine spray and should be dry before night.
● Do not use the sprays too close to the plant.
● Follow all advice given by the manufacturer about toxicity, risk to health, and the protection of groundwater and bees for the sake of the environment. Insecticides which are dangerous or not dangerous to bees, as the case may be, should state so on the packaging.
● After using spraying devices, clean them meticulously with water, adding a squirt of dishwashing liquid. Do not let rinsing water run away into the main sewage, use it for watering!

My tip: The dosages of plant protection agents are often indicated as a percentage. They may be expressed in grams (g), milliliters (ml), or cubic centimeters (cm^3), although all these measurements are almost identical. Convert as follows:
● 0.02% means 0.2 g/ml/cm^3 plant protection agent to 4 cups (1 liter) water;

Changes in leaves due to fungal infections

Black spot: Cool nights after rainfall favor this condition. The star-shaped dark spots will appear from the second month of summer onward, often even on young wood. Consequence: loss of all leaves.

Powdery mildew: This covers leaves, shoots, and buds with a gray white, powder-like film. Cause: unbalanced fertilizing, warm, dry air.

Rose rust: Pinhead-sized blisters on the undersides of the leaves, containing orange red dust (spores of the fungus), which then turn black from the last month of summer onward.

Leaf spot disease: This occurs more often in damp positions. The leaves are covered in variously shaped spots. If the infestation is severe, total loss of leaves may result.

Sooty mold: This fungus colonizes the sticky secretions (honeydew) of aphids and scale insects and forms a dirty black film.

What to do

Fungal infections seldom disappear by themselves. The causes are not always poor care or a tendency inherent in the variety. Varying weather conditions from year to year play an important role too. If the roses are extremely badly infested, it is worth removing all the leaves in the fall, even from the ground. In the spring, spray the plant and the ground with mare's tail brew and garlic brew or with a non-toxic fungicide (ask in your local garden center). In the case of an acute infestation with black spot, mildew, or other fungal infections, try repeat spraying with fungicides specifically formulated for roses. Sooty mold fungi will not disappear until the aphids have been eliminated.

● 0.06% means 0.6 g/ml/cm³ to 6½ pints (3 liters) water or 2 g/ml/cm³ to 2½ gallons (10 liters) water;
● 0.1% means 1 g/ml/cm³ plant protection agent to 4 cups (1 liter) water, 3 g/ml/cm³ to 6½ pints (3 liters) water or 10 g/ml/cm³ to 2½ gallons (10 liters) water.

Changes to the buds

Decaying buds are caused by a *Botrytis* fungus which may also infest leaves and leaf stalks. Control: remove all infested parts.
Nibbled buds: This is caused by an insect. Control: not necessary as the problem only occurs sporadically.
Holes made by insects feeding: Control: not necessary as the problem occurs only sporadically.
Stunted buds: The cause is thrips. The buds do not completely unfold and become crippled. Control: cut off infested parts and spray with an insecticide.

Changes in the shoots

Blind shoots: These are caused by insects (e.g. gall midges). The shoot stops growing and does not form any flowers. Remedy: cut the shoot back to the next healthy buds.
Deformed shoots: Two or three shoots grow together by becoming flattened. The cause is thought to be a hormonal disturbance. Remedy: not necessary, as the general growth is not affected.
Cracks in the bark: Caused by frost, radical pruning or overfertilizing with nitrogen. Remedy: damaged shoots should be pruned in the spring.
Tumors: These are caused by bacteria which invade or are accidentally introduced and are then able to develop due to an unfavorable position.

Control: remove infested parts immediately. Spray frequently with garlic brew to strengthen the plant. If necessary, replant the rose in completely fresh soil.

Scale insects: These sit underneath whitish-yellow to brown waxy scales and live off the sap of the leaves. Control: scratch them off, or spray with special oil (ask at your garden center) in the case of severe infestation.

Withering shoot tips: The cause is the rose borer (*Ardis*) whose larvae bore into the pith. Control: immediately cut back infested shoots and branches. The eggs are located at the shoot tips and base of leaves! Paint the cut surfaces with tree sealant. Repeatedly spray the plant with insecticide.

Changes to the flowers

Red to brownish spots on the petals: This is caused by long-term rainfall. The flowers are unable to dry off and develop spots. Best prevention: choose varieties which are known to be rain-resistant for regions with much rain. Avoid positions which are not well-aired. We recommend immediately cutting off spotty roses in order to encourage the formation of new flowers.

A rose bud appearing out of a rose flower: This phenomenon was once a source of wonder to Goethe! A new shoot grows out of the center of the rose. This happens more often in small-flowered varieties and is no cause for alarm. Just cut them off.

Tattered petals: Either a feature of the variety or caused by hungry insects like earwigs. Take immediate steps to control the problem.

Damage caused by salt

Rose beds which are situated in front gardens near to a sidewalk are often at risk in winter from salt strewn to prevent people from slip-

Changes in leaves caused by pests

Owlet moth caterpillars: The clutches of eggs deposited on the top sides of leaves do not harm the plant. However, when the caterpillars have emerged, you have a potentially harmful situation. The caterpillars hide in the flowers and eat the petals.

Leaf wasp: Its green larvae, ⁵⁄₁₆-³⁄₈ in (6-10 mm) long, turn the leaves into skeletons. Often buds and shoots are eaten too. In some years infestation is particularly severe.

Sawflies: This seems to occur suddenly. The feeding canals on the uppersides of the leaves are caused by the larvae. Infested leaves drop off prematurely.

Aphids: Roses are infested by greenfly. They damage the young shoots, buds and leaves, which become crippled. Cause: warm, dry weather.

Small rose-leaf wasp: The wasp, which grows up to ¼ in (5 mm) long, lays its eggs along the edges of the leaves, which then roll up into tubes and are no longer able to function properly.

What to do

Depending on the degree of severity, remove the leaves, pinch off the egg clusters, cut away webs, and collect the beetles and caterpillars or wash the aphids off with a strong stream of water. If none of this helps, repeatedly spray the plants against biting and sucking insects with insecticides, meticulously following the manufacturer's directions (ask for products specifically formulated for roses).

Warning: Do not spray during flowering time with agents that are toxic to bees. Repeat the treatment according to the manufacturer's directions as one treatment alone will not eliminate the "rearguard" action of these pests.

ping in icy weather. The full effects are not noticed until the spring. The symptoms of soil that is polluted with salt vary greatly and include falling leaves, crippling of parts of plants, discoloration of the leaves, and impaired growth. A great deal of rainfall may dilute the concentration of salt in the soil and it will also help if the water is able to run off into deeper layers of the ground.

Damage by wildlife

If you live in the country or at the edge of a town near a wood or fields, you may find yourself confronted by damage such as nibbled buds. Rose buds and fresh green shoots are a regular delicacy for deer. If the garden is not fenced in, the only thing to do is to employ substances which drive off wildlife by their odor. These agents are sprayed on the plants or old rags are soaked with them and then hung at a height of 30 in (75 cm), spaced about 16-20 ft (5-6 m) apart, near the roses. Please try to make sure that these agents are non-toxic to bees.

Some agents may not be used in areas where the groundwater is protected by law.

Where else to find advice

If you just cannot figure out what is the matter with your roses, you can turn to your local rose-growing club or write to the troubleshooting column of a gardening periodical. You should receive an answer within two weeks if you enclose a stamped, self-addressed envelope.

Changes in leaves due to pests

Vine weevils will often consume leaves, shoot tips and buds overnight, without leaving much. The larvae are worse as they even gobble up the roots.

Leaf-cutting bee: Holes and irregular chunks eaten out of young leaves point to this pest. This damage generally occurs in the spring and is usually only sporadic.

Red spider mites: The worst rose pest. They suck the sap out of the leaves until they wither and drop off. Plants in extremely hot, sunny positions are most at risk.

Rose cicada: Light-colored, winged, jumping insects which suck the sap from the leaves and cause whitish-yellow spots. They occur more often in dry, warm positions.

Rose tortrix moth: At first, a small, brownish caterpillar appears, which nibbles at the leaves and petals and then spins webs on the leaves where the larvae form chrysalises.

My tip: Vine weevils can now be controlled using biological methods such as nematodes (eelworms) which can be ordered through garden centers. The best time for this treatment is the end of the first month of fall to the middle of the second month, or from the end of the second month of spring to the beginning of the second month of summer, always in the evenings. The larvae-consuming nematodes require sufficient moisture in the soil for their development and soil temperatures of more than 54°F (12°C). This method will be unsuccessful in cold weather. Obviously, you do not wish to create an infestation of nematodes so you must implement such a method with care.

Pink roses are everyone's favorite

When leafing through a rose catalog, it seems that, after red, pink is
the most frequent color for roses.
Pink appears in countless shades,
ranging from silver rose to baby
pink, apricot pink, shocking pink,
and coral pink right across the
palette to deepest purple. You
might even say that pink is the
characteristic color of the entire
genus and deeply entrenched in its
genetic programme. It is known that
very many wild roses, the ancestors
of our modern varieties, have
flowers in shades of pink: *Rosa gallica*; *Rosa rubiginosa* – the sweet-
briar or eglantine rose; *Rosa
rugosa;* and *Rosa canina* – the dog
rose; to name just a few. The color
pink is predominant among the old-
fashioned roses and even in modern cultivars. The new English roses
by David Austin display lovely pastel
shades that have never been seen
before. "Trier 2000," the youngest
prize-winning Kordes cultivar, has
pink flowers, as does "Manou
Meilland" (photo, right), demonstrat-
ing that this color will always appear
in ever more fascinating new variations in the future.

*One variety – many shades of
color*
*Whether in bud, half open, com-
pletely open, or almost faded, this
bedding rose "Manou Meilland,"
with a delicate lemony scent,
displays a different shade of pink at
every stage.*

498

The rose grower's ambition

What would you do if you discovered a rose which is thought no longer to exist in the garden of a friend? Perhaps you would like to grow extra roses of a particular variety. It is not impossible to propagate your favorites. The simplest method is from cuttings – the more tricky one is by grafting.

Roses can be propagated in different ways:
- from seeds;
- from shoots growing out of roots;
- from shoots which hang down and take root (layering);
- from cuttings;
- by grafting.

Propagating from seed

This is only possible with wild or pure species roses which have not been grafted; in other words, whose splendid flowers are derived from the same stock as the roots. As most cultivated roses are grafted, they cannot be propagated from seed because the new plants that would grow from the seed would look nothing like the one you had intended to propagate. Propagating from seed is only carried out if you wish to obtain a robust and healthy stock for grafting purposes. These "wild plants" can be obtained from tree nurseries. The best known grafting stocks come from varieties of the dog rose, *Rosa canina* "Intermis" and "Pfänders."

Propagating from shoots

This is only possible with roses which produce long, trailing shoots, for example, *Rosa nitida*, *Rosa omeiensis* "Pteracantha," *Rosa rugosa* and its varieties "Alba" and "Hansa," *Rosa spinosissima* (Scotch rose or burnet rose) as well as *Rosa gallica*.
The long shoots can be chopped off with a sharp spade and planted in the desired position.

Propagating from hanging shoots which take root (layering)

Roses with pliable branches are suitable for this method. A long shoot can be buried 8 in (20 cm) in the soil in spring or summer with just the tip still visible. The part which is deepest in the soil should be stripped of leaves and have a long slice cut off beneath one bud. Dust the cut with rooting powder and keep it open with a small wedge the size of a matchstick. The shoot can be anchored to the ground with pieces of wire bent into U-shapes.

Fill the hole with moistened soil mixed with peat and press this down lightly. Mark the rooting position with a stone. Prop up the end of the shoot that is sticking out above ground with another stone. Rooting will take place during the fall. Do not separate the shoot from the mother plant until the following spring. Then cut it with a sharp spade.

Creating your own roses

This can be a fascinating adventure as you never know in advance exactly what the result is going to be. The aim when crossing plants is always to retain the best features of the two different roses which serve as the father and mother plants and unite them in a new variety. If you are lucky, you may obtain a rose with a completely new color, a particularly handsome appearance, and a subtle scent.

My tip: It is best to choose several plants as mother plants so that you have more available seed.

First step: Choose a father and mother rose. The flowers should be just beginning to open up.
Second step: Cut a flower stem approximately 6 in (15 cm) long from the father plant and stand it in water in a vase. Then choose a mother rose and pull off all the petals.
Third step: Using tweezers, remove all the stamens from the mother flower so that auto-pollination cannot occur. Use a magnifying glass if necessary. Place a paper bag over the flower to avoid any outside influence.
Fourth step: Remove the paper bag next day and have a look at the stigma. If they feel slightly sticky, they are ready to receive the pollen. Check, using a magnifying glass,

whether the father flower is ready to release the pollen. If so, gently wipe the stamens across the stigma of the mother flower.

Fifth step: Make sure that the yellow-orange pollen grains are adhering to the stigma. If not, repeat the pollination procedure.

Sixth step: Place a paper bag over the mother flower; it can be removed again after a week. If pollination was successful, the base of the flower will swell and grow into a rose hip.

Seventh step: After a few months have passed, the rose hip can be snipped off. It should be ripe, but not yet wrinkled.

Eighth step: Bed the fruits in a dish containing damp peat and do not forget to attach a label with the names of the parents on it. Stand the container outside for the winter. Do not protect it from frost, as the seed should be frozen!

Ninth step: In the last month of spring, move the dish of rose hips inside. Extract the seeds from the hips and place them in a dish of water. Seeds which float will be infertile. Only choose seeds which sink to the bottom. Use seeding compost.

Tenth step: As soon as the young plants display their first tiny leaves, they should be pricked out in individual pots.

Small rose varieties were created for balconies and patios.

Grafting

Propagating from cuttings

From the middle of the last month of summer to the middle of the first month of fall is the best time for this type of propagation. The rose shoots are just right for taking cuttings: they should be nice and firm but not completely woody.

First step: Cut off as many healthy shoots as you need. The cuttings should be at least 6 in (15 cm) long and about 12 in (30 cm) would be even better, as longer shoots have been observed to form roots more easily. Remove the flowers and the shoot tip above a cluster of five leaves (see illustration 1).

Second step: Remove all the leaves with the exception of the two lowest ones (see illustration 2).

Third step: Immerse each cutting first in water, then in rooting powder. Push the cuttings so far down into the soil that a finger-long piece with one bud is left poking out (see illustration 3). It is possible to insert the cutting into the ground in a sheltered spot in the garden in a mixture of garden soil, peat, and sand or in pots of seeding compost. Place the cuttings in individual small pots or in groups of three in larger pots.

Fourth step: Press the cuttings down firmly and water them. If they are planted in pots, a transparent plastic bag should be pulled over the pot and the pots should be placed in a bright, but on no account sunny, position. If they are planted outside, make sure the cuttings do not become too wet or, conversely, dry out. Protect them with conifer branches before the start of frosty weather.

Fifth step: Rooting has taken place if new shoots begin to grow – often after eight to ten weeks. If the cuttings are in pots, now is the time to remove the plastic bags, separate the groups of three cuttings and place them in individual pots containing compost.

Budding a rose

Among the many methods of grafting roses, the following has proved itself time and again. Here a bud is removed from a chosen hybrid tea variety and tightly bound to the bare cambium of the wild stock so that it can continue growing there. The layer of tissue called cambium is situated immediately beneath the top layer of bark and consists of cells which are constantly replicating themselves. As plenty of warmth and light are required for this operation, it is best carried out towards the end of the second month/beginning of the third month of summer. Preparations for the procedure should have been made as early as the previous fall or spring.

First step: Obtain the desired number of wild stock plants in spring or fall and plant them in the positions in which they are intended to remain.

If there are no tree nurseries near you, just push a few cuttings of wild dog rose into the soil in the fall. They will root very easily. In the spring, you should let only the strongest main branch remain.

Second step: During the second to third months of summer is the time for budding.

Propagation from cuttings
1. Take cuttings and remove flowers and shoot tips. The cuttings should be about 6 in (15 cm) or, better still, 12 in (30 cm) long.
2. Remove all leaves apart from the two topmost ones.
3. Dip the cutting in water, then in rooting powder and push it into the ground until only a finger-long piece is above ground.

Water the wild stock thoroughly a week beforehand. The ensuing flow of sap will enable you to loosen the bark more easily.

Third step: Expose the neck of the roots of the wild stock and wipe the soil away cleanly. In the case of standard and cascade roses, the grafting procedure should, of course, be carried out at the desired height, not as low as the neck of the root.

Fourth step: Thoroughly clean your hands and the budding knife with hot water and do not later touch the exposed cut surfaces with your hands. Cleanliness is the first pre-requisite for success.

Fifth step: Cut off one or several shoots from each rose that you would like to propagate. Remove all the thorns and leaves, the leaf stalks should remain (see illustration 1).

Sixth step: Find the fattest buds in the middle of each shoot. Using the razor-sharp budding knife, cut these off ¾ in (2 cm) above and below the bud together with a thin layer of bark which should also include a piece of the wood. Then remove the woody piece, leaving the bud undamaged (see illustration 2).

Seventh step: Now, using the budding knife, cut a long T into the bark of the neck of the root of the stock (see illustration 3). The cross of the T should reach halfway round the stem.

Eighth step: Gently loosen the flaps of bark of the T from the tissue underneath using the tapered end of the knife blade.

Ninth step: From above, gently push the piece of bark with the bud underneath the two flaps of bark in the T, so that the bud is peeking out at the top. The piece protruding above the T should be cut off (see illustration 4).

Tenth step: Tie gardener's raffia

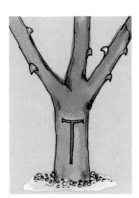

Grafting a rose

1. Cut a 12-in (30-cm) long, healthy shoot from the chosen rose.
2. Choose the fattest bud from the middle of the shoot and cut it out ovally, together with a piece of leaf stalk above and below the bud.
3. Cut a T-shape.
4. Push the grafting bud beneath the two flaps of bark.
5. Wind raffia around the grafting point. The bud must be exposed.

firmly around the grafting point or use a grafting band, covering the bark both above and below the piece of bark. Only the bud should be left poking out (see illustration 5).

Eleventh step: After the budding operation, the soil should be slightly heaped up around the budding point, but leaving the bud free.

Twelfth step: If the bud is still green after four weeks, is becoming fatter, and the remaining leaf stalk drops off if touched gently, the stock and the bud should have fused together. Now cut the binding but do not remove it yet.

Thirteenth step: The following spring, cut off the crown of the wild stock ¾ in (2 cm) above the grafting point. Use your sharpest gardening secateurs for this procedure, as it is of immense importance for the future development of the rose that the crown is removed with a single, clean cut. When the grafted buds have produced plenty of shoots, the shoot tips above the third and fourth leaves can be pinched out with your fingertips. This will promote the growth of new shoots.

503

A brief history of rose cultivation

Anecdotes and record breakers

Fossil evidence proves that the rose has existed for something like 40 million years. For thousands of years it was a common plant in the northern hemisphere. Around 1800, when the first attempts at crossing native European roses with Asian roses were successful, the rose gained greatly in variety and splendor.

A brief history of roses

During the course of human history, hardly any other flower has been so loved, cherished, and sung about as the rose. In antiquity, it was considered to be a symbol of beauty and love. Christianity associated the rose with the delicate loveliness of the Virgin Mary; the Chinese worshipped the rose as a divine being. The first known artistic representations of roses are depicted on a fresco that is over 3,500 years old and can be found in the remains of a Minoan palace at Knossos on Crete. Sappho, a Greek poetess of the eighth century BC, is the first person known to have written a poem about the rose. Poets like Anacreon and Pindar followed her example. In the ancient garden culture of China roses were first planted in beds. Long before our period of reckoning, the Persians are known to have discovered how to make distilled rose water and extract rose oil, and it is thought that the cradle of the European rose

is to be sought in Persia. The Romans spent veritable fortunes on buying roses for decorative purposes for feasts and celebrations. They also used roses for medicinal purposes.

After the collapse of the Roman Empire, the rose seemed to be forgotten until Charlemagne revived an interest in it. Thereafter, the rose was cultivated, mainly for healing purposes, in monastery gardens. Famous artists such as Leonardo da Vinci, Michelangelo, Botticelli, and Pieter Brueghel the Elder captured its beauty in marble and on canvas. Such famous physicians and botanists as Walafrid Strabo, Otto Brunfels, Leonhart Fuchs, Hieronymus Bosch, Tabernaemontanus, Clusius, and Lonicerus all described the rose species known in their times.

In 1752, the first Asiatic rose, *Rosa chinensis*, was brought to Europe from Canton in China. This became the foundation plant for all the European garden roses.

Two hundred years of cultivating roses

"Modern" roses have actually been around no longer than this. To begin with, the East Asian roses were simply planted alongside the native ones and gardeners would wait to see if they cross-pollinated successfully. Finally, at the beginning of the nineteenth century, more scientific cultivation was undertaken. The French rose gardener Desportes had a total of 2,562 different roses in his catalog in 1829. Then the first hybrid Chinese rose was created. From then on, the cultivation of new roses was unstoppable. France led the field, to be exact the French First Lady, Empress Josephine. She was responsible for speeding up the progress of the cultivation and crossing of roses as no other person before or after her. Her gardener, André Dupont, is thought to have been the first to cross-pollinate by hand. Her rose garden at Malmaison made the hobby of raising new rose cultivars popular all over Europe. In France itself, the first Remontant roses were created (1837), followed by hybrid teas (1867) and Polyantha roses in 1875. Later, these were overtaken by English and German cultivating activities. Countless varieties have been created all over the world to date, without the main aims of cultivation having changed a great deal. These are: good health, weather resistance, unusual flower colours and shapes, and, of course, as many different scents as possible.

Roses in cuisine

What is pleasing to your sense of smell ought to taste good too.

Rose punch: Sprinkle 10 ounces (300 g) scented, fresh rose petals with ⅔ cup (150 g) sugar, gently pour 2 teaspoons (10 ml) Grand Marnier over them, cover, and leave to soak in the refrigerator for an hour. Then pour 4 cups (1 liter) dry white wine over this and let it stand in the refrigerator for another hour. Pour through a strainer and, just before serving, add chilled champagne. Float a few fresh flower petals on top for decoration (serves about eight).

Roses for beauty and health

If you like making your own beauty preparations, you can create bath salts, creams, massage oils, and perfumed shampoos or prepare a delicately flavored tea out of scented roses from your garden. Pick the flowers in the morning when the dew has dried, pluck off the petals carefully, and spread out to dry on a clean cloth. Or place on a plate and dry at medium heat for one to two minutes in a microwave oven.

Rose tea: 1 handful of dried flower petals. Pour 3 cups (750 ml) of boiling water over the petals and leave this to draw for ten minutes. The tea can be drunk hot, sweetened with honey, or cold with lemon juice. The substances contained in the petals help to soothe the heart and fortify the liver and gall bladder.

Rose face tonic: Pour 6 tablespoons (100 ml) organic white wine over 1 cup (5 g) rose petals and leave this in a dark container for two weeks. Strain the liquid well. Let the rose wine run through a coffee filter paper and mix it with 4 tablespoons (50 ml) rose water purchased from a pharmacy. Excellent for dry, sensitive skins.

The Gallica rose variety "Rosa mundi" grew in the twelfth century.

"Bonica 82," a modern, versatile rose of the 1980s.

505

NOTES

Author's note

This book deals with the care of roses on balconies, patios and in the garden. Roses have thorns which can easily cause injuries. Always disinfect any wounds to prevent blood poisoning or infection, even it it is just a scratch. If in doubt, consult a doctor immediately. I strongly recommend that everyone who works regularly in the garden should have a tetanus injection for protection. Discuss this with your doctor. Please make absolutely sure that all plant protection agents, even biological ones, are kept in a safe place that is inaccessible to children and pets.

This edition published 1996 by Landoll,
Inc.
By arrangement with Merehurst Limited
Ferry House, 51-57 Lacy Road,
Putney, London SW15 1PR

© 1990 Gräfe und Unzer GmbH, Munich

Text copyright ©
Merehurst Limited 1994

Spring Flowers

KARIN GREINER

Series Editor:
LESLEY YOUNG

Introduction

Each year, as if to signal the end of winter, the arrival in our gardens of delicate snowdrops, graceful narcissi and bright crocuses announces that spring is here again! The first glimpses of spring color in the garden or balcony tubs is, however, just a faint shadow of the splendor that spring is about to present to us. With a little imagination, you can make full use of the beauty and variety of the huge range of spring flowers to clothe your garden, balcony, or patio with color. This guide will help you to choose the ideal plants for you by providing information on a selection of enchanting plants with easy-to-follow tips on their care. Plant expert Karin Greiner explains the correct way to plant spring flowers, how to care for them, and how they can be propagated. Color photographs introduce many of the most beautiful plants, among them the ever-popular bulbs and colorful perennials, many of which are ideal for a wild garden. Detailed instructions on care, as well as an overview of planting times in the fall and spring, will ensure that everything flourishes and blooms both inside your house and out in the garden from the last month of winter through the first month of summer. Planting ideas for flower beds, borders, lawns, balcony boxes, pots, and bowls will enable you to make the most of spring with hardly any effort. In addition, there are tips on planting combinations using your favorite colors.

Contents

Pheasant's eye (Adonis vernalis).

Parrot tulip.

Christmas roses (Helleborus niger) are among the first harbingers of spring.

The author
Karin Greiner is a biologist with a special interest in ecology. She has worked at the Institute for Botanical-Ecological Advice in Munich since 1984 and has published numerous papers on gardening topics, in particular on bulbous and tuberous plants. She is an expert on garden design, specializing in wild gardens, with particular emphasis on maintaining environmental stability.

Acknowledgments
The author and publishers wish to thank Angelika Weber of the Institute for Botanical-Ecological Advice for her invaluable and practical comments on the original text.

Nature awakes

Garden crocus.

No other season creates such feelings of hope as spring. After the endless gloomy, gray skies of winter, the awakening of nature seems like a miracle: the shoots of bulbous plants and hardy perennials seem to appear from nowhere and, over the span of a few weeks, will turn your garden into a sea of color.

Even by late winter some spring shoots are beginning to reach out toward the first, warming rays of the sun. Snowdrops and crocuses announce the arrival of spring in gardens and on balconies. At first, only a few flowers unfold their petals but soon the entire neighborhood appears to explode into an incomparable firework display of shapes and colours. By the time the tulip blossoms are slowly fading and the apple trees are in full bloom, spring is already coming to an end.

Spring flowers in myth and legend
No other group of plants is so surrounded by myths, fairy tales and legends as spring flowers. Their names are associated with countless stories in folklore.
The narcissus received its name in Ancient Greece and is featured in one of the legends of Greek mythology. This plant, which likes to grow on the banks of a pond or stream, bears the name of a Greek youth called Narcissus who thought himself to be quite beautiful. One

day, Narcissus was bending over a pool, enchanted by the sight of his own reflection in the water. When he reached out to embrace the image, he fell in and drowned. Vanity and self-obsession were his downfall. However, the gods took pity on him and transformed his dead body into a narcissus plant, which still casts its lovely reflection on the water even today.
The wild cowslip (Primula veris) is one of the first wild flowers of spring. Its charming umbels are reminiscent of the golden keys to the heavenly gates carried by St. Peter. According to legend, St. Peter opens the gates every spring and, such is his joy at the sight of all the new life, that he drops his keys which fall to Earth. There they are transformed into golden flowers which keep on blooming as if St. Peter never again wishes to close the gates of Heaven after the harsh days of winter.
"Forget-me-not!" say the sky blue flowers of the plant of the same name just as the spring is coming to an end again. As a symbol of fidel-

ity, the forget-me-not (*Myosotis*) represents the hope of humankind that spring will return again next year.

The star among spring flowers
In past times, many spring flowers were considered to be very precious by the peoples of central Europe. Tulips, in particular, have a quite spectacular history. The ancestors of our garden tulips originated from Asia Minor and the Near East where, centuries ago, they were highly prized in palace gardens. The first tulips were purchased by the aristocracy of Central Europe as exotic gems treasured by the Moguls, Indian rulers in the sixteenth century. Soon these exotic plants were flowering in the gardens of the west. The great enthusiasm engendered for this unusual flower led raisers to experiment with new shapes and colors. In the Netherlands, in particular, still the leading country for tulips, a form of "tulip mania" broke out at the beginning of the seventeenth century, when a single bulb could be worth a small fortune. The tulip became an object of market speculation until legislation and an overabundance of tulips finally caused the market to collapse.
There is scarcely another spring flower that offers such a wealth of shape and color as the tulip. Of some 4,000 possible varieties, only a few hundred are still on the market. Every year new cultivars are introduced, most of which soon disappear again. Few new introductions manage to assert themselves against the old, well-tried, and much loved varieties.

Crocuses are an excellent source of nectar for honey bees (Apis mellifera).

Botany

A basic knowledge of botany is one of the tools of every successful gardener. If you are familiar with the natural growth processes of the plants you choose, you will be able to avoid mistakes when you are caring for them.

Survival strategies among spring flowers

Plants have developed various techniques for survival in unfavorable climatic conditions.

Biennial herbaceous plants, like pansies and wallflowers, have extended their growth cycle to cover two years. During the first year they conserve their energies, and then flower and produce seeds during the second year. If the seeds of such plants are sown in summer, many will grow into strong, healthy plants by the fall and will bear masses of flowers the following spring. Many biennials are still capable of producing flowers for several more years but the flowers become increasingly sparse, so it is usual to discard them after their first flowering and sow fresh seed.

NB: Annual plants do not produce flowers in spring as their development always begins in spring.

Herbaceous perennials

(Illustration 1)
Perennials are resilient plants whose above-ground parts often die down every year. The rootstock survives in the soil and the plant renews itself from its shoots. Among the early-flowering herbaceous perennials are aubrieta, bleeding heart (*Dicentra* spp.) and primulas.

Bulbs and tubers are also considered to be perennials which have developed special, underground storage organs to ensure their survival through difficult times. When climatic conditions are right, new plants will grow from the bulbs and tubers.

Bulbs

(Illustration 2)
Bulbs consist of several fleshy layers which enclose the part out of which the shoot, leaf and flower will develop and which supply the developing plant with sustenance. The outer skin, which is tough and dry, protects the bulb from drying out and from damage. Roots grow from the bottom of the bulb.

Tubers

(Illustration 3)
Tubers are the "larders" of plants and are formed out of roots or shoots. They form more or less homogeneous masses, surrounded by a tough, protective layer. Tubers come in different shapes:

● In root tubers (e.g. anemone), the swollen roots are bunched together like claws.

● Shoot tubers (e.g. winter aconite) are usually fat and rounded. The new shoots grow out of the "eyes."

The bulb tuber is an in-between form, in which the fleshy scales fuse into a firm, lumpy mass, with roots sprouting in a crown. There are round bulb tubers or longish ones (bulbous iris).

The life cycle of bulbous plants

(Illustration 4)
The example of the tulip can be used to demonstrate the life cycle of a bulbous plant. The cycle of the tuberous plants is very similar.

2. Bulbs are underground storage organs.

Around the second month of the fall, the bulb, now in its dormant phase, is planted in the soil. A month later, a hard shoot tip will form, which is capable of piercing through quite compact layers of soil in spring. At the same time, roots begin to grow out of the

1. Herbaceous perennials like this cowslip will flower for many years.

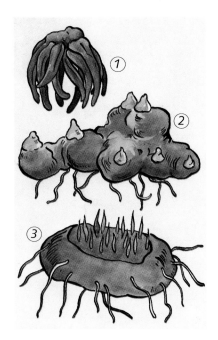

*3. **Tubers:** 1. anemone; 2. winter aconite; 3. cyclamen.*

bottom. These take over the function of water supply and also provide nourishment to the plant. Protected by the soil, the tulip survives the winter in this state.

Around the first and second months of spring, increasing warmth and moisture trigger the further development of the plant. By about six months after planting, the tulip will have produced fully developed leaves and flowers which have been sustained by the stored nutrients. The bulb itself shrinks more and more. Before it disappears completely, however, new little bulbils will begin to form in the axils of the innermost segments. These new bulbs will ensure the growth of new plants the following year.

The foliage will continue to store reserve nutrients for quite a long period after flowering is over. These substances will provide the necessary energy for new bulbs to form.

Finally, after another three months, in late summer, the entire development cycle is completed and the new bulbs enter a dormant phase.

Botanical names

The common names of many flowers are often confusing and may even be different in different regions of a single country. For example, people in different areas often confuse the names snowdrop and snowflake, or bluebell and harebell. A plant can only be classified properly by the use of an official botanical name which provides information about its relationships to other plants of the same type and its special characteristics. Each plant has its own first and second name: a genus name and a species name.

The genus name is the first part of the name. It is written in italic script, with an uppercase (capital) letter, and is often the same for several closely related plants. For example, *Tulipa* is the generic name for all tulips.

The species name is the second part of the name and is always written in italic script, with a lowercase (small) letter, for example, *Tulipa kaufmanniana.*

The variety name (if there is one) is a third name that is given to the plant by the raiser of that particular garden variety. It is enclosed in quotation marks. It often describes an important characteristic of the variety, for example, "The First."

NB: When speaking of "botanical" species, we usually mean wild species and their descendants. For example, "botanical crocuses" are all wild crocus species and the varieties bred from them, except for the large garden crocuses (*Crocus vernus*).

My tip: When choosing plants, take note of their botanical names. This is the only way to ensure that you have bought the right species. Variety names are important if you are looking for a particular cultivar, for example, a tulip of a special color or petal formation.

*4. **Growth cycle of a bulbous plant:** The growth cycle from planting through flowering to the formation of bulbs takes nine months.*

A place in the sun

Flower bulbs.

The warm rays of the sun are needed to coax spring flowers out of their winter sleep, so it is not surprising that so few of them flourish in shady places. If you take account of the position required by such plants, you will be able to save a lot of time and effort.

The right position

Even with the best care, a plant will display feeble growth if it is planted in the wrong place. When choosing a position for your plants, it is a good idea to consider the prevailing conditions of the site. You must look at all the external influences that will interact around the plant. Among these are light, warmth, moisture, and type of soil.

Light and warmth

Most spring flowers prefer positions in full sunlight or mostly sunny positions which also receive plenty of warmth. Warmth is the single most significant trigger for growth following the cold winter period. Cooler positions, which are generally shadier, are only suitable for a few plants with special requirements, like the Christmas rose (*Helleborus niger*) or *Hepatica nobilis*.

Many spring-flowering plants are quite happy planted under deciduous trees and bushes. As the trees are still bare in the springtime, sunlight can easily penetrate to the ground beneath. The spring flowers will have finished blooming by the time the leaves start appearing.

Moisture

The right degree of moisture is particularly important for bulbous and tuberous plants.

Sufficient moisture is essential *in the spring*, during the plants' main growth phase. If there is not enough rain, they will need watering.

In the summer, on the other hand, bulbous and tuberous plants require dry soil so that their underground parts can ripen properly. If they are in constantly wet positions during summer, they will tend to decay.

My tip: When you plant bulbs, etc., insert a water-permeable drainage layer. Water-sensitive species can be protected with a sheet of polyethylene if there are long periods of wet weather.

The right kind of soil

Light to medium-heavy, neutral soils which are water permeable are optimal for tuberous and bulbous plants (which make up the larger percentage of spring flowers). A few spring flowers require acid or lime-rich soils. Soils that are too light or too heavy can be treated before planting.

Checking the soil

The following factors are important:
Consistency: Determining the consistency of your garden soil is quite simple. Take a handful of soil and crumble it between your fingers. The following rules apply:
● Light soil is sandy and will trickle through your fingers.
● Medium-heavy soil is loose and crumbly.
● Heavy soil is full of clay and can be squeezed into a sticky ball.

pH factor (degree of acidity): You can measure the pH value of your garden soil with the help of simple measuring devices. Various products are on sale in garden centers at reasonable prices.
● neutral soil has a pH value of 6.5-7.5;
● acid soil has a pH value of less than 6.5;
● alkaline soil has a pH value of more than 7.5.

My tip: You can send soil samples away to be analyzed (inquire at your local garden center).

Looking good together: Cyclamineus narcissi, double tulips and Brodiaea laxa.

Tips on laying out your garden
Spring flowers can brighten any part of the garden with their glowing colors. Their own particular shape of growth and flower arrangement will determine where they will look best. The more splendid, dominant types will be most effective in flower beds and borders, while plants with small flowers do better under a group of trees or bushes or in a rockery. The following lists contain some recommendations for the positioning of different species of spring flowers.

For shrubberies: garden tulips, garden narcissi, hyacinths, fritillaria, ranunculus, leopard's bane, primroses, and bergenia.
In the rockery: botanical tulips, botanical narcissi, crocuses, fritillaria, winter aconites, grape hyacinths, irises, dog's tooth violets, cyclamen, pheasant's eye, pasqueflowers, primroses, all cushion-forming perennials.
Under trees or bushes: species of narcissus, crocuses, snowdrops, winter aconites, snowflakes, glory of the snow, scillas, anemones,

Ornithogalum, snake's head fritillaria, bleeding heart, Christmas rose, Caucasian forget-me-not, violets.
Along the edge of a pond or stream: narcissi, snowflakes, marsh marigolds (kingcups).
For the lawn, meadow or wild garden: Crocus tommasinianus and other botanical crocuses, glory of the snow, snake's head fritillaria, snowdrops, grape hyacinths, Poeticus narcissi, scillas, and Kaufmann tulips.

519

Planting

What kind of things should one watch out for when buying spring plants? When and where should they be planted?

Tips on buying

Only choose species and varieties of spring-flowering plants that you know are going to be suitable for the conditions that prevail in your garden. Always check that the colors and shapes of the flowers you are about to buy will look right with the existing plants in your garden.

Bulbs and tubers: The larger the girth of the bulb or tuber, the larger the flowers (and the price). Good plants should be undamaged, compact and firm, without signs of disease (soft or discolored places), and should not be dried up. The overall appearance of the plant should be healthy.

Perennial herbaceous plants:
These are most often sold as pot or container plants. They should look well developed and have several strong, healthy shoots. The roots should not be growing out of the pot and the soil should be free of weeds.

Warning: Some spring flowers are toxic.

Preparing the soil

Loosen up the soil in the places where you intend to plant and remove all weeds, stones, and old roots. Improve the soil with mature garden compost. Loosen up heavy soil by adding and mixing in sand. Conversely, very light soil can be improved by the addition of some loam to hold it together better.

Planting bulbs and tubers

Planting times: The species that flower in spring can be planted from late summer to mid-fall. The best planting time is the first month of the fall. The earlier the bulbs are

2. **Drainage:** *Fill the bottom of the hole with sand or grit to form a flat mound.*

placed in the soil before the beginning of frosty weather, the more time they will have to settle and the better they will survive the winter. Species which need a relatively long time to form proper roots should be planted by the first month of the fall at the latest. This goes for snowdrops (*Galanthus*), snowflakes (*Leucojum*), narcissi (*Narcissus*), crocuses (*Crocus*), scilla (*Scilla*) and fritillarias (*Fritillaria*). All other species can still be planted as late as the second month of fall.

NB: Bulbs and tubers should be bought just before they are planted to avoid unnecessary storage!

Tips on spring planting: Bulbous plants that have been brought on early by a gardener or in your own greenhouse, can be planted outside during the first and second months of spring as soon as the soil is no longer frozen. You can fill gaps in your flower beds or decorate a small, empty bed with these "forced" plants. The only drawback is that such a quick crop of beautiful flowers will cost much more.

1. **Planting depths of some bulbous and tuberous plants:** *1. grape hyacinth; 2. crocus; 3. winter aconite; 4. snowdrop; 5. iris reticulata; 6. ranunculus; 7. botanical tulip; 8. garden tulip; 9. dog's tooth violet; 10. narcissus; 11. hyacinth; 12. fritillaria (crown imperial).*

Planting depth
(Illustration 1)

General rule: Bulbs and tubers should be planted in the soil at a depth that equals three times their height. In light, sandy soils, the planting depth should be a little more, and in heavy soils a little less.

Spacing of plants: Plants need room to develop properly. Plant small bulbs/tubers (up to walnut size) about 2-3 in (5-8 cm) apart; larger bulbs 4-6 in (10-15 cm) apart.

Planting and drainage
(Illustration 2)

Large bulbs (larger than walnut size) should be planted farther apart (make a separate hole for each one). Small bulbs can be planted with a special bulb dibble which creates a cylindrical hole that will accommodate two to three bulbs.

3. Planting bulbs in a basket: Ensure that the planting depth and spacing are correct.

My tip: Winter aconites, crocuses, and other small tubers or bulbs that are to be planted in lawns or patches of grass, can be scattered randomly and then planted where they have fallen. This kind of distribution will appear more natural than deliberately planting them in groups.

Drainage: Bulbs do not thrive in waterlogged conditions, so you may need to insert a drainage layer to provide adequate drainage at the bottom of the planting hole.
- If the soil is light and loose, a flat, approximately finger-thick layer of sand beneath the bulbs will be sufficient.
- If the soil is very dense, very moist or heavy, the following procedure is recommended. Dig a hole about 2-4 in (5-10 cm) deeper than usual. Then scatter pebbles, fine gravel, broken pot shards or grit, and sand in the hole. Place the bulbs on top of the drainage layer, then fill in the hole with soil, and finish by watering the bulbs well.

Planting bulbs in a basket
(Illustration 3)

Tulips, narcissi, and other bulbs that have to be removed from the soil every few years can be placed in planting baskets. These flat baskets can later be removed from the soil quite easily, along with the bulbs they contain. The baskets thus facilitate digging up the bulbs and, at the same time, protect them against rodents. They can even be used for storage.

Perennial and biennial plants
Planting times: Plants bought in pots can be planted at any time during the vegetation phase of spring plants. Plants that are not in pots should be planted in early fall, so that the roots will have time to spread out into the soil properly before the beginning of winter.

Planting depths: Perennials, biennials, and bulbs should be planted at the same depth as they were in their pot. Planting them too deep

4. Plant shrubs at the same depth as before.

can lead to decay of the neck of the stem; planting them too shallow will cause them to dry up.

Spacing the plants: Perennials like bergenias, which take up quite a bit of space, will require more growth area than, for example, small forget-me-nots.
Correct spacing:
- small perennials 6-8 in (15-20 cm) apart;
- large perennials 10-16 in (25-40 cm) apart;
- cushion-forming perennials 10-14 in (25-35 cm) apart;
- biennials 6-8 in (15-20 cm) apart.

Planting
(Illustration 4)

Make the planting hole a little larger than the diameter of the rootstock, then loosen up the soil at the bottom of the hole. Set the plant in the hole, fill the hole with soil, and press the rootstock down firmly. Water thoroughly.

Fertilizing

Plants need a balanced, well-regulated supply of nutrients to ensure their well-being. The most important plant nutrients are nitrogen, phosphorous, potassium, and lime, as well as trace elements such as manganese, zinc, iron, copper, and magnesium. Depending on the type and consistency of the soil, such nutrients will be available in various amounts and concentrations. If your garden soil is of good quality, you will not need to worry about the nutrient supply as the soil will contain sufficient nutrients for the growth of plants for several years. When the plants no longer flourish, it is time to improve the soil, but it is necessary to give the matter some thought beforehand. Soil analysis can provide accurate information about the nutrient content of your soil (inquire about such a service at your local garden center). Before you use a fertilizer, take account of the specific nutritional needs of your plants, supply only those nutrients that are really needed and give them in the correct amounts.

Basic rule for fertilizing: Supplying too many nutrients is often more harmful than giving too few. Overfertilizing can lead to problems in growth development, sparse flowering, susceptibility to disease, and a loss of hardiness. The best method is to enrich the soil with organic, natural substances before planting. This will eliminate the need to resort to mineral fertilizers that can be harmful to the environment.

The nutrient requirements of spring flowers

● Wild species, like botanical crocuses, *Scilla* or fritillarias, can manage on few nutrients. Only really poor, nutrient-deficient soils will need to be improved for these species.

● Large tulips and narcissi, as well as short-lived biennials like pansies, are grateful for a plentiful supply of nutrients.

How to improve soil organically

Poorer soils should be treated with organic fertilizer before planting. Ripe garden compost or controlled-release fertilizer, like bone chips or bonemeal, should be sprinkled on, or mixed with, the soil. In the case of large planting areas, or if time is short, the soil can be covered with a thin layer of compost which will also serve as winter protection.

Fast fertilizing

In the case of poor soils and plants that need lots of nutrients, like garden tulips, the nutrient supply in the soil may be almost exhausted by the time of maximum growth. If you were not able to treat the soil beforehand with organic fertilizer, you can resort to fast-acting fertilizers which will provide an instant supply of nutrients for the plants. In addition to mineral fertilizers, organic, fast-dissolving, and liquid fertilizers are all available (such as nettle brew or a liquid fertilizer made from turnips).

Warning: Before using commercial fertilizers, read the directions thoroughly and avoid overdosing! Just like mineral fertilizers, ordinary garden compost and other organic fertilizers can also have a harmful effect if the doses are too large or are applied too often. Overfertilizing is detrimental to the soil and pollutes the groundwater. All responsible gardeners should realize that they have a duty to make only sparing use of fertilizers in order to prevent unnecessary damage to the environment.

Warning: Make sure that fertilizers are stored in a place that is inaccessible to children and pets.

Watering

Water requirements will vary depending on the time of year and the developmental stage of the plants.

After planting, thorough watering is particularly important so that the plants get a good start.

In spring, spring-flowering plants need larger amounts of water, as do all plants at the time of their most rapid growth and flower formation. Usually, however, there is already plenty of water in the soil during spring, following the rainfall of winter. As soon as the soil dries out, however, you will have to start watering.

In summer, during their dormant phase, spring-flowering bulbous or tuberous plants will require only a little water. It is more important to avoid waterlogging at this time. Herbaceous perennials will require plenty of water, even in summer.

Pruning and removing dead heads

The removal of faded flower heads is not a sign of exaggerated tidiness but – depending on the species of plant – a very necessary gardening technique.

In the case of **garden varieties** of tulips, narcissi, hyacinths, and some perennials, the removal of faded flowers is beneficial to the plants as it prevents the formation of seeds, which would use up the plant's energy unnecessarily. Make a point of removing the dead heads as soon as the flowers fade.

A romantic corner of the garden with Darwin tulips and forget-me-nots under a blossoming cherry tree.

The pure white flowers of the snowflake (Leucojum vernum) stand out against the dark, wintry soil.

In the case of **wild species** that are left to grow naturally, the formation of seed is desirable as it will ensure prolific propagation. There is no need to remove dead flowers from these plants.

In the case of **cushion-forming perennials**, cutting back will rejuvenate them. After flowering, cut all shoots back by about a third. Use a large pair of scissors to cut the entire cushion into shape. The plants will then form plenty of new shoots and remain compact without becoming bare in the center.

Dying back

Many spring flowers seem to vanish completely by early summer. First the foliage turns yellow, then, over time, the leaves disappear completely. Only the underground organs of the plant remain viable. This process is called dying back.

Perennials: Make sure to mark the positions of plants that die back early, like bleeding heart (*Dicentra spectabilis*), pheasant's eye, and pasqueflowers, so that you can avoid damaging their roots when digging. The gaps above ground will soon be filled by later-flowering neighboring plants.

Bulbs and tubers: Even though the slowly withering foliage is not very attractive, it should not be removed until it is completely yellow or dried out. With the help of these leaves, bulbous and tuberous plants build up important reserves of vital nutrients which are then held in underground storage organs to provide energy for the next year's growth.

NB: Lawns that contain bulbous plants should not be mowed until the end of spring or in the first month of summer.

My tip: The skilled planting of species that produce lots of fast-growing foliage will help to hide the fading leaves of narcissi and tulips.

Lifting and storing bulbs and tubers

You can remove the bulbs and tubers from the flower beds if you wish to make room for summer plants. The following points should, however, be noted.

Make sure the **foliage has dried up and turned completely yellow** before carefully lifting the bulbs or tubers out of the soil with a garden fork. Foliage that has not yet withered can now be cut off. Remove any loose soil from the bulbs or tubers and let them dry off in a shady place for a few days. Diseased or damaged bulbs and tubers, or those that are too small, should be discarded.

If the foliage is still upright but you need the space for new plants, the removed plants must be given an opportunity to complete their cycle in another position. Remove the bulbs or tubers from the soil, together with the foliage, and lay them out in a shady place in the garden. Cover the bulbs with loose soil and leave them to "rest" until the foliage has withered.

Storage

After lifting the bulbs and tubers, it is important to store them properly before replanting them in the fall. If they are left out of soil for a long time, they risk drying out or becoming infested with fungi and molds.

Proper storage: You will need a wooden box or tray. Cover the bottom of the box with a layer of peat, sawdust, or wood shavings.

The bulbs/tubers should be laid loosely on this layer (they should not touch) and covered with another layer. Keep the box in a cool, dry, dark place (e.g. a cellar) until replanting time in the fall.

NB: Fritillaria and *Erythronia* spp. do not have a protective layer of skin around their bulbs, so they can only be stored in moist peat or some similar medium for a short time.

My tip: New bulbs or tubers should not be bought until shortly before you intend planting, to avoid unnecessary storage.

Warning: Make sure children or pets do not eat bulbs or tubers! Some of them are toxic and most can cause severe health problems.

Winter protection

Many species of bulbs and tubers originate from mountainous regions that are covered by a protective layer of snow during the winter. In regions with little or no snowfall, such species may sometimes be damaged by frost. Sensitive species, like jonquils, *Narcissus bulbocodium* and some *Fritillaria,* will need some form of winter protection. The same goes for cushion-forming plants, sensitive perennials like bleeding heart (*Dicentra spectabilis*), and many biennials. All newly planted bulbous plants are grateful for some extra protection from the cold.

Good protection is provided by a layer of dead leaves or twigs, which can be spread over the plants in late fall. This layer will have an insulating effect and will prevent deep penetration of frost. A few conifer banches or something similar can be laid over perennials. A layer of garden compost, spread over the plants in late fall, will protect them and, at the same time, improve the soil and provide nutrients.

The layer of winter protection should be removed in early spring when the first shoots appear. The best time to remove the covering is on a cloudy, mild day. The delicate young leaves should still be protected from bright, direct sunlight.

My tip: If sunlight is very intense, the plants can be protected by covering them with a piece of sacking, a conifer branch ,or twigs.

Warning: Store bulbs in a place that is inaccessible to children and pets as some bulbs are toxic.

Bulbs/tubers stored correctly:
The best way to store bulbs and tubers is in a wooden box lined with a thick layer of peat, sawdust, or wood shavings.

Propagation

If you want more and more spring flowers in your garden, sooner or later you will wish to try your hand at propagating your own plants. Some spring flowers are able to multiply quite happily without any help from the gardener, but others need assistance. How to propagate spring flowers is explained on the next few pages.

Propagating from seed (generative propagation)
This propagation method is not necessarily successful for all spring flowers. For many of the species covered in this book, in particular the bulbous plants, propagation from seed is tedious and long-winded. Many varieties cannot be propagated at all in this way as they do not produce seed. In addition, the seedlings of many species can take from three to six years to become capable of bearing flowers.
Sowing seed is worthwhile for all biennials, particularly pansies, and some perennials, such as primulas, pasqueflowers, and lungwort. It is recommended that you use only pure species. Some cultivated varieties can lose their characteristic features through generative propagation, so they are best propagated by division.
Sowing seed: The seeds can be sown in boxes of seeding compost during the summer. In the case of dark-germinating plants, like pansies and forget-me-nots, the seed should be covered with a layer of compost (about ¼ in/5 mm thick), while the seed of light-germinating plants can be lightly pressed into the soil.
The seeds should be watered with a fine spray. Stand the seed tray in a warm, bright, but not too sunny, position and ensure even moisture, but avoid wetting the soil too much. Covering the seed tray with a transparent plastic hood or PVC sheet will create a favorable atmosphere for germination.
Pricking out: As soon as the seedlings have formed two to four proper leaves, they should be pricked out. Choose strong, well-developed young plants for careful replanting in small pots or boxes containing seeding compost. Leave enough space between the plants (about 2-4 in/5-10 cm). Throw away any weak plants. After two to four weeks, you can replant them again, if you wish, to ensure that the plants flourish, although this is not absolutely necessary.
Planting out: Strongly developed young plants can be toughened up in late summer/early fall and then planted in their final positions outside.
NB: Plants that germinate in cold conditions, like pheasant's eye, Christmas rose, winter aconite, saxifrage, and bleeding heart, need the trigger of a cold temperature to germinate. Seeds of these species should be sown in the last month of fall, placed in a cool position or

1. Break off the bulbils and plant them. Check the planting depth.

even outside during the winter, and then brought back into a warm place in the last month of winter.
My tip: Many bulbous plants, like snowdrops, and some perennials, like violets, form plenty of seed and look after their own propagation. While self-sowing is desirable in plants that are growing wild, it can be a nuisance in rockeries, where

2. Remove the tiny offsets from the mature tuber and plant them, making sure they are at the correct depth.

you will have to remove the flower heads or seedpods before the seeds are dropped.

Vegetative propagation
Many spring flowers can be propagated in this way without any fuss. Some of the possible methods of vegetative propagation are described below.
NB: Vegetative (non-sexual) propagation means that you will obtain offspring that are identical to the mother plant as no mingling of genetic material from two parents has taken place, which is the case with generative reproduction. If you want to propagate varieties successfully in their original, typical form, you should only propagate using the vegetative method.

Propagation from bulbils
(Illustration 1)

Nearly all species of bulbs form tiny bulbils. Some produce many, others only a few. Narcissi, for example, produce only one or two but these are nearly as large as the original bulb. Grape hyacinths produce lots of little bulbils. Hyacinths, on the other hand, very rarely form any bulbils at all.

The bulbils are very simple to use in propagation. The mother bulb should be removed from the soil after the foliage has died back. The bulbils are then carefully broken off and planted in a propagation bed or back in the same place. Make sure they are planted at the right depth and with the right spacing.

After one or two years, you should have plants that are capable of flowering. In some species, however, this can take up to four years – or even six years in the case of the crown imperial fritillaria or dog's tooth violet (*Erythronium denscanis*).

Propagation from offsets
(Illustration 2)

Tuberous plants, like ranunculus and anemones, form offsets which you can treat in the same way as described above for bulbils. You can expect plants capable of flowering after two to four years.

Propagation from divided tubers
(Illustration 3)

Species such as *Eranthis* (winter aconite) and *Ranunculae* can be propagated quite easily by dividing the tuber. Choose only larger tubers for propagation and proceed as follows. Lift the tuber from the soil after the foliage has died right down and cut it into several pieces with a clean knife, making sure that each portion still has at least one bud, from which a shoot will grow. The cut surface should be dipped in

3. Cut the tuber into several pieces which should all have one or more shoot tips. Plant the pieces with the shoot tips pointing upward.

charcoal powder (obtainable from garden centers) to protect it against decay or fungal infection. Then, plant the pieces with the shoot tips uppermost.

Propagating shrubs by division
(Illustration 4)

The simplest method of vegetative propagation is division. It is possible for many perennials, such as marsh marigold, blue-eyed Mary (*Omphalodes verna*), aubrieta, and dwarf phlox.

Remove the plant from the soil after flowering and either break it up by hand or split it with a knife or hand trowel into fist-sized pieces. Each part should still have a few buds that are able to shoot. The parts must be planted in accordance with the requirements of the species.

Propagation from cuttings

Some cushion-forming perennials can be propagated from cuttings, for example, *Alyssum, Arabis, Iberis,* and bleeding heart (*Dicentra spectabilis*). Cuttings can be taken from the parent plant in the spring or early summer.

Taking cuttings: Using a sharp knife, cut off finger-long pieces of shoot, with four to six leaves, immediately above a bud or node in the stalk.

Rooting in water: Stand the cutting in a glass of water. When roots have formed, plant it in a seeding tray or a small pot filled with seeding compost.

Rooting in compost: Plant several cuttings in a pot or small tray filled with seeding compost. Stand them in a bright, warm position and cover the pot or tray with plastic sheeting to ensure high humidity. When roots have formed, slowly toughen up the plant (remove the plastic cover for longer and longer periods) and, eventually, plant the cuttings outside.

My tip: If you dip the cut surface of the cuttings in rooting powder (obtainable from garden centers), they will form roots much faster.

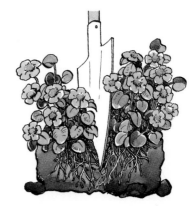

4. Remove the plant from the soil to divide it.

Garden crocus with golden "powder puffs" set in delicate flower cups.

Spring flowers indoors

Tazetta narcissi, hyacinths, and other bulbous plants can be used to bring a scent of spring into the house as early as Christmas. Light and warmth will awaken these plants early from their winter sleep. *Method:* You will need a wide, shallow bowl and a mixture of sand, gravel and bulb compost (mixed in equal parts).

● Fill the bowl with the compost mixture and set the bulbs on top, merely pushing them down very gently but using very little pressure.

● Soak the compost with water so that the bottom of the bulb is immersed in water.

● Stand the bowl in a cool, dark place.

● Make sure there is sufficient water as the growing roots should always be in water.

● When the first shoots start appearing, gradually move the bowl into a brighter position, so that the plants can slowly become accustomed to the light and increasing warmth, until they rapidly produce flowers in bright sunlight.

NB: Hyacinths can also be brought on early in special hyacinth jars (obtainable from garden centers and some florists).

My tip: In addition to Tazetta narcissi, hyacinths and garden crocuses, many varieties of single and double early tulips, Kaufmann and Fosteri tulips, *Iris reticulata*, and winter aconite are all quite suitable for bringing on early.

Pests and diseases

Healthy plants develop immunity

Unfortunately, the warmth of the spring sun not only coaxes flowers into growth but also encourages pests and diseases. Observe your plants during the growth period and also check stored bulbs and tubers so that you can step in with preventive measures before infestation occurs.

Viridiflora tulip.

Promoting natural immunity

The more you meet the needs of your plants with respect to choice of position, the more immunity they will develop toward pests and diseases. Weakened plants which grow feebly in the wrong position are the ideal prey for pests. The better that the plants' requirements for correct light, soil, and nutrients are met, the more easily they will resist parasites and diseases. The best preventive measure is to take a good look at all possible positions and plant the right spring plants in the right places.

In spite of such preventive measures, however, you will occasionally be confronted with aphids, gray mold, mice or even diseases caused by viruses or bacteria, but do not be put off by these possibilities. If you act quickly enough, you will be able to put matters right and continue to enjoy your spring flowers.

My tip: Take a frequent look at your plants so that you will note any changes or abnormalities and get to the bottom of the problem. The

sooner you recognize trouble, the better your chance of success in getting rid of it.

Common problems of bulbous plants

Unfortunately, most of the pests and diseases that attack bulbous plants are so stubborn that they can only be defeated by tough measures, i.e. chemical plant protection agents.

Remedy: In the most severe cases, such as an infestation with narcissus fly or a virus that is causing the deformation of parts of the plant, the best and simplest action to take is to destroy the infested plants immediately. This is really the only way to avoid any further spread of the problem. As bulbous plants are generally not expensive to buy, replacing the lost bulbs is often cheaper than spending money on elaborate forms of plant protection.

My tip: Infested plants should never be thrown on the compost heap, as pests and disease-inducing microorganisms can often flourish there. Throw them onto a bonfire or wrap and put in the garbage can.

Plant protection agents

The use of toxic sprays to combat diseases and pests is no longer recommended. Indeed, in some countries in Europe, local district authorities have prohibited the use of such insecticides and herbicides. If the use of plant protection agents is unavoidable (e.g. in the case of bacterial decay or nematode infestation), extreme caution is advised. Make absolutely sure you read the directions for use throroughly and then follow them meticulously as these substances damage our environment more than they benefit it.

Biological protection agents, which are less harmful to the environment, are always preferable. There are a number of gentle, natural methods to combat pests and diseases. Some of them are described in the following paragraphs. If you want more information on natural, organic gardening, you should make inquiries at your local garden center or seek out gardening publications that promote organic methods.

Warning: Store all plant protection agents, even biological ones, in a place that is inaccessible to children and pets!

Animal pests

Quite a few animals that we normally like and enjoy watching fall under this heading. On the one hand, there are several animal "vandals" who will spoil the beauty of your flowers.

On the other hand, however, such creatures cannot be exterminated from their rightful place in the natural order. It is, therefore, best to employ gentle, but effective, methods to discourage these animal pests. Here are a few tips.

Mice, voles and rabbits
These nimble, elusive rodents view your flower bulbs and tubers as delicacies and will often inflict great damage on plants. They are very hard to combat or chase away.
Counter-measure: Protect your plants by:
● Planting bulbs and tubers in planting baskets made of plastic or wire netting (obtainable from garden centers, etc.) This makes them practically inaccessible to rodents.
● Plant crown imperial fritillarias. These are considered by voles to be very nasty on account of their unpleasant smell, so these particular rodents will stay well away.

Blackbirds and sparrows
These birds in particular will go to great lengths to gobble up whole groups of crocuses, leaving behind sad, tattered petals.
Counter-measure: Attach aluminum strips to sticks pushed into the ground or set up scarecrows. This should frighten the birds away without harming them.

Slugs and snails
The young, delicate leaves of narcissi, tulips, and many perennials are a favorite meal of slugs, which, particularly in a mild spring, can suddenly appear in hordes overnight.
Counter-measure: there seems to be no natural remedy against these arch-pests. The only way to limit the damage they create is by:
● setting up beer traps or snail fences (obtainable from garden centers);
● spraying with a brew made from fern (*Pteridium aquilinum*) (see below);
● surrounding the plants with dry bran or shavings, which slugs dis-

like crawling across.

Thrips and nematodes
Thrips, namatodes and narcissus flies are tiny, inconspicuous pests. Thrips, which look like minute transparent blisters on foliage and petals, suck the sap of the plants. Affected plants generally fade and die. There are no cures for infestation by nematodes and narcissus fly.

Counter-measure: Only preventive measures can bring any relief. The reproductive cycle of these pests, which overwinter in the soil, can be disturbed through intensive working of the soil. This involves carefully loosening the soil every few weeks and crumbling it up with a hand rake or something similar, working in compost to obtain a high content of humus and avoiding overfertilizing.

Fungal diseases
Microscopic fungi cause great damage to spring flowers every year. Gray mold, root and stem decay, dry rot, wet rot, rust, and leaf burn are only a few members of the huge range of fungal diseases.

Biological sprays
You can obtain the dried ingredients for these sprays from specialized horticultural or herbal suppliers, or from some pharmacies.

To combat mildew
Mare's tail brew (Hippuris vulgaris): You will need 18oz (500g) fresh or 1 cup (75g) dried mare's tail to 1¼ gallons (5 liters) of water.
● Bring to a boil and simmer for about 30 minutes. If using the dried herb, first soak in the water for about 24 hours.
● Let the brew cool, strain it, and dilute it with water in 1 part brew to 5 parts water.
● Spray the whole plant with the brew and then also water it with the same.

Garlic tea (when infested): You will need 6 (25 g) garlic cloves to 5½ quarts (5 liters) of water.
● Crush the cloves and pour on 4 cups (1 liter) of boiling water.
● Strain the tea and let it cool.
● Do not dilute. Spray the whole plant with the tea.

To combat slugs and snails (as a preventive measure or when infested)
Fermented fern brew (Pteridium aquilinum): You will need 18 oz (500 g) fresh or ¾ cup (50 g) dried fern to 5½ quarts (5 liters) of water.
● Stir well, let stand and stir daily.
● After five to seven days, when fermentation begins (small bubbles will begin to rise), strain, dilute as 1 part brew to 10 parts water and use immediately.
● Spray or water with a fine spray (both plants and soil).

To combat aphids and for a general strengthening of the plants' immunity to disease
(as a preventive measure or when infested)
Stinging nettle brew: You will need 18 oz (500 g) fresh, non-flowering plants or 1¾ cups (100g) dried leaves to 5½ quarts (5 liters) of water.
● Let it soak for 24 hours, boiling it once.
● When it has cooled, dilute it as 1 part brew to 4 parts water and spray the whole plant with the liquid.

Counter-measures: There are few remedies for fungal infections. If bulbs or other plants are infected, you should avoid planting other members of the same species in the same soil for several years as the spores of the fungi will remain viable for a long time.

Gray mold occurs fairly frequently on bulbous flowers. Various species of gray mold have a fondness for particular plants and will produce characteristic signs of damage on the plants. In tulips, one form of typical damage is called tulip fire; in narcissi, you may often find narcissus fire (see illustration, top right).

Mildew appears most often on perennials and biennials, for example, primulas, wallflowers, and Christmas roses. A flour-like dusting on the leaves and flowers is an unmistakable sign of infestation. To prevent this from spreading, do not site the plants too close together, make sure the soil is loose and water permeable, and water in good time when conditions are very dry.

● Cut off infested shoots and leaves and spray the plant with mare's tail brew or garlic tea.

Common diseases of bulbous and tuberous plants

Gray mold (Botrytis): brown stalk and surfaces of leaves, gray mold patches, the leaves are small and often tattered, the flowers look deformed. Occurs in tulips (tulip fire), snowdrops, hyacinths, narcissi (narcissus fire), and scilla. Cut out infested parts and destroy any infested bulbs.

Basal rot: mold infestation occurs in stored bulbs. Light brown, depressed patches, the bulb decays, and the inside displays a chocolate-brown discoloration. Occurs in narcissi and tulips. Infested bulbs should be destroyed immediately and the infested site should not be used again for bulbous plants for several years.

Nematodes: deformed growth, yellowish lumps in the leaves, no flowers. Brown rings in the bulbs. Occurs in narcissi, tulips, snowdrops, hyacinths, and bulbous irises. Infested bulbs should be destroyed immediately and infested areas should not be used again for planting bulbous plants for at least two years.

Narcissus fly: the shoots are weak, curly and grass-like, or there are no shoots at all. Fat, dirty-white grubs bore holes in the bulb and the bulb begins to decay from the bottom up. Occurs in narcissi, less often in tulips and hyacinths. Destroy soft bulbs in the fall and eaten bulbs in the spring.

Virosis: malformation of the stems, leaves, flowers; patchy, mosaic-like patterns along the veins of the leaves. Occurs in almost all bulbous plants (symptoms vary). Destroy any infested plants immediately. Avoid infestation with aphids as they are carriers of the virus.

Viral and bacterial diseases

Diseases caused by bacteria and viruses are every gardener's nightmare.

Bacteria cause a wettish, decaying rootstock and various diseases. Viral infections can be identified by deformed growth and mosaic-like patterns.

Counter-measures: Diseases caused by bacteria or viruses are incurable. The infested plants should be destroyed as quickly as possible.

NB: Some of the more unusual types of tulip varieties, like Rembrandt or Chamaeleon tulips, were created thanks to viral attack. These plants, which have flame-patterned, striped or veined flower petals in contrasting colors, carry a virus that causes these extraordinary color displays. It is not known how these varieties manage to survive this viral attack. When infected, other tulip varieties generally die.

My tip: Rembrandt or Chamaeleon tulips should be kept well isolated from any other tulips to prevent cross-infection.

Kingcups (marsh marigolds) are ideal plants for the moist edge of a pond. Their reflections in the water makes them look twice as abundant. Trumpet daffodils and Poeticus narcissi grow from the bank right into the meadow.

Splendor on your balcony

Garden tulip.

There is no reason why the balcony should remain bare in spring while your garden is filled with beautiful displays of flowers. Many spring plants flourish in balcony boxes, flowering profusely and bringing all the beauty of spring right up to your door.

The season for balcony flowers does not really begin until the last month of spring, after the last cold snap of the season. Before then, the worst of the winter weather can do great damage to balcony flowers. On the other hand, the flowering season on your balcony can be extended by about three months if you plant some of the less cold-sensitive spring flowers. Spring on your balcony can be just as versatile and colorful as spring in the garden. In addition to biennials like pansies, daisies, and forget-me-nots, many species and varieties of bulbous and tuberous plants, and small perennials can be planted in tubs. If you choose the right species and varieties and note their requirements for care, these charming plants will grace your balcony right through until it is time to plant summer flowers.

Tips on choosing plants

Many spring flowers grow perfectly well in the limited space of flower boxes.

Choosing the right plants

Choose only small plants, such as low-growing wild species and varieties that will grow to a height of about 12 in (30 cm). Flowers that grow very tall will not have enough support and will tend to fall over in the slightest breeze.

Depending on the variety, plants of the same genus may grow to quite different sizes.

Among the tulips and narcissi, the tall-growing varieties can be knee-high. The long, slender stems of Darwin tulips and trumpet narcissi, as well as the heavy flowers of peony tulips, are unsuitable for balcony conditions. Their rather grand-looking flower heads look out of place on a balcony anyway.

In the case of wallflowers, anemones, and narcissi, you should also think about their final height when choosing species. Some wallflower varieties, in particular those intended for use as cut flowers, may attain heights of around 28 in (70 cm) and are, therefore, totally unsuited to balcony positions.

NB: Make sure you pick the right varieties when you are buying seeds and bulbs! Read the information on the package or ask a sales assistant for advice. If you still wish to plant flowers that grow tall, you will have to give them some form of support, especially in windy positions.

How long will flowers last in a spring tub?

There seems to be a general opinion that planting spring-flowering tubs is hardly worth the effort because spring flowers often bloom for such a short time. The result of this is that many a gardener foregoes much of the pleasure to be derived from spring flowers. In actual fact, the flowering period of a balcony tub can last all spring. The trick is to choose species and varieties that flower both simultaneously and in sequence. For example, several varieties of tulip flower one after the other from the first to the last month of spring. The Kaufmann or water lily tulips (*Tulipa kaufmanniana*) flower very early, so you can follow them with single early tulips and end up with cottage tulips. If you plant double daisies between them, there will be no break at all in the flowering sequence.

A balcony box containing late tulips, forget-me-nots, red and yellow wallflowers, and daisies.

Spacing of plants

Plants require a certain amount of room to thrive. With the limited space available in a tub or large container, the number of plants you choose will have to be carefully worked out.

In ordinary balcony boxes (obtainable in garden centers, etc.), which are approximately 8 in (20 cm) deep and 6 in (15 cm) wide, you should plant only really small plants. The space will fill up quickly with very few plants. If you plant them too close together, the roots will compete for growing space and the plants will not be able to develop properly.

A general rule for planting in balcony boxes is to leave a space of two to three fingers' width between the larger bulbs, although smaller bulbs can be set closer together. Leave about a hand's width of space between perennials.

You will have much more room at your disposal with ***large tubs or containers*** that are permanently fixed features. As they are much deeper and wider, they can accommodate more plants (even taller ones). Tall tulips can thus be planted in wind-sheltered positions without falling over at the first gust. Even spring-flowering shrubs, such as rhododendron varieties, and ornamental cherry trees can be planted in these large containers.

Balcony gardening

Much work is required before you can sit back and enjoy a display of colorful spring flowers on your balcony. Caring for these plants is not difficult, however, and the end result is worth all the time and effort.

Preparing the plant containers

Whether you decide to plant in the fall or spring and whether you choose bulbs, tubers, or perennials, the following rules apply.

Compost: The most suitable compost is good quality potting compost which will not form lumps or become heavy but remain water-permeable. Many different brands are obtainable from garden centers. Good potting compost will contain a basic reserve of nutrients which should last for the entire period of growth of your spring flowers. You can also make your own compost using garden soil (or well-sieved, clean, used soil from summer plants), bark humus, and potting compost mixed in equal parts. Add a few handfuls of coarse river sand.

Suitable containers: roomy boxes (at least 6 in/15 cm wide and 8 in deep/20 cm deep), large containers, or large bowls. It does not matter much what material they are made of but drainage holes are essential so that any surplus water

2. *In spring, fill any gaps between the bulbous flowers with small herbaceous plants like daisies or pansies.*

can run away. Clean any used boxes thoroughly before starting.

Drainage: Spread an approximately 2-in (5-cm) thick layer of clay pellets or gravel in the bottom of the pot.

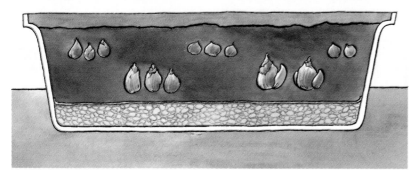

1. **Bulbs in a box:** *The bulbs have been planted at the right depth in a small box containing a drainage layer and compost.*

Place a layer of interfacing fabric over this (obtainable from garden centers, etc.). This will prevent soil being washed into the drainage layer when watering.

Fall planting of bulbs and tubers

(Illustration 1)

Bulbs and tubers should be planted from the end of the first month of fall until the end of the second month of fall at the latest.

Depth of planting: The bulbs of species that are suitable for growing on balconies are naturally quite small. They can be planted 2-3 in (5-8 cm) deep. Larger bulbs, for example those of tulips, should be planted about 4-6 in (10-15 cm) deep in the soil. It is possible to plant them at a more shallow depth in boxes than in a garden bed.

Method

● Lay a drainage layer in the pot or box and cover it with interfacing fabric.

● Fill the container with compost to a depth of about 2 in (5 cm).

● Place the larger bulbs on the compost.

- Fill the container with more soil until you have reached the depth needed for the smaller bulbs and tubers. Place them on the compost and fill up the container to about ¾ in (2 cm) from the edge.
- Press the soil down lightly and water thoroughly so that the soil is moist but not wet.

NB: If you plant bulbs in the fall, they will overwinter in the box and should be protected from frost.

Planting perennials in the fall

Perennials can be planted at the same time as bulbs and tubers in the fall.

3. Tall, bushy plants can be supported by two sticks driven crossways into the soil.

- Place a drainage layer in the container and cover it with interfacing fabric. Pour in soil to about a hand's width deep.
- Set the plants on the layer and add more soil. The plants should sit just as deep as they did in their last pot. Press the soil down well around the roots.
- Add the bulbs and tubers: make holes in the soil with the handle of a trowel or a dibble, pop the bulbs/tubers into the holes, and fill them with soil. Water well.

Planting in spring

Bulbs and tubers that are sprouting can be planted in the first month of spring. The same goes for perennials and biennials. Planting is best done on a mild, cloudy day so that the plants are not subjected to extreme cold or intense sunlight.

- Boxes that contain a layer of drainage material are filled 4 in (10 cm) deep with soil.
- Carefully remove the plants from their pots.
- Place the plants about 2-4 in (5-10 cm) apart and fill the rest of the container with soil. Press it down round the roots and water thoroughly.

Further spring planting

(Illustration 2)

If you only planted bulbs and tubers in the fall, you can create more luxuriant growth in your balcony tub the following spring by planting biennials between the other plants.

- Carefully dig holes in the soil between the bulbous plants.
- Remove the plants from their pots and plant them in the holes; fill them with soil and press it down.
- Water well.

Care in the spring

The first leaves and buds will start appearing when the days get longer and the weather milder.

Watering: The flowers will need plenty of moisture to develop properly. The soil should always be moist but not wet. You can check this by pushing a finger into the soil.

4. Tulips or other long-stemmed flowers should be supported so that they do not fall over.

You only need to water if the soil feels dry at a depth of about 1½ in (3.75 cm).

Protect the plants from frost: A light frost (to about 23° F/-5° C) will not harm your plants very much but the lower that temperatures drop, the more protection they will need. Hoods made of transparent plastic (bubble pack or gardeners' PVC) or folded "hats" made of newspaper can be placed over the plants to keep them a few degrees warmer.

Protect them from the weight of snow: A thin layer of snow will not harm the plants but heavy showers of sleet or slush can cause the stalks to snap. Again, use protective hoods.

Support tall plants

(Illustrations 3 and 4)

- In the case of flowers with very long stalks, push thin sticks into the soil and tie the stems to them with raffia.

Planting times in the fall and spring

Bulbous and tuberous plants can be planted either in fall (bulbs or tubers) or in spring (as shooting plants). Perennials can be planted in the fall but must then be well protected from frost.

Planting in spring is generally safer. *Planting in fall* is cheaper but involves more work as the boxes have to be overwintered. The advantage of planting in the fall is that you have a greater choice of species and varieties because lots of bulbs are for sale, whereas the supply of shooting plants is not always very large in spring.
NB: Make sure you choose good quality bulbs and tubers.
Planting shooting bulbous and tuberous plants in spring is simpler but more expensive. At that time (during the first and second months of spring) you can also plant smaller perennials (container plants) and biennials, for example, pansies and forget-me-nots.
NB: Buy plants with clearly visible buds that have not yet begun to shoot. At this stage of growth, the plants can cope very well with transplanting and will flower for a long time.

Choosing colors for your balcony

The following examples suggest various plants to use for creating attractive combinations of color. The possibilities are limitless!

Yellow, red and blue: This simple trio of colors has a cheerful effect and is eye-catching.
● Suitable plants: yellow cyclamineus narcissi "Peeping Tom" and yellow ranunculus. Red Kaufmann tulips "Scarlett Eleganz." Blue forget-me-not "Amethyst." This grouping includes large, dominant

flowers which blend perfectly with the tiny blue flowers of the forget-me-nots. The tulips will produce long-lasting blooms and create bold splashes of color.

Blue, yellow and white: bright, cool spring colors.
● Suitable plants: blue grape hyacinths (*Muscari armeniacum*) "Blue Spike" and pansies (*Viola* x *wittrockiana* hybrids). Golden crocus (*Crocus ancyrensis*) and yellow double narcissi "Van Sion." White double early tulips "Schoonoord." The first to bloom are the glowing golden crocuses, followed by the tassel-like flowers of the narcissi. The pansies provide a blue carpet right from the beginning until the end of the flowering period and the finale is supplied by the shining white double tulips.

Pink, blue and white: This is a very elegant color combination which works even for very simple plantings.
● Suitable plants: pink double early tulips "Peach Blossom." Blue forget-me-not "Compindi." White cushion-forming primula. This box will flower for weeks on end. Set off by the white of the cushion primulas, the pink tulips harmonize beautifully with the intense sky-blue of the forget-me-nots.

Pastel shades: The main role is played by soft, delicate colors.
● Suitable plants: globe primulas (*Primula denticulata*) "Grandiflora" in a light shade of violet. Yellow cowslips (*Primula veris*). Light blue glory of the snow (*Chionodoxa luciliae*). Violet (*Viola cornuta*) "Bambini mixture" in various pastel colors. Harmonizing shades of the same colors give the planting a charm that is further enhanced by the delicate flowers. The cheerful little faces of the miniature violets peek

out among the primulas and bloom tirelessly until it is time for summer planting.

Shades of blue: Blue gives an optical illusion of depth and shimmers in cool, fresh hues. Blue flowers in different shades and shapes can be delightful and subtle.
● Suitable plants: forget-me-nots; hyacinths "Delfts Blauw" and "Bismarck;" cushion-forming primulas; *Scilla siberica* "Spring Beauty."

White and red: This combination works because of the contrast created between the strong shades of red and shining white.
● Suitable plants: cushion primulas in shades of red and white. Red *Tulipa praestans* "Fuselier." Red hyacinth "L'Innocence."
The small tulips produce several blooms, while the primulas form thick cushions at their feet. The "baroque" hearts of the hyacinths complete the picture. The box will remain in full bloom for several weeks.

Flowers on the balcony all spring long

This planting plan was designed for a box 40 in (1 m) long, 6 in (15 cm) wide and 8 in (20 cm) deep, and shows just how colorful and long-lasting spring can be on a balcony. Various species form eye-catching features one after another, framed by masses of blossom. The early tulips bloom in the first month of spring, producing brilliant red flowers. They are accompanied by the small, pretty cyclamineus narcissi, which bear two to three graceful blooms per stalk. By the time the first flowers have faded, the next buds are already appearing amid the foliage. Little spires of grape hyacinths create magical points of blue light; the yellow tufts of double early tulips draw the eye, while the delicate blooms of the jonquils spread their sweet scent in the last month of spring. From the beginning to the end of spring, the cushion primulas and pansies provide a constantly flowering ground cover.

List of species and varieties — Flowering time
(Figures 1-4 = number of weeks)

Species and varieties	1st month of spring				2nd month of spring				3rd month of spring			
	1	2	3	4	1	2	3	4	1	2	3	4
5 water lily tulips, *Tulipa kaufmanniana* "Showwinner" (glowing scarlet red)			█	█	█	█						
3 double early tulips "Monte Carlo" (glowing yellow)							█	█	█			
7 cyclamineus narcissi, *Narcissus cyclamineus* "Tête à Tête" (golden yellow)		█	█	█	█	█						
5 jonquils, *Narcissus jonquilla* "Baby Moon" (golden orange yellow)							█	█	█	█	█	█
2 cushion primulas, *Primula vulgaris* hybrids (white)		█	█	█	█	█	█	█	█	█	█	█
5 grape hyacinths, *Muscari armeniacum* "Heavenly Blue" (sky blue)		█	█	█	█	█						
2 pansies, *Viola* x *wittrockiana* hybrids "Crystal Bowl Blau" (blue) or other blue varieties			█	█	█	█	█	█	█	█	█	█

Care after flowering

After the last cold spell of late spring, when it is time to plant your balcony boxes for summer, you will have to remove the remains of the spring flowers.

Bulbs and tubers cannot be left in the tubs for several years as they will be unable to store enough energy to go on flowering in a box. If you have a garden, remove the plants from the box, lay them in bunches, together with any remains of leaves, in a shady place, and cover them with compost. When the foliage has turned completely yellow, clean off the bulbs and tubers and store them (see temporary storage of bulbs and tubers). In the fall, they can be planted out in the garden. Particularly well-developed large bulbs and tubers can be reused for balcony boxes. If you have no garden, you can heel in the bulbs and tubers in a shallow box with some of the soil from the planting box and let them ripen in a shady place on the balcony (if the sun is strong, cover the bulbs with twigs). When the leaves have turned completely yellow, store

Winter protection for a balcony box: A box made of wood or polystyrene and a thick layer of wood shavings or dead leaves will protect the bulbs from freezing temperatures.

the bulbs. The healthiest-looking bulbs and tubers can be replanted in the fall (fill up gaps with new plants). If this is incon-venient for you, give the plants to a garden owner or throw them out.

After flowering, **perennials** can remain in the box if it is large enough and if there will still be enough space for summer flowers, or else they can be moved to suitable positions in the garden. If you have no garden, perennials can be transplanted into another tub to continue growing on the balcony until they are required again in the spring. Otherwise, they will have to be thrown away.

My tip: The old soil/compost can be used for soil improvement in the garden (remove large roots, sprinkle the compost onto the beds and rake it in lightly). If you mix the used compost in a ratio of 2:1 with seasoned, ripe garden compost, you can use it again in a balcony box for summer plants.

Overwintering balcony boxes

The cold and frost are much more harmful to balcony plants than to flowers in the garden. If you wish to see a splendid show of blooms each spring, it is essential that bulbs and tubers grown on a balcony are well protected during the winter. For this reason the boxes should be prepared well before the first frosts of winter.

Overwintering in the garden

If you have a garden, you can place the planted boxes of bulbs and tubers in a sheltered place outside for the winter. To protect them from freezing right through, the boxes should be sunk into the soil by about two-thirds or surrounded by thick bundles of twigs or conifer branches.

Overwintering indoors

The boxes can also be overwintered in the house in a position that is cool and frost-free. Light is not necessary. An unheated stairwell or a cool cellar is suitable for overwintering.

Overwintering on the balcony

(Illustration bottom left)

If you have no other facilities, you will have to prepare the boxes in situ on the balcony. The plants can cope with temperatures several degrees below freezing but if there are long periods of freezing weather, there is a danger of the soil in the boxes freezing right through, which would kill the plants. Frost protection is absolutely essential on **unprotected balconies**. An "over-box" will probably prove to be the best solution.

● The box should be 2-4 in (5-10 cm) larger than the planting box and can be made out of wood, polystyrene sheets, or strong cardboard.

● Stand the balcony box in the "over box" and fill the gaps with wood shavings, paper, or other insulating material.

● Cover the box with a thick layer of conifer branches. The plants will survive fairly cold winters if they are protected in this way.

If the balcony is sheltered or you live in a region with mild winters, it will be sufficient to wrap the box in a thick layer of newspaper, wood shavings, strips of fabric, or old pantyhose, tied up in string, and encased in bundles of conifer branches or twigs.

A terracotta container with wild tulips, cyclamineus narcissi, crocuses, and scilla.

Stand the boxes on the floor and then slide a small plank or small pieces of wood underneath it to lift the box off the cold floor. As soon as the days become milder, you can remove the coverings and layers of insulation.

My tip: If the container is very large, you can provide winter protection, even before planting, by lining the inside of the container with polystyrene sheets or bubble pack (leave the drainage holes free).

Watering in winter
After planting, the box should be watered once thoroughly but the soil should not be left soaking wet. This moisture will generally be sufficient for the next few weeks if the boxes are not placed in a position that is too warm. Mild weather will bring the bulbs to life, however, and growth will often begin as early as late winter. The sprouting bulbs will require moisture, so you may have to provide water so that the soil is just damp, even though it is still only late winter. Further watering will only become necessary when the soil has dried out again. For boxes that are overwintered indoors, dryness of the soil will have to be checked for more regularly. The soil should always feel slightly moist, never wet. Whenever it becomes completely dry, gently add a little more water.

Flowering magic in spring

Poeticus narcissi.

From elegant beauties in dazzling colour to humble little gems – the range of spring flowers is enormous. The following pages will introduce you to a selection of enchanting spring flowers and give useful notes on their care.

These short descriptions of the plants, together with the accompanying photographs and helpful tips on their care, should make it easier for you to choose suitable plants for your garden and balcony from the wide range of most commonly available and popular spring flowers, including tulips, narcissi, hyacinths, snowdrops and both sun-loving and shade-loving perennial and biennial herbaceous plants. In addition to the many plants featured here there are, of course, many more flowers that bloom during the months of spring but lack of space makes it impossible to mention all of them. The varieties mentioned here are merely representative of the great number of further extremely interesting varieties in some groups and species.

Glossary of keywords
The botanical name: gives an exact description of the plant.

Family: gives the taxonomy of the plant.
Flowering time and height: refer to the plant being described and may vary according to the variety. Please ask your supplier about any other particular variety.
Warning: supplies information on the toxicity of a plant or states whether it may cause a skin irritation.
Requirements: information on the optimal requirements (light, warmth, moisture, soil).
Care: details important measures of care.
Planting: here you will find ideal planting times, depths and spacing.
Use: the positions where the plant will do particularly well and look effective.

Elegant colours in the garden:
Towards the end of spring, parrot tulips are still in full bloom as the first summer flowers, such as bearded iris, begin to open. Lacy forget-me-nots close the gaps between tall-growing perennials.

An interesting contrast is created by combining single early tulips with candytuft as an underplanting.

Tulips

Tulips lend color to the spring garden. From elegant white to rich red, the countless species and varieties display a wealth of colors and beautiful flowers.

Botanical name: Tulipa.
Family: Liliaceae.
Flowering time: mid-spring to early summer.
NB: according to international classification, tulips are divided into four groups containing a total of fifteen divisions.
Warning: tulip bulbs are toxic and may irritate the skin!

Early tulips
Flowering time: from the middle to the end of the second month of spring.
Height: about 8-10 in (20-35 cm). To this group belong the single early tulips (12 in/30 cm), with flowers that are often scented; also the double early varieties, a shorter-stemmed group with voluptuous flowers.

Lily-flowered tulip.

Viridiflora tulip.

Greigii tulips with decorative leaf patterns.

Medium early tulips

Flowering times: mid- to late spring.
Height: about 14-20 in (35-50 cm).
These medium early-flowering tulips comprise the Mendel tulips, robust varieties which can cope with long periods of rain without coming to any harm, and the often two-colored Triumph tulips, which are also weather-hardy. Also included in this group are the Darwin hybrid tulips, the largest, most splendid varieties of all garden tulips; their flowers grow on firm, knee-high stalks and offer brilliant colors.

Late tulips

(Photographs above and below left)
Flowering times: late spring to early summer.

Height: 16-28 in (40-70 cm).
The Lily tulips, Darwin tulips and Parrot tulips all belong to this group. Cottage tulips are often the very latest flowering tulips of all and are prized for their soft shades. Viridiflora tulips are also counted among this group. Double late tulips resemble peonies in appearance but are sensitive to wind and rain. Rembrandt tulips display an exotic range of colors.

Wild species

(Photograph above right)
Flowering time: mid- to late spring.
Height: 4-16 in (10-40 cm).
The fourth group comprises all wild species and their hybrids, also called "botanical tulips." Among them are the *kauffmanniana* tulips, also called water lily tulips because of the shape of their flowers. *Fosteriana* tulips have the largest blooms of all tulips. *Greigii* tulips also have attractively colored foliage. Among them are a number of attractive species, such as the dwarfs, for example, the luxuriant

yellow-flowering *Tulipa tarda,* as well as tall-growing species, like the Weinberg tulip (*Tulipa sylvestris*).

Tips on the care of tulips

Requirements: sunny to slightly shady, neutral to slightly alkaline sandy or loamy soil. Cannot stand acid or overfertilized soil.
Care: cut off faded flowers immediately. Remove garden tulips from the soil every few years and replant them in a different position. Every fall, fertilize them with garden compost. Wild species need a dry position in summer; fertilize sparingly.
Planting: the best time is early to mid-fall, about 2-4 in (5-10 cm) deep with a spacing of about 4-6 in (10-15 cm). Do not forget a drainage layer as protection against waterlogging.
Use: for specially attractive borders use garden tulips; botanical tulips for rockeries or nature gardens. Single early tulips and the wild species are well suited to balconies.

Narcissi

Easter is daffodil and narcissus time. This genus has a lot more to offer than just the ever-popular daffodil with its glowing golden trumpets. There is a truly astonishing range of varieties.

Botanical name: Narcissus.
Family: Amaryllidaceae.
Flowering time: early spring to early summer.
Warning: narcissi are toxic and the plant's sap may cause skin irritation!

The name Lent lily proves that this plant is firmly established in folklore. The classic Easter flower is the pure yellow trumpet narcissus which forms just one group of the prolific genus of *Narcissi*. There are about 10,000 varieties divided into eleven divisions, which include large and small garden narcissi as well as wild narcissi.

The basis for their classification is the shape of the flower and its origin.

The flowers of narcissi consist of outer petals arranged in a star shape and inner petals which come in varying shapes.

Large garden narcissi

(Photograph right)

Lovers of elegant flowers will much appreciate the group of large garden narcissi. The shape of the inner petals has given the two groups their names.

Daffodils (Lent lilies) have inner petals that are fused into a trumpet-shape that can be as long as the outer petals but may be even longer.

Flowering time: early to mid-spring.

Daffodils are symbols of Easter and spring.

Height: 16-20 in (40-50 cm).

Cup narcissi have bowl-shaped inner petals which are shorter than the outer petals.

Flowering time: mid- to late spring.
Height: 12-18 in (30-45 cm).
Popular varieties: "King Alfred" and "Golden Harvest" among the daffodils, and "Fortune," "Flower Record," and "Ice Follies" among the cup narcissi.

These two groups can have outer and inner petals that are yellow or white, the inner petals may even be red.

Small garden narcissi

Enchanting flower shapes and delicate beauty are the main features of this small garden narcissus.

Double narcissi present an unusual picture as their complicated inner petals resemble those of orchids.

Flowering times: mid- to late spring.
Height: 12-20 in (30-50 cm).

Angel's tears or Triandus narcissi are graceful, delicate garden flowers. The stalk usually carries several pendulous flowers with petals that curl back.

Flowering time: mid- to late spring.
Height: 10-24 in (25-60 cm).

Cyclamen or Cyclamineus narcissi are particularly graceful harbingers of spring. They have been given this name because their petals are turned back like those of cyclamen.
Flowering time: early to mid-spring.
Height: up to 16 in (40 cm).
Jonquils or scented narcissi have several sweetly scented, delicate flowers on each stalk. Jonquils must be planted in a warm, sheltered position and require winter protection.
Flowering time: late spring to early summer.
Height: 10-20 in (25-50 cm).
Tazettas or Poetaz narcissi produce several small, pleasantly scented flowers. They are excellent for propagating. They will require winter protection in the garden.
Flowering time: mid- to late spring.
Height: 12-18 in (30-45 cm).
Poeticus or poet's narcissus present an incomparably beautiful sight, particularly if the white, scented flowers are left to unfold in long grass. The inner petals are very flat and are often edged in red.
Flowering time: late spring.
Height: up to 16 in (40 cm).

Wild narcissi

Wild narcissi are mainly delicate plants. The robust species are suitable for growing outside as well as in bowls. One of the most striking species is the hoop petticoat narcissus (*Narcissus bulbocodium*) whose yellow flowers look just like tiny ballerinas.

Other narcissi

The last group encompasses all narcissi which do not belong in any of the previously mentioned groups on account of their unusual appearance. Worth mentioning are the split-corona and the orchid-flowering narcissi.

Tazetta narcissi are charming dwarf narcissi for the rockery.

Tips on the care of narcissi

Requirements: sunny to semi-shady positions. Any normal, not too heavy, garden soil that is free of waterlogging, even acid soils.
Care: very easy to cultivate; will flower regularly every year without being replanted. Remove dead flower heads.
Planting: in early fall at the latest; large garden narcissi 6-8 in (15-20 cm) deep; smaller species 4 in (10 cm) deep.
Use: large narcissi for flower beds or in groups, at the edges of groups of trees or bushes; small wild species in rockeries or at the edge of a pond. All small varieties are suitable for the balcony.

Poeticus narcissi.

A profusion of popular varieties of garden crocus.

Crocuses

Crocuses are some of the first flowers of spring and always attract attention with their cheerful, brightly colored flowers. A lawn covered in multi-colored crocuses is a lovely sight.

Botanical name: Crocus.
Family: Iridaceae.
Flowering time: last month of winter to mid-spring.
Height: 2¼ -4¾ in (6-12 cm).
NB: In addition to the many spring-flowering species, the genus *Crocus* also includes some fall-flowering species which are not covered here.

Garden crocuses
(Photograph above)
Without doubt, the most striking crocuses are the brilliantly colored, large-flowered garden hybrids. Their large, funnel-shaped flowers appear before the long, narrow leaves and open wide in the warm spring sun. The dominant colors are white, yellow and violet, but some varieties have striped flowers. These varieties are derived from *Crocus chrysanthus* and *Crocus vernus*, proliferate

well by themselves and are also suitable for planting in a bowl.
Popular varieties of garden crocuses are shown:
"Pickwick,"
"Remembrance," "Jeanne d'Arc," "Haarlem Gem," "Early Perfection," "Vanguard," and "Purpureus Grandiflorus."

Wild species

(Photographs right and below)
The wild crocuses cannot quite compete with the giant flowers of the garden crocuses but they are not far behind in growth and splendid color. *Crocus tomasinianus* is sometimes called the "elf crocus" and is highly recommended for its long flowering time (late winter to early spring). The species has lavender blue flowers but there are also white and purple varieties. The Ankara crocus (*Crocus ancyrensis*) and the early spring crocus (*Crocus chrysanthus*) provide a display of beautiful, complementary colors in the company of *Crocus tomasinianus*.
Crocus imperati and *Crocus sieberi* bloom even earlier. In the last month of winter, the first warming rays of the sun coax their delicate flowers from the earth. The latter, in particular, is considered to be one of the most beautiful crocuses for the garden. The gold crocus (*Crocus flavus*) produces glowing golden flowers. It will proliferate well by itself. The name alone conjures up the beauty of the gold brocade or wallflower crocus (*Crocus angustifolius*). A similarly apt name is that of the silver brocade crocus (*Crocus versicolor var. picturatus*) whose white flowers display a tracery of violet-colored veins.

Crocus tomasinianus and Crocus ancyrensis.

Tips on the care of crocuses

Requirements: they will thrive in full sun in humus-rich, well-drained soil.
Care: in summer, the small corms (bulbs) need dry soil to ripen properly and it is necessary to make sure that the soil is well drained at all times. Crocuses flower better on poor soil, so fertilizing is not necessary.
Planting: in the second month of fall, 2-4 in (5-10 cm) deep, spaced 2-4 in (5-10 cm) apart and covered with a layer of ripe garden compost.
Use: in flower beds and lawns. Wild crocuses can also be planted under deciduous trees; they will not be in shade because their flowering time is so early. All species are suitable for balconies, *Crocus vernus* particularly so.
Special note: birds can be a nuisance, although they only peck at the yellow flowers. The only counter-measure is to do without yellow species and varieties. Sometimes birds can be frightened away by toy windmills on sticks placed among the crocuses.

Crocus albiflorus.

NB: green areas (lawns, etc.) covered in proliferating crocuses should not be mowed before the end of spring as it takes that long for the narrow, grass-like crocus leaves to store enough reserves to give the following year's growth the necessary strength.

Fritillarias

This name includes both the large-flowered species like *Fritillaria imperialis* and its delicate relatives, such as the snake's head fritillaria (*Fritillaria meleagris*).

Crown imperial
Botanical name: Fritillaria imperialis.
Family: Liliaceae.
Flowering time: mid- to late spring.
Height: 36-40 in (90-120 cm).

The best known species, out of almost 100 species of the genus *Fritillaria*, is the crown imperial (*Fritillaria imperialis*). Glowing, colored bells hang in a ring below a spiky head of leaves, and golden yellow stamens protrude from each bell. The regal elegance of these plants has always been popular in rustic gardens and it is one of the oldest garden plants. The fiery orange flowers have been the source of many legends. This plant was reputed to have been rebuked for its arrogance by Christ in the Garden of Gethsemane; ever since then it has hung its head and tears fall from its flowers.
Requirements: sunny position; loose, nutrient-rich soil.
Care: if necessary, fertilize when it starts shooting; cut off faded flowers and leaves.
Planting: late summer to early fall, 8-10 in (20-25 cm) deep, slightly tilted on a bed of sand, so that no moisture can accumulate at the stem neck or at the bottom of the bulb.
Use: in borders and flower beds.
Special note: the bulbs give off an unpleasant smell which is effective in frightening off voles. This makes this plant very useful for controlling voles in the garden.

Crown imperial fritillaria, one of the oldest garden flowers.

The original fritillaria had orange-red flowers but red and yellow varieties also exist. "Rubra Maxima," "Lutea," and "Aurora" are popular for the garden. Fritillaria raddeana, which originates from Iran, is very similar but more delicate and has greenish-yellow flowers.

Snake's head fritillaria is a good name for this graceful plant.

Fritillaria acmopetala.

Snake's head fritillaria
Botanical name: Fritillaria meleagris.
Family: Liliaceae.
Flowering time: mid- to late spring.
Height: 8-12 in (20-30 cm).
Warning: this plant is toxic!

The snake's head fritillaria is humbler than its tall cousin, at a height of only 8-12 in (20-30 cm). It has a characteristic and unusual checked pattern on its bell-shaped flowers. These plants can sometimes be found growing wild in damp meadows but you should never dig up plants in the wild as it is a protected species! This means that neither the plant nor its seed may be removed from its natural habitat. You will find a number of beautiful varieties in the gardening trade, for example, the pure white "Aphrodite," the purple green "Artemis," or the large-flowered "Poseidon" in shades of reddish-purple. Snake's head fritillarias are very easy to care for if they are planted in the right position. One thing to note is that the soil should be free of chalk or lime.

They thrive particularly well in marshy ground or at the edge of water where the soil is always damp. They propagate from bulbils and, in time, large groups will form.
Requirements: a sunny to semi-shady position in moist, humus-rich, lime-free soil.
Care: fairly undemanding. The bulbs are not easy to store.
Planting: late summer/early fall; 2-4 in (5-10 cm) deep.
Use: at the edges of groups of trees or bushes, watersides, balconies.
Special note: snake's head fritillarias are much loved by bees which will visit them to seek nectar.

Other fritillarias
Botanical name: Fritillaria species.
Family: Liliaceae.
Flowering time: early to late spring.
Height: 6-16 in (15-40 cm).

Many other attractive species can be grown in the garden, for example:

● The very undemanding *Fritillaria acmopetala* produces knee-high stems with nodding flowers in surprisingly beautiful shades of olive green and reddish-brown during mid- to late spring.

● The almost black flowers of *Fritillaria camtschatcensis*, a species which abhors lime, have a special charm of their own.

● The pale yellow flowers of the exotic *Fritillaria pallidiflora* are most attractive.

● The Persian fritillaria (*Fritillaria persica*) exudes a wonderful scent from its plum-colored flowers. It is relatively easy to cultivate but propagates very slowly.
Requirements: sunny to semi-shady position, in humus-rich soil.
Care: needs winter protection.
Planting: early fall, 2¾ -3 in (7-8 cm) deep.
Use: rockeries; *Fritillaria pallidiflora* will also do well on balconies.

The first signs of spring

The snow may not even have quite melted and the icy hand of Jack Frost may still linger as the winter aconites, snowdrops, and snowflakes open their delicate flowers.

Snowdrops
Botanical name: *Galanthus* species.
Family: *Amaryllidaceae.*
Flowering time: late winter to early spring.
Height: 2-8 in (5-20 cm).
Warning: this plant is toxic!

The snowdrop features in many old stories, for example, Eastern European peasants were once thought to dig up the bulbs as soon as the snow melted, so that witches and wizards could not put spells on the cows to make their milk dry up. This practice is not recommended as the plant is toxic but perhaps the power thus ascribed to snowdrops has something to do with the name *Galanthus*, which means "milk flower." Snowdrops were known 2,000 years ago and were hailed as messengers of spring. It is hard to believe that they are related to the majestic *Hippeastrum* as their green-edged flowers are nothing like the conspicuous flowers of that species. Snowdrops have their own special charm, however, and should be included in every garden.
● The most widespread species of snowdrop, which grows wild in some parts of Europe, is *Galanthus nivalis*. It soon produces seeds in semi-shady positions and establishes large colonies. This

The botanical name Galanthus means "milk flower".

species gave rise to many cultivated varieties, including double types.
● *Galanthus elwesii* is much larger and stronger and sometimes produces its large, striking flowers as early as the second month of winter.
Requirements: sunny to semi-shady position in humus-rich, loose soil; plenty of moisture in spring; dry in the summer. *Galanthus elwesii* likes a sunny position.
Care: do not fertilize; let the foliage dry out after flowering.
Planting: first to second month of fall; 2-3 in (5-8 cm) deep in small groups.
Use: along the edges of trees or in informal lawns.

Eranthis hyemalis (winter aconite).

Winter aconite
Botanical name: *Eranthis* species.
Family: *Ranunculaceae.*
Flowering time: late winter to early spring.
Height: 2-6 in (5-15 cm).

The winter aconite, with its golden inflorescences, opens its petals early in the last month of winter. If you plant all the different varieties together, the flowering time, which is quite short for each individual variety, can be extended to many weeks. The winter aconite (*Eranthis hyemalis*) is the first to flower in late winter; then, in early spring, it is followed by the Cilician winter aconite (*Eranthis cilicica*) and finally by *Eranthis* x *tubergenii* which can bloom right up into the second month of spring.
Requirements: sunny to semi-shady position; humus-rich, loose soil, neutral to slightly alkaline.
Care: very undemanding.
Planting: early fall, 2-3 in (5-8 cm) deep, spaced at 2-4 in (5-10 cm); let the tubers soak in tepid water overnight before they are planted.
Use: under trees or bushes, in rockeries or lawns.

Snowflakes have been planted in gardens since the fifteenth century.

Snowflakes
Botanical name: *Leucojum vernum.*
Family: *Amaryllidaceae.*
Flowering time: early to mid-spring.
Height: about 8 in (20 cm).
Warning: this plant is toxic!

This flower strongly resembles the snowdrop in that its flowers display similar colors and markings. The natural occurrence of this plant in the wild has fallen drastically in recent years but thriving colonies can be found in gardens.
During the first and second months of spring their creamy white flowers, with their green petal tips, stand out even at a distance. The strap-like leaves are dark green and die back after flowering.
● *Leucojum vagneri*, the Hungarian snowflake, is considered to be particularly robust and striking. Usually, two flowers, with yellowish-green tips, appear on each stalk, forming a very attractive arrangement.
Requirements: semi-shady position; humus-rich, evenly moist soil.

Care: the plants should not be cut back too early so that the seeds can ripen and propagation is assured.
Planting: in early fall, about 4 in (10 cm) deep, in small groups.
Use: edging for trees and bushes; along the banks of ponds, etc.

553

Hyacinth beauties in shades of white and pink, blending with similar shades of primulas and daisies.

Hyacinths

The colors are beautiful, the scent is glorious, and they lend a special magic to the springtime garden.

Botanical name: Hyacinthus orientalis.
Family: Liliaceae.
Flowering time: mid- to late spring.
Height: about 12 in (30 cm).
Warning: Hyacinths may cause skin irritation in some sensitive people.

The plump flower heads of hyacinths are admired by many for their fresh colors and bewitching scent.
In the Middle Ages it was believed that merely gazing at a hyacinth could free one from all the sufferings of body and soul. In the language of flowers they represent joy and gentle love.
Whether in the garden, on a balcony or patio, or grown as an indoor plant, hyacinths create an attractive picture that is hard to ignore.

Many varieties

Early varieties of hyacinths did not display the dense flower heads we know today, as their star-shaped, individual flowers hung loosely from the stem.

Just like tulips, these flowers were once objects of financial speculation and were sold for high prices. Over the years, the great interest that developed in cultivating them gave rise to a wide range of different varieties.

The spectrum of colors extends from pure white through yellow, pink, apricot, red, and orange to darkest violet and black. The varieties are not only distinguished by color but also by their flowering time. Early varieties bloom in mid-spring, medium early ones toward the end of the second month of spring, and late varieties in the last month of spring. The Multiflora hyacinths, which have been around since 1912, bloom very early. They form several inflorescences which have very few flowers. Bushy growth is obtained by cutting out the main inflorescence.

Requirements: the position should be sheltered and sunny; the soil humus-rich with plenty of nutrients. Make sure the soil is well drained.

Care: provide protection from frost with a layer of dead leaves or twigs, particularly in regions with harsh weather. The hyacinths can be left in the ground for several years in favorable positions but eventually the inflorescences will become less robust and more open. You can also dig up the bulbs after flowering and store them in a dry place until they are planted again in the fall.

Planting: the larger the bulbs, the more luxuriant the flowers. Slightly smaller bulbs (about 2 in/5 cm in diameter and 6 in/15 cm in circumference) are suitable for planting outside. Plant the bulbs in early to

A colourful bowl of hyacinths, tulips, crocuses, and snowdrops.

mid-fall, about 3-6 in (8-15 cm) deep and spaced 6-8 in (15-20 cm) apart.

Use: they look best in conspicuous positions where their plump flower heads will be in full view. Always plant groups of five or more specimens. They are also well suited to balcony boxes and bowls, and look good combined with other bulbous plants.

Special note: hyacinths propagate easily. Large bulbs, with a diameter of at least 7 in (18 cm), should be used.

Two medium-early hyacinth varieties: pale yellow "Yellow Hammer" and blue "Concorde." The blue "Bismarck," the pure white "L'Innocence," the light pink "Anne-Marie," and the dark pink "Pink Pearl" are also very popular.

Blue spring-flowering plants

All of the following flowers are graceful in appearance and have an undemanding nature. They also compete with each other to produce the most brilliant shades of blue, like precious gems amid abundant foliage. Most species form dense colonies which carpet the ground.

Scillas and Kaufmann tulips in harmonious combination.

Tips on care

The following details apply to all of the flowers mentioned on these two pages.

Requirements: sunny to semi-shady positions; in humus-rich soil.

Care: undemanding.

Planting: first and second months of fall; 3 in (8 cm) deep, in groups.

Use: along the edges of trees, rockeries, in the lawn, in balcony boxes, and bowls.

Warning: scilla are toxic!

Scilla

(Photograph top right)

Botanical name: Scilla species.

Family: Liliaceae.

Flowering time: first and second months of spring.

Height: 2-8 in (5-20 cm).

Warning: this plant is toxic!

The most important of these species is Scilla sibirica which forms dense mats of clear blue, star-shaped flowers. "Spring Beauty" has the most intense shade of blue and the largest flowers. The flowers of Scilla mischtschenkoana, by comparison, shine like delicate porcelain and begin to open at the same time as snowdrops and winter aconites. Pale blue, turquoise, or azure are the shades of the flowers of the two-leafed Scilla bifolia; white and pink sports are also seen.

Grape hyacinths

(Small photograph, right)

Botanical name: Muscari species.

Family: Liliaceae.

Flowering time: early to late spring.

Height: 4-12 in (10-30 cm).

Grape hyacinths produce flowers that seem to reflect the blue of the sky. Their slender spires give any flower bed a slightly Far Eastern flavor. Many of the 50 or so species of the genus Muscari are suitable for growing in the garden and all are undemanding and tough. Muscari armeniacum, for example, forms prolific colonies. Muscari botryoides blooms in the second and third months of spring and has cylindrical flowers. Lovers of seductive scents will soon come to appreciate Muscari neglectum. The feather

Grape hyacinth (Muscari botryoides).

hyacinth (Muscari comosum "Plumosum") will delight you with its pretty, feathery, bushy flowers.

Bluebells

Botanical name: Endymion species.

Family: Liliaceae.

Flowering time: second to third months of spring.

Height: 8-16 in (20-40 cm).

Brodiaea laxa (syn. Triteleia laxa) is a rarity in the garden. The flowers are very elegant and are often used as cut flowers.

The Spanish bluebell (Endymion hispanicus) in a wild garden.

Chionodoxa sardensis.

The bluebell or wild hyacinth (*Endymion non-scriptus*) and the Spanish hyacinth (*Endymion hispanicus*) were once ascribed to the genus *Scilla*.

Glory of the snow
(Photograph, bottom right)
Botanical name: *Chionodoxa* species.
Family: *Liliaceae.*
Flowering time: first to second months of spring.
Height: 4-8 in (10-20 cm).

The common name of *Chionodoxa*, glory of the snow, is a most poetic description of this charming little plant which flowers early,

sometimes just as the last snows are melting. *Chionodoxa luciliae* is the most popular species for planting in the garden. The stem carries about ten shining, blue, star-shaped flowers with white centres. Some varieties are pink. *Chionodoxa gigantea* has lavender blue flowers; those of *Chionodoxa sardensis* are gentian blue.

Iris

Small and delicate best describes these iris species. Their distinctive flowers in many lovely colors make these graceful plants an extravagant treat in the garden or on a balcony.

Botanical name: Iris species.
Family: Iridaceae.
Flowering time: late winter to late spring.
Height: 4-16 in (10-40 cm).
Warning: iris bulbs are toxic!

In Ancient Greece, Iris was the golden-winged messenger of the gods and the goddess of the rainbow. She gave her name to the many-colored plant genus *Iris*, which comprises some 200 species, with several thousand varieties. These exotic flowers are also sometimes called the "orchid of the north." Under the name fleur-de-lys or Bourbon lily, the iris is probably the most famous of all heraldic plants and the old flag of France bore several stylized fleurs-de-lys on a plain background until it was replaced by the tricolor. The flowers, consisting of three falls (hanging petals) and three standards (inner petals) form unique shapes, with their colors providing further charm. Within this large genus the spring-flowering species – in particular the bulbous ones – play a special role.

Iris bucharica forms beautiful clumps.

Gems for your rockery
(Photograph above)
Iris bucharica, which is about 16 in (40 cm) tall, has a most unusual-looking head. The scented flowers are yellow and white, appear in late spring, and resemble stag antlers, which is why it is sometimes called the antler iris. It belongs to the group of Juno irises whose standards (inner petals) are not upright but protrude sideways. This group also includes some rarer species, for example, *Iris graeberiana*, a delicate, lavender blue plant which flowers in late spring and grows about 12 in (30 cm) tall. The Juno iris is very similar to *Iris reticulata*, one of the bulbous irises.

The bulbous irises
The season of flowering irises begins as early as the last month of winter when the flowers appear on 4-8 in (10-20 cm) tall stems. Their blue or yellow petals flutter in the breeze (hence the name "flag") and make an eye-catching feature in the garden.
Tried and tested species and varieties
The canary yellow flowers of *Iris danfordiae* have olive green markings and a very pleasant scent. *Iris histrio* appears in the striking costume of a harlequin, which gives it its botanical name. *Iris histrioides* is not to be outdone in its equally fashionable "outfit." Depending on the variety, the flowers are light blue, dark blue, or violet blue with yellow, orange, or violet-black markings.

Iris reticulata flowers very early.

Dwarf iris "Three Smokes."

Dwarf iris "Lady."

The shoots often push through the thawing snow and they reach their peak of flowering during the last month of winter and the first month of spring. The inconspicuous, grass-like leaves appear after the flowers are over.

Iris reticulata is named for its bulb which is enveloped in a net-like sheath. This plant is easy to care for. The flowers of its many different varieties come in all shades of blue. "Harmony" is a sky-blue variety with petals sporting a shining yellow central stripe. "Katharina Hodgkin" is a hybrid with unusual colors; its delicate yellow flowers are tinged with a breath of cream and blue.

NB: many bulbous iris species or varieties make wonderful cut flowers which will stay fresh in a vase for a very long time.

Requirements: sunny to semi-sunny position in permeable, poor, stony to loamy, slightly chalky soil.

Care: waterlogging must be avoided.

During the summer, the bulbs require dry soil for ripening. If the summer is wet, protect the plants from too much moisture by covering them with glass or plastic sheeting.

Planting: the bulbs should be planted in the second month of fall, 2-3 in (5-8 cm) deep, preferably in a sand-loam mixture.

Use: in rockeries, on tops of dry-stone walls, in balcony boxes, and bowls. Propagates easily.

Warning: these plants are toxic!

Dwarf bearded iris

(Photographs, center top and right) Most people are familiar with the dignified little bearded iris in a summer flower bed. In contrast to the species described above, the bearded iris does not grow from a bulb but from a rhizome, which is a thickened underground stem. Short representatives of this group only grow about 10 in (25 cm) tall and flower as early as mid- to late spring. Their flowers are brilliantly colored and just as splendid as their tall summer relatives. There is an over-whelming range of varieties and the spectrum of colors includes almost all shades. The beards on the falls (outer, hanging petals) are often in a contrasting color to the rest of the petals and create flowers of great visual interest.

Popular varieties: the light lemon-colored "Lemon Puff," the bronze "Gingerbread Man," the dark violet "Cyanea," the ruby red "Little Rosy Wings," and the white and blue veined "Knick Knack."

Requirements: full sunlight, in dry, permeable, neutral to slightly alkaline soil.

Care: propagate from division of the rhizomes. Avoid waterlogging.

Planting: the rhizomes should be planted in shallow holes in the fall. Dig a shallow, circular hole. Place the rhizome in the slightly raised center, carefully spread out the roots, and cover with a thin layer of soil. Do not forget to provide a drainage layer!

Use: in rockeries or on a patio, in large bowls or containers between clumps of grass, cushion-forming plants, and bulbous flowers.

The plump, many-colored flowers of Ranunculus planted together in one large bowl.

Spring rarities

Alongside the ever-popular flowers like tulips and nar-cissi, we must not forget to mention some of the rarer beauties of spring. There is a large choice of many graceful as well as decorative species.

Ranunculae and anemones (Photograph above).
Botanical name: Ranunuculus asiaticus and *Anemone* species.
Family: Ranunculaceae.
Flowering time: late winter to late spring.
Height: 4-12 in (10-30 cm).
Warning: Ranunculae, Anemone nemorosa and *Anemone blanda* are toxic!
Requirements: Ranunculae in sunny to semi-shady positions;

Anemone species in semi-shady to shady places in fresh, humus-rich, lime-containing soil.
Planting: plant *Ranunculae* tubers in a sheltered spot in the first month of spring and let them shoot. Anemones can be planted in colonies in the first and second months of summer, 2-3 in (5-8 cm) deep.
Care: undemanding, provided they are planted in the right position.
Use: Ranunculae in flower beds and bowls; anemones under trees.

Anemone blanda flowers from the first to second month of spring in shades of violet, pink, or white. It is self-sowing and forms vigorous colonies.

Windflowers or wood anemones (*Anemone nemorosa*) love to grow under deciduous trees and form extensive carpets of white flowers. This is the variety "Robinsoniana" with delicate lavender blue flowers.

Cyclamen, the small relatives of the popular indoor plants, are charming, hardy garden flowers that are always much admired.
Botanical name: *Cyclamen* species.
Family: *Primulaceae.*
Flowering time: first to second months of spring.
Height: 2-8 in (5-20 cm) tall.
Warning: these plants are toxic!

Cyclamen coum, one of the spring-flowering species, is a dwarf among cyclamen, at a height of only 2-4 in (5-10 cm). The flowers are white, pink, or carmine red and rise above deep green, roundish leaves. Other species are *Cyclamen libanoticum*, a scented species with shaded flowers, and *Cyclamen repandum*, a prostrate species with a scent of violets.

Dog's tooth violet (*Erythronium*) is a graceful plant for the garden.
Botanical name: *Erythronium* species.
Family: *Liliaceae.*
Flowering time: first to last month of spring.
Height: 4-16 in (10-40 cm).

Purple-spotted leaves and pink, gracefully curving flower bells are characteristic of the dog's tooth violet (*Erythronium dens-canis*). The flowers of *Erythronium revolutum* change color after opening in

shades that graduate from cream to pink. The bells of *Erythronium tuolumnense* are a brilliant yellow.
Requirements: semi-shady position, in loose, fresh, slightly acidic garden soil.
Planting: the last month of spring, 4 in (10 cm) deep, spaced 4 in (10 cm) apart.
Care: fairly undemanding if positioned correctly.
Use: around the edge of trees and bushes, in rockeries.
(**The photographs:** Left, yellow "Pagoda;" right, pink "Purple King.")

Requirements: sunny to semi-shady position in neutral to slightly alkaline soil.
Planting: in the first month of fall, about 2 in (5 cm) deep.
Care: undemanding if placed in the right position.
Use: along the edges of trees or bushes, in rockeries, particularly attractive in wild gardens.

Sun-loving perennials

Herbaceous perennials that like plenty of sunlight will endow your garden with a wealth of colorful flowers. Some of the most prolific flowering plants are the primulas, which come in so many colors that one has to watch out when choosing plants in case the garden becomes too colorful!

When the sun's warming rays penetrate the wintry soil, plants quickly spring to life. The golden cups of pheasant's eye (*Adonis vernalis*) open as early as the last month of winter on sunny slopes of rockeries, together with the nodding heads of the pasqueflower (*Pulsatilla* species) and the golden bells of *Primula veris.* Leopard's bane (*Doronicum*), *Bergenia,* and bleeding heart (*Dicentra spectabilis*) do not begin to flower until spring has well and truly arrived.

Tips on the care of sun-loving herbaceous perennials
These perennials are all easy to grow and will flower without a lot of time-consuming care. Only bleeding heart is a little more demanding and will take several years to develop into a flourishing plant.
Requirements: with few exceptions, all the species mentioned here will manage in ordinary garden soil.
Planting: see planting perennials, and planting times.
Care: always remove dead heads as soon as possible. Large colonies should be rejuvenated every few years by dividing them.

Bergenia species, family *Saxifragaceae*, flowering time first to last month of spring, are also called elephant's ear because of their large leaves. They are suitable for rockeries or a dry pond edging. Some species have vivid green leaves; others have vividly colored foliage in the fall. The flowers come in all shades of pink to red.

Pheasant's eye, *Adonis vernalis*, family *Ranunculaceae*, flowering time last month of winter to second month of spring, requires poor, chalky, dry soil. Suitable for dry and stony beds. *Adonis amurensis* is another pretty species with very decorative foliage.
Warning: this plant is toxic!

Leopard's bane, *Doronicum* species, family *Compositae*, flowering time from the second to third month of spring, bears intensely golden yellow daisy-like flowers. Both single and double varieties are available. They go well with red tulips or blue cushion-forming perennials in borders and beds.

Pasqueflowers, *Pulsatilla* species, family *Ranunculaceae*, flowering time from the first to second month of spring, are fuzzy beauties that will only grow on permeable, poor-ish soil. Some species require acid soil. They should never be fertilized.
Warning: these flowers are toxic!

Kingcups or marsh marigolds
(*Caltha palustris*) belong to the family of *Ranunculaceae,* flower from the second to third month of spring and are easy-to-care-for perennials for the edge of a pond or stream. The soil should contain some lime and plenty of nutrients.
Warning: this plant is toxic!

Primulas are inseparable from the concept of spring. When the yellow flowers of the wild cowslip appear in the meadows, you know winter is really over.
Botanical name: *Primula* species.
Family: Primulaceae.
Flowering time: early to late spring.
Height: 4-16 in (10-40 cm).
Warning: may cause skin allergies in sensitive people!

Primulas offer a rich variety of shapes and colors.
● Border primulas create colorful clumps of flowers in many brilliant colors, some with contrasting white edges.
● *Primula denticulata*, with its round flower heads, thrives in moist soil. These plants produce glorious globes of white, violet, pink and red.
● Candelabra primroses can be obtained in strong colors.
● Carpet primulas (*Juliae* hybrids) are also called Carnival primulas. They come in any number of shades from pastel colors to strong, brilliant colors. They proliferate at a fast rate in the garden.
● Auriculas are splendid flowering

beauties that include the Alpine auricula (*Primula auricula*) with its striking golden yellow flower bells.
● The cowslip is a genuine wild primula (*Primula veris*) with scented yellow flowers, while the wild meadow oxlip (*Primula eliator*) bears unscented sulphur yellow flowers.
Primulas look just as good in balcony boxes and bowls as in the garden. The border primulas, in particular, can be planted here late in the spring.
Requirements: sunny to semi-shady position; fresh to moist, humus-rich soil.
Care and planting: undemanding. Short-lived border primulas should be fertilized a little at the time of flowering. Propagate from seed or by division. Plant in the fall or spring.
Use: flower beds, edges of trees, water's edge, bowls, and boxes.

Bleeding heart (*Dicentra spectablis*) belongs to the family of *Fumariaceae* and flowers in the last month of spring. It should be planted in a shallow hole in permeable, nutrient-rich soil and then left to grow undisturbed.

Shade-loving herbaceous perennials

Far from living in the gloom, these plants flourish in positions that are shady or semi-shady. Some of them are particularly charming, others are conspicuous for their luxuriant growth.

Many herbaceous plants require the refreshing coolness of the shade for protection against the hot rays of the sun. On the one hand, the sun is a welcome source of warmth, but on the other hand it may burn the sensitive foliage of many plants and dry out the soil too fast, so that the plants quickly die. In the summer, the sun would have an even more lethal effect and heat-sensitive plants would suffer considerably. The effect of the sun is softened in the semi-shade, the soil retains moisture, and the temperature differences are not quite so extreme.
Tips on care: The plants introduced here are all easy to grow and care for as long as they are planted in the right positions. The less deep the shade, which means the more light the plant receives, the more moisture is needed in the soil. You might have to water the soil occasionally.

Caucasus forget-me-not and golden strawberry (*Duchesnea indica*) are two flowers that go well together.

Two species that are reminiscent of forget-me-nots, with tiny, sky-blue flowers, are:
● Blue-eyed Mary (*Omphalodes verna*), family *Boraginaceae*, flowers from mid- to late spring.
● The Caucasus forget-me-not (*Brunnera macrophylla*), family *Boraginaceae*, also flowers from mid- to late spring.
● Both are charming plants for the edge of trees or in the rockery. They quickly form well-developed stands. From mid- to late spring they are covered in a myriad pretty little flowers. These plants are extremely undemanding and require hardly any care at all. It is a good idea to plant the Caucasus forget-me-not under cherry trees. The resulting blue carpet of flowers at the foot of the flowering cherry tree is an unforgettable sight.

Hepatica nobilis has various common names. The leaves appear after the flowers.
Warning: this plant is toxic!

Jerusalem cowslip or lungwort (*Pulmonaria officinalis*). The blue lungwort (*Pulmonaria angustifolia*) has flowers that change color from pink to blue.

Violets (*Viola* species) like to live modestly in the shade. One of the most popular species is the scented violet (*Viola odorata*) which has a sweet perfume.

Christmas roses (*Helleborus niger*) are some of the first flowers to defy winter. They may flower as early as the first month of winter (around Christmas time in the northern hemisphere), but certainly by the first month of spring. They need an undisturbed position in chalky, humus-rich soil for many years in order to develop properly. Do not fertilize.
Warning: this plant is toxic!

Epimedium species (barrenwort or bishop's hat) are the ballet dancers among the spring flowers. Their other common name of elf flower says much about the graceful attitude of these little flowers, which seem to dance above their beautifully shaped and colored foliage. Their rhizomes spread rapidly throughout large areas and cover the ground with metallic shiny leaves. Cut back faded foliage.

Other Dicentra species, the sisters of bleeding heart (*D. spectabilis*), look almost as graceful and elegant as the *Epimedium* described left. Whitish, yellow to cherry red flowers, shaped like hearts, cover the plants with their finely slit foliage. The sensitive, rather brittle rootstock has to be handled very carefully when it is planted in shallow, humus-rich soil.

Cushion-forming herbaceous perennials

What would spring be without aubrieta, candytuft, etc.? The stunning effect of these plants is created by the multitude of tiny individual flowers which entirely cover the clumps of foliage. Bordering a path or tumbling over the top of a wall, in a rockery or on the edge of a patio, they are one of the wonders of spring.

Alyssum saxatile and *Alyssum montanum* grow about 8 in (20 cm) tall and are covered with golden yellow to sulphur yellow flowers. Their intense scent entices many insects to visit them. They prefer to grow on humus-rich, sandy, stony soil and can be sown straight into the ground where they are intended to grow.

Aubrieta hybrids prefer a sunny, warm position.
Botanical name: *Aubrieta* hybrids.
Family: *Cruciferae.*
Flowering time: mid- to late spring.
Height: about 4 in (10 cm).

Aubrieta deltoidea is one of the most popular cushion-forming perennials. During the middle and last months of spring it flowers in shades of blue, pink, or even red.
Requirements: sunny, lime-containing sandy or loamy soil.

Care: always keep the soil sufficiently moist. Only fertilize when in flower. After flowering, cut the cushion back by about a third.

Candytuft shines white to pink in large cushions.
Botanical name: *Iberis sempervirens, Iberis saxatilis.*
Family: *Cruciferae.*
Flowering time: mid- to late spring.
Height: about 4 in (10 cm).

Candytuft owes its name to the colorful white, pink and red shades of its flowers. This bushy little plant is evergreen, so it retains its foliage all year round.
Requirements: cut back after flowering; propagate from cuttings.

NB: *Arabis* species should be included among the cushion-forming perennials. Like the candytufts, they belong to the family *Cruciferae.* In addition to white species and varieties, some pink varieties can now be obtained. The cushions should be divided every two to three years so that they do not deteriorate and become bare from the center.

Saxifrage or rockfoil (a red species is seen in the photograph above)
Botanical name: *Saxifraga* x *arendsii.*
Family: *Saxifragaceae.*
Flowering time: mid- to late spring.
Height: about 4 in (10 cm).

All shades, from white to pink to red, are produced by the many varieties of saxifrage. Compact cushions, with leaves that are formed out of closely packed individual rosettes, create a closed cover from which 8-in (20-cm) tall, wiry stalks rise up, bearing cup-shaped flowers during the second and third months of spring.
Requirements: light semi-shady, but also fairly sunny, position in humus-rich, loamy to sandy soil.
Care: after flowering, cut off the flower stalks just above the cushion. Fertilize sparingly. Propagate from cuttings in the fall.

Clouds of forget-me-not surrounding tulips, bleeding heart, and saxifrage.

Biennial spring-flowering plants

All these popular, short-lived, spring-flowering plants are suitable for underplanting with bulbous flowers.

Forget-me-not
(Photograph above)
Botanical name: *Myosotis sylvatica.*
Family: *Boraginaceae.*
Flowering time: early to late spring.
Height: 4-16 in (10-40 cm).
The pure, shining blue of the forget-me-not seems to reflect the color of the sky and will catch the eye in many positions. Clouds of blue flowers are the best kind of setting for brightly colored tulips but even on a balcony they look wonderful as an accompaniment to other, larger flowers.
Requirements: sunny to semi-shady position; humus-rich soil.
Planting and care: sow seed in early to midsummer, cover the seed with soil. Prick out the young plants and plant them out in early to mid-fall. They will need some form of winter protection.

A deep gold wallflower.

Faces full of expression.

White powder-puff daisies.

Wallflower
(Photograph, above)
Botanical name: *Cheiranthus* spp.
Family: *Cruciferae.*
Flowering time: mid- to late spring.
Height: 8-28 in (20-70 cm).
Warning: wallflowers are toxic!

Wallflowers were very popular at one time, although they seem to be less fashionable now. However, the very sweet scent of their yellow, orange, or brownish-red flowers still charms gardeners just as it has always done. The present-day selection offers a multitude of colors and sizes. Some varieties grow up to 28 in (70 cm) tall and are very much in demand as cut flowers.
Requirements: sunny to semi-sunny position; nutrient-rich, chalky, humus-rich soil.
Planting and care: cover the seed with soil in the last months of spring, keep an even degree of moisture, then prick out. Plant out the seedlings in early to mid-fall and give some protection during the winter.
Special note: overwintering can take place in a cold frame, then plant out in the first and second months of spring.

Pansies
(Photograph, above)
Botanical name: *Viola* x *wittrock-iana* hybrids.
Family: *Violaceae.*
Flowering time: early to late spring.
Height: 4-6 in (10-15 cm).

Pansies come in a multitude of shapes and sizes. The early-flowering varieties lift their faces up to the sun from early to late spring; they display the dominant colors of white, yellow, and blue. The late varieties (flowering from mid- to late spring) are often multi-colored, with warmer shades and faces full of expression.
Requirements: sunny to semi-shady position; permeable humus soil, not too rich in nutrients.
Planting and care: sow seed in early to midsummer, cover with soil, then prick out when ready. Plant out in early to mid-fall. Do not fertilize.
Use: pansies can be used universally – as an underplanting, as an accompaniment, or alone. They are all suited to planting in bowls and boxes; the small-flowered varieties, the miniature pansies, look particularly good in small spaces.

Daisies
(Photograph, above)
Botanical name: *Bellis perennis.*
Family: *Compositae.*
Flowering time: first and second months of spring.
Height: 4-6 in (10-15 cm).

Garden daisies and related species are the cultivated descendants of the plain wild daisy. Their flowers are thickly beset with petals and the individual flower head is larger than the wild daisy. Some varieties have flowers resembling small pincushions, others look more like powder puffs. The range of colors extends from pure white to pink to dark red.
Requirements: sunny to semi-shady position; in all soils.
Planting and care: sow seed from late spring to midsummer, protect the young plants from too much sunlight, then prick out. Plant out from midsummer. Use bunches of twigs, etc. as winter protection.
Special note: ready-bought plants can still be planted in the spring.

NOTES

Having your soil analyzed

If you wish to have a soil analysis made, you will have to submit a sample of mixed soil. Choose several spots in the garden and, using a spade, take specimens from a depth of 8-12 in (20-30 cm). You can take a smaller specimen by scraping soil off the blade of the spade with a spoon. The individual specimens should be mixed up thoroughly in a bucket. About 10-18 ounces (300-500 g) of soil, without any large roots or stones, can be sent for analysis in a plastic bag. Inquire at your local garden center for the address of a laboratory that will provide a soil analysis for you.

Author's note

This book is concerned with the care of spring flowers. Some of the species described here (the entire plant including bulbs/tubers) are more or less toxic! The section of the book giving descriptions of the plants points out which plants are toxic. You must make absolutely sure that children and pets do not eat any part of these plants. Some of the plants also secrete substances which may irritate your skin. If you have sensitive skin or suffer from contact allergies, you should make sure that you wear gloves when handling these plants. If you suffer an open cut or other injury while working with soil, visit your doctor to discuss the possibility of having a tetanus injection! All fertilizers and plant protection agents, even the organic or biological ones, should be stored in a place that is inaccessible to children and pets. These agents should not be allowed to come into contact with your eyes. If you are preparing large vats or containers of herbal brew (for spraying, etc.), cover the top of the container so that small children or animals cannot climb in.

NOTES

NOTES